London
The Complete **Residents'** Guide

Passionately Publishing...

EXPLORER

London Explorer 1st Edition   ISBN 13 – 978-976-8182-96-8   ISBN 10 – 976-8182-96-2

Copyright © Explorer Group Ltd 2007

Front Cover Photograph: Victor Romero

Printed and bound by Emirates Printing Press, Dubai, United Arab Emirates.

Explorer Publishing & Distribution
PO Box 34275, Zomorrodah Bldg, Za'abeel Rd, Dubai
United Arab Emirates

Phone	(+971 4) 335 3520
Fax	(+971 4) 335 3529
Email	Info@Explorer-Publishing.com
Web	www.Explorer-Publishing.com

Welcome

You've just made living in London a whole lot easier by buying this book. In the following pages you'll find out everything you need to know to get settled into – and then get the most out of – your new life in one of the world's greatest cities. From insuring a car to buying a kettle, or crooning at karaoke, we can tell you how and where to do it.

The **General Information** chapter fills you in on London's history, geography and culture, and provides details of how to get around and where to stay when you first arrive.

The **Residents** chapter takes away all the headaches involved in setting up your new home. With information on visas, residential areas, schools and red tape, this section will tell you how to deal with all the formalities.

After settling in, take a look at **Exploring**. This chapter guides you through the capital's different neighbourhoods, telling you all about London's world-famous (and less well-known) museums, galleries and parks, and detailing annual festivals and where to go for weekend breaks. There's also a checklist of must-dos. If you've still got time on your hands, move on to **Activities**. Here you'll find out where to play football, how to join a drama group, and which are the best lessons for learning languages. If you'd prefer to indulge, there's also a wealth of well-being options to digest, from acupuncture to yoga, with a bit of spa in between.

Now that you're living in London, you'll also have full access to all the retail that arguably the world's best **Shopping** city has to offer, and we've got a whole chapter dedicated to helping you discover the top markets, department stores and high streets in which to splash the cash.

Don't spend it all in the shops though – save some for the evening. Our **Going Out** chapter gives you a detailed run-down on London's premier places for eating, drinking and partying.

We've also included detailed **Maps** to help you get around, from taking the tube to navigating London's maze of streets by foot.

And if you think we have missed something, please let us know. Go to www.explorerpublishing.com, fill in the Reader Response form, and share the knowledge with your fellow explorers.

The Explorer Team

Explorer online

Life can move pretty fast so make sure you keep up at www.explorerpublishing.com. Register for updates on the latest happenings in your city, or let us know if there's anything we've missed out with our reader response form. You can also check out city info on various destinations around the world – whether you're planning a holiday or making your next big move, we've got it covered. All our titles, from residents' guides to mini visitors' guides, mini maps to photography books are available to purchase online so you need never be without us.

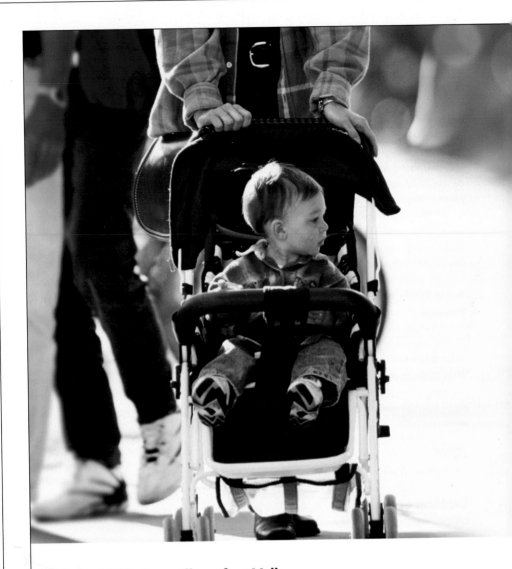

Only 6 295 days till my first Volkswagen.

It gets me. I can't quite say why I'm so madly attracted to my Volkswagen. It's like we share an uncommon passion. Sure, it feels so safe and sound on the road, while also looking sleek and styled on the outside. It also feels nice and comfortable on the inside, too!

But it's really more than all that. It's another dimension. A real connection – it's like a soul mate. I guess I can say it's the ONE for me. So why do I always go for a Volkswagen? Because it simply gets me.

For the love of automobiles

Hashim MM
AKA: Speedy Gonzales

They don't come much faster than Hashim – he's so speedy with his mouse that scientists are struggling to create a computer that can keep up with him. His nimble fingers leave his keyboard smouldering (he gets through three a week), and his go-faster stripes make him almost invisible to the naked eye when he moves.

Jane Roberts
AKA: The Oracle

After working in an undisclosed role in the government, Jane brought her super sleuth skills to Explorer. Whatever the question, she knows what, where, who, how and when, but her encyclopaedic knowledge is only impressive until you realise she just makes things up randomly.

Helen Spearman
AKA: Little Miss Sunshine

With her bubbly laugh and permanent smile, Helen is a much-needed ray of sunshine in the office when we're all grumpy and facing harrowing deadlines. It's almost impossible to think that she ever loses her temper or shows a dark side... although put her behind the wheel of a car, and you've got instant road rage.

Jayde Fernandes
AKA: Pop Idol

Jayde's idol is Britney Spears, and he recently shaved his head to show solidarity with the troubled star. When he's not checking his dome for stubble, or practising the dance moves to 'Baby One More Time' in front of the bathroom mirror, he actually manages to get some designing done.

Henry Hilos
AKA: The Quiet Man

Henry can rarely be seen from behind his large obstructive screen but when you do catch a glimpse you'll be sure to get a smile. Lighthearted Henry keeps all those glossy pages filled with pretty pictures for something to look at when you can't be bothered to read.

Kate Fox
AKA: Contacts Collector

Kate swooped into the office like the UK equivalent of Wonderwoman, minus the tights of course (it's much too hot for that), but armed with a superhuman marketing brain. Even though she 's just arrived, she is already a regular on the Dubai social scene - she is helping to blast Explorer into the stratosphere, one champagne-soaked networking party at a time.

Ieyad Charaf
AKA: Fashion Designer

When we hired Ieyad as a top designer, we didn't realise we'd be getting his designer tops too! By far the snappiest dresser in the office, you'd be hard-pressed to beat his impeccably ironed shirts.

Katie Drynan
AKA The Irish Deputy

Katie is a Jumeirah Jane in training, and has 35 sisters who take it in turns to work in the Explorer office while she enjoys testing all the beauty treatments available on the Beach Road. This Irish charmer met an oil tycoon in Paris, and they now spend the weekends digging very deep holes in their new garden.

Ingrid Cupido
AKA: The Karaoke Queen

Ingrid has a voice to match her starlet name. She'll put any Pop Idols to shame once behind the mike, and she's pretty nifty on a keyboard too. She keeps us all ticking over and was a very welcome relief for overworked staff. She certainly gets our vote if she decides to go pro; just remember you saw her here first.

Ivan Rodrigues
AKA: The Aviator

After making a mint in the airline market, Ivan came to Explorer where he works for pleasure, not money. That's his story, anyway. We know that he is actually a corporate spy from a rival company and that his multi-level spreadsheets are really elaborate codes designed to confuse us.

Kiran Melwani
AKA: Bow Selector

Like a modern-day Robin Hood (right down to the green tights and band of merry men), Kiran's mission in life is to distribute Explorer's wealth of knowledge to the fact-hungry readers of the world. Just make sure you never do anything to upset her – rumour has it she's a pretty mean shot with that bow and arrow.

Abdul Gafoor
AKA: Ace Circulator
After a successful stint on Ferrari's Formula One team Gafoor made a pitstop at our office and decided to stay. He has won our 'Most Cheerful Employee' award five years in a row – baffling, when you consider he spends so much time battling the traffic.

Andrea Fust
AKA: Mother Superior
By day Andrea is the most efficient manager in the world and by night she replaces the boardroom for her board and wows the pants off the dudes in Ski Dubai. Literally. Back in the office she definitely wears the trousers!

Ahmed Mainodin
AKA: Mystery Man
We can never recognise Ahmed because of his constantly changing facial hair. He waltzes in with big lambchop sideburns one day, a handlebar moustache the next, and a neatly trimmed goatee after that. So far we've had no objections to his hirsute chameleonisms, but we'll definitely draw the line at a monobrow.

Cherry Enriquez
AKA: Bean Counter
With the team's penchant for sweets and pastries, it's good to know we have Cherry on top of our accounting cake. The local confectioner is always paid on time, so we're guaranteed great gateaux for every special occasion.

Claire England
AKA: Whip Cracker
No longer able to freeload off the fact that she once appeared in a Robbie Williams video, Claire now puts her creative skills to better use – looking up rude words in the dictionary! A child of English nobility, Claire is quite the lady – unless she's down at Jimmy Dix.

Ajay Krishnan R
AKA: Web Wonder
Ajay's mum and dad knew he was going to be an IT genius when the found him reconfiguring his Commodore 64 at the tender age of 2. He went on to become the technology consultant on all three Matrix films, and counts Keanu as a close personal friend.

David Quinn
AKA: Sharp Shooter
After a short stint as a children's TV presenter was robbed from David because he developed an allergy to sticky back plastic, he made his way to sandier pastures. Now that he's thinking outside the box, nothing gets past the man with the sharpest pencil in town.

Alex Jeffries
AKA: Easy Rider
Alex is happiest when dressed in leather from head to toe with a humming machine between his thighs – just like any other motorbike enthusiast. Whenever he's not speeding along the Hatta Road at full throttle, he can be found at his beloved Mac, still dressed in leather.

Enrico Maullon
AKA: The Crooner
Frequently mistaken for his near-namesake Enrique Iglesias, Enrico decided to capitalise and is now a regular stand-in for the Latin heartthrob. If he's ever missing from the office, it usually means he's off performing for millions of adoring fans on another stadium tour of America.

Alistair MacKenzie
AKA: Media Mogul
If only Alistair could take the paperless office one step further and achieve the officeless office he would be the happiest publisher alive. Wireless access from a remote spot somewhere in the Hajar Mountains would suit this intrepid explorer – less traffic, lots of fresh air, and wearing sandals all day - the perfect work environment!

Firos Khan
AKA: Big Smiler
Previously a body double in kung fu movies, including several appearances in close up scenes for Steven Seagal's moustache. He also once tore down a restaurant with his bare hands after they served him a mild curry by mistake.

Anna Smith

Shopping trips to London were the highlight of Anna's childhood, and so as soon as she was old enough she moved to the city to begin a career in journalism (and professional shopping). Anna specialises in travel and entertainment writing, and is a regular contributor to many of the UK's leading titles including *Sight and Sound* and *Empire*. She lives within a stone's throw of Oxford Street, and loves being right in the heart of such an active, cultural capital.

Catherine Jarvie

Catherine first arrived in the capital from her native New Zealand while on a gap year and immediately fell in love with the vibrancy of the city; 16 years later she's still there, and very proud to call London home. After a stint pulling pints on Portobello Road, she eventually settled at the BBC before leaving to work as a freelance journalist in 2000. She writes features for publications including *The Guardian*, *The Observer* and the *Independent on Sunday*.

Janetta Willis

Arriving in London at the age of 4 via Belfast and Edinburgh, Janetta soon progressed from learning her ABC to obsessively perusing the *A-Z* and now knows the capital like no other. She is a regular contributor to *Broadcast* magazine and author of *The Newcomer's Handbook for London*. When she's not searching for the missing apostrophes of the metropolis, she's avoiding the potholes of the Seven Sisters Road on two wheels.

Nadia Pendleton

After an initial stint in PR, Nadia decided to follow her passion for food and restaurants. She now juggles a career as a food writer, food stylist, cook and reviewer, which has seen her work as a duty manager in some of London's top restaurants and appearing on UKTV Food. Her new cookbook *The Melting Pot: The World in Your Kitchen* celebrates multicultural food in the UK, and nowhere is this more exciting and diverse than in London. Nadia has lived in Bloomsbury for the past six years.

Debra Waters

Debra was attracted to London from her native Yorkshire in 1992, and believes it's impossible to get bored with the city's vibe and rich history. Having swapped arts and charity PR for freelance journalism, Debra has written for *Time Out* and *The Big Issue* among others. She cites urban walks (including longingly gazing through the windows of hugely expensive houses) as her favourite activity.

Thanks...

The biggest thank you must go to the *London Explorer* authors, whose tireless research, unfailing commitment and insider knowledge has ensured that this book is the most comprehensive guide to London life available. Thanks also to Becky Lucas, Ben Robards, Gemma Exley, Helga Becker, Jane Bryan, Nik Taylor, Rania Adwan, and Wenda Oosterbroek for their words and pictures. Last but not least, thanks to everybody in the Explorer office for their support.

"It's that Volkswagen feeling!"
It Gets Me.

I can't quite say why I'm so madly attracted to my Volkswagen. It's like we share an uncommon passion. Sure, it feels so safe and sound on the road, while also looking sleek and styled on the outside. It also feels nice and comfortable on the inside, too!

But it's really more than all that. It's another dimension. A real connection – it's like a soul mate. I guess I can say it's the ONE for me. So why do I always go for a Volkswagen? Because it simply gets me.

For the love of automobiles

Residents' Guides

All you need to know about
living, working and enjoying life
in these exciting destinations

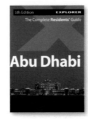  

＊ Covers not final. Titles available Winter 2007.

Activity Guides

Drive, trek, dive and swim... life will never be boring again

Mini Guides
The perfect pocket-sized
Visitors' Guides

✳ Covers not final. Titles available Winter 2007.

Mini Maps
Wherever you are,
never get lost again

✳ Covers not final. Titles available Winter 2007.

Photography Books
Beautiful cities caught through the lens

Contents

Contents

moving?

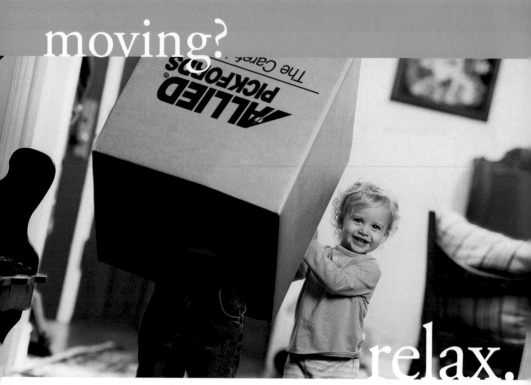

relax.
we carry the load. _{SM}

Door to door moving with Allied Pickfords

Allied Pickfords is one of the largest and most respected providers of moving services in the world, handling over 50,000 international moves every year.

We believe that nothing reduces stress more than trust, and each year thousands of families trust Allied Pickfords to move them. With over 800 offices in more than 40 countries, we're the specialists in international moving and have the ability to relocate you anywhere anytime. Move with Allied to Allied worldwide.

www.alliedpickfords.com

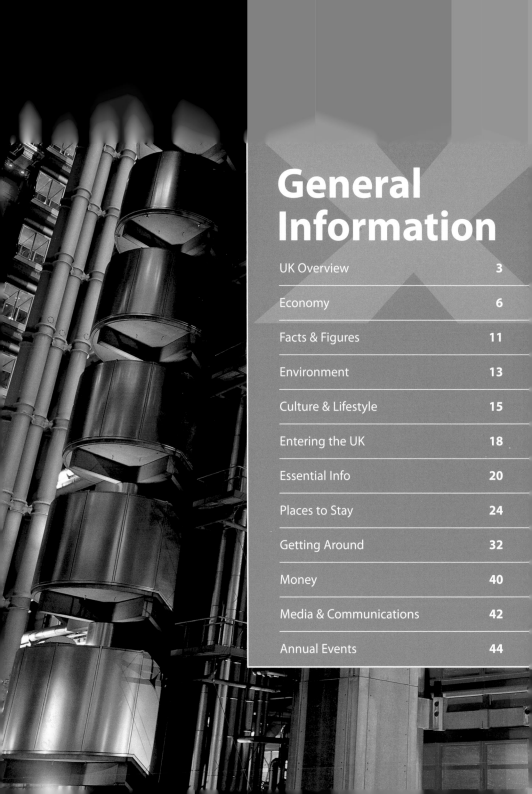

General Information

General Information

Geography

The geopolitical make-up of the UK can be somewhat confusing, even to those who were born and bred there. The two islands (and many smaller ones) that lie off the north-west coast of mainland Europe are commonly referred to as the British Isles – but this is a geographical rather than political term. The largest is Great Britain, while the smaller, westerly island is called Ireland. Politically these are divided into two countries: the United Kingdom of Great Britain and Northern Ireland, (the UK), and the Republic of Ireland. The UK is made up of four constituent countries: England, Scotland and Wales (Great Britain) and Northern Ireland (a sixth of the island of Ireland), plus several smaller territories. The Republic of Ireland, which is fiercely independent of the UK, consists of the remaining five-sixths of the island of Ireland. London is the capital of both the UK and England, while Scotland, Wales and Northern Ireland also have their own capitals (respectively Edinburgh, Cardiff and Belfast).

Physical Geography

Several seas of the North Atlantic surround the UK, and its coastline touches the North Sea, Irish Sea, Celtic Sea and English Channel. The only land border is between Northern Ireland and the Republic of Ireland, although the Channel Tunnel under the English Channel connects the UK by rail to continental neighbour France. The UK is 94,526 square miles (244,820 sq km) in size, with England accounting for more than half of that area. Large parts of Scotland, Northern Ireland, Wales and north-west England are mountainous, although in world terms these peaks are not particularly big (Ben Nevis in Scotland, at 1,343m, is the highest). The Pennines, a range of hills known as the 'backbone of England', runs south through from the Scottish border to the Peak District in central England, forming a natural divide between east and west, with the eastern side of the country generally flatter. The lower-lying areas are generally given over to rolling countryside, which is mainly farmland or, where it remains, woodland. There are also 14 national parks that preserve areas of particular beauty or interest.

London

Most of the UK's 60 million population is concentrated in densely packed cities and urban conurbations. Greater London, in the south-east of England, is by far the biggest in terms of size and population (7.5 million people). It's also one of the largest cities in the world by area, covering more than 600 square miles, and can broadly be defined as everything within the M25 orbital motorway. The Thames river is the most distinctive geographical feature. It flows east some 200 miles from its Gloucestershire source, cutting through London and dividing the city into north and south, before making its way to the North Sea. The capital's main business, administrative and tourist centres are situated on and around the Thames, with residential areas radiating outwards for several miles in all directions. The city's highest natural point is in north London's Hampstead Heath, at 134m above sea level, while Shooters Hill is the highest point south of the river (132m).

Tunnel Vision

Much as they like to be kept apart, the English and French were joined in 1994, when the Channel Tunnel opened. After £12 billion and more than eight years of construction, the tunnel, 38km of which is underwater, reunited the UK with mainland Europe. And thanks to the new Channel Tunnel Rail Link at St Pancras, passengers can travel between London and Paris in a little over two hours.

History

History and London go hand in hand – millions of visitors from around the world come to the UK's capital to get a slice of the tradition and heritage for which the city is renowned. Despite the periodical destruction of large chunks of London across the ages, through fire and attack, much of that history is in evidence today – from palaces and parliament to cathedrals and cobbled streets, there's plenty of it left to see. London's story stretches back 2,000 years to Roman times, when invaders expanding their empire westwards settled on the banks of the Thames. Over the next 300 years, despite being razed by rebel Queen Boudicca in AD61, the settlement grew to become Londinium, capital of Britainnia and home to an estimated 60,000 inhabitants. As with the rest of the Roman Empire, Londinium's prominence began to fade until it was eventually abandoned in the 5th century, but fragments of the town's wall are still visible amid the modern day offices in London's financial district, and the names of Aldgate, Bishopsgate, Ludgate and Newgate can all be traced to these times.

The Missing Millennium

The legacy of life over the following 1,000 or so years in London is pretty scarce. After the Romans, London, like the rest of Britain, was the subject of settlement, invasion and resettlement. Saxons, Vikings and Normans all came to the island's shores and the site of the capital was occupied intermittently to varying degrees, both within the old Roman city boundaries and without them to the west. But the propensity to build things very close together and out of wood meant fires often destroyed large swathes of the town. One of the more notable remnants from this period is Westminster Abbey. Edward the Confessor, the last Anglo-Saxon king of England, had a huge stone church built in the 11th century on the site of a wooden monastery two miles west of the city. He didn't last long enough to enjoy the fruits of his workers' labours however, as he died a few days after the church was consecrated. A little less than a year later, in 1066, Norman conqueror William was coronated there, beginning a new chapter of English history and starting the royal lineage that, to some degree, continues today. The abbey that stands there now is not the original – Henry III had it rebuilt in the Gothic style a couple of hundred years later – but parts of it can be seen in the arches and columns of the cloisters. William was also responsible for ordering the construction of part of the Tower of London, another of the capital's oldest remaining monuments. Other significant buildings from this era are few and far between. An overcrowded, dirty and disease-ridden London was effectively wiped out in 1666 by the Great Fire.

A Plague on all the Houses
Rotting animal carcasses, dirty water and general squalid conditions in medieval London made outbreaks of infectious disease a common occurence, including several bouts of the deadly plague. The last plague epedemic in the city, in 1665, was brought to an abrupt halt by the Great Fire.

St Paul's and The City

The five-day inferno had started in a baker's shop. What sprung out of the ashes does form a very distinctive part of today's city though. The architect Sir Christopher Wren was the major figure in London's reconstruction, designing many of the churches that are dotted around the city, including the iconic St Paul's Cathedral. The fire also meant new houses were needed; these were built to the west, paving the way for the wealthier residential areas that exist on that side of town.

What the Dickens?

The grim reality of life for the less well-off in Victorian London is captured and characterised in the works of celebrated novelist Charles Dickens. Books such as Oliver Twist, Bleak House *and* Little Dorrit *paint grim portraits of the hardships of the time, and serve as strong social commentaries on the treatment of the poor in the 19th century.*

Industrialisation

London's development and urbanisation gathered pace during the 18th and 19th centuries, with the population increasing, and polarising, rapidly. The rich got wealthier as the industrial revolution and empirical expansion transformed Britain into the major world superpower of the age. At the same time the gap between the haves and have-nots became more marked than ever as the city grew at an unprecedented rate (the population swelled from around one million to six million between the start and end of the 1800s). Plush residential squares and large terraced townhouses were built to accommodate the well-off, and no expense was spared on building pioneering scientific and academic establishments (the museums and institutes around South Kensington demonstrate this), while the poor struggled to get by in slum areas of the city and East End. Crime rates soared, eventually leading to the formation of the Bow Street Runners, the embryo of the Metropolitan Police. A significant Victorian contribution to today's London was the development of public transport, the city's arteries. The first subterranean train route, between Paddington and Farringdon Road (the Metropolitan line), was opened in 1863, and the first underground electric track was in place less than 30 years later, along a stretch of what is now the Northern line.

Twentieth Century

The start of the 20th century marked a change in attitude from the straight-laced Victorian era, with entertainment and glamour taking a foothold in the capital. New cafes, theatres, and hotels including The Ritz, played host to a lively social scene. Like the rest of the country, Londoners were hugely affected by the first world war (bombing raids by air ships resulted in about 600 casualties). But the war also accentuated the frivolity of the upper classes in the 'Roaring 20s' as those who could made the most of a return to normality. Once again though it was a divided city; as one half partied, the other half struggled. Poor post-war economic conditions brought housing and labour difficulties to much of the working-class population, with strikes and civil disturbances prevalent.

Things only worsened with the economic depression of the early 1930s. As the decade progressed, however, the city's population grew to record levels – about 8.5 million – and the combination of housing shortages and the advent of the motor car saw the city grow to the north and west as huge swathes of suburbs were created.

Millennium Bridge

The second world war brought modern-day London's darkest hour – the Blitz of 1940 and 1941 – during which aerial bombardment by German bombers destroyed huge areas of the city, mainly the East End, and killed thousands. By the time the war was over in

4

1945, large chunks needed to be rebuilt. The urgency with which this was required combined with the country's hugely depleted resources saw the gaps filled with cheap temporary housing, high-rise estates and stark, concrete offices. Many of these pockets still stand out, sitting uneasily amid more upmarket residential and commercial surroundings.

Killer Fog

In 1952, a smog (fog filled with soot) engulfed London for four days, bringing the capital to a standstill. Caused by the combination of excessive coal burning and freezing temperatures, the air quality was so poor that it is estimated to have caused the deaths of about 4,000 people. Vehicles were abandoned, shows were cancelled, and people were forced to stay indoors. The crisis led to the imposition of laws to phase out 'dirty fuels' and black smoke.

Post-War Years

The austere post-war years were lit up by the staging of the Olympics at Wembley in 1948, and the Festival of Britain in 1951 (which led to the development of the South Bank area as a cultural centre). As Britain returned to relative prosperity in the 1950s, labour shortages brought about a policy of attracting immigrants to the capital. Transport workers were recruited from the Caribbean, particularly Jamaica and Trinidad, and Indian, Pakistani and Bangladeshi migrants also came to London, transforming the city's society into a multi-ethnic one. Different groups settled into different areas – West Indians in Notting Hill and Brixton, Bangledeshis in the East End and Indians in the west London suburbs. Although London prides itself on its diversity, settlement and acceptance was anything but easy for most new communities, and tensions have periodically flared up in the form of riots, notably in Notting Hill in the 1950s and Brixton in the 80s.

London in the 1960s has taken on a legend of its own: the hip areas of Kings Road and Carnaby Street, a burgeoning music, film and party scene, and the World Cup victory all helped to create the 'Swinging 60s' label. While the reality of life in this decade may not quite match the hedonistic image, London's reputation as a cutting-edge place for arts and fashion was born. The party scene didn't carry over into the 70s though; harsh economic conditions led to civil unrest, and political disputes in Ireland spilled over to mainland Britain as the IRA began bombing campaigns in the capital, which would last for the next 30 years. But like the 60s the mood of the era manifested itself in music, with the discontent and aggression of the time spawning the punk movement.

Margaret Thatcher's heavy handed rule in the 1980s did little to ease the public mood, as her government's right-wing economic and social policies once again widened the gap between rich and poor. Riots broke out periodically, unemployment peaked, and battles with trade unions were fierce. Thatcher also abolished the Greater London Council, meaning London's administrative independence was diminished. As in previous eras, however, it was boom time for some; plans to redevelop part of the rundown Docklands area in east London were put in place. Although the project did not run smoothly – a property crash in the early 1990s and an IRA bomb in 1996 threatened the development – the outcome was Canary Wharf, an area of high-rise office space for international banks that now dominates the skyline.

A New Era

A healthy economic climate has seen other innovative buildings spring up, including 30 St Mary Axe ('the Gherkin'), while the new millennium saw projects such as the London Eye, Millennium Bridge and Tate Modern (plus the much-maligned Millennium Dome) added to London's list of attractions. The year 2000 also saw the introduction of the position of London mayor. Ken Livingstone was elected (he's still there today), and his major impact has been to introduce the Congestion Charge for drivers in central London (p.154). He also backed the city's successful bid to host the 2012 Olympics, which is expected to provide jobs, investment and regeneration.

The day after London was awarded the games, in July 2005, four suicide bombers blew up three tube trains and a bus, killing 52 people, and injuring hundreds more. While the attacks had a sobering impact on the lives of all residents, resilient Londoners determined to carry on with 'business as usual'. As on many occasions over the last 2,000 years, London has picked itself up, and the story of this remarkable city is set to keep on unfolding.

UK Overview

The UK has the second-largest economy in Europe, after fellow EU member Germany, as well as the fifth-largest gross domestic product (GPD) in the world in terms of market exchange rates, and the sixth-largest by purchasing power parity.

In recent times, the British economy has seen its longest period of sustained economic growth for more than 150 years, with low interest and unemployment rates. However, the distribution of wealth has long been an issue – the UK has one of the highest levels of income inequality within the EU, with 1% of the population possessing 21% of the wealth. Official figures show that the average household had a gross income of £24,000 per annum in 1999-2000, the most recent year for which the information is available. By comparison, the figure is £22,000 in the United States and just £700 in China.

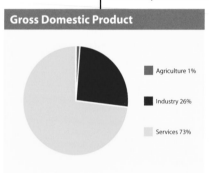

Gross Domestic Product

Agriculture 1%

Industry 26%

Services 73%

Although British GDP grew by 1.8% in 2005, this was slower than expected – something chancellor Gordon Brown attributed to the high price of oil, the easing of house price increases and the subsequent slowdown in consumer spending. It is expected to increase in the near future. Primary energy production in the UK accounts for 10% of GDP, one of the highest shares of any industrial nation. The country has large coal, natural gas and oil reserves, and, thanks to the North Sea oil fields, the UK became a net hydrocarbon exporter during the 1990s.

Some of the UK's leading companies are based in this sector including BP, Royal Dutch Shell, Cairn Energy, Centrica and Anglo American. Cars, trains and aircraft are among other important industrial exports.

London Overview

London has Europe's largest city economy and, along with New York and Tokyo, is a major global powerhouse. Domestically, it accounts for about one-fifth of the country's GDP. On the international stage, London has many advantages that give it the edge over other economic centres, including Britain's friendly relationship with the US, the widespread use of the English language and law throughout the business world, and the capital's positioning as a major aviation hub. London's multiculturalism – one of its main selling points – is another attraction for international businesses.

Employment

At present, the British economy is buoyant, growing by approximately 2% every year – and London plays a major part in this success. The city has a workforce of 3.4 million and with wages about 20% higher than in the rest of the country, it is no surprise that so many people are attracted to the capital. Salaries range from an average of £20,000 for manual jobs to six-figure pay packets for some City workers. The inflated wages of those in the financial sector skew the average salary for non-manual occupations, which is £37,000. The downside for London earners is the high cost of living; rental and housing costs, which, in an already overinflated national market, can be up to twice as much as elsewhere in the country. The knock-on effect is that 750,000 people commute to work from outside the capital each day.

Leading Industries

Finance is London's largest industry. Over half of the UK's top 100 listed companies (the FTSE 100) and more than 100 of Europe's 500 largest companies are based in the capital, most within the City of London. The modern development of Canary Wharf

6

now acts as a second finance centre, and includes the worldwide headquarters of companies such as HSBC, Reuters and Barclays. Finance may be the largest industry, but London's booming creative sector is one of the most significant, especially when compared with other countries; it generates more than £14 billion in annual sales and employees over 400,000. It's a highly competitive area and there is a scrabble for jobs in advertising, architecture, design, fashion, film, music, publishing, radio and TV. The BBC is the largest media employer, but other broadcasters also have headquarters around town. Most national newspapers are edited in London, even if the printing presses are now scattered around the country.

Tourism is the other big business in London, with more than 350,000 workers employed full-time thanks to the regular stream of visitors who spend £9 billion in the city annually. Around 3 million of Greater London's population work in service industries, with another half a million employed in construction and manufacturing.

London Developments

London is the place to be if you work in construction; there have been massive developments in recent years, particularly within the transport and leisure industries. The rebuilding of Wembley Stadium, England's national football arena, has been one of the major construction projects in the capital over the past decade (see p.8). Something of a controversial affair, coming in way over schedule and budget, it has reportedly cost more than £750 million so far, and has had more bad press than the England manager. On the plus side, the scheme has included significant upgrading of transport infrastructure in north-west London.

Another sporting project set to preoccupy the country for the foreseeable future is the preparation to stage the Olympics in the capital in 2012. London beat rival bids from Paris, New York and Madrid to host the event, and in doing so created a major opportunity for local industries and communities. Deprived parts of east London, including Stratford, are set to benefit from investment in facilities, property and transport, and other areas slated to host minor Olympic events should also prosper. The games are expected to create thousands of jobs across a range of sectors; bus drivers, architects, engineers, IT specialists, electricians, bricklayers, journalists, printers, drivers, caterers, tour guides, choreographers, and even hairdressers will all be needed. Despite this, reports about the various projects being over-budget and behind schedule have already begun to circulate, so expect more of the same over the next five years.

Trafalgar Square

National Stadium, National Fiasco

In 2000 England played their last football match at the old Wembley. Shortly afterwards, the ground was demolished to make way for a brand new state-of-the-art national stadium – and the project has been dogged by problems ever since. The controversy began before the last ball was even kicked when other considerably cheaper proposals to build the stadium in the Midlands and northern England were overlooked. From the design, what to do with the old stadium's famous twin towers, constant delay, a huge overspend and protracted wrangles between the constructors, Multiplex and owners, the Football Association, it's been a rocky ride. After several postponements, the latest prediction is that the 2007 FA Cup final will 'definitely' be played at Wembley – when football fans will be able to see for themselves whether it's been worth the wait.

Part of the Olympic project includes the development of a shuttle train to run from Stratford to central London, which will tie in with the Channel Tunnel Rail Link. This high-speed rail service to the British side of the tunnel will see the shifting of the Eurostar terminal from Waterloo to St Pancras in 2007, and will also include a stop at Stratford. As well as the employment and investment created by the building of the line, the King's Cross area around St Pancras station is set to benefit from a major facelift (see p.79). Other proposed transport projects include the East London line extension, which will link Highbury & Islington in the north with south-east London (the first phase is set to open in 2010), and the Crossrail connection of west and east London – although this is some years off as it is still in the planning stage. A fifth terminal at Heathrow airport is scheduled to open in 2008.

One noticeable indicator of London's strong economy is its changing skyline; several new examples of modern high-rise architecture have sprung up in and around the City over the last few years, and there are more in the pipeline. Developers plans' include the Shard London Bridge, which at 310m will be almost twice the height of the recently built Gherkin when it is finished in 2011, and will house a Shangri-La hotel, office space and residential units. Other projects set to loom large over London include the 35 storey City Road Basin in Islington and a 48 floor tapered glass building on Leadenhall Street in the City.

Tourism

Tourism makes a major contribution to the capital's economy, not to mention its day-to-day life. According to Visit London, an estimated 24.5 million visitors were drawn to the city in 2005 – more if you include domestic daytrippers – by London's heritage, iconic landmarks and cultural attractions, spending about £9 billion in total.

On top of this, tourism is responsible directly or indirectly for creating nearly 350,000 jobs in London.

The capital's tourism industry has, however, been hit by various political and natural events this decade, from 9/11, the invasion of Iraq and the London bombings of 2005 to the outbreaks domestically of foot and mouth disease and, internationally, Sars. The weakening of the dollar against the pound has also lessened the appeal to US travellers, which is by far the UK's most substantial overseas market. While visitor numbers have still not returned to the levels of 2000 – estimated at 31.6 million – both domestic and international tourism remain strong, supported by the rising number of cheap European flights in the last few years.

Recent additions to London's list of attractions, including the London Eye (p.217) and Tate Modern art gallery (p.196), have proved incredibly popular. The investment in infrastructure ahead of the Olympics in 2012, and the opening of a fifth terminal at Heathrow in 2008, should help to increase the numbers of international visitors.

Government & Politics

Britain is a constitutional monarchy, whereby the monarch acts as head of state while an elected parliament makes and passes legislation. The present sovereign is Queen Elizabeth II, who has held the throne since 1952 when she succeeded her father, George VI. The heir is Charles, Prince of Wales, the eldest of the Queen and Prince

Philip's four children. The Queen is also head of state of the 15 other Commonwealth Realm countries, which include Canada, Australia and New Zealand, and 14 overseas territories, as well as being head of the Commonwealth. The monarch's powers may appear to be significant but they don't hold much weight in terms of law or policy making; ambassadorial duties and providing fodder for tabloid stories are the royal family's principal public roles today.

Parliament and the Prime Minister

The Queen generally acts on the advice of the prime minister, whose party is democratically elected every four or five years by the public. The current ruling party is Labour, which has been in power since 1997. Tony Blair is party leader, and therefore prime minister, although he has indicated he will hand over leadership within the party in 2007 (the open secret is that this will be to the present chancellor, Gordon Brown). Parties gain power by having a majority of representatives elected by the public to sit in the House of Commons as members of parliament (MPs) for local constituencies – at the last general election, in 2005, Labour retained power by winning 355 'seats', compared with the Conservative party's 197 and the Liberal Democrats' 62. There is a second chamber of parliament, the House of Lords, which studies legislation passed by the Commons and is also the highest court of appeal in the UK. Unlike the Commons, the House of Lords is not democratically elected; its members are appointed by the Queen, Church of England, or internal elections.

The Mayor

Greater London is divided into 74 local constituencies, with an MP representing each one in the House of Commons. The city also has its own administration, which is coordinated by the Greater London Authority (GLA). The principal figure of the GLA is a mayor, who is democratically elected every four years and has executive powers covering London's planning, transport, policing, economic development and cultural activities. The London Assembly, also part of the GLA and elected by the public, has the authority to approve and question various elements of the mayor's work.

The GLA was formed in 2000, 16 years after Conservative prime minister Margaret Thatcher abolished the largely left-wing Greater London Council and gave much of the authority for the running of the city to central government. When the Labour Party came to national power in 1997, it pledged to hand some form of self-governance back to London, and the GLA was formed three years later. Ken Livingstone, who was a Labour member at the time, wanted to stand for mayor but was overruled by Tony Blair, so he controversially quit the party to run as an independent candidate. He subsequently won the election, and remains the mayor today – although he was readmitted to Labour before his re-election in 2004, a somewhat embarrassing about-turn for his seniors. Undoubtedly Livingstone's most high-profile move has been to introduce the Congestion Charge to cut traffic in central London, a move welcomed by some but highly criticised by others.

There are also 32 local boroughs within London, which have elected councils to take responsibility for running their own local planning, schools, social services and refuse collection.

The Houses of Parliament

International Relations

The UK is the only state that is a member of the G8, EU, Nato, the Commonwealth and the UN Security Council, putting it in a unique position on the global stage. It is also a member of the Organization for Security and Cooperation in Europe and Council of Europe. The UK has been a member of the EU since 1973 and is subject to laws passed by the European Parliament, although it has so far declined to ditch the pound in favour of the euro. Its economy may be smaller than those of Germany or Japan, yet the UK plays a larger role than either of those countries on the international scene, both militarily and diplomatically. Democracy, humanitarianism and respect for human rights are claimed to be top priorities for the current government, but these ideals have been questioned following the UK's involvement in the Iraq war and the fight against terrorism. The government has also increased the political bridging role it plays between Europe and the US, leaving it open to much criticism from other political players and the public. In 2003, when the US pushed to invade Iraq, the UK government pledged its support despite the fact that Britain's Stop the War Coalition held the largest demonstration in the country's history, when up to two million protesters marched through London.

Hay's Galleria

The Lloyd's Building

Tower Bridge and City Hall

Westminster

Facts & Figures

Ethnic Diversity
According to the Office of National Statistics, the most ethnically diverse areas in the UK are the London boroughs of Brent and Newman, where there's an 80% chance that two people chosen at random would be from an ethnic minority group.

Population

London's population grew rapidly during the 19th and 20th centuries – it was the most populated city in the world until it was overtaken by New York in 1925. There are now an estimated 7,517,700 people living in the Greater London area. However, the capital's wider metropolitan area is home to closer to 12 million people. London is also host to one in eight of the UK's population and has three million households. More recently, the demography has altered considerably; more than a quarter of London's population is now from an ethnic background, the largest non-white population of any European city. London has more women than men and its population is younger when compared with the rest of the country; 47% of the population is aged between 16 and 44. The average life expectancy in some of the city's more affluent boroughs, such as Chelsea and Kensington, is 82 for men and 86 for women, which is noticeably higher than the national average of 76 and 81.

Population Age Breakdown

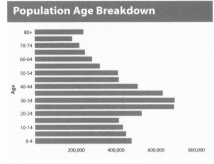

Source: Office of National Statistics

National Flag

The Union Flag, commonly called the Union Jack because it was flown from the jack staff of naval ships, is the national flag of the United Kingdom. It is made up of the crosses of the patron saints of England (St George), Scotland (St Andrew) and Ireland (St Patrick); England is represented by a red cross on a white field, Scotland is represented by a white diagonal cross on a blue background and Northern Ireland is represented by a red diagonal cross on a white field. Wales, although part of the United Kingdom, is not featured in the flag. When the flag was first created in 1606, Wales was part of England and not, as it is now, a separate principality. Each constituent country of the UK also has its own individual flag. The Union Flag is flown on government buildings on various dates considered important, such as the birthdays of members of the royal family and national or state celebrations and events.

Education Levels

Level 1: 1+ 'O' level passes, 1+ CSE/GCSE any grades, NVQ level 1, Foundation GNVQ

Level 2: 5+ 'O' level passes, 5+ CSEs (grade 1). 5+ GCSEs (grades A-C), School Certificate, 1+'A' levels/ AS levels, NVQ level 2, Intermediate GNVQ

Level 3: 2+ 'A' levels, 4+ AS levels, Higher School certificate, NVQ level 3, Advanced GNVQ

Level 4/5: First degree, Higher degree, NVQ levels 4 and 5, HNC2, HND, Qualified Teacher status, Qualified Medical Doctor, Qualified Dentist, Qualified Nurse, Midwife, Health Visitor

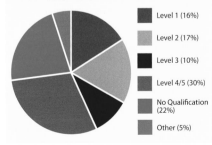

- Level 1 (16%)
- Level 2 (17%)
- Level 3 (10%)
- Level 4/5 (30%)
- No Qualification (22%)
- Other (5%)

Source: Office of National Statistics

Local Time

The UK is in the zone of UCT (Universal Coordinated Time, which is the same as Greenwich Mean Time, or GMT). Clocks go forward one hour ahead of UCT on the last Sunday of March. On the last Sunday in October, the clocks go back again to UCT. The period in between is known as British Summer Time (BST). The time changes at 01:00 on both days. The table (left) lists time differences between UCT and various cities around the world, not incorporating daylight saving time in any country.

Social & Business Hours

Many offices in London work a rigid Monday to Friday 09:00 to 17:30 week – you only have to be on the tube during rush hour to realise how many people live by this schedule. But business hours elsewhere in the city vary greatly; shops in central London are generally open until at least 19:00, Monday to Saturday, and until 18:00 on Sunday. Many larger shops are open until 20:00 and 21:00 on Thursdays. Some local grocery stores and petrol stations are open 24 hours.

Banks in central London are usually open from 09:00 to 17:00, Monday to Friday, but most are closed on Saturday afternoons and all are closed on Sunday. Post office opening times vary, but most are open from 09:00 to 17:00 Monday to Saturday.

Time Zones

Abu Dhabi	+4
Athens	+2
Auckland	+12
Bangkok	+7
Beijing	+8
Berlin	+1
Canberra	+10
Cape Town	+2
Colombo	+5.5
Denver	-7
Dubai	+4
Dublin	0
Helsinki	+2
Hong Kong	+8
Johannesburg	+2
Manila	+8
Muscat	+4
Los Angeles	-8
Mexico City	-6
Moscow	+3
New York	-5
Paris	+1
Perth	+8
Prague	+1
Rio de Janeiro	-3
Rome	+1
Santiago	-4
Singapore	+8
Sydney	+10
Tokyo	+9
Toronto	-5
Wellington	+12

School Holidays

Britain's workers may be restricted to just eight public holidays and about 20 to 25 days annual leave, but the UK's schoolkids (and teachers) get a better deal – most state schools get 13 weeks of holidays, including a whopping month and a half off in July. Those at private schools get even more.

Public Holidays

The UK has relatively few public holidays, often called 'bank holidays', compared with its European neighbours. As the alternative name suggests, banks close on public holidays, but the majority of shops tend to remain open (apart from on Christmas Day when virtually everything closes). Attractions and businesses that normally shut on Sundays will probably do so on public holidays too. There are currently eight permanent public holidays in England, with days in lieu awarded when they fall on weekends. The dates of Good Friday and Easter Monday vary each year, but are always at the end of March or early April. School holidays include the Easter and Christmas public holidays, although others may fall within term time (private school holidays tend to differ from those of state schools). See the Department of Trade and Industry's website for more details on public holidays (www.dti.gov.uk).

Public Holidays

New Year's Day	Jan 1
Good Friday	Apr 6 (2007); Mar 21 (2008)
Easter Monday	Apr 9 (2007); Mar 24 (2008)
May Day	May 7 (2007); May 5 (2008)
Spring	May 28 (2007); May 26 (2008)
Summer	Aug 27 (2007); Aug 25 (2008)
Christmas Day	Dec 25
Boxing Day	Dec 26

12

Hotting Up
*Four of the five
warmest years since
weather records began
in 1772 took place
after 1990. The
highest temperature
ever recorded in the
UK – 38.5°C – occurred
in Faversham in
August 2003.*

Climate

The stereotype of a Brit moaning about the UK's unpredictable weather – there's always too much rain or not enough – is largely a fair one. Unexpected changes in temperature and conditions are common, although locals still seem surprised, bemused and mildly annoyed.

The phrase 'April showers' has become synonymous with the weather during spring. This is probably the most unpredictable time of year: the average rainfall during the month is 6mm and the lowest temperature on record for the United Kingdom was recorded in April, but it has also been known for London to reach as high as 29°C in spring (temperatures range from an average low of about 7°C to an average high of 15°C).

Recent summers have seen record temperatures; the summer of 2005 was one of the hottest on record for Britain and much of Europe. Typically, temperatures range from an average low of about 14°C to an average high of 23°C in summer. Autumns have also been unseasonably hot in recent years. Of course, there's no guaranteeing these high temperatures, something for which regular tube users are grateful – the London Underground network has no air conditioning. In winter, London is one of the warmest places in the

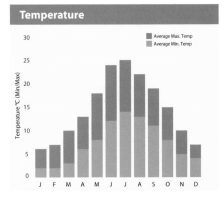

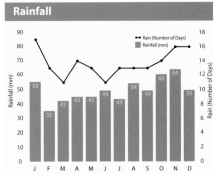

Source: Office of National Statistics

country, meaning there's little chance of snow, but it's still advisable to dress warmly (temperatures range from an average low of 2°C to an average high of 8°C in winter). These extremes and rises in temperature have, as in other cities, being blamed on global warming. However, other meteorologists have been quick to dismiss such suggestions, stating the UK has always had a variable climate. Regardless, it's sensible to have an umbrella or waterproof jacket to hand, whatever the season. For an up-to-date five-day forecast visit the Met Office website at www.met-office.gov.uk

Flora & Fauna

Suprisingly for such a huge city, with its seemingly ceaseless sprawling urban streets, nearly 40% of the capital's total area is green. It's possible to enjoy the sights and sounds of nature without leaving the city centre. As well as seven Royal Parks, plenty of trees flourish in the urban environment thanks to wind protection and heat from buildings. In south-west London, Richmond Park (p.215) has large areas of grassland, complete with lakes, rivers and grazing deer. These habitats support a fantastic array of wildlife, giving a sense of the countryside in the middle of the city. Even in the formal landscapes of the city's parks you can find butterflies and many other small creatures.

Birds

The mixture of trees, shrubs and grassland found in London's parks provides shelter, nest sites and foraging for birds such as green woodpeckers, stock doves, tawny owls, jays and robins. Many species of waterbird also breed on lakes, and others use London's parks as stopovers during migration. Away from the greenery of the parks, linnets, blackbirds, thrushes, and finches are frequent visitors to back yards – although they often fall victim to predatory cats. Not so much of a natural wonder in the city are pigeons, seen on most streets and squares, often in their hundreds. Their scrawny feathers and general unhygienic ways means they are often referred to as 'rats with wings'.

Marine Life

London's river Thames was declared 'biologically dead' as little as 50 years ago due to the level of water pollution. However, environmental controls have vastly improved the situation and the river is now awash with wildlife, including 120 species of fish. The river is now ranked among the cleanest metropolitan tideways in the world. More than 130 seals were spotted in 2006, bottlenose dolphins have also been seen upstream of London Bridge, and a whale even visited the river in early 2006, much to the fascination of Londoners and the world's media. Sadly it didn't survive the jaunt, dying during a rescue attempt, and his skeleton is now in the custody of the Natural History Museum (p.207).

Environmental Issues

London bears the pressure of millions of visitors and residents creating waste, consuming electricity and driving cars – all of which have a negative impact on the environment. However, the current mayor is committed to making the city much greener through a number of initiatives, including the Congestion Charge and encouraging recycling.

Ecosystems

A number of environmental organisations are looking to improve London's open spaces, preserving their ecosystems while making them more accessible to residents. The London Biodiversity Partnership aims to protect and improve the capital's habitats and species for future generations, while the London Wildlife Trust manages 26 nature reserves in Greater London.

Pollution

Poor air quality is estimated to cause 1,600 premature deaths in the city each year. However, it is being cleaned up considerably with the introduction of a Low Emission Zone, which will ban polluting lorries, buses, coaches and taxis from London's streets. The mayor's energy strategy will see London switch production from fossil fuels to renewable sources over the next 10 years.

Recycling & Waste

The waste produced by Londoners would fill an Olympic-size swimming pool every hour, but waste management and disposal have improved over the past 25 years as a result of higher standards and tighter controls. At the moment, about 11% of household waste is recycled, although it is estimated that the figure will rise to 25% by 2008. Each London borough provides paper, glass and aluminium recycling services and facilities for its residents – some pick up from doors, while others provide communal recycling bins.

Water

In comparison to other European cities, London's water is incredibly pure. Two major sewage treatment works have also opened in recent years, both of which contain advanced generators with the ability to convert human waste into power.

Culture

Few cities can boast a more vibrant mix of people and cultures than London. It is one of the most diverse capitals in the world – the 2001 census revealed that 29% of the city's population was from a minority ethnic group. And perhaps because of this it is hard to talk about one overall, dominant cultural way of life. From the huge Bangledeshi population in east London to the Portuguese stronghold of Stockwell, London's ethnic communities are large and varied. Some of these communities, such as the post-war Caribbean immigrants, are now up to third generation and are firmly embedded as Londoners – indeed, one of the city's major festivals, the Notting Hill Carnival, is deeply rooted in the Afro-Caribbean culture. Sizeable pockets of temporary migrants, such as young Australians and South Africans and, with the recent enlarging of the EU, eastern Europeans, also form significant communities across the capital.

Rise Up
The mayor, Ken Livingstone, underlined his liberal credentials soon after he was elected by creating the city's first festival celebrating multiculturalism. Now called Rise: London United, the mix of music, comedy and dance attracts around 100,000 people to a central London park each July.

Liberal but Anonymous

It is not just people from overseas who are drawn to the city either – a large number of the city's population, particularly people in their 20s and 30s, are drawn to London from elsewhere in the UK for professional reasons, especially to work in the finance or media sectors. Among this group, the most popular cultural practice is mainly a social one – most young people tend to go out to bars and restaurants with friends and colleagues after work and at weekends.

There is a substantial percentage of 'born and bred' Londoners too, on the whole white working-class people whose family history connects them to the area in which they live. These are not necessarily cockneys though – that distinction officially only applies to people from the East End of London.

Despite, or perhaps because of, London's liberal nature, it can also be an anonymous place in contrast to smaller towns or cities, and the transient nature of many residents means a sense of community can be hard to foster.

It would be incorrect to say London is a totally harmonious place – race-related tensions do occur and manifest themselves in violent incidents, and immigration is also a sensitive subject on the wider UK political scene. Recent events on the international stage, namely the 'war on terror', and the London bombings in 2005, have put a sharp focus on Muslims in British society too. But on the whole, Londoners are proud of their city's diversity and the fact that it remains one of the most tolerant and welcoming places to live in Europe.

Language

Other options **Language Schools** p.261

English is London's primary language, although approximately 300 others are now spoken in this multicultural city. It's not out of the ordinary to hear people ordering breakfast in Italian, chatting on the tube in Urdu, asking for coffee in Arabic or talking on their mobile in Turkish. While it may be the second language for a number of residents, nearly all instructions and signs are written in English and hundreds of language schools are regularly full of overseas students getting to grips with the universal vernacular.

Slang

Cockney rhyming slang is famous for its humorous slant on the English language. Its origins date back to the East End of the 19th century, evolving as a way for locals to communicate with each other without outsiders catching on to the meaning. To the uninitiated it can be very confusing; it works by replacing words with short phrases that rhyme with them. In its simplest form, terms such as 'boat race' are used instead of 'face', but it gets more complicated to understand when, to quicken speech, the phrase is abbreviated to only the first word or syllable. Therefore, 'plates' is used to mean 'feet' (from 'plates of meat'), and 'bees' means 'money' (from 'bees and honey'), removing the rhyming element. Today, London slang is veering away from the traditional as the recent influx of other cultures exerts its influence. Research shows that many London youths have taken on a dialect combining Bengali and cockney phrases – words such as 'nang' (meaning good) and 'creps' (trainers) have been incorporated into the local lingo. Linguists and academics may be writing reports on such developments, but these are unnecessary for most locals, who will hear the dialect first-hand from teenagers at the back of most buses.

Religion

As with language, the mix of faiths in London is incredibly diverse, with all major world religions represented. Historically, however, the city has been dominated by Christianity – which is evident from the large number of churches in the capital. The majority of British people are nominally Christian, although the number of those that attend church services on a regular basis has been falling for many years, and is significantly low.

Anglicanism is the main denomination of Christianity in the UK, and is led by the Archbishop of Canterbury, whose main residence is Lambeth Palace. The bishop of London oversees most parts of north London from St Paul's Cathedral (p.202), while churches south of the river are administered from Southwark Cathedral (p.188).

The largest Roman Catholic place of worship in England and Wales is Westminster Cathedral, from where the Archbishop of Westminster leads the English and Welsh

The Priory Church of Saint Bartholomew the Great

Catholic church. Other Christian denominations also have headquarters in the city, including the United Reformed Church, Salvation Army and Quakers.

London is the most important centre of Islam in the United Kingdom, with the boroughs of Tower Hamlets and Newham having the highest proportions of Muslims in the UK, with the London Central Mosque a well-known landmark on the edge of Regent's Park.

Over half of the UK's Hindu population lives in London, making make up a fifth of the communities in Brent, Harrow and Southall, and Neasden is home to one of largest Hindu temples in Europe. Followers of Hare Krishna are sometimes seen in London, particularly near the Radha Krishna temple in Soho. More than two-thirds of British Jews live in the capital, with significant Jewish communities in parts of north London including Stamford Hill and Golders Green.

National Dress

Unlike the Scottish, who have kilts, the English don't really have a traditional national dress. In fact, during one Miss World pageant the English contestant came out wearing a beefeater's costume in honour of the Tower of London's famous guards, such is the lack of a fitting alternative. However, due to the city's multicultural mix, it's common to see residents wearing the national dress of their native countries – although Jack Straw, Leader of the House of Commons, prompted strong debate in 2006 by stating that he would prefer Muslim women not to wear full veils as it was a 'visible statement of separation and difference'.

Food & Drink

Other options **Eating Out** p.372

Michelin Meals
London has more
Michelin-starred-
restaurants than any
other city apart from
Paris. The capital now
has 43 establishments
with the coveted
accolade (five more
than New York), led by
Gordon Ramsay's
eponymous restaurant
in Chelsea – the only
eatery in the capital
with three stars.

London's culinary reputation has taken a turn for the better in recent years. Long thought of as a place that served bland and stodgy fare, the capital is now home to some of the most diverse and high-quality eateries in Europe. According to the *Zagat Survey 2005*, London is one of the top four cities in the world in which to eat out. There are plenty of Michelin-starred fine-dining restaurants to choose from, but the city caters for all price brackets and palates. From African to Afghan and Polish to Peruvian, every type of cuisine is represented. New restaurants and bars spring up constantly as the capital picks up then drops the latest trends. In recent years canteen-style noodle bars, Thai cafes, Turkish grills and Spanish tapas bars cropped up, only to be replaced by authentic burger joints, hummus and even risotto restaurants.

There has also been a much-heralded revival in British food and local produce. The *Good Food Guide 2006* identified this growth in modern British cooking and a trend for restaurants to credit their producers, suppliers and breeds of animal – so you'll often see labels such as 'local', 'seasonal', 'well-sourced' and 'organic'. Perhaps the most commmon British cooking practice, both in the home and at restaurants, remains the traditional Sunday roast. A joint of beef, lamb, pork or chicken is roasted, accompanied by potatoes (also roasted), assorted vegetables, gravy and a yorkshire pudding, and is a firm Sunday fixture on most pub menus, where it's often washed down with a pint of beer. The other traditional British staple, fish & chips, is still sold, wrapped in newspaper, from 'chippies' across town. At the other end of the scale, the more delicate afternoon tea remains a popular, if quintessentially English, tradition at upmarket hotels such as The Ritz. Chinese food in London has been a constant over the years. Although the quality of restaurant and ingredients can vary greatly, Chinatown remains one of the most popular places to head for a late-night bite in central London. And no Londoner should have difficulty finding an English curry house; Brick Lane in the East End and Southall to the west have some of the best in the UK.

Home Cooking

The city's independent stores and markets are a food lovers' haven. Borough Market (p.368) attracts hordes of foodies for seeking its range of fresh meats, fish, bread and cheeses. There are also plenty of specialist stores, including Chinese supermarkets, Italian delicatessens, and French patisseries, not forgetting the upmarket Fortnum & Mason department store (p.356) and the foodhalls at Selfridges (p.333) and Harrods (p.332). Most major supermarkets stock a wide range of high-quality produce; Tesco, Sainsbury's, Asda and Waitrose are the big names to look out for on the high street.

Drink

The only real restriction on alcohol in the UK is how much your body can take – which is not necassarily a good thing. You can buy beer, wine and spirits from supermarkets or any number of national and local off-licence stores – you'll find at least one on most high streets – while restaurants, pubs, clubs and entertainment venues all serve alcohol, many until the early hours (see p.313). Tea and coffee are both widely consumed by most of the population.

17

You May Enter
*For a quick check on
whether you need a
visa to enter the UK,
visit the government's
website at
www.ukvisas.gov.uk*

Visas
Other options **Residence Visa** p.55, **Entry Visa** p.52

Citizens of EU countries plus Iceland, Liechtenstein, Norway and Switzerland can live and work freely in the UK. Citizens of the USA, Canada, Australia, South Africa and New Zealand only require a valid passport for a visit of up to six months, but are prohibited from working unless they secure a work permit. They must also prove that they are able to support themselves during the visit and intend to return home. A 'leave to enter' form will be given upon arrival. Citizens of Commonwealth countries who are aged between 17 and 30 and have no dependents can apply for a two-year working holiday visa prior to visiting the UK. This allows them to spend up to 50% of their trip in employment, leaving plenty of time to travel around the whole country. If you apply for this visa, your main interest in the UK must be a holiday and any work taken must be to support your travels. You will need to apply to your British High Commission before you leave your home country.

Short-term visitors from the majority of countries, including most English-speaking nations, are able to enter the UK as **visitors** and do not need to have a visa. If you enter in this way you need to be able to support yourself financially as you will not be permitted to work legally. This does not apply to the following **visa national** countries, whose citizens require a visa whatever their length of stay: Afghanistan, Albania, Algeria, Angola, Armenia, Azerbaijan, Bahrain, Bangladesh, Belarus, Benin, Bhutan, Bosnia-Herzegovina, Bulgaria, Burkina Faso, Burma, Burundi, Cambodia, Cameroon, Cape Verde, Central African Republic, Chad, China (excluding Hong Kong and Macao), Colombia, Comoros, Congo, Cuba, Cyprus, Djibouti, Dominican Republic, Ecuador, Egypt, Equatorial Guinea, Eritrea, Ethiopia, Fiji, Gabon, Gambia, Georgia, Ghana, Guinea, Guinea-Bissau, Guyana, Haiti, India, Indonesia, Iran, Iraq, Ivory Coast, Jamaica, Jordan, Kazakhstan, Kenya, Kuwait, Kyrgyzstan, Laos, Lebanon, Liberia, Libya, Macedonia, Madagascar, Malawi, Mali, Mauritania, Moldova, Mongolia, Morocco, Mozambique, Nepal, Niger, Nigeria, North Korea, Oman, Pakistan, Palestinian Authority, Peru, Philippines, Qatar, Russia, Rwanda, Sao Tome & Principe, Saudi Arabia, Senegal, Serbia and Montenegro, Sierra Leone, Somalia, Sri Lanka, Sudan, Surinam, Syria, Taiwan, Tajikistan, Tanzania, Thailand, Togo, Tunisia, Turkey, Turkmenistan, Uganda, Ukraine, United Arab Emirates, Uzbekistan, Vatican City, Vietnam, Yemen, Zambia and Zimbabwe.

Student Visas
To gain a student visa you need to be enrolled in a full-time course of at least 15 hours a week of weekday, daytime study at a single educational institution. However, EU citizens can enter the country to study without formalities. For Americans, one easy way of obtaining a work permit is with Bunac, the British Universities North American Club. It assists students in obtaining work permits for the UK, as well as a few other countries. This permit is only valid for six months per lifetime, and is not extendable, but you can work in any job for that time. With a Bunac work permit, you can also obtain a National Insurance number. See www.bunac.org for more information.

Visa Extensions
Those entering the country as visitors can only extend their stay in emergencies, such as the death of a relative or serious accident. To extend your stay in the UK, ring the Visa & Passport Information Line on 0870 6067766 before your current visa expires. Some visas, such as student visas, can be extended by simply travelling in and out of the UK. This is not always the case though; most extensions involve queuing at the Immigration & Nationality Bureau in south-east London, so always check first.

Health Requirements

The UK has high sanitation levels, but shares the same common health problems as other developed nations. Visitors from certain countries who plan to stay for longer than six months will need to be screened for tuberculosis. A new government programme permits this screening to be done in the applicant's home country before coming to the UK. There are plans to increase the list of countries on the TB screening list to include the likes of South Africa and China. See www.ukvisas.gov.uk to check your home country's status.

Customs

Like other EU nations, the UK has two customs systems; one for goods bought in another EU country, where taxes and duties have already been paid, and one for goods bought in the rest of the world. There is no limit to the amount of goods you bring to the UK from the EU – you won't be required to pay tax, as long as tax was included in the original price and the goods are for personal use. If a customs officer has any reason to suspect that goods have been bought for commercial purpose, he or she is likely to ask questions. This can result in goods being seized and, if you are found to be selling unlicensed alcohol or tobacco, it could result in up to seven years in prison. From elsewhere in the world, there are limits to the amount of duty-free products you can bring with you. Unlicensed drugs, offensive weapons, indecent and obscene material featuring children, counterfeit and pirated goods, meat, dairy and other animal products are prohibited from being brought into the UK from any destinations. Firearms, explosives and ammunition, pornography, live animals, certain plants and their produce and radio transmitters are also restricted from being brought into the UK from any destination.

Cigarettes & Alcohol

For goods purchased at airports or on ferries outside the EU, you are allowed to import either 200 cigarettes, 50 cigars or 250g of tobacco; two litres of still wine; one litre of spirits over 22% or another two litres of fortified wine, sparkling wine or liqueur; 60cc of perfume; 250cc of eau de toilette; and other goods to the value of £145.

Leaving the UK

Check-in opens three hours before departure for all long-haul flights from the UK and two-and-a-half hours before for short-haul flights from Heathrow and Gatwick. Short-haul flights from other UK regional airports open for check-in 90 minutes before departure. This might seem like a lot of waiting around, but it's often necessary due to all the additional security checks that are now in place. Getting to the airport early also increases your chances of being able to choose your seat. Most major airlines don't require reconfirmation after booking, but this does depend on the destination and, even if the airline does not stipulate that you have to reconfirm, it is still advisable for you to do so in case flight times have changed. The frequency of children travelling by themselves has led many airlines to set up specific services for what they call 'unaccompanied minors'. This covers children between the ages of 5 and 11. You'll also need to be aware of the destination country's visa and customs regulations before you travel.

E-tickets

These days, e-tickets are issued as standard on most flight routes meaning you don't have to wait to receive your ticket in the post or collect at the ticket desk – you are simply emailed confirmation of your booking. It is also possible to check in using self-service machines or online from home with many airlines (over 15 operate this service at Heathrow, including British Airways and Virgin). If you use any of these options you still need to arrive at the airport in good time to catch your flight, and also bring the credit card that was used to make the booking.

In Emergency

If the worst happens, dial 999 to call the police (free from any phone). This number will also put you in touch with the fire or ambulance services. To report non-urgent crime, contact your local police station.

In case of an accident, most major hospitals have 24 hour Accident and Emergency (A&E) departments (see p.20). Free emergency treatment is open to EU nationals, nationals of non-EU European countries upon production of a passport, and UK residents of over 12 months. NHS Direct is a confidential 24 hour helpline and website available to anyone to help diagnose medical complaints. Call to speak to a nurse for advice at any time of day or night, or see www.nhsdirect.nhs.uk.

Emergency Services

Emergency Services (Police, Fire, Ambulance)	999	Emergencies
Anti-terrorist Hotline	0800 789321	Security
EDF Energy	0800 0280247	Electricity
National Grid	0800 111999	Gas
NHS Direct	0845 4647	Medical advice
Thames Water	0845 9200800	Water
Transport for London	0845 330 9882	Lost property

Crime & Safety

Central London's crime rate isn't considered to be especially high; the violent crime rate is 22.2 per 1,000 people. Gun crime is creeping up, although this has so far been restricted to inner-city areas.

Much of central London is covered by CCTV and there is a big police presence, but sensible precautions should still be taken. Petty crime is the biggest problem that you're likely to encounter so take care when using an ATM and check that no one is looking over your shoulder. Stick to well-lit areas and don't flash money or expensive items around, and be discreet with maps and guidebooks, which can make you appear vulnerable. Never use unlicensed minicabs and have your wits about you on public transport. You should also be wary about when you wear headphones, especially white ones, as iPod theft is a common occurrence. Listening to music can affect your ability to hear potential trouble and traffic too – in 2006, 216 people were killed and 3,953 people were seriously injured on the capital's roads. Pedestrians accounted for almost half of these deaths. Generally women should have few problems travelling alone, although it's still important to be cautious, especially after dark. Common sense tells you to be observant when waiting at isolated tube, train and bus stops late at night. The taxi firm Ladycabs (7254 3501) has female drivers and caters for women travelling alone.

Police

London's police force is the Metropolitan Police, known colloquially as 'The Met'. There are over 30,000 officers operating in the capital, including members of the British Transport Police, who are responsible for preventing crime on trains and the London Underground. The Met also has a division that patrols the Thames in speedboats, and operates a floating police station near Waterloo Bridge.

The City of London has its own police force, over 1,000 strong, which is responsible for policing the Square Mile. The forces are separate, but wear similar navy blue uniforms, as do Police Community Support Officers (PCSOs), who patrol mainly on foot. Since the terrorist bombings of July 2005, the presence of police officers in central London has noticeably increased, but they remain a rarer sight in residential streets, where PCSOs are more visible.

Police Community Support Officers As part of the Metropolitan Police's 'safer neighbourhood' scheme, Police Community Support Officers have been recruited in growing numbers to reassure Londoners. These officers patrol on foot, and although they don't have the power of full police officers, they can issue fixed penalty notices, confiscate alcohol and disrupt anti-social behaviour.

Embassies & Consulates

Name	Telephone	Area
Argentina	7318 1300	W1
Australia	7379 4334	WC2
Austria	7235 3731	SW1
Belgium	7470 3700	SW1
Brazil	7499 0877	W1
Canada	7258 6506	W1
China	7299 4049	W1
Denmark	7333 0200	SW1
Greece	7221 6467	W11
Finland	7838 6200	SW1
France	7073 1000	SW1
Germany	7824 1300	SW1
India	7836 8484	WC2
Iran	7225 3000	SW7
Italy	7312 2200	W1
Japan	7465 6500	W1
Jordan	0870 0056952	W8
Lebanon	7229 7265	W8
Malaysia	7235 8033	SW1
Mexico	7499 8586	W1
Norway	7591 5500	SW1
Oman	7225 0001	SW15
Pakistan	7664 9200	SW1
Russia	7229 8027	W8
South Africa	7451 7299	WC2
Spain	7235 5555	SW1
Sri Lanka	7262 1841	W2
Thailand	7589 2944	SW7
Turkey	7591 6900	SW7
United Arab Emirates	0870 0056984	SW7
United States	7499 9000	W1

Dos & Don'ts

Several London boroughs, including Hammersmith & Fulham, have introduced blanket bans on anti-social public drinking. This doesn't mean you can't enjoy a glass of wine with a picnic or outside a pub, but it does give the police and council officers power to stop anyone drinking alcohol if they think it is causing a nuisance or distress to others. After much political and public debate, smoking in public will be banned from July 1 2007. This means lighting up will be outlawed in all enclosed public places in England, including pubs and restaurants. Smokers having a cigarette in public face on-the-spot fines of £50. Don't expect premises to turn a blind eye – they will be fined up to £2,500 if anyone is caught smoking. Several London boroughs have laws allowing them to impose on-the-spot fines of £50 on someone caught dropping litter. The same fine stands for dog owners who allow their pets to foul in public.

Lost/Stolen Property

Stolen or lost possessions should be reported immediately to the police. If you are unfortunate enough to have your passport stolen, you should also report the matter to your country's embassy in London. Enquiries about items left on trains or at overland stations can be made by calling 7928 5151. Alternatively, for belongings lost on the bus or tube, visit Transport for London's lost property office at 200 Baker Street (0845 3309882 or www.tfl.gov.uk). It receives over 600 items each working day so your chances of being reunited with your valuables are fairly good.

Travelling with Children

With its crowds, traffic and complex transport system, London might seem like a hostile place for children, but if you do your research, it can be a delight. The mayor has introduced a campaign to make the capital a more child-friendly city. All children under the age of 16 can travel free on buses and trams throughout London at any time, while children under the age of 11 may travel free on the tube from 09:30 on weekdays and at any time during weekends and public holidays (provided they are accompanied by an adult). Children under the age of 5 can travel free on London transport at anytime. There are plenty of hotels that offer family rooms, based on two adults sharing with two children. Premier Travel Inn, Travelodge and Novotel all offer this service, and Novotel also offers free breakfast for children.

Family-orientated restaurants and cafes are also common, with some offering child menus, and even free food for certain age groups. The Natural History Museum (p.207) and the Science Museum (p.207), are great fun for children, with hands-on exhibits to keep them engaged – the free admission is an added bonus.

Area Dialling Codes

Belfast	028
Birmingham	0121
Bristol	0117
Cardiff	029
Edinburgh	0131
Glasgow	0141
Leeds	0113
Liverpool	0151
London	020
Manchester	0161
Newcastle upon Tyne	0191
Nottingham	0115
Sheffield	0114

Disabled Visitors

Thanks to the Disability Discrimination Act of 1995, all new tourist attractions and hotels now make full provision for wheelchair users, and access to public places has greatly improved. Many older buildings such as museums make extra efforts for individual requirements. This can include free wheelchair hire, induction loops and braille guides.

The tube network has been hard to modernise as access to most stations is via escalators and steps. Newer routes, such as the Jubilee line, have more stations with lift services though, and almost all London buses are wheelchair accessible.

The national Blue Badge scheme, which allows special parking access for disabled car users, has only limited application in Westminster, the City of London and parts of Kensington, Chelsea and Camden, where badge holders are not allowed to park on yellow lines during the day.

However, badge holders can make a one-off payment of £10 and will then be exempt from paying the Congestion Charge. See www.london.gov.uk for more information.

Electricity

The standard voltage throughout the UK is 230-240V AC, 50Hz. Plugs have three square prongs. Adaptors for European, Australasian and American electrical items are available at most airports and good electrical stores.

Telephone & Internet

London's traditional red phone boxes are now tourist attractions in their own right – most have been replaced by much less attractive modern boxes. With the rise of mobile phone use, pay phones aren't the necessity they used to be and as a result some are more commonly used as public toilets. If you can hold your breath, most take coins, phone cards and credit cards. Pre-paid phone cards, sold in denominations of £5, £10, £15 and £20, can be bought from selected newsagents.

British Telecom has pinned its hopes for the survival of the public phone on the fact that it is now possible to check and send emails from them, but it can be expensive.

London is generally very net-friendly – many hotel rooms have internet access and there are a huge number of internet cafes across the city. The biggest and easiest to use are easyEverything (www.easyeverything.com), which has various branches in central London. Rates start at £1 for 30 minutes. Keep an eye on your belongings while you surf though as pick-pocketing does occur when people are distracted. For laptop users, most of the large hotels offer free Wi-Fi access. Larger coffee shop chains charge for the service, but several smaller cafes and pubs offer it for free to attract custom.

Post & Courier Services

Post in the UK is generally efficient, but you can't rely on its speed, while post offices can be chaotic with lengthy queues. Stamps can be bought at post offices, vending machines, supermarkets and newsagents; you can find your nearest post office at www.royalmail.com.

Items weighing under 1kg can be sent either by first or second class post; first class mail aims to deliver your letter or packet the next day (apart from Sundays, when there is no delivery) and currently costs 32p for standard-sized letters and small items weighing up

Courier Companies

CitiPak	0870 0661866	www.citipak.co.uk
City Bikes	7735 5888	www.citybikes.biz
City Sprint	7880 1000	www.citysprint.co.uk
CourierNet	8830 1413	www.couriernet.co.uk
DHL	0870 1100300	www.dhl.co.uk
ecourier	0870 0853333	www.ecourier.co.uk
Online Courier	0800 600006	www.online-couriers.co.uk
TNT	0808 2620808	www.tntpost.co.uk
UPS	7491 0022	www.ups.com

to 100g. Second class post is a slower service normally delivered within three working days, but is up to a third cheaper than the first class service. A new facility offered by Royal Mail allows you to print your postage from your PC with a pre-paid account so you'll never run out of stamps again – again, see www.royalmail.com for details. Airmail starts at 44p for a postcard or letter weighing up to 20g and takes on average between three and seven days to deliver. The UK's iconic red post boxes can be found on pavements around the capital, and also outside all post offices.

Alternatively, courier companies offer delivery services ranging from the filing of business papers at administrative offices to the immediate transporting of items across the city, whether by messenger bike or parcel van (see p.22).

Drinking Water
The DWI (Drinking Water Inspectorate) says tap water is safe to drink in London, although excess air can sometimes make it appear cloudy when you first fill a glass.

What to Wear

One of the things you can rely on in London is the unreliability of weather. While the UK's climate can hardly be called extreme compared with some other parts of the world, the unpredictability means it's advisable to be prepared for most possibilities when dressing. It can get very cold in the winter, with temperatures in low single figures, so it's sensible to wrap up in warm clothing, including a hat and scarf. Summers, while not consistently sweltering, tend to have several hot spells, where temperatures can reach the high 30s. The main thing to be prepared for, however, is rain – it can pour down at a moment's notice, whatever the month. The key to being comfortable is layering – so you can adjust to temperature changes – and having a waterproof jacket and umbrella to hand.

Tourist Information

The capital's main tourist office is the Britain and London Visitor Centre at Lower Regent Street (0870 1566366), near Piccadilly Circus tube. It's open seven days a week, from 09:00 to 18:30 on weekdays (09:30 on Mondays), and from 10:00 to 16:00 at weekends (09:00 to 17:00 on Saturdays from June to September). The shop provides free information, travel and destination advice for visitors to London and Britain, and can help with booking tickets, accommodation and transport. Staff are multilingual, meaning that queries can be answered in French, German, Italian, Russian and Japanese, among others. The London Information Centre in Leicester Square (7292 2333) provides a similar service, and is open from 08:00 to 23:00 on weekdays and 10:00 to 18:00 on weekends. There are several other local tourist information offices around town, see www.visitbritain.com for locations.

Overseas Information

VisitBritain, the official agency for promoting travel to the UK, operates a network of over 20 overseas offices which are useful for planning your visit before you travel. Around 60% of VisitBritain's staff are based overseas with the remainder in London. Visit London (www.visitlondon.com) is a useful resource for events listings, tickets, maps and downloadable guides to eating and shopping.

VisitBritain Overseas Offices		
Australia	Sydney	+61 293774400
Belgium	Brussels	+32 26463510
Canada	Toronto	+1 4169256326
Denmark	Copenhagen	+45 33339188
France	Paris	+33 144515621
Germany	Frankfurt	+49 692380711
Ireland	Dublin	+353 16708000
Italy	Rome	+39 0668806821
Netherlands	Amsterdam	+31 206855051
New Zealand	Auckland	+64 93031446
South Africa	Johannesburg	+27 113250342
USA	New York	+1 2129862200

23

Places to Stay

Although London can be pricey, it is packed full of accommodation options for every taste and budget. According to the latest figures from Visit London, there are 564 hotels in London and 165,846 beds, with occupancy rates high enough to make advance booking recommended. At the top end of the market there are several world-renowned five-star hotels such as The Ritz, The Savoy, The Dorchester and Claridge's. For those with a lighter purse, hostel accommodation in London has improved greatly, with cheap digs appearing more regularly in recent years. Prices are more competitive than they used to be, but it's always best to compare various online sources before booking.

Hotels

Hotel accommodation in London used to suffer similar criticism to that of the rest of the capital – it was cramped, overpriced and came with shocking customer service. If you did find something to suit your taste it was then unlikely to fit your budget. But thankfully times have changed. London's hotel options are now as varied and plentiful as the rest of the city's attractions, and more competitively priced. The city's world-famous luxury hotels have been joined by an increasing number of stylish boutique and budget hotels, as well as innovative bed and breakfasts, and 'pod' hotels for those who want a place to sleep and little else. Places to stay are also starting to crop up outside of traditional tourist spots; good news for those looking for some peace and quiet, and to explore beyond the city's main sights.

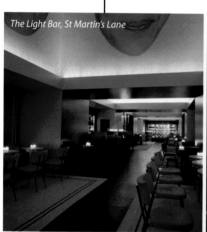
The Light Bar, St Martin's Lane

Renaissance Chancery Court London

Claridge's

Main Hotels

Claridge's

Brook St
W1
⊖ Mayfair

7629 8860 | www.theclaridgeshotellondon.com

This elegant hotel is a London institution. For over a century it has enjoyed the company of illustrious guests and various royal families, all attracted to the hotel's huge, plush rooms, and art deco flourishes. There are 203 of them, as well as luxurious suites. The hotel's Gordon Ramsay restaurant, a recent addition, has become an attraction in its own right (see p.395).

Covent Garden Hotel

10 Monmouth St
WC2
⊖ Tottenham Court Road

7806 1000 | www.firmdale.com/covent.html

Situated in the heart of London's theatreland, this stylish hotel, which was once a hospital, has become a major hangout for the film crowd, who often make use of the hotel's screening rooms. There are 58 individually designed bedrooms and suites, mostly with huge windows overlooking the rooftops of central London.

The Dorchester

Park Lane
W1
⊖ Marble Arch

7629 8888 | www.thedorchester.com

A stone's throw from London's most exclusive shopping districts and with suites that overlook Hyde Park, The Dorchester isn't shy of claiming that it was built on 'the most prestigious acre and a half of real estate in the world'. Its 250 luxury rooms are fit for those with only the fattest of wallets.

Great Eastern

Liverpool St
EC2
⊖ Liverpool Street

7618 5000 | www.london.greateastern.hyatt.com

Now part of the Hyatt chain, the Great Eastern sits next to Liverpool Street station in an historic Victorian building. Redevloped by Sir Terence Conran a few years back, it's now a slick sanctuary of modern art, design and fine dining. It has 267 rooms, six restaurants and bars, and eco-friendly water systems in its bathrooms.

Hazlitt's

6 Frith Street
W1
⊖ Oxford Circus

7829 9888 | www.rookeryhotel.com

Situated right in the heart of Soho, Hazlitt's occupies three Georgian houses in Frith Street which date from 1718. Famed for its good old-fashioned service and plain old furniture, Hazlitt's is a slice of English eccentricity in the heart of one of the city's most cosmopolitan districts.

25

81 Great Eastern St
EC2
⊖ *Old Street*

Hoxton Hotel

7550 1000 | *www.hoxtonhotels.com*
This hotel's sleek decor, mod-cons and plump bed linen should impress most visitors – especially as its prices are more than reasonable. Small rooms cost from £59 a night with free water, fresh milk, free Wi-Fi and phone calls charged at standard rates. Its location, a short hop from both the City and Hoxton's hipster bars, make it popular with both businessmen and tourists.

Cadogan Place
SW1
⊖ *Victoria*

Jumeirah Carlton Tower

7235 1234 | *www.jumeirahcarltontower.com*
The owners of the 'seven-star' Burj Al Arab in Dubai and Essex House in New York now have two properties in London. This 220 roomer overlooking Cadogan Place is a short stroll from Harrods and Harvey Nichols and is hugely popular with business travelers and shoppers. The Peak Health Club & Spa on the ninth floor offers spectacular views to counter all that unpleasant sweating.

Richmond Way
W14
⊖ *Shepherd's Bush*

K West

0870 0274343 | *www.k-west.co.uk*
Nestled in Shepherd's Bush, K West has become an unlikely late night hang-out for debauched Londoners – passing rock stars can often be spotted staggering to their rooms. For those of a more healthy persuasion, the hotel's K Spa is undoubtedly one of the most stylish places in the city to relax and unwind.

1 Aldwych
WC2
⊖ *Covent Garden*

One Aldwych

7300 1000 | *www.onealdwych.co.uk*
Handily placed for both The City and West End, One Aldwych has racked up the awards in its relatively short life. Housed in a renowned Edwardian building that dates from 1907, the hotel is arguably the most cutting-edge and contemporary in the capital. It has a collection of more than 400 works of contemporary art - there is a piece in each of the 105 rooms - and the swimming pool plays music.

252 High Holborn
WC1
⊖ *Holborn*

Renaissance Chancery Court London

7829 9888 | *www.renaissancehotels.com*
This landmark structure, built by the Pearl Assurance Company in 1914, has only recently been turned into a hotel. And so striking is the building that it has been featured in numerous film and TV productions. But if the grand architecture doesn't floor you, the high-class facilities, including a very swish spa and restaurant, definitely will.

26

The Ritz

150 Picadilly
W1
Picadilly Circus

7493 8181 | *www.theritzlondon.com*
London's most famous hotel is a tourist attraction in its own right. Standing proud at 150 Picadilly since 1906, The Ritz is ridiculously opulent (it has its own line in fine jewellery) – and expensive. Although its world-famous afternoon tea is a more reasonable, if similarly luxurious, proposition. The Ritz prides itself on having two members of staff per guest room.

The Rookery

Cowcross St
EC1
Farringdon

7336 0931 | *www.rookeryhotel.com*
Located near the winding lanes of Old Smithfield, known as 'rookeries' due to the high proportion of crooks and criminals which frequented them, The Rookery is crammed full of antiques, sumptuous bedrooms and cosy public rooms. Arguably the most romantic place to stay in the city.

The Sanderson

50 Berners Lane
W1
Oxford Circus

7300 1400 | *www.sandersonlondon.com*
The listed 60s office block that houses the Sanderson doesn't have the most elegant facade, but Ian Schrager, the king of New York style, has, in partnership with Phillipe Starck, worked his magic. The hotel comes complete with a bamboo-filled roof garden, a large courtyard, spa, restaurant and several uber-cool bars.

The Savoy

The Strand
WC2
Covent Garden

7836 4343 | *www.fairmont.com/savoy*
Now part of the Fairmont chain of hotels, The Savoy vies with The Ritz as London's most prestigious hotel. Guests have included Winston Churchill, Marilyn Monroe and various members of the Royal Family since the hotel was opened on The Strand in 1889. Some of the hotel's 250 rooms offer great views of the Thames, and its signature restaurant, The Savoy Grill, has a Michelin star.

St Martins Lane

45 St Martin's Lane
WC2
Covent Garden

7300 5500 | *www.stmartinslane.com*
The brightly coloured revolving doors of St Martins Lane stop passersby in their tracks, and combined with the lobby's light installations, set the (modern) arty tone. Another successful partnership between Ian Schrager and Phillipe Starck, St Martins Lane has 200 rooms over nine floors. The garden rooms on the first floor have landscaped patios; something of a rarity in this part of town.

27

Hotels

Five Star	Phone	Website
Baglioni	7368 5700	www.baglionihotels.com
The Berkeley	7235 6000	www.theberkeleyhotellondon.com
The Berners Hotel	7666 2000	www.thebernershotel.co.uk
Blakes Hotel	7373 6701	www.blakeshotels.com
Brown's	7493 6020	www.brownshotel.com
Charlotte Street Hotel	7806 2000	www.charlottestreethotel.com
Claridge's	7629 8860	www.theclaridgeshotellondon.com
The Connaught	7499 7070	www.theconnaughthotellondon.com
Covent Garden Hotel	7806 1000	www.charlottestreethotel.com
The Dorchester	7629 8888	www.thedorchester.com
Dorset Square Hotel	7723 7874	www.dorsetsquare.co.uk
Goring Hotel	7396 9000	www.goringhotel.co.uk
Grange City Hotel	7863 3700	www.grangehotels.co.uk
Grange Holborn Hotel	7242 1800	www.grangecityhotel.co.uk
Great Eastern	7618 5000	www.great-eastern-hotel.co.uk
Grosvenor House	7499 6363	www.marriotthotels.com
Halkin	7333 1000	www.halkin.co.uk
The Hempel	7298 9000	www.the-hempel.co.uk
Hilton London Canary Wharf	3002 2300	www.hilton.co.uk/canarywharf
Hilton London Docklands Riverside	7231 1001	www.hilton.co.uk/docklands
Hilton London Euston Hotel	7943 4500	www.hilton.co.uk/euston
Hilton London Green Park	7629 7522	www.hilton.co.uk/greenpark
Hilton London Hyde Park Hotel	7221 2217	www.hilton.co.uk/hydepark
Hilton London Metropole	7402 4141	www.hilton.co.uk/londonmet
Jumeirah Carlton Tower	7235 1234	www.jumeirahcarltontower.com
Jumeirah Lowndes Hotel	7823 1234	www.jumeirahlowndeshotel.com
Knightsbridge Hotel	7584 6300	www.charlottestreethotel.com
The Lanesborough	7259 5599	www.lanesborough.com
Le Méridien Piccadilly	7734 8000	www.starwoodhotels.com
London Marriott Country Hall	7928 5200	www.marriott.com
London Marriott Hotel Grosvenor Square	7493 1232	www.marriotthotels.com
London Marriott Hotel Kensington	7973 1000	www.marriotthotels.com
London Marriott Hotel Park Lane	7493 7000	www.marriotthotels.com
London Marriott West India Quay	7093 1000	www.marriotthotels.com
Metropolitan	7447 1000	www.metropolitan.como.bz
myhotel Chelsea	7667 6000	www.myhotels.com
Number Five Maddox Street	7647 0200	www.living-rooms.co.uk
One Aldwych	7300 1000	www.onealdwych.com
The Park Lane Hotel	7499 6321	www.starwoodhotels.com
Radisson Edwardian May Fair Hotel London	0800 374411	www.radissonedwardian.com/mayfair
Renaissance Chancery Court London	7829 9888	www.renaissancehotels.com
The Ritz London	7493 8181	www.theritzlondon.com
Royal Garden Hotel	7937 8000	www.royalgardenhotel.co.uk
The Sanderson	7300 1400	www.sandersonlondon.com
The Savoy	7836 4343	www.savoygroup.co.uk
Sheraton Belgravia Hotel	7235 6040	www.starwoodhotels.com
Sheraton Park Tower	7235 8050	www.starwoodhotels.com
The Soho Hotel	7559 3000	www.charlottestreethotel.com
St Martins Lane	7300 5500	www.stmartinslane.com
Tower Thistle	7481 2575	www.thistlehotels.com

28

Hotels

Four Star	Phone	Website
Ambassadors Hotel in Bloomsbury	7693 5400	www.ambassadors.co.uk
The Chamberlain	01895 259809	www.fullershotels.com
City Inn Westminster	7630 1000	www.cityinn.com
The Clarendon Hotel	8318 4321	www.clarendonhotel.com
The Colonnade	7286 1052	www.theetoncollection.com
Corus Hotel Hyde Park	0870 6096161	www.corushotels.co.uk
Crown Moran Hotel	8452 4175	www.crownmoranhotel.co.uk
Danubius Hotel Regents Park	7722 7722	www.danubiuslondon.co.uk
Durrants Hotel	7935 8131	www.durrantshotel.co.uk
Express By Holiday Inn City	7300 4300	www.hiexpress.co.uk
Express By Holiday Inn Earl's Court	7384 5151	www.hiexpress.co.uk
Express By Holiday Inn Hammersmith	8746 5100	www.hiexpress.co.uk
Express By Holiday Inn Limehouse	7791 3850	www.hiexpress.co.uk
Express By Holiday Inn Southwark	7401 2525	www.hiexpress.co.uk
Express By Holiday Inn Stratford	8536 8000	www.hiexpress.co.uk
Express By Holiday Inn Swiss Cottage	7433 6666	www.hiexpress.co.uk
Express By Holiday Inn Victoria	7630 8888	www.hiexpress.co.uk
Express By Holiday Inn Wandsworth	0870 7201298	www.hiexpress.co.uk
Five Sumner Place	7584 7586	www.sumnerplace.com
Gainsborough Hotel	7957 0000	www.hotelgainsborough.co.uk
Grange White Hall Hotel	7580 2224	www.grangehotels.com
Hazlitt's	7434 1771	www.hazlittshotel.com
Hilton London Islington Hotel	7354 7700	www.hilton.co.uk/islington
Hilton London Tower Bridge	3002 4300	www.hilton.co.uk/towerbridge
Holiday Inn Brent Cross	0870 4009112	www.hiexpress.co.uk
Holiday Inn Camden Lock	7485 4343	www.hiexpress.co.uk
Jurys Clifton Ford Hotel	7486 6600	www.jurysdoyle.com
Jurys Great Russel Street	7347 1000	www.jurysdoyle.com
Jurys Kensington Hotel	7589 6300	www.jurysdoyle.com
La Suite Executive Hotel	7487 8100	www.lasuitehotel.com
The Lennox Hotel	0870 8503317	www.pemct.co.uk
London Bridge Hotel	7855 2200	www.london-bridge-hotel.co.uk
London Marriott Hotel Maida Vale	7543 6000	www.marriotthotels.com
London Marriott Hotel Marble Arch	7723 1277	www.marriotthotels.com
London Marriott Hotel Regents Park	7722 7711	www.marriotthotels.com
Number Sixteen	7589 5232	www.charlottestreethotel.com
Park Lane Mews Hotel	7493 7222	http://london.park-lane-mews-hotel.tobook.com
The Pelham Hotel	7589 8288	www.charlottestreethotel.com
The Portland	7580 7088	www.grangeholbornhotel.com/the_portland_hotel
The Portobello Hotel	7727 2777	www.portobello-hotel.co.uk
Radisson Edwardian Mountbatten Hotel	7836 4300	www.radissonedwardian.com/mountbatten
The Rookery	7336 0931	www.rookeryhotel.com
The White House	7387 1200	www.solmelia.com
The Zetter	7324 4444	www.thezetter.com
Three Star	Phone	Website
Basil Street Hotel	7581 3311	na
Bedford Hotel	7636 7822	na
Brompton Hotel	7584 4517	www.bromhotel.com
City Hotel	7247 3313	www.cityhotellondon.co.uk
Cranley Gardens Hotel	7373 3232	www.cranleygardenshotel.com
Elizabeth Hotel	7828 6812	www.elizabeth-hotel.com
Gresham Hotel	7580 4232	www.greshamhotellondon.com
Harlingford	7387 1551	www.harlingfordhotel.com
Jurys Inn Chelsea	7411 2200	www.jurysdoyle.com

29

Hotel Apartments

Hotel apartments offer a cheaper alternative to hotels for families, large groups or those on short-term work contracts. Not only that, but they also allow visitors the chance to feel more at home; most come complete with kitchens, linen and dining areas. Apartment accommodation ranges from luxury serviced suites such as the Athenaeum in the heart of Mayfair (www.athenaeumhotel.com), to shared options such as Alexander Fleming House (www.studystay.com) in Hoxton, which is comprised of self-contained flats.

Bed & Breakfasts

Bed & Breakfasts	
Aster House	www.asterhouse.com
B&B Belgravia	www.bb-belgravia.com
Bulldog Club	www.bulldogclub.com
Guesthouse West	www.guesthousewest.com
Jesmond Dene Hotel	www.jesmonddenehotel.co.uk
Lime Tree Hotel	www.limetreehotel.co.uk
Luna & Simone Hotel	www.lunasimonehotel.com
The Boulevard Hotel	www.boulevardhoteluk.com
The Lord Jim Hotel	www.lgh-hotels.com
The Main House	www.themainhouse.com

Bed & Breakfasts

Most bed and breakfasts (B&B) are housed in former residential properties, which means rooms can be small. However, they normally include the same amenities as hotels, including TVs, tea and coffee-making facilities and telephones, but at a fraction of the price. B&Bs also normally offer a more 'intimate' experience, with plenty of chat in communal areas – which can be a plus or downside, depending on your point of view.

Budget Accommodation		
Astor Victoria	7834 3077	www.astorhostels.com
Astors Museum Inn	7580 5360	www.astorhostels.com
easyHotel	7373 1977	www.easyhotel.com
Goldsmiths House	7387 4501	www.hostelworld.com
Hyde Park Inn	7229 0000	www.hydeparkinn.com
Kipper Projects	8980 1401	www.kipperproject.org.uk
My Pad	7262 4471	www.mypadlondon.co.uk
Palmers Lodge	7483 8470	www.palmerslodge.co.uk
Piccadilly Hostel	7434 9009	www.piccadillybackpackers.com
St Christopher's Village	7407 1856	www.st-christophers.co.uk
YHA London Thameside	7232 2114	www.yha.org.uk

Budget

Although London has a reputation for being expensive, its budget options and hostel accommodation has improved greatly. The constant influx of international travellers means that there are cheap, stylish and modern digs appearing in nearly every location – including central options. Most offer dormitory-style accommodation as well as private rooms, and some come with en-suite bathrooms. They also offer a ready-made community, ideal for lone travellers bored of their own company.

King's College,
The Strand
WC2
⊖ Charing Cross

King's College London Halls of Residence

7848 1700 | www.kcl.ac.uk

Relive your school years in style by staying at this university's halls of residence. Only available in the summer months, the four different residences at Hampstead, Waterloo, London Bridge and Denmark Hill offer B&B or room-only en suite accommodation from £19 per night. It would be very hard to find somewhere cheaper in central London than this.

12 Sherwood St
W1
⊖ Picadilly Circus

Piccadilly Backpackers

7434 9009 | www.piccadillyhotel.net

In this giant warren of a hostel, which has 700 beds, conventional dormitories with each having been converted into capsule-style pods – six in each room in a two-up, three-across formation with stepladders – giving much more privacy than some shared hostel rooms. At around £18 a night, the rooms, which contain sinks and lockers, are a bargain for central London.

MOTO**RAZR** *maxx* **V6**

Move faster with 3.5G HSDPA high speed mobile broadband, external touch music keys and a 2 mega-pixel camera with flash. **The new MOTORAZR maxx V6. Cutting-edge speed for cutting-edge style.**

hellomoto.com

Getting Around
Other options **Maps** p.78, **Exploring** p.162

It might look like an initmidating sprawl, but once divided into north, south, east and west, London is surprisingly easy to navigate, despite not having the grid layout of other cities. The public transport system gets a hard time, sometimes deservedly so, but

it is generally reliable; a TripAdvisor survey recently judged the city to be the best overall for public transport, ahead of New York and Paris. Further improvements are promised in the run-up to the 2012 Olympic Games, including expansion of the underground (or tube, as it is commonly known) in London's currently neglected East End, and a tram system running from north to south.

There is a dense network of buses, including routes that operate through the night, and this can be a cheap and convenient option – once you figure out which one goes where. There are extensive roadworks planned over the next few years, making driving in the capital not particularly adviseable – most people soon find that the tube is the quicker option. Parking restrictions (policed by over-zealous wardens and accompanied by high penalties), coupled with the Congestion Charge, make motoring even less appealing.

Cycling on the streets of the city centre can be a slightly stressful experience, but it's certainly practical for many commuters – the number of cyclists in London has rocketed in recent years. Those who like the feel of a free-wheel might find a pedicab journey more rewarding; around 200 three-wheel rickshaw-style cabs have been operating in London's West End for several years and it's an enjoyable ride, especially after a drink or two, although the fee should be agreed upon before boarding. The same goes for minicabs, which must be booked in advance; black cabs, however, operate metered fares and can be hailed from the street.

Transport for London's extensive website provides up-to-the-minute information on all modes of London transport and its Travel Information Centres are located at stations throughout the city, including Piccadilly Circus, Victoria and Liverpool Street, plus Heathrow airport. The website's Journey Planner feature (www.tfl.gov.uk/journeyplanner) tells you the best routes to and from specific locations, by rail, tube, bus, bike, or on foot.

Air
Other options **Leaving the UK** p.19

International flights to London arrive at either Heathrow (LHR), 15 miles west of London; Gatwick (LGW), 27 miles to the south; Stansted (STN), 35 miles north-east; Luton (LTN), 30 miles to the north; or City (LCY), which is by the Thames in east London.

Heathrow is the world's busiest international airport and second busiest cargo port. More than 90 airlines have made it their base, and over 62 million passengers pass through the airport each year. Heathrow currently has four terminals, with a fifth terminal set to open in 2008. Terminals 3 and 4 handle transatlantic flights (the UK national airline, British Airways, uses Terminal 4). A shuttle bus operates between the terminals, and the Heathrow Express is free between terminals 1,2,3 and 4.

Gatwick is London's second gateway and has two terminals, North and South. The airport has rapidly expanded in recent years and now has 21 scheduled flights to US

Airlines

Air France	0870 1424343	www.airfrance.com
Air India	7565 7979	www.air-india.com
bmibaby.com	0871 2240224	www.bmibaby.com
British Airways	0870 8509850	www.britishairways.com
easyJet	0871 2442366	www.easyjet.com
Emirates Airline	7808 0033	www.emirates.com
KLM Royal Dutch Airlines	8750 9200	www.klm.com
Lufthansa	0870 8377747	www.lufthansa.com
Olympic Airlines	0870 6060460	www.olympicairlines.com
Ryanair	0871 2460000	www.ryanair.com
Singapore Arilines	0870 4146666	www.singaporeair.com
United Airlines	0845 8444777	www.ual.com
Virgin Atlantic	0870 3802007	www.virgin-atlantic.com

destinations, as well as several charter flights, which use the South Terminal. A shuttle train operates between the terminals.

City, Luton and the state-of-the-art Stansted (designed by Sir Norman Foster), are mainly served by European airlines, and no-frills carriers such as Ryanair and easyJet. London has excellent bus and train connections between its airports and the centre. Trains can be quick, especially the Gatwick and Heathrow Express services, but you'll have to get yourself and your luggage to the carriage. Airport link buses (generally operated by National Express) may ease the luggage hassle and drop you closer to central hotels, but they're at the mercy of London traffic. Taxis can be more convenient than buses, but are much more expensive.

Airport Bus Services

There are several bus companies and routes that operate from London's airports. Journey times vary, and are dependent on the state of the busy traffic. Also, if you have an early morning or late night departure or arrival you should confirm what time the services start and finish. It is worth booking a seat at peak times in case the bus fills up.

From Heathrow – National Express runs coaches to Victoria station from early morning to late night; check for times. The journey takes about 40 minutes and costs £10 one-way, with a coach leaving approximately every 20 minutes. See www.nationalexpress.com for more information and booking details. For late night arrivals or departures, the N9 night bus runs every half hour to Trafalgar Square – check out www.tfl.gov.uk/buses for route and time details.

From Gatwick – National Express coaches take about 80 minutes from Gatwick into town and cost £6.60 one-way. Services leave the airport for central London (Victoria coach station) every hour. See www.nationalexpress.com for further details.

From Stansted – Terravision Express operates two services per hour to Victoria coach station. The single fare is £8.50 and the journey takes roughly 75 minutes. Go to www.lowcostcoach.com for further information.

From Luton – easyBus runs every 40 minutes to Baker Street. It's a cheap service – fares cost from £1 and the journey takes just under an hour. See www.easybus.co.uk.

From City – since the opening of the Docklands Light Railway, City airport has moved away from using mainly airport shuttle bus services and now utilises the trains. The DLR goes directly to Bank station. The fare is £3 one-way and takes just over 20 minutes. See www.tfl.gov.uk/tube for more information.

33

Boat

In the past five years, riverboat piers have opened at Millbank, Blackfriars, Woolwich Arsenal, Bankside, Poplar and Waterloo, making commuting by Thames a much more viable option. Services are popular with visitors and commuters alike; since the terrorist attacks on the tube in July 2005, traffic on the river has soared by a whopping 40%.

However, for a more relaxing cruise, there are many leisurely services, offered by various companies, which go as far as Hampton Court in the west and Greenwich in the east, as well as lunch and dinner cruises. Go to www.tfl.gov.uk/river for more information.

> ### London is Your Oyster
> If you're planning on using public transport fairly frequently, you should consider getting an Oyster card. These electronic swipe cards, available from tube stations, can be loaded with either credit or a weekly, monthly or annual travelcard, and will save you money on the single fare. They are vaild on tube, bus and some train services, and give discounts on boat services.

Bus

Any Requests?
A lot of bus stops are 'request' only, so if you don't stick your hand out to hail the bus you want, it will invariably sail past without you and you'll have to wait for the next one.

London's network of buses can seem quite complex, but once you get used to hopping on and off it's quite easy to negotiate and a great way to get around. The majority of the capital's buses are distinctive red double-deckers – although they're all now modern versions, as the famous Routemasters went out of service in 2005.

In some areas, such as parts of east London where the tube service isn't available, certain bus routes are essential for commuters and can therefore get quite busy. This also means that a lot of effort has gone into running a reliable service – and on some streets buses are more frequent than taxis.

Tickets must be purchased before boarding in central London (Zone 1) and are available for £1.50 from machines at bus stops, although it can be easier and cheaper to buy a bus pass, carnet tickets (a pack of six costs £3.90) or credit on an Oyster card. These are available at Travel Information Centres, some bus stops, and newsagents (look for the bus symbol in the window).

Most services operate from 05:00 to 00:30, with certain routes now operating 24 hour services. A network of night buses is also available. These are generally reliable, but journeys from the West End can get pretty rowdy at weekends.

Car

Other options **Transportation** p.153

Having a car in the capital can be a headache. Many parts of central London are designated for residents-only parking, and where meter or pay-and-display spaces are available they're not cheap. Rates can be as high as £4 per hour, although parking is usually free after 18:30 and at weekends. Penalties for illegal parking are high and

wheel clamps are widely in use, so avoid parking on double yellow lines and red routes (which signal priority bus lanes). Another expense is the Congestion Charge, which aims to tackle the problem of central London's overcrowded roads (see p.154). It currently covers the area from the City in the east to Chelsea, Kensington and Knightsbridge in the west. There are also plans to bring in a higher levy for those with four-wheel-drive vehicles. Anyone driving into the zone from 07:00 to 18:30, Monday to

Car Rental

Alamo	0870 4004562	www.alamo.co.uk
Avis	0870 0100287	www.avis.co.uk
Budget	0870 1565656	www.budget.co.uk
Europcar	8897 0811	www.europcar.co.uk
Hertz	0870 8460006	www.hertz.co.uk
National Car Rental	8897 3232	www.nationalcar.co.uk
Thrifty	7391 4600	www.thrifty.co.uk

Friday, is charged a fee of £8, which is payable at any time up to midday the day after your journey (although a £2 surcharge is added from 22:00 to discourage late payments). Visit www.cclondon.com or petrol stations to make advance payments. Anyone who fails to pay the charge before the deadline is required to pay £100 (reduced to £50 if the fine is made within 14 days of the date of the notice).

Speed Limit

The UK has similar speed restrictions to other European countries. Limits are 70mph (113kph) on motorways, 60mph (97kph) on single-lane main roads and 30mph (48kph) in built-up areas, although central London's slow-moving traffic means it's rare you'll get the chance to exceed this. Look out for red circular signs displaying the limit for the road you're on.

Pedal Power
You can hire a bicycle from various pick-up points in London (and drop it off again), simply by keying in a pin number to a locked up bike. See p.249 or call OY Bike Systems on 8955 6800.

Cycling

Cycling has become an increasingly popular mode of transport in the city – there has been a reported 20% increase in bike journeys since the terrorist attacks in 2005, with an estimated 450,000 cyclists taking to the capital's roads each day. Cycling in the city centre is not for the faint-hearted, but it's certainly a quick, cheap and healthy way to get around. Ongoing efforts have been made to make cycling in London easier and more enjoyable, including the introduction of additional cycle lanes. For information on routes and printed guides and maps covering the whole city see www.tfl.gov.uk/cycles. Although it isn't the law, it is advisable to wear a helmet and, because of traffic pollution, some people also opt for facemasks. Strong lights and visible clothing are also essential, as is a sturdy lock (preferably two) and insurance; bicycle theft is common throughout the capital.

Motorcycles

The number of motorcyclists on London's roads shows that riders aren't put off by any dangers faced – the risks posed are about the same as anywhere else in the UK.

Filtering between lanes is allowed but it's illegal to ride in bus lanes, many of which now have enforcement cameras. It is normally possible to find a parking space in the City and West End during peak hours, although at times it can take some patience. Some local authorities allow motorcycles to park free of charge in residents-only parking spaces, and there are bike bays with anchors for attaching a heavy-duty chain. Motorcycles are not subject to the Congestion Charge.

35

The Knowledge ◀
London's black-cab drivers aren't street savvy by chance. Each driver has to learn 'The Knowledge' – at the very least 300 routes across the city and the whereabouts of all major landmarks. They also have to tackle a written test, followed by interviews where they must give the shortest journey between two given points, before they can hit the road.

Taxi

London's famous black cabs, which can now be seen in a variety of colours, are an institution in the city. A yellow light above the windscreen indicates that the cab is available; if you see one just stick your arm out to signal it. Late at night cabs are more scarce, so be bold and grab one when you can; if you're not at a designated taxi rank, there's no etiquette. London's cabbies are generally happy to strike up conversation and are renowned for their knowledge of the city. This means they will know the shortest route between any two points in the capital, so you shouldn't need to give directions. Fares are metered, with a minimum charge of £2.20, and increments of 20p for each 219 metres. This can prove expensive even if you're travelling short distances. Be aware that some drivers will refuse to take you if your destination is deemed too far from the centre – or in many cases, their home. As a tip, most people round up to the nearest pound.

Legally, minicabs can't be hailed on the street – they must be hired by phone or directly from one of the many 24 hour minicab offices around the city. These minicabs display their licenses in their car – don't be afraid to ask to see one. Minicabs don't have meters, so it's essential to fix a price before you get in the car. Addison Lee (7387 8888) is a reputable firm with a fleet of cars all over the city. However tempting, unlicensed (and therefore illegal) minicab drivers touting for fares should be avoided, particularly by those travelling alone.

Taxi

A1 Express	W2	7262 7282	–
Ace Cars East	E3	7790 9999	–
Addison Lee	W2	7387 8888	info@addisonlee.com
Blueback	W1	0870 7711711	bookings@blueback.com
Brucar	E3	0870 608 5500	bookings@brunel.com
Camberwell Cars Limited	SE5	7703 4461	camberwellcars@btconnect.com
Chepstow Cars	W2	7229 0076	–
Chequers Transport	SW1	7730 6789	admin@chequerstransport.co.uk
Covent Garden Cars	WC2	7240 1040	–
Greyhound Cars	SW6	7384 2300	–
Hackney Road Fleet Cars	E2	7739 4080	–
Handicars	SE13	8852 2211	info@handicars.co.uk
Hoxton Cars 2	E1	7739 3030	–
London Radio Cars	NW1	7916 5555	info@lrcars.co.uk
Matrix Connections	SW6	7107 0700	bookings@matrixmoves.com
Meadway Radio Cars	NW11	0845 456 8000	bookings@meadway.com
Premier Airport Cars	N16	7249 9999	info@premierairportcars.com
Putney car service	SW16	8677 1111	bookings@thekeengroup.co.uk
RS Cars	EC1	7250 0027	–
Swiss Cottage Car Services	NW3	7433 1000	raj@swisscottagecars.freeserve.co.uk
Wyndhams Cars	W3	8752 8000	darren@cdsgroup.co.uk

Dry Cleaners p.74
Divorce Lawyers p.108

Written by residents, these unique guidebooks are packed with insider info, from arriving in a new destination to making it your home and everything in between.

Explorer Residents' Guides
We Know Where You Live

Train

Overland trains are useful for reaching places that are not served by the tube. There are a number of overland lines that cross the capital, including the North London Line, which runs from Richmond in the west to Woolwich in the east, and Thameslink, which runs from Brighton on the south coast through to Bedford, via London Bridge and King's Cross. These services tend to be less regular than the tube and some are not covered by the Oyster card system (see p.34). For more information on timetables and routes see www.tfl.gov.uk/rail.

Mainline stations that offer services to other parts of the country include Waterloo, London Bridge and Victoria, which serve south and south-east England; Paddington, which serves the west and south-west; King's Cross, St Pancras and Euston, which serve the north; and Liverpool Street, which serves the east. Tickets must be bought before boarding; with longer journeys, the further you book in advance, the cheaper the ticket. See www.thetrainline.com for more information.

Escalating Tensions

It may sound petty but it pays to observe the unwritten rule of the underground. Stand to the right of escalators and walk up the left and you won't be in trouble. London commuters are hard-nosed when it comes to tube etiquette, so you'll soon know if you've put a foot wrong.

Underground

Despite constant grumbling by passengers about overcrowding, delays and steep fares, the tube, as the underground is universally known, is usually the quickest and easiest way of getting across London. There are 12 underground lines, plus the Docklands Light Railway and interconnected overland stations, all marked in different colours on Harry Beck's famous map. Any train heading from left to right on the map is designated as eastbound, and any train travelling from top to bottom is southbound. This rule can get a little tricky on the Circle line, but there are indicator boards on station platforms. If your departure and destination stations are not on the same line, you need to find the nearest station where lines intersect.

The network is divided into six zones. If you're travelling several times in one day, or through a couple of zones, you should consider a Travelcard or Oyster card. A single ticket within Zones 1 to 4 costs £3 (£1.50 to £2.50 when using an Oyster card), while travelling from Zone 5 or 6 to Zone 1 will cost £4 (£3.50 with an Oyster card).

If you're caught without a valid ticket (which includes crossing into a zone that your ticket doesn't cover), you're liable for a £20 fine.

The first tube train operates at around 05:00 from Monday to Saturday, and 07:30 on Sundays. The last trains leave central London between 23:30 and 00:30. The network can get extremely busy and uncomfortable during rush hour. For more information and to plan your journey, visit www.tfl.gov.uk/tube. Pocket tube maps are also available free of charge at all tube stations.

Walking

Travelling by foot can be an excellent way to get around central London and often saves time compared with using public transport – it's surprising how close some landmarks and areas are to each other. Finding your way round is fairly straightforward with a *London A-Z* street map, available from bookshops, supermarkets, petrol stations or Tourist Information Centres.

The city is committed to becoming one of the most walking-friendly cities in the world and plans are already under way to improve the pedestrian environment.

Cars drive on the left in the UK so make sure you look in the correct direction when crossing the roads. The city's Royal Parks, which include Hyde Park, Regent's Park and Kensington Gardens (see p.213), make pleasant thoroughfares, taking walkers from central London to Notting Hill or Camden. London's canal network also offers a different, though not always scenic, route through the city (see p.218).

King's Cross

Liverpool Street

London Bridge

Canary Wharf

Victoria

Blackfriars

Money

Cashback

Most supermarkets and petrol stations offer 'cashback' – effectively a bank withdrawal from a cash register. When you're paying for an item with a debit or credit card you can ask for cashback of up to £50. You'll be given the cash and the amount will be debited – as well your original purchase – from your account, at no charge.

Most shops, restaurants and hotels will accept payment by credit or debit cards – look out for a sign displayed in the window or at the desk or till. In an attempt to prevent fraud and misuse of cards, a new protection system has been introduced called 'chip and pin', where you type your card's pin number into a handheld machine rather than sign for your purchase.

The increase in ATMs has meant travellers' cheques are now slightly out of fashion, but they are still changed at banks, post offices, hotels and bureaux de change. The most commonly accepted are American Express, Visa and Thomas Cook, and cheques issued are likely to be one of these three brands.

Local Currency

Although the UK is a member of the European Union, the country has retained the pound sterling and pence as its unit of currency rather than committing to the euro. One hundred pence make one pound sterling (£1). Coins come in denominations of £2, £1, 50p, 20p, 10p, 5p, 2p and 1p, while paper notes come in denominations of £5, £10, £20 and £50. The different notes are quite similar in size and appearance, so be careful. It's not very common to have a £50 note, so they are often scrutinised when you use them. Scottish banks issue their own notes, but they are valid in England. Something that costs £1.50 is often described as being 'one fifty' rather than 'one pound fifty'.

Exchange Rates

Foreign Currency (One Unit)*	FC to £	£ to FC
Australia	0.41	2.46
Bahrain	1.38	0.73
Bangladesh	0.008	132.91
Brazil	0.25	4.05
Canada	0.44	2.26
Cyprus	1.18	0.85
Denmark	0.09	10.87
Euro	0.69	1.46
Hong Kong	0.07	15.02
India	0.01	84.87
Malaysia	0.15	6.75
New Zealand	0.36	2.79
Norway	0.08	11.84
Oman	1.35	0.74
Pakistan	0.009	116.74
Philippines	0.01	93.40
Russia	0.02	50.28
Singapore	0.34	2.95
South Africa	0.07	14.38
Sri Lanka	0.005	210.53
Sweden	0.07	13.57
Switzerland	0.43	2.34
Thailand	0.02	67.34
United Arab Emirates	0.14	7.06
US	0.52	1.92

*Rates from March 2007

Banks

Every area of London has at least one of the big high-street banks; the names to look out for include Barclays, NatWest, Lloyds TSB, HSBC and Royal Bank of Scotland. The opening hours for most are Monday to Friday from 09:30 to 16:30, although some major branches are open until 17:00 during the week, as well as on Saturday mornings. Several of these banks have international status, or at least affiliation with equivalent banks abroad, and you can generally exchange travellers' cheques and currencies for a fairly low commission.

Opening a bank account in the UK is fairly straightforward, and it can be done with a little patience and lots of paperwork. See p.66 for more information.

ATMs

You'll find ATMs (cash machines) all over the capital, most of which accept Visa, MasterCard, Cirrus or Maestro cards. Most are situated outside banks and are accessible 24 hours a day, although you should be wary when using them late at night. Cloning of debit and credit cards – when skimming devices have been attached to ATMs – is also on the increase, but with the advent of chip and pin cards, it is now very difficult to use cloned cards for retail sales. However, it is still possible to use them to obtain cash from ATMs, so you should check the machine carefully before using it and shield your hand when entering your pin. ATM machines can also be a cheap way of obtaining British currency because they work on a good exchange rate; there will probably be a 1.5% fee for credit cards used this way.

Exchange Centres	
American Express Europe	0870 6001060
HSBC	0845 7404404
Post Office	0845 7223344
Thomas Exchange Global	7240 1214
Travelex	7400 4000

Money Exchanges

You can change cash and travellers' cheques at banks, post offices, large travel agents, some Tourist Information Centres, American Express and bureau de change outlets throughout the city. Banks and travel agents will usually charge a fixed fee, about 3% with a minimum fee of £2.50, but post offices don't charge any interest. If it's not convenient to go to a post office, TTT Foreign Exchange Corporation (7836 0528) and Thomas Exchange Global (7240 1214) both have several branches in the city centre.

Credit Cards

Most hotels, shops, restaurants and supermarkets in London accept major credit cards such as MasterCard, Visa, American Express and Diners Club – not surprising given that in 2005, more money (£89 billion) was spent by British people on debit cards than with cash. Your card will also allow you to withdraw cash from most ATMs, as well as get cashback from leading supermarkets. In smaller shops and restaurants, it's worth checking whether they accept credit cards before ordering.
If a credit card has been lost or stolen, or you discover it has been used without your permission, let your card issuer know immediately; once you have done this, you won't be liable for any subsequent misuse of the card.

Tipping

Although there are no set rules, tipping in London is common practice. If you're pleased with the service you've received in a restaurant, cafe or hotel, it's normal to leave 10 to 12.5% as a tip. In most restaurants and hotels, you can leave this on your credit card, although if you give cash directly to your waiter or waitress it's more likely that they'll directly benefit. However, sometimes the bill will include a service charge of 10 to 15%, in which case you needn't add any further tip. With taxi drivers, it's usual to round up to the nearest pound if the final fare is under £10, or give 10% if more. Bar staff don't expect tips, but it's a nice gesture to offer to buy them a drink if they've been especially helpful.

Inn the Park

41

Newspapers/Magazines

The UK has a huge number of media companies, most of which are based in London – a situation that leads to occasional accusations of 'London bias' in the national press. The national daily newspapers are divided into 'broadsheets' and 'tabloids'; while this was originally a size-based distinction, it is now more of a quality reference as virtually all the papers have become tabloid-sized. Broadsheets (including *The Times, Guardian, Daily Telegraph* and *The Independent*), have extensive foreign coverage as well as home news, and tabloids (including *The Sun, Mirror, Daily Express, Daily Mirror* and *Daily Star*), while still covering major news stories, tend to focus on celebrity, scandal and entertainment. These newspapers, which are widely available from newsagents, shops and news stands, all cost less than £1 during the week, although the price rises on Saturdays when many supplements are included, such as TV guides and glossy magazines. Several sister papers of the dailies are published on Sundays, and these are even weightier.

Tabloid Tales
The UK's biggest-selling daily newspaper is also its most infamous. The Sun has been responsible for a string of controversial headlines, salicious exclusives and elaborate stings over the years. Still, that combination hasn't helped recent sales, which threaten to dip below three million copies a day.

London also has four city-wide daily newspaper titles; the paid-for *Evening Standard* (sister paper of the *Daily Mail*), plus three free papers, *Metro, London Lite* and *The London Paper*, all of which are available on the streets and tube and railway stations. Competition is fierce between the latter two, which are both available from mid-afternoon, with rival vendors vying to give you a copy of their paper. There is also a large number of local newspapers in London, which often provide the best source of news for your area.

The independent weekly listings magazine *Time Out* has been providing concert, film, theatre and arts listings for almost 40 years and is a valuable source of information. You'll find a good selection of magazines in most newsagents and supermarkets. Borders on Oxford Street (p.317) has an excellent range, while for older copies head to the Vintage Magazine Store (7439 8525).

American and European newspapers are available in central London at good newsagents and the larger news stands and cost a bit more than at home. Australians have their own UK-based weekly magazine, *TNT*, which contains home news as well as London job and accommodation listings and is available outside many central tube stations.

Further Reading

London is the subject and setting of an infinite number of books, both fact and fiction, many of which can help you navigate your way around the city and discover its hidden charms. First and foremost, the *London A-Z*, which comes in a variety of shapes and sizes, is something no London resident or visitor should be without. *Time Out* publishes a series of recommended guides on London walks, pubs and restaurants. *The London Compendium* by Ed Glinert delves into the dark stories of some of London's best-known streets, while *London: The Biography* by Peter Ackroyd dissects London's 2,000 year history. *London Orbital* by Iain Sinclair is an introspective account of the author's journey by foot along the M25 road that circles the capital, while Tim Moore's highly amusing *Do Not Pass Go* explores the streets made famous by the Monopoly board. *The Likes of Us: A Biography of the Working Class*, by Michael Collins, analyses life as a white inner-Londoner, and for a good contrast try *The Lonely Londoners*, a novel by Sam Selvon based on the experiences of the first wave of Caribbean migrants to the capital in the 1950s. Monica Ali's *Brick Lane* is a more recent take on being part of London's large East End Asian community. Jake Arnott's fictional trilogy featuring Soho underworld character Harry Starks (*The Long Firm, He Kills Coppers* and *Truecrime*) is an entertaining mix of Soho-based gangster violence and cultural commentary on London from the 1960s through to the 1990s.

Media & Communications

Websites

There are numerous websites on living in London, with new ones appearing all the time. Both residents and tourists rely on them, whether it's for practical purposes or for entertainment. Some are put together by huge organisations while others are run by individuals. The table below lists some of the most useful ones.

Blogs

Featuring the musings and observations of individuals, blogs can provide a good insight into real London life, and many are updated on a daily basis. The irreverent http://london.metblogs.com and www.londonist.com have a worldwide following, while http://london-underground.blogspot.com is a witty and painfully accurate read about travelling on the tube.

Websites

Business & Industry

www.cityoflondon.gov.uk	Local government services for the City of London
www.london-fire.gov.uk	London Fire Brigade news and information
www.met.police.uk	Home of the Metropolitan Police
www.parkingticket.co.uk	Guide to parking regulations in London

City Information

www.london.gov.uk	Website of the mayor and Greater London Authority
www.londonvoices.com	Information on London neighbourhoods
www.streetmap.co.uk	Find your way around the capital
www.tfl.gov.uk	Up-to-the-minute public transport information
www.visitlondon.com	Guidance for tourists in London

Culture

www.ltmuseum.co.uk	London's Transport Museum
www.museumoflondon.org.uk	Museum of London
www.nhm.ac.uk	Natural History Museum
www.npg.org.uk	National Portrait Gallery
www.royalacademy.org.uk	Royal Academy
www.tate.org.uk	Tate art galleries
www.thebritishmuseum.ac.uk	The British Museum
www.vam.ac.uk	V&A

Directories

www.118118.com	Directory of business addresses and numbers
www.yell.com	Search engine providing access to business information

Living and Working

www.gumtree.com	Free classified ads including jobs, dating and flats to rent
www.london.craigslist.org	Classified and personal ads for the London area

News and Media

www.bbc.co.uk/london	News, sport, weather and community information
www.thelondonpaper.com	London's latest news and headlines
www.thisislondon.co.uk	London news from *The Evening Standard* plus listings, reviews and ticket booking

Nightlife

www.fancyapint.com	Pub guide to the capital
www.timeout.com/london	*Time Out*'s listings website
www.whatsoninlondon.co.uk	Entertainment information

Online Shopping

www.net-a-porter.com	High-end fashion delivered via courier
www.roomservice.co.uk	Takeaway service from over 80 of London's top restaurants

Restaurants

www.london-eating.co.uk	Restaurants rated by the public
www.squaremeal.co.uk	Reviews of London's top restaurants
www.toptable.co.uk	Book last minute and discount tables at leading restaurants

London Annual Events

London Boat Show

Royal Victoria Docks
*www.london
boatshow.com*
January

The London Boat Show at ExCeL offers curious visitors the chance to view everything from the latest millionaire yachts and cutting-edge powerboats to dinghies, narrowboats and surfboards. Those just browsing can navigate their way through 800 stalls and several high-tech demonstrations.

Chinese New Year

Chinatown
*www.chinatown
chinese.co.uk*
February

This is the largest Chinese New Year celebration outside of China and includes events in and around Trafalgar Square, Leicester Square and Chinatown. More than 200,000 people turn up to enjoy the parades, concerts and food stalls spread throughout the streets, with the highlight being the spectacular fireworks in Leicester Square.

London Fashion Week

Natural History Museum
*www.london
fashionweek.co.uk*
February/September

Twice a year top designers dust off their sewing machines as London Fashion Week comes to life. Even if you're not lucky enough to bag yourself a front-row invitation, this is your opportunity to find out who the new names to look out for are; more than 170 exhibitors use London Fashion Week as a showcase for their work.

St Patrick's Day Parade & Festival

Various locations
*www.london.gov.uk/
stpatricksday*
March

London's Irish community celebrates St Patrick's Day in the traditional manner, with music, dancing and plenty of Guinness. The parade itself has floats from every Irish county, with hundreds of stalls along the route. There's also a stage in Trafalgar Square with live performances and an Irish food market in Covent Garden.

The Boat Race

Thames
www.theboatrace.org
April

The Oxford and Cambridge Boat Race, contested each year between the UK's most revered universities, has been going since 1829. Now a major event on the sporting calendar, it draws millions of TV viewers worldwide, plus thousands of spectators who line the banks of the Thames from Putney to Mortlake to watch the action unfold.

London Marathon

*Greenwich to
St James' Park*
*www.london-
marathon.co.uk*
April

This gruelling 26.2 mile run is the largest race of its kind. Each year, more than 30,000 runners take part, and enthusiastic crowds take to the streets to watch some of the world's finest athletes and bravest amateur runners complete the route, which passes some of London's most recognisable landmarks.

Chelsea Flower Show

*Royal Hospital,
Chelsea*
www.rhs.org.uk
May

The Chelsea Flower Show is the Royal Horticultural Society's flagship event. Every year, visitors flock to see the best of garden design and horticulture, and to seek inspiration for their own patches. It also gets extensive television coverage on the BBC.

Open Garden Square Weekend

Various locations
www.opensquares.org
June

The only time of the year when London's elegant, and normally private, square gardens are opened to the public. Around 130 take part, including the School of African and Oriental Studies' Japanese roof garden and Southwark Cathedral's monastic churchyard.

Pride London

Central London
www.pridelondon.org
June

Pride has firmly established itself in London over the last 30 years and is the biggest event in the gay calendar. The carnival transforms central London with a flamboyant parade of floats representing every aspect of the gay and lesbian community.

Taste of London

Regent's Park
www.tasteoflondon.co.uk
June

Set in the lush surroundings of Regent's Park, this four-day celebration of posh nosh and fine wine features 40 of London's most prestigious restaurants and their celebrated chefs, who serve sample-sized signature dishes for visitors to try. There are also demonstrations and workshops for budding cooks.

Wimbledon Lawn Tennis Championships

Wimbledon
www.wimbledon.org
June and July

Tennis fever grips the capital during Wimbledon fortnight as the leading players compete on the famous grass courts in what is arguably the sport's biggest tournament. Most tickets are sold through a public ballot but some are available during the tournament; demand is high and queuing for hours has become something of a tradition – as have strawberries, Pimms and the occasional downpour.

Hampton Court Palace Flower Show

Hampton Court Palace
www.rhs.org.uk
July

Probably the second most well-known horticultural show in England after the Chelsea Flower Show, the Hampton Court Palace Flower Show gives visitors an opportunity to see gardens designed and built by both prominent and new designers, set in the idyllic parkland of Henry VIII's favourite palace.

Lovebox Weekender

Victoria Park
www.lovebox
weekender.com
July

With DJ tents, live arenas and all manner of fun (including graffiti demonstrations, circus workshops, a fun fair and comedy shows) this event is a must for music fans with their finger on the dance pulse. With capacity for 10,000 people each day, this summer weekend has attracted big name such as Jamiroquai, Roots Manuva and Groove Armada, that band that is the brains behind the mini-festival.

Outdoor Concerts

Twickenham
www.picnicconcerts.com
July and August

Marble Hill in Twickenham, plus Audley End and Battle outside London, play host to a series of outdoor classical, opera and pop concerts, finished off by fireworks on selected weekends and evenings during the summer. Hundreds of people gather to sit on the grass and deckchairs and take in the heady atmosphere.

Summer Gigs

Somerset House
www.somerset-
house.org.uk
July and August

Forget getting muddy at Glastonbury; the Courtyard of Somerset House is surely the most idyllic music location in the summer. The line-up usually includes a mixture of up-and-coming artists and more established acts; Erykah Badu, Bloc Party and Goldfrapp have all appeared in recent years.

Coin Street Festival

South Bank
www.coinstreet
festival.org
July to September

This free festival on the South Bank features music, dance, performance and art from members of London's refugee communities. There are also art and craft workshops for children and roving street theatre shows. The food and drink stalls place an emphasis on fair trade.

Proms

Royal Albert Hall
www.bbc.co.uk/proms
July to September

This eight-week summer season of daily classical music concerts held annually in locations across the capital, including the Royal Albert Hall, was founded over 100 years ago. Now, with each season consisting of over 70 concerts, it's the biggest classical music festival in the world., and televised by the BBC.

Notting Hill Carnival

Notting Hill
ww.londoncarnival.co.uk
August

One of Europe's biggest street festivals, the Notting Hill Carnival is the high point of the London cultural calendar. Established in 1964 as a Caribbean festival, the carnival is now a huge celebration of costume parades and traditional calypso and modern dance music. It takes place over two days at the end of August and is a full-on, action-packed experience.

Brick Lane Festival

Brick Lane
www.bricklanefestival.com
September

Focusing on this area's rich multicultural elements, Brick Lane Festival boasts a craft market, live music, fun-fair rides and a carnival procession. It usually runs in conjunction with the Banglatown International Curry Festival, which showcases Indian, Bangladeshi and Pakistani foods.

Great River Race

Thames
www.greatriverrace.co.uk
September

The Great River Race is one of London's most spectacular water-based events; each year up to 300 traditional boats, including wherries, war canoes, Cornish gigs and Chinese dragonboats, compete in a 22 mile race from Richmond to Greenwich.

The Mayor's Thames Festival

Westminster Bridge
to Tower Bridge
www.thamesfestival.org
September

Over half a million visitors are estimated to attend this annual event, which boasts a flurry of free activities including street theatre and workshops, live music, a riverside bazaar, spectacular night carnival and food stalls. The festival has grown to become the capital's largest free, open-air arts event since its inception in1998.

Open House London

Various locations
www.londonopen
house.org
September

Open House London gives members of the public the chance to nose around some of the capital's landmark properties. Over one weekend, more than 600 buildings open their doors and show off rooms that are hidden from view for much of the year, including ambassadors' residences, government buildings, private clubs, medical centres and media offices.

Regent Street Festival

Regent Street
www.regentstreet
online.com
September

Once a year, Regent Street closes for this extravaganza, which sees two stages host live music and theatre productions. Many of the street's famous shops have special offers and demonstrations, while restaurants and bars produce special menus and provide a rare opportunity for alfresco dining.

Frieze Art Fair

Regent's Park
www.friezeartfair.com
October

Now one of the most important fixtures on the art calendar, The Frieze Art Fair brings together some of the world's most exciting contemporary art galleries. There is also a lively discussion programme for those who want to share their thoughts or just learn more from the artists, dealers, curators and collectors who attend.

London Film Festival

Various locations
www.lff.org.uk
October

The star-studded London Film Festival presents the very best of new film from the full spectrum of cinema, with an extensive schedule of advance screenings and lectures at theatres across the capital. One of the year's major films normally opens the event.

Bonfire Night

Various locations
www.bonfire.org
November

Every year across the UK on November 5 there are massive celebrations to commemorate the failure of the 1605 'gunpowder plot', led by Guy Fawkes, to blow up the Houses of Parliament. This uniquely British commemoration sees the capital stage scores of blazing communal bonfires, traditionally with an effigy of Guy Fawkes thrown on top, and pyrotechnic displays attract huge crowds to 'ooh' and 'aah'.

Children's Film Festival

Barbican Centre
www.london
childrenfilm.org.uk
November

This innovative festival offers an educational programme of world-class events and films to children and families over 10 days. From workshops to animation, film premieres to sing-a-longs, it is a fun addition to the Barbican Centre's repertoire.

Christmas Lights

West End
www.westend
london.com
November to January

Christmas lights illuminate the capital's shopping streets, particularly Oxford Street, Bond Street and Regent Street, filling the winter gloom with much-needed festive sparkle. London's various displays are world famous and the lighting-up ceremonies are popular public events, especially as celebrities are usually hired to flick the switch.

Somerset House Ice Rink

Somerset House
www.somerset
houseicerink.org.uk
November to January

The grand 18th century courtyard of Somerset House provides one of the most impressive ice skating backdrops in London. There's also a skate school for those with wobbly legs and an upmarket cafe serving hot drinks for less energetic spectators.

Open House London

Thames Festival

AES INTERNATIONAL

Individual Solutions...

...for individual clients

- Savings and Investments
- Offshore Banking
- Foreign Exchange
- Financial Planning
- Tax and Legal Advice
- Corporate Services

info@aesfinance.com   www.aesfinance.com

14 Rue Maunoir, 1207 Geneva, Switzerland, TEL:+41 22 534 9474

Residents

Overview

As one of the world's foremost cities and the capital of one of the wealthiest nations on the planet, London has long been a magnet for migrants of all kinds, whether fleeing persecution, seeking to join family or looking for new opportunities and a better life. The capital is so huge and made up of so many different elements that the slogan 'the world in one city', currently being used by the London 2012 Olympic organisation, is certainly apt. But people's perceptions of the place tend to vary widely. Some see a dog-eat-dog environment, where life is hurried and hassled, some see opportunities to make their name, fortune or both, and some are simply drawn by the incredible mix that gives London its edge in terms of fashion, food, music and nightlife. There's certainly no shortage of people queuing up to give it their best shot. Few entry restrictions apply to European Union nationals coming to the UK, but immigration rules for everyone else have been tightened up noticeably (and are subject to constant change). If you plan to come to the city for more than six months, the chances are you'll need to apply for a visa before you set off.

Considering London

London offers a vast range of opportunities in terms of work and play, but is not without its downsides. The cost of living is high and it can be hard to find your feet, especially if you do not have vast reserves of cash. But armed with a few good tips you can quickly discover how to get hold of massively reduced theatre tickets, eat fabulous food on the cheap, and take advantage of sales, markets and discount stores. One major drawback of living in London is that it's full-to-bursting; if you're keen on the quiet life, it's unlikely to be the place for you. Getting around is a constant battle as it's rare to live and work in the same area, and the daily commute certainly grinds some down.

Covent Garden

If, however, you embrace an environment of constant change, you're not going to find many places that offer such variety: a great history; ambition to be at the forefront of innovations in architecture and business technology; and nightlife and leisure options of every conceivable variety. If you come from outside the European Economic Area you usually need a permit to work legally in the UK, which must be applied for on your behalf by the company you are going to work for. You will then be able to apply for a visa. There are a handful of professions and schemes that offer exceptions to the work permit stage, but you will still require a visa (see p.18). Permit-free occupations tend to reflect particular shortages in the UK labour market – doctors, scientists and engineers, for example – so if you belong to one of these professions, you may well find that the red tape is comparatively easier to get through.

**'London is dangerous
– you'll get mugged'.**
*As with most major
cities, crime is an issue
and usually tops any
poll of residents'
concerns. Statistics vary
widely from year to
year, but the city tends
to have a higher-than-
average rate of street
robberies. The better
news is that there is a
relatively low incidence
of gun and knife crime.*
'It's always raining'.
*Not true – in 2006 the
lack of rainfall in
London and the south-
east led to severe water
shortages and hosepipe
bans were introduced.*
'It's grey and dull'.
*London has a surprising
range and quality of
greenery, from ancient
woodlands such as
Highgate Wood to
reinvented spaces such
as Mile End Park (see
Exploring, p.162).*

Before You Arrive

Things worth doing before you leave include:

Passports – make sure your passport is up to date and all official documents and certificates are to hand. Stock up on passport photographs.

Property – if you live in your own property, make arrangements to sell or rent it. Both storage and shipping are expensive so you may want to consider selling some of your less-precious belongings.

Utilities – have your utilities disconnected or taken out of your name, and make sure all bills are up to date and avoid leaving any debts or loose ends.

Shipping – you could need to arrange shipping well in advance, depending on the distance you're travelling. Transporting your possessions from Australia, for instance, may take up to 12 weeks.

Finances – make sure your bank and other financial institutions are aware of your move. Consider switching to online banking to keep track of your accounts while moving around. Investigate what your situation will be in the UK regarding tax, national insurance and pensions.

Research – estate agents' websites carry details of property to rent and buy, while websites aimed at newcomers, such as www.gumtree.com, will give you an idea of what is available on the flat-share front. If you are bringing children, schools can be researched via government website www.direct.gov.uk and the schools inspection service Ofsted (www.ofsted.gov.uk).

When You Arrive

Once you arrive in London, there are a number of things you'll need to do quickly to help you get settled:

Accommodation – your first priority is likely to be finding somewhere to live. Most lets are furnished, so a trip to IKEA is unlikely to be a must initially (see p.336).

Phones – get a mobile phone as soon as you can – it'll make sorting out everything else a lot easier (see p.339).

Utilities – gas, electricity, water, phone and internet may all need to be connected or at least transferred to your name (see p.135).

Transport – if you intend to drive, you can make arrangements to transfer your licence. Driving in the capital can be an expensive and fraught affair, however, with parking fees and the Congestion Charge all adding up (see p.154). Nearly half of London households do not have a car, and private vehicles are the main mode of transport for only 10% of people travelling to central London to work.

Emergencies – note the location of your country's embassy, register with it if possible, and find out what help it can offer you in the case of an emergency (see p.20).

Social – making new friends is a great way to help you settle quickly. Consider joining a team or social group (see Activities, p.234).

Essential Documents

To ease your passage through bureaucracy make sure you have access to your official documents. You're almost certain to need the following in your first couple of months:
Passport
Work permit
Birth certificate
Marriage or **civil partnership certificate**
Proof of employment to secure accommodation
Proof of address to open a bank account, or join the library or DVD store
Driving licence

When You Leave

If and when you decide to pack up and leave London behind, there are a number of things you need to take care of before you take off:

Accommodation – if you are renting, make sure you give the required notice to the landlord (normally a month) and leave the property in good order to ensure the return of any deposit.

Utilities – have your utilities disconnected or taken out of your name, and pay any outstanding bills.

Possesions – consider what you want to do with your belongings. Arrange shipping to your next destination or storage if you are intending to return.

Car – if you have a car, make arrangements to sell it (see p.155).

Documents

Whether applying for a visa or arranging a wedding, it's always wise to get an idea of how long any administrative procedure will take and leave plenty of time for bureaucratic machinations. Applications can sometimes be fast-tracked, but this will nearly always cost you. If you are coming to the UK to take up a pre-arranged job, your company may well pitch in to help with finding accommodation and the settling-in process.

Entry Visa

Other options **Visas** p.18

EU Expansion
As the EU expands, nationals of more recent member countries may find themselves subject to some restrictions, such as being required to register as a worker. You can check this at www.working intheuk.gov.uk.

The government website www.ukvisas.gov.uk contains a useful tool for determining whether or not you need a visa to enter the UK based on where you are coming from, the purpose of your visit and your proposed length of stay. You can also download application forms and check the latest regulations here. Remember that you need to sort out the paperwork with your nearest British embassy or diplomatic mission before you leave your home country, although the application forms can usually be filled in and payment made online. The processing fees for visas vary depending on the type you are applying for, but expect to pay upwards of £100. The Home Office website www.workingintheuk.gov.uk contains information about work permits and other entry schemes, while the Immigration and Nationality Directorate (www.ind.homeoffice.gov.uk) deals with immigration queries once you are in the UK.

European Citizens

If you are a citizen of one of the 27 European Union member states, or Iceland, Liechtenstein, Norway or Switzerland, you do not require a visa to enter the UK, whether it's to live, look for work or claim benefits. You'll still need to have a valid passport to travel, however.

If you intend to stay in the UK on a long-term basis, you should apply for a residence permit from the Immigration and Nationality Directorate once you are in the country. This will allow you to stay for five years, and means any dependants who are not themselves EU or European Economic Area nationals can then apply to enter the country to be with you.

Visitor Visas

Short-term visitors from the majority of countries, including most English-speaking nations, are able to enter the UK as 'visitors' and do not need to have a visa. If you enter in this way you need to be able to support yourself financially as you will not be permitted to work legally. This does not apply to the following **'visa national'** countries, whose citizens require a visa whatever their length of stay: Afghanistan, Albania, Algeria, Angola, Armenia, Azerbaijan, Bahrain, Bangladesh, Belarus, Benin,

Bhutan, Bosnia-Herzegovina, Bulgaria, Burkina Faso, Burma, Burundi, Cambodia, Cameroon, Cape Verde, Central African Republic, Chad, China (excluding Hong Kong and Macao), Colombia, Comoros, Congo, Cuba, Cyprus, Djibouti, Dominican Republic, Ecuador, Egypt, Equatorial Guinea, Eritrea, Ethiopia, Fiji, Gabon, Gambia, Georgia, Ghana, Guinea, Guinea-Bissau, Guyana, Haiti, India, Indonesia, Iran, Iraq, Ivory Coast, Jamaica, Jordan, Kazakhstan, Kenya, Kuwait, Kyrgyzstan, Laos, Lebanon, Liberia, Libya, Macedonia, Madagascar, Malawi, Mali, Mauritania, Moldova, Mongolia, Morocco, Mozambique, Nepal, Niger, Nigeria, North Korea, Oman, Pakistan, Palestinian Authority, Peru, Philippines, Qatar, Russia, Rwanda, Sao Tome & Principe, Saudi Arabia, Senegal, Serbia and Montenegro, Sierra Leone, Somalia, Sri Lanka, Sudan, Surinam, Syria, Taiwan, Tajikistan, Tanzania, Thailand, Togo, Tunisia, Turkey, Turkmenistan, Uganda, Ukraine, United Arab Emirates, Uzbekistan, Vatican City, Vietnam, Yemen, Zambia and Zimbabwe.

Working in the UK

If you are from outside Europe and are being posted to London by your company, or have secured employment in advance, your firm needs to apply for a **work permit** on your behalf via Work Permits (UK), part of the Home Office. Once you have a permit you must then apply to your nearest British embassy or diplomatic mission for a visa. To make a visa application you will need a valid passport, passport photo, work permit, and a non-refundable processing fee. Dependants of permit holders, spouses, partners and children under 18 can accompany the permit holder on the basis of their relationship, but need visas in their own names so must apply separately (using the above documentation as well as a marriage or civil partnership certificate or birth certificate as appropriate). For further information, visit www.workingintheuk.gov.uk or approach the British diplomatic mission in your country.

Once in the UK you may be required to register with the police (you will be notified via a stamp in your passport if this is the case). To register, take your passport and two passport-size photographs to the Overseas Visitors Records Office, Brandon House, 180 Borough High Street between 09:00 and 16:30, Monday to Friday (7230 1208). If you're outside London, your local police station can inform you of the nearest registration point.

There are several other options for working in the UK that may be applicable to you:

Highly Skilled Migrant Programme – this is a points-based system, also administered by Work Permits (UK), which allows those with high levels of education and experience to apply for a visa and then enter the UK to look for work for a period of up to two years. Go to www.workingintheuk.gov.uk for further information.

Training and Work Experience Scheme – this programme allows foreign nationals to gain a visa to enter the UK to train towards a professional qualification or to undertake short spells of work experience, typically one year at the most.

53

Permit-free occupations – just to complicate matters, there are a number of professions that don't require a work permit, including: those seeking to establish a business (handled by the Business Case Unit, see www.workingintheuk.gov.uk); ministers of religion; journalists; artists; sole representatives of overseas firms; employees of overseas governments; airline ground staff; doctors; dentists; science and engineering graduates; and seasonal agricultural workers. You do still need to get a visa, however. Investors and retired people of independent means also only need to apply for a visa.

Working Holidaymaker Scheme – this is how many young people from countries such as Australia, New Zealand and South Africa who want to live and work in London on a temporary basis or as part of a round-the-world trip get their hands on a visa. Anyone between the ages of 17 and 30 from a country on the list below is able to apply for a visa to stay in the UK for up to two years without the need for a work permit.

Working holidaymakers are not supposed to work for more than 12 months out of the two years, but are allowed to take up most jobs apart from setting up a business or working as a sports professional. Anyone you travel with, including partners or spouses, needs to qualify under the same criteria.

Dependant children can only travel with you if they will be under five when your holiday is over. When you apply for a visa under this scheme you may be asked to prove how much money you have. This is to check that you have sufficient funds to support yourself for at least two months after you arrive as you will not be able to claim any state benefits.

You can't extend your two-year stay, but after a year you can apply to switch to a work permit (if the job you have is classed as a 'shortage occupation' – see www.workingintheuk.gov.uk for a full list and the latest information) or, if you have the necessary qualifications, the Highly Skilled Migrant Programme (see above).

All Commonwealth countries are covered by the Working Holidaymaker Scheme. These are: Antigua and Barbuda, Australia, The Bahamas, Bangladesh, Barbados, Belize, Botswana, Brunei Darussalam, Canada, Cyprus, Cameroon, Dominica, Fiji, The Gambia, Ghana, Grenada, Guyana, India, Jamaica, Kenya, Kiribati, Lesotho, Malawi, Malaysia, Maldives, Malta, Mauritius, Mozambique, Namibia, Nauru, New Zealand, Nigeria, Pakistan, Papua New Guinea, St Kitts and Nevis, St Lucia, St Vincent and the Grenadines, Samoa, Seychelles, Sierra Leone, Singapore, Solomon Islands, South Africa, Sri Lanka, Swaziland, Tanzania, Tonga, Trinidad and Tobago, Tuvalu, Uganda, Vanuatu and Zambia.

UK Ancestry visas – if you're from a Commonwealth country (see above) and one or more of your grandparents was born in the UK, then you've hit the jackpot. A UK Ancestry visa enables you to live and work unrestricted in the UK for up to five years, and then apply for permanent residence. Partners, spouses and children under 18 can gain visas on the basis of your Ancestry visa.

Students – in order to enter the UK on a student visa you must have been accepted into a full-time course at a publicly funded or recognised private institution, and be able to meet the costs of your course fees and living expenses of yourself and any dependants.

Need Some Direction?

The *Explorer Mini Maps* pack a whole city into your pocket – and once unfolded make excellent navigational tools for exploring. Not only are they handy in size, with detailed information on the sights and sounds of the city, but their affordable price means that they won't make a dent in your holiday fund. Wherever your travels take you, from the Middle East to Europe and beyond, grab a Mini Map and you'll never have to ask for directions.

Blue Card – US students in full-time education or recent graduates can apply for a Blue Card, a special entry visa allowing them to live and work in the UK for up to six months. The Blue Card must be obtained before leaving home. For further information visit www.bunac.org.

Gap-year students – overseas students who have finished secondary education and are taking a gap year before starting a degree course can apply for a visa to enter the UK to work temporarily in a school. You need an invitation from a school and a confirmed place on a degree course to qualify.

Residence Visa

Other options **Visas** p.18

If once you are in the country you wish to extend your stay or apply for permanent residence, known as 'leave to remain', you'll need to approach the Immigration and Nationality Directorate (www.ind.homeoffice.gov.uk). In some circumstances you may need to leave the country and re-enter after applying for a different visa to the one you originally came in on. After being settled in the UK on a long-term basis (three years if you are married to a British citizen or five years if not), you can apply for naturalisation as a British citizen. This involves taking a 'Life in the UK test' or attending English language and citizenship classes, and finally attending a citizenship ceremony where you make an oath (see www.lifeintheuktest.gov.uk).

ID Card

The UK is currently in the process of rolling out a National Identity Scheme which is intended to lead to the biometric data of all UK residents over the age of 16 being stored on a national register. Everyone will then be issued with an ID card, including foreign nationals who are resident in the country for longer than three months. The first ID cards are slated to be introduced in 2008 or 2009, and it will eventually become compulsory to have one – although at this stage it is not envisaged that people will have to carry them on their person. The introduction of ID cards in the UK is certainly not without controversy, with some civil liberties groups campaigning vigorously against them. In the meantime, when asked to provide proof of identity, people typically use their passport, driving licence or birth certificate.

Driving Licence
Other options **Transportation** p.153

European Citizens
If you're from the European Union or European Economic Area you can drive any vehicle for which your home country licence is valid. Once a UK resident, you can drive cars and motorcycles until you are 70, or for three years, whichever is the longer period. You can drive lorries, minibuses or buses until you're 45, or for five years if you are between 45 and 65. If you wish to continue driving outside these limits you must obtain a British licence (see Exchanging your Licence, below).

If you hold a licence with a vocational entitlement, you need to register your details with the Driver and Vehicle Licensing Agency (DVLA). See www.direct.gov.uk or call 0870 240 0009. Stricter eyesight standards apply for vocational drivers, and you must tell the DVLA about any health conditions that may affect your ability to drive. Car and motorcycle drivers can also register with the DVLA, which allows you to take advantage of the fixed penalty system for road offences rather than having to go to court.

Other Countries
Britain has licence exchange agreements with Australia, Barbados, British Virgin Islands, Canada, Falkland Islands, Gibraltar, Hong Kong, Japan, Mexico, New Zealand, Singapore, South Africa, South Korea, Switzerland and Zimbabwe. Visitors from these countries with full driving licences can drive for up to 12 months, as can new residents. To carry on driving beyond a year, you must exchange your licence for a British one within the 12-month period. You can still exchange your home country licence for up to five years after becoming a resident, although you can't drive in the interim period. New residents must pass the relevant driving test in order to qualify to drive large or passenger-carrying vehicles.

Visitors and new residents from the rest of the world can drive as long as their existing licence is valid for a year from the date of entering the UK, but to keep driving you must apply for a British provisional licence and pass a driving test before this period is up (see Learning to Drive, overpage). As long as you do this within 12 months, you will not need to display learner plates or be supervised by a qualified driver. Leave it too late though and you'll default to the regular provisional licence conditions.

Exchanging Your Licence
In order to exchange your licence you must be a resident with a permanent UK address, and your home country licence must be valid (international driving permits are not exchangeable). You'll also have to give up your original licence, which will be returned to the issuing authority in your country of origin. You need to fill in and return a form (D1), which you can order from the DVLA website or pick up from Post Offices. Note that Canadian licences can only be exchanged for ones covering automatic vehicles, upgradeable with proof of having passed a manual test or by taking a test in the UK. Japanese and Korean licences must be surrendered with an official translation from, respectively, to the Consulate General of Japan (7465 6500) and the Embassy of the Republic of Korea (7227 5505).

Driving Schools

Name	Area	Phone	Web
AA Driving School	Various locations	0800 5870087	www.theaa.com/drivingschool/index.html
Britannia Driving School	Various locations	0800 252692	www.britannia-driving-school.co.uk
BSM	Various locations	0845 7276276	www.bsm.co.uk
Chevron Driving School	Various locations	0800 526436	www.chevrondrivingschool.co.uk
Driver Education Centre	N1	7241 3322	www.declondon.com
Holborn School of Motoring	EC1	7837 9707	www.holborndrivingschool.co.uk
Learners UK	Various locations	0800 7317655	www.learners-uk.co.uk

Learning to Drive

In Great Britain (Northern Ireland has separate a licensing process, although the licences are valid in the rest of the UK) the legal age for driving cars and motorcycles is 17. For medium-sized vehicles it is 18 and for large lorries and buses it is 21.

In order to learn to drive a car, moped or motorcycle, you must first apply for a provisional driving licence from the DVLA. You can apply online or by filling in the D1 application form, available from any Post Office. You'll need proof of identity, a passport-size photograph and a fee of £38. You should receive your provisional licence within three weeks of applying, and then you can begin to learn to drive. While in possession of a provisional licence you are only allowed to drive if accompanied by a qualified driver, and must display L-plates on your vehicle when on the road. While in possession of the provisional licence, you must take a test, to which there are two components: practical and theory. To find test centres in your area or to book a test online, go to www.direct.gov.uk/motoring.

Birth Certificate & Registration

Any birth in the UK must be registered in the district where the child was born within 42 days. Registration is usually done at the hospital where the child was born (staff will guide you through the process), or at a register office (see www.gro.gov.uk to find your nearest one).

If you can't get to the register office nearest to where the birth took place, you can go to another one and they will send your details to your local office. When you sign the birth register you will receive a 'short' birth certificate (a full version with all relevant details on can be ordered for £10) and a registration card, which will enable you to sign your child up with an NHS doctor. If the parents of the child are married either one can register the birth, but if you're not married and you want the father's details to be recorded both parents need to go. If the father can't attend with the mother, his details can still be included if he fills in a form confirming his paternity. The form (16) is available from the General Register Office website (see above). If the mother is unable to go, she must fill in the same form to confirm the identity of father so that he can register the birth.

Where parents are married, both automatically have legal parental responsibility of the child, and if they are unmarried parental responsibility is also conferred by the father's name being recorded on the birth register. If the father's name is not recorded in the first instance, it is possible to re-register a birth at a later date. If neither parent is able to register the birth, it should be done by someone who was present at the birth or who is responsible for the child. The same registration rules apply to stillbirths (defined as a baby born with no sign of life after 24 weeks of pregnancy).

Where one of the parents is a British citizen or 'ordinarily resident' in the UK – that is they are legally in the country, have been here several years and have indefinite leave to remain – the child automatically has British citizenship. If both parents are in the UK on temporary visas then the child is not a British citizen at birth, but may become one later if either parent becomes a British citizen or settles permanently before the child reaches 18. Alternatively if a child lives in the UK until the age of 10, they may be eligible to become a British citizen.

Passports

Babies and children under 16 must have their own passports in order to travel, which can be applied for by a parent through www.passport.gov.uk or by picking up an application form at a main Post Office. Child passports are valid for five years before they must be renewed, but children under 16 cannot get adult passports – so, for instance, a 15-year-old will be issued with a child passport which will still be valid for five years.

The fee is £45 and it can take up to three weeks before you receive the passport. If you need it sooner call 0870 521 0410 to arrange an appointment at a passport office, where you can pay more for either a fast-track (one-week) or premium (same-day) service.

For non-urgent applications, you can get help filling in passport application forms by paying for the 'Check & Send' service available at Post Offices and Worldchoice travel agents, which costs about £7. If you're in the UK on a temporary basis, you should consult your embassy in order to arrange getting a home country passport for your baby.

Although the registration of births, deaths and marriages takes place at a local level in the UK, the General Register Office holds all the deeds, and it is this office you should approach if you need to replace lost certificates or track down records.

The Price of Love

If you're not sufficiently alarmed by the fact that the average cost of a wedding in the UK is around £16,000, it seems wedding guests don't escape the expense, typically spending around £400 on each wedding they attend. On top of that, around 1.3 million guests each year stump up a whopping £1,300 each to attend weddings held overseas.

Adoption

If you are settled in the UK and considering adopting a child, you should approach the adoption agency in your local authority. You'll need to go through a formal application and preparation process, during which you'll be assessed to see if you are suitable. If accepted as a potential adopter you then face a wait before you are matched with a child, which can take anything from a couple of weeks to a year or more. Married couples, co-habiting couples of any sexuality, civil partners and single people can all apply to adopt, regardless of race or religion. Once a child has been settled, an adoption order will be made that ends legal ties with the child's birth family. Fostering a child is usually a more short-term prospect, with carers providing a temporary home for children whose families are not able to look after them for a time. Where the country in question allows it, and it is in line with international law, it is possible to adopt a child from abroad and have it registered with the General Register Office.

Christenings & Naming Ceremonies

Apart from the formal registration of a birth, many people toast the new arrival with family and friends. If you want to have your child christened you should approach your chosen church. The ceremony is a formal one, which generally includes the naming of godparents who, along with the parents, pledge to bring up the child according to religious teachings – although many people whose faith is not very strong still have their children christened. A non-religious alternative is to hold a naming ceremony instead. These can take whatever form you choose – www.humanism.org.uk is a good source of inspiration for such events.

Marriage Certificate & Registration

Marriage and Civil Partnership

The traditional confetti-strewn white wedding remains a common Saturday morning sight on the steps of London's churches – but there are many ways of getting hitched in the modern metropolis, from low-key register office ceremonies to exchanging vows dressed as Elvis on the London Eye. Since 2005, same-sex couples have been able to register their partnerships in much the same way as traditional marriages and have not been slow to do so (although any religious blessing will be subject to faith rules). The legal bit of tying the knot can take place at the local register office or a venue otherwise recognised for civil marriage or partnership (see www.gro.gov.uk for a list of venues, including restaurants, historic buildings, town halls, theatres and football grounds), as well as, for heterosexual marriage, at a church or religious building that is authorised to carry out wedding ceremonies. See p.352 for a list of wedding services.

Certificates & Licences

Civil Partnerships

Since 2005, lesbian and gay couples in the UK have been able to have their relationships legally recognised as 'civil partnerships', which have the same status as marriage in terms of tax, benefits and immigration status. Civil ceremonies can be held in the same venues as marriages, with the exception of religious buildings (you'll need to refer to the particular religious institution to see if it has any provisions for same-sex blessings). For a civil partnership to end you must fill out a petition, which will lead to the official dissolution of the partnership. This is the equivalent of a divorce, but can only happen after one year.

The Paperwork

Getting married or registering a civil partnership in the UK is a fairly straightforward matter. The legal age for union is 16, although those under 18 need the consent of a parent or guardian. The only restriction is that both parties need to have lived in the district covered by the register office for seven days prior to registering for the marriage – you'll need to show your passport and proof of address to the superintendent registrar.

If you have been married or registered a civil partnership before you have to provide official documentation of the divorce or dissolution, or the death of your spouse or partner.

Anyone who has settled status or indefinite leave to remain can get married in the UK – otherwise you are not permitted to marry unless your visa specifically allows it or you have obtained a certificate of approval from the Immigration and Nationality Directorate (www.homeoffice.ind.gov.uk). The authorities are empowered to act against anyone they believe is using marriage or civil partnership to get around immigration controls.

To get married, you need to give at least 15 days' notice at the register office or other approved venue, where notices of your marriage or civil partnership are displayed. Once you have given notice, you then have a window of a year to tie the knot. The costs of registering a marriage or civil partnership are fairly minimal: to give notice at a register office, approved premises or religious building (other than Church of England) is £30 per person, while the price of a register office ceremony starts at £40. For approved premises the cost is set locally and is likely to be a bit higher, and there will be a further charge made by the owner of the building. The fees are also set locally for a religious ceremony in a Church of England building, but religious ceremonies in other premises usually involve the additional charge of £47 for a registrar to attend. Lastly you'll have to find £3.50 for the official certificate.

If you wish to get married or register a civil partnership abroad, you should approach the embassy or high commission of the country in which you are intending to wed.

Very Civilised
According to official figures, there were 15,672 civil partnership ceremonies in the UK between December 2005 – when they were recognised by law – and September 2006. A quarter of these took place in London, with Sir Elton John and his partner David Furnish among the first to tie the knot.

Changing Your Name

There is no legal bar from changing your name (unless you are doing so to commit fraud) – all you need to do to effect the change is start using your new name. For official purposes it might be necessary to prove your change of name, in which case a letter from a responsible person such as a doctor, solicitor, MP or priest confirming that they have known you by both names will usually suffice. If you're getting married and choose to change your name the formalities will be included in the marriage registration process. There are also two more formal ways of changing your name, for which you will need to enlist legal help: by statutory declaration or by Deed Poll (see www.ukdps.co.uk).

Death Certificate & Registration

If the death of a relative or friend is expected, happens in hospital or while the person is under medical supervision a hospital doctor or the deceased's doctor should be called. They will then issue a medical certificate stating the cause of death. If there is any uncertainty about the cause, the doctor or police will inform the coroner (see below). The deceased's next of kin should be told as quickly as possible, and arrangements made with a funeral director, who, as well as organising the funeral or cremation, will act as a guide through the process of registering the death.

Registering a Death

A death must be registered within five days at the register office in the district where it happened. This is usually done by a relative of the deceased, but if there is no relative available to do it the death can be registered by the person who found the body, someone who was present at the death, or the person in charge of overseeing the funeral arrangements. If necessary you can register a death at an office other than the local, although this may take a day or two longer and delay the funeral or cremation (see www.gro.gov.uk to find your nearest office). When you go along you need to take the medical certificate of the cause of death and provide a number of details about the deceased: date and place of death; full name of deceased and maiden name; date and place of birth; occupation; date of birth of spouse or civil partner; address; and pension particulars. Where relevant, the death cannot be registered until the coroner has given approval.

The person registering the death is able to buy more death certificates, for about £10 each, which will probably be needed in order to sort out the deceased's affairs. You can order further copies of the death certificate from the register office for up to 28 months, and from the General Register Office after that.

You'll also receive a certificate that you are required to give to the funeral director. If the death has been reported to the coroner, they may issue one of these certificates so the funeral or cremation can go ahead even if the death has not yet been registered. In addition a certificate for social security benefits will be issued so any state benefits or pensions can be sorted out, along with a booklet called *What to Do After a Death* which provides useful information and advice on issues that may need attending to.

Investigation

If there are any unusual circumstances surrounding a death the register office will report it to the coroner before registering it. These include circumstances where a doctor has not issued a certificate of the cause of death; where the cause of death is unknown or suspicious; and where death has occurred during an operation. The coroner will then rule on whether further investigation is required, and the death cannot be registered until this is done.

Returning the Deceased to Country of Origin

If the body needs to be moved out of the country the district coroner must be informed – you can do this by filling in a form, which the coroner or register office can supply. The certificate for burial or cremation should also be given to the coroner. The coroner will usually give permission four days or so after receiving the forms, although the process may be speeded up in urgent circumstances.

Organ Donation

At any given time there are some 8,000 people in the UK waiting for an organ transplant, but only around 3,000 operations are carried out each year due to a shortage of donors. If you want to be a donor, you should make your wishes known by signing up to the NHS Organ Donor Register at www.uktransplant.org.uk or by phoning 0845 606 0400.

Explorer Online

No doubt now that you own an Explorer book you will want to check out the rest of our product range. From maps and visitors' guides to restaurant guides and photography books, Explorer has a spectacular collection of products just waitiing for you to buy, you genius! Check out our website for more info. *www.explorerpublishing.com*

Working in London

There's no doubt that London's economy and services would quickly grind to a halt without the massive contribution of foreign workers. Incomers perform crucial roles in all realms of employment, from cleaning and childcare to medicine and education. While the work permit system is designed to protect British workers, in reality most sectors are open to expats who have either secured a job in advance or belong to one of the visa categories that allow them to enter the UK and then look for work. Some professions, such as teaching and social work, are constantly struggling with staff shortages so any qualified person stands a good chance of finding work in these areas.

London Weighting

London has many attractions as a place to work: it is the centre of many British industries; a wide range of multinationals have a presence; the City serves as Europe's

financial centre; and, as a major tourist and business destination, there is a huge hospitality and service industry. The Olympics in 2012 (see p.7) will provide thousands of new jobs in fields such as construction, transport, entertainment and leisure, the service sector, IT, telecoms, and hospitality and catering. But as you explore this land of opportunity, it's important to remember that London is always hovering around the top 10 most expensive cities in the world to live in, so even if you get a foot in the door and find a job, the expense of day-to-day living may be a strain on your resources. The cost is acknowledged in that most jobs in the capital pay more than their equivalents in other parts of the UK – 'London weighting' – but you may still find that salaries do not necessarily keep pace with London prices.

Setting Up Business

If you are thinking about coming to the UK expressly to set up a business, you need to consult the Business Case Unit of the Immigration and Nationality Directorate (www.workingintheuk.gov.uk), and you should do the same even if you are already in the country as it may have implications for your immigration status. Depending on the kind of business you have in mind, you will have to address tax issues (as a self-employed person you are taxed differently to an employee) and will almost certainly need to use an accountant to guide you through the process. This is even more important if you are hiring other people, in which case you must also take out employer's liability insurance and sort out income tax and National Insurance contributions (see p.64). Other kinds of insurance, such as for public liability, may also be necessary. If you are thinking of running your business from home, you should check that your tenancy agreement, mortgage conditions or title deeds do not place any restrictions on business use, and, again, additional insurance will probably be necessary. If you are renting or buying premises for business use they must have been approved for this purpose by the local authority, and in some cases you may need to seek planning permission.

Workers in Britain toil away for the longest hours in Europe, but without any gains in terms of productivity. According to the Trades Union Congress more than five million workers in the UK put in an average of 7.4 hours in unpaid overtime each week. Many workplaces rely on a culture of staying late and employees doing over and above their contracted hours. However, the notion of achieving a 'work-life balance' is growing. Employers already have a legal duty to give serious consideration to any request for flexible working from employees with children under the age of six.

Working Hours

For most office-based jobs the working week is Monday to Friday, 09:00 to 17:00, with some variations depending on company policy or the demands of the position. There are, of course, a whole range of jobs for which different hours apply, especially in the retail and service sectors where many people work evening and weekend shifts. The number of hours you can work per week is governed by the Working Time Directive, a piece of European legislation designed to protect workers. It puts a ceiling of an average of 48 hours on the working week, but at the moment individual employees can choose to opt out of this, and some professions, such as the police, are exempt. Night workers have additional protection, with a limit of an average of eight hours in 24 and the right to free health assessments. Workers are entitled to at least one day off per week and statutory leave is four weeks per year. This can include public holidays, although typically it doesn't. A standard company will offer 22 to 25 days leave per year plus public holidays, while public sector organisations, such as councils, tend to be more generous with around 30 days. There are usually eight public holidays in England and Wales each year (see p.12).

Business Councils & Groups		
American Business Council	7467 7400	www.babinc.org
China-Britain Business Council	7802 2000	www.cbbc.org
Commonwealth Business Council	7024 8200	www.cbcglobelink.org
The India Business Group	7836 8484	www.hcilondon.net
Japan Business Council in Europe	–	www.jbce.org

Finding Work

With thousands of people coming to London every year to try to make a living, competition for jobs can be high and wages low for entry-level positions, especially in areas such as the media where opportunities are limited. In some fields, the people-hungry service and retail sectors in particular, there are always openings, but with the cost of living you may find it difficult to get by on the minimum wage if you do not have some money in reserve. In general, unless you are coming from a European Economic Area country, or are on a spousal, working holidaymaker or ancestry visa, you will have secured a work permit before you have come to the UK (see Visas, p.18). If you are being posted or transferred to London by your company or have been recruited internationally, relocation costs and help with practicalities will typically form part of the deal.

Looking For Work

There are a multitude of recruitment websites that allow you to search vacancies in London, register your details and upload your CV. These include, but by are by no means limited to, www.justlondonjobs.co.uk, www.secsinthecity.co.uk, www.cityjobs.com, www.fish4.co.uk, www.gisajob.com and www.monster.co.uk. For work of a more casual nature, websites such as www.gumtree.com list hundreds of jobs on a daily basis, and there are a number of recruitment agencies (see p.63). National newspapers carry job adverts, the majority of which tend to be based in London. *The Guardian* is particularly good as it contains daily dedicated recruitment sections – media, arts, PR and marketing on Monday; education on Tuesday; society jobs on Wednesday; science and environment on Thursday; IT on Friday; and graduate and general jobs on Saturday. All vacancies that appear in the paper can also be viewed at www.guardian.co.uk. London's *Evening Standard* carries job adverts too.

You can approach companies directly, but cold calling to ask about job opportunities is generally likely to meet with a frosty reception – it's usually safer to email or post your CV then try a follow-up phone call if you don't receive a response. The more targeted your approach, such as finding out specific names and job titles, the better your chances of success. The application process for advertised posts varies according to the job and the recruiter. For most public and voluntary sector positions, it will involve filling out an application form, a process that can often be done online. In the private sector, it is more common for job adverts to request that you post or email a CV and covering letter, and possibly examples of your work. Always make sure you follow to the letter any guidelines on how to apply – many vacancies attract a high number of applications, so those that fail to follow instructions are often the first to find their way into the bin.

Recruitment Agencies

Adecco	8307 6000	www.adecco.co.uk
Blue Arrow	0800 0855777	www.bluearrow.co.uk
Brook Street	0172 7848292	www.brookstreet.co.uk
Elect Recruitment Ltd	8582 0110	www.electrecruitment.co.uk
Euro London	7583 0180	www.eurolondon.com
Hays Accountancy Personnel	0800 716026	www.hays.com
Manpower	7831 6868	www.manpower.co.uk
Phee Farrer Jones	0870 0489100	www.pfj.co.uk
Recruit Employment Services	8221 2011	www.recruitemployment.co.uk
Reed	7220 4775	www.reed.co.uk
Reed Accountancy	7638 1021	www.reed.co.uk
Select	7600 8582	www.select.co.uk
Teaching Personnel	8221 4547	www.teachingpersonnel.com
Telepower	7630 6496	www.telepower.co.uk

Volunteer Here
One of the most popular volunteer organisations in the UK is the VSO. Many experienced professionals pack in their jobs and join the charity for two-year placements in some of the world's poorest countries. The volunteers' aim is to pass on their skills, be it in teaching or marine biology, for the long-term benefit of local people. VSO pays for flights and living expenses. For more information, see www.vso.org.uk.

Voluntary & Charity Work

Volunteering can be an excellent way of gaining experience, learning new skills and making contacts – at the same time as getting that warm glow from doing something worthwhile. It may also lead to being offered a paid position. Alternatively you may simply wish to volunteer in order to meet like-minded people or because you have spare time you feel could usefully be offered to a cause you hold dear. A great many national charities are based in London, from wildlife and conservation campaigns to helping the homeless or staffing crisis phonelines. Once you've decided on the kind of work you'd like to do, contact the organisations that interest you directly. The websites www.timebank.org.uk and www.do-it.org.uk offer searchable databases of volunteer opportunities by region. Openings also arise with local campaigns and events – check websites and look out for notices in public libraries, bookshops and cafes. It is possible to enter the UK solely to do voluntary work if you make arrangements with a specific charity, or to stay on to do such work after entering for another reason – check www.ind.homeoffice.gov.uk for more information.

Working as a Freelancer/Contractor

Being your own boss is a dream scenario for many, but setting up as a freelance in any profession takes a lot of dedication and groundwork. However, in fields such as broadcasting production, journalism, PR, design and even social work and healthcare, freelancers with the right skills can certainly thrive in London. Successful freelancers have often spent many years building up their skills base so someone new to the scene will have a lot of ground to make up. Online discussion groups can be useful ways of getting a feel for the sort of contracts available and rates paid, with individuals often willing to pass on work opportunities they are unable to take up themselves. There are also many industry-specific recruitment agencies that may be able to help you find short-term contract work (see p.63).

In terms of taxation, you will need to inform the Inland Revenue that you are self-employed (see www.hmrc.gov.uk). Income tax and National Insurance are payable on the money you make through freelance work, so be sure to account for it in your budget. You will be able to claim back certain expenses from your tax bill, so keep hold of any receipts. For those entering the UK from outside the European Economic Area, a visa will not normally be granted specifically to work as a freelancer but it is certainly possible for those on spousal, working holidaymaker or ancestry visas, for instance, to work on a freelance basis.

Minimum Wage

The National Minimum Wage sets out the legal minimum amount workers must be paid per hour (which can work out as an hourly average over a week or month). There are three rates: for workers 22 and over the rate is £5.35 per hour (rising to £5.52 in October 2007); for workers between 18 and 21 it is £4.45 (£4.60 from October 2007); and for those aged 16 and 17 the rate is £3.30 (£3.40 from October 2007). The exceptions to the minimum wage are: those under 16; some apprentices and trainees; au-pairs and nannies where accommodation and meals form part of the deal; the self-employed; members of the armed forces; and voluntary workers. If you think you are not being paid the minimum wage, phone the National Minimum Wage Helpline on 0845 6000678.

Employment Contracts

The letter of an offer of employment should set out the job you are taking up and supply basic details. Under UK law you are entitled to a written statement, within two months of starting a job, which sets out the central terms of your contract: job title, hours, salary, leave entitlement, sick pay, pension provision, notice period and the company or organisation's grievance and disciplinary procedure. It should also state whether the job is of a fixed-term nature or permanent.

There are certain rights that cannot be overwritten by an employment contract, including: receiving an itemised pay slip; being paid at least the national minimum wage; having at least four weeks' paid leave; maternity leave of 26 weeks and the right to return to work after this (see p.144), and/or paternity, adoption and unpaid parental leave; freedom to ask for flexible working; union representation; weekly and daily breaks; the right not to be discriminated against on the grounds of sex, race, disability, religion and sexual orientation; and various other rights associated with notice periods and dismissal, depending on the length of your service. Most employees working regular, part-time or full-time hours are also entitled to statutory sick pay.

Many organisations operate a probationary period of around three months – if this is the case it should say so in your contract. During this time the notice period will typically be a week as opposed to a month. With some positions the amount of notice you need to give if you leave will increase with your length of service.

UK law also stipulates a statutory minimum disciplinary and dismissal procedure, which must consist of, at the least, a written statement, a meeting and an appeal meeting. Individual organisations' procedures may include more elements than this, such as a system of verbal or written warnings. At disciplinary meetings you have the right to be accompanied by someone you work with or a trade union official, and you must be given time to respond to any allegations made against you. Your employer must also have a grievance procedure in place which consists of the same three steps and allows you to make an official complaint if you are unable to resolve any problems informally.

Employees have considerable protection under UK and European law and, if you have any suspicion that you are being treated unequally, have been denied statutory rights or dismissed unfairly, you should seek knowledgeable advice. You may be able to build a case that you can then take to an employment tribunal – the legal body that enforces working rights. Trade unions provide specialised help and cover all spheres of work, and employees have the right to join or not join a union as they see fit. Alternatively, approach the Citizens Advice Bureau, which offers free independent advice. To find your local office go to www.adviceonline.org.uk.

Changing Jobs

A job for life is an outdated concept in the UK, and in London in particular, with many workers changing companies or positions regularly for career advancement, personal circumstances or just a fresh challenge. However, if you are tied to a particular job by a work permit you cannot change jobs without approval from the Immigration and Nationality Directorate, which in reality means your new employer applying for a new permit. Aside from this, your employment contract will set out the amount of notice you need to give before leaving a job, and as long as you follow this you should not encounter any problems or complications. When you leave a job you will receive a P45, a tax document that you need to hand over to your next employer.

Company Closure

There is a considerable amount of legislation governing redundancy, not least stating that you cannot be made redundant on a discriminatory basis and that the company must investigate if there are any other vacancies it could consider you for. If you have been with an employer for two years or more before you are laid off then you are entitled to redundancy pay. This also applies if the company you are working for folds. If the company has ceased trading but is not insolvent, you should attempt to claim the redundancy from it in the first instance; if the firm does not respond, is insolvent, in receivership or in liquidation, you need to contact the National Insurance Fund on 0845 145 0004.

If you are in the country on a work permit obtained by your company and it subsequently closes, you will need to find a new UK employer to sponsor you if you wish to stay. This also applies if you want to leave your job for any other reason. After five years of continuously working in the UK, however, you will gain the option of applying for indefinite leave to remain, removing the need for any further work permits.

Canary Wharf

The Complete **Residents'** Guide

Bank Accounts

The major banks and building societies in the UK, known as the 'high-street banks', all offer a comprehensive range of financial services including current accounts, savings accounts, credit cards, mortgages, loans and insurance. In addition to the UK-based banks, some of which offer foreign currency accounts, there are branches of some international banks such as Citibank in central London. All banks offer online and telephone-banking as a matter of course, and there are various internet-only accounts available, which may make sense if you are moving around a lot.

Typically you can only open a bank account with proof of address and proof of earnings. It is customary for banking to be 'free' in the sense that there are no automatic monthly charges levied, with charges instead made for going beyond an agreed overdraft limit or for certain other services. Premium accounts, which offer a wider range of benefits, usually incur a monthly charge and may require a minimum deposit every month. Most banks offer special accounts for those under 16 and for full-time students. Banking hours are generally Monday to Friday, 09:00 to 17:00, with some variations. Note that only a few banks are open on Saturdays. Once you open an account you'll receive a chequebook and a debit card that allows you to withdraw money without charge from a network of ATMs and for a fee from other ATMs (if there is a charge it will be stated on-screen).

A Nation of Shopoholics

It's undeniable that as long as you have a regular income and a bank account, getting credit or an unsecured personal loan presents few obstacles and, with many banks offering 0% interest to start with and a tempting range of other incentives, it can be hard to resist the urge to sign up and hit the shops. However, a credit card habit can quickly get you into financial difficulties as monthly payments mount up, creating a vicious cycle where servicing your debts necessitates further borrowing. If you find yourself getting out of your depth, seek free confidential advice on managing your debts from the Citizens Advice Bureau, www.adviceonline.org.uk, or from the National Debt Line (www.national debtline.co.uk; 0808 8084000).

Financial Planning

Bearing in mind London's high cost of living, the prospect of having enough disposable income to put money aside for the future may seem rather remote. Still, all banks and building societies offer a range of savings accounts with different interest rates and access terms for those looking to save. Some banks even offer current accounts which will automatically transfer money to a savings account once your credit balance reaches a certain level.

Financial advice in itself is big business and there are no shortage of companies, comparison websites and financial pages of newspapers offering advice, tips and predictions. Banks and building societies also offer a range of investment options, including offshore opportunities. For an impartial take on the available options contact the government's financial watchdog, the Financial Services Authority (www.fsa.gov.uk/consumer). Here you can search for an FSA-accredited financial advisor in your area.

The consistent climb in property prices over the last 20 years has led to property being widely considered a wise investment, with 'buy to let' a favoured option for many with money to invest. Note that if you buy property in the UK, you are immediately considered resident in the UK for tax purposes. For more on buying property, see page.75.

Main Banks

Name	Phone	Web
Abbey	0800 5872758	www.abbey.com
Allied Irish Bank (GB)	01895 272222	www.aibgb.co.uk
Barclays Bank plc	0800 400100	www.barclays.co.uk
Halifax	0845 7203040	www.halifax.co.uk
HSBC ▶ p.149	0845 7404404	www.hsbc.co.uk
Lloyds TSB Bank plc	0845 3000000	www.lloydstsb.com
NatWest	0800 200400	www.natwest.com
Royal Bank of Scotland	7409 0599	www.rbs.co.uk
Woolwich	0845 0700360	www.woolwich.co.uk

Cost of Living

Item or Activity	Price/Cost
Apples (per kg)	£1.69
Bananas (per kg)	90p
Bottle of house wine (restaurant)	£13
Bottle of wine (off licence)	£6
Burger (takeaway)	£2.50
Bus (10 km journey)	£1.10
Camera film	£5
Can of dogfood	49p
Can of Soft Drink	50p
Cappuccino	£1.80
Car rental (per day)	£140
Carrots (per kg)	50p
CD album	£11.99
Chocolate bar	40p
Cigarettes (per pack of 20)	£5
Cinema ticket	£9
Dozen eggs	£1 (battery); £2 (free range)
Film developing (colour, 36 exp)	£7
Fresh beef (per kg)	£10 to £17
Fresh chicken (per kg)	£2.75
Fresh fish (per kg)	£14
Golf (18 holes)	£20
Haircut (female)	£40
House wine (glass)	£3.50
Large takeaway pizza	£12
Loaf of bread	85p
Local postage stamp	32p
Milk (1 litre)	64p
Mobile to mobile call (local / minute)	20p
New release DVD	£19.99
Newspaper (international)	65p (The Times)
Newspaper (local)	40p
Orange juice (1 litre)	£1 (longlife); £1.80 (fresh)
Pack of 24 paracetamol tablets	£1.50 (generic)
Petrol (gallon)	£4
Pint of beer	£2.50
Postcard	75p
Potatoes (per kg)	50p (cheapest)
Rice (1kg)	£2
Salon haircut (male)	£25
Six-pack of beer (off licence)	£6
Strawberries (per punnet)	£1.50 (in season); £2.99 (out of season)
Sugar (2kg)	£1.57
Taxi – licensed black cab (10km)	£19
Text message (local)	10p
Tube of toothpaste	£1.50
Water 1.5 litres (restaurant)	£3.50
Water 1.5 litres (supermarket)	60p

Pensions

If you have an existing pension in your home country, you may want to continue to pay into it, especially if you plan your stay in London to be temporary. Many UK employers offer a pension scheme as part of their terms of employment. A pension scheme usually consists of monthly contributions deducted from your pay and matched by your employer, which are then paid into a pension fund made up of investments. Individual plans vary considerably, with public sector pensions typically the most generous.

It is also possible to pay into a pension fund separate from your employment. You can find out about these through the usual sources of financial advice – websites, newspapers, money magazines and financial advisers. In addition to any occupational pension, women over 60 and men over 65 are entitled to the State Retirement Pension if they or their married partner or civil partner have paid sufficient National Insurance contributions (NICs) (see p.64) during their working life. The UK has bilateral social security agreements with various countries including the USA, which exempt you from paying UK NICs and allow you to continue to pay into your home country's state provision. Special provisions often also apply to those from Australia, New Zealand and Canada – consult the website www.thepensionservice.gov.uk for more information.

Taxation

The UK tax system, administered by HM Revenue and Customs, operates under the principle of taxing all income generated in the UK, with your personal level of income taxed determined by how much you earn (if you earn very little, you may not be liable to pay any tax at all). For income tax purposes you are considered 'ordinarily resident' if you are in the UK with the intention of staying for three years or more (students are exempt).

Owning property in the UK also puts you in the 'ordinarily resident' bracket. The other main tax category you may fall into is 'resident', in which case you may have a 'domicile' other than the UK. You are treated as resident in any given tax year (running from 6 April one year to 5 April the next) if you are here for 183 days or more. As ordinarily resident or resident you are liable to pay UK income tax on all your earned income including pensions and investments, and capital gains tax, which applies to the disposal of major assets. You will also be liable if you come to the UK regularly over a number of years and spend an average of 91 days or more each year in the country. The UK has double taxation agreements with various countries, including the USA, Canada, Australia, New Zealand, South Africa, and Ireland, which could give you tax exemption or partial tax relief. Your employer or embassy may well able to help you out with these matters, or visit the HM Revenue and Customs website (www.hmrc.gov.uk). You should also have a look at this website if you think you might be entitled to claim tax back; if for instance you have paid for a period in which you were not in the country.

Income tax is deducted from your salary by your employer's payroll department before it reaches your paypacket, with details provided on your payslip. If you are working on a freelance or self-employed basis, you are responsible for your own tax calculations via a system called self-assessment. Again see the HMRC website, www.hmrc.gov.uk or www.direct.gov.uk, for guidance through the necessary tax returns. Government help in the form of tax credits is available to low-paid residents, but not usually to those in the country temporarily.

There is a sales tax on most items you buy in the UK called value-added tax (known as VAT), plus additional duties on alcohol, cigarettes, fuel and gambling.

Council tax is a local charge which pays for the services which your local authority supplies; the amount you pay depends on the band your property falls and which borough you live. If money is tight it may be worth investigating the amount you will be liable for as it can vary. The majority of private renters as well as owner-occupiers are responsible for their council tax, with discounts for single-occupant dwellings.

Legal Issues

The law in England and Wales is based on parliamentary democracy. The judiciary is independent from Parliament, which makes the laws of the land. The main courts in operation are: the county court, which deals with civil cases including landlord and tenant disputes, consumer disputes, personal injury claims, discrimination cases and debt; the magistrates court, which deals with some civil cases but mainly with criminal cases known as 'summary offences' where the defendant is not entitled to trial by jury and the maximum penalty is six months' imprisonment and/or a fine of up to £5,000. In some cases the defendant can choose to have their case heard in a magistrates court rather than go to trial by jury.

The crown court mainly deals with serious criminal offences tried by judge and jury. The High Court, the Court of Appeal and the House of Lords deal with appeals and complex cases of various natures. The jury system allows those accused of serious criminal offences to be tried by their peers (jury members are chosen at random from the population at large). The accused also has the right to legal representation, and may be eligible for help with legal costs if on a low income. As the UK is a member state of the European Union and required to comply with European legislation, those in the UK have the ultimate recourse to the European Court of Justice. Penalties in UK law range from fines and community service to suspended prison sentences and prison sentences. There is no death penalty.

Drink-Driving Laws

Driving under the influence of drugs or alcohol is illegal in the UK, with the legal limit being 80 milligrammes of alcohol in 100 millilitres of blood. Government statistics suggest that nearly one in six deaths on the road involve a driver over the legal limit. Regular hard-hitting advertising campaigns add to a growing societal disapproval of drink-driving. If stopped by the police on suspicion of drink-driving it's in your interests to cooperate as it's an offence to refuse a breathalyser or specimen test.

Divorce

To get divorced in England and Wales, your marriage must be recognised by UK law and you must meet residence rules. If both partners agree to the divorce then it is known as an 'undefended' divorce and can be dealt with relatively straightforwardly. If one partner does not want a divorce then it is a 'defended' divorce and solicitors will be involved. To start divorce proceedings you need to fill in certain forms which you can get from a divorce court – in London undefended divorce is generally dealt with by the divorce registry. If there is no agreement over childcare and finances the courts will arbitrate. Either party can pursue a claim for maintenance through the courts (you should seek legal advice if you wish to do this).

The financial support of children remains the responsibility of both parents, even if they are unmarried, and claims for maintenance can be pursued via the Child Support Agency (www.csa.gov.uk). The civil partnership equivalent of divorce is dissolution, and is dealt with by the courts in a very similar way, although the grounds on which you can apply for dissolving your partnership vary slightly.

Law Centres

Londoners are subject to the legal system of England and Wales – Scotland has a different system of law. In London there are a number of law centres that provide free legal advice to those unable to afford a solicitor. These can often offer expert advice in areas such as immigration, employment and housing. See www.lawcentres.org.uk for more information.

Making a Will

Making a will is a way of ensuring your wishes are respected after your death. Bear in mind that unmarried couples or same-sex couples who are not in a civil partnership do not automatically inherit from each other unless a will has been drawn up to this effect. You may also be able to limit the amount of inheritance tax payable by making a will. In order for a will to be legal it must be made voluntarily by someone aged 18 or over. The will must be in writing and signed by the person making the will in the presence of two witnesses, who must also sign the document. Your witnesses should not stand to gain from the will. A will does not have to drawn up in the presence of a solicitor to be legally valid, although it is good practice to have it looked over or written up by a solicitor who specialises in will-making, especially if the will is complicated or the care of children is involved. When making a will, take into account what your possessions and money consist of (encompassing property, bank accounts, insurance policies, pensions and shares) and who you wish to benefit from the proceeds, including any charities. You also need to consider who you would like to act as guardians for any children under 18. The people you appoint to oversee the sorting out of your estate and carrying out the wishes outlined in your will are known as 'executors' and you can choose up to four executors. People often pick relatives, friends, solicitors or bank representatives to be their executors, but make sure you check with them that they are willing to assume the responsibility. For straightforward changes to a will you can add a codicil, a further written statement setting out the new terms. If you are making major changes then it is better to draw up a fresh will that expressly revokes the previous one.

Adoption

If you are settled in the UK and are considering adopting a child, you should approach the adoption agency in your local authority in the first instance to find out more. You will need to go through a formal application and preparation process during which you will be assessed and your background checked to see if you can meet the needs of an adoptive child. If accepted as a potential adopter, you then face a wait to be matched with a suitable child, which can take any time from a couple of weeks to a year or more. Married couples, co-habiting couples of any sexuality, civil partners and single people can all apply to adopt, regardless of race or religion, and your suitability will be assessed according to both national and local policy. Once a child has been settled with you, an adoption order will be made that ends any legal ties with the child's birth family. For more information, contact the British Association for Adoption and Fostering (www.baaf.org.uk).

69

Anti-social Behaviour Orders (Asbo) were introduced in 1998 to reduce the level of petty crime in local communities, and have since gained something of a notorious reputation. An Asbo is a civil order issued against someone who has harassed or distressed people in their community, and usually bans them from carrying out that particular activity again. The range of offences includes intimidation, noise-making, rubbish-dumping and vandalism – although there have been some more, rather bizarre orders dished out over the years. These include a woman banned from answering the door dressed only in her underwear; a 60-year-old barred from feeding bread to the birds; and an 87-year-old man prevented from making sarcastic remarks to his neighbours. You have been warned…

Crime

According to the Home Office, 23% of the UK's population were a victim of some kind of crime during a 12-month period in 2005-06 – which, although a high figure, is significantly down from a peak of 40% in 1995. In London, levels of crime are uniformly higher than the national average, although generally falling at the same rate. Of course statistics and trends do not tell the whole story, and fear of crime is a major issue for the city's population – it's liable to top most people's list of social concerns. London is served by two police services, the City of London Police, a small force which covers the Square Mile, and the Metropolitan Police, which deals with the bulk of the city.

Safety Tips

Your personal perception of risk will probably depend on various factors, such as where you live, when and how you travel, and the level of dodgy behaviour on the streets around you. To protect yourself when out and about after dark stick to well-lit routes and avoid run-down areas or red-light districts. If using public transport try to sit close to the front of the bus or train and choose a well-populated carriage if possible. Avoid using ATMs in quiet corners and try not to display expensive phones or MP3 players when on your own at night (remember too that listening to music can dent your awareness of what is going on around you).

Women in particular should avoid unlicensed minicabs as there have been many cases of rape and sexual assault involving this mode of transport. Always book minicabs in advance from a licensed firm and, if possible, have someone see you into the car. It is illegal for minicabs to tout for business on the street, and the only cab you should hail is a licensed black taxi.

In crowded shopping areas, restaurants and bars, pickpocketing and bag-snatching is a fairly common occurrence. To prevent this: avoid putting wallets or valuables in your back pocket; carry handbags in front of you rather than behind; and in bars and restaurants try to keep all your belongings within your line of vision.

Arrest

The police can arrest you if they have reasonable grounds to believe you are guilty of a crime, are in the middle of committing one, or preparing to carry one out. If you are arrested, you will be cautioned and taken to a police station. Once in custody, you have the right to let someone know of your arrest by making a phone call, and the right to talk to a solicitor (at any police station there will be a duty solicitor to whom you can talk free of charge). Those under 17 should not be interviewed without the presence of a parent or guardian. If you are not British you should consider contacting your embassy as it may be able to offer you additional help. Once you've been arrested the police must either charge you within 24 hours or release you (which they may do if they consider the offence too minor to merit prosecution, or if they have insufficient evidence), unless they get special permission to hold you without charge for longer. For arrests relating to terrorism, however, the police have greater powers of detention. Once charged, you will appear at a magistrates' court, which may result in your release on bail or detention in custody until your trial. The police are governed by extensive codes of practice and you have the right to make a complaint if you believe they have not followed them.

Criminal Record

Records of prosecutions and cautions, reprimands or final warnings made in England, Wales and Scotland are kept on a central database by the Criminal Records Bureau. Job application forms may request information about convictions here or abroad and employers can apply for disclosure of applicants' criminal records, particularly for

positions that involve working with children or vulnerable adults.

A national sex offender register keeps tabs on the movements of all those convicted of, or cautioned for, sexual crimes in the UK since 1997, which schools, community organisations and some employers have access to. Even if employers cannot access foreign criminal records, they will be very stringent about checking references and employment history. Having a criminal record in your country of origin can also affect your eligibility for a UK visa.

Drugs Possession

It would be pointless to pretend that illegal drugs are not widely available in London. It's also the case that the police are so overstretched trying to catch dealers and break up drugs rings that individual occasional users are not terribly likely to be caught and prosecuted unless they are being particularly conspicuous or their drug use forms part of wider criminal activity. Illegal drugs fall into three main classifications – A, B and C, with A carrying the highest penalties for using or dealing. Class A includes heroin, methadone, cocaine, ecstasy, LSD, amphetamines prepared for injection, and magic mushrooms prepared for use. Possession can lead to seven years in prison, while a conviction for dealing could lead to life in jail. Class B drugs are mainly amphetamines and barbiturates, while Class C includes cannabis, anabolic steroids and tranquillisers such as Valium and Temazepam that have not been prescribed for you, plus some milder amphetamines. Maximum penalties for possession are five years in prison for Class B and two for Class C, and 14 years in prison for supply for both categories.

Motoring Offences

If you are found guilty in court of a motoring offence such as speeding or dangerous driving, you could incur between 3 and 11 penalty points on your licence, usually in conjunction with a fine. Depending on the offence you can apply to have the points removed after a certain length of time. You'll be disqualified from driving if you chalk up more than 12 points over three years, and for more serious driving offences your licence can be immediately disqualified for a prescribed length of time.

Traffic Accidents

If you are involved in a traffic accident, make sure you stop at the scene. As the driver you should remain with your vehicle and give your name and address and vehicle registration number, and the details of the owner of the vehicle if different, to anyone involved in the accident. If someone has been injured, the driver will also need to produce a valid insurance certificate. If they don't have this about their person they should present it to a police station within seven days. When an accident has resulted in damage to vehicles the driver must be prepared to give their insurance details to anyone who may wish to make a claim against them. It is important to establish who is liable for the accident – in some cases this will be straightforward, but if there is any doubt then the presence of a witness will be crucial. Whatever happens you should get in touch with your insurance company as soon as possible, and remember you may be able to get free legal advice from the firm or any motoring organisation you are a member of. For more on vehicle insurance, see p.156.

Housing

Finding a place to live in London can be a draining experience, physically, emotionally and financially; so much so that it has been known to put people off the city entirely. But while there is undoubtedly a lot of work and a good bit of luck involved, firm ideas about your requirements and sound advice about London's key residential areas will make the task easier. Whether you choose to rent or buy, there's no getting away from the fact that accommodation is likely to take a fair chunk of your monthly earnings. House prices are high and renting may save you money in the short-term, but if you plan to stay in London on a long-term basis you may want to consider the possible benefits of buying property. Below is a guide to London's most popular neighbourhoods and details of the renting and buying process in the capital.

Renting in London

Council Tax

Council tax is a charge which pays for the services that your local authority supplies; how much you pay depends on the band your property falls into and which borough you live in. If money is tight it is worth investigating the amount for which you will be liable as it can vary greatly. The majority of private renters, as well as owner-occupiers, are responsible for their council tax, with discounts for single-occupant dwellings.

Residential rents in London are high and tend to be on a slightly upward trend (they are less susceptible to the more dramatic rises of house prices, however). How much you have available to spend per month has major implications for which areas and which type of accommodation you will be able to consider. The quality of individual property also plays a part in how much rent is asked. There's rarely much negotiation involved in rent prices as landlords have little difficulty finding tenants.

Finding a Home

When looking for accommodation, some choose to use a letting agent who deals professionally with the renting out of properties. Most high-street estate agents that sell properties also act as letting agents. Letting agents deal mostly with entire flats and houses, so simply looking in their windows or trawling their websites will give you a feel for the kind of property on the rental market in any particular area.

The advantages of using them are that they can take some of the hassle out of the search for accommodation and that their procedures for setting up tenancies are standardised and hopefully efficient. The downside is that you will probably pay slightly more in rent than you would if you rented directly from a landlord. Some letting agents charge tenants if they successfully find them somewhere or have some kind of paid registration scheme, while others only charge landlords. Letting agents who have signed up to the National Approved

Letting Scheme (www.nalscheme.co.uk) have agreed to maintain certain standards, including having a complaints procedure in place, so these are the best ones to use. If you are more interested in joining a flat- or house share, you will find these widely advertised on the internet, on dedicated flatsharing websites such as www.spareroom.co.uk or http://uk.easyroommate.com, or on community and listings websites such as www.gumtree.com. See p.73 for more property websites.

Housing

What's Included in Rent

It is slightly unusual to find an unfurnished let in London; rented accommodation generally comes complete with main kitchen appliances such as a fridge and washing machine, plus bedroom and living room furniture. Rent can either be 'inclusive' or 'exclusive' of bills. When a place is advertised with bills inclusive, it generally means the rent covers the price of gas, electricity and water. Council tax, a monthly payment to the local authority (see p.72), may or may not be included so make sure you check. Telephone bills will almost always be the tenant's responsibility. Houses or apartments which come with a dedicated parking space are not very common and will command a premium in terms of rent. Likewise, it is only the properties at the most expensive end of the market which are likely to have facilities such as air conditioning, door staff or an on-site gym. Major repairs to the property are the landlord's responsibility, as is the upkeep of gas appliances, which, by law, must be serviced annually. Tenants, for their part, have a duty to keep the property they are renting and its contents in good general order.

Flat Broke

According to the latest figures from the Land Registry of England and Wales, the cheapest area to buy a flat in London is the borough of Barking and Dagenham, where the average price of a flat is £129,081. The most expensive area in which to buy remains the Borough of Kensington and Chelsea, at an average price of £677,543. The average cost of a flat in the Greater London area was £275,267 in January 2007.

Deposits and Leases

In the UK it is standard to put down a refundable deposit of at least one month's rent and pay one month's rent in advance before you move into a new place. You then continue to pay your rent in advance at monthly intervals. If you are renting a self-contained property on your own or as part of a group you will probably be asked to sign a legally binding agreement called an 'assured shorthold tenancy'. This kind of tenancy covers a minimum of six months, with the agreement being renewable after this time. Within the initial six months the landlord or tenant must give one month's notice if they wish you to leave, and two months' notice once the contract has been extended beyond this time (unless the two parties come to a mutual agreement). The rent should not go up during the first six months unless the tenancy agreement has a clause allowing for this or you agree to the increase. After this time you may well be subject to rent increases and you have little recourse (other than moving out) if you consider them unfair. The majority of houseshares fall into a category called 'houses in multiple occupation' and are governed by additional health and safety regulations, which are enforceable by the local council. If you are sharing accommodation with the person who owns it however, you have far fewer rights.

Landlord-Tenant Disputes

If you have any problems with your landlord, you should consider approaching the Citizens Advice Bureau (www.citizensadvice.org.uk), a free advice service with local offices. Each local authority also has a tenancy relations officer who can intervene in landlord-tenant disputes. You can contact them via your local authority website, or via

Estate Agents

Name	Phone	Web	Areas Covered
Alex Neil	7537 9859	www.alexneil.co.uk	East
Chard	7244 7711	www.chard.co.uk	West
Foxtons	0800 1386060	www.foxtons.co.uk	All areas of London
Harrison Ingram	8312 4111	www.harrisoningram.co.uk	South-east
HouseWeb	0845 1235181	www.houseweb.co.uk	All areas of London
Keatons	8525 7788	www.keatons.com	East and North
Kinleigh Folkard & Hayward	8780 3535	www.kfh.co.uk	South-west, South-east, West, North-west, North, East
Lauristons	8994 4433	www.lauristons.com	All areas of London
Ludlow Thompson	7480 0120	www.ludlowthompson.com	All areas of London
Marsh & Parsons	7368 2480	www.marshandparsons.co.uk	Brook Green, Chelsea, Holland Park, Kensington, Notting Hill
Martyn Gerrard	8346 0102	www.martyngerrard.co.uk	North
Winkworth	7240 3322	www.winkworth.co.uk	All areas of London

73

Housing Abbreviations

Apt	Apartment
B/R	Bedroom
C/H	Central heating
D/G	Double glazing
D/W	Dishwasher
Dec	Decorated
Dep req	Deposit required
F/F	Fully fitted/Fully furnished
F/H	Freehold
Furn	Furnished
G/F	Ground floor
Gch	Gas central heating
Gdn	Garden
Incl	Including bills
L/H	Leasehold
M/F	Male/female
M/W	Microwave
Osp	Off street parking
Pmc	Per calendar month
Pw	Per week
Refs req	References required
U/F	Unfurnished
W/F	Washer dryer
W/FLRS	Wooden floors
W/M	Washing machine

www.direct.gov.uk. There are a great many laws and regulations which landlords must comply with, especially governing health and safety, discrimination and harassment, so it is always worth seeking advice if you believe you are being treated unfairly.

Housing Help

It is fairly unusual for assistance with accommodation to be provided by employers in London, and such practices tend to be restricted to employers paying for temporary accommodation while new arrivals find their feet. More help with relocation and in-country orientation may well be on offer with more senior roles. However, there is state provision for help with finding affordable housing, either to rent or buy, for those employed in 'key worker' professions such as the police, the health service and social work – measures which were brought in to stop such workers being priced out of London. For more information about affordable housing schemes as well as emergency housing assistance, see www.shelternet.org.uk.

Main Accommodation Options

Renting a Flat or House

Taking the lease on a whole property may be your preferred option if you're looking for your own space or are arriving in London with family or colleagues in tow. Houses and flats, usually furnished, can be rented directly from individual landlords or from estate agents acting on their behalf. The standard tenancy is a six-month contract, but most estate agents also cater to those looking for shorter-term lets.

Renting a Room in a Flat or House Share

A popular choice for young people and students on a budget, this involves joining an existing set-up where a group of tenants are renting a flat or house from a landlord or agency. You would normally have a bedroom to yourself and share communal areas such as the bathroom, kitchen and living room. A flatshare or houseshare is often an attractive option for those first moving to London, both because it tends to be a cheaper alternative than renting a whole property yourself and because it can offer the chance to get to know new people and build a social life.

Renting a Room as a Lodger

This works in a similar way to a houseshare, except you are sharing facilities with the owner of the property and as such may have less of a say in household matters.

Renting From a Social Landlord

If you are in housing need you may be able to apply for subsidised rented accommodation, which is typically owned and managed by a local council or a housing association.

Buying

The restrictions on buying your own place in London are generally financial, but if you have the funds and the commitment to go through the purchasing process, this can offer a degree of control and security difficult to find in rented accommodation.

Part Buy/Part Rent
Various affordable housing schemes allow those without the financial means to buy a property outright to purchase part (usually starting at 25%) of a housing association property while paying a subsidised rent on the remaining portion.

Other Rental Costs
When moving into rented accommodation you should be prepared to pay the deposit and a month's rent in advance. If you are using a letting agent which charges tenants, make sure you know how much their fee is and when it is payable. If your rent is exclusive of bills, find out how often you will be paying utility and water bills and how much council tax (p.72) you will be charged (council tax can be paid annually or monthly).

Buying Property
Getting on the property ladder has become something of an obsession in the UK, and in London in particular, over the last 20 years. Overall, house prices have risen at an extraordinary rate since the beginning of the 1980s, with the exception of one big blip at the outset of the 1990s. At the end of 2006, the average price of a flat in London was £270,964, while a terraced house would set you back an average of £349,478, and a detached house £678,915. Despite the fact that these prices leave many struggling to get a foot on that ladder, the consensus is that the large annual bonuses paid to those working in London's financial sector mean that such high prices are sustainable. There are no residency restrictions on buying property either, which has encouraged overseas property investors. Due to many years of price rises, property in London is widely regarded as a sound investment, although of course there is no guarantee that prices will continue to grow indefinitely. Those who buy when regeneration plans or new transport links are first mooted, for instance when King's Cross station got the go-ahead for the construction of the high-speed rail link to Paris, are likely to make a profit in several years' time when an area reaps the benefits of new investment. Previously undesirable areas within east London – which will play a major role in hosting the 2012 London Olympics – are experiencing a massive surge of interest. But such property speculation inevitably involves a lot of guesswork and patience, while living in an area undergoing a vast amount of building work and change presents challenges of its own.

The Process
The basic sequence of events runs as follows: find a property you like; secure the funds to pay for it, usually by agreeing a mortgage; make an offer; get a survey done; complete conveyancing (the legal business of transferring a property from one party to another); exchange contracts with the seller; and 'complete' the purchase before moving in. Some of the most common frustrations and delays arise when a 'chain' is involved; this means that the buyer and/or the seller are dependent on other sales going through in order to move themselves. For this reason first-time buyers are often looked upon favourably by sellers, as they are not involved in selling a property themselves.

Buying to Rent
Buying a property in order to let it out is a popular choice for people looking for a reliable source of income, and most of the high-street lenders now offer special 'buy to let' categories of mortgage. But while it may seem like a lucrative option, you need to be aware of your legal responsibilities as a landlord in terms of the maintenance of the property. A significant investment may also be needed initially to bring the property up to a standard to be let out. And if you decide to hand over the day-to-day management of the property to an agent, their fees will of course eat into your profits.

Mini Marvels
Explorer *Mini Visitors' Guides* are the perfect holiday companion. They're small enough to fit in your pocket but beautiful enough to inspire you to explore. With detailed maps, visitors' information, restaurant and bar reviews, the lowdown on shopping and all the sights and sounds of the city, these mini marvels are a holiday must.

Selling Property

After deciding to sell their home, and deciding which fittings such as carpets and curtains to include in the sale, most people approach several local estate agents to get a range of valuations of the property (most estate agents will do quick free valuations with more thorough formal valuations incurring a fee). You can then decide what you believe to be a sensible asking price and can try and arrange a sale privately, although the vast majority of people employ an estate agent to advertise the property, send out details to potential buyers and show them around the property. The estate agent's commission is usually worked out as a percentage of the selling price, typically between 1.5% and 2.5%. There are likely to be additional charges, for expenses such as advertising and VAT, all of which should be detailed in your initial contract and some of which may well be payable even if you end up selling to a buyer who was not found by that estate agent. You can entrust the sale to one estate agent under a 'sole agency' contract, or several under a 'joint agency' or 'joint sole agency' agreement, something that will usually cost more as it maximises your chances of making a quick sale. Agents who have signed up to the Estate Agents Ombudsman Scheme (OEA, www.oea.co.uk) have agreed to abide by a code of practice, which gives you a fair measure of recourse in the event of any disputes.

Mortgages

Unless you have sufficient funds to make a purchase outright, buying a property will require arranging a mortgage, a large-scale loan where your home is offered as security. There are two main types of mortgage:

Repayment – this is the most common type of mortgage where an amount of capital is borrowed and repaid over a set term (usually 20 or 25 years) in monthly instalments together with variable interest charges.

Endowment – the idea behind endowment mortgages is that you take out a loan in conjunction with an endowment policy with an insurance company. Monthly payments go towards paying off the interest on the loan and you also pay a monthly contribution to the policy. At the conclusion of the mortgage term the policy should have matured sufficiently to provide a lump sum to pay off the loan. There is risk attached to this type of policy as it is investment-based, and as a result it's becoming less popular in the UK.

Mortgage Providers

Provider	Phone	Website
Abbey	0800 555100	www.abbey.com
Alliance & Leicester	0800 0563254	www.alliance-leicester.co.uk
Hadenglen	0846 2264757	www.hhfplc.co.uk
HSBC ▶ p.149	0800 1696333	www.hsbc.co.uk
Lloyds TSB	0800 7833534	www.lloydstsb.com
NatWest	0800 0969527	www.natwest.com
UK Mortgagelink	0800 3765120	www.ukmortgagelink.org
Woolwich Open Plan	0845 0705090	www.woolwich.co.uk
Yorkshire Building Society	0845 1200100	www.ybs.co.uk

Mortgages are available from banks, building societies, finance houses, mortgage companies and, in the case of endowment mortgages, insurance companies, on examination of your finances and the lender making an assessment of your risk. You can go directly to a lender to arrange a loan or employ a broker to sift through the deals available and approach lenders on your behalf. As well as dedicated mortgage brokers, some estate agents also act as brokers. The amount you can borrow usually depends on how much you earn, with a standard maximum amount being three times your annual salary. The increasing discrepancy between salaries and house prices in London, however, has led lenders to consider lending up to five times your salary. It's usual to put down a cash deposit on your property of 5% to 10% of its total price, but it can be possible to negotiate 100% or even 120% mortgages.

All lenders have a standard variable rate (SVR) of interest which applies to mortgages but offer many deals based on different rates of interest. For instance 'tracker' mortgages are tied to the Bank of England's base interest rate, 'fixed rate' mortgages allow you to pay at a stable rate of interest for a proscribed time, and 'discounted rate' mortgages offer an interest rate below the SVR, but tacked to it.

Other Purchasing Costs

Ground rent and service charges – properties bought on a freehold basis include the land on which it is built as well as the building itself. However, if you are buying a property on leasehold terms, which is particularly common with flats in London, someone else owns the freehold and you will be liable to pay ground rent (something that does not usually run to more than £200 per year). More costly is the service charge for the upkeep of communal areas in your building. Service charges can amount to more than £1,000 per year, with additional costs cropping up for major repairs.

Survey and valuation fees – mortgage lenders will value the property you intend to buy before lending you the money. You'll also need to have your own survey done; this can either be a basic inspection or a more detailed report on the condition of the property – a wise investment if you are buying an older property or have any doubts about its structural soundness.

Stamp duty – this tax runs at the rate of 1% of the purchase price for properties between £125,000 and £250,000, 3% for those costing between £250,001 and £500,000, and 4% for those costing over £500,001.

Mortgage Payment Protection Insurance – this covers you if you are unable to make your mortgage repayments due to illness or redundancy.

Mortgage broker and/or mortgage lender fees – some lenders offer no fee deals, others will charge a fixed fee of a few hundred pounds.

Solicitor fees – a solicitor is needed to draw up, process and verify all the documents involved, and fees will typically cost you upwards of £500.

Land Registry fee and local authority search fees – small charges for standard administration.

Real Estate Law

Once you have made an offer on a property, the offer has been accepted and the survey has been satisfactorily completed, the legal business of transferring the property from one party to another, known as conveyancing, gets underway. One point to note is that even if a buyer has accepted your offer, there is nothing in law to prevent them from then accepting a higher offer from someone else. This practice, known as 'gazumping', can mean a lot of time wasted, not to mention considerable distress – although you can try and protect yourself by requesting that the property is taken off the market when your offer is accepted. Both buyers and sellers traditionally engage solicitors to deal with the rather tortuous steps involved in conveyancing on their behalf. Solicitors arrange for contracts to be exchanged, any deposit to be paid and set a date for the 'completion' of the sale. Completion is the date at which the legal transfer details and mortgage agreements are sent to the Land Registry and the property legally passes into the possession of the buyer.

77

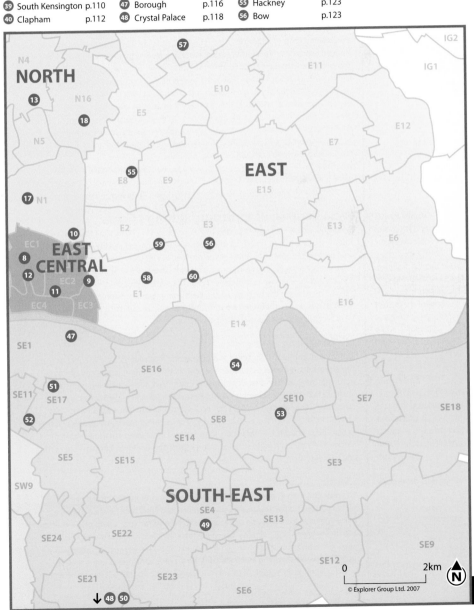

Residential Areas
Other options **Exploring** p.162

It's on the Map
The map on page 78
shows the location of
London's main residential
areas, and the boundary
of each postcode area.
For a full postcode
map, see p.458.

There is a good deal of snobbery among London's estate agents about what counts as a desirable location, but the realities of affordability and space mean that all kinds of people live in all sorts of places and that even the most unpromising corners of the city have their passionate adherents.

In a city where it's not unheard of for people to commute two hours to work, you need to consider how you are going to get to your place of work or study and how long you are prepared to spend doing it.

Some of London's more intensely urban areas may be fine for those who like bustle and excitement, but less suitable for those with a family who, along with those who hanker after a garden, tend to gravitate towards more suburban areas in the outer boroughs of London. If you have school-age children you will also want to look at the performance of local schools as they can vary dramatically. Apart from the very pressing matter of how much money you have at your disposal, other things which may affect your choice include: nearby parks and open spaces; leisure amenities such as gyms and swimming pools; shopping facilities; nearby bars and restaurants; and proximity to the centre of town.

Wherever you fall on the income scale or what you hold to be important, the following guide is intended to provide a snapshot of the capital's main residential neighbourhoods, their charms and idiosyncrasies, their plus points and their downsides.

West Central: Bloomsbury & King's Cross

Good Points
With its elegant squares
and venerable academic
institutions, Bloomsbury
is leafy and dignified,
while being only
moments away from
some of the busiest
shopping streets in
London – and a
train to Paris.

Bloomsbury covers an area bounded by Euston, Gray's Inn Road, High Holborn and Tottenham Court Road, and is full of academic institutions set in leafy squares. The academic theme continues north of Euston Road in King's Cross, where the British Library resides (see p.200). King's Cross, once known only for its station and seedy red light district, has been massively overhauled, boosted by the conversion of St Pancras into the terminus of the high-speed rail link to Paris. Existing Victorian crescents and streets have been rediscovered and previously derelict or industrial land has begun to be covered in new retail and residential development.

Accommodation

Bad Points
King's Cross is in the grip
of a redevelopment frenzy,
and noise and disruption
is likely to affect residents
until at least the end of
the decade.

Overview map, p.78

With its concentration of colleges and educational institutions, Bloomsbury has many student residences so its population is mainly youthful, international and often transient. There are also a lot of cheap and mid-priced hotels, meaning tourists gravitate here too. Permanent residents live in tall converted townhouses in distinctive Georgian squares, or in the occasional mansion block. King's Cross was once an extremely grubby area, but now any of its period residential property is likely to have been bought for renovation. In the spaces inbetween, smart new apartment blocks are flying up. A large social housing estate, Somers Town, lies between Euston and Camden Town.

Shopping & Amenities

The West End, with its endless possibilities for shopping, nightlife and sightseeing, is easily accessed from here. More locally the renovated Brunswick Centre occupies a prime spot in Bloomsbury and has a range of upmarket fashion outlets, plus a Waitrose and the Renoir arthouse cinema. Elsewhere there are plenty of local grocery stores, newsagents and bookshops, and Lamb's Conduit Street has a stretch of more quirky stores. A massive shopping and hotel complex is being constructed in the shell of George Gilbert Scott's gothic Midland Hotel building, which fronts St Pancras station.

I ⊙ beautiful music

Music now looks as beautiful as it sounds. The new W880i
Walkman® phone with up to 900 songs, it's just as
beautiful on the inside.

sonyericsson.com/walkman

Sony Ericsson

University facilities aside, Bloomsbury has a number of private gyms and two retro bowling alleys (see p.240) and its many squares give it a leafy feel, although there is no large park in the area. The British Museum (p.205), with its enormous collection of artefacts from across the globe, is at the heart of Bloomsbury, and there are a number of other smaller museums dotted around such as the Charles Dickens Museum.

Eating & Drinking
Euston Road is lined with fairly anonymous coffee shops, pubs and restaurants that provide sustenance for those passing through the stations. Close to Euston, Drummond Street has a vibrant strip of Indian restaurants, while the gentrification of King's Cross has led to the advance of chain restaurants and tarted-up boozers. Bloomsbury too has many cafes and pubs, primarily catering for office workers, students and tourists, with pizza and pasta-orientated chain restaurants on Southampton Row and the area around Holborn tube. The smaller streets encircling the British Museum offer rather more intimate options. Fitzrovia, between Tottenham Court Road and Marylebone Road, and Charlotte Street in particular, has a good selection of restaurants, covering Indian, Thai, Spanish and Italian. There are a number of big club venues around King's Cross such as Scala, but Bloomsbury, dominated by traditional-style boozers which shut at 23:00, is fairly quiet in the evening. Lamb's Conduit Street is the best bet for trendy bars, gastropubs and innovative restaurants.

Education
There are a couple of primary schools in Bloomsbury, including St Joseph and St George the Martyr, while several primary and secondary schools in the boroughs of Islington (www.islington.gov.uk), Camden (www.camden.gov.uk) and Westminster (www.westminster.gov.uk) are accessible from the area. There is a selection of private schools in the City and Westminster.

Transport
Euston, King's Cross and St Pancras form a formidable triumvirate of mainline stations offering routes to the Midlands, the north of England, Scotland and the continent. Several tube lines feed into these: the Victoria and Northern lines pass through Euston and King's Cross, and the Circle, Hammersmith & City and Metropolitan lines also stop at King's Cross and Euston Square. In Bloomsbury, the Piccadilly line stops at Holborn and Russell Square (plus King's Cross), and the Northern line calls at Goodge Street.

Safety/Annoyances
While King's Cross is losing its rough edges, it is still noticeable for housing a red-light district, drunks and drug-dealers, especially around Pentonville Road and some of the back streets. While there are plenty of clubs and bars in the area, it's preferable to know where you're going and not to linger.

Good Points
A great central location with a pleasant neighbourhood feel and access to Oxford Street.

West Central: Marylebone, Bayswater & Paddington
On one edge of Marylebone is Oxford Street's Selfridges (p.358), while on the other is the scary, four-lane traffic of Marylebone Road and the equally frightening lines of tourists queuing to enter Madame Tussauds. Connecting these two mainstream attractions is Marylebone High Street, which, with its designer boutiques, pavement cafes and jolly locals, appears blissfully unaware of the urban melee at either end. Beyond Edgware Road, Bayswater and Paddington are less gentle environs, with a mix of hotels, bed-and-breakfast accommodation, expensive lets and grand townhouses. All these areas attract international buyers and provide temporary bases for wealthy travellers and permanent settlers.

Residential Areas – West Central

Bad Points
Pollution, traffic and crowds.

Overview map, p.78

Accommodation

Marylebone, Paddington and Bayswater are all densely populated. Marylebone has plenty of desirable property – mansion blocks, garden squares and runs of Georgian and Victorian townhouses, with private homes standing next to embassies and medical practices. A similar pattern continues along the western side of Edgware Road into Bayswater, where many large, expensive residences blend into a mix of bed and breakfasts and flats towards Notting Hill. There's also a high density of B&Bs, hotels and guesthouses around Paddington station in the north. Paddington Basin is a new development of apartment blocks next to a small tributary of Regent's Canal. On the north side of the Marylebone flyover are extensive tracts of flats built as social housing, much of which is now in private hands. Prices reflect the West End location, although they are not as ridiculous as the dizzy heights of Belgravia and Mayfair.

Shopping & Amenities

Marylebone High Street acts as an appealing village centre to this area, a focal point that other parts of central London lack. It has a selection of stores offering designer clothes,

Paddington

luxury home accessories, kitchen gadgets, chocolate and toiletries. Side roads such as Blandford Street and Moxon Street hold further delights in the shape of bakeries, organic butchers, cheese shops and delicatessens. The Waitrose and Tesco Metro on Marylebone High Street meet the grocery needs of locals, with a farmers' market held on Sundays off Moxon Street. On the hectic Edgware Road Middle Eastern groceries snuggle up to Woolworths, Marks & Spencer, and a Somerfield supermarket. The department stores and crowded pavements of Oxford Street are a short walk away, and Regent's Park and Hyde Park are also easily accessible. Tourists flock to Madame Tussauds and Baker Street for the Sherlock Holmes association, but residents tend to give these a wide berth. To the west of Marylebone High Street, around Harley Street, is a concentration of private doctors and healthcare practitioners.

Eating & Drinking

Cafes and bars spill out on to Marylebone High Street, where a range of chain pubs, wine bars and eateries dominate, and there are more options in the surrounding streets, including Persian and Swedish restaurants on Crawford Street. Edgware Road has a flurry of Middle Eastern takeaways, shisha cafes and juice bars, many of which are open 24 hours. Away from the traffic, St Christopher's Place, tucked between Oxford Street and Marylebone, has large branches of Carluccio's, Pizza Express and others, all with outdoor tables. Baker Street offers more tourist-orientated fare.

Education

State primaries in the area tend to be church schools and come under the auspices of Westminster borough (www.westminster.gov). Private options include Connaught House School for children up to 10, and International Community School and Queen's College London (girls only), which cater for all ages. State secondaries are equalled in number by private schools such as Portland Place College and the all-girls Francis Holland, with more up the road in St John's Wood and Maida Vale.

The Complete **Residents'** Guide

Transport

Transport options are many and various. Paddington has a high-speed rail link to Heathrow as well as overland trains to west London and beyond. It is also on the Bakerloo, District, Circle, and Hammersmith & City tube lines, as is Edgware Road, while Baker Street also has links to Greenwich and Docklands via the Jubilee line. Marylebone offers overland trains to the north-west suburbs as well as being on the Bakerloo line. Buses from Edgware Road and Baker Street run to Oxford Street and Marble Arch in one direction, and King's Cross and Liverpool Street in the other.

Safety/Annoyances

The Marylebone Road is a multi-laned pedestrian nightmare, and the roar and pollution are not for the faint-hearted.

Good Points
Party animals will relish living here – it's all on your doorstep.

Bad Points
Noise, litter, and uncouth crowds out for a good time mean peace and quiet is in short supply.

Overview map, p.78

West Central: Soho & Covent Garden

Soho, a compact area roughly bounded by Oxford Street, Charing Cross Road, Shaftesbury Avenue and Regent Street, is one of the most notorious, complex districts of London. Depending on where you're coming from it can mean any number of things; within it is the heart of the UK's film and TV industry, a red-light district, a jazz scene, the centre of gay London, plus any number of businesses, offices, restaurants, bars and clubs. Covent Garden, extending the other side of Charing Cross Road towards Bloomsbury, is primarily a shopping and tourist destination.

Accommodation

Flats to rent or buy in Soho tend to be above shops or businesses in Victorian conversions, with only a handful of houses or modern blocks of apartments available. There are a few more purpose-built apartments in Covent Garden. Space is at a premium and you have to be pretty determined – or lucky – to find somewhere in these areas.

Shopping & Amenities

The shopping meccas of Oxford Street and Covent Garden are on the doorstep, complete with flagship branches of high-street fashion stores. Tottenham Court Road is the place to look for electrical goods and home furnishings. In Soho itself, the stalls on Berwick Street Market (p.367) offer reasonably priced fruit, vegetables and cheeses, and the road is notable for its independent record shops. For everything oriental, visit the stores in Chinatown – a small but very busy run of streets between Shaftesbury Avenue and Leicester Square. There are also a number of Italian delicatessens and restaurants dotted around, a legacy of the area's past as a hub of Italian immigration. Famous too are Soho's sex and fetish shops. In Covent Garden, which is permanently awash with tourists and shoppers, there's a covered market that sells all manner of arts, crafts, clothes and jewellery. The central plaza is surrounded by big-name fashion retailers that extend all the way down Long Acre, while Neal Street is dominated by shoe shops. The area is rich culturally – Covent Garden is the home of the Royal Opera House, the English National Opera is around the corner on St Martin's Lane, and the National Gallery and National Portrait Gallery are in Trafalgar Square. London's Theatreland is concentrated around the Strand and Drury Lane. Soho Square is a rare patch of green in the area, but St James's Park and Green Park are within walking distance.

Eating & Drinking

Soho offers a dizzying range of nightlife spots packed into a very small area. Atmospheric old-school boozers such as The Coach and Horses and French House (see p.422), and the exclusive Groucho Club, have been in the area for decades and are populated by Soho 'characters', while jazz clubs such as the Wag Club and Ronnie Scott's continue to keep the trumpet solo alive. The partially pedestrianised Old Compton Street is the centre of the gay scene, with many more bars and shops in the surrounding streets. Throughout the area there is an ever-changing parade of restaurants and bars which reflect the fashions in food and drink.

Education

The idea of raising children in the centre of the West End, particularly Soho, is not something on most parents' agendas. Still, it does have a primary school, Soho Parish, with 150 pupils. On the other side of Charing Cross Road on Drury Lane is St Clement Dane's primary school, and St Joseph's and All Souls primaries are just on the edge of Bloomsbury. Queen's College London private school on Harley Street takes girls from 3 to 18, while the private Westminster Abbey Choir School offers a choral-based education to boys aged 7 to 14. The boroughs of Westminster (www.westminster.gov.uk) and Camden (www.camden.gov.uk) cover west central London, and there are more schools available within the region.

Transport

The tube map converges on this area so there is no shortage of options, and many destinations are walkable. The Piccadilly line stops at Piccadilly Circus, Leicester Square, Covent Garden and Holborn; the Victoria, Central and Bakerloo lines stop at Oxford Circus; and Embankment tube is on District and Circle lines. Mainline station Charing Cross, serving areas of south London, Kent and Sussex, is adjacent to Trafalgar Square, while Waterloo lies just south of the river Thames.

Safety/Annoyances

The West End is not primarily a residential area so creating a sense of community is not easy. Otherwise, it has all the pitfalls you'd expect of a home in the heart of a major city.

West Central: Other Areas

Westminster & Pimlico

Westminster stretches south of St James's Park to Vauxhall Bridge Road, bordering with Pimlico to the west. The area is home to the Houses of Parliament and numerous government departments and residences, meaning any available property tends to be occupied by officials, diplomats or wealthy older professionals. Garden squares are usually accessed only by keyholders. The immediate area surrounding Victoria station is grubbier, with a high density of offices and mid-range to downmarket hotels. The pretty terraced streets and decent ex-social housing of Pimlico provide weeknight accommodation for MPs and homes for young City workers. A boat service shuttles from The Tate Britain to the London Eye and Tate Modern.

Mayfair & Belgravia

Mayfair, famous as the most expensive street on the Monopoly board, is a square of land bounded by Oxford Street, Regent Street, Park Lane and Piccadilly, while Belgravia is a rectangle between Sloane Street, Knightsbridge, Green Park and Buckingham Palace Road. These are both exclusive areas dominated by grand regency white stuccoed houses and imposing terraces, which are variously diplomatic residences, luxury short-let apartments and the homes of the super-rich.

East Central: Clerkenwell

Good Points
Top drawer restaurants and trendy bars make this a happening spot.

Nestling in between the City, King's Cross and Islington, Clerkenwell is a trendy Zone 1 location with many faces: a neighbourhood for both fashionable young professionals and a long-standing working-class population; a haunt of artists, writers and minor celebrities; a clubbing centre; and a place of work for thousands.

Bad Points
Kids from the local estates are lively and take delight in burning the Vespas of 'hip' media workers.

Accommodation

Property is a three-way split between attractive Victorian townhouses and squares, loft-style apartments and council estates. Some of the estates, such as those built by the Peabody Trust in Clerkenwell Close, are better examples of social housing with flats which have little trouble attracting interest when they come onto the market. The area bounded by Rosebery Avenue, King's Cross Road and Pentonville Road has appealing and quiet Victorian squares and circuses. Things are more complex on the south-side, with live-work units, small offices and artists' studios mixed with flat-fronted terraced houses, low-rise estates and loft conversions.

Overview map, p.78

Shopping & Amenities

Exmouth Market is lined with trendy niche shops selling gifts, flowers, jewellery alongside a weekly food market on Fridays and Saturdays. Small supermarket Budgens caters to more mundane needs, while there is a Tesco Metro on St John Street. Leather Lane market has stalls offering a good selection of fruit and vegetables, as well as discount clothes and household items. Islington (see Exploring, page.162), with its range of supermarkets and high-street stores, is a 10-minute walk. With a buzzy and engaged local community, Clerkenwell holds annual architecture and literary festivals, and there are frequent readings by local authors at Metropolitan Books on Exmouth Market. Sadlers Well Theatre on Rosebery Avenue is world famous for its dance productions. Green space is mainly churchyards, small parks and squares, such as the lovely shady Wilmington Square. Ironmonger Row Baths is unique as the only public-owned leisure facility in London which offers Turkish baths.

Eating & Drinking

Clerkenwell boasts a multitude of bars, gastropubs and restaurants, which cluster around Exmouth Market, St John Street, Clerkenwell Road and Farringdon Road. Clerkenwell is often credited (or blamed, depending on your point of view) with launching the gastropub craze which has so comprehensively swept London. The Eagle on Farringdon Road and The Peasant (p.427) on St John Street continue to do brisk business, despite the legions of imitators and competitors they have spawned. Other Clerkenwell restaurants, such as Moro, with its Spanish-Moroccan food, and St John's (p.383) famous for its use of offal, have national reputations. The area around Farringdon station and Charterhouse Street is known for its cutting-edge bars and clubs.

Chop, Chop ▶
Try the genuine one-off that is The Quality Chop House on Farringdon Road. Here you can sample no-nonsense British dishes such as liver and bacon and steak and kidney pie, just as the working class did in the late 19th century.

Education

State primaries Clerkenwell Parochial, Hugh Myddelton, Christopher Hatton, Moreland and St Peter and St Paul RC fall under Islington (www.islington.gov.uk/education). Private options include The Charterhouse Square School, as well as the independent schools in and around the City and Westminster. The closest state secondary is Central Foundation Boys' School.

Transport

Farringdon (Hammersmith & City, Circle and Metropolitan lines) is the nearest tube to Clerkenwell, although Angel (Northern line) is only a 10 minute walk from Exmouth Market. The overland line passing through Farringdon goes to King's Cross as well as Gatwick and Luton airports. King's Cross is also within striking distance, opening up the Piccadilly, Victoria and Northern lines, as well as, tantalisingly, Paris, via the new high-speed rail link. Buses from Farringdon Road and Rosebery Avenue go to King's Cross, Tottenham Court Road, Piccadilly and Waterloo.

Safety/Annoyances

Charterhouse Street and Farringdon Road are invaded by clubbers well into the small hours at weekends, which can cause problems.

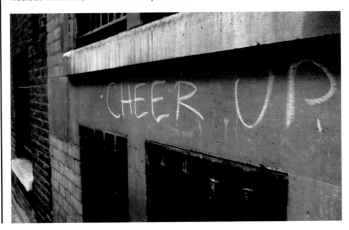

Good Points
If it's hip and it's happening, then it's here.

East Central: Shoreditch & Hoxton

Hoxton and Shoreditch, once largely grim areas, have been transformed over the past 10 years. Now a magnet for the arty and the trendy, the area is considered one of Europe's hottest clubbing spots. In the midst of numerous small design enterprises, media companies, clubs and restaurants, residential property is a collection of council estates and new loft apartments, while a set of graceful and well-preserved Georgian terraced streets off Brick Lane house the most desirable property in the area.

Bad Points
Shoreditch is famous for attracting a self-consciously cool crowd – read into that what you will.

Overview map, p.78

Accommodation

A large amount of social housing is increasingly hemmed in by new residential and office developments. Hoxton and Shoreditch were some of the first areas to popularise New York loft-style living in London in the late 1990s, so there are plenty of converted warehouses, ex-industrial buildings, and high-density apartment blocks to cater to young professionals. Georgian and Victorian properties in the area are precious rarities.

Shopping & Amenities

There is little in the way of everyday practical food shopping, although there is a Somerfield supermarket by Old Street roundabout. A stroll away on Bishopgate is a Tesco while Liverpool Street station has a Marks & Spencer Food Hall next to branches of WH Smith, Boots and The Body Shop. The Broadgate Circus complex spreading out around the station houses a number of upmarket boutiques and, more excitingly, an ice rink. Worth seeking out is an enclave of boho and vintage at the shops and stalls of Old Spitalfields Market (p.369), where you can also stock up on organic food at the weekends. Brick Lane's famous Sunday street market offers fruit, vegetables, cheap clothes, bric a brac, while Columbia Road (p.368) is a spectacularly colourful flower market. There is little green space in the area, with the exception of the delightful Spitalfields City Farm, the rather less inspiring Shoreditch Park and the odd garden square. The Regent's Canal runs through the north of the area, taking you to Victoria Park (p.216) if you stick to the towpath for long enough. The Britannia Leisure Centre on Pitfield Street has a public swimming pool and sports facilities.

Eating & Drinking

Hoxton, Shoreditch and the surrounding areas are bursting at the seams with bars and restaurants. The ultra-trendy Hoxton Square is the area's focal point and its immediate vicinity is home to several restaurants, bars and clubs. Nearby is celebrity chef Jamie Oliver's Fifteen (p.399) and original hip Hoxton hangouts Cantaloupe (p.409) and Home (p.435). A rash of aircraft-hangar-style bars have sprung up around the junction of Great Eastern Street and Shoreditch High Street to cater to the clubbing crowds. The Spitz in Old Spitalfields Market serves up food, drink, art and live music, while among the diverse daily takeaway stalls you can find falafel, curry, traditional pies and burgers. Brick Lane, with its unique mix of curry houses and fashionista bars, is another popular local destination. A number of Vietnamese restaurants cluster at the southern end of Kingsland Road, while Columbia Road has sprouted bars and cafes alongside its flowers.

Hoxton Square

Education

Schools in the area fall under the local boroughs of Hackney (www.hackney.gov.uk), Islington (www.islington.gov.uk) and Tower Hamlets (www.towerhamlets.gov.uk). St Monica's Roman Catholic Primary School is in Hoxton Square, while the religiously affiliated St John The Baptist Voluntary Aided Church of England (CofE), St Luke's and St Matthias primary schools are all nearby. The private primary The Lyceum at Kayam House is on Paul Street. The main state secondaries are divided between the same three boroughs.

Transport

If you work in the City or its fringes you can probably walk to work. Otherwise, Liverpool Street is on the Central, Metropolitan and Hammersmith & City lines and its overland station offers commuter services to Essex and Kent. Old Street is on the Northern line and also has an overland link to Essex Road, Highbury and Islington and Finsbury Park.

Safety/Annoyances

The major through routes of Old Street, Great Eastern Street, Shoreditch High Street and City Road can lend the area a rather grimy aspect, and the influx of determined party-goers at the weekend is not to everyone's taste.

Good Points

The City is a heavily built-up area, but there are some 200 open spaces to explore – historic burial grounds, bowling greens, rose gardens among them.

Bad Points

Visitors and commuters outnumber residents by almost 50 to one.

Overview map, p.78

East Central: The City & Barbican

The City is the financial heart of London – and Europe. Packed into the Square Mile are the country's major financial institutions and trading floors.

The majority of the City's residents live in one place – the Barbican, a mixed residential development and major arts centre. Built on a bombsite in the late 1960s and opened in 1976, it has been reviled as somewhere to live and as a venue. However, in the way of these things, it was awarded Grade II listing status in 2001 and is now regarded with fondness and even admiration by many.

Accommodation

The Barbican has around 2,000 flats providing homes for upwards of 4,000 residents. You will know pretty quickly whether living here is for you. Some see the echoing walkways and blank concrete facades nothing short of depressing, while others find solace in the absence of traffic and are bewitched by the cubby-hole flats with their panoramic views and innovative use of space. All the flats are in private hands and prices are high for reasons of location, prestige and quality. The adjacent Golden Lane Estate, built earlier by the same architects, Chamberlin Powell and Bon in much the same style, if slightly less brutalist, has another 640 flats. Originally made up entirely of social housing, some Golden Lane flats are still in public hands and are let out at affordable rents to key workers and those in housing need. A sprinkling of other apartment blocks have been built in recent years, and the very occasional row of terraced houses survives.

Shopping & Amenities

A topsy-turvy world exists in the City, with the streets full to bursting during the week and eerily deserted at the weekend. Traditionally the vast majority of businesses have been closed at weekends though increasingly the chains and the coffee shops on major routes around Bishopsgate, Moorgate and St Paul's open up to catch passing tourists. A smart Waitrose supermarket enlivens an otherwise drab shopping centre off Whitecross Street. The Barbican (p.174) has a major gallery, small and large performance spaces, arthouse cinema and a fantastic indoor garden. The Museum of London is also here.

Eating & Drinking

Catering to the City's 330,000 workers are sushi bars, fast-food takeaways, and seemingly a Pret-a-Manger on every corner. The snack bars and coffee bars cluster around Liverpool Street, St Paul's and thoroughfares such as Bishopsgate and Moorgate and bright gastropubs rub shoulders with crusty old wine bars full of middle-aged businessmen. Many pubs serve food to cash in on City trade but few are worth a special trip. The Barbican has bars attached to its auditoriums and cafes with outdoor tables. The best restaurants are to be found slightly beyond the City's boundaries towards Spitalfields Market, Hoxton and Clerkenwell.

Education

The solitary state school within the City of London is Sir John Cass's Foundation Primary, although some of the schools on the City fringes of Islington, Camden and Hackney are very close. Nearby private primaries include St Paul's Cathedral School, The Charterhouse Square School and Dallington School. Slap bang in the middle of the Barbican is the private City of London School for Girls, which takes pupils upwards of age 7, while, for the boys, City of London School is on Queen Victoria Street. Catering to pupils with special needs of all ages is Richard Cloudesley PH School on Golden Lane. Private stage school Italia Conti Academy of Theatre Arts takes pupils from the ages of 10 to 16.

Barbican

Transport

As befits the financial centre of Europe, the City is well-served by tube and overland stations. Liverpool Street, Barbican, Moorgate and Farringdon all have stops on the Hammersmith and City, Circle and Metropolitan lines. The Central line stops at Chancery Lane, Liverpool Street, Bank and St Paul's and the District line at Mansion House, Cannon Street, Monument, Tower Hill and Aldgate East. From Barbican, Moorgate and Farringdon, the Thameslink service links to King's Cross, south to Gatwick Airport and Brighton and north to Luton Airport. Further commuter services are available from Fenchurch Street. Bus routes criss-cross the Square Mile, but can be overcrowded and slow.

Safety/Annoyances

The City is overwhelmingly a commercial and financial centre, which means many of the more personal aspects of living in a residential neighbourhood are missing.

Good Points ◀

Regeneration cash has poured into Finsbury Park over a number of years so the area is likely to continue to improve, and its range of transport options is excellent.

North: Finsbury Park, Stroud Green & Crouch End

Finsbury Park is a major transport hub that has undergone a comprehensive makeover. The streets fanning out around the station, known as Stroud Green, have begun to shake off a somewhat dowdy reputation to develop a personality of their own. Over the hill, Crouch End is a well-established desirable neighbourhood, which combines a busy village centre and wide tree-lined residential streets. Crouch End's appeal for those with babies and young children is boosted by being within easy reach of Alexandra Park, Priory Park and Highgate Wood.

Bad Points
The area still has some very grimy corners, and grimy characters hanging round some insalubrious pubs. Football traffic from the nearby Emirates Stadium regularly causes traffic mayhem.

Overview map, p.78

Accommodation

Finsbury Park has a mixed bag of social housing, privately rented accommodation and owner-occupied houses and flats. Streets of expansive Victorian houses have traditionally been ruthlessly converted into downmarket flats or bedsits but are now increasingly being turned into large spacious apartments, or else converted back into extremely generous family homes. Gaps in terracing are filled by social housing and new luxury developments. Stroud Green's streets offer more flats in modestly sized houses which provide homes for couples and groups of students and young workers. The huge, mostly late Victorian, houses lining Crouch End's wide leafy streets have often been split into spacious flats that are eagerly snatched up by aspiring young couples and older professionals alike. Families with older children tend to head further north towards areas such as Muswell Hill and Bounds Green, where there are more reasonable family sized dwellings available. New developments of one and two-bedroom flats provide additional options in Crouch End for those not too attached to period features.

Shopping & Amenities

The bustling Stroud Green Road is full of bargain cosmetics outlets (if you need a wig, this is the place to go), Halal butchers and dirt cheap grocery stores piled high with mangoes, avocadoes and other exotic fare. A Tesco supermarket provides more traditional groceries. Over the hill, Crouch End Broadway has several small supermarket branches – Marks & Spencer Food, Tesco and Budgens – as well as excellent independent baker Dunns. This compact shopping area also boasts a healthfood store, butchers, fishmongers, bike shop and branches of upmarket off-licences Nicola and Oddbins, while music stores, bookshops and art shops do a brisk trade with the area's arty crowd. Finsbury Park itself has a boating lake, children's play area, running track and cafe, and plays host to a number of events and festivals in the summer. Priory Park is another pleasant green space and the nearby local authority-run Park Road Pools has an outdoor swimming pool, tennis courts and playing fields.

Eating & Drinking

Locals are kept nourished by a cheerful and reasonably priced selection of cafes and restaurants on Stroud Green Road, including a couple of very good pizzerias and bargain Indian vegetarian restaurant Jai Krishna. Cosy corner pub The Faltering Fullback on Perth Road is always busy and is a more attractive option than the rather grimy boozers on the main drag. The large Old Dairy bar and restaurant at the start of Crouch End Hill is another neighbourhood stalwart. Crouch End itself has numerous neighbourhood restaurants and gastropubs, such as the child-friendly brasserie Banners, the Italian-influenced Florians and excellent gastropub The Queens Pub and Dining Room on Broadway Parade. Indian, Vietnamese, Turkish, Spanish, noodle, pizza and kebab restaurants and takeaways can all be found near the Broadway, Topsfield Parade and Park Road.

Education

The state schools in Crouch End come under the Haringey local education authority (www.haringey.gov.uk), while those further south fall under Islington (www.islington.gov.uk). Private primaries include Holly Park Montessori School and North London Rudolf Steiner School. For secondary age children there is Hornsey School for Girls, Highgate Wood Secondary and the Church of England Greig City Academy, as well as the specialist Islington Arts and Media School near Finsbury Park.

Transport

Finsbury Park offers an excellent range of transport options: stops on the Piccadilly and Victoria tube lines; buses to the West End and City; plus a quick overland rail link to Moorgate and Old Street. Crouch Enders rely on buses, which can get very packed at peak times, to take them to Finsbury Park or King's Cross where they can then pick up the tube. Residents to the west of Crouch End are within reach of Highgate tube on the Northern line. Crouch Hill station on the Stroud Green side is a stop on the overland North London line.

Safety/Annoyances

With hordes of football fans descending on the streets and takeaways before and after big Arsenal games at the nearby Emirates Stadium and crowds of music fans crushing into the tube when festivals are on during the summer, the sheer pressure and noise of people can be off-putting. The groups of men congregating around the cafes on Blackstock Road can also seem intimidating and the area is still regarded as a bit edgy.

Good Points

A safe neighbourhood with plenty of character and period charm.

Bad Points

Highgate's settled older demographic and villagey atmosphere make it unsuitable for those who enjoy the variety and excitement of urban life.

Overview map, p.78

North: Highgate

Perched on a hill with panoramic views across the city, Highgate is one of London's most aesthetically pleasing areas. An upmarket London village full of ladies who lunch and settled residents who find that they need rarely stray from the local area, Highgate has a rarefied inward-looking quality which will appeal to those looking for peace and quiet.

Accommodation

Highgate's large houses and pretty Georgian and Victorian cottages are highly prized and often occupied by long-term residents. To the south of Waterlow Park, the wide sloping terraced streets known collectively as Dartmouth Park offer more prime real estate. There is comparatively little in the way of rented accommodation, especially for those on more modest budgets; what there is tends to be upmarket lets of houses and flats. You will still find, however, the odd elderly and eccentric Highgate writer taking in lodgers.

Shopping & Amenities

Highgate High Street has the usual favourites of London's faux village centres: expensive delicatessens and other outlets offering posh nosh, plus a bookshop, bistros and, of course, estate agents. A nearby Waitrose in Holloway Road provides a wider selection of upmarket groceries. Jacksons Lane Arts Centre is a buzzy local venue mounting plays and offering classes.

Parks and green space are the area's main draw with Highgate Wood perfect for a Sunday stroll, while Waterlow Park, off Highgate Hill, is a well-kept and pleasing spot with duckponds and plenty of space for children to play. Next door to Waterlow is Highgate Cemetery, perhaps the most famous graveyard in London, which provides a fascinating glimpse into the personalities that have inhabited London down the centuries. To the north of the area lies Highgate Golf Course. In addition to this abundance of genteel greenery, Hampstead Heath, with its bathing ponds, football pitches, cafes and dramatic expanses of open space, is very easily accessible.

Eating & Drinking

Highgate Village has plenty of cafes, brasseries and pubs as well as branches of Pizza Express, Strada, Zizzi and small Chinese dim-sum chain Dim T Café. North Hill has the area's best gastropub, The Bull. Swains Lane, near to the Highgate entrance of Hampstead Heath, has a variety of cafes and ice-cream parlours. The Pavilion Cafe in the middle of Highgate Wood does a roaring trade in coffee, snacks, ice-cream and more substantial meals.

Education

State primary provision falls under Camden and Haringey local authorities (www.camden.gov.uk and www.haringey.gov.uk). State secondary schools include the boys Catholic school St Aloysius College on Hornsey Lane and girls Catholic Mount Carmel Technology College. The major Camden secondaries such as Parliament Hill, William Ellis and Acland Burghley tend to be popular with Highgate's residents. Not surprisingly for such a well-to-do area there are a number of private options, such as Avenue Nursery and Pre-Preparatory and the boys-only Highgate School.

Transport

Tube stops on the Northern line at Highgate and Archway go to the City and West End. Buses travel to Holloway and Islington and then to the City, and drivers can follow the same major arteries of the Holloway Road and Upper Street towards the West End. To the south of the area, Upper Holloway has a stop on the overland North London line.

Safety/Annoyances

The main issue for Highgate's potential residents is expense. Unless you are particularly lucky, you will need patience and an above average income to find even a short-term berth here.

Good Points

With peaceful garden squares lying just a few minutes away from tube stops and roads into the City and central London, Islington is an area with a huge amount of cachet.

Bad Points

The chain pubs and tacky restaurants invading Upper Street make for a raucous and sometimes aggressive atmosphere on Friday and Saturday nights.

Overview map, p.78

North: Islington

Known as a property hot-spot and notorious for its enclave of wealthy residents working in the arts, the media and politics – Tony Blair lived here before his move to Downing Street – Islington holds a special place in the national consciousness as a byword for a type of left-leaning highbrow professional. However, it's a far more mixed area than its reputation might suggest, with young City professionals rubbing shoulders with the middle-class old guard, a long-established working-class population and recent immigrants.

Accommodation

Property for sale in Islington tends to be elegant townhouses or conversions, which command very high prices. The residential heartlands either side of Upper Street, around Canonbury Square and Barnsbury Street, offer charming streets of large villas and flat-fronted Georgian terraces. A sprinkling of new developments of luxury apartments have sprung up over the last 20 years, especially around the busy Angel and Essex Road  intersections and in Highbury. There is a surprisingly high proportion of social housing too, and any accommodation for sale or rent on these council estates will be significantly cheaper than elsewhere in the area.

93

Shopping & Amenities

The compact N1 Centre at Angel houses high-street outlets such as Mambo, Gap, Borders, HMV and French Connection. Nearby, the cheerful Chapel Market has stalls offering fruit and veg, fish, bargain clothes and household goods, complementing the standard supermarket selection of goods at Sainsbury's and Marks & Spencer on Liverpool Road. As Upper Street extends towards Highbury & Islington tube station, there are more upmarket boutiques, bakers, delicatessens, gift stores and homeware shops, as well as a huge number of estate agents. On Sundays, a popular farmers' market behind the town hall offers an excellent selection of seasonal produce, while Camden Passage antiques market is a great place for second-hand collectibles. The plain Highbury Fields is the area's largest green space and has tennis courts and football pitches, and there are many attractive small garden squares in the area, which are open to the public. Pleasant walks can be had along Grand Union Canal and in the small nature reserve around the Islington Ecology Centre at the top of Drayton Park. The Crafts Council on Pentonville Road houses an art gallery, and there are several excellent local theatres, including at the King's Head and Hen & Chickens pubs (see p.425), the high-profile Almeida Theatre, and the sweet Little Angel puppet theatre in Dagmar Passage. The Islington Carling Academy in the N1 Centre is an established middle-sized venue on the gig circuit, and the Vue cinema has several screens. Down the road, Screen on the Green puts on more leftfield releases.

Eating & Drinking

Islington's residents never want for eating and drinking options. There are a huge number of bars, pubs, restaurants, takeaways and cafes, and the length of Upper Street continues to offer fresh choices. All the big chains such as Pizza Express, Wagamama, Yo! Sushi, Carluccio's, Walkabout and Starbucks are represented, as are cuisines from Thai and Indian to modern European and Afghan. If you fancy a tipple, there are gay bars, straight bars, boozers, gastropubs and cocktail lounges in abundance. There are quite a few more watering holes on Liverpool Road, as well as the very pleasant Drapers Arms on Barnsbury Street and the Duke of Cambridge organic bar and restaurant on St Peter's Street.

Education

A good selection of popular and well-run state primary schools can be found in Islington, with a further concentration in Highbury (www.islington.gov.uk). In contrast, Islington's state secondaries have gained a fairly dire reputation, with many middle-class parents doing their best to smuggle their kids to schools in the neighbouring borough of Camden. However, the schools are making a big effort to improve their image, with better results beginning to be achieved by the mixed Islington Green and Highbury Grove schools, and girls' Highbury Fields, which has a special focus on science. The centrally located Samuel Rhodes MLD and The Bridge both offer special needs provision, while St Paul's Steiner is a private primary.

Transport

The City branch of the northern line stops at Angel, which, along with an overland rail link at Essex Road, provides quick access to the financial district. The Victoria line has a stop at Highbury & Islington with a journey time to Oxford Circus of around 15 minutes. The overland North London Line also stops at Highbury & Islington. Various bus routes head to the City and the West End as well as north and east London.

Safety/Annoyances

Safety/Annoyances

The pavements and highways around Angel are packed more or less all the time – as well as the many people who come here to work every day, many others come to shop and others to eat, drink and dance. Late at night the area can seem a bit frantic, with crowded nightbuses and the odd fight.

Good Points

A loyal local community ensures 'Stokey' has plenty of character and a buzzing, happening feel.

North: Stoke Newington

With its mixture of street credibility and cuteness, Stoke Newington is an area with considerable appeal. The absence of a tube meant the area used to be something of a well-kept secret but, although the cat is now out of the bag and it is no longer cheap to buy in the area, Stoke Newington is still more reasonably priced than many of its north London neighbours.

Bad Points

Depending on where you work, Stoke Newington can present transport issues due to overcrowded buses and slow-moving traffic.

Overview map, p.78

Accommodation

A wide range of accommodation runs the gamut from shoddy conversions and council estates to large Victorian family homes and luxury penthouse apartments. The area's closely packed Victorian terraces, concentrated to the south of Church Street, attract buyers, often couples with young children, and groups of renters. Overlooking the park, Queen Elizabeth's Walk contains the most expensive houses in the area with some generously sized, attractive villas.

Shopping & Amenities

Stoke Newington Church Street, which curls up from Clissold Park, has a homely yet interesting collection of shops including a baker, bike shop, toy store, organic food outlet, Fresh & Wild, plus various second-hand bookshops, alongside a fair few places to stop off for a cappuccino. On Saturday mornings a small farmers' market is held in the grounds of William Patten School on Church Street. If you tire of shopping, you can seek a bit of spiritual solace in the lovely overgrown Abney Park Cemetery, where nature walks are regularly organised. On Stoke Newington High Street you will find slightly more everyday grocery stores and takeaways, a Woolworths, fishmongers and a bargain sports shop. Clissold Park has tennis courts and a playground, and is popular with dog-walkers, joggers, Sunday footballers and troops of local toddlers. Its outdoor cafe has several tables and is extremely p[oBeyond the park are two reservoirs where you can get active at an indoor climbing wall and a watersports centre. There are also several private gyms plus many local alternative healthcare practitioners. An excellent independent cinema, The Rio, is located on the border of Stoke Newington and Dalston.

Eating & Drinking

A colourful selection of restaurants on Church Street span Turkish, Italian, fish and chips and Mexican, while Keralan restaurant Rasa serves up top-notch vegetarian food. Cheap curry houses and kebab joints jostle for punters alongside pubs such as the Three Crowns on the busy corner of Church Street and High Street. Around the corner is the huge Thai eaterie YumYum, while the residential streets to the south of Church Street contain many well-frequented pleasant local pubs, such as The Londesborough and The Prince. Further gastronomic adventures can be had at Newington Green and the Kurdish and Turkish-influenced area of Green Lanes, where you can experience some of the best kebabs in the capital.

95

Education

Although the local education authority, Hackney (www.hackney.gov.uk), has had its problems down the years, Stoke Newington has plenty of well-regarded state primary schools, the majority of which are mixed and have nursery provision. There's also a Jewish primary school, Simon Marks. The main local state secondary, Stoke Newington School, is a typically large culturally mixed inner-city comprehensive with some 1,500 pupils. To the north of Stoke Newington, where there is a huge Hasidic Jewish community, there are many private Jewish primary and secondary schools, most of which are single-sex. The Horizon School provides state special needs education to both primary and secondary-age children.

Transport

Several bus routes to the City, Islington and the West End run from Stoke Newington High Street and Newington Green, with journey times of 30 minutes to an hour depending on traffic flow. Overland trains from Stoke Newington station reach Liverpool Street in 20 minutes, but the nearest tubes, Manor House (Piccadilly line) and Finsbury Park (Piccadilly and Victoria lines), are a bus ride away for most residents. A new link to the tube network is set to materialise in 2010 in the shape of the East London line extension at Dalston Junction.

Safety/Annoyances

If you have a low tolerance for yummy mummies and their squealing toddlers, this may not be the neighbourhood for you.

Switched On
The huge mast which dominates the south of Alexandra Park made televisual history in 1935 when it was used for the first high-definition TV transmissions by the BBC. The future of the transmitter is uncertain, however, as the government plans to switch off the analogue signal and go digital by 2012.

North: Other Areas

Wood Green, Muswell Hill, Bounds Green & Palmers Green

Wood Green offers a welter of mid-priced rental accommodation and terraced houses and conversions for sale at prices low by London standards. A massive if rather downmarket shopping centre, Wood Green Shopping City, provides a wide range of fashion outlets and high-street names, as well as two multiscreen cinemas and some barn-sized pubs. The area's trendier inhabitants head for The Chocolate Factory arts development where there is an upmarket restaurant and the occasional gentrified pub. The more northerly neighbourhoods of Muswell Hill, Palmers Green and Bounds Green are far more suburban in character, attracting a high number of families and those looking to settle down. There are good selections of local shops and restaurants, plus small branches of high-street chains, at both Muswell Hill and Palmers Green. Muswell Hill is without a tube and residents often use Wood Green which, like Bounds Green, has a Piccadilly line stop. Alexandra Park is handily placed for residents of all these neighbourhoods.

Archway & Tufnell Park

Tufnell Park and Archway have both grown in popularity latterly, with new bars and restaurants opening along Junction Road to serve the newcomers. Although in the throes of regeneration, Archway, situated around the major traffic intersection of Archway Road, Highgate Hill, Holloway Road and Junction Road, retains its rougher edges and bargain basement shopping opportunities. However, the area's residential streets have perfectly decent terraced housing. Tufnell Park has some very attractive tree-lined streets and is within easy reach of Kentish Town and the Nag's Head shopping centre on Holloway Road. There are Northern line tube stops at Archway and Tufnell Park and various buses beetle up and down Holloway Road, Brecknock Road and Tufnell Park Road.

Good Points

Camden's youthful and hedonistic atmosphere make it a great choice for music fans in particular, and there are plenty of opportunities to develop a social life in the local area.

Bad Points

The market and the night spots mean the area is massively crowded at weekends, making it difficult for locals to get around.

Overview map, p.78

North-West: Camden Town & Kentish Town

Home to a huge network of markets that are apparently irresistible to black-clad teenagers from all over the globe, Camden Town is arguably better known as place to get your nose pierced than somewhere to put down roots.

That said, the area has some appealing residential corners and is a convenient base for the West End. Next door Kentish Town is a calmer and more purely residential prospect, but with a bustling high street of its own and good transport links it is steadily gaining in popularity.

Accommodation

Elegant Georgian townhouses on streets off Parkway and Victorian terraces behind the main drag of Camden High Street are much sought-after, while there are houseshares in the area offering rented accommodation to groups of students and young workers. Ex-local authority property on the area's many estates offer cheaper options.

Moving along Regent's Park Road towards the enclave of Primrose Hill, the houses, and the prices, get more substantial. Kentish Town's tall terraces offer stacks of houses and conversions in varying conditions to rent and buy, with the best property found in the large terraced homes of the Dartmouth Park neighbourhood west of Fortess Road. New apartment blocks targeted at young professionals continue to spring up on any vacant land.

Shopping & Amenities

Camden market has outgrown its original site at Camden Lock and fills additional sites on either side of Camden High Street and Chalk Farm Road. The markets are at their busiest on Saturdays and Sundays although there are some stalls open for business every day. Paintings, crafts, candles, second-hand books and leatherwork are on offer at the Lock site, while the markets towards the tube on Camden High Street and in the Electric Ballroom have an emphasis on clothing and accessories. Stables Market and Camden Canal Market off Chalk Farm Road are good hunting grounds for vintage clothes and retro fixtures and fittings for the home. There are high-street shops, including Gap and Boots, lining Camden High Street and Parkway.

Fruit and vegetables are on offer daily at stalls along Inverness Street, while a large Sainsbury's on Camden Road covers the basics. A multiscreen Odeon cinema on Parkway shows all the latest releases, and Camden is renowned for its many music

Camden High Street

venues both large, such as The Jazz Café and Koko (p.442), and small, such as Barfly and The Dublin Castle. Down by Camden Lock is the popular Jongleurs comedy club.

Regent's Park is the area's lungs; its manicured lawns and fabulous flowerbed displays provide a welcome break from the hustle and bustle. For outdoor pursuits enthusiasts the Jubilee Waterside Centre in Camley Street offers courses in kayaking, canoeing and rock climbing. Kentish Town Road has grocery shops, as well a good fishmongers, florist and bookshop. The Kentish Town Forum is a major gig venue, with lesser known bands playing the Bull & Gate pub next door. Kentish Town City Farm, which has the distinction of being London's first city farm, is on Cressfield Close.

Market Meals

Shoppers will never go hungry in Camden. The weekend markets are full of takeaway stalls offering everything from fresh orange juice and falafel to hot dogs and curry.

Eating & Drinking

Camden has a bunch of near-legendary live music pubs, including The Enterprise, The Dublin Castle and The Good Mixer. On and around the High Street is a more generic range of chain pubs, with the odd more intimate option such as The Crown and Goose gastropub on Delancey Street. With its buzzy global-themed bars and cocktail lounges, Inverness Street is also a night-time draw. Greek and Portuguese family run restaurants can be found tucked away on side streets such Pratt Street and Bayham Street and on Eversholt Street, around the corner from Mornington Crescent tube, is authentic Japanese restaurant Asakusa (p.401) and long-standing local favourite tapas restaurant El Parador. Down towards Camden Lock, chain restaurants, including Wagamama and Pizza Express, provide more familiar fare. The expansive Garden Cafe in Regent's Park offers snacks and more substantial meals at indoor and outdoor tables. A number of pleasant neighbourhood pubs and bars also cater to the locals of Kentish Town unwilling to travel down the road to Camden proper.

Education

Camden in particular is perhaps not an obvious choice as a place to live for parents with small children, but there are plenty of large local state primaries with nursery provision, all of which come under Camden Borough (www.camden.gov.uk). The L'Ile aux Enfants on Vicars Road is a French-speaking private primary, while there are a number of other private options, both single-sex and mixed, in the nearby areas of Hampstead and Primrose Hill.

The area's large state secondary schools, including single-sex Camden School for Girls, Parliament Hill School (girls) and William Ellis (boys), as well as the mixed Haverstock School are well regarded and often preferred by parents in neighbouring boroughs over more local provision. Special needs education is supplied by Jack Taylor and Chalcot Schools.

Transport

Situated in Zone 2 at the meeting point of all four branches of the Northern line, Camden Town tube is handy for the City and the West End but, due to the market-bound hordes, is a major hassle to use at weekends. Mornington Crescent, Kentish Town and Chalk Farm, all also on the Northern line, offer less hectic alternatives. Buses from Hampstead Road can get you to the West End within 15 minutes. Kentish Town also has a handy overland train link to Farringdon, Barbican and Moorgate.

Safety/Annoyances

The chief drawback of living in Camden is its slightly sleazy aspect, which becomes apparent after dark. It is not uncommon to be approached by drug dealers as well as harangued by drunks on the street. People chomping kebabs and reeling around the streets after pubs shut can be pretty unpleasant, with the accompanying noise and litter having a particular impact on residents.

98

Good Points

*A Hampstead address
is bound to impress.
West Hampstead still
has kudos but remains
affordable.*

Bad Points

*The rather cramped
tube stations and
narrow roads in both
Hampstead and West
Hampstead can
become crowded at
peak times.*

Overview map, p.78

North-West: Hampstead & West Hampstead

With its fine literary heritage and celebrity dinner parties, Hampstead is one of London's more exclusive areas. West Hampstead, the area to the west of Finchley Road around West End Lane, is a popular and less staid neighbourhood, which has plenty to offer young professionals without commanding the heights in prices and prestige of its older brother.

Accommodation

With grand houses on streets often blocked to outside traffic, Hampstead guards its exclusivity closely and there's no doubt that to buy a house in the area requires close to millionaire status. Accommodation to rent in the area is also at the higher end of the price scale, often aimed at overseas visitors for whom money is no object. Although not cheap, West Hampstead is a more realistically priced prospect and has a higher number of flats, both conversions and purpose-built, available to rent and buy. Houses in West Hampstead tend to be modest two and three-bedroom terraces.

Shopping & Amenities

The centre of commercial Hampstead huddles around the junction of Heath Street, Holly Bush Vale and Hampstead High Street. Here there are small tasteful branches of high-street stores next to upmarket delicatessens and home accessory shops. The Everyman Cinema on Holly Bush Vale is one of London's most luxurious independent auditoriums. Eclectic local attractions include the Freud Museum (complete with couch) on Maresfield Gardens and Keat's House on Keat's Grove. West End Lane is West Hampstead's main thoroughfare and shopping area, where there are local groceries and gift shops. Hampstead Heath is the best park in London in terms of sheer size and variety, its 789 acres offering plenty of opportunity for sporting activities – including swimming in its bathing ponds – as well as room to run, walk and lounge. Kenwood House (p.199), an 18th century manor house within the Heath, stages classical music events during the summer.

Eating & Drinking

Hampstead High Street has branches of the higher-end restaurant chains, including Carluccio's, Pizza Express, dim T café, Paul, Giraffe and Hamburger Union. Heath Street has more of a range with Indian, Japanese and North African eateries, as well as fish restaurant Pescador Two and Horseshoe, a gastropub with its own on site microbrewery. Places to drink include modern bar and restaurant Toast, gay pub The King William IV and cosy traditional boozer Ye Olde White Bear. American-style diner Tinseltown offers food, drink and milkshakes into the wee small hours. Over in West Hampstead's West End Lane and Fortune Green Road, there is an ever-shifting array of bars, cafes and restaurants, few of which seem to stick except chains such as Gourmet Burger Kitchen and (yet another) Pizza Express. A more notable local is the Czech Bar and Restaurant, attached to a long-standing Czech and Slovak cultural centre. The Brew House cafe at Kenwood House on Hampstead Heath provides tea and snacks for those enjoying a walk in the park, while the popular park pub The Spaniards Inn (8731 6571) caters to those who fancy something a bit stronger.

Education

Local education in Hampstead is dominated by private provision and includes a number of preparatory schools for primary-age children, both mixed and single-sex. Major private secondary schools include, for girls, Royal School Hampstead and South Hampstead High School, and for boys, University College School.

99

State primary and secondary schools come under the control of the London Borough of Camden (www.camden.gov.uk) and tend to serve neighbouring Camden and Highgate as well. Swiss Cottage School has special needs provision.

Transport
A Northern line tube stop at Hampstead goes to the West End and the City but gets rather crowded. Likewise legions of commuters descend on West Hampstead tube in the mornings taking the Jubilee line to the West End and Docklands, while an overland stop on the Thameslink line allows quick access to King's Cross and further afield to Gatwick and Luton airports.

Safety/Annoyances
Hampstead is largely inaccessible to those on modest budgets and can seem rather snobbish. The high number of four-wheel drive vehicles and people-movers clogging up the roads detract from the area's villagey pretensions.

Good Points

Both these neighbourhoods are spacious and prestigious, with beautiful houses and excellent access to green space, which make them particularly suitable for families.

Bad Points

A lack of cheap places to shop, eat and drink is likely to exact its toll on your wallet.

Overview map, p.78

North-West: Primrose Hill & Belsize Park

Primrose Hill is a star-studded neighbourhood, close to the earthiness of Camden Town and the grandiosity of Hampstead, but with a classy yet bohemian edge of its own. The cosy area tucked between Hampstead and Primrose Hill is Belsize Park, built as a suburban estate of houses on the site of a manor house in the second half of the 19th century, with flats added after the Second World War. It is another highly desirable enclave of property, with Gwyneth Paltrow and Chris Martin heading a list of celebrity residents.

Accommodation
Belsize Park's attractive large white stucco houses and pretty mews cottages command Hampstead-style prices, with red-brick mansion blocks offering generously sized flats for the wealthy man or woman about town to rent or buy. Property tends to be yet more expensive in leafy Primrose Hill, with the delightful multicoloured houses on Chalcot Square the most sought-after. Opportunities to rent are fairly minimal and are at the upper end of the market.

Shopping & Amenities
There's a solid range of local stores on Haverstock Hill and England's Lane, including a bookshop, banks, charity shops, gift shops, florists, dry cleaners, plus the usual grocery stores and newsagents. Regent's Park Road is Primrose Hill's high street with a fabulously upmarket range of designer boutiques, perfumeries, and home accessory and furniture stores supplying the local celebs with plenty of opportunities to offload their cash. The area also has that badge of a desirable neighbourhood – a farmers' market. Primrose Hill itself has wonderful panoramic vistas across London and is the perfect place to watch the city's fireworks fizzle across the sky on Bonfire Night. Regent's Park, which has a zoo and acres of space in which to play sport (or sunbathe), lies to the south of Primrose Hill, while Hampstead Heath, lying to the north of Belsize Park, is well within reach.

Eating & Drinking
Haverstock Hill and England's Lane have a good number of cafes, bars and restaurants, while 35 varieties of the clear stuff are available at Polish vodka bar and restaurant Zamoyski on Fleet Road. Primrose Hill is known for large expensive bars such as The Engineer and The Lansdowne, which attract the odd celebrity (as well as a fair amount of flak for poor service and overpriced food), but there are a good number of less pretentious pubs scattered about the main drag of Regent's Park Road. Not many local restaurants are highly rated but there's a massive amount of choice in nearby Camden and Hampstead.

Education
Primrose Hill and Belsize Park families have much the same choice of schools, with an emphasis on private options, as those living in Camden (p.97) and Hampstead (see p.99).

Transport
Belsize Park has a station on the Northern line, and stops on the overland North London line at Hampstead Heath and Gospel Oak are close by. Primrose Hill's residents have the option of using Chalk Farm or Camden Town tube stops, also on the Northern line. Buses from Primrose Hill go around Regent's Park to reach the West End in minutes.

Safety/Annoyances
The area is not always very welcoming to those of modest means, with property investors, shops, cafes and restaurants all striving to make the most of a wealthy clientele.

Good Points

The area has good transport links and benefits from its proximity to Westminster.

Bad Points

Kilburn High Road is a somewhat uninspiring and overcrowded shopping street with limited nightlife options.

Overview map, p.78

North-West: Queen's Park, Kilburn & Kensal Rise
The neighbourhoods of Queen's Park, Kilburn and Kensal Rise occupy a slice of north-west London. Queen's Park, with its large Edwardian-era villas and suburban feel, holds obvious attractions for wealthy residents. The previously more down-at-heel Kilburn and Kensal Rise have both risen in popularity in the past 15 years due to their stocks of terraces ripe for gentrification and the relative ease of commutes from here to the City and West End; all three areas have underground stations in Zone 2.

Accommodation
Queen's Park has plenty of red-brick houses on spacious leafy streets, which are popular with well-to-do families. The best of these, the five or six-bedroomed houses on the east side of the park, sell for millions. Tucked away behind the hectic Kilburn High Road and interspersed with various council estates, the streets of Victorian terraced houses and conversions in Kilburn provide a reliable supply of houses and flats to buy and rent. Many of the streets lying off both sides of the High Road are pleasantly tree-lined and boast good-sized terraces, especially in the Brondesbury conservation area to the north. In Kensal Rise, the houses and flats are a mixed bag, but there is a good supply of Victorian terraces.

Shopping & Amenities
The bustling Kilburn High Road, a stretch of the ancient Roman route of Watling Street, has a hotchpotch of pound shops, branches of chains such as Primark, Boots and Sainsbury's, and plenty of Caribbean-influenced grocery stores. The Tricycle Arts Centre, with its theatre, cinema and gallery, has plenty to offer the culturally minded. Queen's Park's main shopping street is Salusbury Road where you can find a range of upmarket bakeries and delis, boosted by the recent addition of a farmers' market at Salusbury Road School on Sunday mornings. Queen's Park itself is an award-winning 30-acre green space with pitch and putt golf, tennis courts, a cafe and children's play area. Kensal Green Cemetery, close to Harrow Road, is one of London's most historic burial grounds and houses the graves of writers William Makepeace Thackeray and Anthony Trollope.

Eating & Drinking
Kilburn High Road still has its fair share of scruffy boozers amid its sprinkling of new gastropubs. Eating options on the High Road are largely confined to kebab, pizza, Chinese and Indian takeaways alongside cheap high-street stalwarts such as McDonalds and Nando's. Popular and reasonably priced brasserie Little Bay (p.389) caters to slightly more sophisticated palates. Those with more adventurous tastes might find more to

interest them in Queen's Park, where there are a number of pleasant if expensive local restaurants and gastropubs on Salusbury Road and Lonsdale Road. Kensal Rise's Chamberlayne Road has a good range of local pubs, cafes and restaurants.

Education

Schools within the boroughs of Brent (www.brent.gov.uk), Camden (www.camden.gov.uk) and Westminster (www.westminster.gov.uk), with their range of cultural traditions and income brackets, are accessible from Queen's Park, Kilburn and Kensal Rise. Alongside a good range of state primaries, encompassing Church of England and Catholic schools, there are a number of Muslim schools nearby including the state-funded Islamia Primary in Queen's Park, which was founded by Yusuf Islam, previously known as the pop star Cat Stevens. Two private Montessori primaries are also close at hand, plus a number of Jewish schools. State secondaries in Westminster and Camden tend to be more convenient for those at the Kilburn end than Brent's schools.

Transport

Kilburn and Willesden Green stations on the Jubilee line provide a link to Westminster and beyond to Southwark and Docklands. The Bakerloo line also stops at Kilburn Park, Queen's Park and Kensal Green. An overland stop at Kilburn High Road gives swift access to Euston, opening up the City and Islington. The North London line, with stops at Kensal Rise, Brondesbury Park and Brondesbury, provides a link with Camden, Islington and Hackney. Kilburn is also a handy location for Notting Hill, Kensington and the West End by bus.

Safety/Annoyances

A number of high-profile murders near Kensal Rise and in neighbouring Harlesden and Willesden have given rise to a rather dicey reputation. There is perhaps a residual uneasiness between the older inhabitants of the area's estates and newer wealthier incomers.

North-West: Other Areas

St John's Wood & Maida Vale

Evening Sessions
Maida Vale is perhaps most famous for its studios, which have hosted live performances from some of the world's top rock and pop acts, as well the late, legendary DJ John Peel's eponymous sessions. It's a small, intimate venue, which means that tickets are few and far between. See the BBC's website, www.bbc.co.uk, for upcoming shows.

St John's Wood and Maida Vale are highly desirable, exclusive and very central residential areas of London (both are in the borough of Westminster), with semi-detached and detached houses and grand mansion blocks lining wide boulevards. St John's Wood has a large American population (there is an American school here), and is a favoured destination of wealthy settlers from overseas. St John's Wood High Street has all the shopping mainstays of a prosperous neighbourhood. Maida Vale has another stash of graceful and large properties on generously proportioned streets, some of which curve around communal gardens. Running through the area is a pretty stretch of the Grand Union Canal known as Little Venice where houseboats are moored. Properties are fairly scarce and priced in line with their size, location and status.

Swiss Cottage

Swiss Cottage on Finchley Road represents a boundary area between Camden and the suburban areas of Finchley (its unusual name dating from a Swiss-style chalet inn built in 1826). The Swiss Cottage section of busy Finchley Road has large branches of supermarkets Waitrose, Sainsbury's, as well as a Habitat, a multi-screen Odeon cinema and a wide range of high-street outlets. Property covers the spectrum from Victorian terracing to council blocks and new apartment developments.

West: Ealing, Acton & Chiswick

All the positive aspects of suburban living – abundant green space, comprehensive shopping areas, decent schools and plenty of local amenities – make Ealing a reliable choice for the family orientated.

If you find suburban life a touch stifling and bland, then Ealing may seem on the quiet side. Long journey times can make trips into central London arduous.

Overview map, p.78

A residential district developed during the second half of the 19th century around the major transport links in the area – the road from Oxford to the centre of London, the Grand Union Canal and the Great Western Railway – Ealing was established as a favourite London suburb of the middle classes by the 20th century. The borough of Ealing was formed in 1965 and covers the suburb and surrounding districts. Central Ealing, roughly bounded by Hangar Lane, Western Avenue, Argyle Road and Gunnersbury Park, is a solidly respectable, self-contained area with plenty of green space and leafy streets. Acton and Chiswick extend to the east and south, with both neighbourhoods supplying further tracts of suburban housing. Those who choose to live here often do so because of its high standard of living, abundance of green space, good schools and a strong local infrastructure. Well-established Polish, Japanese, Greek and Iranian communities lend international influences.

Accommodation

Impressive semi-detached and detached family homes with large gardens dominate on the streets closest to Ealing Broadway station, a proportion of which have been converted into flats and are available to rent. The grand houses on the streets surrounding Walpole Park and Ealing Common are some of the most desirable. Several handsome mansion blocks dating from the early 1930s can be found alongside council estates, which tend to be of a reasonable standard too. Towards Acton, Northfields, Hanwell and Greenford, terraced streets with mainly three or four-bedroom houses take over. The Poets' Corner part of Acton, north of Churchfield Road, contains smaller cottage-style houses and maisonettes, which are very popular, while the South Acton estate is the largest social housing development of its kind in west London. Acton's cheaper rented accommodation attracts young travellers. Chiswick has a further range of attractive housing including the Victorian garden-suburb style Bedford Park, plus some attractive Edwardian and 1930s domestic architecture in the Grove Park area.

Shopping & Amenities

A large mall, the Ealing Broadway Centre, meets most shopping needs with the usual host of high-street stores, while a smaller mall on the corner of The Broadway and Springbridge Road has more of the same. A Saturday farmers' market occupies a site on Leeland Road, and quirky independent shops, delicatessens and a garden centre can be found on Pitshanger Lane. Major supermarkets include Waitrose and Sainsbury's in West Ealing, and a massive Tesco is housed in the former Hoover building on Western Avenue. Chiswick High Road is another major retail centre, as is Acton's High Street, but for a more eclectic selection of shops it's worth heading for Churchfield Road. A jazz festival is held every summer in Walpole Park, which also has children's play areas, ponds and an animal enclosure. The Questors Theatre overlooking the park is one of Europe's largest amateur theatres. Other generous green spaces, such as Lammas Park and Gunnersbury Park, are also of a high standard. As well as playgrounds, sports pitches and tennis courts, Pitshanger Park and Brent Valley also both have golf courses. Public sports facilities include Gurnell Leisure Centre and Acton Swimming Baths. Chiswick's Strand on the Green, south of the M4 motorway and next to a stretch of the Thames, is a very pleasant spot for a Sunday wander with Georgian buildings housing attractive pubs which spill out onto the riverside.

Eating & Drinking
The options in Ealing Broadway are extensive, with a wide range of coffee shops and pizza, pasta, tapas, noodle, Greek and Indian restaurants lining Uxbridge Road, Bond Street and Ealing Green. The Broadway also has a fair few barn-sized chain pubs which do a brisk trade at weekends. More homely local restaurants and cafes are tucked away on Pitshanger Lane. The Ealing Park Tavern in Northfields has a reputation as one of the better pubs in the area. Hanwell has a couple of very upmarket restaurants in its centre, and Southall has myriad curry houses and Indian sweet centres. Acton's Churchfield Road has become a local hot-spot with an abundance of gastropubs, restaurants and trendy cafes, while a significant population of young Australians and South Africans ensure a vibrant atmosphere. Chiswick High Road and Turnham Green Terrace, meanwhile, have dozens of popular wine bars and restaurants, including established chains such as Zizzi, Strada and Nando's.

Education
The borough of Ealing's (www.ealing.gov.uk) education provision is well regarded across all levels, and parents here benefit from a good choice in both the state and private sectors – although competition for places at the most popular schools is fierce. State primaries are numerous, as are private ones – Aston House is mixed, Durston House and Clifton Lodge are boys-only, and Falcon School for Girls, Harvington School and St Augustine's Priory are all-girls options. Chiswick's state schools come under Hounslow borough (www.hounslow.gov.uk). Private secondary schooling is offered by Ealing College Upper School and St Benedict's (both boys), plus, for girls, the Notting Hill & Ealing High School (ages 4 to 18). There is a private Japanese school in Acton, plus other private options in the nearby boroughs of Hammersmith & Fulham and Richmond.

Transport
The Central line from Ealing Broadway offers a direct journey of around 30 minutes into Oxford Street, and then on to the City. A useful overland rail line, stopping at Ealing Broadway and Acton, will take you to Paddington in a matter of minutes (it travels to Slough and Reading and beyond). The Piccadilly line has several stops across the area, including South Ealing, Northfields and Acton Town. Acton, in particular, is well-served by public transport with several District and Piccadilly line stops supplemented by overland stations. There are a clutch of stations in the Chiswick area on the District line.

Safety/Annoyances
Ealing has become increasingly car-dependent, with locals putting up strong opposition to plans to bring trams to Uxbridge Road – something which would benefit the environment and residents without cars.

Good Points
Some of the loveliest streets and squares in London combined with a youthful and globally inspired energy.

West: Notting Hill & Holland Park
Once an overcrowded landing place for poorer immigrants and the generally down-at-heel, Notting Hill has emerged in the past 20 years as one of London's top-flight neighbourhoods. The gentrification gathered pace very quickly, putting the area's best properties beyond the reach of most. Large white stucco houses on grand sweeping crescents, pretty garden squares and mews cottages – as seen in the film *Notting Hill* – are the area's most distinctive architectural features, although life in the area spans a far greater range than this. Beyond the major traffic artery known as the Westway, North Kensington has a high density of council estates, and the diverse cultural traditions of the whole area are highlighted in the annual Notting Hill carnival and Portobello Market (see p.46 and 369). South of Notting Hill, Holland Park has always been exclusive, with tracts of large Victorian houses within the means of only the most wealthy buyers or renters.

Bad Points ◀
Swift gentrification and escalating prices threaten the very qualities that made Notting Hill so attractive in the first place, while Holland Park is strictly for millionaires only.

Overview map, p.78

Accommodation

Many of the houses on Notting Hill's crescents that fan out from Ladbroke Grove have been restored as family homes after years of being carved up into bedsits, and now attract wealthy City, media and showbiz types. Property south of Holland Park Avenue becomes increasingly grand towards the Kensington borders. Prices are lower towards Shepherd's Bush to the west and North Kensington to the north as the standard of accommodation drops, although new apartment blocks are being built to cash in on Notting Hill's popularity. Trellick Tower, a 31-storey council block off Golborne Road, illustrates the change in the area's fortunes; once considered a symbol of everything ugly and bleak about modern social housing, its flats are now keenly fought over on the open market.

Shopping & Amenities

Portobello Market stretches most of the length of Portobello Road, with antique shops at the Notting Hill Gate end giving way to a motley selection of stalls under the Westway selling everything from vintage clothing to antique glass bottles. The legendary independent shops on and around Portobello Road wage a constant battle against high-street homogenisation as the chains try to move in, while around Notting Hill Gate and Pembridge Road you'll find various chain stores, plus a cache of second-hand shops. Westbourne Grove and Ledbury Road have a range of fine delicatessens and gift shops. Upmarket shopping can be found on Kensington Church Street, which leads to the useful mix of designer boutiques, high-street staples and supermarkets on Kensington High Street. A large Sainsbury's supermarket near the Ladbroke Grove and Harrow Road junction serves the north of the area. For outdoor space, the compact Holland Park has an orangery, Japanese garden and the odd peacock strutting around, while the massive expanses of Kensington Gardens and Hyde Park are a stroll away. The Westway Sports Centre has clay and indoor tennis courts, football pitches and basketball courts (see p.293), and there are plenty of private gyms in the area.

Eating & Drinking

Choice abounds, with upmarket French restaurants neighbouring Caribbean takeaways. Chain coffee shops, gastropubs and pizza restaurants cluster around Notting Hill Gate tube, interspersed with interesting independents. The restaurants and bars on Kensington Park Road and Ledbury Road are a good bet for fine dining and wine quaffing, with Westbourne Grove boasting a good few lunch spots. Ladbroke Grove has many popular bars including the Fat Badger. Portobello Road has a massive number of coffee shops, cafes, British boozers, bars and all manner of restaurants. An influx of refugees into the area around the time of the Spanish civil war leaves its mark with a number of Spanish restaurants and tapas bars dotted around, while Golborne Road is renowned for its Portuguese cafes and patisseries. There's a lively nightlife scene too, with a number of clubs and live music venues including the Notting Hill Arts Club (p.444) and Neighbourhood.

Education

Private education establishments cater for offspring of wealthier residents, with the Notting Hill Preparatory School taking children up to the age of 11 and the Southbank International School serving all school ages. Wetherby Preparatory School caters for primary-age boys and the neighbouring Pembridge Hall School is for primary-age girls, while private secondary schools include the mixed David Game College and Tabernacle School and the boys-only Wetherby School. There are many more small-scale private alternatives in nearby Westminster. State schools largely come under the authority of Kensington and Chelsea (www.rbkc.gov.uk). Schools in the adjacent local education authority of Hammersmith & Fulham (www.lbhf.gov.uk) are also within reach. The Instituto Espanol Vicente Canada Blanch on Portobello Road is a private bilingual Spanish and English school.

Transport

Notting Hill Gate and Holland Park both have stops on the Central line, with Oxford Circus just minutes away. Ladbroke Grove and Westbourne Park are on the Hammersmith & City line. Paddington station is close by, offering express access to Heathrow and trains to the south-west of the country. The Westway and Harrow Road are major traffic routes through the area.

Safety/Annoyances

The annual Notting Hill Carnival – three days of live music, parades and partying in the street over the August bank holiday – is a world-famous celebration of the area's Afro-Caribbean cultural heritage, but the influx of revellers is not welcomed by all residents. Although rates of Carnival-related violence have fallen recently, some locals still feel the area is less safe (as well as more noisy) during this time.

West: Shepherd's Bush & Hammersmith

Good Points

Down-to-earth with a lively local social scene, these are bustling neighbourhoods with much to offer those new to London.

Bad Points

A number of major traffic routes run straight through both areas, and a general lack of greenery and open space affects Shepherd's Bush in particular.

Overview map, p.78

Shepherd's Bush and Hammersmith are conveniently placed neighbourhoods that extend south from Uxbridge Road to the Thames. Both areas have a spread of reasonably priced accommodation which encourages young renters to pitch up here, with expensive family homes available for the better-off to buy in the more picturesque pockets of Hammersmith. There are large retail centres in both areas and plenty to keep you occupied, with major cultural amenities in the shape of the Lyric Theatre, Riverside Studios, Shepherd's Bush Empire and Hammersmith Apollo (see p.449).

Accommodation

Hammersmith has some posh enclaves such as Stamford Brook and Brook Green, where there are some large, grand properties, while Shepherd's Bush is dominated by more standard terraced streets and housing estates, which huddle around the major roads that converge on the area. Both neighbourhoods have steady supplies of rented accommodation, often occupied by groups of young people from Australia, South Africa and New Zealand. The massive BBC Television Centre on the northern edge of Shepherd's Bush, plus a colossal new retail development, ensure there are plenty of media professionals and speculators keen to buy property in the area.

Shopping & Amenities

A range of groceries, off-licences and takeaways line Shepherd's Bush Green, with a shopping centre on the east side of the triangle the place to find high-street stores. Running between Uxbridge Road and Goldhawk Road, Shepherd's Bush Market is one of London's most cheerfully multicultural, with a fascinating range of African, Caribbean, Polish and Asian stalls offering exotic fruit, vegetables, spices, meat and fresh fish, alongside fabrics, CDs, DVDs and jewellery. About to muscle its way in, however, is Westfield London, a new retail development of some 270 outlets slated to open in 2008. The Kings Mall on King Street in Hammersmith has high-street favourites, including Marks & Spencer, Habitat and TK Maxx, with a good few shops also to be found in the arcade around Hammersmith tube. There are some well-respected entertainment venues in the area, ranging from the massive Hammersmith Apollo to the smaller Riverside Studios art centre. The Lyric Hammersmith has an attractive Victorian interior, while the Bush Theatre stages work by new writers. This part of town is a little light on park life though, with Holland Park the closest green space to Shepherd's Bush. Further south, Hammersmith's stretch of the Thames lies just beyond the traffic roaring along the Great West Road, with pretty Barnes and the London Wetland Centre nature reserve a stroll away over Hammersmith Bridge. West of Hammersmith, where things become less hectic and more leafy, is the family orientated Ravenscourt Park.

Eating & Drinking

Wining and dining options in Shepherd's Bush have expanded beyond grubby takeaways and unappealing pubs in recent years to encompass a wider range, with Goldhawk Road featuring vegetarian, Polish and European restaurants. Large pubs on Shepherd's Bush Green fill up nightly with a young cosmopolitan crowd swapping backpacking tips before heading for gigs at the Shepherd's Bush Empire. Westfield London will add significantly to the number of chain restaurants within reach, while hopefully not having too much of a detrimental effect on local businesses elsewhere. Hammersmith has a good number of large pubs around the station and King Street, which usually serve food. The western end of King Street is less hectic and has a modest selection of cafes and restaurants. The best pubs are to be found on The Mall next to the river, such as The Dove, while Brook Green also has some upmarket bars and restaurants.

Education

State schools are administrated by the Hammersmith & Fulham local education authority (www.lbhf.gov.uk), with some in neighbouring Kensington and Chelsea (www.rbkc.gov.uk) also close at hand. There are numerous private schools in the area, including French language Ecole Francaise Jacques Prevert, where the One World Montessori Nursery is also located, all-girls Bute House Preparatory, and the mixed Norland Place (all three are primaries). Hammersmith is home to several private secondary schools too, including St Paul's Girls' School, The Godolphin and Latymer School (also girls) and the mixed Latymer Upper School. Places that provide special needs education include Jack Tizard, Cambridge and Woodlane schools.

Transport

The Central line serves Shepherd's Bush as well as the BBC at White City, providing a quick journey into the West End and City, while the Hammersmith & City line stops at Hammersmith, Goldhawk Road, Shepherd's Bush and Latimer Road. Hammersmith is also on the District and Piccadilly lines, the latter offering easy access to Heathrow. All the area's stations are in Zone 2. A new Hammersmith & City line stop at Wood Lane is currently under construction.

Safety/Annoyances

With busy transport intersections, main roads and shopping areas, all but the most exclusive parts of Shepherd's Bush and Hammersmith are thoroughly urban, and the rough and tumble of daily life will not suit everyone.

West: Other Areas

Earls Court & Barons Court

Earls Court sits between Old Brompton Road and Cromwell Road and is dominated by the Earls Court Exhibition Centre, where major trade fairs, conferences and concerts are staged. The area is known for cheap and mid-priced hotels and bed-and-breakfast accommodation, and is handy for the major museums of South Kensington, as well as Knightsbridge and central London. Its location and price has made Earls Court a firm favourite for budget travellers – it's dubbed 'Kangeroo Court' due to the number of Australian and New Zealander backpackers that call it their (temporary) home. Its stock of rental property, however, has largely been converted from the down-at-heel, pokey bedsits of the 1970s into luxury flats. It was once the gay centre of London too, and still has a number of gay venues and residents. To the west of Earls Court is the Barons Court/West Kensington area, a more residential prospect than its neighbour with flats to rent and buy in converted Victorian houses, mansion blocks and council estates. The amenities of Fulham are close at hand, and both areas are well-connected with stops on the Piccadilly and District lines.

Barnes, Richmond, Kew & Kingston

The spacious, prosperous and leafy suburbs of Barnes, Richmond, Kew and Kingston have plenty of desirable property, in particular large family homes. The presence of the Thames gives these suburbs an extra draw, and access to the countryside from these areas is also relatively easy. Kingston has the largest shopping mall in the area, with a comprehensive spread of high-street names, while Richmond has a smaller but still bustling hub. Kew and Barnes have pretty village centres with attractive independent shops. Deer roam the huge expanse of Richmond Park, while Kew Gardens (p.219) draws visitors from all over for its collection of global flora and fauna. The major drawback is that it can be a trek into town – these areas are served by either overland trains or the rather slow District line.

Show Offs

If you've got an interest in beer, bathrooms or British rock bands, the chances are that you'll end up at one of Earls Court's exhibition centres. Earls Court One and Two, plus Olympia, host some of the UK's biggest shows, conferences, award ceremonies and gigs. A Turkish travel show, wrestling and speedboats are among the attractions planned for 2007. The venues are also set to play a part in the 2012 Olympics. For more information, see www.eco.co.uk.

Good Points ◀

*Regeneration money and
the efforts of the local
community have eased
the area's problems.*

Bad Points ◀

*Brixton is noisy and non-
stop, and the crime rate,
while falling, is still high.*

Overview map, p.78

South-West: Brixton & Stockwell

Brixton, along with bordering areas such as Tulse Hill and Herne Hill, emerged as a workaday suburb in the latter part of the Victorian era. Today, however, it is best known as a centre for the UK Afro-Caribbean community, a result of the influx of Jamaican immigrants to London in 1948. Caribbean-influenced shops and nightlife are at the core of the Brixton vibe, although many other communities now make their homes here too. With several major estates in the area, not to mention a relatively recent history of riots and civil unrest fuelled by poverty and racism, it is an area with more than its share of deprivation. That said, its vivid street life and mix of cultures give it a special place in the hearts of many. Further north, Stockwell is similar in its variety of its population and accommodation but lacks a real centre.

Accommodation

Brixton's large Victorian terraces provide a wealth of houses and converted flats for rent. Historically this has been a fairly inexpensive place to live but more and more properties are being done up and sold off to young professionals. Stockwell has a mix of council estates, terraces and, in Stockwell Park, Regency houses.

Shopping & Amenities

The daily Brixton Market on Electric Avenue, around the corner from the tube, offers a dizzying array of products from around the world, with Caribbean, African, Far Eastern and South American stalls offering exotic fruit, vegetables, pigs' trotters, dried piranha, incense, fabrics and much more. There are several sports shops too, plus high-street supermarkets such as Sainsbury's and Iceland. For outdoor escapism, Brockwell Park has a great lido for summer swimming and community get-togethers. Brixton's Ritzy Cinema shows all the latest releases as well as playing arthouse offerings and staging film festivals.

Eating & Drinking

Caribbean snack stalls and African restaurants abound, as do the familiar fast-food outlets, takeaways and kebab shops. In recent years more upmarket venues have opened up including noodle bars and gastropubs. Brixton offers plenty of opportunities for clubbing and live music, with the renowned Brixton Academy and superclub The Fridge leading the way (see p.442). There are plenty of bars to choose from, plus an increasing number of lounge-style venues such as the Ritzy Cinema's cafe and bar. More intimate choices include The Windmill (close to the actual Brixton Windmill), Jamm, The Effra Tavern and The 414. The intersection of Stockwell Road and South Lambeth Road is home to numerous lively cafes and tapas bars owned and frequented by members of the large local Portuguese community. Things become a bit more laid-back towards Herne Hill where there is a cheerful selection of local eateries around Half Moon Lane.

Education

As tends to be the pattern with inner-city boroughs, parents who are in a position to do so often go to extreme lengths to get their children into schools they feel are better. Others, however, will staunchly defend local schools in the state sector. Private schools, such as Streatham and Clapham High (girls) and Dulwich College are located in more affluent areas of south-east and south-west London. Special needs education is offered by Turney Primary and Secondary Special School and Elm Court School, while The Orchard is a state-funded Muslim school. State schools come under Lambeth LEA (www.lambeth.gov.uk).

109

Transport
Brixton tube is in Zone 2 at the end of the Victoria line, giving swift access to Victoria, Oxford Circus and King's Cross. Stockwell is the next stop on the Victoria line and has an interchange with the Northern line, which also stops at Oval and Kennington. Overland stops at Herne Hill, Tulse Hill and Loughborough Junction offer a direct route to the City, while overland trains from Brixton travel to Victoria.

Safety/Annoyances
The sheer press of people on Brixton's streets can make life uncomfortable. As with any area where youth culture rules, crime and drugs is an issue.

Good Points ◀
Fashion label queens will be in seventh heaven in Chelsea.

Bad Points ◀
High-street homogenisation has driven the spark of originality from King's Road, and every other vehicle seems to be a petrol-guzzling 'Chelsea tractor'.

Overview map, p.78

South-West: Chelsea, Fulham & South Kensington

Oscar Wilde, the Pre-Raphaelites, the swinging 60s, punk rock, Russian billionaires – the area extending from Sloane Square along King's Road and down to the Thames has seen plenty of action down the years, although Chelsea's mystique is less potent today than it used to be. Escalating house prices and rents have meant variety has been largely sacrificed as the area becomes the exclusive haunt of millionaire playboys, rock stars, diplomats and the infamous 'Sloane rangers'. Once a working-class stronghold, neighbouring Fulham is now firmly upper middle class. South Kensington to the north is primarily a tourist district, with major museums and many hotels of varying standards. There are also several international institutions and schools that give the area a European flavour.

Accommodation
The freehold of large tracts of Chelsea property is in the hands of one landowner, the Earl of Cadogan, while international property investors take a keen interest in any remaining opportunities. On the rare occasions that these properties do come on the market, they are largely inaccessible to rent or buy to all those except the most rich and determined. What was a slightly less glamorous area by the river, the site of the former Lots Road power station, has been extensively redeveloped into large luxury apartment complexes. Fulham's property market is slightly less other-worldly, although its former working-class Victorian terraces now command prices significantly more than they would elsewhere in London. South Kensington is a mixed bag, with townhouses and flats, often aimed at the short-term high-rent international market, sharing streets with hotels and businesses.

Shopping & Amenities
Although famous as a chic, innovative shopping destination, King's Road nowadays has little to distinguish it from any other high street. All the major fashion chains are here (no one else could afford the rents), alongside branches of Habitat, Heal's and Espacio for furnishing that dream pad. The reasonably priced Peter Jones department store is at the Sloane Square end of the road, while Terence Conran's designer shop at Bluebird is at the other. A large Sainsbury's is west of the exclusive Chelsea Harbour development. Chelsea's emphasis has long since shifted away from cutting-edge fashion to designer clothing – you could do serious damage to your bank balance in an hour on Sloane Street before you even make it as far as Harvey Nichols and Harrods on Knightsbridge. Fulham Broadway is home to slightly more ubiquitous chain stores, while further west along Fulham Road and New King's Road is an interesting selection of independent shops. There's a cheery street market on North End Road, and antique hunters find much to interest them on Lillie Road and Parsons Green Lane. For culture buffs, the Royal Court Theatre on Sloane Square has an unrivalled reputation, and every May, thousands of green-fingered types make the pilgrimage to the Chelsea Flower Show in the grounds of

10

the Royal Hospital Chelsea (see p.44). Multiplex cinemas are plentiful, while the Chelsea Cinema on King's Road is an excellent independent. Museum-hoppers will find much to delight them in the area, from the blue-plaque heritage of Chelsea to South Kensington's 'big three' museums: Science, Natural History and Victoria & Albert (see p.205). There is no shortage of private gyms and health clubs in the area, especially in the new developments towards the river.

Eating & Drinking

King's Road has fast-food outlets and no end of branded cafes and restaurants catering for tourists, shoppers and office workers. Celebrity chefs and restaurateurs grace the area including Terence Conran's Bluebird Dining Room on King's Road and Gordon Ramsay on Royal Hospital Road. Off King's Road the streets of Chelsea are punctuated with venerable, expensive brasseries and restaurants. There is a further clutch of chain eateries on Fulham Broadway, Fulham Road and Wandsworth Bridge Road (three Pizza Expresses at the last count), interspersed with a few more individual options. Elsewhere the museum cafes in South Kensington are good spots for lunch, with Old Brompton Road a reliable bet for eating out in the evening.

Education

Unsurprisingly, private schooling is popular in these parts. Redcliffe School, Cameron House, Kensington Preparatory School for Girls and Falkner House are among the options for primary-age children, and there are Muslim and French-language schools in the vicinity. Parayhouse School and The Moat School both offer private special needs education, and the Lycee Francais Charles de Gaulle in South Kensington teaches a French primary and secondary curriculum.
State schools come under two boroughs – Kensington and Chelsea (www.rbkc.gov.uk) and Hammersmith & Fulham (www.lbhf.gov.uk) – with the well-regarded Catholic boys' London Oratory a standout option.

Transport

Chelsea and Fulham rely primarily on the District line, one of the slower tube branches, with stations at Sloane Square (which is also on the Circle line), West Brompton, Fulham Broadway and Parsons Green. Both the District and Piccadilly lines stop at South Kensington, with another Piccadilly line stop at Knightsbridge. There are several major bus routes into central London.

Safety/Annoyances

Fulham has two football clubs, Fulham (p.183) and the hugely popular, mega-rich Chelsea (see p.288). Stamford Bridge, Chelsea's ground, is next to Fulham Broadway and home matches have a noticeable impact on traffic and public transport in the area. Pubs and restaurants also groan under the weight of sometimes rowdy 'Blues' fans.

11

South-West: Clapham & Battersea

In the 18th and early 19th centuries Clapham was favoured by the upper classes, who built grand houses overlooking its common. The Victorian era brought the railways and the area morphed into a typical commuter suburb. It remained that way until the 1990s when Clapham rose significantly in popularity and prestige as buyers became seduced by its mix of urban grittiness, period charm and decent transport links. Battersea, meanwhile, has more of an industrial history, symbolised by the iconic chimneys of Battersea Power Station (which is due to be redeveloped as a residential and retail centre). A significant amount of social housing was built during the 20th century, and it is only recently that an upturn in fortunes at the riverside has begun to turn Battersea into a thriving quarter.

Accommodation

The most desirable residential areas of Clapham are to the north and south of the common, where period properties of all vintages and sizes, from four and five-bedroomed Victorian houses to small rented flats, can be found. Professional couples and singles have moved en-masse to the area surrounding Clapham High Street. The wide terraced streets between Clapham and Wandsworth commons have become known for their appeal to middle-class families, earning it the nickname 'nappy valley'. Despite Battersea's industrial heritage, its riverside location meant extensive residential building was inevitable. The stretch of ground between Albert and Wandsworth bridges is now dominated by smart apartment blocks. Further south, older mansion blocks can be found overlooking Battersea Park, and there are attractive Victorian cottages on Shaftesbury Estate.

Shopping & Amenities

There is a good range of shops on Clapham High Street, including a Sainsbury's supermarket, independent grocery shops and chain stores. Abbeville Road is a more intimate local centre with gift shops and boutiques. To the western side of the common, in the middle of 'nappy valley', Northcote Road has a classy selection of antiques shops, delicatessens, butchers and bakers. The hulking remains of Battersea Power Station are set to be transformed into an enormous shopping and entertainment centre over the course of the next decade, although the project has been doged by controversy and delay. As well as the wide open space of Clapham Common, there is the equally large Battersea Park (p.213). Culture-wise the Clapham Picturehouse is a fine local cinema and the Battersea Arts Centre on Lavender Hill puts on a varied programme of plays and performances.

Eating & Drinking

Clapham High Street hums with life as bars and restaurants get packed at the weekend. Chains such as Strada and Bierodrome have moved in to clean up on the booming market, while on the curving Venn Street there are a variety of bistros and brunch spots. Other local favourites include pizza favourite Eco and popular pub Bread and Roses on Clapham Manor Street, which holds comedy, cabaret and DJ nights. There is no shortage of cafes dolling out cappuccinos to yummy mummies along Northcote Road and Abbeville Road. Travelling east along Lavender Hill or north along Queenstown Road will reward you with another wide selection of wine bars, cafes and restaurants.

Education

A wide selection of primary schools serve the vast number of families in the neighbourhood, including several state-run options plus private boys-only Thomas's Preparatory, The Dolphin and Parkgate House. In common with other inner-city areas, secondary schools, under the control of local education authority Lambeth (www.lambeth.gov), have a rather mixed reputation and parents choose carefully. Private secondary schools include Streatham and Clapham High School for girls and Emanuel School.

Transport

Clapham Junction is claimed to be the busiest railway junction in the UK, and trains go from here to Victoria, Waterloo and Kensington. Other overland stations can be found at Clapham High Street, Battersea Park, Queenstown Road and Wandsworth Road. The Northern line extends to Clapham North, Clapham Common and Clapham South, providing the area with good tube coverage (all stations are in Zone 2). Buses also converge on the area and offer routes in all directions. Should you ever need it, the London Heliport is situated on the Battersea riverside.

Safety/Annoyances

In common with other areas that have been buoyed by affluent new residents and gained a reputation as a going out destination, Clapham High Street can be annoyingly busy, hassled and boisterous at the weekends.

Good Points

Enormous houses in a family friendly neighbourhood.

Bad Points

The obnoxious traffic of Trinity Road and the depressing fortress of Wandsworth prison.

Overview map, p.78

South-West: Putney & Wandsworth

Putney is a classy neighbourhood in an appealing location on the southern banks of the Thames. It is similar to Chelsea in its demographic make-up, perhaps slightly more family orientated, although it doesn't have the same level of glamour. Also firmly respectable and conservative is neighbouring Wandsworth, another of south London's desirable and spacious areas.

Accommodation

The most coveted properties in the area are the spacious detached houses in the streets to the west of Putney Hill. East Putney's Victorian and Edwardian terraces are not on the same scale, but they sit on clean, quiet streets, attracting well-off middle-class families. Wandsworth too has a good deal of luxurious property to offer. Some of the most impressive houses are located in the wide streets off Baskerville Road – with their massive gardens and the occasional swimming pool, they're practically mansions by London standards. A great deal of social housing in Wandsworth was sold off during the 1980s and is now in private hands, while most of the Putney stretch of riverside is lined with new-build apartments. On top of this are the older mansion blocks – mostly one and two-bedroom units aimed squarely at wealthy young professionals. Property to let also tends to be targeted at the luxury end of the market.

Shopping & Amenities

The Putney Exchange shopping centre close to Putney Bridge has a Waitrose supermarket and high-street clothing stores, and there is a comprehensive shopping mall in the town centre at Wandsworth High Street plus a large sports centre. An upmarket run of small boutiques, delicatessens and gift shops can be found on Bellevue Road along the southern edge of Wandsworth Common. Generous green space is on the doorstep at Putney Heath, Barnes Common and Wandsworth Common, with the many leisure pursuits of Richmond Park and Wimbledon Common also appealingly near. You can walk, jog, cycle, drink, eat or meander along Putney's riverside, which is also home to several rowing clubs (see p.271).

11

Eating & Drinking
Putney has the usual variety of chain restaurants that pop up in well-to-do areas serving pizza, noodles, Italian, gourmet burgers and Greek, with restaurants and bars clustering around Upper Richmond Road, Lower Richmond Road, Putney Bridge Road and Putney High Street. There is also a fine choice of wining and dining in pleasant surroundings in Putney's riverside quarters. Bellevue Road is Wandsworth's location for trendy and upmarket restaurants, with gastropubs located on the corners around the common.

Education
The St Michael Steiner School and Roche School are prominent private primary institutions in Wandsworth, as is Prospect House in Putney. The private girls' Putney High School and the mixed Putney Park School are both combined primary and secondary establishments. State schools fall under the control of Wandsworth borough (www.wandsworth.gov.uk), with special needs specialists including Garratt Park and Linden Lodge, and the private Centre Academy. The private schools of Hammersmith & Fulham and Richmond are also close at hand, as is, for the twinkle-toed, The Royal Ballet School.

Transport
A branch of the District line heads south at Earls Court towards Wimbledon, stopping at Putney Bridge on the north side of the river and East Putney on the south. An overland train links Putney and Wandsworth Town with Clapham Junction and Waterloo, while Wandsworth Common is connected to Victoria. The South Circular road takes a massive volume of traffic through the area.

Safety/Annoyances
The busy, noisy Trinity Road and South Circular cut through Wandsworth, leaving it somewhat disjointed.

South-West: Wimbledon, Southfields & Earlsfield
The tantrums of McEnroe, the shorts of Navratilova and the tears of Federer – Wimbledon is known most of all for tennis, with fans from all corners converging here every summer for the premier grass court championships. But for the rest of the year, away from the spotlight, Wimbledon is a quiet, green and thoroughly suburban neighbourhood extending south of Putney and Wandsworth. Southfields and Earlsfield are largely residential sub-divisions of Wimbledon, separated by the river Wandle.

Accommodation
Wimbledon's millionaires' row lines the hilly streets bordering the common, with the houses around Wimbledon Park less exalted but still highly desirable. Further south, the fashionable Wimbledon Village has a spread of period houses, luxury apartments and new developments. The least expensive property is close to Wimbledon Broadway where modest suburban development accompanied the arrival of the railways. Southfields contains large Victorian terraces, supplying family homes and flats to rent and buy at prices a notch lower than Wimbledon, with Earlsfield having similar tracts of property.

Shopping & Amenities
Wimbledon's main shopping street is Wimbledon Broadway, where there is a substantial mall called, inevitably, Centre Court. The High Street in Wimbledon Village has a pricier range of stores. Wimbledon and Putney commons are expanses of heathland extending for well over 1,000 acres, and offer plenty of opportunity for

Good Points
Bucolic green space, a genteel suburban environment and a good tram service.

Bad Points
The commute to the north or east of London is arduous.

Overview map, p.78

rambling, cycling and horse-riding. For tennis fans a visit to the Wimbledon Lawn Tennis Museum is highly recommended (see p.291).

Eating & Drinking

High Street and The Broadway both offer the tried and tested selection of chain pubs and restaurants, with family friendly options including Giraffe and Pizza Express. Garratt Lane is where you'll find Earlsfield's restaurants, wine bars and pubs. For those enjoying a morning stroll, the cafe attached to the windmill on Wimbledon Common is legendary for its hearty breakfasts. A night of greyhound-racing in an excitable atmosphere at Plough Lane is in stark contrast to the area's more staid and suburban charms (see p.289).

Education

There is a good range of schools in and around Wimbledon, although the area's state secondary schools are unusual in being predominantly single-sex institutions. Wimbledon comes under the umbrella of Merton borough (www.merton.gov.uk), and of the state schools Garratt Park offers special needs provision. Private primary schools for boys include Willington, Wimbledon College Preparatory and Wimbledon Common Preparatory, while the choice for girls includes The Study Preparatory School and Wimbledon High School, which takes secondary-age pupils too. Private secondaries include King's College School (boys), Hall School Wimbledon (mixed) and the small Norwegian School in London.

Transport

Tube stops at Wimbledon, Wimbledon Park and Southfields are in Zone 3 and all on the District line. Overland stops at Wimbledon, Earlsfield and Raynes Park give quick access to Waterloo, and there is a tram service to other south London areas, such as Mitcham, Croydon and Beckenham.

Safety/Annoyances

The tennis championships has a massive impact on residents in terms of bringing crowds and traffic into the area, making school runs and shopping trips a challenge.

South-West: Other Areas

In at the Deep End
During the summer, south Londoners like to take a dip in the recently refurbished Tooting Bec Lido. It's open from 06:00 until 20:00 from 27 May until 31 August and has a paddling pool and cafe. From October to March, it's only open to members of the South London Swimming Club (www.slsc.org.uk).

Tooting

Tooting is a cheerful, easy-going neighbourhood with plenty of charms, which it doesn't shout about. Drawn in by cheap but decent rented accommodation and a refreshingly unpretentious vibe, many young workers have made their homes here. Tooting High Street – the focal point of the area with a Northern line tube station at either end – has a range of high-street chains, market stalls and local shops. Curry houses and Asian groceries are plentiful too. There is a good-sized open space, Tooting Common (which is officially two separate entities, Tooting Graveney Common and Tooting Bec Common). Here you'll find the Tooting Bec Lido, the largest outdoor swimming pool in Europe (see p.215).

Balham

The south London neighbourhood of Balham grew from a country area into a railway suburb after a station opened here in 1856. Situated between the commons of Clapham, Wandsworth and Tooting, and with a tube stop on the Northern line offering access to the City and West End, Balham was ripe for the gentrification that took hold of the area during the 1990s. Du Cane Court, a 676-strong apartment complex, supplements a stock of terraced houses. Around Balham High Road there is a Waitrose, an organic supermarket, independent bookshop, bars and restaurants. A local Polish community, established in the 1950s and reinvigorated by recent immigration, centres on the White Eagle Club which has a restaurant and regular entertainment events.

South-East: Borough

Good Points
Enough tourist attractions on your doorstep to keep your entire family and circle of friends entertained.

The varied and exciting area of Borough extends back from the South Bank between Waterloo and Tower Bridge, and encompasses such delights as the Tate Modern, the National Theatre, City Hall, the best food market in London, smart new residential developments, and spectacularly reinvented industrial buildings.

Accommodation

Bad Points
Shops and restaurants used to catering to tourists may not always offer the best prices or service.

Overview map, p.78

Borough has plenty of warehouse conversions and apartment blocks, many of which have been built in the past 15 years. Happily, in contrast to Docklands, they tend to include a percentage of affordable housing, allowing for a broader social mix to settle in the area. The surviving cobbled streets and Georgian houses around Guy's hospital are sought-after examples of period architecture. To the east of Borough is Bermondsey, a much poorer area largely made up of huge council estates and social housing.

Shopping & Amenities

Some of London's greatest modern landmarks and top cultural attractions are on your doorstep here – all under the gaze of the all-seeing London Eye (p.217). The Southbank Centre is home to the National Theatre, National Film Theatre, Hayward Gallery and Royal Festival Hall (see p.449). Down the way the Tate Modern, spectacularly housed in a converted power station, continues to draw the crowds after its triumphant opening in 2000 is highly recommended, and its art bookshop is comprehensive (see p.196). Smaller galleries crop up throughout the surrounding streets, with the Design Museum close to Tower Bridge. A stroll across the Millennium Bridge, meanwhile, brings you to St Paul's Cathedral and the modern shopping plazas that surround it. The Old Vic theatre on The Cut, which has Kevin Spacey as its artistic director, stages high-profile productions of classics, while along the road the renovated Young Vic puts on work by new writers. Down by London Bridge station is the gruesome but perennially popular London Dungeon and the meticulous reconstruction of Shakespeare's Globe (p.450). Borough Market (p.368) is credited with kickstarting the trend for farmers' markets, and it's a

Borough Market

paradise for the culinary inclined with stalls full of fresh, organic produce. The Oxo Tower has several small design enterprises with shops attached, and Hay's Galleria has high-end boutiques and craft stalls. More workaday shops are less common – there's a Marks & Spencer and a few other grocery stores dotted around London Bridge station. As well as riverside strolls, residents can take the air in Bermondsey's Southwark Park or try out something more adventurous at Surrey Docks Watersports Centre.

Eating & Drinking

The enormous popularity of Borough Market, which has takeaway stalls offering delicious organic chicken wraps and chorizo burgers, has resulted in a surge of restaurant activity in the surrounding area. This ranges from the exclusive, such as Oxo Tower, to chains such as Wagamama, fish!, The Real

116

Greek and Tas. At the Waterloo end, The Cut is the street to head for with numerous pubs and restaurants, while back on the river Gabriel's Wharf offers a good few cafes and restaurants with outdoor seating for summer lunches. The riverside east from the Southbank Centre is lined with pubs, sandwich bars and coffee shops, and the arts complex itself has chains such as Giraffe and Eat. The National Film Theatre has a bar, coffee shop and self-service cafe, with benches outside, and there are more coffee stops and restaurant facilities in the Tate Modern. The cavernous Vinopolis houses a bar, restaurant, shop and wine-tasting visitor attraction dedicated to the pleasures of the grape (see p.314), while several other large wine bars soak up the area's many office workers. For a quieter pint, more intimate pubs can be found on the dinky riverside streets towards Rotherhithe. In the shadow of Tower Bridge is Hay's Galleria, and its smart wine bars and eateries, while there are two Conran restaurants nearby.

Education

There are several centrally located schools in the Borough area, split between Southwark (www.southwark.gov.uk) and Lambeth (www.lambeth.gov.uk). Snowsfields primary incorporates the Tim Jewell Unit for Children with Autism. Prominent state secondaries include Notre Dame and St Olave's girls' schools, Archbishop Michael Ramsey Technology College and Bacon's College. The high-performing private schools of Dulwich are also within reach.

Transport

Waterloo and Waterloo East stations are the destinations for commuter trains coming from south-western areas of the UK. Waterloo International station, which housed the channel tunnel rail link when it originally opened in 1994, will be closed from November 2007 when the new terminus opens at St Pancras. As a tube stop Waterloo is on the Northern, Bakerloo and Jubilee lines. London Bridge offers southbound overland rail options and Northern line tube connections, and Borough is also on the Northern line. The spacious Jubilee line stations of Waterloo, Southwark, London Bridge and Bermondsey, built in the 1990s, make using the tube in these areas less of a trial than elsewhere, and provide a fast link to Docklands and the West End. A good selection of buses go north from London Bridge and Waterloo, while the City is quickly accessible on foot over the various bridges.

Safety/Annoyances

Crowds of tourists – and residents – in high season means a simple walk to the shops can become a major effort, and the neighbourhood doesn't always feel as if it belongs to locals.

11

South-East: Crystal Palace, Brockley & Sydenham

The interlocking neighbourhoods of Crystal Palace, Brockley and Sydenham cover a wide area, which contains some of the residential heartlands of south-east London. With plenty of open spaces, tracts of housing covering a spectrum of styles, plus decent journey times into town, their increasing popularity among a wide demographic is assured. Bordering on the area is Dulwich, which although too upmarket for some to afford, has amenities which can be enjoyed by all.

Accommodation

The meandering streets sloping away from Crystal Palace Park towards Sydenham Hill are wide, quiet and green with some massive houses, often divided up into generously proportioned flats. Plenty of new-build flats and houses are also in evidence. Forest Hill and Brockley offer huge amounts of affordable rented accommodation in a more urban, densely packed environment – mostly in terraced houses. Flats and smaller houses tend to be reasonably priced, making good starter homes, with prices for the larger period houses steeper. The streets of Dulwich Village, around the genteel College Road, are in a different league and price bracket altogether.

Shopping & Amenities

Small-scale collections of shops can be found on Sydenham Road as it curls away from Sydenham station, and around the junction where Forest Hill station is situated. London Road, running from Forest Hill to East Dulwich, has a Sainsbury's next to local shops. New Cross Gate, which has a retail park, and Lewisham town centre, a major shopping destination, are within easy reach by bus. Dulwich Village, with its upmarket groceries and boutiques, is also close by. Green space is abundant, from the attractively landscaped Dulwich Park to the more functional Crystal Palace Park, whose attractions include Victorian-era life-size model dinosaurs looming out of the undergrowth. All that is left of Crystal Palace itself, which was built for the Great Exhibition of 1851 in Hyde Park, painstakingly relocated in Sydenham Hill (thus conferring its name on the area) then destroyed by fire in 1936, are the slightly spooky remains of its grand terraces. The National Sports Centre, with an indoor arena, tennis courts, sports pitches and an athletics track, is also within the park's confines (see p.236). These facilities have begun to look slightly weary but are set to be updated in the run-up to the 2012 Olympics. The Horniman Museum on London Road, with its dusty, slightly macabre cases of stuffed animals, offers a somewhat dated exhibition experience, although it does have pretty gardens.

Eating & Drinking

Westow Hill – one side of the increasingly trendy 'Crystal Palace triangle' – to the west of Crystal Palace Park boasts a clutch of pleasant restaurants and bars, some with beer gardens and terrific views, while the upmarket establishments of Dulwich Village and Lordship Lane in East Dulwich are within striking distance. There are few pubs or restaurants of any particular note in Forest Hill or Sydenham, but plenty of local cafes, kebab shops and pizza takeaways.

Education

Schools in several local authorities – Lewisham (www.lewisham.gov.uk), Lambeth (www.lambeth.gov.uk), Southwark (www.southwark.gov.uk) and Bromley (www.bromley.gov.uk) – all take pupils from the Crystal Palace, Sydenham and Dulwich areas. Private schools incude Springfield Christian School (primary), Alleyn's School and St Dunstan's College (all ages), pluss the well-known Dulwich College, which serves ages from 2 to 16. Brent Knoll School and Bredinghurst School cater for special needs.

Transport

There's a reason for the area's reasonable pricing – the lack of tube coverage. However, frequent train services run into London Bridge and Victoria from Crystal Palace, Sydenham Hill, Forest Hill and Crofton Park, with journey times of 15 to 30 minutes. Transport links are due to improve soon with the extension of the East London line, which will run from Crystal Palace through the East End and on to Shoreditch, Dalston and Highbury & Islington. Buses are plentiful, linking to other parts of south London as well as north into the West End and City. The main thoroughfare of the South Circular Road carries traffic through the area.

Safety/annoyances

Traffic can be heavy on the roads that break up the area, with busy intersections sometimes creating a slightly barren feel.

Good Points ◀

A well-connected part of south London that is only going to improve.

Bad Points ◀

It hasn't been made over yet – move in now and you can look forward to several years of noise and disruption.

Overview map, p.78

South-East: Elephant and Castle & Kennington

Once dubbed the 'Piccadilly Circus of south London', Elephant and Castle was in Victorian times a hive of commerce and entertainment, with dapper department stores and popular music halls. The area today is unrecognisable from that era due to being flattened during the Blitz and rebuilt as an expanse of concrete and roads – the main features now are a notoriously ugly pink shopping centre hemmed in by an unpleasant conflagration of busy roads and grey buildings. Today it's a cheap place to live, popular with low earners and students (there is a major arts and media university, the London College of Communication, based here), but that is not likely to be the case for too much longer. The area's central location means it was never going to elude the forces of regeneration for ever, and, with £1.5 billion being bandied about, building work has already started in earnest. In a few years expect the area to be rebuilt, relandscaped, regenerated – and unrecognisable. South of Elephant the brighter neighbourhood of Kennington has townhouses and hidden squares.

Accommodation

Much of Elephant's poorly designed and hastily constructed post-war social housing is slated to go, to be replaced by a mixed development of social housing and private apartments with landscaped green space and pedestrianised areas. New public transport links will ensure these apartments have no trouble being bought or let, although it will probably take a few years before prices match those in Borough and Docklands. The disruption caused by the building works will probably mean that cheap rented accommodation, something the area has always offered a good deal of, continues in the short-term at least. Metro Central Heights, a complex of apartment blocks originally designed as an office space by 1960s architect Erno Goldfinger, is one the few examples of modernist architecture in the area that has been deemed worth saving. Further south along Old Kent Road, property is dominated by council estates. Kennington, on the other hand, has some grand property; mainly terraces and pretty squares of townhouses and apartments around Kennington Park Road and Kennington Road. It is popular with MPs and workers due to its position across the river from the Houses of Parliament.

Shopping & Amenities

The current shopping centre, with its dank dangerous pedestrian tunnels, run-down interior and shabby collection of shops, is due to bite the dust in 2010, to be replaced by 800,000 square feet of spanking new retail indoor and outdoor space and a multiscreen cinema. Latin American settlers have brought much-needed life to a corner of the shopping centre, opening cafes, groceries and social centres, and it is to

119

be hoped that these small businesses will find a place in the new development as small-scale streets and units are built to break up the current dominance of large roads and thundering traffic. A grand food market is also planned for the area to the east of the railway viaduct. The Imperial War Museum on St George's Road offers a broad and challenging range of exhibitions and permanent displays (see p.206), and the South Bank Centre is only a few minutes away. To the south, Kennington Park has a welcome expanse of green space.

Eating & Drinking

Until the new development arrives there are a handful of Latin American eateries, plus a huge selection of bars and restaurants in Borough within easy reach. Kennington Lane also has a good range of restaurants of its own, and the West End, Clapham and Brixton are not far away. The massive Ministry of Sound nightclub is on Gaunt Street (see p.443) and there are a selection of gay clubs and bars towards Vauxhall.

Education

Elephant & Castle shares much the same choice of schools as Borough (see p.116), with state options split between Lambeth (www.lambeth.gov.uk) and Southwark (www.southwark.gov.uk). The selective Dulwich College, James Allen's Girls' School and Alleyn's School are the nearest private institutions.

Transport

Despite its ungainliness, Elephant has remained a major transport hub used by those in surrounding areas, and, for a south London location, it is well-served by the tube with Zone 1 stops on the Bakerloo and Northern lines. Revamped, the facilities will only improve. The Northern line also stops at Kennington and Oval. Buses travel outwards in all directions from here as several major roads converge on the roundabouts.

Safety/Annoyances

While the prospects for Elephant & Castle are undoubtedly good for the area, major building work is likely to last for the best part of a decade.

Good Points
Lots of expansive open space, and Blackheath is a real find.

Bad Points
You may feel outnumbered by the tourists that flock to maritime Greenwich.

Overview map, p.78

South-East: Greenwich

Greenwich is an attractive locale – think grand Georgian houses, green swards, market stalls and boat trips – and a sunny weekend will bring out the crowds to enjoy everything the riverside and bustling centre has to offer. The Greenwich peninsula, site of the ill-fated Millennium Dome, is set to get another chance at life as it forms the centre of the 'river zone' of the 2012 Olympics. Beyond Greenwich Park, the neighbourhood of Blackheath is a well-kept secret, with gorgeous houses and a pretty village centre rewarding those who dare to venture this far south.

Accommodation

Parts of Greenwich, notably streets such as Crooms Hill that overlook the park, and Blackheath have some striking examples of Georgian architecture, though these highly prized period homes come with highly inflated price tags. The eastern end of the Greenwich waterfront is mostly former industrial land, and is being redeveloped with the sort of luxury riverside apartment blocks of which London is becoming accustomed. Close to the Dome on the Greenwich peninsula is Millennium Village, a much-trumpeted environmentally friendly development of about 1,400 homes of all sizes. Further south lies the typical jumble of estates and modest terraced streets. Blackheath Park is an exclusive estate with a range of large family homes dating from the late 19th and early 20th centuries.

Shopping & Amenities

The National Maritime Museum, Royal Greenwich Observatory and the Cutty Sark (see p.207) ensure a steady stream of tourists into the area, and the gift shops, restaurants, coffee shops and cafes of Greenwich Church Street cater well for this crowd. The presence of Greenwich's famous market is an additional draw – it is open from Thursday to Sunday with stalls selling art, jewellery, collectibles, antiques, retro home accessories and food. Of further use to locals is a large Sainsbury's supermarket at Bugsby Way close to North Greenwich station. The same complex houses Boots, B&Q and the multiscreen Odeon Greenwich. Blackheath's thriving village centre has a range of useful local stores and amenities, as well as gift shops and purveyors of posh nosh. There is also a farmers' market on Sunday mornings. Blackheath Halls, a medium-sized concert venue, puts on an interesting programme, and the Arches and Waterfront leisure centres, with pool and gym facilities, are both centrally located in Greenwich. Greenwich Park, which has the Royal Observatory in its midst, is an attractive space with stunning views across the river towards central London. Equestrian, modern pentathlon riding and running events will be held here during the Olympics, while the reworked Dome is to become a 20,000-seat indoor arena. The expanse of Blackheath, dramatically overlooked by stunning sweeps of Georgian houses, is another excellent green space.

Eating & Drinking

Both Greenwich and Blackheath boast a fine array of eating and drinking establishments. In Greenwich there is everything from tea rooms and fine dining to chain pasta places and noodle bars. Blackheath's pubs and restaurants, centring on the delightfully named Tranquil Vale, are a quieter prospect but, with a wide choice of cuisines covering Spanish, Thai and European, there is plenty to explore. There are branches of all the fast-food high-street favourites next to Greenwich's Odeon in Bugsby Way.

Education

The borough of Greenwich (www.greenwich.gov.uk) extends south of Blackheath to include some large residential outer London areas, so the local authority's schools are many and diverse. The private Riverston School is in the southern reaches of nearby Eltham.

Transport

The millennium building frenzy led to substantially improved public transport in Greenwich, with a tube link at North Greenwich on the Jubilee line bringing the area closer to the West End, Docklands and Stratford. The Docklands Light Railway also makes its way under the river with stops at Cutty Sark, Greenwich and Deptford Bridge. You can make the same journey on two legs by walking the Greenwich Foot Tunnel, or take one of the many boats along the Thames from Greenwich Pier. Overland rail trips from stops at Maze Hill and Blackheath to London Bridge take less than 20 minutes.

Safety/Annoyances

Greenwich has rather too many kitsch cafes of the 'olde English' variety, and the hordes of tourists can be an irritant to locals.

121

South-East: Other Areas

Camberwell

Camberwell is another of inner south London's railway suburbs, its defining period of development and major population growth occurring during the second half of the 19th century. Estate agents in the 1990s were alerted to the previously overlooked area by the well-preserved Georgian terraces along Camberwell Grove and Grove Lane, although most of Camberwell's accommodation consists of more mundane Victorian terracing and a good few tower blocks. Its residents are a mix of ethnic groups and income brackets – there are large Afro-Caribbean and African communities, and students who attend the Camberwell College of Arts and nearby King's College. The hub of the neighbourhood is Camberwell Green, but with its hurtling traffic and nose-to-tail buses, it's not noticeably green. There is no tube in the area and the nearest overland stations are at Loughborough Junction and Denmark Hill, so buses are the public transport staple, with journey times into central London of about 25 minutes (traffic permitting).

East Dulwich

Although not as rigorously upmarket as neighbouring Dulwich Village, which has country house-style residences and a rural ambience, East Dulwich is thoroughly gentrified. Lordship Lane, with its grand red-brick Victorian buildings, is where most of the area's pubs, restaurants and delicatessens can be found. A small market on North Cross Road on Fridays and Saturdays sells books, antiques and foodie goodies. Dulwich Park is a particularly attractive neighbourhood open space, and you can hire bicycles to get around. Trains from East Dulwich station on Grove Vale will take you to London Bridge in 12 minutes.

East: Docklands

Good Points
A fresh, bright and modern environment where quaysides and wharves have been reinvented to spectacular effect.

Docklands is a bright, shiny new world of water, glass, granite and steel. Once the largest port in the world, the London docks faded away in the 1960s with the advent of containers and many local residents lost their livelihoods. In the 1980s a bold and vast regeneration project was undertaken to breathe new life into what had become an unloved backwater. Huge new skyscrapers, extensive and high-tech business premises and shopping plazas plus mile upon mile of warehouse conversions, modern apartment blocks and luxury riverside developments, have now created a quite unique new quarter of London – the closest the capital has to Manhattan.

Accommodation

Bad Points
Tie shops, pricey paninis, bento boxes and Belgian beer dominate, robbing the area of any individuality – or any chance of a bacon sandwich.

Accommodation is heavily dominated by blocks of luxury pads, with private gyms, river views and off-street parking. Property prices are high, but there is a constant supply of one and two-bed apartments to rent. Towards Wapping, housing becomes more picturesque with converted warehouses and wharves. In the far south end of the Isle of Dogs is a stretch of council estates, which mixes slightly uncomfortably with new developments. Houses are in short supply throughout, although development is continuing apace in the east of the area.

Overview map, p.78

Shopping & Amenities

The retail centres and plazas surrounding Canary Wharf are comprehensive, with supermarkets and a wide range of upmarket clothing and accessory chains. There's a multiscreen cinema at West India Quay, and The ExCel Centre, a few stops east of Canary Wharf, is a massive conference and exhibition space with the London Arena concert arena adjacent. Mudchute Park has a city farm, and a foot tunnel under the Thames allows easy access to the many attractions and markets of Greenwich.

Eating & Drinking

You're guaranteed to find a shiny branch of your favourite chain restaurant somewhere here; sushi bars, pizza restaurants, juice bars and expensive sandwich shops are plentiful. Large waterside bars encourage outdoor drinking in a refreshingly car-free environment at West India Quay. Individuality and quirkiness, however, are at a premium as rents are too high for all but the big brands to afford. The Prospect of Whitby at Wapping is the best example of the few traditional pubs in the area.

Education

There are a surprisingly high number of state primaries in the Docklands vicinity, both religious-affiliated and not. There's a small private primary, River House Montessori, at Heron Quay. Close to Wapping are St Peter's London Docks and Hermitage primary schools. Secondary schools can be found in the main part of Tower Hamlets to the north (see Whitechapel, Bethnal Green and Stepney Green, page. 126), or over the river in Southwark (see Borough, page 116).

Transport

Docklands' singularity is confirmed but its very own transit system, the Docklands Light Railway, most of which is in Zone 2. Stops on this dinky railway are frequent and comprehensive, linking with the tube at Bank and Tower Gateway in the City to the west and Stratford to the north. Canary Wharf is also a tube stop on the Jubilee line, which offers a roundabout but quick route to Westminster and the West End.

Safety/Annoyances

The Docklands development was parachuted into this area with little consultation or thought for the needs of the existing local community, and there are still uncomfortable contrasts between the haves and the have-nots.

Good Points ◀
Hackney is a right rollicking cultural rollercoaster of a neighbourhood.

Bad Points ◀
Parts of the neighbourhood are considered rough, if not downright dangerous.

Overview map, p.78

East: Hackney & Bow

Hackney carries a lot of baggage in terms of crime and deprivation, but its charms – a melting pot of cultural influences, a fascinating past of immigration and political agitation, vibrant green spaces – continue to win over many a doubter. South of Victoria Park and bounded by the Blackwall Tunnel Northern Approach, the Limehouse Cut canal and Grove Road/Burdett Road, lies Bow, another East End neighbourhood that has been greatly gentrified over the past 20 years.

Accommodation

Hackney and Bow have some splendid examples of English architecture, such as Clapton Square, Sutton Square and Tredegar Square, which all have well-preserved Georgian terraces. Fine as these properties are, they are expensive and in fairly short supply. There are many streets of dilapidated Victorian terraced houses. These have traditionally been carved up to provide cheap rental accommodation but increasingly they are being refurbished to a higher standard or even turned back into family

homes. Gentrification is particularly noticeable in the attractive streets surrounding the open space of London Fields, the trendy Broadway Market area and in the roads bordering Victoria Park. In between the older council estates, a good number of mixed development apartment blocks have been built over the past 15 years providing accommodation for the lower-waged and key workers. The Clapton area, between Lea Bridge Road and Homerton High Street, has a further run of Victorian terraced streets, providing plenty of flats and houses to rent or buy. The 2012 Olympics will affect the north-east end of Hackney and is already impacting favourably on house prices.

Shopping & Amenities

Hackney's main street, Mare Street, has an array of shops including Primark, Woolworths and many local grocery stores, with a large Tesco superstore on Morning Lane. Broadway Market has a flurry of independent art shops and a farmers' market on Saturdays. The redeveloped area around Hackney Town Hall has a coffee shop, library and local history museum. Next to the Town Hall is The Hackney Empire, a theatre dating from 1901 which had fallen into disrepair. A concerted fundraising campaign eventually led to it being thoroughly restored and it triumphantly reopened in 2004. It's now a leading variety venue staging theatre, comedy, dance and a rocking annual pantomime. Live music is on offer at the next door Marie Lloyd Bar, which stays open until 01:00. Bow has less to offer, but there's a Tesco at Bromley by Bow for groceries and Hackney Downs, London Fields and Hackney Marshes for fresh air. Victoria Park (p.216) separates Hackney and Bow and its acres afford many opportunities for dog-walking, football and kite-flying.

Eating & Drinking

Broadway Market, with its fine selection of bars, gastropubs and not one, but two, Argentinean restaurants, is the current hot-spot for trendy eateries and watering holes. The Inn on the Park is well-placed to supply refreshment to those enjoying a sunny afternoon in Victoria Park, while Lauriston Road nearby has a concentration of brasseries and restaurants. There are some good cheap Vietnamese restaurants on Mare Street as well as the usual range of takeaways. Towards Dalston and Stoke Newington are many excellent Turkish and Kurdish kebab restaurants.

Education

Common with many inner-city areas struggling with high demand and limited resources, Hackney and Bow's schools have taken a bit of a criticism for their standards over the years. As always, individual schools vary enormously and results can improve dramatically and quickly so it's best to get as much up-to-date information as you can before making any decisions. Contact Tower Hamlets education authority for more details (www.towerhamlets.gov.uk). State primaries are plentiful and busy (schools such as London Fields and Sebright have over 400 pupils apiece). There are few private primaries locally, one exception being the Gatehouse School on Sewardstone Road, close to Victoria Park. Secondary state schools include Cardinal Pole Roman Catholic, Hackney Free and Clapton Girls' Technology College.

Transport

Hackney's doesn't have a tube station, but for those who work in the City, the area is handily placed – it takes just 15 minutes to Liverpool Street from stations at London Fields, Hackney Downs and Clapton. Stops on the overland North London line at Hackney Central and Homerton link with the transport hub at Stratford and so open up Docklands and the wider tube network.

Bow is better placed for the tube, with Bow Road (District and Hammersmith & City), Bow Church (Docklands Light Railway) and Mile End station (Central, District and Hammersmith & City lines) at the western end of Bow Road and Mile End Road.

Safety/Annoyances

Hackney has a bit of an edge, and parts of it can seem rather chaotic and intimidating. A stretch of Clapton Road in particular has a reputation as 'murder mile' due to a spate of drug-related gun crime. While these events are distressing and frightening, the chances of getting caught up in them are slim.

Good Points

Walthamstow is reliable, cheerful and always improving, with plenty of local green space.

Bad Points

There is a distinct lack of decent local restaurants and pubs.

Overview map, p.78

East: Walthamstow

At the opposite end of the Victoria line from Brixton, Walthamstow has begun to shake off its 'end of the line' reputation. A shopping centre, street market, a good range of property at reasonable prices, access to the countryside and decent transport links all make it a newly attractive proposition.

Accommodation

Walthamstow has an abundance of small to medium-sized Victorian houses and conversions within walking distance of the tube. The most sought-after location is the village, to the east of Hoe Street, where there is a conservation area and picturesque Victorian cottage-style houses. A constant supply of reasonably priced rented accommodation in shared houses and flats keeps up the numbers of students, recent immigrants and young professionals, while family homes bring in middle-class families on modest incomes.

Shopping & Amenities

Walthamstow has a daily street market on High Street which is often cited as the longest in Europe. The range of produce doesn't quite live up to the hype but is basic and useful – fruit, vegetables, cheap household accessories and toiletries. The nearby Selbourne Walk Shopping Centre has all the familiar high-street names. The Bakers Arms junction has a further concentration of shops. There are good leisure facilities (Waltham Forest Pool and Track on Chingford Road, the exotically named Leyton Leisure Lagoon on High Road) plus the soon-to-be Olympically enhanced indoor and outdoor sporting facilities of the Lea Valley. The Vestry House Museum in the Village traces the local history of the area, while the William Morris Gallery on Forest Road celebrates the life and work of the 19th century designer in the house where he was born. Behind it Lloyds Park is a pleasant local park and playing area. Epping Forest and Wanstead Flats are also nearby.

Eating & Drinking

Aside from the usual takeaways, the High Street and Hoe Street end of Walthamstow do not offer much in the way restaurants. Pubs also tend towards the large and anonymous, although there are a few more appealing spots in the Village. The Lea Bridge Road also has a few places to eat out. A drive east finds a better selection around Wansted High Street. For an exciting and cheap (assuming you're not a gambling addict) local night out, head for Walthamstow Stadium (p.289).

Education

Numerous state primary and secondary schools come under the control of the Borough of Waltham Forest (www.walthamforest.gov.uk). Several religious schools include St Mary's Walthamstow, St Patrick's and St Mary's Catholic Junior School. Walthamstow Montessori School and the Islamic Shakhsiyah Foundation school are two of the few private primaries in the area. Barn Croft Primary offers special needs provision, as does Whitefield Schools and Centre, which takes children up to the age of 19. The private Forest School in College Road takes some 1,200 pupils from 4 to 16.

Transport

Walthamstow Central and Blackhorse Road are on the fast Victoria line so offer very reasonable journey times to King's Cross, Oxford Street and Victoria. Walthamstow Central offers services to Hackney and Liverpool Street as well as in the other direction to Essex. Other overland stops at Blackhorse Road and Walthamstow Queen's Road connect with the outer branch of the North London line. Buses go towards Hackney and Tottenham, but journey times are lengthy.

Safety/Annoyances

Walthamstow's increasing popularity means the tube and rail stations are frantically busy in the mornings with long queues and any delays resulting in overcrowded platforms.

Good Points
Relatively cheap central areas to live that come with bags of history and character but are constantly reinvigorated by change and new waves of immigration.

Bad Points
Heavily built-up with some bleak overcrowded estates.

Overview map, p.78

East: Whitechapel, Bethnal Green & Stepney

These neighbourhoods, which still have much of the traditional working class East End about them, are strung out along Whitechapel and Mile End Road from Aldgate on the edge of the City to Mile End Park. Heavily bombed during the Second World War, the area has great tracts of social housing dating from the 1960s some of which have become rundown, overcrowded and crime-ridden. However, regeneration, redevelopment and the expansion of student accommodation at Queen Mary University have seen the dynamics of the area change dramatically since the 1980s. Encouraged by easy access to both the City and Docklands young professionals have moved into new apartment blocks and loft conversions.

Accommodation

In between student residences and warren-like housing estates are a scattering of still-standing Victorian terraces and the occasional square, which tend to house the most appealing property in the area. Alongside these remnants are new apartment blocks, built on former industrial land and by the Regent's Canal to entice City workers. There are plenty of reasonably priced shared houses and flats to rent.

Shopping & Amenities

Markets and shops along Bethnal Green Road, Roman Road and Whitechapel Road supply locals with cheap fruit, vegetables, household goods and toiletries, and there's a large Sainsbury's supermarket where Whitechapel Road turns into Mile End Road. The more exciting markets and malls of Spitalfields, Petticoat Lane and Brick Lane are within easy reach (see Shoreditch and Hoxton, page. 88). Columbia Road, with its flower market and arty shops, just sneaks into the north-west corner of Bethnal Green. As well as Brick Lane and Cheshire Street's proliferation of small galleries, fashion boutiques, bespoke furniture-makers and home accessory stores, Whitechapel Art Gallery (p.197), standing close to Aldgate East tube, mounts major exhibitions and has a cafe and an art bookshop. The once bleak and uninspiring length of Mile End Park was thoroughly re-landscaped in 2000 with new playgrounds, gardens, an electric go-kart track, an Ecology Park complete with wind turbine and a flower-covered pedestrian bridge linking its two halves. Its current minimal running track facilities are being considerably expanded to include a new pool and leisure centre. There is also an indoor climbing wall at Mile End (p.243). Mile End Genesis multiscreen shows mainstream film releases.

Eating & Drinking
The traditional East End boozer is alive and kicking in these parts, with the most infamous being The Blind Beggar on Whitechapel Road, the scene of a murder carried out by one of notorious 1960s gangsters, the Kray Twins. Some of these remain resolutely dingy, unwelcoming and occasionally sinister, while others are cheerful and unpretentious with a mixed clientele. Otherwise, you'll never want for takeaways and cheap curry houses on Whitechapel Road and Bethnal Green Road, but more upmarket options are in shorter supply. The western end of the Bethnal Green Road and the gentrified area around Globe Road has the best supply of bars and restaurants. The Leman Street area to the south of Whitechapel has a good selection of Indian restaurants as does, of course, Brick Lane (p.395), which is famous for its curry houses.

Education
There are dozens of state primaries and secondaries in the area, including Church of England and Catholic-affiliated schools, many of which are juggling the needs of children from widely differing backgrounds. All come under the control of Tower Hamlets (www.towerhamlets.gov.uk). George Green's School (humanities) and Langdon Park Community School (sports), have special focus status. The two Bishop Challoner Catholic Collegiate schools provide single-sex education. Private options include several Muslim schools, both primary and secondary, serving the area's large Bangladeshi community. State special needs education is provided by the Stephen Hawking School (primary) to the south of the area near Limehouse Road, and Beatrice Tate School (secondary).

Transport
The Central line stops at the heart of Bethnal Green and Mile End servicing the City and the West End. The District and Hammersmith & City lines also stops at Mile End, Whitechapel and Stepney Green. The Docklands Light Railway can be picked up at Tower Gateway, Shadwell and Limehouse. The soon-to-be extended East London Line also travels through the area with stops at Shadwell and Whitechapel.

Safety/Annoyances
These areas can still have a bit of an edge with high levels of deprivation and social exclusion on run-down estates. Periodically (often around election time) there is social and political tension between different ethnic groups.

East: Other Areas
Huge amounts of regeneration money have been pumped into the Stratford area over the last 10 years as it has been transformed into a major transport hub on the back of the Channel Tunnel Rail Link. Next to the new station, which is on the Docklands Light Railway, the Central and Jubilee lines, is a refurbished shopping centre, cinema, arts centre and new residential apartment blocks. Their buyers and those who have snapped up property in the area's previously dowdy terraced streets are banking on one thing – the 2012 Olympics. Nearby Leyton and Leytonstone are generally unremarkable areas, but with stops on the Central line and a great deal of cheaply priced rental accommodation, they can make convenient bases.

Setting up Home

Once you've found a place to live, signed your name on the dotted line and collected your keys, chances are you'll want to move in and get settled as soon as possible – especially if the alternative is sleeping on someone's floor. What you need to shop for depends on whether you are buying or renting and how long you envisage your stay in the UK will be. Most rental accommodation in London is already furnished with major items such as a bed, wardrobe, living-room furniture and kitchen essentials. Smaller everyday items such as bed linen are unlikely to be included, and of course it's the little things you add yourself that will make your new place feel like home. If you're moving at the behest of your company, you may be offered relocation help. Relocation companies, often hired by employers, can help with things such as in-country orientation and schooling.

Moving Services

If you are moving to the UK from overseas, there are many shipping companies who will pack and transport your belongings for you (www.intlmovers.com is a good place to source a suitable company). Premium services will organise every last detail of your move – but it's an expensive business, and if your stay is likely to be a short-term rental it makes sense to bring as little as possible as you're unlikely to need to buy major items of furniture. If you are settling in for a long stay or buying a property, shipping the large items of furniture you already own may well be cost effective. Firms that belong to the British Association of Removers (www.removers.org.uk) comply with codes of conduct, which include cover for loss or damage. The cost of a professional move of a small flat's worth of stuff in London starts at around £250, with additional charges for services such as storage and packing. Unregulated 'man with a van' type services are advertised widely in local papers and on the internet. They tend to be cheaper, but you may find yourself with little protection or recourse should anything go wrong. Alternatively, car rental companies will hire out vans by the day (you'll need your driving licence and a deposit) if you feel confident enough to move your own belongings.

Relocation Companies

Alexanders Removal & Storage Specialists	0845 0096633	www.gotoalexanders.co.uk
Bishop's Move	7498 0300	www.bishopsmove.net
Budget Shipping	0800 6528980	www.budget-shipping.co.uk
Crown Relocation	02920 501101	www.crownrelocation.co.uk
Excess International Movers	0800 7831085	www.excess-baggage.com
Pro-Move Relocations Ltd	8501 2614	www.promoverelocations.co.uk
Sargents	8320 5590	www.sargents.co.uk

Removal Companies

Amber Moves	8201 5488	www.ambermoves.com
Britannia	0845 6006661	www.britannia-movers.co.uk
Capital Moves & Storage	0800 6522192	www.capitalmovesltd.com
Clockwork Removals	8870 6176	www.clockworkremovals.co.uk
The Collectors	8961 9398	www.collectors-london.co.uk
Crispins Removals	7739 0303	www.crispins-removals.co.uk
Doree Bonner International	8303 6261	www.doreebonner.co.uk
Monarch UK & European Movers	0800 9546474	www.monarch-movers.com
Movin' uk	0800 7317682	www.movinuk.com
OIS Removals	0800 7835702	www.oisremovals.co.uk
Pickfords	8219 8200	www.pickfords.co.uk
R C Russ Group	0800 9171408	www.rcrussgroup.co.uk
Russell Fewins	0800 7837795	www.rf-domesticremovals.com
Trek Removals	7473 4759	www.trekremovals.com

Go Second-Hand

Some of London's markets, such as Brick Lane, have many stalls offering second-hand furniture and household items of varying quality and prices, while areas such as Holloway Road have concentrations of shops selling furniture from office and house clearances. Also look out for car-boot sales in your local area, widely held on Saturday and Sunday mornings and advertised at the venue or on noticeboards in the local area. Charity shops can be a good source for inspiration too. Many people now sell any unwanted items they have on the internet at eBay (www.ebay.co.uk) and other auction sites, while on www.freecycle.org community-spirited people offer unwanted items for free if you can arrange to pick them up.

Furnishing Your Home

Most rental accommodation in London is let furnished and typically has items including a bed, sofa, table, chairs, washing machine, cooker and refrigerator. Other items such as a TV, desk and bookcases may or may not be included. If you are looking specifically for an unfurnished let, be aware that this is not the norm in the capital so you should specify this requirement as soon as possible when contacting letting agents and landlords.

If you need to buy furniture, London offers options for every budget. For major purchases the most inexpensive tends to be Swedish flat-pack emporium IKEA, but if you don't have access to a car and opt to use the delivery service it may not work out quite as cheap as you may think – you also have to put whatever you buy together yourself. Many furniture retailers offer interest-free credit deals, which enable you to pay for major items over a stipulated time, but again, remember to factor in the delivery charge. Reasonably priced furniture outlets on the high street include Habitat, Cargo and Argos. For a wide selection of beds and sofas, take a look at the stores along the Warren Street end of Tottenham Court Road.

If all you need are soft furnishings, your choice is even wider. High-street stores such as Woolworths, BHS, Marks & Spencer, Habitat and Peacocks all have reasonably priced ranges of lamps, towels, bed linen, cushions, vases, candlesticks and kitchen utensils. Large branches of supermarkets are good places to look for cheap deals on small items of furniture, kitchen gadgets, storage boxes and electronic goods. See p.328 in Shopping for more details.

Household Insurance

When it comes to burglary rates, London tends to hover in the top three of the most-afflicted cities in Europe. It's wise to keep security in mind from the outset and to look out for obvious risk factors such as badly fitted windows or inadequate locks when viewing properties. However, even the most fortified home can fall victim to thieves, so insurance is a sensible and reasonably priced precaution. Basic cover of your belongings starts from around £15 a month to insure you against burglary, flood, fire, vandalism, burst pipes and storm damage, with additional premiums to cover accidental damage and incidences such as bicycle or portable computer theft outside the home. You may be able to get special deals from your existing bank, building society or the provider of your car insurance or breakdown cover, as well as

Household Insurance

A Quote Insurance	0800 0923935	www.aquote.co.uk
AA	0800 1976169	www.theaa.com
Abbey	0800 670660	www.abbey.com
Asda Insurance	0800 0155547	www.asdafinance.com
AXA	7702 3109	www.axa.co.uk
Churchill	0800 200326	www.churchill.com
Direct Line	0845 2463564	www.directline.com
Endsleigh Insurance Services	0800 3892011	www.endsleigh.co.uk
Halifax Home Insurance	0800 1693668	www.halifax.co.uk
NatWest Home Insurance	0800 0515450	www.natwest.com
Norwich Union	0800 0683662	www.norwichunion.com
Post Office Home Insurance	0800 7830362	www.postoffice.co.uk
Privilege	0845 2460515	www.privilege.com
Royal & SunAlliance	0800 300660	www.royalsunalliance.co.uk
Saga	0800 0154752	www.saga.co.uk
Zurich Home Insurance	0800 868686	www.zurichinsurance.co.uk

129

from dedicated insurance agents such as Direct Line or Churchill. Companies including Endsleigh specialise in low-cost insurance deals for students living in halls of residence and shared accommodation. Note that mobile phones are rarely covered by home contents deals and it's usual to buy insurance direct from your phone operator.

Laundry Services

It is standard for rented accommodation to have a washing machine unless the property is so small that there is no room for one. The only time you are likely to come across shared laundry facilities is in student halls of residence or the occasional mansion block. If your let is unfurnished or does not have a washing machine (or, more likely, your washing machine breaks down) then a coin-operated launderette is generally to be found where there's a collection of local shops. Most have attendants who will provide change for the machines, and will do service washes for an additional charge.

> **Made to Measure**
> If you're fussy about your furnishings, or your house has oversized rooms or windows, you may prefer to get your home decorations tailored rather than pay for off the shelf products. Specialist furniture outlets sell made-to-measure curtains, blinds and carpets, while department stores including John Lewis and House of Fraser also offer bespoke services. For more information on tailoring services, see p.350.

Domestic Help

With the tendency for London flats and houses to be on the small side, and bearing in mind the city's already high cost of living, employing a cleaner may seem something of a luxury – but as Londoners find their time increasingly squeezed by work and social commitments, it is catching on in some parts. If you live in a shared house or flat then clubbing together to get a cleaner may make for a more pleasant living environment, and won't cost a fortune. As it is a position that demands a certain level of trust, hiring a cleaner from a personal recommendation is a good idea if at all possible. Plenty of domestic cleaning agencies exist too, which you can find listed in phone directories or at www.yell.com, Gumtree (www.gumtree.com/london) although these are generally more expensive. Cleaners tend to charge by the hour and duties will be a matter of negotiation, but usually cover general cleaning, floor-mopping, vacuuming, washing-up and dusting. Most will

> **Find a Tradesman**
> Despite the number of plumbers, electricians and decorators offering their services in the capital, residents often struggle to find a tradesman that they can trust. To be sure of any individual's or company's credentials, check these websites:
> **www.londontradesman.co.uk**
> **www.trustcorgi.com/findinstaller/findaninstaller.htmx**
> **www.iphe.org.uk**

undertake ironing and laundry if asked too. Live-in maids and nannies are the preserve of the wealthy and those with big enough houses. The only live-in help that is common in London is an au-pair - young people from overseas who help out around the home and with childcare for a set number of hours a week in return for board, meals and a modest allowance. UK immigration rules have a special au pair category for nationals of the following countries: Andorra, Bosnia-Herzegovina, Croatia, Faroe Islands, Greenland, Macedonia, Monaco, San Marino and Turkey (people who come from within the EU plus Switzerland are free to work as an au pair in line with standard regulations, see p.53). Many agencies exist to help match au pairs and employers, and most have an online presence.

Babysitting & Childcare

London does not always feel like the easiest setting in which to bring up children. Only a handful of gyms, department stores, shopping malls, superstores and workplaces have creches, but you can expect to find baby-changing facilities in any large museum, gallery, chain restaurant or station. But there are significant resources and avenues of help available:

Parent and toddler groups – these are for under-fives and their parents or carers (you cannot leave your child here unaccompanied). The groups are either free or you pay a minimal charge of £3 per session - your council website will hold details of all those in your local area. Other child-centred activities you can take the little ones along to include playbuses, toy libraries, baby massage and music groups – all great ways to keep the kids occupied and meet other parents. Watch out for parent and baby screenings at local cinemas too.

Babysitting & Childcare		
The Babysitting Company	7385 0055	www.thebabysitting.co.uk
Hopes and Dreams Babysitters	7833 9388	www.hopesanddreams.co.uk
Kiddikare	01483 271241	www.kiddikareuk.co.uk
Safehands	0870 8446688	www.safehandsnetwork.com
Sitters	0800 3890038	www.sitters.co.uk
Top Notch Nannies	7259 2626	www.topnotchnannies.co.uk

Childminders and day nurseries – each council has a list of registered childminders and day nurseries, which you can access online. All premises must have been inspected, and individuals need to have provided references and undergone police checks.

Nannies – if you are considering full-time home-based help with childcare, you may wish to approach one of the many recruitment agencies that specialise in placing nannies with families. Using an agency will incur a hefty fee, but the peace of mind may be worth the expense. Alternatively you can look for advertisements by nannies offering their services in magazines (*The Lady* is a good place to start) or place an ad yourself.

Babysitters – finding a babysitter is no easy task, and many London parents rely on informal networks of friendly parents who 'sit' each other's kids. Nanny agencies do sometimes have babysitters on their books, otherwise personal recommendations are the best way forward.

Domestic Services

In rented accommodation, your landlord is obliged to take care of any major repairs and you are spared the hassle of organising it yourself. Plumbers, handymen, electricians and carpenters in your area are listed in telephone or online directories, and given the sheer number of them and the many horror stories it's always best to go on personal recommendation. That said, even people who have lived in London for many years have difficulty finding reliable individuals or firms. If you know the nature of the work needed, one approach is to phone or email a few companies and ask for a quote for cost and timescale.

A typical price for straightforward jobs such as fixing leaks, installing washing machines, laying flooring or tiling starts at around £45 for the first hour, with each additional hour at another £35. Expect to pay at least double for evening, night-time and weekend call-outs. If a gas appliance is involved, it is essential for your safety that you choose an operative who is CORGI-registered, which means they have been properly trained. For gas and electricity, bear in mind that utility companies offer service plans where you pay a monthly charge and receive an annual service and repairs, depending on the terms of the particular deal.

Pest Control

It is common to experience problems with mice, rats, or squirrels, especially in London's older properties, and for those with balconies, pigeons can be a real nuisance. The occasional manifestation of cockroaches, wasps or other creepy-crawlies is also a possibility which you should be prepared for. If the problem is more than your hardware shop can help with, then local authorities may be able to provide free pest control services for outside or communal areas, but they will often only treat inside for a charge. There are also plenty of private pest control agencies to choose from. If you are in rented accommodation, talk to your landlord as they can be expected to tackle infestation as part of their responsibilities. In the case of fleas, which seem to an endemic problem for pets and their owners in London, prevention is better than cure so ask your vet about pre-emptive strikes.

Local Libraries

Public libraries often have a wide range of films, DVDs and videos available to rent for a week or longer at cheaper rates than high-street stores. Joining your local library requires two proofs that you live in the borough. Once you have a card you can use any of the area's branches.

DVD & Video Rental

Most local high streets have a film rental store, and membership is ordinarily free on the production of a couple of proofs of name and address, and perhaps credit card details. As videos fall by the wayside, it is increasingly common for stores to deal solely in DVDs. Prices are generally around £3.50 for a new release for one or two nights, less for older films. Rental chain Blockbuster, which has branches throughout London, also hires out an extensive range of computer games. Online DVD borrowing is becoming more popular too, offered by the likes of Amazon (www.amazon.co.uk), Sofa Cinema (www.sofacinema.co.uk) and LoveFilm (www.lovefilm.com). You pay a monthly subscription which allows you to order DVDs online and have them delivered by post, and you can generally keep them for longer periods.

Pets

The UK likes to think of itself a nation of animal lovers, and many homes have at least one pet. Cats, dogs, rabbits, guinea pigs, hamsters, budgies, fish, even snakes and reptiles, you name it, Brits keep it. When choosing a pet you have to think carefully about your ability to provide an environment in which it can thrive. It's an ongoing expense too – you'll need enough money to cover veterinary care, food and toys, plus an aquarium, hutch or cage where appropriate. Animals such as dogs thrive on companionship and may not be suitable for those who work long hours. If you are renting accommodation, check with your landlord as it is common to have a 'no pets' rule, or to stipulate which animals they will allow.

Cats & Dogs

Dogs and cats are widely kept in the UK, although they are only generally suitable for those living in houses or ground-floor flats with garden access. Dogs must be kept on

leads in the street, and are not permitted to foul the pavement. You should carry a stock of plastic bags with you and use the red dog-waste bins that are provided in most parks. While it is acceptable to allow your dog off its leash in parks and open spaces, always remember that some people, especially small children, can find dogs frightening (it is common for children's play areas to be designated as dog-free zones). Battersea Dogs & Cats Home (www.dogshome.org) rescues and rehouses London's stray or unwanted animals, while

Dangerous Dogs Act
The Dangerous Dogs Act came into force in 1991 following a number of high-profile cases of dogs attacking children. This bans people from owning four main types of dog – pit bull terrier, tosa, dogo argentino and fila brasiliero – without specific court exemption. Any that are exempted need to be registered, microchipped and muzzled, and kept on a leash in public. The breeding and sale of these dogs is also prohibited, although it is commonly acknowledged that there is a large black market in illegal dogs.

Cats Protection (www.cats.org.uk) is a UK-wide organisation, with local branches, that finds homes for stray cats. In both cases you'll be assessed for your ability to provide a suitable home, and the animal will be microchipped and have had some jabs. You'll also be asked for a donation. Another option is to buy a puppy from a breeder registered with The Kennel Club (www.the-kennel-club.org.uk). To help keep down the numbers of strays, animal welfare groups tend to recommend having your cat or dog neutered.

Birds & Fish

Keeping fish or birds is an option if you have insufficient space for a larger animal. For fish keepers, the main distinction is between freshwater and tropical fish. Freshwater fish, such as goldfish, can be kept in either aquariums or ponds, whereas tropical and marine fish need tanks with special equipment that mimics their natural environment. You can buy fish from pet shops, aquatic centres, breeders and some garden centres. Alarm bells should ring if you see tanks where the water is dirty, the fish are overcrowded, or there are dead fish. If you are buying tropical or marine fish, check their source as the trade in wild fish, as opposed to ones bred in captivity, is damaging to the environment and many die in transit. Pet birds too vary widely in their needs, so make sure you are fully informed about the species you opt for. Budgies and canaries, for instance, are social birds and should be kept in groups in large aviaries, whereas some parrots may be more suited to life in a house or flat.

Pet Shops

Pet shops are not the best place to buy puppies or kittens, as the animals have often been separated from their mothers prematurely and kept in conditions likely to encourage disease. Pet shop trade can also encourage the cruel practice of puppy farming. It is far better to adopt a pet from an animal rescue centre, such as Battersea Dogs & Cats Home (see Cats & Dogs), or from the litter of a dog or cat owner you either know, has been recommended to you, or whose house you have visited in order to see the conditions the animals are kept in. It is unusual to see pets on sale on market stalls, and buying from this source is not recommended.

Vets & Kennels

There are plenty of veterinary practices of all sizes and specialities in London. The Royal College of Veterinary Surgeons, the UK's regulatory body for vets, administers a

Animal Theft

Although urban myths abound about pets being stolen for animal research or the fur trade, such rumours have little to substantiate them – it's more likely that many animals that go missing have been killed on the road rather than stolen. Most pet theft is opportunistic and targeted at animals presumed to have a high value, such as pedigree dogs and cats. To minimise the risk, have your pet microchipped by a vet and put a tag on its collar to show that this has been done. Try to keep cats in at night (this also helps protect them from the dangers of the road) and do not let dogs roam unsupervised.

Pet Boarding/Sitting

A Furry World	N1	0870 3500508	Boarding, petsitting
Cats, Dogs & Peace of Mind	W5	7987 2017	Petsitting
Happy Hounds & Cooler Cats	E11	8558 4427	Petsitting, dog boarding, dog walking
One O One Pet Care	NW1	7691 4896	Petsitting
Walkies & More	SE18	8854 1018	Petsitting, dog walking
Westend Dogs & Pur-Fect Cats	WC1	7405 4111	Petsitting

Practice Standards Scheme, and vets that have been accredited undergo regular inspection. Use the postcode search facility at www.rcvs.org.uk to find a list of practices in your area. Vets' bills can be steep, however, and it's worth considering pet insurance to guard against the possible costs (see box). If you really cannot afford to take an animal to a vet, or if you find an injured animal, contact the People's Dispensary for Sick Animals (www.pdsa.org.uk) or the Royal Society for the Prevention of Cruelty to Animals (www.rspca.org.uk), both of which run free local animal clinics and rescue centres.

Pets Grooming/Training

A Furry World	N1	0870 3500508	Grooming
Absolutely Animals Grooming Centre	SE12	8857 2888	Grooming, training
Cool Canines	SW20	8287 0055	Grooming
Curracloe	W5	0785 7038303	Grooming
Fluff Fluffs Your Canine Beautician	E17	8243 0000	Grooming
Pet Pavilion	SW3	7376 8800	Grooming
Primrose Hill Pets	NW1	7483 2023	Grooming
Scruffs 2 Crufts	SE9	8850 3990	Grooming
Southfields	W4	8995 2060	Grooming

If you are going on holiday and don't have anyone who can look after your pet while you are away, you'll need to use a kennel or cattery. For space requirements, most of these tend to be in outlying areas of London or beyond. It's worth visiting your local establishment in advance to satisfy yourself that your pet will be well cared for. Other pet services include dog and cat grooming parlours, dog walking companies, and dog training and behaviour consultants, all of which will be listed in your local phone directory.

Bringing Your Pet to the UK

After many years of operating a strict six-month quarantine policy aimed at keeping rabies out, the UK has now adopted the Pet Travel Scheme (PETS), whereby cats and dogs can enter the UK from the EU and a number of other designated countries, including Australia, New Zealand, the US, Canada and the United Arab Emirates, if certain procedures have been followed. The pet has to be microchipped, after which it must be vaccinated against rabies. The pet then needs to have a blood test and a vet's certificate confirming that it is free of rabies. All this has to be done at least six months in advance of any journey. Finally, 24 to 48 hours before you tuck Tiddles under your arm and head off, your pet must be treated against ticks and tapeworm. As for the journey itself, this must be undertaken on an authorised carrier (see www.defra.gov.uk). Slightly different rules apply to rabbits, ferrets and other rodents. If you skip any part of the process your pet is likely to be put in quarantine. Once your animal has fulfilled the criteria of the PETS scheme it will be able to move within the designated countries, again using authorised carriers.

Veterinary Clinics

Barrier Animal Care Clinic	SE7	8293 6580
Battersea Veterinary Clinic	SW11	7924 5350
Citivet	E1	7790 4599
Companion Care Veterinary Surgery	E6	8507 3904
David Cuffe & Associates	SW8	7498 6363
The Dragon Veterinary Clinic	N19	7272 3354
Elizabeth Street Veterinary Clinic	SW1	7730 9102
Goddard Veterinary Group	E15	8534 1948
Heath Veterinary Practice	NW5	7284 4344
The Hyde Park Veterinary Centre	W2	7723 0453
John Hankinson Veterinary Surgery	SE14	8692 3030
Mayow Veterinary Surgery	SE26	8659 4496
Village Veterinary Practice	NW3	7794 4948
Tom The Cat Place	W9	7289 1000
Zasman Veterinary Clinic	N8	8347 5200

134

Saving Energy

It is within everyone's power to minimise their personal carbon footprint. Consumer energy prices are high and subject to quite stiff hikes from time to time, so it is also financially worth your while to save as much energy as possible. Buying low-energy lightbulbs, not leaving appliances on standby and investing in good insulation and draught-proofing are all easy steps to start with. Contact the Energy Saving Trust at www.est.org.uk for more information.

Gas & Electricity

While some houses and flats only have electricity supplies, gas is widely used for central heating and cooking as it tends to be more energy-efficient. Once only the province of nationalised companies, the gas and electricity markets have been opened up to competition since the 1990s. There are now about 15 firms to choose from, including some that specifically use renewable energy sources or make other environmental pledges. You can choose to buy gas from one source, electricity from another, or take both from the same company. You can also switch companies, all of which are constantly competing for your custom by offering different price deals and tariffs. When you move into a property, unless you are the first occupier, you'll be taking over gas and electricity accounts from previous residents. You will need to get in touch with the property's existing energy suppliers to let them know your address and meter number. Take a meter reading on the day you move in to ensure your first bill is

Gas & Electricity Suppliers		
British Gas	www.house.co.uk	0845 9555510
Countrywide Energy	countrywidefarmers.co.uk	0800 4047961
EDF Energy	www.edfenergy.com	0800 0962270
Npower	www.npower.com	0845 7906050
Powergen	www.powergen.co.uk	0800 4046272
ScottishPower	www.scottishpower.com	0845 2700700

correct (meters are often located in built-in cupboards in flats or houses, or in communal areas in apartment blocks or converted properties). It is unlikely that you will find a gas or electricity supply unconnected unless a property has been vacant for a substantial length of time – but if you do, contact the energy company as soon as possible to arrange reconnection, before you move in if possible. Ways of paying your bill are flexible, with discounts often available if you opt to manage your account online or pay by direct debit.

Occasionally rental properties have been fitted with gas and electricity meters that are operated by a prepayment system. In this instance your landlord should give you a prepayment key or card, which can be topped up at designated shops or petrol stations. You should also ensure that your gas boiler has passed a safety test – if you're buying you should arrange this through British Gas or your supplier, and if you're renting your landlord should be able to show you an up-to-date safety certificate.

Water

When you move into rented accommodation, the water supply should already be connected – UK citizens have a legal right to a supply of safe drinking water. London tap water is fine to drink and is required to comply with standards set by both national government and Europe (although for reasons of taste, some people choose to use water filters or buy bottled water). The company responsible for the water supply in most of London is Thames Water, which also maintains the city's water mains and sewers (if you see a burst pipe in the street, they are the people to call). When you move into an unoccupied property, you'll need to contact Thames Water, which can be

Water Suppliers	
Southern Water	0845 2780845
Thames Water	0845 9200888
Three Valleys Water	01737 764444

done online at www.thameswater.co.uk, to register your details. In properties that have water meters, you'll be billed on the basis of the volume of water you use, otherwise it will be a rateable amount dictated by the size of your property. If your house or flat does not have a water meter you can request one to be fitted. Bills are sent out once or twice a year, with various options for payment. The water company is legally prohibited from cutting off your supply of water, and if bills go unpaid it must take action through the courts to recover the debt.

Sewerage

London's massive underground network of sewers was built in the late 19th century as the result of a grand engineering project conceived to address the problem of London's 'Great Stink'. Before the construction of the drains system, effluent and waste would simply flow from open sewers into the River Thames, eventually giving rise to a smell so vile that Parliament was appalled into action. Today the Victorian sewers are still sturdily doing their job, with the proviso that sudden downpours can occasionally overwhelm the system and lead to sewage discharging into the river. Upkeep of London's sewers comes under the remit of the water companies and the cost is covered in your water bill.

Rubbish Disposal & Recycling

Rubbish disposal is the responsibility of your local authority, which organises weekly collections from domestic properties. There will either be a wheelie bin outside your house or a communal dustbin area where you should put your rubbish. Given the volume of rubbish that London produces, it is becoming more and more important to recycle. All councils now offer some kind of doorstep recycling scheme; typically this is a green plastic box in which you collect recyclables such as glass, paper and cans and leave out for collection once a week. Depending on the council, you may also have a brown bin for kitchen waste. In addition, there are many communal recycling points, with separate banks for different materials, which you can find by

consulting your local council website or via www.direct.gov.uk. If you are getting rid of a large item, such as refrigerator or mattress, you can arrange for the council to collect it for free from outside your home and dispose of it.

Telephone

Public Phoneboxes
You can find public BT phoneboxes on every street corner in London, where you can pay for calls by cash or credit card. Other operators can also install phone points and phone boxes, which are operated in a similar way. Emergency calls to 999 are always free.

The dominant player in the UK's telephony network is BT, which has universal coverage. The vast majority of properties come with a BT landline already installed (look for a wall socket with a BT logo). To get connected all you need to do is get a phone and call BT to sign up for one of its tariffs. BT also sells and rents out phone equipment and offers many extras such as additional lines, call waiting, and answering services. Charges consist of a flat rate of line rental, plus whichever call package and extras you choose (see www.bt.com for more information). If there is no existing line in your property, BT will install one for a fee. BT also offers dial-up and broadband internet packages. The main competitor to BT in London is the cable company Virgin Media (formerly NTL Telewest), which offers a triple package of landline telephone,

Telephone Companies

BT (British Telecom)	0800 800150	www.bt.com
SwiftCall	7507 0005	www.swiftcall.co.uk
TalkTalk	0870 4420698	www.talktalk.co.uk
Virgin Media	0845 8407777	www.virginmedia.co.uk

digital TV and broadband internet. There are various competitor services you can sign up to, such as Talk Talk (www.talktalk.co.uk), which can significantly cut the cost of calls while you pay only line rental charges to BT.

Mobile Phones

Mobile phones are available on a pay-as-you-go or contract basis from around six commercial operators. With pay-as-you-go, you buy a mobile from a phone shop or store such as Woolworths, and then buy credit to make calls by topping up a card at newsagents and high-street outlets. With a contract, many phones are free if you sign up (usually the minimum term is at least one year). There are a huge variety of contracts and special offers on the market at any given time, which can be signed up to at authorised dealers on the high street or direct from the service operators in their shops, by phone or via the internet. To get a contract you will need to provide identity and bank account details and the company may well run a credit check, but for pay-as-you-go phones there are no restrictions. A typical contract works out as a monthly charge, which includes a set number of minutes worth of calls or number of texts or combinations of both, with additional charges for usage beyond this. You can also pay an additional amount each month to

Mobile Service Providers

O2	0870 6003009	www.o2.co.uk
Orange	0800 0792000	www.orange.co.uk
T-Mobile	0845 4125000	www.t-mobile.co.uk
Virgin	0845 6000070	www.virgin.net
Vodaphone	0870 0700191	www.vodaphone.co.uk

have your phone insured. This is something it may be wise to consider especially as mobile phone theft very common in London, and if you sign up to a contract you will be obliged to continue to pay the minimum monthly charge until the tied-in period expires. To take your number with you when you change providers, you need to get something called a 'PAC' code which your outgoing provider can give you to pass on to the new company.

Cheap Overseas Calls

The cost of making international calls has fallen in recent years, but by using an international calling card you can significantly cut the costs. Cards can be purchased from newsagents and allow you to make cheap international calls from a BT line by dialling an initial code which connects you to the cheap call provider. International call centres and shops with phone booths inside are a common sight among local parades of stores. While they are not the most salubrious of places, they offer calls to different global destinations at flat rates per minute. In addition you can make international calls via broadband internet by downloading certain software. The most popular free software, Skype, allows you to make calls to other Skype users all over the world for no charge, with calls to non-users also available at greatly reduced costs.

Internet Service Providers

AOL	0870 3202020	www.aol.co.uk
BT (British Telecom)	0800 800150	www.bt.com
Demon	0800 0273737	www.demon.net
Easynet	0800 0534343	www.uk.easynet.net
HomeChoice	0800 0724454	www.homechoice.co.uk
Mistral	0870 4936300	www.frontier.net.uk
Orange Broadband	0870 9090666	www.orange.co.uk
Pipex	0845 0772455	www.pipex.net
TalkTalk	0870 4420698	www.talktalk.co.uk
Tiscali	0870 7449966	www.tiscali.co.uk
Virgin Media	0845 8407777	www.virginmedia.co.uk

Internet

London has a huge number of internet service providers to choose from, offering both dial-up and broadband services. Dial-up packages require a modem and software which your chosen ISP will supply. As well as dedicated ISPs more and more mobile phone operators and cable and satellite companies offer a broadband service, and offer discounts if you sign up to more than one of their product packages. Broadband services offer fast downloads, unlimited time online and sometimes free national and international calls as part of the deal. Prices start from $10.99 per month for unlimited access.

Internet cafes are everywhere. They charge for access by the hour, usually at very cheap rates such as £1 an hour. Many public libraries also offer free internet access, although you may need to book a time slot.

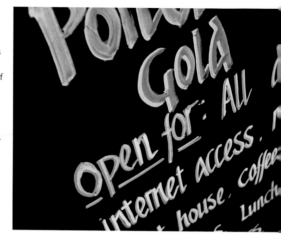

Bill Payment

Phone and internet charges are usually monthly, and you can pay using various methods. The most common is direct debit – you fill out a direct debit instruction online or on paper and the company deducts the bill amount at an agreed time each month. Otherwise pay by debit or credit card over the phone or internet, or by cheque or card through the post. Some bills can also be paid at the Post Office, in which case they can be paid by cash. All major service providers now facilitate and indeed encourage (as it cuts down their postal and stationery costs) you to manage your account online or by phone.

Sometimes a straightforward registration process is required or sometimes you are automatically assigned a log-in and password. Often you will get a slight discount if you choose to manage your account online, something which also allows you to keep close tabs on calls, usage and transactions. In the case of mobile phones, there will be a number you can call to check how many of that month's free minutes you have left.

Counter Productive?
The closure of many post offices, especially in rural areas, has caused anger and much controversy in the UK. Plans to close a further 2,500 have been opposed by the mayor who claims that local communities in London, especially older and disabled people, will be greatly disadvantaged.

Post & Courier Services

The UK postal system can generally be relied upon. Letters and packages up to a certain size can be sent either first class or second class. A letter sent by first class will probably arrive the next day or else the day after. Second class letters usually take two or three days, but could take up to a week or so. Smaller letters can be posted at post boxes, which you'll find on streets throughout the capital.

Postal services in the UK are available on the high street from the Post Office. Post offices sell stamps and will weigh your item to allow you to pay the correct postage. The price of postage is decided by the weight, size of your letter or package, and whether its destination is national or international. Various premium delivery options, such as next-day delivery or recorded delivery, can be bought for an additional fee. The Post Office also offers a range of other services including bill payment and currency exchange and is the place to pick up passport and driving licence applications. First class and second class stamps for letters and postcards are available from many newsagents and supermarkets. UK postal delivery is handled by the Royal Mail, a publicly owned company, which makes door-to-door deliveries to domestic addresses once a day. Larger parcels are delivered by Parcelforce, with the Post Office again the place to access the service.

Couriers

Careering courier vans, motorbike despatch riders and cycle couriers are familiar sights on the streets of London. Courier companies will pick up an item from one address and promise to get it another within a couple of hours, the same day or next day depending on the destination and the service you choose. Most couriers operate an international service. For courier companies local to you, consult the phone book or online directories. International courier companies such as UPS and DHL all have London bases.

Radio

London has a wide range of radio stations, some of them national and some local, run by public service broadcaster, the British Broadcasting Corporation (BBC) and a number of licensed commercial operators. The BBC's output covers pop music stations Radio 1 and Radio 2, classical music station Radio 3, the speech-based Radio 4, BBC World Service, and sports-orientated speech and live commentary station Radio 5 Live. There is also a BBC local radio station, BBC London, which is particularly useful for traffic and public transport updates in the capital. Commercial stations cover the entire spectrum of musical genres across rock, pop, indie, urban, jazz and classical. All these stations are available on traditional FM/AM radio, received through analogue signal, but are also on digital radio (DAB). Additional stations are available only on digital radio, which can be accessed via digital TV set-top boxes (see Television, below), DAB digital radio sets or stereo systems with a DAB tuner. If you are buying a new radio it makes sense to buy a DAB one as there are plans to turn off the analogue radio signal by 2012. Many illegal pirate radio stations can be picked up on analogue radio sets, and can interfere with licensed stations; another reason to go digital.

TV Licence

If you watch TV in the UK you must pay an annual television licence fee – it is this cash which funds public service broadcaster the BBC. Even if your TV is rented you must still get a licence, but one licence covers all the sets at any private address, and if you move mid-way through a licence period you can transfer it to your new address. The cost of the TV licence is set by the government and in 2007 it was £131.50 for 12 months (it is free to those over 75 and half price to those who are registered blind). You can pay the whole lot or sign up to pay in monthly instalments by direct debit at www.tvlicensing.co.uk.

Television

The UK currently has five national terrestrial TV stations freely accessible by all televisions: BBC1 and BBC2 (public service channels operated by the BBC, which is funded by the licence fee, see left); ITV1 and Five, commercial broadcasters with some public service obligations; and Channel 4, a public service broadcaster which is self-financing through advertising and other commercial activity. All of these channels offer a mix of programmes which encompass news, documentary, reality, drama, comedy, US imports and entertainment. Between 2008 and 2012 the analogue TV signal in the UK is being switched off by region and the country is moving over to entirely digital TV transmission, something which will greatly increase the number of channels available to everyone. Digital TV can currently be accessed via existing aerial sockets by buying a set-top box, known as a 'Freeview' box, which plugs into your television set and allows you to access around 30 free-to-air channels of all kinds (including the original five). Televisions and personal video recorders (PVRs) which have in-built digital capacity are also now on the market. In addition, you can get free-to-air digital TV by cable or satellite (see below) services or by broadband.

Satellite TV & Radio

You can get a wide range of channels free-to-air with Freeview. If you have a digital TV these channels will be built-in. If you have an analogue set, you will need to buy a small set-top box, which costs from £20, to receive them. Certain channels such as those showing some football, cricket and other international sporting events, adult channels, movie channels and TV on-demand, are only available by subscription. The main providers of paid-for channels in London are satellite company Sky (www.sky.com) and Virgin Media (ww.virginmedia.com). When you sign up you are supplied with all necessary equipment and can choose from a range of options which include different channels, starting from around £5 for the most basic package of channels and pay-per-view facilities up to £45 a month for those offering the lot.

Satellite/Cable Providers

HomeChoice	0800 0724454	www.homechoice.co.uk
Sky TV	0870 5800874	www.sky.com
Virgin Media	0845 8407777	www.virginmedia.co.uk

139

General Medical Care

Britain's public-funded National Health Service (NHS) was established in 1948 on the principle of free healthcare for all. Most citizens use the NHS as their primary health resource, with private practitioners the choice of only a small percentage (who usually have private health insurance). If you've been in the country legally for at least six months, you will usually be entitled to free treatment. Also, if you have come to the country to take up a job, to study or are on a spousal visa, you should have no trouble using the NHS. Emergency treatment is free for all no matter how or why they have entered the country, and so are the following services: family planning; compulsory psychiatric treatment; HIV testing; treatment for some communicable diseases including tuberculosis, cholera, food poisoning, malaria and meningitis.

NHS Numbers

People born in the UK are automatically assigned an NHS number, which is used as a way of keeping track of records when you switch doctors or move around the country. You do not need an NHS number to receive treatment, but as a new resident you will be given one when you register with a GP.

NHS Walk-In Centres

These are centres which you can go to for advice and treatment of minor problems from qualified staff without making an appointment. Centres tend to be open long hours, and you can use them even if you are not registered with a doctor. Contact NHS Direct or visit www.nhs.uk to find your nearest one.

Registering with a Doctor

General practitioners (GPs) are NHS doctors who work in surgeries to provide a service in local communities. Doctors' surgeries are overseen by a local Primary Care Trust (PCT), which you can find details of on www.direct.gov.uk. The majority of services are free to those who qualify for treatment under the NHS, including consultation, diagnosis, advice and physical examinations, but fees are sometimes charged for doctors' notes or for some vaccinations for going abroad. You will also need to pay a standard fee of £6.65 for any prescribed medication, although there are exemptions to the charge, including pensioners, students and people on benefits. To find a local doctor, consult a directory or approach your PCT which will have a list of those in your area - then simply phone a surgery and ask to register. Some may refuse you on the basis that their patient list is full or you live too far away, but there are many surgeries in any given area so you should not have too much trouble finding one willing to register you. It is possible to change the surgery you are registered with and move to another one if for any reason you are not happy.

Emergency Services

In the case of a medical emergency, call 999. This is the number to dial to request an ambulance, fire engine or the police. You will be asked which service you require and be put through to the relevant operator, who will take details of where the ambulance is needed and what the emergency situation is. You should expect an ambulance to arrive in 10 minutes or less. There is no charge for calling an ambulance.

40

Pharmacies

Even the smallest parade of shops tends to have a pharmacy (or dispensing chemist) where you can pick up the medicines prescribed to you by a doctor. Many medicines and drugs are also available without a prescription, and pharmacists can be useful sources of advice or information about common medical complaints. Pharmacies are often located near to or affiliated to a doctors' surgery; opening hours vary but tend be later than some shops. Zafash Pharmacy (7373 2798) on Old Brompton Road near Earl's Court is open 24 hours.

Prescription Charges

Although a visit to your GP is free, if the doc prescribes medicine you will be asked to pay a charge of £6.85 per item at the pharmacy. Children, pregnant women, people on state benefits and those with certain conditions are exempt from the charges.

Screening Programmes

The NHS runs three targeted screening programmes aimed at cutting the rates of cervical cancer, breast cancer and bowel cancer. All women between 25 and 64 are entitled to free cervical cancer screening, consisting of a simple smear test which can be carried out by your GP or at a sexual health clinic. If you are registered with a GP, you should receive an invitation for a smear test once you reach the age of 25, and then at three-yearly intervals until the age of 50 when the frequency of invitations drops to every five years. If you are not registered with a GP and want to have a free test, get in touch with your nearest family planning or sexual health clinic, which will carry one out. Women between 50 and 70 are invited for mammograms to screen for breast cancer every three years at a local screening unit, again through being registered with a GP. Women over 70 can make an appointment for a mammogram at any time, and those under 50 can talk to their GP or phone NHS Direct on 0845 4647 if they have any concerns. Bowel cancer screening is offered every two years to men and women between the ages of 60 and 69. Although a test for prostate cancer is available, there is no programme for men to be routinely screened. Again, if you have any worries or believe you need to be tested, talk to your GP or staff at a sexual health clinic. For more information on any kind of cancer worry and for advice on self-examination, go to www.cancerbackup.org.uk or phone free on 0808 800 1234.

NHS Direct

For 24 hour free confidential medical information from experienced nurses, call NHS Direct on 0845 46 47 or go to www.nhsdirect.nhs.uk. Calls are charged at a local rate. It can be a useful service if your GP is closed or you have to wait for an appointment.

Health Insurance

Health insurance is sometimes offered by employers as a perk, but this is by no means common, especially in smaller firms. As a result, many individuals also take out private policies (often to guard against long NHS waiting lists). Should you wish to take out private health insurance in the UK, there are a wide range of plans from dedicated private healthcare companies such as BUPA and Nuffield, which have their own clinics, hospitals and specialists, to consider.

Health Insurance Companies

Aspen Healthcare Ltd	72560 6111	www.aspen-healthcare.co.uk
AXA PPP healthcare	0870 6080850	www.axa.co.uk
BMI Healthcare	7009 4500	www.bmihealthcare.co.uk
BUPA	0800 600500	www.bupa.co.uk
Capio Healthcare UK Ltd	7847 2850	www.capio.co.uk
HCA International Ltd	7616 4848	www.hcainternational.com
PHS Private Health Service	0800 0420555	www.privatehealthservice.co.uk
Standard Life Healthcare	0800 333350	www.standardlifehealthcare.co.uk

Donor Cards

Donor cards, which give your consent for your organs to be used after your death to save the lives of others, can be picked up from hospitals, doctors and libraries. While a donor card is of great help in expressing your wishes, it can get lost so for a permanent record sign up to the NHS Organ Donor Register (www.uktransplant.org.uk). It is also important to let your relatives know of your wishes.

Giving Blood

An estimated 2.1 million blood donations are needed every year to keep pace with demand, which makes giving blood one of the simplest yet most valuable things you can do to help save lives. As the regular government advertising campaigns put it: 'Do something amazing today'. The National Blood Service is tasked with recruiting donors and maintaining blood stocks. Blood donor sessions are held regularly in venues such as hospitals, schools, colleges and community centres. You do not need an appointment; just turn up to register. You will be asked a few questions regarding your general health and possible exposure to infectious diseases before the donation is taken. Donating a pint of blood will take little more than 10 minutes. Go to www.blood.co.uk or phone 0845 7711 711 to find a session near you.

Giving Up Smoking

Coughing Up
Smokers in the UK should be under no illusions about how their habit is perceived by the government. Not only is lighting up banned from all public places (from July 2007), but each packet of cigarettes comes printed with 'smoking kills', and other such friendly warnings. If that wasn't enough, a packet of 20 is likely to cost you at least £5.

Smoking is the biggest single cause of illness and death in the UK, with more than 120,000 people dying from smoking-related diseases every year. It is even considered so hazardous to the health of others that it is banned in public places (as of July 2007). If you are having trouble quitting smoking, nicotine replacement therapy (NRT) can more than double your chances of success. NRT is available in many forms, including nicotine patches, gum, lozenges and nasal spray. These are available from high-street chemists and supermarkets without prescription, although your GP can also prescribe them. Your GP can prescribe other drugs and refer you for counselling if you continue to have difficulty. Many areas are also covered by an NHS Stop Smoking Service, which can put you in touch with a trained advisor and group support. Go to www.gosmokefree.co.uk, or ring the NHS Smoking Helpline on 0800 1690 169.

Government Hospitals

If your doctor refers you for hospital treatment, you have the right to choose which one you are admitted to. You can discuss the options with your GP, who should offer you the option of at least four NHS hospitals. There are more than 35 hospitals in London, and things to consider are location, reputation and facilities (you can find more information at www.nhs.uk). Some forms of treatment require specialist units that may not be available at all hospitals – again, your doctor can advise you on this.

Emergencies

If you become seriously ill or require urgent treatment, many – but not all – NHS hospitals have Accident and Emergency departments. This is the part of the hospital where an ambulance on an emergency call-out will take patients, but you can also admit yourself. A&E works on a priority basis – more serious circumstances are attended to ahead of lesser complaints so you could be in for a long wait, particularly on Friday and Saturday nights when the nation's penchant for alcohol over-indulgence takes its toll on hospitals. If your predicament is less severe – say a sprain or cut – a better option is to go to your nearest Minor Injuries Unit. As with A&E you don't need to make an appointment, but because they don't treat emergencies, waiting times are much shorter. If you're unsure of which department is most appropriate, call NHS Direct (0845 4647). You'll also be advised on the location of your nearest unit.

In England and Wales abortion is legal up until the 24th week of pregnancy if two doctors agree to it. Further to this, an abortion can be performed at any time if two doctors agree that it is necessary to save the life of the mother, prevent long-term damage to her physical or mental health, or if there is a high risk the baby will be born with a serious disability. To get a free NHS abortion you need to be referred by a GP or a doctor, a family planning clinic (www.fpa.org.uk) or a Brook Centre (Brook Advisory Centres is a voluntary network offering free and confidential sexual health advice and services to the under 25s, www.brook.org.uk). Women can also refer themselves to a private clinic; it costs from around £350 up to £750 for a late abortion. Contact the British Pregnancy Advisory Service on 0845 7304030 or go to www.bpas.org.uk for details of private clinics and advice on other options in the event of unplanned pregnancy.

Private Healthcare

It is becoming more common for employers to offer private health insurance or health check plans as part of a package of benefits, while many individuals opt to pay for their own cover as they consider private facilities to provide more personalised, comfortable and swift levels of service than the heavily burdened NHS. Private rooms and treatment are available at many NHS hospitals as well as at entirely private hospitals and clinics, which are often run by large healthcare companies such as BUPA, BMI and Nuffield (see below). There are a large number of private establishments in London running the full gamut of medical services, including acute care, health assessments, well-woman and well-man health screening, travel injections and cosmetic surgery. Your healthcare provider or insurer will direct you to suitable hospitals, or see www.privatehealth.co.uk. The Medicentre chain, with clinics based at several major London stations, offers walk-in consultations with a doctor or nurse.

Private Healthcare Providers

Aspen Healthcare	7256 6111	www.aspen-healthcare.co.uk
AXA PPP Healthcare	0800 333311	www.axappphealthcare.co.uk
BMI Healthcare	7009 4500	www.bmihealthcare.co.uk
BUPA	0800 600500	www.bupa.co.uk
HAS	0800 0721000	www.hsa.co.uk
Medicentre	0870 6000870	www.medicentre.co.uk
Nuffield Hospitals	0800 688699	www.nuffieldhospitals.org.uk

Maternity
Other options **Babywear** p.316

Most mothers give birth to their baby in the maternity wing of an NHS hospital, where they have access to medical support and pain-relieving drugs if required. There are also some dedicated NHS birth centres, which may offer a more personal level of care than a large hospital wing. It is also entirely possible to give birth at home attended by a midwife. Maternity care is free on the NHS and once you have been confirmed as pregnant you can nominate a hospital maternity unit where you wish to give birth (you can change your mind at a later stage). Ante-natal care is then arranged around this.

If you'd prefer to give birth in a private hospital, contact the individual institution to find out about prices and levels of service. There are only two dedicated private maternity facilities in the city: they are the Portland Hospital for Women and Children on Great Portland Street, close to Oxford Circus (www.theportlandhospital.com) and The Hospital of St John and Elizabeth (www.hje.org.uk) near St John's Wood underground station.

When thinking about a hospital or centre to choose, consider not only the level and sort of care you want, but also the distance you are prepared to travel for ante-natal appointments and for the birth itself. An obstetrician will tend only to be involved if there are complications in the pregnancy.

If you are opting for a home birth, ante-natal care can be given by a community midwife or GP (but not all GPs have facilities for this). You can also enlist the help of an independent midwife, for whose services you would pay. In hospital, you are generally allowed up to two people to be present with you during labour and birth; they can be your spouse or anyone else you care to nominate. In terms of a hospital birth itself, you can elect to have a baby by vaginal birth or by caesarean, or a caesarean may be performed in an emergency.

Children with Disabilities
Children with disabilities should be given any support and treatment they need through the NHS, and there are a vast number of support groups and charities out there to help. It is illegal for schools to treat children with disabilities unfavourably. For more information contact the Council for Disabled Children (www.ncb.org.uk).

Ante-Natal Care

The level of NHS ante-natal care you receive depends to a great extent on the particular maternity unit you nominate. At the bare minimum you will be offered ante-natal classes and various check-ups and scans during the course of the pregnancy to check the physical health of the baby, its size and position in the womb, and to determine whether you are expecting more than one baby. You may also be offered screening tests for conditions such as spina bifida and Down's syndrome if, for instance, you are over a certain age. The level of choice you have in other matters, such as induction and pain relief, is quite high but does depend on the hospital so it's always best to make enquiries or raise any particular concerns. If possible ask other mothers about their experiences as they are usually the best source of knowledge about the pros and cons of different hospitals in your area.

Post-Natal Care

If there are no complications around a hospital birth, you may be able to return home within a couple of days. Post-natal care is provided by the midwife in hospital and then at home for up to 28 days after the birth (although they can extend this if necessary). The midwife will help you with breastfeeding, check stitches and offer advice on common post-pregnancy problems, and will visit on a regular basis during the first 10 days after birth. If there are no complications the midwife will usually sign your care over to a health visitor (usually attached to a GP's surgery) who will continue the post-natal care on a less intensive basis. If your baby is born premature or there are any complications for either of you, you will be cared for in hospital for as long as is necessary.

Maternity Rights

Pregnant women are protected by the law at work and have a guaranteed minimum list of rights, such as the right to take time off for ante-natal care. Expectant mothers are also protected against being dismissed or treated unfairly on the basis of their pregnancy and have the right to return to work after they have had the baby. All pregnant women employed in the UK also have the right to take 26 weeks of maternity leave, which can begin any time in or after the 11th week before the baby is due. You need to inform your employer of your pregnancy, due date and the date you wish your maternity leave to start before the end of the 15th week before the due date. If you have worked for the same employer for 26 weeks at the beginning of the 15th week before the due date, you are entitled to an additional 26 weeks. You are also entitled to statutory maternity pay for 26 weeks at a percentage of your average gross weekly earnings if you have worked for the same employer continuously for 26 weeks at the beginning of the 15th week before the due date. Many employers offer enhanced maternity benefits to these legal minimums. Fathers also have the right to one or two weeks' paternity leave, subject to the length of time they have been with their employer.

Contraception & Sexual Health

Condoms are available on the shelves of pharmacies, supermarkets, many general grocery stores and from vending machines in public toilets. Emergency contraception ('the morning-after pill') is available over-the-counter at pharmacies. If you wish to be prescribed the birth control pill or other forms of contraception you should approach your GP or a family planning clinic (www.fpa.org.uk, 0845 1228690). If you think you may have a sexually transmitted disease, are not registered with a doctor or feel uncomfortable talking to your doctor, you may prefer to consult a family planning clinic or sexual health clinic. Sexual health clinics (also known as GUM or STD clinics) are usually attached to NHS hospitals and have drop-in sessions. They offer an expert and confidential service, including diagnosis, HIV testing and treatment.

Paediatrics

Your baby's jabs and check-ups are organised and held by your GP or local child health clinic, and you should expect to be sent notice of appointments soon after your child is born. The immunisation schedule is comprehensive and includes:

Polio – injections are needed at two, three and four months.

Diptheria, tetanus, whooping cough and Hib – one injection required at two, three and four months.

Meningitis C – injection at two, three and four months.

Measles, mumps and rubella (MMR) – the first injection is given shortly after the child's first birthday. Due to the controversy surrounding this combined vaccine, which some claim can lead to autism, some parents opt for their children not to have it. Booster jabs are given between the ages of three and five, and once your child is at school they will be immunised there. Flu jabs and the pneumococcal vaccine may be recommended to children with certain medical conditions.

Dentists/Orthodontists

The NHS provides basic dental treatment at a reduced cost, or free to children, those who are on certain benefits and pregnant women. Dentists are either private or take a mixture of NHS and private patients. Because the range of treatments in private practice is greater, including cosmetic dentistry, Botox, whitening and some specialist treatment, those who can afford it tend to opt for private status. To find a dentist in your area willing to take NHS patients, phone NHS Direct on 0845 46 47 or go to www.nhsdirect.nhs.uk. For private treatment simply phone a dentist of your choice and arrange an appointment.

Opticians & Opthamologists

London has chains of opticians (such as Specsavers and Dolland & Aitchison) as well as many independent opticians, with larger branches of high-street chemist Boots also offering an optician service. Opticians carry out eye tests (usually costing £25), draw up prescriptions and sell prescription glasses, sunglasses and contact lenses. You can also buy contact lenses here, or from many online suppliers, while solutions are widely available from pharmacies

Opticians & Opthamologists		
Boots Opticians	0845 1204343	www.bootsopticians.co.uk
David Clulow	0208 5156700	www.davidclulow.co.uk
Dolland & Aitchison	0121 7066133	www.danda.co.uk
Optical Express	08702 202020	www.opticalexpress.co.uk
Specsavers	–	www.specsavers.co.uk
Vision Express	0844 4771177	www.visionexpress.co.uk

and supermarkets. If your job involves a lot of screen work, your employer should offer free eye tests and contribute towards the cost of glasses if you need them for VDU use.

Cosmetic Treatment & Surgery

Cosmetic surgery is swiftly gaining popularity and the gory gamut of procedures on offer is vast. Liposuction, breast enlargement or reduction, tummy tuck, nose-reshaping, facelifts and more, are available at a huge number of private London clinics, including private hospital chains such as BUPA.

All clinics and hospitals are regulated and inspected by the Healthcare Commission; if you are in any doubt about the authenticity or standards of an institution you should ask to see their latest report or go to www.healthcare.org.uk. Some non-surgical cosmetic procedures, such as microdermabrasion, are also available from some beauty salons and spas, which are the best bet for more everyday treatments such as waxing, facials and manicures. Dentists can also give botulinum toxin (Botox) injections.

Alternative Therapies

Alternative therapies are a booming business in London with therapists offering treatments including acupuncture, shiatsu, aromatherapy, kinesiology, lymphatic drainage, Indian head massage, homeopathy, osteopathy, reflexology and Reiki. There is a big crossover between beauty treatments and what might be considered alternative therapies so if you are looking for help to address a specific medical problem, it is worth doing your research and finding a qualified practitioner. Alternative therapies tend to be expensive; you can expect to pay at least £50 for an hour's massage and they are rarely available on the NHS.

Acupuncture/Acupressure

Acupuncture is a branch of traditional Chinese medicine and a popular alternative treatment offered by specialist acupuncturists, doctors and physiotherapists. You will also find trained practitioners at alternative health clinics and Chinese medicine centres.

Acupuncture, which usually involves the insertion of needles into specified points in the body, is used to address many common ailments. There are plans to regulate who can practise the therapy in the UK, but be aware that at the moment anyone can set themselves up an acupuncturist; the nature of the treatment and possible risks of non-sterile equipment make it particularly important to check qualifications. In addition, some high-street Chinese medicine centres have dubious reputations and are sometimes linked with products from endangered species. The British Acupuncture Council (www.acupuncture.org.uk) maintains a register of acupuncturists who have completed three years of training, while the British Medical Acupuncturist Society (www.medical-acupuncture.co.uk) is a professional body for existing healthcare professionals who have usually taken shorter courses. Members of both organisations have been assessed and hold suitable insurance. For a private session of around 30 minutes you should expect to pay at least £35, with courses of treatments usually recommended.

Official Bodies

The British Complementary Medicine Association
www.bcma.co.uk

Institute for Complementary Medicine
www.i-c-m.org.uk

The Research Council for Complementary Medicine
www.rccm.org.uk

Massage Therapy & Reflexology

Massage therapy works by movement on the skin to promote healing, relaxation and general wellbeing. All kinds of massage, including reflexology, Swedish, sports, shiatsu and Indian head massage, are undertaken by practitioners in London and a range of treatments is on offer at the capital's health centres, spas, sports clinics and beauty salons. In addition many masseurs work on a freelance basis and are equipped to come to your house – look for adverts in the press or notices in leisure centres and health food shops. Check the website of Massage Therapy UK (www.massagetherapy.co.uk) for a database of practitioners. There are a great number of qualifications but one of the most widely accepted is the ITEC diploma. The cost of a full-body massage lasting an hour is upwards of £40, with cheaper rates sometimes offered by those still in training.

Aromatherapy

Aromatherapy is the therapeutic use of essential oils and is often used in conjunction with massage. Other techniques can involve the inhalation of oils by way of vapourisers, compresses, diffusers or baths, and the treatment is often chosen to aid relaxation or relieve anxiety. Essential oils can be bought in health food shops and pharmacies, while aromatherapy massage is a common treatment at complementary

Reflexology/Massage Therapy

Alternative Medicine London North Stoke Newington	Various locations	7690 8044
The Greenwich Natural Health Centre	SE10	8691 5408
The Healthy Living centre (HLC)	N1	7704 6900

Health

health centres and beauty clinics. The self-regulatory body for aromatherapists is the Aromatherapy Council (www.aromatherapycouncil.co.uk) and should be contacted on 0870774 3477 for advice on recommended practitioners. Prices are comparable with other kinds of massage.

Homeopathy

Healthy Advice
Despite the popularity of celebrity nutritionists on TV in the UK, debate continues over the qualifications – or lack of – of certain practitioners. A respected source of information is the British Nutrition Foundation. For more details, see www.nutrition.org.uk.

As with many alternative therapies you will find that there are a bewildering number of homeopaths advertising their services in London, with qualifications – and quality of service – varying widely. The Society of Homeopaths is a professional grouping of homeopaths who have attained certain educational standards, are insured and have signed up to a code of ethics and practice. Check its online search facility at www.homeopathy-soh.org to find practitioners in your neighbourhood. It is possible, if not common, to get homeopathic treatment on the NHS; ask your GP if you can be referred to the Royal London Homoeopathic Hospital on Great Ormond Street, which is the main NHS resource for complementary medicine in the capital. A smallish range of homeopathic remedies is on offer in most pharmacies, but for a more comprehensive selection try one of Neal's Yard Remedies (www.nealsyardremedies.com) stores across London or Nelsons Homeopathic Pharmacy (www.nelsonshp.com), near Bond Street tube.

Rehabilitation & Physiotherapy

Whether you've picked up a slight strain from playing sport or are recovering from a more serious injury or accident, the NHS provides a range of physiotherapy treatment. As with most specialist services, you will have

Rehabilitation & Physiotherapy		
Camden Physiotherapy Clinic	NW1	7424 8668
Josephine Lawson Physiotherapy Clinic	EC3	7929 0983
Kensington Physiotherapy	W1	7603 0040
Physio4Life	SW15	8704 5998
Physiotherapy London	E14	7093 3499
Portland Physio	WC1	7436 8960
Pure Sports Medicine	Various locations	0870 2000878
Sprint Physiotherapy	W8	7938 1350
Vanbrugh Physiotherapy	SE10	8293 5454

to be referred by your GP in the first instance. Alternatively, there are a number of private and sports injuries clinics operating in the capital. Check whether they are registered with Health Professions Council (www.hpc-uk.org) before going any further.

Nutritionists & Slimming

The press in the UK is routinely filled with stories about the nation's problem with obesity. And the journalists may have a point – the NHS concludes that 'people in England generally eat too much food, and too much of their diet contains an excess of fat, salt and sugar'. If you're looking to shed a few pounds or seeking sensible dietary advice, speak to your GP in the first instance.

Nutritionists & Slimming			
Body 4 Life	W2	7402 8999	www.body4lifehealthcare.co.uk
BodyCHEK	EC1	7256 9377	www.bodychek.co.uk
The Joseph Clinic	E18	8989 7569	www.nimbiz.com/TheJosephClinic
Lorraine Wilder	NW11	8455 0721	www.tri-nutrition.co.uk
Nutritional Therapy	SW12	8767 3893	na
Richmond Diet Clinic	Various locations	0800 591615	www.richmonddietclinic.co.uk
Weightwatchers	Various locations	0845 7123000	www.weightwatchers.co.uk
Wimpole Therapeutics	W1	7491 7767	www.wimpoletherapeutics.com

Back Treatment

According to the NHS, lower back pain – which is the most common back complaint – affects 7 in 10 people at one stage in their lives. As most problems heal themselves, a GP will only refer you for tests if your pain lasts longer than

Back Treatment		
The Back Clinic	W1	7486 7711
Gonstead Clinics UK	W1	7637 2920
The Lister Hospital	SW1	7730 7733
The London Back Clinic	SE1	7089 0627
London Physio Centre	W1	0800 0850682
Pure Sports Medicine	Various locations	0870 2000878
The Wellington Hospital	NW8	7586 5959

six weeks or if he or she suspects other reasons for the pain. The charity BackCare (www.backcare.org.uk) has some useful advice on preventing back pain. There is also a variety of chiropractic clinics operating in the capital. The British Chiropractic Association (BCA), founded in 1925, represents over half of UK chiropractors. All BCA-affiliated members will have undergone a minimum of four years' training and will also be recognised by the General Chiropractic Council. See www.chiropractic-uk.co.uk for more information.

Counselling & Therapy

Counselling and therapy is available through the NHS for free, with the caveat being that these services are in tremendous demand so you may face a wait of weeks or possibly months for a referral. If you suffer from depression, discuss the matter with a GP, who can prescribe anti-depressants either on their own or in conjunction with counselling. If you are not registered with a doctor, the Depression Alliance (www.depressionalliance.org) offers a wide range of free self-help information and can put you in touch with local support groups. For more serious problems you may be referred to the psychiatric unit of an NHS hospital or to a dedicated unit that specialises in a particular issue. Outside of the NHS there are hundreds of private counsellors and therapists to choose from, covering a variety of therapeutic disciplines.

Addiction Counselling		
Alcoholics Anonymous	www.alcoholics-anonymous.org.uk	0845 7697555
Narcotics Anonymous	www.ukna.org	7730 0009
Gamblers Anonymous	www.gamblersanonymous.org.uk	7384 3040
Samaritans	www.samaritans.org.uk	0845 7909090

Addiction Counselling & Rehabilition

Whatever addiction you may have a concern about, you will find dedicated organisations, phonelines and websites able to offer help and advice. There are also any number of support groups, both informal and formal. Check the website www.helplines.org.uk for a searchable database of helplines in the UK.

Support Groups

The number of people in London can give rise to that 'alone in a crowd' feeling, and if you have just arrived in the country, meeting new people and making friends can seem a daunting prospect. But the flip side of this is that London has an enormous network of social groups, sports clubs and support groups covering just about everything you can think of. From gay choirs to Australian Rules football teams, it's all here and ready to be enjoyed.

London also has plenty of social groups, activities and social centres catering to expat communities and different nationalities, see Social Groups (p.276). If you are depressed or know someone who is, contact the Campaign Against Living Miserably (0800 585858), or the Samaritans (08457 909090).

Relate

The charity Relate offers advice, relationship counselling, sex therapy, mediation, consultations and support, face-to-face, by phone and online for couples and families. There is a charge for face-to-face courses and counselling sessions, but you can expect it to be far less than most private counsellors. See www.relate.org.uk or call 0845 1304016.

48

Education

In common with the principle of free healthcare, the principle of free education is a central pillar of British society. Following their fifth birthday all children in the UK are required to receive full-time education up to the age of 16, which usually means they will attend school (although it is possible to teach your child at home if you can satisfy the authorities that you are capable). Each area in London is covered by a local education authority (LEA) and it is the responsibility of the LEA to find a free school place for your child – this includes all children who have come from abroad to live here either on a temporary or permanent basis. It must also provide a further full-time education place to anyone between the ages of 16 and 19 who wants to continue studying.

The Reading Room at the British Museum

State primary and secondary schools follow the National Curriculum, which determines which subjects must be taught and in what way, with pupils working towards GCSE qualifications. From here they can decide to study for A-Levels for the next two years, which, depending on their grades, will gain them entry to university – where free education stops.

All schools are also subject to regular inspections by the Office for Standards in Education (Ofsted) and their examination results are published in league tables.

Education in London is a very fraught issue, with places at high-performing schools hotly contested – parents have even been known to move house or take up a religion to try and get their kids into a particular school. If you are prepared to pay for your child's education, there is an extensive range of independent private schools to choose from. Independent schools do not have to follow the National Curriculum, and nearly always have selective admissions policies.

Nurseries & Pre-Schools

All three and four-year-olds living in London are entitled to a free early education place, which should be for at least two-and-a-half hours, five days a week, during term time. 'Early years' education can take place in nursery schools, nursery or reception classes in primary schools, playgroups and private day nurseries and schools. The minimum provision is free, but if you wish your child to attend for extra hours you may have to pay. Contact your local school or nursery directly, or approach your local education authority to find out what is available in your area. ChildcareLink (www.childcarelink.gov.uk) is also a useful resource for finding nurseries or other childcare facilities near to you.

Primary & Secondary Schools

State primary and secondary schools that are free to attend come in various forms, but all have a governing body which deals with day-to-day running and sometimes has a say in admissions policy. These are the main types:

Community schools – this type of school is owned, funded and the admissions policy set by the LEA.

Voluntary-controlled and voluntary-aided schools – schools owned by a voluntary organisation, typically a church.

Foundation schools – owned and run by a governing body but funded by the LEA.

City technology colleges – these schools operate independently of the LEA and are funded by commercial sponsors and the Department for Education and Skills.

Education

Ofsted
All schools, in both the private and state sectors, are regularly assessed by the government's school inspection body Ofsted. For inspection reports, go to www.ofsted.gov.uk, where you will also find a list of outstanding providers.

Specialist schools – these schools have a special focus (such as sports or arts); although they still follow the National Curriculum.
Academies – publicly funded independent schools which provide free education to local pupils.
Special schools – schools for pupils with special educational needs.

Parents have the right to express a preference as to which school they would like their child to attend and the LEA must try and comply with their choice, although this may not always be possible. Schools in London, especially secondary schools, can have varying results and reputations, which often leads to those considered the best becoming over-subscribed, with the result that some parents will have to be disappointed.
Depending on the school you choose you will need to contact it directly or go via the LEA and fill in an application form. Admissions policies include things such as: whether your child has a sibling already at the school; how far you live from the school and if this area is in its 'catchment' area; if it is religious school, whether your child follows that religion; whether the school gives preference to those who favour single-sex or co-ed schools; whether your child has been excluded from other schools. Some state schools also select all pupils, or a proportion of them, by academic ability. If your child is denied a place at a school of your choice, you must be told why, either by the school or the LEA, and given the opportunity to appeal the decision. To apply to an independent school, contact the school directly. To find your nearest state school visit www.yourlondon.gov.uk/maps/fynschool.jsp.

Higher Education

London's universities and colleges of further education attract students aged 18 upwards from all over the world. Admissions policies are set by the individual institutions and typically involve reaching certain standards and attending an interview. For UK students funding comes from a system of student loans, which are repaid gradually when the student starts employment. To come to London from another country in order to study, you need to secure a place on a course, pay the relevant fees and apply for a student visa (see Entry Visa, p.52).

Universities

London attracts students from all over the globe by virtue of its rich academic traditions, the mind-expanding variety of its teaching establishments and of course the wealth of social and cultural resources the city offers.
Tuition fees vary from institution to institution, but international students should expect to pay from around £8,800 a year for undergraduate and postgraduate arts courses, rising to £14,000 for the first year of medical degrees – with living expenses to be considered on top of this. Most universities offer a limited number of scholarships that overseas students can apply for – check the website of the relevant institution.

151

Universities		
University of London	www.lon.ac.uk	7862 8000
London Metropolitan University	www.londonmet.ac.uk	7423 0000
London South Bank University	www.lsbu.ac.uk	7815 7815
University of the Arts London	www.arts.ac.uk	7514 6000

The Open University

The biggest university in Britain is the Open University, which provides distance learning opportunities to degree level and beyond. Teaching makes use of printed course materials, TV programmes and online resources, supported by tutors and staff at regional centres. The majority of courses have no entry requirements and students are usually in full-time employment (with employers often paying course fees). To get an idea of the massive number of courses offered, see www.open.ac.uk.

University of London

Central in attracting overseas students to the capital, both at undergraduate and postgraduate level, is the University of London, a federation of 31 largely autonomous colleges and institutions, which share some joint facilities in Bloomsbury such as the huge Senate House library and the social and sports centre at the University of London Union (ULU) – both on Malet Street. Among the university's most prestigious specialist institutions, which can lay claim to such illustrious alumni as Mahatma Gandhi, John F Kennedy and Archbishop Desmond Tutu, are the London School of Economics, the School of African and Oriental Studies, the London School of Hygiene and Tropical Medicine, the Central School of Speech and Drama, the Royal Academy of Music and the London Business School.

Of the multi-faculty colleges, Goldsmiths' College, based in south-east London, is particularly renowned for its fine art department boasting alumni such as Vivienne Westwood, Lucian Freud and Damien Hirst. University College London, in the heart of Bloomsbury, has an emphasis on medical disciplines, while Queen Mary University in east London has a strong arts faculty. Birkbeck College offers part-time degrees aimed at those with existing daytime commitments. Major medical schools include Barts and The London School of Medicine and Dentistry, part of Queen Mary University, the Royal Free and University College Medical School, and the Royal Veterinary College. The schools all have their own administrations and admissions policies so check individual websites to order prospectuses or find out about research possibilities.

Other Universities

Outside of the University of London other higher education establishments include London Metropolitan University, with campuses in the City and Islington; London South Bank University, which has strong vocational courses in engineering, computing, health and social care, and also houses the National Bakery School; and the similarly vocationally strong Middlesex University, which has campuses in the outer north London area.

The University of the Arts London is Europe largest's university for art, design, fashion and communication. Of its six renowned colleges, The Central Saint Martins College of Art and Design, located around Covent Garden, is one the most famous art and fashion institutions in the world, having nurtured the talents of Gilbert and George, Anita Pallenberg, Stella McCartney and Alexander McQueen – and also contributed incalculably to pop history by being the venue of the Sex Pistols' first ever gig.

Special Needs Education

If your child is having problems with aspects of learning and you believe they have special needs you should have them assessed by the Local Education Authority (LEA) as soon as possible. If the LEA agrees they have special educational needs (SEN) they then have a duty to ensure those needs are met either in mainstream schools or special schools. If there is no suitable provision available locally in the state sector, the LEA may pay for the child to attend a special school. Wherever you are in London you will have access to a local parent partnership service, a statutory agency providing support, advice and education to the parents of children with SEN. To find your local service, go to the National Parent Partnership's website at www.parentpartnership.org.uk.

Transportation

Transportation

Other options **Getting Around** p.32, **Underground** p.38

In a city as big as this, where few people are lucky enough to live close enough to their work to walk, conditions of travel can add or subtract greatly to quality of life. London's biggest transport issue of recent years, and one which divides opinion, has been the Congestion Charge, a daily charge levied on those who drive cars into central London on weekdays. The majority of London's commuters do not drive to work, but use the London Underground (the tube), overland trains or buses, all of which can suffer from overcrowding and cramped conditions. Fares for public transport generally compare unfavourably with other major European cities. As the costs and hassles of both driving and public transport escalate, many people are turning to pedal power.

Tube map
See the inside back cover for a map of the London Underground

Buses

Massive investment in the London bus network boosted the number of bus journeys in the capital by 38 per cent between 1999/2000 and 2004/05, with an estimated six million passengers travelling by bus on any given weekday. The frequency of services has noticeably improved and dedicated lanes allow buses to breeze past some of the worst traffic. For short journeys, buses can represent a cheaper and reasonably swift alternative to the tube, whereas in areas the tube doesn't reach, such as Hackney and parts of south London, they are a necessity. In order to further speed up bus journeys passengers have been strongly incentivised away from paying for fares in cash: it now costs double if you pay by cash rather than pre-payment Oyster card (see p.34). Even if paying a cash fare, many buses in the middle of town require you to buy a ticket before boarding by using coin-operated ticket machines at bus stops, where you will also find maps of bus routes. It's possible to buy one-day, weekly and monthly bus passes, but it is generally simpler to get yourself an Oyster card which covers you for tubes, trams and the DLR as well. Those over 60 or registered disabled can claim a Freedom Pass, which gives them free travel on London's public transport, with under-16s and 16 and 17 year-olds in full-time education also entitled to free bus journeys. More and more buses are designed to be accessible to wheelchair users and those with buggies, although lack of space can present difficulties. Regular bus routes operate until around 00:00, with some routes running 24 hours, and special Night Bus routes covering the rest of the network. For details about routes, times and how to apply for passes, contact Transport for London (7222 1234, www.tfl.gov.uk/buses).

Now Boarding
Double-decker buses should be boarded by the front door and your Oyster card passed over the reader by the driver, your travelcard or ticket shown to the driver, or your fare paid to him. The long single-decker buses, popularly known as 'bendy buses', can be boarded at any door along their length if you have an Oyster card, travelcard, or pass, which should then be passed over one of the on-board card readers.

Cycling

Once the province of whippet-thin courier riders in lycra and the occasional fearless old lady, cycling's popularity in London has soared over the past 10 years. Inexpensive, healthy, green, quick, reliable: its logic is pretty convincing, despite anxieties about traffic, bike thieves and the occasional downpour. Mountain bikers and Tour de France wannabes aside, most commuters find that a basic hybrid or road bike adequate for their requirements, with prices starting at around £200 at London's many bike shops. Some employers also offer interest-free loans for bike purchase, in the same way as they do for travelcards. Get yourself some lights, which you must have by law to cycle at night, a helmet, a stout lock, a puncture repair kit and maybe a bit of fluorescent kit and off you go. Dedicated cycle paths are the exception rather than the rule in London, and not always well-maintained, but there are many backstreets, park, canals and cut-throughs cyclists habitually use to avoid particularly hairy roads. Useful cycle maps covering the entire city are produced by Transport for London, order them from www.tfl.gov.uk or you can pick them up in bike shops or libraries. Another good source of advice and know-how is the London Cycling Campaign, www.lcc.org.uk.

153

Congestion Charge

If you drive in the Congestion Charge zone in central London between 07:00 and 18:00 on weekdays, you've got to pay the Congestion Charge. The charge is £8 if you pay on the same day you stray into the zone, or £10 on the following day. Payments can be made at many newsagents as well as online at www.cclondon.com, where you will also find details of the Congestion Charge zone's boundaries (which are expanding all the time).

Taxis & Minicabs

London's official black cabs, with yellow 'For Hire' or 'Taxi' signs on the front are the only type of cabs that you can pick up at taxi ranks or hail on the street. Drivers of these taxis have passed a test on their knowledge of London's geography and each cab has an official number, a visible meter and a minimum charge of £2.20 (more if you book by phone or start your journey at an airport). When taxi signs are lit it means the car will usually stop for you when waved at. Black cabs work out as an expensive form of transport and many people use them only if in a particular hurry, it is late at night, they are out on special occasion – or if someone else is paying. Black cabs can be booked in advance by calling 0871 8718710.

Licensed minicab firms, whose cars you can book either on the spot in one of their offices or by calling their individual number, tend to offer a slightly cheaper service, but their drivers are not always fully up-to-speed about roadworks and the best routes to take. It is illegal for any cab driver to tout for business by approaching people on the streets and it is potentially dangerous to get into any taxi unless you are sure the driver belongs to a licensed firm.

Minicabs do not have meters, so ask for a fare estimate before setting off. Cab firms advertise by delivering cards door-to-door, or when you are out and about text HOME to 60835 to have the number of a local licensed firm sent to your mobile. Chauffeur services and executive car services are readily available, but are mostly only used by those in particularly high-powered positions. Limousine hire, on the other hand, is considered a bit tacky and mainly the preserve of gaggles of teenagers on birthday sprees. Black taxis, minicab firms and all other sorts of private vehicle hire are regulated by the Public Carriage Office, part of Transport for London, and in the event of problems or complaints phone 0845 602 7000 or email coms

Driving in London

There may be plenty of cars on London's roads but it's common for younger people, and new residents especially, not to own cars or else to have a car which they use sparingly. Further out, there's a higher level of car ownership and car journeys.

The hassles of parking in central London and the likelihood of traffic jams mean that for many driving is simply impractical and undesirable. The price of petrol, which is heavily taxed, is around 86.5p a litre; expensive compared with the US and other European countries.

While driving in London is on the whole lawful, it can be quite tense, especially on busy routes. You will also quickly realise the importance of being aware of pedestrians crossing, not necessarily at official crossing points (this is not illegal; there is not a concept of 'jaywalking' in the UK), and cycles and motorbikes weaving in and out of traffic. Also be aware of the 'school run'; congestion on the streets around 09:00 and 15:30 as parents drop off and pick up their kids from school.

Traffic Updates

Regular traffic updates can be caught on London's many local radio stations, such as Capital Radio and BBC Radio London. Television text services, Teletext and Ceefax, are also good sources of up-to-date information, as is the Transport for London website (www.tfl.gov.uk).

Transportation

Hands-Free?
One recent traffic law to be aware of is a ban on using a handheld mobile phone when at the wheel (hands-free equipment is acceptable). This legislation was initially widely flouted – until the standard penalty for violation was raised to a £60 fine and three penalty points on your licence.

Driving Rules & Regulations

The speed limit for driving in residential areas is 20 miles per hour (mph) or 30mph, where you will often encounter traffic-calming measures such as speed bumps. Outside of built-up areas speed limits vary between 40mph and 50mph, with 70mph on motorways, but are always clearly signed. Driving under the influence of drugs or alcohol is illegal in the UK; the legal limit is 80 milligrammes of alcohol in 100 millilitres of blood, but many people avoid alcohol entirely if they plan to drive. The penalties for driving or attempting to drive over the limit or when under the influence of drugs are fierce, carrying a maximum of six months' prison sentence, a fine up to £5,000 and a driving ban of at least one year, with a maximum of 14 years in prison if a death is caused. It is also worth remembering that an endorsement for drink-driving also remains on your driving licence for 11 years. Wearing a seatbelt is compulsory in both the front and back of cars, as well as in minibuses and coaches if seatbelts are provided. Safety seats are also compulsory for children with rules governing the ages and heights at which different restraints, or booster seats, must be used. Motorcycle riders and their passengers are legally obliged to wear approved crash helmets. For more details, see www.thinkroadsafety.gov.uk. For a comprehensive overview of driving rules get a copy of The Highway Code, a government-sponsored guide which is available inexpensively from bookshops and large newsagents.

Parking

Parking is notoriously expensive and limited. It is unusual for properties to have garages or off-street parking, and many streets have insufficient space for their residents to all park their cars. This of course can lead to considerable inconvenience. Many local councils have brought in CPZs (community parking zones) which allow only local resident permit-holders and their visitors to park. Fees for parking in the centre of town are high, with most streets having restricted parking or parking meters which charge by the hour. NCP (National Car Parks) also runs several large underground and multistorey car parks in the centre of town, which are reliable, if expensive, places to park. Violations of parking regulations are rigorously enforced, with a typical penalty charge of £50 if you pay quickly, going up to £100 after a certain number of days, with the risk of your car being clamped or towed if it is left in the wrong place for too long.

Vehicle Leasing

Car and van rental is available from the familiar international companies you see at airports such as Hertz, Avis, Sixt and Europcar, as well as numerous companies local to the UK and London, which often beat them for price. Prices start from around £25 a day for the smallest class of car, rising by engine capacity and size of vehicle. Vehicles are hired out by the day, with discounts sometimes on offer for longer rental periods.

Buying a Vehicle

You can buy a car new from a dealership or secondhand from a used car dealer or from an individual. You should have no problem locating the car of your choice as all the major brands are represented in London – one thing to bear in mind when choosing to buy a car is that the more gas-guzzling they are the more tax you will be liable to pay (see Registering a Vehicle, p.156). Dealerships offer finance terms, subject to your credit status, but you may wish to compare interest rates with bank loans as they may offer a better deal.

Vehicle Insurance

You have to be insured to be able to drive legally in the UK. There are three main types of policy available, the minimum requirement being third-party cover, which pays out to other parties if you are involved in an accident. You can top that up with

155

The Complete **Residents'** Guide

New Car Dealers

Aircool	7272 5014	www.aircool-garage.co.uk	Audi, Volkswagen
AMC	8944 9966	www.amclondon.com	BMW, Mercedes
Beadles	0845 6080560	www.beadles.co.uk	Volkswagen, Nissan, Toyota, Land Rover
Chiswick Suzuki	8560 1718	www.fulton.suzuki.co.uk	Suzuki
Elite Motors	8461 2000	www.mazda.co.uk	Mazda
Fiat	0080 034280000	www.fiat.co.uk	Fiat
Finchley Road Audi	0845 8039003	www.m25audi.co.uk	Audi
Ford	8534 7661	www.ford.co.uk	Ford
H R Owen	7736 8481	www.alfaromeo.co.uk	Alfa Romeo
Hendon	8200 4040	www.hendon-honda.co.uk	Honda
HL Austin & Son Ltd	8874 6262	www.hlaustin.co.uk	Skoda
Humming Bird KIA	8346 0101	www.kia.co.uk	KIA, Mitsubishi
Mercedes-Benz	7351 4000	www.mercedesretail.co.uk	Mercedes
Mini Park Lane	7495 9500	www.miniparklane.com	Mini
Porsche Centre Mayfair	7514 0900	www.porsche.com	Porsche
Renault UK Ltd	0800 0723372	www.renault.co.uk	Renault
Rolls Royce Motor Cars London	7491 7941	www.rrmc-london.com	RollsRoyce
SEAT	0800 262622	www.seat.co.uk	SEAT
Stratstone Land Rover	7514 0400	www.stratstone.com	Land Rover
Stratstone of Mayfair	7629 4404	www.stratstone.com	Aston Martin, Cadillac, Corvette, Jaguar
Toyota	0845 1213646	www.toyota.co.uk	Toyota
Waters Group Hertfordshire	0845 3311927	www.waters.co.uk	Peugeot, Renault
West London Nissan	8280 0665	www.westlondonnissan.co.uk	Nissan

Second-Hand Cars

As well as the huge number of used-car dealers throughout London, second-hand cars are widely advertised for sale in classified papers such as Auto Trader, Exchange & Mart and Loot. Always ensure the seller can provide you with the car's service history and relevant documentation. You can research the MOT history of the vehicle you are thinking of buying at www.motinfo.gov.uk, or contact your breakdown association which, for a fee, will check the car before you buy it.

fire and theft, which will cover your vehicle if it is stolen or torched, while fully comprehensive covers pretty much everything, including damage to your own vehicle regardless of who caused the accident. On top of this there are countless variables, such as whether you want to pay 'excess' (a part payment on any claim you make in return for a cheaper premium), add other named drivers, or be covered for driving in Europe. Insurance companies – of which there are many – also offer a no-claims bonus as a reward for not claiming on the policy; the longer you go without using your cover, the cheaper the cost of the policy. Make sure you get a detailed description of exactly what is covered before you sign up. Below is a list of some of the major insurers. There are also some useful price-comparison services around such as www.moneysupermarket.com and www.pricechecker.co.uk.

Registering a Vehicle

The Driver and Vehicle Licensing Agency (DVLA) is the official body responsible for registering cars in the UK. Every vehicle, bar those which are registered in foreign countries, must have a registration document from the DVLA (www.dvla.gov.uk) detailing the specifications of the vehicle and the identity of its owner. When you buy a car, the DVLA must be told so that this registration document can be sent to you. For a car to be on the road it must also have a current Vehicle Excise Duty disc (tax disc) displayed in the front windscreen. Tax can be renewed every six or 12 months online at www.vehiclelicence.gov.uk by phone or at a Post Office once you have the registration document, insurance document and MOT certificate (see below). The amount of tax you pay for your car is related to its CO_2 emissions. No tax is payable on electric cars, with the tax bill for traditional cars ranging from £50 to £210.

Vehicle Insurance

AA	0800 1976173	www.theaa.com
Barclays	0800 0156585	www.barclaysgeneralinsurance.co.uk
Budget	0800 0289044	www.budgetinsurance.com
Churchill	0800 200326	www.churchill.com
Cornhill Direct	0800 3288831	www.cornhilldirect.co.uk
Diamond (women only)	0800 362436	www.diamond.co.uk
Direct Line	0845 2463761	www.directline.com
Elephant.co.uk	0870 0131072	www.elephant.co.uk
Endsleigh	0800 7836414	www.quotes-endsleigh.co.uk
Esure	0845 6037874	www.esure.com
First Alternative	0845 6070380	www.firstalternative.com
Halifax	0800 9175764	www.halifax.co.uk
Marks & Spencer	0800 1071823	www6.marksandspencer.com
NatWest	0800 0515405	www.natwest.com
Norwich Union	0800 0929561	www.norwichunion.com
Post Office	0800 7830357	www.postoffice.co.uk
RAC	0800 0517820	www.rac.co.uk
Senior Car Insurance UK	0870 0133044	www.senior.i4m.co.uk
Zurich	0800 333800	www.zurichinsurance.co.uk

Traffic Fines & Offences

The majority of more minor driving offences, such as driving while using a handheld mobile phone, running a red light, and not wearing a seatbelt are usually punishable by a fixed penalty notice (FPN). A FPN is a fine starting at £30 which you must pay within 28 days in order for the offence to be considered spent and no record to be kept. If you feel the fine is unwarranted you can ask for a hearing, but if you do not respond by either paying up or appealing within 28 days the fine is automatically doubled. Offences which are considered more serious, such as speeding or driving without insurance, are known as 'endorsable' – meaning that on top of a fine of anywhere between £60 and £200, between three and 11 penalty points are recorded

on your licence. If you clock up 12 points on your licence within three years, your licence will be disqualified for at least six months. Drink driving offences result in automatic disqualification. If your car has a mechanical fault which has resulted in a traffic offence, then you may be issued with a vehicle defect rectification notice which means you will have to present proof, such as a garage receipt, to a police station that the problem has been fixed (as well as paying the fine). The most serious driving offences, death by dangerous driving and the like, are punishable by long prison stretches.

Parking Fines

Parking in a restricted zone or outstaying a parking meter will spark a 'penalty charge notice' (more commonly known as a parking ticket) which will be stuck onto your windscreen by a parking attendant. The fine for a PCN is £100, or £50 if you pay within 14 days. As with FCNs, you can appeal but risk paying the higher rate of £100 if your appeal is unsuccessful. If your car is wheel-clamped for being left in the wrong place, a bigger fine will need to be paid before the clamp will be removed and you can reclaim your vehicle – full details of what you need to do

157

will be posted on your car. If your car has been towed away for being illegally parked, you need to phone the TRACE service on 7747 4747, who will be able to tell you where your car has been taken and how much the release fee is.

Breakdowns

The majority of drivers in London take the wise precaution of breakdown cover. The Automobile Association (AA) and the Royal Automobile Club (RAC) are the two most widely used organisations (www.theaa.com and www.rac.co.uk). If your car breaks down in the city, stay with your vehicle unless it is dangerous to do so and call your breakdown company immediately. If you break down on a motorway, walk to the nearest freephone (they appear at regular intervals by the side of the road) – this will connect you to the transport police who will call your breakdown company or tow the vehicle off the motorway if you are not covered. Use your mobile phone if you feel it is unsafe to leave your vehicle, especially if you're a woman alone at night.

Seatbelts

Seatbelts are compulsory in both the front and back of cars, as well as in minibuses and coaches if they are provided. Tight regulations govern the use of safety seats for children, with different restraints or booster seats necessary depending on the ages and heights of the children on board. See www.thinkroadsafety.gov.uk for detailed information.

Traffic Accidents

If you are caught up in a traffic accident, the important thing to do is to stop at the scene. As the driver you should remain with your vehicle, and give your name and address, the name and address of the owner of the vehicle if it isn't yours and the vehicle registration number to anyone involved directly or indirectly with the accident. If someone has been injured, the driver will also need to produce an insurance certificate. If they don't have this with them they should report to a police station as soon as possible and present the insurance certificate to the station within seven days of the accident. When an accident has resulted in damage to vehicles rather than people then the driver must be prepared to give their insurance details to anyone who may wish to make a claim against them. For insurance purposes it will be important to establish who is liable for the accident – in some cases this will be straightforward but if there is any doubt then the presence of any witnesses will be crucial. Whatever happens you should get in touch with your own insurance company as soon as possible, and remember you may be able to get free legal advice through your insurance company or any motoring organisation you are a member of. If you are verbally abused by another driver, it's probably best (if not always easy) to ignore it in case the incident escalates. Any physically threatening or violent behaviour should be reported to the police and, again, get the names of witnesses if you can.

Vehicle Repairs

All cars over three years old must pass an annual Ministry of Transport test (MOT), which checks the road-worthiness and emissions of vehicles. MOTs cost about £50 and are carried out at official test centres in garages displaying a blue 'three triangles' logo. If your vehicle fails the MOT, you will need to get the faults repaired and then have it re-examined (some centres offer a free re-test within 14 days, but you need to check this first). For everyday repairs, there are a wide choice of garages in London, from fast-fix chains such as Kwik-Fit (0800 222111) to authorised centres that deal in specific makes of car. Most manufacturers recommend taking your car in for a service twice a year to keep it running smoothly. Insurance companies offer 'no-claims bonuses', and the value of the discount increases with the number of years you go without claiming so check the impact of drawing on your insurance to cover minor repairs. New cars that break down should be covered by a warranty for a limited period – check your policy details for the exact terms.

Babywear p.98
Bank Loans p.22

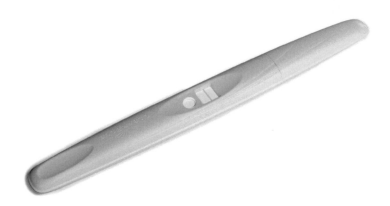

Written by residents, these unique guidebooks are packed with insider info, from arriving in a new destination to making it your home and everything in between.

Explorer Residents' Guides
We Know Where You Live

Raw power, refined.

The new Chevrolet Tahoe refines the raw power of a 355 horsepower Vortec V8
engine and couples it with smooth handling and a quiet ride. Examine Tahoe's
luxuriously appointed interior and you'll find refinement in every detail.

CHEVROLET

TAHOE

Tahoe 2007

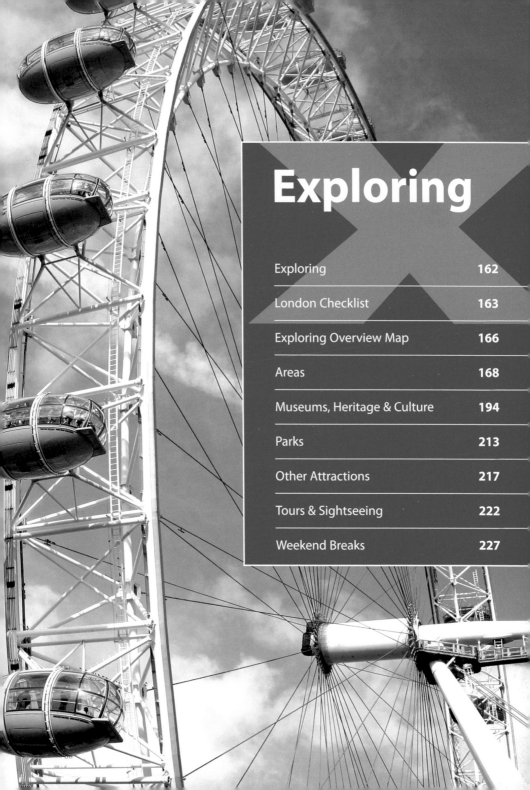

Exploring

Exploring

A Full Calendar

Unlike many places in the world, there's no 'best season' to visit London – on top of its year-round attractions, you'll find a full calendar of special events. From outdoor ice rinks in winter to blooming flowers at Kew and Chelsea in spring, and the carnival in Notting Hill in the summer to proms and parades in autumn, there's an array of events to entertain residents and visitors alike (see p.44).

Exploring

It's often said by the people who live here that London isn't really representative of England – that it is an entity entirely unto and of itself. On the surface this comment seems fair enough. After all, on appearances alone, 21st century London is a vibrant, multicultural metropolis that has more in common with New York than the old city of York 200 miles up the road. But scratch below the surface and it quickly becomes apparent that this 'new' London is merely an extension that sits comfortably alongside the old. 'Old' London is, of course, the home of Big Ben and Piccadilly Circus, the royal family and those familiar red double-decker buses. But it's also a heritage that stretches back over hundreds of years. Pre-Roman settlements have been discovered along the Thames, but London, as a united settlement in its own right, was established following the Roman invasion in AD43. The first coins found from Londinium, as it was known then, date the foundation of the capital back to AD50. The heart of Londinium was the area we now know as the City – the capital's financial quarter – and traces of the Roman era can still be seen today amid the skyscrapers, glass and expensive suits. London is described as being made up of a series of villages and it's true that many neighbourhoods within the capital's 32 boroughs possess a character that is distinctly their own, be it the reggae-infused street culture of Brixton, the elegantly refined charms of leafy Hampstead or the gritty urbanity of central London itself. In broader terms, however, London is very clearly a city of two halves; a geographical definition that's come about by the way the river Thames roughly splits the capital in two. It's a standing joke among Londoners that those who live north of the river rarely travel south, but in truth the divisions between London's two geographical characters are now largely anecdotal – urban regeneration crossed the river a long time ago, while the northern half of the city is home to its fair share of council estates and gritty neighbourhoods.

It is most likely that anyone wanting to explore will begin in the centre, where the energy of Soho and Chinatown, the world-famous Theatreland and the almost tangible history of the newly regenerated East End evoke the rich vibrancy and variety of the capital's ancient and modern history.

London Pride

What really captures visitors' imaginations, however, is the powerful iconography of the city, from the pomp of Buckingham Palace to the ceremony of the Houses of Parliament. Mix in the sheer joyful playfulness of the architectural wonders of the new skyline, of which the giant observation wheel, the London Eye, is the unqualified winning example, and you have that heady mix of traditional and modern that 'new' London does so well. One reason the capital continues to entice and fascinate lies in its multifaceted appeal. Whatever you're coming for, you'll find it here. The City of London is the UK's financial hub, attracting an endless stream of international business travellers. London's heritage, history and reputation as both a top party destination and the gateway to the rest of the UK and western Europe continues to draw tourists and longer-term residents from every corner of the globe. And when they get here their preconceptions are confounded again by a city that isn't just tall buildings and ancient monuments, but one filled with more beautiful and accessible green spaces than any other city of its size in the world. Londoners – whether born and bred or one of the many thousands who relocate to the capital each year – are justifiably proud of the city they live in. They may have a practical cynicism about aspects of the city's infrastructure, especially its overworked transport system, but ask almost any one of its residents and they will say that London's heritage, cosmopolitan cultural mix, world-class shopping, arts and entertainment and broadly egalitarian views make this a place that always fascinates and surprises.

Take a Double-Decker Bus
London's buses are a great way to get the lie of the land and are far cheaper than black cabs. The hop-on, hop-off bus tour companies based around Marble Arch and Baker Street, while geared to tourists, are surprisingly popular with residents. For the purist, travelling a 'heritage route' on one of the old Routemaster buses is a good alternative. Take the number 15 from Trafalgar Square to Tower Hill, complete with views of Big Ben and St Paul's, or the number 9 from the Royal Albert Hall to Aldwych, via Piccadilly Circus.

Cruise the Thames p.223
A river cruise along the Thames by day or night is a spectacular way to see the city's great landmarks, from the Houses of Parliament to 30 St Mary Axe (known locally as 'the Gherkin') just along from Tower Bridge. The cheery Tate to Tate boat (painted in a kaleidoscope of multicoloured spots designed by artist Damien Hirst) runs every 40 minutes between Tate Britain in Pimlico and Tate Modern on the South Bank.

Get off the Tube Map
Tucked away in the heart of London are a series of 'villages' that tend to stay well off the tourist path for the simple reason that they're not serviced by the tube. However, enclaves such as Wandsworth, Stoke Newington and Dulwich Village, with their local art galleries, boutique shopping, spacious parks and great neighbourhood restaurants, are worth making the effort to explore.

Step Back in Time
There's more to this city than its great Edwardian, Georgian and Victorian architecture and landmarks from Westminster Cathedral to the Albert Memorial. Visit one of the many historic houses dotted throughout the city that are open to the pubic, from the magnificence of Kenwood House (stunningly located on Hampstead Heath) to Dennis Severs' House, a so-called 'living museum' providing a snapshot of life in the late 18th and early 19th centuries.

Dance in the Streets p.209
Every August bank holiday, the streets of west London come alive to the Caribbean rhythms of the Notting Hill Carnival. Europe's biggest street party takes place over two days, regularly drawing up to one million revellers to what is now one of London's most exclusive neighbourhoods. Other highlights of the city's annual festivities include the rich, aromatic fancy of Chinese New Year in Soho and Baishakhi Mela, Brick Lane's celebration of all things Bangladeshi.

Explore the City's Canals
If the river Thames is at the very heart of London, then its many canals and waterways are its arteries. From Roman times until the 18th century, there was only one bridge across the Thames, and so for over 1,000 years travel by water was the best way to navigate the city. London's many canals are no longer integral to transport and commerce, however they are much loved by residents as picturesque places for a stroll or a gentle day of barge-dwelling.

Glide across the Ice
London has started to look like something out of the closing scene of Richard Curtis's *Love Actually* in recent times – all twinkling lights and pretty locals taking to the ice amid a picture-perfect backdrop of freshly fallen snow. While the snow may be lacking, anyone looking for beautifully lit outdoor ice rinks will not be disappointed. Somerset House, Alexandra Palace, the Natural History Museum and Kew Gardens have all hosted outdoor rinks in recent years.

Enjoy a Curry p.395

Tourists might still believe a Londoner's top feast is fish & chips, but locals know that curry is in fact king. You will find Indian curry houses on every high street but for a particularly memorable meal try visiting the so-called 'curry corridor' on Tooting High Street and nearby Upper Tooting Road, or head slightly out of town to Southall, where the strong Asian community means that curry is a very local dish.

Go Horse Riding in Hyde Park p.214

There's nothing quite like a gentle trot through the city's largest park on a crisp morning to get a fresh perspective on the city. The local stables offer opportunities for all levels of rider, hiring out horses to those with enough experience to explore the park at their own pace as well as fully guided lessons for beginners, individually or in small groups.

Go to a Gig p.449

Whether your chosen beat is rock, garage, jazz, hip-hop or folk, there will be a live performance to cater to your tastes somewhere in London on any night of the week. Wembley Arena, Brixton Academy, Ronnie Scott's and Camden's grungy indie mecca Barfly are just some of the venues, great and small, catering to international and home-grown musical talent.

Watch Some Sport p.286

Whether your tastes run to an adrenaline-fuelled night of betting at Walthamstow's famous dog track or a more leisurely perusal of Wimbledon's on-court action over strawberries and cream, there's always something for the avid sports fan. If it's pure pleasure you're after, however, you won't do any better than joining the crowds at the annual University Boat Race or London Marathon. Supporters line the routes (and fill the pubs) shouting encouragement to the teams and participants as they pass.

Go to Church p.197

St Paul's Cathedral and Westminster Abbey are justifiably London's best-known churches and you can avoid both the crowds and the entry fee by visiting them during service. But don't overlook other magnificent places of worship in the city, such as Westminster Cathedral near Victoria station and South Kensington's Brompton Oratory.

Visit a Street Market p.367

Camden for furniture and goth-hippy chic, Portobello for antiques and fashion and Borough for every foodie's dream – London's street markets are some of the best and most diverse in the world. But it's not just the big, world-renowned markets that are worth a visit. Almost every neighbourhood has somewhere selling bargain pots and pans or boutique bread (quite often in the same place). London's markets are the hub of a local community; find a good one and you'll never want to visit a supermarket again.

Make your Debut in the West End

Not while there's a show on, obviously, but a number of the larger theatres do offer regular guided backstage walks that let punters experience the thrill of preparing for curtain up. The Royal Opera House, Albert Hall and Shakespeare's Globe tours are particularly fascinating, not least because the buildings themselves are so spectacular. In the West End proper, the Theatre Royal Drury Lane offers the UK's first interactive theatre tour.

Take a Walking Tour p.225

A good way to get some bite-sized historical context for parts of the city you might not visit every day is to try one of the many guided or solo walking tours available. Join an organised group such as the famous Ripper Walks in and around Whitechapel or pick up one of the Blue Plaque walking guides that allow you to follow in the footsteps of a neighbourhood's famous residents.

Lose Yourself in a Museum p.205

The number of must-see galleries and museums in London is too numerous to be individually name-checked. Suffice to say that whether your interests lie in archaeological treasures (British Museum), the history of art and design (Victoria & Albert Museum) or just great art (National Gallery and Tate Modern and Britain), London is the place for you.

Stroll the South Bank p.186

Long dismissed as a concrete monstrosity, the Southbank Centre, home to theatres and the Hayward Gallery, is enjoying a revival. To get there, walk up-river from Tower Hill, taking in 'the Gherkin', Shakespeare's Globe and Tate Modern. From there it's an easy stroll past the street performers and teenage skateboarders. Enjoy a drink at the pleasant open-air National Film Theatre bar, before finishing your journey at the foot of the London Eye.

Swim Outside p.215

Londoners are a hardy bunch and that's never more apparent than when witnessing their love of outdoor swimming pools. One of the most famous is Brockwell Lido, endearingly known among locals as 'Brixton Beach'. For those who like their water a little more au naturel, the bathing ponds on Hampstead Heath have been drawing in the crowds for at least 180 years. Pop down on Christmas Day, when the nip of the near-freezing water is countered with post-swim celebrations of mulled wine and mince pies

Have a Pint with the Locals p.420

You still might not be able to get a decent cup of coffee in some parts of the city, but you can pretty much guarantee you'll find a decent pub, whether it's a preserved old Victorian boozer converted into a fashionable gastropub or a spit-and-sawdust number where the same old geezers have been propping up the bar for years. Cheers!

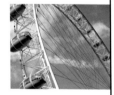

Take a 'Flight' on the London Eye p.217

Since opening on the South Bank at the turn of the century, this giant observation wheel has become one of the great, iconic symbols of the capital. Housing 32 giant, sealed walk-on pods, the Eye offers breathtaking views for up to 25 miles in all directions across the city. Try it just as night falls and watch as London's grey exterior is replaced by shimmering lights.

Discover a Secret Garden

This is a favourite horticultural haven. Or you might choose to hang out in one of the capital's many squares. These little patches of green tucked away in the heart of the city are a great way to escape. Whether you choose the bustling vibe of Soho Square with its office workers and cycle couriers or the surprising quiet of Russell Square, you're in for a peaceful (re)treat.

165

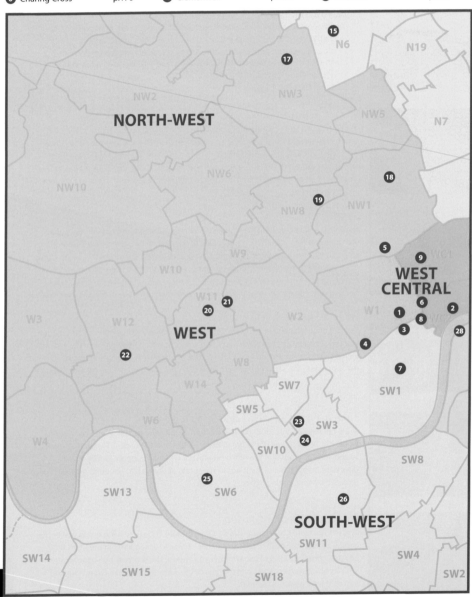

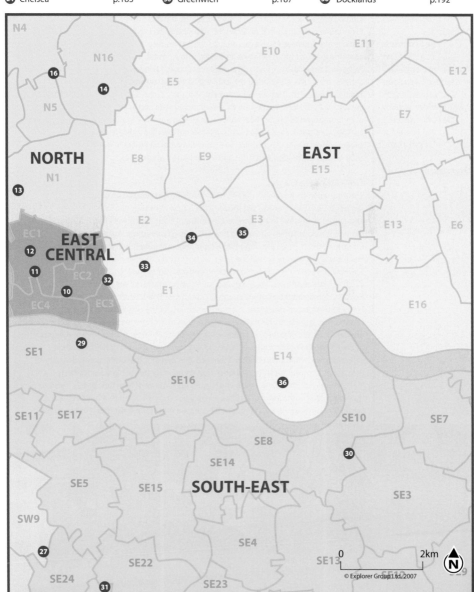

West Central

Soho, Covent Garden, Charing Cross – they're some of the city's more evocative locations, regarded by visitors as the heart of London for decades. But these parts of the capital are more than just sightseeing destinations. Both Soho and Covent Garden, for example, sustain vibrant local communities, while Marylebone's pretty, village-like streets and quiet squares are one of London's less-familiar treats. At the area's eastern edge, Holborn is caught between the glitz of Theatreland and the sobriety of its place as the traditional home to the city's legal profession. On the region's northern edge is King's Cross, where St Pancras is soon to become the main terminal for the high-speed Channel Tunnel Rail Link. This neglected part of the city has for years been famous for stations and seediness, but it can also lay claim to some pretty waterside developments, and, slowly but surely, is being redeveloped into a desirable locale.

As fascinating as these less-discovered parts of central London are, however, there is no denying that anyone exploring this area will be drawn towards the main attractions. Trafalgar Square, the Houses of Parliament, Piccadilly Circus – they're all here, and are as impressive in the flesh as they are on the cinema screen and in the imagination. What's even more surprising is just how concentrated into a small area they are. But there are also pleasant discoveries to be had in unexpected quarters – the genteel calm of the streets around the British Museum in Bloomsbury; blissful peace of London's garden squares; and the hidden museums and lesser-known art galleries.

Soho & Covent Garden

The reputation for seediness may remain, but Soho has cleaned up its act. Once most famous for its strip bars and sex shops, Soho is now almost better known, at least among those who live in London, as the centre of both the capital's film industry (around Wardour Street) and as the heart of its gay community (focused on Old Compton Street). It has also long had a reputation as being home to a particularly louche arts and literary scene. The tale that poet Dylan Thomas lost his manuscript of *Under Milk Wood* after overdoing it at drinking institution The French House (7437 2799) is just one of many you'll hear about Soho's characterful old boozers.

Roughly demarcated by Oxford Street, Charing Cross Road, Shaftesbury Avenue and Regent Street, this is one of the most bustling parts of the city. Whereas other parts of London may be famous for the attractions within them, here the attraction is Soho itself. And it's not all pubs and nightlife either – Berwick Street offers the twin delights of the city centre's only authentic fruit and veg market and some of the best fabric shops in town, while an afternoon spent in Soho Square is one of the great pleasures of the capital. Look out for the park bench that commemorates the late singer Kirsty MacColl, famous for her duet with The Pogues on *Fairytale of New York*, or pay a visit to the House of St Barnabas (7437 1894), a lovely Georgian building that has been a hostel for homeless women for over 150 years, on one of the few times it opens to the

public throughout the year. Golden Square, a little further west, provides a similar green space but without the atmosphere.

Just over Shaftesbury Avenue is London's Chinatown. Don't let the gimmicky pagodas fool you into thinking that this area is anything but authentic - Chinese families settled the area in the 1950s, opening the first of the many restaurants the district is now famous for, and the surrounding streets are at the heart of the capital's Chinese New Year celebrations. Nearby Charing Cross Road was once famous for its antiquarian bookstores, most of which have now disappeared, although the huge Foyles (see p.318) bridges the gap between old and new.

Shaftesbury Avenue itself is the heart of London's Theatreland. Bargain hunters can pick up half-price tickets to a selection of West End shows from the 'tkts' booth in Leicester Square (see p.450). The real centre of old London theatre, however, is Drury Lane, where the Theatre Royal (7494 5091) offers interactive tours of the premises. Nearby, the Royal Opera House (7304 4000), which overlooks Covent Garden piazza, also offers tours of its splendid, revamped building. The backstage visits are a treat – you may even catch sight of The Royal Ballet (which is also based here) in training, and you can take advantage of the sweeping new terrace to enjoy a coffee overlooking the piazza. Across the square is St Paul's Church, which is known as the 'actors' church' – plaques inside commemorate departed stars of stage and screen.

Despite its charms, Covent Garden is labelled as one of London's tourist blackspots, which is more than a little unfair. Look beyond the bustling piazza, with its weird and wonderful – and sometimes downright awful – array of street performers, and the vast but uninspired covered market (on the former site of the old Covent Garden Flower Market, which moved to Nine Elms in 1973), and there is much to charm the visitor. A highlight is Neal's Yard (see p.365), with its famous cheese shop, wholefood sellers and slightly hippyish feel, while Seven Dials is sleek and chic, home to a lovely selection of boutiques and cafes. For something that doesn't involve shopping, visit London's Transport Museum (7565 7299), which offers an interesting insight into the history of the capital's tube and bus network. It's a particular winner with children, and is scheduled to reopen in November 2007 after refurbishment. A short stroll away, The Photographers' Gallery (7831 1772) is an interesting place to while away an hour.

Piccadilly Circus, Mayfair & Marylebone

The golden art deco interior of the Criterion restaurant on Piccadilly (0871 2238045) is stunning, and is perfect for a pre-theatre cocktail or two. Outside, the neon brashness of Piccadilly Circus is one of the capital's most famous landmarks. It is always heaving with traffic and tourists milling around the legendary Statue of Eros. A little further along Piccadilly, the food hall at historic department store Fortnum & Mason (see p.356) never fails to delight, but if it's views you're after head to Waterstone's. The 5th View bar and cafe (7851 2433) on the top floor of Europe's largest bookshop offers a sweeping vista across London and is a perfect place to unwind after pounding the galleries of the nearby Royal Academy of Arts (see p.195).

North of Piccadilly is Mayfair, where the genteel environs of one of the capital's most exclusive residential neighbourhoods almost brings things to a standstill. Away from the shops of New Bond Street and its immediate vicinity there is little for the casual visitor to explore, although the cobbled streets around Shepherd Market by the eastern edge of Hyde Park have a number of small boutiques and independent shops, plus a few restaurants and traditional pubs. Across the frantic, bustling Oxford Street another attractive oasis awaits. The main focus of Marylebone Village is the lovely run of shops, art galleries, cafes and bars along pretty Marylebone High Street.

One of its most famous residents is Daunt Books (see p.362), a dedicated travel bookshop in a beautiful Edwardian setting. Another local favourite is the weekly

---

farmers' market that takes place between 10:00 and 14:00 on Sundays in nearby Cramer Street car park (7833 0338). For culture, you can't beat the charms of Wigmore Hall (7935 2141), a wonderful venue for chamber music, and the Wallace Collection in Hertford House (7563 9500), a former private residence that now displays a stunning array of treasures, including works by Rembrandt and Velazquez.

Marylebone is also home to Harley Street. Once renowned for its physicians, today's patients are more likely to be visiting for Botox shots and new-age practices – but the reputation still holds. The Royal Institute of British Architects (7631 0467) is nearby, and its beautifully designed – naturally – RIBA Café and Restaurant is open to the public.

Charing Cross, Westminster & The Strand

Across the road from Charing Cross station is the grand sweep of the pedestrianised Trafalgar Square, overlooked by the imposing National Gallery (7747 2885) and the handsome church of St Martin-in-the-Fields (7766 1100). Dating from 1722, painters William Hogarth and Sir Joshua Reynolds are buried in the churchyard, along with Charles II's mistress, Nell Gwynne. The church's regular lunchtime and evening choir concerts are justifiably celebrated, as is its cosy Cafe in the Crypt.

The thoroughfares off Trafalgar Square all lead to major attractions. Go through Admiralty Arch and down the Mall, past the Institute of Contemporary Art (p.194) and St James's Palace, and you'll reach Buckingham Palace (p.201). Head in the opposite direction from the square, towards the City, and you'll find yourself on the Strand, a famous riverside promenade of the 18th and 19th century (before the construction of the Thames Embankment) that at first glance now looks like just another of London's busy, traffic-choked streets. There are still some gems here though – the beautiful Somerset House, which was the capital's first purpose-built office space, is now home to world-class museum collections (p.208). Down on the river itself, Cleopatra's Needle

Household Cavalry

Nelson's Column

Whitehall

overlooks the water. This pink granite obelisk stood in Heliopolis in around 1500 BC and was given by the viceroy of Egypt to George IV in 1820.

And it doesn't stop there. Going back to Trafalgar Square as a starting point, a trip down Whitehall first offers up the splendour of Banqueting House (0870 7515178), all that remains of Whitehall Palace after it was destroyed by fire in 1698. Now primarily used for official state gatherings, the ceiling of the main hall is adorned with works by Rubens and, functions permitting, is open for the public to explore. Beyond that, a journey past the Cenotaph – where the Queen lays the first poppy wreath every November on Remembrance Sunday in honour of soldiers killed fighting for crown and country – and the Cabinet War Rooms (7930 6961), home to the Churchill Museum commemorating the former prime minister, leads you to Westminster Abbey and the Houses of Parliament (see p.204 and p.202).

Bloomsbury & Beyond

Rather less attractive at first glance are the roads around Euston and King's Cross stations. The spectacular British Library (see p.200) is the biggest draw, although King's Cross is one of the capital's neighbourhoods most frequently tipped as being 'on the up'. While it's still pretty grimy, there's a definite feel that something positive is in the air in this quirky area. Canvas nightclub (7833 8301) operates a nice sideline as a roller disco on Thursday and Friday nights, while Konstam at the Prince Albert (7833 5040) is a gastropub, located in a lavishly transformed Victorian boozer, that sources all its food from within the M25. Less than 10 minutes' walk away lies another pleasant surprise: Camley Street Natural Park (7833 2311), two acres of pretty green space in the middle of an otherwise relentless urban jungle. Back around King's Cross station, the beautiful Grade I-listed Midland Grand Hotel beside St Pancras is currently being restored after many years of neglect and uncertainty about its future. This glorious 19th century gothic revival building (which pop fans will recognise as the location of the Spice Girls video *Wannabe*) will once again operate as a hotel.

Easier to pin down is the pretty area of Bloomsbury, which has long been a favourite haunt of London's literary crowd. Writers Virginia Woolf and EM Forster, among others, were part of the famous Bloomsbury Group, while Charles Dickens once lived in Tavistock Square. These days, famous faces still abound – Ricky Gervais, creator of cult sitcom *The Office*, is just one of the well-known media types settled around here today. The biggest attraction in this part of town is the impressive British Museum (p.205). It would take a lifetime to pay proper attention to everything in the museum's vast collection, but luckily entry is free so you can return again and again. Just around the corner, The Cartoon Museum (7580 8155) is another hidden gem, as is the wonderful Renoir arthouse cinema in Brunswick Square (7837 8402). For something completely different, head to the fabulously kitsch All Star Lanes on Bloomsbury Place (p.240), a small, luxury 10-pin bowling venue complete with diner and swanky cocktail bar, all kitted out in a retro-American style.

Bloomsbury is rich in manicured gardens, such as those at Bedford and Russell squares, but a little further south in nearby Holborn is a real open-air treat. Lincoln's Inn Fields is London's largest garden square and is home to the wonderful Sir John Soane's Museum (see p.208). The architect designed and built his house in the late 18th century, both as somewhere to live and as a place to show off his collection of art and antiquities to the public.

Holborn in general has a restrained feel. The area is the heart of the city's legal profession. The four ancient Inns of Court, including the imposing Lincoln's Inn, are impressive structures, steeped in history and atmosphere. They are closed to visitors, but anyone with an interest in how the country's legal profession works can attend the public galleries of the Royal Courts of Justice on the Strand (7947 6000).

171

Roman ruins, the Tower of London and St Paul's, the modern 'Gherkin' office block – London's complete architectural history is here.

The Essentials
Tell a secret in the Whispering Gallery in St Paul's, take in the view from Rhodes 24, join in the procession at the annual Lady of Mount Carmel festival in Clerkenwell.

Overview map, p.166

East Central

The City of London sits on the site of Londinium, the urban colony founded by Roman invaders in the middle of the first century AD. Now the financial heart of capital and country, the City gleams with startling new architecture, such as 30 St Mary Axe (affectionately dubbed 'the Gherkin'). Most new buildings are high-rise office blocks that house the international banking fraternity, but there's more to the City than money; the area is awash with history.

On its southern edge lies the Tower of London, a fortress dating back to medieval times. Move forward several hundred years and you're in Dick Whittington's London. The famous mayor took office four times between 1397 and 1419 and was popular for his commitment to the capital's poor, introducing innovations such as public conveniences and drinking fountains. Sadly the church he was buried in was destroyed in the Great Fire in 1666, which wiped out about four-fifths of the City and led to an extensive reconstruction project under the directorship of Sir Christopher Wren. Many of the capital's landmark buildings, including St Paul's Cathedral (see p.202), are a legacy of this renowned architect.

The modern-day City is often accused of being soulless, an atmosphere critics say is embodied by the stark modern lines of the Barbican Centre, which has divided opinions since it was built in the 1960s. Certainly for anyone who visits after business hours or on weekends, the area, stripped of its half-million office workers, resembles a ghost town. But it can be fun to wander peacefully through a part of London that normally teems with life. Areas around the City proper, such as Smithfields and Farringdon, have become popular choices for urban homeowners in recent years, although it's unlikely that the City will turn into the Oxford Street of the east on a Saturday any time soon.

The City

The City of London is roughly defined by the remains of the old Roman wall that once encircled it. Though the destruction and subsequent rebuilding after the Great Fire brought London's standing as a walled city to a fairly abrupt close, fragments of it are still in evidence. You can see remnants of the original wall at the Tower of London (0870 7566060), originally built in the 11th century just outside the City boundaries, and its line clearly runs from there along Vine Street to Aldgate and beyond.

The area around London Wall also offers potential for Roman-ruin spotting. After a visit to the splendid Museum of London (see p.206), where the full history of the capital from pre-Roman times to the present day is revealed through a fascinating series of interactive displays, head to nearby Bastion Highwalk for a glimpse at a segment of the original wall itself. Better still, the Guildhall Art Gallery (see p.206) contains Londinium's original Roman amphitheatre, which dates from the second century AD.

Remains of the wall's original architecture are also woven into the fabric of the city itself. You can see it in the churchyard of St Botolph's Aldersgate on the corner of Little Britain and King Edward Street in EC1, where John Wesley converted to Methodism. The adjacent Postman's Park, a pretty patch of green where posties at the former General Post Office used to go for lunch, contains a touching 19th century memorial to ordinary Londoners who died while performing heroic acts of bravery. The brainchild of George Watts, a Victorian painter and philanthropist, it commemorates individuals and their deeds on a series of porcelain plaques.

Nearby is the Old Bailey (named after the street that followed the line of the fortified wall or 'bailey'), which sits next to what was the notorious Newgate Prison. Rebuilt in 1673 after the Great Fire and extensively added to since, London's main criminal law court is most famous for the distinctive gold statue of Justice, who stands on top of the building with her sword in one hand and scales in the other. Trials in session can be viewed from the public gallery (7248 3277).

It was the Great Fire that really redefined the landscape of the City. Starting in Pudding Lane and ending in Pye Corner, the fire burned for three days, destroying 87 churches and over 13,000 homes (some Londoners believed it was an act of retribution against their collective gluttony). The Wren-designed Monument (7627 2117) is the world's tallest single stone column. Built in 1677 to commemorate the fire, it sits 202 feet from where the fire started and offers magnificent views from over the city from the top. Across the City on Cock Lane, the Golden Boy of Pye Corner (a statue of a child, known as 'The Fat Boy', set into the wall) marks the place where it ended. But it is St Paul's Cathedral that is the greatest legacy of the Great Fire and remains Sir Christopher Wren's architectural masterpiece. The world's second-largest cathedral (after St Peter's in Rome), it celebrates its 300th birthday in 2008.

The City of London's current status as a financial powerhouse has forced huge changes on London's historical centre. The imposing Bank of England building on Threadneedle Street, which has a free museum accessed from Bartholomew Lane (7601 5491), has occupied the same site since 1734 – but other longstanding institutions haven't been so lucky. Old Billingsgate Fish Market existed on Lower Thames Street since the Middle Ages until it was moved to a new location on the Isle of Dogs in 1982 to make way for more shiny new office buildings, while Fleet Street's identity as London's home of journalism was slowly laid to rest after Rupert Murdoch moved his titles (including *The Times* and *The Sun*) to Wapping in the late 1980s. You can, however, still visit the house on nearby Gough Square where one of Fleet Street's most famous men of letters, Dr Samuel Johnson, lived and wrote the first edition of the English dictionary (7353 3745).

Cannon Street

Tower Bridge

Blackfriars Bridge

It's not all bad news though. The celebrated Gherkin (or 30 St Mary Axe to give it its correct title), which was built on a site that was badly damaged by an IRA bomb in 1992, is widely seen as a symbol of prosperous 21st century London. It's not open to the public but access is often granted during the annual London Open House architecture festival (see p.211). Alternatively, for a year-round taste of the modern City of London, visit the swanky Rhodes 24 restaurant on – you guessed it – the 24th floor of Tower 42 (see p.381) and combine fine dining with truly breathtaking views.

Barbican

Just outside the old city walls lies the Barbican Centre (7638 8891) in an area that was settled by the Romans ('barbican' means fortified watch tower). As stark a piece of 1960s architecture as the Southbank Centre across the river (see p.217), it too has been equally lauded and reviled by critics. The Barbican was developed as part of a rebuilding project after the area was severely damaged by bombing raids during the second world war. It contains a big residential development (despite – or perhaps because of – the architectural notoriety, its flats are some of the most sought after in central London) as well as a splendid arts centre, complete with galleries, theatres and one of the best cinemas in London.

But even the modern Barbican doesn't shy away from its history. A portion of a bastion of the original Roman wall can be seen above ground in the churchyard of St Giles' Cripplegate, located in the heart of the centre. This historic church was founded in the 11th century and is itself steeped in history. Oliver Cromwell was married in it in 1620 and the poet John Milton buried here in 1674. The church itself survived the Great Fire but was bombed during the second world war, so only the tower and walls now date back to the 16th century.

Close to St Bartholomew the Great's fine medieval church (7656 5171) and St Bartholomew's, London's oldest hospital, which both date back to 1123, is Smithfield Market. It has occupied the site between West Smithfield and Charterhouse Street for over 800 years and is still going strong. Today it employs over 3,000 people, has its own meat market and is legendary among the city's late-night clubbers and night-shift workers as one of the few places with early-opening pubs (an old licensing law stipulates that a pub next to a market can open from as early as 05:30). Check out Smiths of Smithfield (see p.382), an excellent four-storey restaurant complex serving up modern British food, including the finest of what's available from the nearby market.

Clerkenwell

Head a little further north-east and you reach Clerkenwell, another historic part of the city that has recently enjoyed a makeover. It was the site of one of the first big conversions of business space into residential space in the city, and is now full of fashionable bars, restaurants and boutique shops. The area clustered around Clerkenwell Green (also home to the London Masonic Centre) and the lovely cobbled Exmouth Market are particularly good spots, while nearby St John Street is lined with wonderful restaurants, including meat lovers' favourite St John (see p.383).

Local history isn't far away here either. Hatton Garden has been London's jewellery quarter for centuries and is still lined with shops selling gems, even as the surrounding streets have become home to whizzy kids specialising in new media. A stone's throw away, the Lady of Mount Carmel festival has been celebrated on the first Sunday after July 16th every year since 1883. In what was the first Catholic procession of its kind in Britain since the reformation, an effigy of the Madonna is carried through the streets from St Peter's Church in Clerkenwell Road. Today, Italians from all over London are drawn to the festival each year.

Are you always taking the wrong turn?

Whether you're a map person or not, this pocket-sized marvel will help you get to know the city... and its limits.

Explorer Mini Maps
Putting the city in your pocket

Overview map, p.166

North

North London is a mass of contradiction, and its best-known neighbourhood, Islington, is the perfect illustration of this. Adored by the left-wing middle classes who fell in love with the area's many stately Georgian and Victorian properties in the 1970s, and who have populated and popularised it ever since, Islington, like the wider north London community, is also a working-class enclave. High-rise council blocks sit uneasily beside stucco-fronted Edwardian mansions and, for all the area's vibrancy and obvious flash, there's an edge of aggression and decay that isn't going anywhere fast. In short, north London is in equal parts exciting and restful, downbeat and charming. Highgate, for example, is an area of largely quiet refinement, while Crouch End and Muswell Hill are popular with families and, like Islington, boast their fair share of liberal, creative types. Finsbury Park, meanwhile, has little to recommend it to the casual visitor, but its transient reputation means that it has long been popular with a diverse ethnic mix, from Afro-Caribbean to Thai.

Islington

Upper Street is Islington's spine. It runs all the way from Angel, near the City, north to Highbury & Islington station, and can get so busy with traffic and crowds that it moves with a bustle to rival that of Oxford Street. A journey along its length is like a sociological study of north London itself – it shifts from busy to calm, and high street to high-end. Towards Angel, Upper Street is home to supermarkets, chain stores, bawdy late-night boozers and the pleasingly chaotic Chapel Market, just off Liverpool Road. This section of the street is a flat, wide drag that makes it easy to miss the charms of Camden Passage – a discreet collection of boutiques, antique shops and home to a great collectibles market on weekends – which runs parallel to the main road.

Things start to become more refined at Islington Green, where Essex Road splits away from the main artery. Upper Street continues on to the left, the delightful Angel Flowers (see p.330), famous for its statuesque displays, signalling the change in demeanour. Boutiques and quirky furnishing stores nestle alongside treasures such as The Hart Gallery (7704 1131), showcasing modern paintings, sculptures and ceramics, and two feted independent theatres, the intimate King's Head (see p.425), part of the pub of the same name, and the Almeida (7359 4404), which attracts top international actors.

Islington Green

There is more to Islington than Upper Street, of course. To its west are the Edwardian terraces of Barnsbury (defined chiefly by Liverpool Road, on to which the massive Business Design Centre, home to the annual London Design Show, backs) and to its east, past a mixture of Georgian houses and dreary council blocks, lies Canonbury. This pretty, exclusive enclave is one of London's most sought-after addresses, and boasts a number of famous former residences – look out for the Blue Plaque at 17a Canonbury Square, marking the house where social satirist Evelyn Waugh once lived.

Islington isn't blessed with the open spaces that feature in other parts of north London. Highbury Fields, just north of Upper Street, is the area's largest parkland and notable for providing refuge to about 200,000 people who fled the Great Fire of London in 1666.

Stoke Newington

Hot on Islington's heels in the bohemian fashion stakes is the charming Stoke Newington, a little further north on the borders of Hackney. A lack of access by tube means that 'Stokey' will probably never have the cachet of its neighbour but, like Islington, trendy young media types have adopted the area as their own.

As in other parts of north London, rich and poor rub alongside one another in what can, at times, be a somewhat awkward alliance. Stoke Newington High Street, the suburb's other main thoroughfare, is busier and more down-at-heel than Church Street and its buzzing side roads of gastropubs and bric-a-brac shops, although the High Street offers excellent Middle Eastern grocers and restaurants. For the casual visitor, however, Clissold Park, bordered by Green Lanes, Church Street and Elizabeth's Walk, is a particular delight. With its deer enclosure, duck ponds, tennis courts and children's paddling pool, the bump and grind of city life feels a long way away.

Highgate, Finsbury Park & Beyond

If tracing an area's history through its deceased is your thing (and even if it's not), then a visit to London's most famous cemetery at Highgate (8340 1834) is a must. Located on the western borders of north London, Highgate is a leafy residential suburb that has much in common with nearby Hampstead. The cemetery is the resting place of Karl Marx, George Eliot and many more. The older West Cemetery is particularly atmospheric, with its overgrown headstones, wild flowers and extraordinary Egyptian catacombs – but access to this part is by guided tour only.

Rather less salubrious is nearby Finsbury Park. A busy, dirty area that is more thoroughfare than locale, its proximity to Arsenal Football Club's spectacular new Emirates Stadium (see p.287) ensures the tube and train stations get a lot of through traffic, though few visitors pause for more than a pint and a kebab on the way home. For those who want to linger, Gillespie Park, next door to the stadium on Gillespie Road, is home to the excellent Islington Ecology Centre (7354 5162) – a development of former railway land complete with wetlands, meadows and ponds. But the area is best known for Finsbury Park itself, which is a regular concert and festival venue (the annual Irish Fleadh and the Big Gay Out are both held here). A Sunday market takes place there every week, and its tennis courts and boating lake are popular with locals. North of Finsbury Park lies leafy Crouch End, a middle-class haven swarming with what are semi-affectionately known as 'yummy mummies' – well-educated 30-somethings who have dedicated themselves to full-time motherhood with a zeal that ensures their children are as fashionably dressed and accessorised as they are. Residents of Crouch End and neighbouring Muswell Hill often talk of a 'village' atmosphere (a feeling no doubt connected to the lack of tube access to the area), but these are very urbane villages, full of high-end, specialist delis and cute designer boutiques. Crouch End Broadway's redbrick clock tower is, literally, a striking monument dating from 1895. As the focal point of the area it's a great starting place for browsing the shops of Crouch Hill, Tottenham Lane and Park Road, the last of which leads directly up to Muswell Hill. Muswell Hill Golf Club (8888 1764) is a private 18 hole course that welcomes visitors during the week and has limited spaces on weekends. But it is nearby Alexandra Palace (8365 2121) that is the area's most visited attraction. Set within 196 acres of parkland and with great views over central London, 'Ally Pally' is an exhibition venue that was first opened in 1873 as a recreation centre for Victorian London (the original building was destroyed by fire only 16 days after it opened, but was rebuilt again by 1875). Alongside its ever-changing roster of events, the Palace is home to a spectacular indoor ice rink (see p.260), a delightful conservation area and a beautiful if somewhat dilapidated Victorian theatre, currently a pet restoration project for local actors including *Truly, Madly, Deeply* star Juliet Stephenson.

The Lowdown ◀
*Literary and eccentric,
popular with families,
and home to London's
largest uncultivated
parkland at
Hampstead Heath.*

The Essentials
*Enjoy a pint at the
Spaniard's Inn, where
legendary highwayman
Dick Turpin was said to
have been born. Take
a dip in Hampstead
Heath's bathing
ponds, and watch
cricket at Lord's.*

Overview map, p.166

North-West

It's been said that north-west London is tolerant of eccentricity, and nowhere is that more true than in Camden Town, with its bustling market, thriving indie scene and, less appealingly, its reputation for drugs, crime and living rough. But eccentricity in varying degrees is a quality found across most of the region.

Lovely, bookish Hampstead, for example, is not only a favourite residence of celebrities and London's intelligentsia, it also has a reputation for being the centre of psychotherapy in the city – Sigmund Freud was one of its most famous residents. Exclusive Primrose Hill, meanwhile, became famous in the 90s for the romantic and hedonistic antics of the so-called 'Primrose Hill set', broadly comprised of actor Jude Law, his then wife Sadie Frost, supermodel Kate Moss and various famous hangers-on who lived in or frequented the area.

North-west London isn't without the social problems of other parts of town though. Camden's earthy ways are arguably a large part of its appeal, while Kentish Town, slightly further north, has a reputation for being rough around the edges, despite its increasing popularity with families. However, the region is also home to some of London's loveliest neighbourhoods, such as the well-heeled St John's Wood and nearby Belsize Park, and boasts acres of beautiful parkland.

Hampstead

This part of London is blessed with more than its fair share of places that people will go out of their way to pay a special visit to, but only Camden, with its hugely popular market, is a bigger draw than Hampstead.

The greatest attraction here is Hampstead Heath (see p.213). Featuring nearly 800 acres of semi-wild parkland, the Heath's highlights include its famous bathing ponds, the spectacular views from Parliament Hill, and the neo-classical splendour of Kenwood House (see p.199). Kenwood is home to a stunning art collection featuring works by Turner, Vermeer and Rembrandt, and its grounds play host to a series of classical and popular concerts – past performers include Elvis Costello, the English National Opera and Abba tribute band Bjorn Again, although there are no concerts planned for 2007. Kenwood's lovely Brew House Cafe is a great spot to stop for a bite or, for a real taste of history, pop into the Spaniards Inn (8731 6571), where rumour has it that legendary highwayman Dick Turpin was born. And Turpin's not the only eminent local – Hampstead has long been associated with famous names. Current residents include George Michael, Boy George and 'M' herself, Dame Judy Dench, but a visit to Burgh House (7431 0144), a Grade I-listed building, reveals others. The house was built in 1704 when Hampstead's reputation was as a spa (drawn from the nearby Wells), and is now home to the Hampstead Museum, featuring displays honouring former residents including painter John Constable, novelist DH Lawrence and artist Stanley Spencer. Other historic houses of note are Keats House Museum (7435 2062), where the great Romantic wrote *Ode to a Nightingale*, and the Freud Museum (7435 2002). The lovely Arts & Crafts building honours the great psychoanalyst – who lived here until his death in 1839 – and even has his famous sofa on display. But if all that analysis gets too much, head to the boutiques lining the pretty cobbled streets tucked off Hampstead High Street and indulge in a little retail therapy instead.

Camden

Camden Town built its reputation in the late 1970s. If King's Road in Chelsea was punk's spiritual home, then Camden provided the elbow grease. Famous venues such as Dublin Castle (7485 1773) nurtured much of the city's music talent – The Buzzcocks and The Clash both played there, and it's where Madness got their big break – and the music scene is as strong as ever today. Other local treats include the Jazz Cafe (7916 6060) and

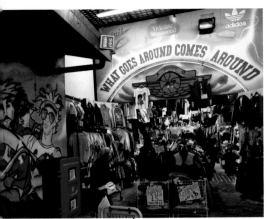

Camden Market

Barfly (p.440), currently *the* indie venue to be seen at, while the recently revamped Roundhouse (7424 9991) across the road celebrates an older, slightly more sedate scene.

If it seems like much of Camden's reputation is built around going out, that's because it is. Bars and restaurants run the length of Camden High Street through to the end of Chalk Farm Road, and are buzzing seven days a week. But the area's main attraction is the internationally famous Camden Market (see p.368), the main site of which was converted from Camden Lock's wharves and warehouses in the 70s. Made up of six different markets, things really get going on weekends when Stables Market, housed in a former horse hospital on Chalk Farm Road, opens its doors.

The amount of people can be pretty unbearable at the height of the weekend throng. A mostly young crowd, made up of goths, indie kids and rockers, swarm the area around Camden Town tube station and nearby Stables Market, picking at the Doc Martens, antiques and bric-a-brac, or hunting out a bargain at the various classic vintage clothing emporia. Even so, it's still possible to get away from the crowds – the quiet calm of Regent's Canal, accessed via the bridges over Camden Lock, is only moments away.

Primrose Hill & Beyond

Geographically, Camden Town and Primrose Hill are close neighbours, separated by little more than a railway line. Spiritually, however, they couldn't be further apart. Whereas the former revels in its rough and ready reputation, and its penchant for indie types and travellers with dogs on strings, Primrose Hill is primarily a leafy, well-to-do residential area that, like nearby Hampstead, has long been associated with creative, arty types – a sort of exclusive bohemia for those with a gold card.

The area is most famous for Primrose Hill itself – a pretty mound of grass set atop a compact park on the northern border of the considerably grander Regent's Park. Up until a few years ago, the space was famous for its annual Guy Fawkes fireworks celebrations (p.47), but overcrowding led to the local authorities putting a stop to that. However, Primrose Hill's fine views over London ensure that it's still a big draw for locals and people that come from further afield – on a sunny day you can hardly move for picnic blankets and frisbees. Back at street level, most of the action takes place along Regent's Park Road, home to good local restaurants, independent shops and boutiques. Designer furniture store Boom Interiors (7722 6622) is a highlight – it began life at Stables Market down the hill 10 years previously, and broke the mould by making a successful transfer from Camden to the 'other side'.

One of the biggest attractions in nearby St John's Wood, however, isn't really an attraction at all. Abbey Road Studios is famous as the workplace for The Beatles, but isn't open to the public. You can take a virtual tour on www.abbeyroad.co.uk, or join the ranks of the thousands of fans who've taken their photo at the famous zebra crossing nearby – but do take care to avoid the passing traffic. The area's other celebrated landmark is Lord's cricket ground (7616 8500). The home of the Marylebone Cricket Club hosts regular matches, from county games to international Tests, and fans can tour the grounds and museum all year round. You can even book a coaching session at the MCC Indoor School based there, or pop into the onsite Lord's Tavern Bar & Brasserie for a pint.

179

The Lowdown
Genteel residential properties, sophisticated cafe culture and monied bohemia.

The Essentials
Join the crowds at Notting Hill Carnival, haggle for a bargain at Portobello Market and tour the canals of Little Venice.

Overview map, p.166

West

Rich with leafy grandeur, fashionability and abundant multiculturalism, west London has long been one of the most desirable parts of the capital to live in. Notting Hill is its shopfront, advertising the best of what's on offer – its famous market, Afro-Caribbean heritage and cool boutiques are calling cards to visitors and city residents alike.

But there is more to see than just Notting Hill. West London is broadly bordered on one side by Hyde Park and Kensington Gardens, and stretches out west towards Heathrow airport. In between, the area is home to the refined watery delights of Little Venice, with its colourful, bobbing canal boats and millionaires' mansions, the itinerant populations of Paddington and Bayswater, and the inevitable pockets of inner-city scrum that are the vibrant, if unlovely, main highways of Shepherd's Bush and Hammersmith. All in all it makes for an eclectic mix, but one that seems for the most part to work rather well.

Notting Hill

It's hard for anyone visiting Notting Hill to imagine it as anything but an exclusive place to live. However, during the 1950s, Notting Hill, with its predominantly West Indian population, was more famous for its race riots than its carnival. Even as late as the 80s and early 90s, W11 was still considered edgy, but an influx of money brought (and bought) stability. The area is distinctly marked by rich and poor parts, but in central Notting Hill the blend of multiculturalism, consumerism and laid-back charm is successful.

The backbone of Notting Hill is Ladbroke Grove. Famous for being a main part of the Notting Hill Carnival parade route (see p.212), Ladbroke Grove's wide sweep runs from Kensal Rise at its top end through the junctions of Lansdowne and Stanley crescents, whose curves nod to a time in the 1830s when Notting Hill was home to a horse-racing track, and into the genteel splendour of Holland Park, one the city's most exclusive addresses.

There's another street in the area, however, that is even more well-known. Portobello Road (where a struggling George Orwell once lived in a bedsit at number 22) is home to the weekly antiques and bric-a-brac market, and is packed solid every Saturday (see p.369). For a quieter alternative, consider visiting on a Friday for the market that takes place directly opposite a run of tasty, cheap eateries, including the splendid S&M Café (p.418) – that's sausage and mash – under the Westway.

Portobello Road runs from Notting Hill Gate to Golborne Road at its upper end where, under the shadow of Erno Goldfinger's infamous Trellick Tower, the area's shabby-chic ethos remains intact. It's also home to a vibrant Portuguese community – the Lisboa Patisserie (8968 5242) is well-served by locals. This is the gateway to the Grand Union Canal too. It's a pretty stretch of waterway that, if followed west, leads directly to the Victorian splendour of Kensal Green Cemetery, which was immortalised by GK Chesteron in his poem *The Rolling English Road*, and where pioneering engineer Isambard Kingdom Brunel is buried.

Considerably more upmarket is the shop frontage around the top end of Westbourne Grove and Ledbury Road, where boutiques and restaurants act as honey to the bee for the monied masses. On any given day you could be sharing aisle space with the many A-listers frequently spotted in these parts, from Gwyneth Paltrow, Kate Moss and Stella McCartney to local Nobel prize-winning author Harold Pinter.

But for all its modish makeovers, the area still exudes a waggish charm. Sure you can sit in

Portobello Road

West

Carnival Chaos

The Notting Hill Carnival is a festival of colour, noise and round-the-clock partying that draws thousands of revellers each year. The downside is that the streets become full-to-bursting, making it impossible to get from one side of Notting Hill to the other in a hurry (you literally can't move in places). If you're meeting friends somewhere in the throng, or trying to get to a particular music stage, it's essential to plan where to enter the fray from. You can access the area from several tube stations, including Westbourne Park, Queensway, Latimer Road and Notting Hill Gate (some close at certain points over the weekend), but pick the wrong one and you could be waving your carnival arrangements goodbye.

the comfort of a plush leather armchair while watching the latest movie at the Electric Cinema (7908 9696), but you can also still rub shoulders with the market traders at Mike's Cafe (7229 3757) on Blenheim Crescent, once a favourite haunt of punk rockers The Clash. For all the real and present worries about Portobello Road turning into yet another high-street clone, classics such as Rough Trade records (p.340) have been feeding the city's taste for alternative music for close to 30 years, while nearby Peoples Sound on All Saints Road keeps the reggae beats alive (7792 9321).

Westbourne Grove, Shepherd's Bush & Beyond

Little Venice is an oasis in the heart of London, tucked away in the otherwise largely residential Maida Vale. Officially occupying the relatively small basin where the Grand Union and Regent's canals meet at the junction of Westbourne Terrace Road and Blomfield Road, this pretty area of water is home to a number of barges and narrowboats, including a cafe, gallery and, in the winter, a children's puppet theatre (7249 6876). It's perfect for a weekend stroll – five minutes west leads you to the fashionable Waterway pub (7266 3557), while the journey east takes you through to Regent's Park and Camden. To the south lies Paddington Basin, where a long regeneration project aimed at transforming the waterway into a desirable urban development is nearing completion. It's a welcome bit of spruce and polish for Paddington, an area that, despite its proximity to the West End, has always remained slightly scruffy and transitory. From here it's just a short hop to the uneasy charms of Bayswater. With its mix of stately white-fronted mansions and a jumble of backpackers' hostels and hotels, Bayswater's proximity to Hyde Park and Kensington Gardens (see p.214) cannot be underestimated as one of its chief draws. The main drag, Queensway, has the air of a rundown outpost of Oxford Street, all cheap chain stores and shops selling union jack tea towels. However, a good mix of ethnic restaurants along Queensway and the easterly end of Westbourne Grove go a long way to redressing this balance. The same goes for The Porchester Centre (see p.300), which features an art deco spa that is no less charming for being slightly old-fashioned, and Whiteleys, an imposing Edwardian shopping centre and multiplex that was London's first department store (p.355). Bayswater Road runs west into Notting Hill Gate and the desirable mansions and shops of Holland Park Avenue. Lidgate butchers (7727 8243) is regularly voted one of London's best, while nearby Portland Road hosts a number of pricey-but-lovely boutiques, including vintage clothing emporia Virginia (7727 9908). Best of all is the neighbourhood's eponymous park. One of the prettiest in London, it features roaming peacocks, a serene Japanese garden, orangery and outdoor theatre, and remains remarkably unbothered by tourists, who rarely make it past Kensington Gardens. Nearby Shepherd's Bush offers few similar charms, although it is trying to improve. Away from the pollution-choked fug of Shepherd's Bush Green, the environs of Goldhawk Road are home to a rising number of upmarket bars and restaurants. There are also two great local entertainment venues – the Shepherd's Bush Empire (8354 3300) and the Bush Theatre (7610 4224). With the BBC Television Centre right on the northern edge of Shepherd's Bush (call 0870 6030304 for studio tours), the area has long been ripe for a media-led middle-class makeover – the only real surprise is that it is taking so long. Neighbouring Hammersmith is even more split in personality – the frenetic rush of the area's main artery, King Street, is in stark contrast to leafy Brook Green and laid-back Hammersmith Grove. The biggest attraction in this part of town, however, is the river. The Dove (8748 5405) on the charming Upper Mall is a tiny, ancient riverside pub in the shadow of the handsome Hammersmith Bridge. This and other pubs on the stretch of the Thames, right the way along to the exclusive houses of Chiswick Mall, really come alive on a summer's evening. It's a great place to enjoy a drink before heading to the nearby Riverside Studios (8237 1111) or a gig at the Hammersmith Apollo (0870 6063400).

The Lowdown
*Sophisticated and
urbane with the best of
London's high and low
culture. Outdoor
spaces in abundance.*

The Essentials
*Get lost in the V&A,
hang out at the
Chelsea Physic Garden
cafe, cool off in
Brockwell Lido on a hot
summer's day.*

Overview map, p.166

South-West

Some of the most charming neighbourhoods in London can be found in the south-west of the city. Chelsea, with its world-famous King's Road, was the centre of all that was cool about the capital for much of the later part of the 20th century, while South Kensington's many museums, monuments and seats of learning have long made it a focal point for education and the arts.

Much of it is very pretty too, as is fitting for a swathe of the city that boasts many of its most desirable addresses. Chelsea is home to row upon row of beautiful white stucco-fronted mansions, as well as an attractive wharf and an exclusive riverfront development, while Clapham and Wandsworth, on the south side of the Thames, are blessed with wide, open commons that have attracted an influx of young professionals over the past decade or so, putting a little buzz into the neighbourhoods.

And let's not forget that this part of town is synonymous with one of the most well-known international sports tournaments. Wimbledon plays host to the legendary tennis Grand Slam tournament each summer (see p.291), livening up what is, for the rest of the year, another leafy part of town. South-west London is by no means all quiet exclusivity and high refinement though – south-east of Clapham lies Brixton, one of the capital's liveliest neighbourhoods.

South Kensington

Just along from Kensington High Street, perched at the far corner of Kensington Gardens, is the golden, gothic spire of the George Gilbert Scott-designed Albert Memorial. This lavish tribute, commissioned by Queen Victoria in honour of her late husband and finished in 1872, marks the gateway to South Kensington – a fitting pointer as much of the surrounding monuments and museums sprang from the artistic and intellectual curiosity of the Victorian age.

Directly across the road from the Albert Memorial lies the rotund Royal Albert Hall (7589 8212), where short daytime tours of the auditorium and backstage are available. Opposite is the Royal College of Art (7590 4444), a world-class postgraduate university that hosts external art fairs and exhibitions in its main gallery (check out its annual Secrets sale, in which postcard-sized works by the likes of David Bailey, Manolo Blahnik and Damien Hirst can be picked up for £35).

Royal Albert Hall

In the streets behind the Albert Memorial lie more educational institutions, including the Royal College of Music and Imperial College, plus a number of international embassies and foundations. The Goethe-Institut (7596 4000) is a cultural centre that promotes the German language abroad and is home to the charming Hugo's organic cafe (7596 4006), while the nearby Institut Francais houses the Cine Lumiere (7073 1350), which shows an excellent programme of French films with English subtitles.

The main attractions in South Kensington, however, are the 'big three' – the trio of world-famous

Walk or Ride?

Some tube stops may be closer together than you think. What looks like a long distance on the underground map is sometimes not quite so far above ground. It takes longer to get the tube from Piccadilly Circus to Leicester Square than to walk it – they are only two minutes apart. Conversely, try to walk from Golders Green to Brent Cross – the same distance apart on the map – and it'll take you at least half an hour. It's always worth cross-checking against an overground map.

museums grouped around the base of Exhibition Road. The Natural History Museum, the Science Museum and the Victoria & Albert Museum are vast monuments to Victorian curiosity that have grown to become three of the world's greatest museums (see p.207).

Aside from educational establishments, the nearby Brompton Oratory (7808 0900) is a magnificent Italianate baroque-style Catholic church that is the exact replica of the Gesu Church in Rome. A very different kind of worship is indulged in nearby Knightsbridge, home to Harrods, the self-styled 'world's most famous department store' (see p.356), and where Sloane Street pays retail homage to the biggest names in fashion design.

Chelsea

For a generation of Londoners there is a part of Chelsea that forever swings, while for another it's an abiding symbol of punk rock. But whichever way you cut it, King's Road is undoubtedly one of the capital's most iconic thoroughfares. The centre of 'Swinging London' in the 1960s, and home to Vivienne Westwood and Malcolm McLaren's groundbreaking shop, Sex, in the 1970s, its special mix of bohemia and wealth has long been part of its attraction.

While a visit to King's Road no longer holds such cultural sway, it still affords a splendid opportunity to peek into the area's social past. The array of English Heritage Blue Plaques cladding its shopfronts and houses includes *Rule Britannia* composer Thomas Arne at 215, while 19th century pre-Raphaelite artist Dante Gabriel Rossetti once lived at nearby Cheyne Walk, the exclusive strip of riverfront housing that was more recently home to Mick Jagger. Today, artist Damien Hirst is the proud owner of one of the many luxury houseboats moored in nearby Chelsea Harbour.

But it's not all famous faces and cultural trends in Chelsea. The Royal Court Theatre (7565 5000) at the Knightsbridge end of King's Road celebrated 50 years of independent theatre in 2006 – John Osborne's *Look Back in Anger* was the first play to be staged there – and its reputation for finding and developing new talent continues to grow. A little further south, on the banks of the Thames, the Royal Hospital Chelsea (7881 5200) is a Sir Christopher Wren-designed architectural extravagance that has been home to veteran soldiers since 1689. The site's extensive grounds play host to the annual Chelsea Flower Show in May (see p.210), while visitors at other times of the year can explore its courtyards, chapel and hall for free, or pop into the onsite National Army Museum (7881 2455).

A short stroll away you'll find the delightful Chelsea Physic Garden (7352 5646). Founded by the Worshipful Society of Apothecaries in 1673, it studies the benefits of botany in relation to medicine. The beautiful garden that was planted at its founding to help apprentices learn to identify plants is one of London's best-kept secrets and a wonderful place to while away a summer afternoon.

Fulham & Beyond

Follow King's Road west and you'll arrive at Fulham. While not quite in the same league as Chelsea in terms of out-and-out wealth, Fulham is still one of London's upmarket boroughs and a popular place for City workers to live. Fulham Broadway is the hub of the action here, with plenty of bars and eateries that attract a young crowd – although it can get rowdy on weekends and evenings and when Chelsea Football Club (whose Stamford Bridge ground is actually in Fulham) play at home. At the other end of the borough, refined Parsons Green is home to the famous White Horse pub (7736 2115). This hugely popular place serves a vast array of beers, and food from an outside grill in summer, although its reputation for attracting

183

Brixton Backlash

Underlying tension between Brixton's Afro-Caribbean community and the Metropolitan Police erupted into violence in April 1981 in some of the worst public disorder the capital has seen. The troubles were blamed on aggressive 'stop and search' tactics and alleged racism among officers. The rioting spread across the country in the following months forcing then Prime Minister Margaret Thatcher to launch a wide-scale enquiry. The landmark findings by Lord Scarman into the Brixton troubles found that huge unemployment and poverty were factors in the unrest and that police had disproportionately targeted black people.

well-to-do patrons has earned it the moniker of the 'Sloaney Pony'. Beyond Parsons Green, the western ends of Fulham Road and New King's Road are home to an interesting range of independent shops, restaurants and bars, including the excellent Nomad Books shop and cafe (7736 4000), while the riverside Bishops Park is a great place for watching the teams of dedicated rowers as they toil up and down the Thames from the boatsheds of Putney on the opposite shore.

For more riverside action, cross the Thames and head south-west to the charming 'villages' of Barnes, Kew and Richmond. Kew is famously home to the exquisite Royal Botanic Gardens (p.219) and is easily reached from London by tube and rail, while the rugged Richmond Park is London's largest Royal Park (p.215).

Still south of the river but further east is Wandsworth, an area popular with young professionals. Historically, Wandsworth Town is known for sheltering Protestant craftsmen from Europe fleeing religious persecution – the Huguenot cemetery can still be seen – and the old-fashioned feel of the area is further enhanced by the sight of ale from the nearby Young's brewery being delivered to local pubs by horse and cart. In recent years, Wandsworth has also become a destination for gourmands from all over the capital – Chez Bruce (8672 0114) by Wandsworth Common is a popular restaurant that serves up Michelin-star food. Nearby Tooting Bec offers people the chance to burn off any unwanted calories in its attractive lido (see p.215), the largest open-air pool in Europe.

Battersea & Brixton

Next to Wandsworth is Battersea, with its sweeping park, monumental disused power station and famous Dogs & Cats Home (7622 3626), and below it lies Clapham. This one-time overlooked part of the capital has come into its own in recent years and is now a draw for families and young professionals. The wide, flat space of Clapham Common, a popular summer venue for outdoor cinema, concerts and events, divides the suburb neatly in half. On one side, Clapham Junction features the bustling Northcote Road as is its focal point. Here you'll find a good range of independent shops and buzzing restaurants and bars. Be sure to stop at the wonderful Hive Honey Shop (7824 6233), a temple to all things honey-related and home to a five-foot-high glass-fronted beehive that houses some 20,000 bees. The excellent Battersea Arts Centre (7223 6557) on nearby Lavender Hill is a thriving independent theatre in what was once the local town hall.

On the south side of Clapham Common, Clapham Park is a chichi enclave, the hub of which centres around the shops and cafes of Abbeville Road. At times it's hard to believe that the ethnic charms of multicultural Brixton are just next door, but a quick stroll up Brixton Hill to Coldharbour Lane brings you into the centre of one of London's most vibrant neighbourhoods.

With its large Afro-Caribbean population, Brixton is to south London what Notting Hill was to west – but the former has so far resisted the level of gentrification that has changed the

face of the latter. The area has an edgy reputation, from the riots of the 1980s to its high crime rate, but there are few parts of the capital with such a buzz. Brixton Academy (7771 3000) is one of London's top live music venues, the Ritzy Cinema (7733 2229) is an independent film fan's dream, and there are pockets of local history everywhere, including the tribute to post-war Caribbean immigrants just off the market in Windrush Square. Browse the bustling street market around Electric Avenue (so-called for being the first shopping street in Britain to be lit by electricity) or cool off on a summer's day in the beautifully restored Brockwell Lido (see p.215).

The world has much to offer.
It's just knowing where to find it.

If you're an American Express® Cardmember, simply visit
americanexpress.com/selects or visit your local homepage, and click on
'offers'. You'll find great offers wherever you are today, all in one place.

selects

Overview map, p.166

South-East

The Lowdown

Sophisticated and cultural, with some of London's most unique 'village' atmospheres at Greenwich and Dulwich Village.

The Essentials

Borough Market on a Friday or Saturday morning, arriving at Greenwich by boat along the Thames, taking in a movie at the NFT, the views across London from the outside balcony of Tate Modern's members' room.

Central south-east London used to be a pretty grim place. The Southbank Centre was a stark, concrete wasteland visited by a cultural elite, Bankside as a destination didn't really exist, and Waterloo was known for little more than being a transport hub and, of course, its bridge. Over the last 10 years, however, all that has changed. London's South Bank is now one of the capital's great attractions, particularly during the summer when the river views and street festivals draw crowds in their thousands.

Elsewhere, the area has livened up considerably too. Borough, a previously unprepossessing part of the city between Waterloo and London Bridge, blossomed as its produce market developed into a Mecca for foodies everywhere, with the nearby Tate Modern helping to draw in the crowds. Further afield, self-contained suburbs such as Greenwich and Dulwich are popular with families, their village-like atmospheres attractive to locals and visitors alike.

Some parts of the area are still beset with problems, however. Elephant and Castle, with its hulking shopping centre and ring roads, never seems to move any closer to a persistently predicted makeover, while neighbourhoods such as Camberwell and Peckham continue to be associated with street crime and disharmony despite regeneration projects and an influx of professional couples and young families. Meanwhile, the lack of tube stations in suburban south-east London means that it's a part of the city that will always remain off the main tourist trail.

South Bank & Bankside

The first of many must-sees here is the London Eye (see p.217). You'll catch sight of it from all over London, but it's actually located just west of Hungerford Bridge, a spectacular construction designed by Isambard Kingdom Brunel in 1841, and renovated in 2000. In the seven years since the London Eye opened, at the turn of the millennium, this stunning observation wheel has become the capital's biggest star – beautiful to look at and fun to ride. Nestling nearby is London Aquarium (p.221), one of the biggest exhibitions of global aquatic life in Europe. It also shares building space with Dali Universe (0870 7447485), where more than 500 of the Spanish surrealist artist's works are on permanent display.

On the other side of Hungerford Bridge lies the Southbank Centre (see p.217), home to such treasures as the National Theatre, Hayward Gallery and the recently renovated Royal Festival Hall. The sharp concrete lines of brutal 1960s architecture make the centre hard to miss and have been the focus of much controversy over the decades. But the general livening up of the South Bank area, including the run of restaurants, bars and cafes that now line the riverbank, have brought the one thing that was needed to soften the area's harsh architecture – people. It also houses the National Film

Listing Logic
Listed building status is awarded as a means of protecting buildings that are deemed to have architectural or historical value. The system is administered by English Heritage, and listed status is classed by grades – either I, II* or II, with Grade I the most important. There are well over 350,000 listed buildings in the UK, the majority of which are older, classic properties, such as the Old Royal Naval College and Eltham Palace, but also include more unusual examples. These include Trellick Tower, the high-rise block of flats in west London once considered a symbol of urban decay but now a desirable residential spot; the entrance to the Blackwall Tunnel; and even the elephant and penguin houses at London Zoo.

Theatre (7928 3232), one of London's best cinemas. It features a programme of classic retrospectives and previews, and is a major venue for the London Film Festival held each November.

Continuing eastwards, Gabriel's Wharf, just past London Television Centre (where programmes such as *The South Bank Show* are filmed), offers a good selection of restaurants, cafes and bars in a pretty, cobbled setting. Next is the Oxo Tower, which separates the South Bank from the area known as Bankside. The Tower's distinctive 'OXO' logo was built into the brickwork to circumvent an order banning advertising on the site. Its eighth-floor restaurant (7803 3888) provides one of London's best views and is a favourite for romantic dates, while the Coin Street area around it is popular with artists. It houses numerous small galleries and artisan shops, and is home to the annual summer Coin Street Festival (www.coinstreetfestival.org).

Bankside is home to the Tate Modern (see p.196), a temple to contemporary art converted from a disused power station. The Millennium Bridge, which spans the Thames directly outside the Tate, was the first new footbridge to be built across the river in over a century, but had to be closed shortly after it opened in 2000 as it swayed when people started to walk across it. Even though that problem has long been resolved, Londoners still affectionately refer to it as the 'wobbly bridge'. Shakespeare's Globe (p.202) is here as well, offering an authentic, if somewhat rarefied, taste of Elizabethan London.

A little further along the river, near London Bridge, this sense of stepping back in time increases. Here, visitors will find a replica of The Golden Hinde, explorer Sir Francis Drake's ship, along with eerie treasures such as The Clink Prison museum (7403 0900), the atmospheric 17th century Old Operating Theatre museum (7188 2679) and, of course, that blockbuster attraction, The London Dungeon (7403 7221).

Borough

Lying in the shadow of Southwark Cathedral, Borough Market is a wholesale fruit and veg market that has been trading on this spot for centuries (see p.368). It's long been a fascinating attraction in its own right, but the boom in organic and 'real' food across Britain in recent years has put Borough on the foodie map – every Friday and Saturday the market teems with Londoners out to get their hands on some of the freshest and finest meat and produce in the capital. The atmospheric streets around the market have also proved a favourite with filmmakers, featuring in hits such as *Bridget Jones's Diary* and *Lock, Stock and Two Smoking Barrels*.

Southwark Cathedral (7367 6700) itself is also worth a visit. The site has been home to places of worship for over 1,000 years, although the main structure of today's church was built over 200 years from 1220. John Gower, one of the fathers of English poetry and a friend and contemporary of the better-remembered Geoffrey Chaucer, is buried here. It's a lovely spot to escape the bustle of the city. Alternatively, pop into the nearby Bramah Museum of Tea and Coffee (7403 5650), a delightfully informative homage to the English love affair with the cuppa.

Greenwich

Considerably further east along the river is Greenwich. Stepping off the train or boat here is rather like entering another world – or another London, at least. This pretty, green neighbourhood is the birthplace of Greenwich Mean Time, has been designated a Unesco World Heritage Site, boasts hundreds of acres of glorious parkland, and is steeped in maritime history.

Highlights within Greenwich Park itself include the Royal Observatory and the National Maritime Museum (see p.207), along with lesser-known attractions just as worthy of a visit. One such place is Ranger's House (8853 0035), an elegant

187

Marathon Journey
Although south-east London is not the capital's first port of call for most when exploring London, some parts of the area may be already familiar to many – thanks to the London Marathon. The first half of the annual event, which is run by thousands and watched on TV by millions, winds its way through the streets of the south-east, taking in Blackheath, Greenwich Park, the Cutty Sark and Bermondsey before crossing the Thames at Tower Bridge. Unfortunately for the runners, there are still another 13 miles – and a lot more pain – to go on the north side of the river…

Georgian villa that, as the name suggests, was once home to the 'Ranger of Greenwich Park' (an aristocratic entitlement rather than a post for a common labourer). The building is now home to the Wernher Collection – a wonderful anthology of over 700 pieces of medieval and renaissance works of art. Also on the edge of the park, the nearby Fan Museum (8305 1441) is the only registered museum in the world dedicated to its subject. Boasting over 4,000 fans dating from the 11th century, it's a delightfully eccentric treat.

The area's other big maritime attraction is the Cutty Sark (8858 3445), a former tea clipper that last sailed commercially in 1922 before being dry-docked in Greenwich in 1954. The ship is currently closed to the public while much-needed renovations on the old girl are carried out, although a temporary exhibition next to the ship is planned to open in early 2007 and will remain there until the boat reopens in late 2008.

The main shopping area around Greenwich Church Street is a great place to browse independent boutiques, but the real retail draw around these parts is Greenwich Market. It's open throughout the week, but this covered market really comes into its own on weekends when day trippers arrive from all over the city to browse stalls selling handicrafts, clothing, collectables and antiques. And while you're there pay a visit to the beautiful Hawksmoor-designed St Alfege Church, built in 1714 on the site where St Alfege, a former Archbishop of Canterbury, was reputedly captured and killed by Danes in 1012.

Of course the centrepiece around here was supposed to be the Millennium Dome, housed a little further away in the light-industrial and rather unlovely North Greenwich neighbourhood. The Dome opened to much fanfare on millennium eve, but was dogged by bad press and bad luck and closed ignominiously shortly after. It is now being converted into the O2 Arena, an entertainment centre due to open in July 2007. A better bet in the meantime is to stroll the Thames Path to the Thames Barrier, where the Information and Learning Centre (8305 4188) offers a fascinating insight into London's flood-defence system.

Dulwich & Beyond

Head south and slightly west from Greenwich and you'll reach Dulwich, an area that offers a taste of village-like charm to visitors unlikely to travel to many of south-east London's other largely residential neighbourhoods – although cricket fans are likely to want to make a trip to Kennington to visit The Oval (see p.287).

Busy Lordship Lane in East Dulwich offers a good selection of bars, boutiques and restaurants – the award-winning organic butcher William Rose (8693 9191) is a particular favourite – and runs towards Dulwich Village, where there are open spaces in abundance. The land around Dulwich College, originally set up in 1619 by Edward Alleyn to offer education for the poor but now an exclusive public school, is host to a good local farmers' market on the fourth Sunday of every month, while at nearby Dulwich Park you can take a spin on one of the recumbent bikes available for hire, or just relax in the pleasant cafe. But perhaps the biggest attraction around here is the Dulwich Picture Gallery (see p.194), one of London's finest.

Further south lies Crystal Palace Park, where the remains of the original Crystal Palace can still be seen. It was built for the Great Exhibition of 1851 in Hyde Park and later transferred to south-east London, but was destroyed by fire in 1936.

The park was the site of the world's first 'theme park' – constructions of then recently discovered dinosaurs were put up to illustrate the process of evolution before the publication of Charles Darwin's *Origin of the Species*, and they still stand there today. Also in the park is the 160ft circular Tea Maze, one of the largest in the country.

Painted Hall, Greenwich

Cutty Sark

Old Royal Naval College

Chapel, Old Royal Naval College

Overview map, p.166

East

The Lowdown
Cool bars, cutting-edge art galleries and vibrant multiculturalism sit alongside some of the capital's poorest and most deprived neighbourhoods.

The Essentials
Visit Columbia Road Flower Market on a Sunday morning, enjoy early-morning bagels and coffee on Brick Lane, enjoy a picnic in Victoria Park, explore Dennis Severs' spooky 'living museum'.

East London has seen some of London's biggest change in fortunes in recent years. Since the 1990s, Hoxton, Shoreditch and Spitalfields have become the capital's cool quarter, home to art galleries, independent boutiques, nightclubs and bars. Elsewhere in the area, slowly but surely, fortunes are changing too. Much of east London is still primarily determined by urban grit – fume-clogged Whitechapel, for example, is still far from a destination in its own right, despite being home to attractions such as the truly groundbreaking Whitechapel Art Gallery. Lovely Victoria Park and its immediate surrounds are a welcome antidote to all that, but while land developments have brought dramatic changes to neighbouring areas such as Mile End and Bow, much of the landscape remains dominated by tower blocks.

The biggest transformations are probably still to come. Rapid building and planning proposals have accompanied the successful bid to host the Olympics in Stratford in 2012, and there's a good chance that this will have a knock-on effect on nearby Leyton and Walthamstow. After all, if you really want to know what an influx of money and corporate power can do to a community, you need look no further than Docklands, the formerly rundown riverside development that now rivals the City of London in terms of commerce.

Shoreditch

An influx of artists seeking cheap studio space saw the former East End slums of Shoreditch soar in popularity in the late 90s, although in truth it was the rise of the dot.com industry at about the same time that really brought money into what had been an otherwise brutally deprived area. Some of the swankiest developments in recent years can be found along the Regent's Canal, including an apartment conversion of the Gainsborough Studios, where Alfred Hitchcock produced *The Lady Vanishes*. While rising prices have meant much of the early art community has moved on, Shoreditch, with its real sense of East End history and modish fashionability, is still a great area to visit. A good place to start any tour is Hoxton Square. It is leafy but slightly down at heel, and on a warm summer evening it still fills with more fashionable young things than you can shake a paintbrush at. It was once the axis around which Shoreditch's new cool swung and is home to the most famous of 'britart' galleries, White Cube (7930 5373). Two other excellent contemporary art spaces nearby are Victoria Miro (7336 8109) and Flowers East (7920 7777). For a more traditional flavour of Shoreditch, visit the bustle of Hoxton Street Market, located on a stretch of road also home to authentic pie and mash shop, F Cooke (see p.190). Nearby Hoxton Hall (7684 0060), an authentic Victorian music hall and the only one of its kind still operating today, offers an alternative glimpse into the area's past with its vibrant musical theatre programme. Elsewhere, The Geffrye Museum (7739 9893) is another local gem, with a series of period rooms showcasing the English domestic interior from 1600 to the present day. Once you're done there, pop into one of the many nearby Vietnamese restaurants that this stretch of the Kingsland Road is famous for.

Shoreditch High Street

Spitalfields

A little further east, the area around Spitalfields and Brick Lane is undergoing a similar transformation to its fashionable neighbour. Nowhere is this more clearly seen than Old Spitalfields Market itself (see p.369). Recently the subject of a multimillion pound design makeover courtesy of architect Sir Norman Foster, you can buy all sorts here - organic vegetables, designer clothes, and everything in between. Sundays are the most vibrant day for a visit, which is handy as this is when the area's other two hugely popular markets also hum with life – the Columbia Road Flower Market (see p.368) blossoms early on Sunday mornings, while the northern end of nearby Brick Lane (p.368) offers up goods ranging from old records to new shoes throughout the day. Spitalfields lies in the shadow of the striking Christ Church, a recently restored Hawksmoor-designed building dating from 1792. The area is currently best-known for its buzzing Bangladeshi community and the run of curry houses in and around Brick Lane. However, Shoreditch has a long history of immigrant communities, including French Huguenots and Jews. The Museum of Immigration and Diversity (7247 5352) aims to tell that history. Located at 19 Princelet Street, the former home of a Huguenot silk weaver, the building needs extensive renovation, but there is some limited access throughout the year.

Elsewhere, the eccentric Dennis Severs' House (see p.198) is a self-styled 'living museum' that recreates a mid-18th to early 20th century house in painstaking detail. On the subject of eccentricity, Spitalfields is also home to cult artistic duo Gilbert and George. Other famous locals include artist Tracey Emin and author Jeanette Winterson, who owns Verde's deli on Brushfield Street. More notoriously, The Ten Bells pub opposite Spitalfields market on Commercial Street was reputedly frequented by Jack the Ripper and his victims, although with fashionably distressed sofas and DJ-led music nights there's little trace of that era now.

However, nowhere in the area is the old and new brought together more than in and around the streets of Brick Lane itself. The Sunday market still bustles, and the area's reputation for cheap curry and fresh bagels from the legendary Brick Lane Beigel Bake (7729 0616) continues to precede it. Alongside this, venues such as The Old Truman Brewery (7377 2899), with its bar, cafe and gallery space, and the fashionable boutiques of nearby Cheshire Street have breathed a new life to an area that, for all its contradictions, seems to work rather well.

Bethnal Green & Bow

The southern end of Brick Lane leads directly to Whitechapel Road, an unremittingly ugly stretch of busy highway. The bustling street market between Valance Road and Cambridge Heath Road, the huge East London Mosque, and the striking glass architecture of newly opened Idea Store public library (7364 4332) are a big draw for locals, but the biggest attraction for non-residents is the Whitechapel Art Gallery (see p.197). This innovative contemporary art space was founded in 1901 and consistently showcases some of London's most exciting exhibitions.

A little further east, the relentless grimness that seems to affect this part of London (helped in no small part by the number of tower blocks erected after the Blitz in the second world war) begins to soften. Infamously home to the Kray twins in the 1960s, Bethnal Green has benefited enormously from the rise of Spitalfields and is home to the charming Victoria & Albert Museum of Childhood (8983 5200), which recently reopened after extensive renovations.

Much of neighbouring Mile End shares the intermittent scruffiness that affects much of east London. However, the spectacular Millennium Project – an ambitious regeneration of Mile End Park complete with an ecology centre, art pavilion, extensive sports and recreation facilities, and the innovative grass-covered 'green bridge' that

191

backs on to the lovely Victoria Park – is well worth checking out. Victoria Park's charms are one of London's best-kept secrets. Much loved by locals, it is the city's third-largest cultivated green space and offers a lake, deer enclosure and delightful cafe. A great way to reach the park from north London is to walk or cycle along the towpath of the Grand Union Canal from Angel, Islington. Travelling south-east from Victoria Park, the canal meanders through Bow down towards Limehouse Basin, a pretty marina with a good heritage trail near the Thames.

Docklands & Beyond

From here it's a short hop along the river to Docklands, where the striking redevelopment of Canary Wharf that was spearheaded by former prime minister Margaret Thatcher in the 1980s is finally coming into its own. Many of the big City banks have offices here, as do a number of national newspapers, including *The Independent* and *The Telegraph* groups. This part of London, with its gleaming tower blocks and identikit loft-style apartments, still really only operates at full scale during working hours, but it is gradually beginning to develop an evening life. Events such as the annual Greenwich and Docklands festivals and better access by tube and light rail have done a lot to open the area up to non-business visitors, while the Museum in Docklands at West India Quay (0870 4443857), an offshoot off the Museum of London, offers an excellent glimpse into the history of life around the docks, while for kids you can't beat Mudchute Park & Farm (7515 5901), the largest city farm in Europe.

Hot on Docklands' heels in the regeneration stakes is the multi-ethnic community of Stratford, whose fortunes are set to soar as the 2012 Olympics draw nearer. The recently opened high-speed Channel Tunnel Rail Link is another feather in the area's cap, and it is hoped that the feeling of prosperity such innovations bring will reverberate to nearby Leyton. If so, there's a good chance that this growing affluence will be felt in Walthamstow too. But until then this area will remain best known for its greyhound racing track (see p.289) and the pretty former childhood home of Victorian designer and craftsman William Morris at Lloyd Park (8527 3782).

Canal boats, Docklands

Is getting lost your usual excuse?

Whether you're a map person or not, this pocket-sized marvel will help you get to know the city like the back of your hand… so you won't feel the back of someone else's.

London Mini Map
Putting the city in your pocket

Museums, Heritage & Culture

One of London's greatest qualities is its ability to assimilate, adapt and evolve; in recent years the city has committed to casting one eye towards the future while keeping the other firmly on the rich diversity of its past. The results of this are plentiful and engaging, and have breathed new life into a city that, for all its great wealth of heritage, was in danger of becoming a cultural dinosaur. Innovative newcomers such as the London Eye, Tate Modern and 'new' British Library now sit alongside traditional treasures such as the Houses of Parliament, Buckingham Palace and St Paul's Cathedral as major international attractions.

The capital's diverse range of heritage and culture is showcased in the hundreds of museums and attractions found across the city. Whether your interest lies in the history of London itself, the pomp and ceremony of its royal heritage, or the unique – and sometimes eccentric – legacies of its former residents, there's so much to learn about. The following section highlights some of the capitals 'must-see' cultural places, attractions and festivals.

Art Galleries

Other options **Art & Craft Supplies** p.315, **Art** p.314

London is justly famous for its wealth of art galleries and the variety of work they display. Whether you'd like to trace the history of western European art through the National Gallery's vast permanent collection, soak up the atmosphere as well as the work in the cathedral-like environment of Tate Modern, or prefer to uncover a rising star of the British contemporary art scene around east London's Hoxton Square, London is the place for you. The galleries listed here offer a comprehensive overview of London's current art scene, from the private treasures of the Wallace Collection to the quirky delights of the Institute of Contemporary Art. Most of the major galleries offer a regular programme of events, ranging from lectures tailored to current exhibitions to family activities and even art classes (keep up to date with what's on by visiting the galleries' individual websites). All of the larger galleries offer membership schemes. Individuals pay an annual subscription in exchange for free entry to exhibitions and other perks, such as access to members' rooms (the one at Tate Modern, with its spectacular views over the Thames, is particularly memorable).

7 Gallery Rd
SE21
⇌ *Tulse Hill*

Dulwich Picture Gallery

8693 5254 | www.dulwichpicturegallery.org.uk

The world's first-ever purpose-built art gallery is a charming neo-classical affair in a leafy corner of south London. Originally designed by Sir John Soane and first opened to the public in 1811 it has recently undergone extensive renovations – and now the best little picture gallery in the world is looking better than ever. Small and perfectly formed, the gallery specialises in classical art, playing host to three international loan exhibitions each year. However, its permanent collection, featuring works by Old Masters including Rembrandt, Canaletto and Rubens is more than enough of an attraction in its own right. Extend your visit on a sunny day by exploring the peaceful gardens in which the gallery sits or soak up the atmosphere in the charming Picture Gallery Café – the perfect spot to while away an hour or two away from the rush of the city centre.

The Mall
SE1
⇌ ⊖ *Charing Cross*

Institute of Contemporary Art

7930 0483 | www.ica.org.uk

The lure of the Institute of Contemporary Art is much more than what's hanging on the gallery walls; this is not so much an art gallery as a bustling, creative, contemporary 'space'. Its setting, in a stately Georgian terrace right on the Mall and within stone-throwing distance of Buckingham Palace, seems faintly incongruous at first. But it's this kind of juxtaposition of setting with function that London does so well. With its film theatres, auditoriums and a bustling cafe bar that is an entertainment destination in itself, the venue attracts a youngish arty crowd every day – and night – of the week. It offers a rotating programme of independent film screenings, talks, performances and club nights and plays host to the annual Beck's Futures contemporary art award. Founded by the anarchist Herbert Read in 1948, the Institute of Contemporary Art might not sit outside the establishment as it once did (Conservative leader David Cameron celebrated his ascension to the head of his party here in 2006), but a quick visit reassures there's plenty of life in the old dog yet.

2 St Martin's Place
WC2
🔵 **Leicester Square**

National Portrait Gallery

7306 0055 | *www.npg.org.uk*

Tucked away on a smallish street to the side of its big sister, the National Gallery, the National Portrait Gallery offers a social history of Britain and the faces that have influenced and shaped it. The gallery was established in 1856 as a place to honour those Britons who, according to founder Earl Philip Henry Stanhope, 'are most commemorated in British history as warriors or as statesmen, or in arts, in literature or in science'. While its scope has broadened rather considerably since then (anonymous sitters occasionally get to jostle for wall space with images of such famous historical figures as William Shakespeare and the likes of David Beckham and Kate Moss) its remit – to create a social record through images of the nation's people – remains the same. Portraits are arranged in chronological order over five floors  of exhibition space, and the gallery hosts a number of annual painting and photographic competitions, including the BP Portrait Award and the Photographic Portrait Prize. Be sure to leave enough time during your visit to pop into the top-floor Portrait Restaurant with its great views over Trafalgar Square.

Burlington House
W1
🔵 **Piccadilly Circus**

Royal Academy of Arts

7300 8000 | *www.royalacademy.org.uk*

Despite being located in the neo-Palladian splendour of Burlington House, the RA has always had a resolutely unconventional streak. This is perhaps best seen in its annual Summer Exhibition, now the largest open contemporary art exhibition in the world. In a tradition that stretches back to the Academy's founding in 1768, around 9,000 artists anonymously submit their work in the hope of being one of the 1,200 selected for display. The result is an intriguingly eclectic assortment of works that is the highlight of the gallery's exhibition calendar. A trip to the Royal Academy lasts as long as you want it to. Aside from the three or four large-scale exhibitions it mounts each year, the Royal Academy of Arts offers an evolving programme of smaller shows alongside its permanent collection, as well as free lunchtime lectures, gallery talks and workshops. On a sunny day, the courtyard is one of the city's finest places to relax.

195

Kensington Gardens ◀
W2
⊖ *Lancaster Gate*

Serpentine Gallery

7298 1515 | *www.serpentinegallery.org*

Since opening in 1970, the Serpentine Gallery has been quietly and steadily building itself a reputation as an international showcase for contemporary art. Nestled discreetly within Kensington Gardens, the gallery was fully refurbished in 1998 and is now one of the jewels of London's art scene. The gallery itself is small – you would be hard-pressed to make a visit last more than an hour – but the calibre of its shows is consistently high and pleasingly experimental, whether a solo effort by the likes of American abstract expressionist Barnett Newman or a group show by emerging British artists. Even if the exhibition programme isn't to your taste, visiting the gallery requires a stroll through Kensington Gardens or Hyde Park, a delight in itself. The summer pavilion, which is temporarily erected beside the gallery for three months each year, has recently become a draw. The 2006 installation, featuring an egg-shaped inflatable canopy, was designed by award-winning architect Rem Koolhaas and was used for exhibitions and film screenings alongside its main function as a cafe.

Millbank ◀
SW1
⊖ *Pimlico*

Tate Britain

7887 8000 | *www.tate.org.uk*

When Tate Modern opened on the South Bank in 2000, the original Tate further up the Thames was reconfigured to display only British art. In reality, it was a return to the gallery's roots – it had first opened as the National Gallery of British Art in 1897, funded by collector and sugar magnate Henry Tate (almost immediately becoming known as the Tate Gallery). Now displaying work from 1500 to the present day, it is home to the world's largest collection of works by revered Romantic artist JMW Turner (housed in the specially constructed Clore Gallery). The Tate also hosts regular exhibitions by British artists of historical note and is a strong supporter of contemporary British art, playing host to the annual Turner Prize, the UK's biggest contemporary art award. But it isn't just the work on the walls that draws punters – its acclaimed events programme includes the likes of Late at Tate Britain on the first Friday of every month. The galleries are open until 22:00, accompanied by a programme of films, music and talks.

Bankside ◀
SE1
⇌ ⊖ *Blackfriars*

Tate Modern

7887 8000 | *www.tate.org.uk*

The astonishing success of Tate Modern since its opening at the turn of the millennium has caused some to accuse it of being more theme park than art gallery. However, to dismiss it in this way is to miss the point. Physically the building is spectacular; housed in a former power station, Tate Modern hugs the Thames and offers picture-postcard views of

London's skyline. But there's far more than setting to this gallery. On Saturday and Sunday afternoons the vast Turbine Hall might be filled with anything from puppet theatre to musical performances. Elsewhere, its movie theatres, auditoriums, comprehensive shop and numerous cafes and restaurants ensure the place is a hive of activity. And that's before we even mention the art – a comprehensive and inspiringly curated romp through the history of modern western art. Tate Modern is unashamedly populist but it's definitely not an artistic theme park, more a contemporary showcase for our times.

Hartford House,
Manchester Square
W1
🚇 *Bond Street*

Wallace Collection

7563 9500 | *www.wallacecollection.org*

Housed in what was once the private residence of its former owners, this stunning collection of 18th and 19th century treasures, including Old Masters by Titian, Rembrandt, Velazquez and Hals'The Laughing Cavalier, is one of the finest collections of ever assembled by one family. Amassed by five generations of Wallaces, it was bequeathed to the nation in 1897. Its intimate setting, tucked away in a quiet residential square, brings the treasures on view to life. Along with the permanent collection, special exhibitions are always on show. A programme of talks and study days, alongside a great package of activities for children make this a great place to return to again and again. And if that wasn't enough, the beautiful courtyard plays host to a great restaurant, while dining rooms are available for private functions. It's also a popular spot for wedding receptions.

80-82 Whitechapel
High St
E1
🚇 *Whitechapel*

Whitechapel Art Gallery

7522 7888 | *www.whitechapel.org*

While the gentrification of London's East End continues apace, some parts seem slower to benefit than others. Busy, dirty Whitechapel High Street, with its endless smoggy traffic jams, is a case in point – but there is one very good reason to visit. Tucked away behind an imposing art nouveau facade is one of London's most innovative contemporary art spaces, the Whitechapel Art Gallery. Founded in 1901 to bring great art to the people of east London, it has been said that the Whitechapel 'taught Britain to love modern art'. Its roster of exhibitions over the years has included international names such as Mark Rothko, Pablo Picasso and Frida Kahlo, along with pioneering UK artists such as Gilbert & George and Lucien Freud, make up the roll call. But for all its big-name clout, the gallery remains a neighbourhood space; it regularly hosts events for schools and the local community and its 'Friday Late Nights' are hugely popular. There are plans to expand the gallery in to the space next door (formerly home to Whitechapel Library). It should be open in 2008. Until then the main gallery remains open as usual.

Historic Houses

London has a fascinating social history, and there's no better way to get close to it than to enter one of the open houses that belonged to former celebrated residents. Private collections make up some of the capital's richest and most varied anthologies of art, antiquities and curiosities. In some cases, such as at Kenwood House or John Soane's Museum, the owners directly bequeathed their collections to the nation. In others, such as Linley Sambourne House, it was more of a happy accident than planning, the result of a building being passed down unchanged through the generations. Some may now feel more like museums or art galleries than private residences, while those belonging to royalty and the landed gentry have always seemed far beyond the reach of the majority of the population. But it's always worth remembering that every one of these buildings was once, first and foremost, a home, and each offers a unique insight.

149 Piccadilly
W1
🚇 *Hyde Park Corner*

Apsley House

7499 5676 | *www.english-heritage.org.uk/apsleyhouse*

Also known as 'Number One London' because it was the first building encountered after passing through the toll gates at the top of Knightsbridge, Apsley House was the home of the first Duke of Wellington. His descendents remain in residence today, making it the capital's last great aristocratic townhouse still in use.

This neo-classical mansion houses the Duke's collection of furniture, silver, porcelain, medals and memorabilia. The art display contains works by European masters such as Velazquez, Rubens and Goya, plus important British paintings. Wellington moved into the house in 1817, two years after his victory at the Battle of Waterloo – so unsurprisingly Napoleon looms large in the collections. Along with the sumptuous Sevres Egyptian dinner service, designed by the French general for his wife Josephine, there is also a colossal nude sculpture of Napoleon by Canova. You can buy a ticket that gives access to neighbouring Wellington Arch, which offers magnificent views over the Houses of Parliament and Hyde Park.

48 Doughty St
WC1
⊖ Russell Square

The Charles Dickens Museum

7405 2127 | *www.dickensmuseum.com*

The only surviving London home of the great English writer has been preserved as a museum in his honour. Charles Dickens lived in the house for just two years, between 1837 and 1839, but it looks like he never left. Along with original manuscripts and rare editions of the Victorian novelist and social commentator's works, there are original pieces of furniture and paintings spread over the four floors of this modest house. Special exhibitions enliven the permanent installations, while a regular programme of events including weekly readings and 'handling sessions' (in which visitors can write with a quill pen that Dickens used, and touch other original items) help bring it all to life. The house also puts on walks that take visitors through David Copperfield and Oliver Twist's London, plus lectures that offer a wider insight into Victorian London.

18 Folgate St
E1
⇌ ⊖ Liverpool Street

Dennis Severs' House

7247 4013 | *www.dennissevershouse.co.uk*

Artist Dennis Severs painstakingly transformed this London residence into a re-creation of an early 18th century home. Severs, who died in 1999, lived in the house, and created a 'living museum' that feels as if the occupants have just popped out. The 10 rooms, each lit by fire and candle, are wonderfully atmospheric; food smells trip the senses, while the creaking of stairways and chiming of clocks all add to the feeling that this is a house in which people actually live. The result is a unique experience, like walking into a painting and being invited to make it home. It's a long way from the studied formality of the city's other historic houses, but if what you're after is a glimpse into a forgotten world, look no further. The 'Silent Night' tours by candlelight are particularly intriguing, and the annual Christmas installation is one of the capital's alternative festive highlights. Opening times are restricted to Monday evenings, and in the afternoon on the first and third Sunday and subsequent Monday of each month. Reservations are necessary for Monday evening tours.

Court Yard
SE9
⇌ Eltham

Eltham Palace

8294 2548 | *www.elthampalace.org.uk*

Eltham Palace is one of the capital's most extraordinary historic houses. The first royal owner was Edward II in the early 14th century, and it was continuously remodelled and extended into one of the country's largest palaces. Despite such heritage (Henry VIII grew up here) the building fell into decline in the 17th century, and remained that way until it was bought by Stephen and Virginia Courtauld in 1933. The pair restored the Great Hall, with its magnificent hammerbeam roof, to its former glory, and built an adjoining art deco home for themselves featuring a lavish circular ocean-liner-styled central room with luxury furnishings. The brilliantly preserved result is a stunning evocation of 1930s London, charmingly juxtaposed against the grandeur of the medieval palace. The buildings are set in 19 acres of gardens, which surround the original moat and offer great views over London – perfect for a picnic in summer.

Hampton Court Palace

East Molesey
Surrey
⇄ *Hampton Court*

0870 7515175 | *www.hrp.org.uk/hampton*

Despite being well outside the centre of the capital, this is one of London's great tourist attractions. For more than 200 years, the palace was one of the country's most significant royal residences. It began life in the 16th century as the official home of Thomas Wolsey, Archbishop of York, but Henry VIII soon ousted him, and its place as a royal favourite was secured. Over the years it went on to become both prison to Charles I and then later home to Oliver Cromwell. In 1737, Queen Caroline, wife of George II, died at the palace and, while it remained a royal residence, it was never used again in full by the royal family. Highlights include Henry VIII's magnificent state apartments, lined with paintings and tapestries, and the stunning gilded ceiling of the chapel. The Tudor kitchens (where guests can take cookery classes), outdoor winter ice rink and world-famous maze, in the stunning landscaped grounds, are all top-draw attractions, even to the most royal-weary of visitors. Entrance costs £12.30 for adults, or £4 for just the gardens. Open daily.

Kensington Palace

Kensington Gardens
W8
⊖ *High Street*
Kensington

0870 7515170 | *www.kensington-palace.org.uk*

When Princess Diana died in 1997, the focus of the world's media turned to Kensington Palace – her residence since her marriage to Prince Charles in 1981 (and subsequent divorce) as thousands turned out to mourn by the palace gates. Floral tributes are still frequently left today, and its significance as a site of memorial to Diana continues. Aside from this association, the palace merits considerable investigation as a building in its own right. Beautifully located in Kensington Gardens, on the western edge of Hyde Park, the former Jacobean mansion has been a favoured home of English royalty for centuries. Queen Victoria was born here, and she first opened the state apartments to the public on her 80th birthday in 1898. It's a tradition of access that has remained intact, on and off, ever since. Visitors can also see the charming royal ceremonial dress collection, featuring items worn by Queen Elizabeth II and Princess Diana. Other highlights include The Orangery and the beautiful sunken garden. Open daily.

Kenwood House

Hampstead Lane
NW3
⊖ *Golders Green*

8348 1286 | *www.english-heritage.org.uk*

This beautiful neo-classical home sits majestically on the northern fringes of Hampstead Heath. Robert Adam redesigned the original building for celebrated judge Lord Mansfield in the 18th century. Brewing magnate Edward Cecil Guinness, the first Earl of Iveagh, bought the house and grounds in 1925, leaving it and part of his art collection to the nation upon his death two years later. Today, the combination of sumptuous interiors and stunning art makes it a London must-see. You can enjoy works by Rembrandt, Vermeer, Turner and Gainsborough, plus Constable's *Hampstead Heath with Pond and Bathers*, painted little more than a stone's throw away. One of the other great attractions of Kenwood is the grounds in which it sits. Beautifully landscaped, they offer visitors lakeside and woodland walks, while The Brew House Cafe (8348 2528) is a favourite spot for strollers to enjoy the hilltop views across London. In summer, a series of outdoor concerts takes place in the bandstand across the lake – a highlight of the city's season of outdoor festivals.

Leighton House Museum

12 Holland Park Rd
W14
⊖ *High Street*
Kensington

7602 3316 | *www.rbkc.gov.uk/leightonhousemuseum*

The former studio and home of Victorian artist Frederic, Lord Leighton is a sumptuous affair that is now as much an art gallery as it is a historic home – the walls are hung with works by the artist, plus pre-Raphaelite contemporaries such as

199

Edward Burne-Jones and John Everett Millais. Leighton, a former president of the Royal Academy, was famous for entertaining his artistic associates, and his home is appropriately extravagant. The heavy Arabic influence of the main salon is typical of the time (the Victorians were fascinated by what they saw as the 'exotic'). A fountain kitted out with a gilt mosaic frieze is the theatrical centrepiece of the Arab hall, a stunning example of Victorian extravagance. A major new education centre is due to be completed and available to the public by mid 2007. Open daily except Tuesdays, entrance is £3 for adults.

18 Stafford Terrace
W8
⊖ **High Street Kensington**

Linley Sambourne House

7938 1295 | *www.rbkc.gov.uk/linleysambournehouse*

Former *Punch* cartoonist Linley Sambourne moved into this Kensington townhouse in 1874 and remained there throughout his 36 year marriage to wife Marion. Upon her death in 1914 (Linley had died four years earlier), the Sambournes' house was inherited by their youngest son, Roy. He made no alterations to the interior, thus preserving it perfectly. Fine period details such as stained-glass windows and imposing fireplaces, along with evidence of money-saving tricks including redecorating around wall-mounted pictures, offer a unique insight into Victorian lifestyles and habits.

The house evidently evolved in decor and style, as any family home does; William Morris wallpaper peeks out from behind its replacement, and original floor tiles can be seen beneath a layer of carpeting. The house also reveals the prolific career of Linley Sambourne himself. Over 1,000 of his cartoons and illustrations survive, along with a huge collection of photographs. Access to the house, which is open between March and December, is by guided tour only. Advance booking is strongly recommended.

Heritage Sites

Other options, **Museums** p.205, **Art** p.314

From the Houses of Parliament to St Paul's Cathedral, London has long enthralled visitors and residents with the depth of history revealed through its architectural sites. Many of the city's ancient buildings are still in use today and this function, as monuments to the present as much as to the past, keeps them very much alive and well maintained.

English Heritage is the organisation entrusted with ensuring the country's architectural heritage remains intact. They 'list' buildings according to a scale (Grade I or Grade II, for example) that protects them as they stand and ensures that any alterations or repairs can only be carried out under strict guidelines. Interestingly, a building doesn't need to be old to be considered of great architectural significance. The 60s-built Southbank Centre, for example, is home to the Royal Festival Hall, a Grade I-listed theatre that has recently reopened having undergone extensive refurbishment.

Most of the sites listed here are open to the public as visitor attractions, at least in part. If there's a building you would particularly like to visit that doesn't offer regular public entry, or you'd like to see more of one that does, the annual London Open House weekend (p.211) offers a chance to do just that.

96 Euston Rd
NW1
⇌ ⊖ **King's Cross St. Pancras**

British Library

7412 7332 | *www.bl.uk*

When the British Library moved to its new site at St Pancras in 1998 it marked the completion of the UK's largest building project of the 20th century. Housing a copy of every publication produced in the UK and Ireland, the British Library collection stands at around 150 million items and includes maps, magazines, music scores and patents as well as books. Treasures include the *Magna Carta* document, the recording of Nelson Mandela's trial speech, Beatles manuscripts and a Leonardo da Vinci notebook. It is one of the greatest collections of human endeavour anywhere in the world. The reading rooms aren't open to casual visitors but the library welcomes guests into its exhibition galleries (which feature a permanent exhibition from the library's extensive collection in the Treasures Gallery along with a number of changing displays elsewhere), bookshop and lovely cafe and restaurant. There is also a good programme of events, lectures and seminars that members of the public can attend. The magnificent red-brick, modernist building also houses some wonderful art specially commissioned and created for the site. Look out for Sir Eduardo Paolozzi's monumental sculpture of Newton (after William Blake) and Anthony Gormley's large-scale polished stones in his Planets series, both of which can be found in the main piazza.

The Mall
SW1
⊖ St. James's Park

Buckingham Palace

7766 7300 | *www.royal.gov.uk*

To all but the most devoted royalists, the Changing of the Guard is probably best left to the throng of tourists hanging at the gates. For anyone interested in London's history, however, a visit inside the palace itself is quite another matter. The Queen's official residence in London is a handsomely imposing building at the south-west end

of the Mall in a former town house owned by the Duke of Buckingham. John Nash, George IV's favourite designer, did much to transform what was previously known as Buckingham House into the 775 roomed extravaganza seen today, using Bath stone to double the size of the original structure in a French neo-classical style. The restructuring continued well into the 19th century and was completed just before the outbreak of the first world war. There are three main areas for visitors to explore. The royal residence opens for a few months over the summer while the Queen is

away; the throne room, state dining room and music room – where four royal babies, including Prince Charles and Prince William were christened – are among the 19 rooms and gardens that are opened to the public and The Royal Mews is a working stable where visitors can watch horses being trained, exercised and fed, and where the splendidly opulent golden state coach, which is used for Coronations, forms part of a permanent display of state vehicles. The Queen's Gallery was reopened in 2002 to show off part of the Royal Collection – an astonishing anthology of treasures, featuring works by Leonardo da Vinci, Rubens and Canaletto. Also on display are lavish furnishings, jewellery, sculptures, ceramics, and works by Faberge. The exhibitions change frequently so art and history lovers may want to return – register on arrival and your ticket will grant unlimited admission for 12 months.

Parliament Square
SW1
⊖ Westminster

Houses of Parliament
7219 3000 | www.parliament.uk

To many, the giant clock tower commonly known as Big Ben isn't just a geographical landmark, but the very symbol of London itself. It might come as a surprise, then, to know that the tower (the name Big Ben actually refers to the bell inside rather than the structure itself) has been a feature of the London skyline for less than 150 years.

In 1834 a fire destroyed most of the Houses of Parliament, leading to the construction of much of the building that stands today, although the site's history as a centre of authority stretches back over 1,000 years. Big Ben sounded its first gong in 1859. All

that remained from before the fire was Westminster Hall, the Jewel Tower and the crypt of St Stephen's Chapel. Charles Barry's bold Gothic structure bore the brunt of a bombing raid during the Blitz in 1941, destroying the House of Commons chamber. Architect Sir Giles Gilbert Scott designed its five-story replacement, which opened in 1950; the structure has remained largely unchanged since then. Despite its history, the building looks remarkably cohesive, its imposing structure looming large over the Thames. Much of the building can be visited – the Jewel Tower and chapel crypt are open year-round – while one-hour tours of the clock tower can be arranged in advance through your local MP. UK residents can also attend parliamentary debates (again, tickets are issued through MPs) and watch judicial hearings and committees (you queue on the day for this), offering a rare insight into British politics in action.

21 New Globe Walk
SE1
⊖ Mansion House

Shakespeare's Globe
7902 1400 | www.shakespeares-globe.org

The reconstruction of the original Elizabethan theatre on the South Bank of the Thames, where the great English playwright worked, was a labour of love for American actor and director Sam Wanamaker, who spearheaded much of the fundraising. Sadly the filmmaker didn't live to see his dream realised, but his efforts are recognised by a Blue Plaque outside the venue. Since opening in 1997, the new Globe has put on plays in its 'wooden O', which faithfully recreates the experience of Elizabethan audiences – right down to the uncomfortable gallery seating (spectators are advised to bring a cushion) and the cheap, standing-only 'bear pit' below. The theatre is open for performances between May and September, and features both the Royal Shakespeare Company and international theatre troupes. A year-round exhibition brings the history of the venue to life. You should make time to join one of the tours (every 15 to 30 minutes) as the guides pass their knowledge on with an infectious enthusiasm.

Ludgate Hill
EC4
⊖ St. Paul's

St Paul's Cathedral
7236 4128 | www.stpauls.co.uk

Designed by Sir Christopher Wren as part of a massive rebuilding project across the capital after the Great Fire in 1666, this famous domed cathedral in the City of London is the fifth structure of its kind on this site – a cathedral dedicated to St Paul has stood here since 604AD. The current St Paul's was built between 1675 and 1710 (the first service took place in 1697), and the architecture is stunning. The Whispering Gallery in the dome is worth a visit even if its magical acoustics are often drowned out by the sheer volume of people trying to put them to the test. Downstairs, the crypt is fascinating – some of its content pre-dates the cathedral – while the main organ, installed in 1695, was once played by the composer Mendelssohn. St Paul's has been the focus of much of the capital's spiritual life since then, from the funerals of Lord Nelson and Winston Churchill to the marriage of Charles and Diana and, more recently, memorial services for those killed in the 2005 tube bombings. As such, it is a church that remains close to the hearts of Londoners; a service is held here every day and all are welcome to attend.

Tower Hill ◀
EC1
⊖ *Tower Hill*

Tower Bridge

7403 3761 | *www.towerbridge.org.uk*

For a long time neighbouring London Bridge was the only connection between the north and south banks of the Thames. Further crossings were added to the west, but it wasn't until the later part of the 19th century that public pressure for ready access to the now densely populated East End resulted in proposals for a bridge to the other side of London Bridge. After much public consultation and over 50 proposed designs, Tower Bridge was officially opened in 1894.

At the time, Tower Bridge was considered to be one of the great feats of modern industrial engineering, the largest and most complex bascule (counterbalanced) bridge ever built. Even today its construction impresses – hydraulic power still opens the bascules, even if, since 1976, oil and electricity rather than the original steam has driven them. A comprehensive account of the bridge's history can be seen in the exhibition in the high-level walkways that had been closed to the public since 1910 following a lack of use (people preferred to wait and watch the bascules rise rather than access the walkways themselves).

Trafalgar Square ◀
WC1
⇌ ⊖ *Charing Cross*

Trafalgar Square

www.london.gov.uk/trafalgarsquare

The 'crossroads of London' was established in the early 18th century. Architect John Nash incorporated the space into his improvement plans for the capital in 1812, envisioning it as a cultural public place, and in 1830 it was named Trafalgar Square. Following the building of the National Gallery the square underwent substantial

St Paul's Cathedral

203

changes. Nelson's column was erected in 1843 (and the bronze guarding lions at its base in 1867), and the square's famous fountains installed in 1845 (although its mermaids, dolphins and tritons were added later). In 1876, the Imperial Standards of Length, which mark the point from which all distances from London are measured, were set in the north terrace wall, although these were moved to sit next to the central staircase when it was added in 2003. In its long history Trafalgar Square has been a focal point for Londoners; it has always been a magnet for rallies, protests and celebrations and was traditionally the place where hardy locals swam in the fountains to welcome in the new year (something mayor Ken Livingstone tries to dissuade people from doing, not entirely successfully). During the 1990s, it was decided that the square's fourth statue plinth, which remained controversially empty for decades, would be used as a rotating platform for modern art. The debates surrounding each decision of what to display next have become as important to the process as the works themselves, but nothing like as controversial as the mayor's decision to remove the familiar pigeons from the square in 2003.

Parliament Square
SW1
⊖ Westminster

Westminster Abbey
7654 4900 | *www.westminster-abbey.org*

A must-see for anyone on London's heritage trail, Westminster Abbey is known as the House of Kings – the place where English royalty is both crowned and buried. The main part of church as it stands today was built in the 13th century, although additions such as the Lady Chapel (built by Henry VIII), with its soaring, vaulted ceiling, continued to be added over the next three centuries. The site was originally a Norman monastery built at the command of King Edward (now St Edward the Confessor, whose remains lie in a magnificent tomb behind the high alter) in 1065, the only remaining traces of which are found in the Cloisters (home to the Abbey Museum). Every monarch since William the Conqueror has been crowned in the abbey, and more than 3,000 are buried there. Poets' Corner is particularly notable as the resting place for some of England's greatest literary figures, including Geoffrey Chaucer, writer of the *Canterbury Tales*, and TS Eliot. Others, including Shakespeare, have had commemorative plaques erected here in their honour. Elsewhere, the grave of the Unknown Warrior, close to the west door, has long been a site of pilgrimage.

For all its history, however, the abbey is very much a functioning place of worship. Services are held every day and a comprehensive line-up of concerts and lectures runs throughout the year. There's nothing quite like attending a carol service to get the full measure of the church in all its glory; revel in wonder as the notes of the choristers soar into the furthest reaches of one of the world's great ecclesiastical monuments.

British Museum

Museums

Other options **Art** p.314, **Heritage Sites** p.200, **Historic Houses** p.197

It's a sign of the city's endearingly eccentric Englishness that if enough objects can be gathered around a particular site or subject to constitute a collection, then a museum created in its honour won't be too far away. Not that this has done the nation's cultural heritage any harm. Indeed, some of what constitute the city's finest collections, including what is now the Natural History Museum (once little more than one man's anthology of curios) started life this way. Londoners love their museums. They are so much more than tourist sites geared to attracting travellers passing through. This is helped in no small part by a substantial injection of government funding over the past decade which has made access to the permanent collections of all the major public museums free of charge. Other incentives include the development of a dedicated, innovative and ever-changing roster of events, lectures and special exhibitions at all of the large (and many of the smaller) sites. The following list covers the city's must-see museums. Specialising in subjects including art, design, archaeology, science and ancient and modern history, they indicate the breadth of knowledge that is waiting to be discovered – and rediscovered – in the city.

Great Russell St
WC1
⊖ **Russell Square**

British Museum

7323 8299 | www.thebritishmuseum.ac.uk

With more than 94 galleries open to the public and one of the world's greatest collections of antiquities (the Rosetta Stone, the earliest known image of Christ and the controversial Elgin Marbles are just some of its many treasures) it's fair to say that a visit to the British Museum should be planned as a day out rather than squeezed into a quick visit. Whether your interests lie in ancient Egypt, Asia or Britain itself, you will find something here to satisfy your tastes. Set in a glorious columned building that dates back to 1857, the interior Great Court was redesigned a few years ago to incorporate a vast glass-and-metal latticed dome, creating the largest covered square in Europe (and now a great place to relax with coffee and a book). However long or short your visit, be sure to pop into the Reading Room, now restored to its former blue, cream and gold colour scheme. Here you'll get a very real sense of it as the place that inspired such great writers as Dickens, Shaw and Eliot.

28 Shad Thames
SE1
⊖ **Tower Hill**

Design Museum

0870 8339955 | www.designmuseum.org

Beautifully situated on the south bank of the Thames in the shadow of Tower Bridge, the Design Museum is housed in a modern glass-fronted building with glorious views of the City and Canary Wharf. Dedicated to 20th and 21st century product design, architecture and fashion, the main gallery is a delightful hybrid of an upmarket sales showroom and a 'serious' exhibition space. It's a showroom because so many of the products on display are, or have until recently been, for sale in department stores and high-end retailers across the world (including, it should be noted, the excellent on-site shop) and a serious exhibition space because this museum takes modern design very seriously indeed. Despite the obvious intellectual approach taken to design, however, the museum presents its knowledge with a light (and light-hearted) touch. Although it's one of London's most interesting and innovative museums it's not one of the largest – a morning or afternoon should give you plenty of time to explore. Younger visitors are offered a free 'design action pack', complete with fun treasure trails. The regular children's workshops are some of the best to be found anywhere in town.

Guildhall Art Gallery & Roman Amphitheatre

Guildhall Yard, off Gresham St EC2
Bank

7332 3700 | *www.guildhall-art-gallery.org.uk*
Guildhall Art Gallery is home to the City of London's extensive art collection (more than 4,000 pieces in total), including works by Millais and Constable. The real gem is the remains of a Roman amphitheatre found on the site in 1988. The City of London incorporated the find into proposals that were then under way to build an art gallery to replace the original one destroyed during an air raid in 1941 and it finally opened its doors to the public in 1999. Dating from the 2nd century AD – a time when London, then under Roman rule, was know as Londinium – the remains also revealed remnants of later Norman and Saxon settlements on the same site.

Imperial War Museum

Lambeth Rd SE1
Waterloo

7416 5320 | *www.iwm.org.uk*
The imposing colonnade of London's Imperial War Museum sets a fitting tone of sobriety for what is a sober subject – the history of war in the 20th century. Serious as the topic is, the museum succeeds in its quest to give a human face to its theme, with exhibitions that are both intelligent and thought provoking. A special exhibition due to run until 2008, for example, reviews the history, impact and effect of the second world war as it was experienced in Britain through the eyes of the nation's children. Elsewhere, the Holocaust exhibition is a powerful yet beautifully restrained demonstration – through the use of historical material including photographs, posters and personal testimonies – of Nazi persecution of the Jews and other groups before and during that same conflict The museum touches on important and very worthy subjects, never failing to inform where it could so easily preach. It's worth two hours of anyone's time, but you could easily spend a whole day here.

Museum of London

150 London Wall EC2
Barbican

0870 4443852 | *www.museumoflondon.org.uk*
Want to learn about the people who lived in the Thames Valley before London became London? Interested in tracing the city's history through events such as the Plague, the Great Fire and the first and second world wars? Keen to find out how the capital became the first world city – a cross-cultural melting pot that still influences London's development today? You'll find all this and more at the Museum of London, quite possibly the most comprehensive city museum in the world. The modern, glass-fronted entrance sits right in the centre of London's business district, the Square Mile, but is not as incongruous as it first seems. This is the heart of Roman London, the city's original settlement. London Wall, the street on which the museum is located, is exactly that: the site of the fortress wall that once surrounded Londinium. The museum is currently undergoing extensive remodelling that will eventually see its exhibition space doubled. Access is limited while this work is being carried out but it's still well worth visiting. Set aside an hour or two, or more if you want to use the interactive facilities, and prepare to be amazed by London's many secrets.

National Maritime Museum & Royal Observatory

Park Row
SE10
DLR *Cutty Sark*

8858 4422 | *www.nmm.ac.uk*

London's lengthy naval history is the focus of this Greenwich museum and is guaranteed to bring out the wannabe sailor in you. Over 30 galleries throughout the museum and observatory reveal one of the biggest collections of boats and navigational equipment in the world. The museum's location as home of the Prime Meridian (they don't call it Greenwich Mean Time for nothing) allows visitors to quite literally straddle the eastern and western hemispheres simultaneously. Also on site is Queen's House, home to the museum's fine-art collection, and a short stroll away lies the Cutty Sark sailing boat, built in 1869 and now permanently housed in dry dock on the riverfront. King George VI formally opened the National Maritime Museum to the public in 1937, and a vast, white classical exterior is the imposing centrepiece of what is now known as Maritime Greenwich (which gained Unesco World Heritage Site in 1997). Make a day of it by spending time exploring the museums and their surrounding picturesque location on the south side of the Thames.

Natural History Museum

Cromwell Rd
SW7
⊖ *South Kensington*

7942 5000 | *www.nhm.ac.uk*

The world-famous dinosaur exhibitions tend to top most people's must-see list at this South Kensington museum and it's no surprise why. The sight of a full-sized diplodocus skeleton flooded by natural light from the ceiling of the imposing cathedral-like

surrounds of the museum's central hall is a sight to cherish – but there's plenty more for visitors to explore and enjoy. The original German Romanesque-style building first opened as the National History Museum in 1881 (it was part of the British Museum collection for over 250 years until the size of the natural history collection grew too big and required its own home). Its purpose-built design features delightful touches such as the terracotta monkeys over the main arches at the museum's entrance. Inside are housed all manner of natural treasures, from giant

specimens of sperm whales to a fascinating history of Earth's geological evolution. One of the museum's recent successes is the Darwin Centre – home to a comprehensive and frankly bizarre collection of bottled animal specimens from around the globe. Be sure to pay a visit to the serene haven that is the Wildlife Centre, a natural garden in the heart of the museum that opens during the summer months.

Science Museum

Exhibition Rd
SW7
⊖ *South Kensington*

0870 8704868 | *www.sciencemuseum.org.uk*

A common misconception is that the Science Museum, rather like the neighbouring Natural History Museum, is first and foremost somewhere best visited by kids, an assumption that couldn't be more incorrect. The museum was set up in 1857 after profits from the success of the Great Exhibition earlier that decade were used to purchase land in South Kensington for the purpose of creating institutions dedicated to the then burgeoning fields of science and technology. Today the same passion for inventiveness that inspired the museum's founding remains apparent. Over the years the building's classical interior has been remodelled to incorporate glass lifts and all the mod cons necessary to create a world-class exhibition space, complete with 'virtual voyages' and an impressive Imax cinema showing science-related films. The Wellcome Wing features the latest developments in science and the fascinating exhibition programme offers ample reason to return again and again. 'Science night sleepovers' and the opportunity for children's birthday parties to be held at the museum might still make it sound like somewhere more for kids than adults to enjoy, but don't believe a word of it – one visit and you'll be hooked.

Sir John Soane's Museum

13 Lincoln's Inn Fields
WC2
⊖ Holborn

7405 2107 | www.soane.org

The spectacular display of art, ornaments and antiquities on display at this former home is no cobbled-together affair. The celebrated 18th century architect Sir John Soane bought this central London townhouse with the intention of displaying his extensive collection, and planned long before his death in 1837 that it would function as a museum after he was gone. The result is a fascinatingly eclectic display offering not only a chance to see the collection, but an insight into the man himself. Important works include paintings by Turner, Watteau and Canaletto, plus Hogarth's famous satirical series, *A Rake's Progress*. But equally fascinating are the smaller exhibits – the stained-glass catalogue is filled with rare examples from European monasteries and convents, while the collection of early 19th century domestic furniture contains everyday items such as book carriers, few of which were preserved for posterity. A lecture tour is offered every Saturday at 14:30 to the first 22 people who purchase tickets after 14:00. Open late on Tuesdays.

Somerset House

The Strand
WC2
⊖ Temple

7845 4600 | www.somerset-house.org.uk

Situated on the Strand, one of central London's main arteries, lies the imposing and beautifully restored 18th century Somerset House, the city's first purpose-built office block. The site is now home to the shiny decorative treasures of the Gilbert Collection (bequeathed to the nation by Arthur Gilbert in 1996) and the Hermitage Rooms – the display of which recreates in miniature the Winter Palace in St Petersburg from which the collection is on long-term loan. Best of all, however, is the jewel-like Courtauld Institute Gallery. Occupying the northern wing of the building is this staggering collection, which includes works by Dutch master Rubens, and Manet's post-impressionist masterpiece, *Bar at the Folies-Bergere*. Other attractions lie away from the house's collections. The Great Courtyard is home to impressive display fountains in the summer and a much-loved winter ice-skating rink, while the terrace offers splendid views over the Thames.

Victoria & Albert Museum

Cromwell Rd
SW7
⊖ South Kensington

7942 2000 | www.vam.ac.uk

Forget spending a day here – you could spend a year at the V&A and still have more to see. This is the most extensive collection of art and design in the world – a glorious, must-visit place. The museum houses over 11km of gallery space, with entire rooms dedicated to glassware and tapestry and others furnished to replicate a period style in every detail, right down to the curtain swags. Visitors arrive through the Grand Entrance and approach an illuminated reception desk under the vast, Medusa-like coils of glass suspended from the striking domed ceiling. This clash of styles works beautifully and is a good metaphor for the museum itself; ever curious in its embrace of great new design while never sacrificing or compromising the past. The museum shop, a great place to pick up thoughtful and slightly unusual gifts, is one of the best in London, and the new John Madejski Garden is a summer gem. Keep an eye on the museum's events programme – musical evenings and high-end craft fairs are particular treats.

Festivals

Like the city itself, London's festivals are an eclectic mix. The biggest, brightest and brashest by far is the Notting Hill Carnival (p.212), which

Victoria & Albert Museum

brings the vibrancy of the Caribbean to west London's streets for a two-day party each August bank holiday weekend. But there are many more from which to choose, each revealing another side to the city's character, history and rich weave of multiculturalism – from the relative refinement of the Chelsea Flower Show to the vibrant colour of the Chinese New Year.

The following list doesn't claim to be definitive (there are far more events across London than could ever be listed here) but it will give you a flavour of the variety and scope of festivals celebrated in the capital. Each borough's local authority monitors and, in many cases, organises community events throughout the year. Visit local government websites for more information or keep an eye out for listings in newspapers to keep abreast of what's going on where.

5 Old Montague St
E1
⊖ Aldgate East

Baishakhi Mela

7539 3411 | www.baishakhimela.com

In less than 10 years, this annual celebration of Bengali arts, music and culture – and the Bangla new year – has grown from a small celebration for Brick Lane's Bangladeshi community into the largest Asian gathering in the UK, regularly attracting more than 80,000 visitors on one Sunday each May. The event opens with a procession featuring music, costumed dancers and children in traditional dress who take to the streets to wish onlookers 'shubho nobo borsho' (happy new year) and lead them to the main event – a celebration of music and dance, from traditional folk through to Bollywood and Bengali rock. Brick Lane itself is turned into a buzzing market place, featuring hundreds of stalls selling handicrafts and traditional Bangladeshi fashion. The area (known locally as Banglatown) is famous for its curry houses, and those lining Brick Lane itself spill into the road, which also features attractions from street performance and henna painting (mehendi) to rickshaw rides. It's a bright, bustling, colourful celebration that offers a glimpse into one of London's most vibrant communities.

Horse Guards Parade
W1
⊖ St. James's Park

Beating Retreat & Trooping the Colour

7839 5323 | www.royalparks.gov.uk

For those with a yen for military pageantry or simply a passion for a 'jolly good show', the annual Beating Retreat by the Massed Bands of the Household Division in Horse Guards Parade is a must. Grounded in the early traditions of chivalry when sounding retreat signalled the end to the day's fighting and a return to camp, the ceremonial interpretation of this has become a major event in the British army's calendar. About

209

300 musicians, pipers and drummers perform the Beating Retreat ceremony in a display of precision drill and extravagant colour. Spirited marches and displays are followed by an evening of music and singing in the annual event, which takes place over two evenings in late May.

If you prefer your military ceremonies with a little less melody, Beating Retreat has been described as being 'like Trooping the Colour with music'. The Queen's annual inspection of her troops also takes place a few weeks later, in mid-June, starting in Horse Guards Parade and moving through to the Mall . The ceremony marks the Queen's official birthday and dates back to the early 18th century.

Various locations

Bonfire Night
www.bonefire.org

'Remember, remember the 5th of November' goes the children's chant in honour of the annual celebration of the failed attempt by Guy Fawkes to blow up the Houses of Parliament in 1605. Traditionally, children would tour their local neighbourhood asking for 'a penny for the Guy' – an effigy that would later be burned at the top of the bonfire. These days Bonfire Night is more commonly marked by fireworks celebrations in every backyard and clearing across London. Every November 5 the air is heavy with explosives and the sk lights up with spectacular displays. One of the biggest and best public displays is the celebration that takes place each year at Alexandra Palace, which features a funfair in the grounds from late afternoon. Clapham Common in the south and Victoria Park (p.216) in the east are two other popular venues. Most local authorities put on some kind of celebration in a local park on the Saturday that falls closest to the night of November 5 – check out local listings information a week or so before the big night.

Royal Hospital
Chelsea
SW3
South Kensington

Chelsea Flower Show
0845 2605000 | *www.rhs.org.uk/chelsea*

Sponsored by the Royal Horticultural Society, the Chelsea Flower Show is the annual event for green-fingered professionals and amateurs everywhere in the UK. The show runs for five days every May in the grounds of the Royal Hospital (it's been held at this site since 1913, although its precursor, the Great Spring Show, was first held in Kensington in 1862) and is open to members of the public on the last three days of the event. There are about 600 exhibitors, including around 50 temporary gardens across 11 acres of grounds and over 100 floral exhibitors in the great pavilion. Exhibitors come from as far afield as Barbados, Sri Lanka and Australia, with medals awarded to winning entries before the show opens. Due to the time of year it's held, Chelsea Flower Show is often cursed by rain. But like Wimbledon in June, the bad weather has become almost as much a part of the event as the actual gardens. Visitors manage to console themselves with the 8,000 bottles of champagne, 20,000 glasses of Pimms and 110,000 cups of tea and coffee that are sold during the week.

Various locations

Chinese New Year
7851 6686 | *www.chinatownchinese.co.uk*

The exact venue may vary from year to year, but there's no doubt that this is one of the most outstanding events on London's festival calendar. Celebrations usually take place on the Sunday closest to New Year's Day (depending on the lunar and solar calendars, it falls between the end of January and mid-February each year) and feature parades, music and fireworks through the streets around Soho's Chinatown. Crowds of more than 200,000 people are not unusual (it's the largest celebration of the event outside China), which in recent years has meant that the main parade, organised by London Chinatown Chinese Association, has been re-routed along Charing Cross Road to

Trafalgar Square. This isn't to say that Gerrard Street (the pedestrian thoroughfare that forms the gateway to Chinatown and the point at which the parade used to start) isn't still at the heart of the action. Every Chinese restaurant in the area opens its doors to a stream of customers – both Chinese and non-Chinese – wanting to partake in a traditional new year feast. Food stalls are set up in every available spare space, there are dragon and lion dances through the streets, and a great fireworks display in Leicester Square.

Various locations

Greenwich and Docklands International Festival
8305 1818 | www.festival.org/gdif.html
This fabulous performing arts festival is a relative newcomer on the London calendar (it celebrated its 10 year anniversary in 2006), but it's already made a big splash. A typical programme consists of awesome acts of street entertainment that are a long, long way from wind-walking a la Marcel Marceau; think a battalion of French drummers suspended from a crane over Docklands, or 10 metre high wheels of colour spinning through the streets of Bow rather than a man spray-painted gold and standing still on a plinth. The action takes place at sites throughout Greenwich and east London, usually on an extended weekend in June or July. It's the thrilling interaction of some of the capital's most iconic landmarks, such as Canary Wharf and the Old Royal Naval College, being used as backdrops to giant stilt walkers and the odd piece of inflatable architecture that really makes the mind boggle. Every year the performances are different but one thing's for certain – you will be left thrilled and amazed.

Various locations

London Film Festival
www.lff.org.uk
While not quite endowed with the cachet of Cannes or the glamour of Venice, the two-week London Film Festival is a must for any cinema-lover. Unlike many of its more starry international counterparts, all the viewings at the event are open to the public and offer a chance to see the best in global cinema, from big-budget studio affairs to independent features and shorts. The festival celebrated its 50th year in 2006 and the organiser (the British Film Institute) has got the programme running like a well-oiled machine. The main action – and glitzy, red-carpet premieres – takes place at the Odeon in Leicester Square, but a number of cinemas around the city host screenings and related events, most notably at the National Film Theatre on the South Bank and the Institute of Contemporary Art (see p.194). For a fortnight it feels like London goes movie mad as Hollywood's big hitters fly into town to promote their latest flicks – a welcome bit of sparkle to those otherwise grey November days. Be sure to book early to get a piece of the action.

Various locations

London Open House
www.londonopenhouse.org
This annual celebration runs every weekend in September and offers members of the public the chance to peek behind the doors of more than 500 of the capital's buildings – many of which are not normally open to the public. Organiser Open House, an independent group working with architects, designers and builders, aims to promote a better understanding of structural design across the capital and encourage its citizens to take pride in the diversity of London's architecture. Previous treats have included a chance to get inside some of the newest additions to the city skyline, such as 30 St Mary Axe (the curvaceous Norman Foster-designed City building that's affectionately known locally as the Gherkin) near Tower Hill, as well as some of its oldest. The Museum of Migration (www.19princeletstreet.org.uk), for example, is the former home of a Huguenot master silk weaver in Spitalfields that conceals a synagogue built over its

garden – the building is not yet restored and therefore only rarely open to the public. The Open House weekend is a chance to unlock the door to this and other buildings in the capital and gain a glimpse into the city's history. Guides to the year's participants go on sale about a month before the event.

Various locations ◄

Notting Hill Carnival

www.carnaval.com

What began as a small street festival by and for local residents to celebrate their Afro-Caribbean culture has, more than 40 years down the line, been transformed into not just the largest in London or even the UK, but the single biggest street event in Europe. More than one million revellers descend on W11 each Sunday and Monday of the August bank holiday weekend. Sunday is traditionally quieter – it's Children's Day, which means that the junior members of the local community lead the bands of steel-drum players and DJs in a rich, vibrant procession that wiggles from Westbourne Grove towards Bayswater, and on to the top of Ladbroke Grove near Kensal Green. By Monday afternoon, the streets inside the parade route are throbbing to sound systems and live performances, food stalls sell the obligatory goat curry and jerk chicken, and impromptu parties seem to spill from every house and flat.

Things have got so congested that in 2006, for the first time, the mayor of London organised a sister celebration, Caribbean Showcase, to take place on the Monday in Hyde Park. Both events were deemed a huge success and it's likely that the mayor's festival will continue to run alongside the main celebrations.

Various locations ◄

Thames Festival

7928 8998 | *www.thamesfestival.org*

First launched in 1997 by the mayor of London, this annual two-day September event has quickly grown to become the capital's largest free open-air arts festival. Located on the river roughly between Westminster Bridge and Tower Bridge, the festival is in the shadow of some of London's most iconic monuments, including the Houses of Parliament (p.202) and the London Eye (p.217). An estimated 500,000 people attend the weekend event, which features street theatre, music, acrobatics and dance on and around the river. The highlight of the celebrations is undoubtedly the night carnival, which brings the festivities to a close on the Sunday evening. Running along the South Bank, it features music, dancing and masquerade, drawing revellers in their tens of thousands and culminating in a spectacular firework display over the Thames. The event is the culmination of the annual Coin Street Festival – a series of cultural and arts displays focused along the South Bank throughout the summer (see p.187).

Parks
Other options **Natural Attractions** p.218

London is blessed with an abundance of parks and open spaces. From the high-maintenance lawns of the Royal Parks in central London to the wilds of Hampstead Heath in the north of the city and Richmond Park on the south-east edge of the capital, there is full and easy access to the great outdoors wherever you might be in the city and at any time of year.

The cram of urban living means that many Londoners live in flats without a garden of their own, and so local – and even central London – parks become like one giant communal backyard. On weekends in particular, the city's green spaces fill up as residents move outdoors to walk their dogs, run, cycle and skate or simply kick a football about in an impromptu game with friends. During the summer, picnics are a popular way to while away a sunny afternoon, and during lunch hours and early evenings the parks and abundance of welcoming squares in the city centre buzz with sunbathing office workers.

London's parks are open during daylight hours and access to public areas is free and open to all. Dogs are usually welcome, but cycling, while mostly encouraged, is generally restricted to roads and designated paths. There are a number of private gardens nestling in squares around some of London's more exclusive neighbourhoods to which access is for residents only. A chance to peek into the city's secret gardens does come around once a year, however, when the Open Garden Squares Weekend allows the public to visit some of the many private and institutional grounds across the city. Visit www.opensquares.org for more information.

Battersea Park
Battersea Park
SW8
South Kensington

8871 7534 | *www.batterseapark.org*

Battersea Park lies on the south side of the Thames between Chelsea Bridge and Albert Bridge, and has been open for almost 150 years. The 200-acre site was first opened by Queen Victoria in 1858 after being landscaped with soil dug out during the construction of Victoria docks. It has recently undergone an extensive £11m renovation programme and is looking better than ever. The largest open space in the borough of Wandsworth, Battersea boasts a boating lake, a children's zoo, an athletics track, an art gallery and magnificent display fountains among its many attractions. Its annual November fireworks display – the largest in central London – attracts crowds of more than 55,000. The enclosed events arena (accessed via Chelsea gate) has hosted everything from craft fairs and wedding shows to theatrical and acrobatic performances and parties, while the smaller boules area is popular for fun days in the summer.

Hampstead Heath
Hampstead Heath
NW3
Highgate

7482 7073 | *www.cityoflondon.gov.uk*

Wild and wonderful Hampstead Heath is one of north London's most treasured assets. Everyone who visits has a favourite feature, be it the views across London from Parliament Hill, the untamed beauty of its bathing ponds (originally dug out as reservoirs to supply water to London in the 17th and 18th centuries), the manicured lawns of the magnificent Kenwood House or simply the acres and acres (791 in all) of semi-wild parkland freely available to be explored.

One of the Heath's lesser-known treats is the Pergola and Hill Garden (behind Inverforth House, off North End Way, NW11), an Edwardian structure as long as Canary Wharf is tall, which offers wonderful views towards Harrow on the Hill. The traditional play area at Parliament Hill is a treat for children, and this part of the heath also boasts an outdoor lido and ice-skating rink (over the Christmas period), along with athletics tracks, tennis courts, a petanque pitch and facilities for playing volleyball. Regular walks and guided nature trails are organised throughout the year, and jazz concerts and fun fairs are some of the features of a full programme of summer events.

Holland Park
W8
⊖ **Holland Park**

Holland Park

7361 3003 | *www.rbkc.gov.uk/parksandgardens*

First-time visitors might be a little taken aback by the sound of some of Holland Park's local wildlife; the mournful cry of the resident peacocks come as something of a surprise. But these exotic birds are just the first of a number of striking treats the park has in store. Thanks to the abundance of foxes, rabbits and squirrels, visitors could be forgiven for thinking they'd stumbled into the (albeit very stylised) countryside – foragers are even rewarded with blackberries in the autumn.

The park's highlights include its beautiful formal garden, complete with sundial and fountains, and the wonderful koi carp lake in the Japanese-inspired Kyoto Garden. Its highly praised season of open-air opera (www.operahollandpark.com) remains one of the capital's better-kept secrets. Be sure to book a place in the covered terrace and Dutch garden lounge for guaranteed weatherproof enjoyment. Elsewhere, The Belvedere, a sumptuous restaurant in what was once the summer ballroom of Holland House, a former 17th century Jacobean mansion, is one of the city's more romantic spots. It is, unsurprisingly, a favourite for couples on their wedding day.

Hyde Park
W2
⊖ **Marble Arch**

Hyde Park & Kensington Gardens

7298 2100 | *www.royalparks.gov.uk*

Probably London's most famous open space, Hyde Park is also one of the capital's finest, offering 350 acres of landscaped gardens in which to watch wildlife, horse ride, rollerblade and row. Henry VIII first used Hyde Park as a private hunting ground for deer after acquiring the land from the monks of Westminster Abbey in 1536, but it wasn't until just over 100 years later in 1637 that Charles I opened the park to the public. Long used for national celebrations (as far back as 1814 a fireworks display was organised by the Prince Regent to celebrate the end of the Napoleonic wars) the park frequently hosts concerts, rallies and events. In 2005 it staged its biggest performance

to date: the Live 8 charity concert event. Elsewhere, Speakers' Corner, near Marble Arch, has been a 'cradle of free speech' since 1866, drawing crowds every Sunday morning as ordinary citizens have their say, while the Serpentine has proved popular for sunbathing and swimming since 1930. Other highlights include the Serpentine Gallery, and the Albert Memorial in neighbouring Kensington Gardens, which backs on to the palace in which Princess Diana lived. Indeed, Kensington Gardens and Hyde Park have become synonymous with the late princess. The Diana Memorial Fountain pays tribute to her memory, attracting around one million visitors a year, while the seven mile Diana Memorial Walk follows a trail through Kensington Gardens, Hyde Park and St James's Park (follow the plaques set into the ground).

Lidos

www.lidos.org.uk

The capital's outdoor swimming pools are a summertime treat, and many of them offer a real sense of community – something that's easy to lose in a big city. Brockwell Lido (7274 3088), for example, offers regular themed barbecues that feel like the whole neighbourhood is in attendance. Parliament Hill (7485 5757), the Serpentine (7706 3422) and the largest outdoor swimming pool in Europe, Tooting Bec (8871 7198), all offer an oasis away from the heat and pollution of the city. For year-round swimming, head to London Fields Lido (7254 9038); newly reopened after a 20-year absence, it now offers the capital's first Olympic-sized heated outdoor swimming pool.

Regent's Park

7486 7905 | *www.royalparks.gov.uk*

This lush, carefully landscaped patch of green lying roughly between Baker Street and Primrose Hill offers the largest outdoor sports area in the capital. Almost a quarter of the park's 410 acres are made up of 'The Hub' – a community sports pavilion and pitches plus other facilities for tennis, netball, and golf coaching. Regent's Park is also one of London's prettiest, designed by architect John Nash in 1811, and the perfect place for a summertime stroll. The stunning Queen Mary's Gardens and Rose Gardens (home to around 30,000 blooms of 400 varieties) are perfectly manicured treats, while areas of woodland and wildflowers continue to attract a wide variety of birdlife, for which the park is particularly famous.

Regent's Park is also one of London's top venues for outdoor summer concerts, featuring everything from Shakespeare in the park at the Open Air Theatre (0870 0601811) to puppet shows and lunchtime and evening concerts in its bandstands. A selection of excellent refreshment places includes the Garden Café in Queen Mary's Garden and The Honest Sausage (voted one of the top five restaurants in parks by London's *Evening Standard*), on the Broadwalk near London Zoo. The zoo, located on the north-western edge of the park, separates Regent's Park from Primrose Hill, a pretty, relatively small patch of central London grassland that offers excellent views across the city from the top of its grassy knoll.

Richmond Park

8948 3209 | *www.royalparks.gov.uk*

At 2,500 acres, Richmond Park is London's largest Royal Park, and famous for its ancient oak trees and roaming deer (Charles I introduced red and fallow deer for hunting when he moved to Richmond Palace to escape the plague in 1615; about 650 remain today). The site is a National Nature Reserve and feels rather more like wild countryside than the carefully cultivated space of the city's other Royal Parks. There's always an exception, however, and here it comes in the form of the Isabella Plantation, near Broomford Hill, a beautifully maintained and organically run woodland garden that was planted post-second world war and is fenced to keep grazing deer out. Home to a national collection of azaleas and rhododendrons, it is particularly beautiful to visit in April and May when the flowers are in bloom (regular guided tours are available). Richmond Park's sheer scale means that it's popular with sports enthusiasts too. Its flat, wide expanse makes it a great place for informal kickabouts among groups of picnickers. In addition, the park offers some of the best stretches of road for designated cyclists in the city and bike hire is available year-round from the Roehampton Gate car park (phone 07050 209249). Would-be anglers can buy a fishing permit (8948 3209) and try their luck at Pen Ponds, and there's even a 'pay and play' 18 hole golf course and driving range (8876 3205).

215

St James's Park
SW1
⊖ **St. James's Park**

St James's Park & Green Park

7930 1793 | www.royalparks.gov.uk

Flanked by Buckingham Palace, St James's Palace and the Houses of Parliament, St James's Park is steeped in royal history. Formerly the site of a 13th century leper hospital, it was taken over by Henry VIII in 1532 (for yet another deer park) and it is still used for royal ceremonies today (most memorably, the annual Beating Retreat in summer, p.209). Its location at the heart of London's tourist trail makes it one of the most visited parks in Europe (around 5.5 million people pass through each year), but St

James's still manages to retain an air of tranquil calm. One of its top attractions is the small colony of pelicans to be found near Duck Island. The birds were first introduced in 1664 as a gift from the Russian ambassador and their daily feed at 15:00 is a much-loved ritual that's frequently enlivened by their brazen mingling with the park's human visitors. Considerably quieter, nearby Green Park's 40 acres of grassland is the link between St James's Park and Hyde Park. While lacking both the pomp and ceremony of its renowned neighbours, the park is not without its historical significance; it was a duelling ground until 1887, and is also famous as the site of a rebellion against the marriage of Mary I to Phillip II of Spain in 1554.

With its mature trees and grassland, the park is a favourite spot for Londoners to escape the bustle of the city centre, and is popular with joggers and sunbathers alike. It is also famous as a site of remembrance for Commonwealth citizens who fought in the two world wars – memorials to Canadian soldiers and servicemen from the Caribbean, Africa and the Indian sub-continent can be found near Constitution Hill.

Victoria Park

Victoria Park
E2
⊖ **Bethnal Green**

8985 1957 | www.londontown.com

London's third-largest cultivated open space remains, somewhat bafflingly, one of its best-kept secrets. Quite why that is, is something of a mystery, for Victoria Park is a verdant oasis in the middle of the East End, complete with picturesque lakes, a deer enclosure, children's playground and the quaint, rose-strewn delights of an old English garden.

Visitors may well be too enchanted with the park's many delights (there are few things more enjoyable than a Sunday afternoon resting in the shade of one of its many trees, watching the cyclists, dog-walkers and five-a-side football players roll by) to be t concerned about the site's history – but the story of Victoria Park's beginnings is a fascinating insight into part of London's past. The park opened in 1845 after a 30,000-strong petition supporting a campaign for a public park to rival those of the Royal Parks in the capital's west was presented to Queen Victoria. The monarch supported the then-common consensus that open spaces were both morally and physically beneficial and granted permission for a park aimed primarily at the working classes in London's East End to bear her name.

The idea of Victoria Park as a kind of 'people's park' has been sustained throughout its history. Not only did it originally have its own 'speakers' corner', but it was renowned for its use as a site for public meetings, from the Chartist rally in 1848 to the Great Dock Strike of 1889. It was a key part of the home front during the second world war and even housed German prisoners of war.

Other Attractions

Westminster Bridge Rd
SE1
⇌ ⊖ *Waterloo*

London Eye
0870 9908883 | *www.londoneye.com*
The London Eye, conceived as part of the country's millennium celebrations, has become the capital's most popular paid-for attraction – an average of 10,000 people visit it every day (over 3.5 million every year). Not bad for what was only ever intended to be a temporary construction (the initial planning permission for the giant observation wheel was for 25 years only). With moves towards an extension in progress, and even talk of listing the structure to preserve its status indefinitely, it's fast looking to become a permanent icon of the city – much like another so-called temporary construction, the Eiffel Tower, which was erected for the Paris Exposition in 1889 and still stands well over 100 years later. Located on the South Bank, the London Eye is the largest observation wheel in the world. It has 32 sealed capsules (one for each of London's boroughs) weighing in at 10 tonnes each, and is able to carry up to 800 passengers per half-hour revolution. On a clear day you can see as far as Windsor Castle, almost 25 miles away. But for all the remarkable statistics, what really impresses about the Eye is its sheer, joyful beauty. Its stylish curve has quickly come to represent all that is forward-thinking about London; the easy grace with which it sits against London's historical architectural icons is symbolic of the capital's willingness to embrace the future while still retaining pride in its past.

Belvedere Rd
SE1
⇌ ⊖ *Waterloo*

Southbank Centre
0870 3804300 | *www.southbankcentre.org.uk*
The Southbank Centre arts complex that dominates the view of the Thames riverbank on either side of Waterloo Bridge dates back to 1951 when the Royal Festival Hall was built in honour of the Festival of Britain. Additional buildings and concert halls were added over the next decade and a half (the Hayward Gallery wasn't built until 1968) and now incorporate treasures such as the National Film Theatre (NFT). The result is a classic example of 60s brutalist architecture that is both loved and loathed by Londoners.
In recent years, however, the tide of opinion seems to be turning in Southbank's favour. Architecturally its future is protected (the Royal Festival Hall has recently undergone a comprehensive renovation project and is now a Grade-I listed building) but what's really placed it in the heart of Londoners is the egalitarian approach that has been adopted to its use. The main halls are the venues for some of the best concerts and theatre the city has to offer, with an eclectic programme that runs from small plays by first-time writers to grandiose staging of the classics, and from classical concerts performed by world-renowned orchestras to alternative music and poetry events, such as those staged in the annual Meltdown festival over the summer.
Outside, meanwhile, people enjoy the riverside cafes and restaurants (there are few better places to enjoy a coffee or a drink on a summer's day than the benches outside the NFT cafe), browse the interesting second-hand book market and take in the street performances as skateboarders show off their stuff underneath the complex's tiers and ramps.

217

With the relatively recent additions of two neighbouring attractions, the London Eye on one side and Tate Modern on the other, the Southbank Centre's future as a cultural magnet is assured. And with all those people breathing new life into the place, its austere lines no longer seem quite so brutal as they once did.

Natural Attractions

Many of London's 'natural' attractions – those that connect the visitor to the city's natural rather than purely architectural beauty – are not, in fact, that natural at all. The river Thames is the capital's defining natural landmark, although its form has been artificially manipulated by the building of the embankment areas in the 19th century. Many of London's smaller natural waterways have also been engineered to create the pretty network of canals evident today. There are of course plenty of parks and open spaces in the city (see p.213), as well as beautiful areas of countryside out of town that are perfect for a weekend away (p.227).

Various locations ◀

Canals and Waterways

01903 201120 | www.british-waterways.co.uk

While not strictly a 'natural' attraction, what remains of London's canal network is the inner city equivalent of the great outdoors. The waters themselves are used largely for pleasure boating while their towpaths are popular with commuting cyclists and Sunday strollers, and these waterways offer a wonderful alternative view on the capital. The Regent's Canal, for example, runs for more than two miles across north London, from Little Venice to Camden Lock, passing through London Zoo and Regent's Park along the way. For a hint of the East End's industrial past, follow the Grand Union Canal through Victoria Park, into the Limehouse basin and on through Bow. A leaflet of canal walks is available from British Waterways (see p.226), but if you simply head to your nearest waterway and explore you're sure to find something to delight.

Various locations ◀

River Thames

www.riverthames.co.uk

The river Thames is without a doubt one of the capital's greatest natural attractions – even if what helps to define it is the wonderful cityscape that has built up around it. In central London, around the South Bank, the river provides the backdrop for some of the city's grandest architectural jewels; travel further out of the city and it's used for fishing, punting and rowing. A kind of scavenging called 'mudlarking' is a popular activity undertaken on its banks at low tide; it's not unknown for treasure hunters to recover ancient coins, artefacts and pieces of pottery, especially in the City area. But for a real taste of how man and nature have combined to create a great wonder, a visit to the Thames Barrier is a must. This spectacular metallic structure crosses a 523m stretch of the river just beyond North Greenwich and is the second-largest movable flood barrier in the world. There's a small museum to give visitors an insight into how it works (8305 4188).

Virginia Water

Wick Rd
Surrey
⇌ Virginia Water

01753 860222 | *www.theroyallandscape.co.uk*

To anyone visiting now it's almost impossible to imagine that Virginia Water hasn't nestled in this quiet corner on the outskirts of Greater London, just beyond the historic royal town of Windsor, since time immemorial – but this picturesque lake was only dammed and flooded in 1753. There are clues, of course, in the follies and temples built around the water's edge that this is a landscape that was once the playground of kings and queens, but a quick dip into the stunning surrounding woodlands dispels any sense that you are anywhere other than in one of the country's loveliest natural environments.

Nature Reserves

There's something quite refreshing about visiting ecological projects and wildlife sanctuaries in the middle of one of Europe's most relentlessly urban cities – the paradox makes it all the more special. The marshy land on which much of the capital was built means that wetlands have been able to be preserved on its edges (and, in the case of the London Wetland Centre, recreated in the city itself), offering a safe haven to native birds, animals and plants. For something a little more manmade, but no less spectacular, Kew Gardens is one of the world's most important centres for plant conservation.

Kew Gardens

Royal Botanic
Gardens, Kew
TW9
⊖ Kew Gardens

8332 5655 | *www.rbgkew.org.uk*

While not strictly a nature reserve, the Royal Botanic Gardens (to use Kew's proper name) is recognised as one of the leading plant conservation centres in the world. Many of its botanical specimens were planted in the 17th and 18th centuries and much of the centre's ongoing research focuses on this extraordinary collection. There is much to see for the casual visitor too. Wildlife and conservation areas include a bee garden, a stag beetle loggery, a biodiversity garden and rare native trees. Visit in spring to see the woodland floor become a lush carpet of bluebells, snowdrops and wild garlic. There are formal gardens too, including rose, Japanese and rock gardens, while the iconic glass-and-steel Victorian Palm House is recognised as one of the finest structures of its kind in the world.

Queen Elizabeth's Walk
SW13
≄**Barnes**

London Wetland Centre

8409 4400 | *www.wwt.org.uk*

The London Wetland Centre is the only project of its kind in the world – a wild expanse of manmade wetlands in the heart of a capital city. It covers 40 spectacular acres and was created on a series of former reservoirs. Local birds and wildlife have taken to it like ducks to water – in 2006 four avocet chicks hatched in the centre, a rarity as these birds tend not to breed inland. The modern visitor centre offers vast expanses of glass windows through which you can see the 180 species of wild birds the site attracts each year. Top spots include peregrine falcons and a breeding colony of sand martins, along with more than half the UK's species of dragonfly and eight species of bat.

Purfleet, Essex
RM13
≄**Purfleet**

Rainham Marshes

01708 899840 | *www.rspb.org.uk*

This nature reserve is the largest remaining wetland in the upper reaches of the Thames Estuary. The land was bought by the Royal Society for the Protection of Birds, and opened in late 2006. It's particularly notable for its wading birds, but is also home to finches, birds of prey and wintering wildfowl, along with wetland plants, insects and one of the highest densities of water vole in the UK. The dashing new visitor centre has been built with the environment in mind – solar panels, rainwater harvesting and optimum use of natural light are just some of its features. The views from the centre are spectacular, but better yet is the chance to explore the marshes themselves. The Wednesday guided walks are popular, and if you can make it out of bed in time, the 'dawn chorus' walks are excellent.

Zoos & Farms

London Zoo may be one of the capital's biggest attractions and a failsafe option for a great family day out, but it's just one of many attractions that allow visitors to get up close and personal with nature's creatures. There are a number of local petting zoos and city farms dotted throughout the capital – Alexandra Palace (8365 2121), for example, has one that's open year-round – while London Aquarium is the largest aquatic centre of its type in Europe. Its huge, walk-through tanks give visitors a hands-on experience that's hugely popular with visitors and locals alike.

1a Goldsmith's Row
E2
⊖**Bethnal Green**

Hackney City Farm

7729 6381 | *www.hackneycityfarm.co.uk*

About 200 years ago, this site was a farmers' market, but it became a brewery and factory before being transformed into a city farm in 1984. As well as housing animals, this farm offers a programme of classes and events, and hosts craft activities including children's dance lessons, pottery, stone sculpture and textile printing. There's a cafe serving organic food (p.415), and afternoon feed-the-animal sessions at 16:00. Open Tuesday to Sunday.

1 Cressfield Close
NW5
≄⊖**Kentish Town**

Kentish Town City Farm

7916 5421 | *www.ktcityfarm.org.uk*

In the heart of a local authority housing project in north London sits a gem in the shape of this city farm – one of the first of its kind to be set up in London, in 1972. Here people can learn different aspects of animal care, and everyone is encouraged to handle the chickens, cows, goats, horses, pigs and sheep, some of which are rare breeds. Entrance is free, although donations are welcomed, as are volunteers wishing to work with animals or children. There's also a classroom, stables, picnic area and gardens. Open Tuesday to Sunday.

London Aquarium

County Hall,
Westminster Bridge Rd
SE1
Waterloo

7967 8000 | *www.londonaquarium.co.uk*
Centrally located on the South Bank in the old County Hall building, the city's aquarium displays one of Europe's largest exhibitions of global aquatic life, in over 2.5 million litres of water. More than 350 species are divided into 14 zones, each of which simulates a different environment. The Pacific section, for example, is home to four species of shark and puffer fish, while mono glide through the mangrove zone. The touch pool is hugely popular – visitors are invited to stroke giant winged rays and other flat fish. A favourite time to visit is during feeding (generally on Mondays, Wednesdays and Fridays from 12:00-12:30) when divers plunge into the main Atlantic tank, while a programme of regular educational talks gives visitors the chance to learn more about the aquarium's commitment to conservation.

London Zoo

Regent's Park
NW1
Camden Town

7722 3333 | *www.londonzoo.com*
The capital's main zoo is a popular year-round family attraction, although its central location can be the cause of the occasional surprise for passers by. In 2006, a dozen cheeky squirrel monkeys scaled the trees in their enclosure to freedom – much to the surprise of people strolling through Regent's Park. The zoo's animal checklist takes in all the big-name favourites, along with rarities such as Komodo dragons, and the curious meerkats and charismatic penguins are perennially popular. The zoo has been accused in the past of not providing enough space for the animals, but renovation projects have improved things. Indeed, London Zoo is a strong supporter of animal conservation and actively encourages visitors to get involved – you can even help by adopting an animal if you take a shine to one.

Mudchute Park & Farm

Pier St
E14
DLR *Mudchute*

7515 5901 | *www.mudchute.org*
Basking in the shadow of Canary Wharf, Mudchute is home to Europe's biggest city farm. Originally a dumping ground for spoil and silt from nearby Millwall Dock, the 'mud chute' grew over and a wild habitat developed. But it wasn't until local residents protested against an application for the proposed building of a high-rise estate on the land that its true worth was recognised. In 1977 the Mudchute Association was formed to protect and develop the area. Animals including horses, goats, sheep, cows, geese, ducks and even llamas have all been introduced, and it's a great place for kids to learn about farm life. The site includes an equestrian and education centre, a garden centre, and small shop and cafe.

Vauxhall City Farm

165 Tyers St
SE11
Vauxhall

7582 4204 | *www.vauxhallcityfarm.org.uk*
A sanctuary amid the jumble of transport links, offices and urban dwellings that make up busy Vauxhall, this small site has horses, sheep and chickens, as well as a therapeutic riding centre, ecology garden, bug house and wildlife pond. There is also a community garden and allotments where local residents produce and exchange their own food. The accent is on training disadvantaged young people, the elderly and those with special needs. Open Wednesday to Sunday.

22

Tours & Sightseeing

Other options **Weekend Breaks** p.227

Everyone knows that London is a big city with a lot to see. Exploring on your own is a great way to get to know it, but sometimes it's just easier and more convenient to leave it to the experts. Whether you're new to the capital, a visitor, or even a long-time resident wanting to learn a little more about the place in which you live, there are people who are only too happy to show you the way.

Tourism is one of London's biggest industries and there are a multitude of sightseeing options to choose from. You can explore on foot, on two or four wheels, or even, in the case of London Duck Tours, by amphibious land-and-sea vehicle. Another reason to choose a tour over going it alone is that many of the bigger operators have special relationships with the most popular attractions, offering fast-track entry and separate guided tours. For a special occasion, a tailor-made bespoke tour is a wonderful way to learn more about London, its history and its treasures. Look out for Blue Badge guides (see p.226), who have to undergo rigorous study and testing in order to qualify.

The following information is an overview of the different type of tours offered, and some of the best companies that operate them.

Sightseeing Tours

Private driven sightseeing tours let you set the pace – days out are arranged around the attractions you most want to see and time can be built in for any extras, such as breaks for visiting shops or sights. Set routes are also an option if you'd like someone else to do the planning. If you want to blend in with the crowd you can take a special taxi or car tour, or if you prefer to be flash you can do your sightseeing by limo.

Various locations

Black Taxi Tours of London

7935 9363 | *www.blacktaxitours.co.uk*

London cabbies are famous for having 'The Knowledge' – knowing the streets of London like the back of their hand (p.36) – so who better to show you around the capital? Opt for a general two-hour sightseeing tour, one of the special tours, such as Secret London or Tales of the Thames, or even customise your own outing. Two-hour tours cost £85 (good for up to five passengers), and there's a £5 supplement on weekends and bank holidays.

Various locations

Capital Limo

0800 1951244 | *www.capitallimo.co.uk*

Fancy having everyone staring at you as you stare at the sights? You and your group can clamber into your choice of stretch limousine and be driven all over town in showbiz style. Prices start at £195 for a three-hour tour, with room for eight to ten people in the limo.

Various locations

Chauffeurs UK

8404 2356 | *www.chauffeur.org.uk*

Chauffeurs UK offers full and half-day private tours of the capital in luxury, understated style. Tailor-make your own excursion, or choose from one of the company's five set tours of central London. Day-long trips outside London are also available. You'll pay from £165 for half a day in a luxury sedan, plus £1.65 per mile.

Bicycle Tours

Combine your sightseeing with a healthy workout by jumping on a bike and powering your own way around the city. Some of the major traffic thoroughfares can be a little hair-raising for cyclists to say the least so if you're going off on your own make sure you take advice from the hire shop when you plan your route, and use a helmet as well. If you've really got the pedal-power bug, you can also get from A to B by flagging down one of the many pedicabs that operate in central London.

Various locations

Capital Sport
01296 631671 | www.capital-sport.co.uk
Capital Sport offers self-guided day trips and short breaks that allow you to explore London and, if you want to escape the city, countryside in regions such as Kent and the Cotswolds. Overnight tours include hotel accommodation and luggage transport. Day trips cost from £35, short breaks from £159.

1a Gabriel's Wharf
SE1
⇌ ⊖ Waterloo

The London Bicycle Tour Company
7928 6838 | www.londonbicycle.com
Located on the South Bank for instant access to the Thames path, The London Bicycle Tour Company gives cyclists the option of pedalling their way through one of three half-day guided tours of the capital's attractions, or just hiring a bike and going it alone. The tours cost £14.95, and bicycle hire is from £2.50 per hour.

Boat Tours

Take to the Thames to get a completely different perspective on some of the capital's most popular landmarks. There are various guided tours to choose from, or use one of the water taxi options to construct your own mini-tour. Many boats provide onboard commentary, and Travelcard holders (see p.38) are generally entitled to discounts of up to 30%.

Embankment Pier
WC2
⊖ Embankment

Catamaran Cruises
7987 1185 | www.catamarancruisers.co.uk
Circular boat-tours depart every 15 minutes from Waterloo, Embankment, Bankside, Tower and Greenwich piers. If you want to make an evening of it, try a dinner cruise – it's a lovely, romantic way to see the city by night. Circular tours cost £9 for adults, and dinner trips start at £69.

Westminster Pier ◀
SW1
⊖ *Westminster*

Circular Cruises
7839 2111
A hop-on, hop-off boat tour that sails from Westminster or Festival Pier (summer only) to St Katharine Dock, near Tower Bridge. Services and running times alter according to the season, so be sure to check before setting out. A one-day adult ticket costs £7.

55 York Rd ◀
SE1
⊖ *Waterloo*

London Duck Tours
7928 3132 | *www.londonducktours.co.uk*
The perfect way to see all the capital has to offer by road and on water without having to change vehicles – if you don't mind being seen in a bright yellow amphibious vehicle that was originally used to take the troops ashore on the D-Day landings in the second world war. A tour costs £17.50 for adults.

Various locations ◀

Tate to Tate
7887 8888 | *www.tate.org.uk/tatetotate*
Runs every 40 minutes between the Tate Britain and Tate Modern galleries (see p.196). It's a great way to get a 'highlights' tour of London by river in a bespoke catamaran – the boat's painted design is by artist Damien Hirst. Sites passed include the Houses of Parliament, the London Eye (where the boat makes a stop) and St Paul's. Single adult fare is £4.30 single, while a 'river roamer' ticket (multiple-use hop-on, hop-off) costs £7.30.

Westminster Pier ◀
SW1
⊖ *Westminster*

Thames River Services
7930 4097 | *www.westminsterpier.co.uk*
A year-round water taxi service that runs along the Thames from Westminster Pier to Greenwich. Boats depart every 40 minutes. If you want to travel a little further an alternative, extended route takes passengers as far east as the Thames Barrier. Adult fares are £7 for a single ticket, £9 for a return (£8.70/£11 for the extended trip).

Bus Tours
Other options **Walking Tours** p.225

One of the best ways to see London is from the top of a double-decker bus. Operators offer one-day hop-on, hop-off tours on several routes through the capital's top attractions, allowing you to set your own pace and see what you want to see. All have onboard commentary (with translations). For those who prefer a more hands-free approach to sightseeing, guided panoramic coach tours are also available. These include options for full and half-day tours in a luxury coach with plenty of photo opportunities and fast-track admission to selected tourist sites.

Various locations ◀

Big Bus Tours
7233 9533 | *www.bigbustours.com*
A 24-hour hop-on, hop-off ticket on one of these open-top double-decker sightseeing tours costs £20. There are two interchangeable routes, and the fare includes a river cruise and guided walking tours. Fast-track attraction tickets are also available. Get on at Paddington Station, Marble Arch, Green Park, Victoria and Trafalgar Square.

Various locations ◀

Evan Evans Tours
7950 1777 | *www.evanevanstours.co.uk*
This long-established tour company offers three London sightseeing trips in luxury coaches, led by a qualified Blue Badge guide. A full-day tour of the best of the capital's attractions, complete with river cruise and a pub lunch, costs from £65 per person. Half-day tours are available from £28.

224

Various locations ◄ ## The Original London Sightseeing Tour
8877 1722 | *www.theoriginaltour.com*

You can buy your tickets on the day for this hop-on, hop-off service, or book online with a discount. Buses leave every 10-20 minutes from Baker Street, Piccadilly Circus, Marble Arch, Victoria and Embankment Pier, and include a free river cruise. Tickets are valid for 24 hours from first use. The on-the-day fare is £18 for adults.

Various locations ◄ ## Premium Tours
7404 5100 | *www.premiumtours.co.uk*

Specialist company Premium Tours offers a range of bespoke bus excursions of the capital. Get ghoulish with the Jack the Ripper tour, which takes you on a drive through the notorious Victorian murderer's old East End haunts followed by a 'terror cruise' of the Thames at night. Adults cost £19.50. Other itineraries include a £35 half-day visit by coach to the capital's top royal attractions, with a private guided tour of the Tower of London – a must for anyone interested in the monarchy.

Helicopter & Plane Tours

For a real treat, you can take to the skies and get a bird's-eye view of the capital. There are a number of companies offering helicopter tours over London, and while most of these take off from outside the capital in neighbouring counties such as Surrey or Kent, it is possible to fly from central London itself. Small planes are a slightly cheaper option, but bear in mind that whatever way you plan to do it the weather and air-traffic control can affect whether or not you'll be able to fly. Most companies offer seats on a set route but if you'd prefer something a little more tailor-made, charter flights are the ultimate luxury option. You can take a chopper ride with Into The Blue (01959 578100) and London Helicopter Tours (8249 6055) for about £120 per person, while Experience Mad (www.experiencemad.co.uk) offers light-aircraft flights from £75.

Walking Tours

Much of London's varied history is wrapped up in the fabric of the capital itself, so a fun way to unlock its secrets is to undertake a walking tour. Whatever your area of interest might be there's a good chance that someone, somewhere has designed a walk that will appeal to you. Choose from self-guided walks and set your own pace, or join one of the entertaining themed walks that reveal everything from haunted sites to historic highlights. Most individual attractions offer comprehensive tours around their own premises, but, for something that covers a wider area, such as a period in history or a favourite London character, nothing beats joining one of the many specific excursions that are on offer. Just make sure you're wearing comfortable shoes.

Show Us Your Badge

If you're considering joining a tour or hiring a private guide, it's worth checking whether they carry a Blue Badge – this means that they are officially registered, have received proper training and should know the city inside out. There are more than 1,000 operating in London (see www.blue-badge.org.uk).

Guided Walking Tours

There are a plethora of guided tours on offer around the capital, covering pretty much every theme or subject you can think of. In the evenings it's not unusual to see groups of people huddled on a street corner, intently listening to the pearls of wisdom being thrown their way by a knowledgeable guide. Original London Walks (7624 3978) is one of the capital's most established walking tour companies, and offers a huge range of itineraries. Whether it's exploring areas such as Mayfair and Little Venice, ghost tours or tracing the old haunts of notables from The Beatles to Jack the Ripper, it's all covered. If the dark and ghoulish side of London is your thing, TV historian Richard Jones also runs Jack the Ripper and ghost tours (8530 8443). City Secrets Walks does spooky tours too, as well as a very good guide to Shakespeare's Elizabethan London (7625 5155). The similarly named Secret London (8881 2933) offers insightful explorations of different parts of town, as well as theatrical, legal and film-themed tours. For a specialist movie-related expedition join film historian Sandra Shevey's tour of locations used in Alfred Hitchcock pictures.

Self-Guided Walking Tours

If you'd prefer to stride out on your own, there are several self-guided options to get you around town. Pick up a free London Wall Walk leaflet from the Museum of London (see p.206), which will guide you through a two-mile tour of the old Roman wall that once encircled the ancient city of Londinium. The Jubilee Walkway is a 14-mile self-guided walk originally created in honour of the Queen's Silver Jubilee in 1977, and extended and updated for her Golden Jubilee in 2002. There are five central London itineraries in total, each dotted with plaques acknowledging important sites along the way. Leaflets are available at www.jubileewalkway.com or from Tourist Information offices. Another plaque-based option is to tour around some of the 800 or so English Heritage 'Blue Plaques' that adorn many of the capital's private residences, marking former homes of famous or notable people. You can design your own walk at www.english-heritage.org.uk/blueplaques or get hold of a guidebook from most bookshops. If you'd like to escape to the water, London's canals offer tranquil settings with great views and some of the city's oldest and most fascinating history. Download one of British Waterways' free walking guides from www.waterscape.com/londonwalks and explore hidden London, including routes from Islington to Limehouse and the pretty area around Little Venice.

Hyde Park

Cheap Fright

Cheap flights to Europe with budget airlines easyJet and Ryanair are hugely popular with Londoners, but be aware that flights don't always land at your destination's main airport. This could add another hour or so – not to mention a fair amount of hassle – to your journey. Always check with the airline before you book.

Weekend Breaks

The rise in low-cost, no-frills air travel in recent years has seen a sharp increase in the number of passengers flying to short-haul destinations from London. Weekend city breaks are particularly popular with top destinations including Barcelona, Amsterdam and Prague, while shoppers love to pop across the pond for a weekend flexing their plastic in New York. Paris is a big hit for couples seeking a weekend of romance, and getting there has never been easier. Eurostar began operating its direct rail service between London and the French capital a little over 10 years ago and the partly operational high-speed rail link from King's Cross (services previously departed from Waterloo) has reduced journey times to less than two and a half hours. That's around the same time it takes to get from London to Manchester by train so it's not hard to see its appeal.

None of this should undermine what's on offer in the UK, however. There are a number of destinations – for day trips or overnight stays – that are easily reached from the capital. Some of the highlights include the pretty countryside of the Cotswolds, including the university town of Oxford and Shakespeare's Stratford-upon-Avon, and the wonderful mix of sweeping Georgian architecture and ancient Roman history in the city of Bath in Somerset.

In summer, Londoners can't get enough of the seaside, and the coastal city of Brighton, less than an hour away by train, is a popular choice. The delights of Devon and Cornwall, in south-west England, make for popular annual summer holidays and longer breaks.

If activity holidays are more your thing, you might want to try a cycling trip in the New Forest or a walking holiday in the beautiful mountains of the Lake District. Breaks to other UK cities are becoming increasingly popular – Manchester in particular is a favourite with clubbers and gay travellers. Most big towns in the UK are within reach by train or coach, but local bus services in smaller towns can be patchy to say the least. For information about timetables and prices to all UK destinations by rail, contact National Rail Enquires (0845 7484950 and www.nationalrail.co.uk). For UK-wide information on long-distance travel by coach try National Express (0870 5808080; www.nationalexpress.com).

Further afield, Scotland's capital city, Edinburgh, is a worthy choice. Its annual arts and comedy festival each August is a particular draw, and attracts well over a million people from around the world.

Explorer Online

No doubt now that you own an Explorer book you will want to check out the rest of our product range. From maps and vistors' guides to restaurant guides and photography books, Explorer has a spectacular collection of products just waitiing for you to buy, you genius! Check out our website for more info.
www.explorer publishing.com

Dublin was for a long time a favourite destination for rowdy groups on stag and hen weekends, but as cheaper destinations in eastern Europe have opened up, the Irish capital has regained its reputation as a spot for a more cultural break (much to the relief of locals).

If you're planning to explore in the UK, hiring a car is probably your best option. The following are some suggestions for a range of trips outside London. Those in the south of England have been selected for their suitability either as daytrips or for weekend breaks, those further afield require at least an overnight stay but can easily be seen in a weekend. It's a far from exhaustive list, however; one of the great joys of the capital is its location as an easy springboard to other places. You could spend years in London without taking in everything there is to see, but with some Londoners even travelling as far afield as Cape Town on extended weekend breaks, it quickly becomes clear that, budget aside, the only limit is your imagination.

22

The Cotswolds

If you're travelling by car it's easy to tour the pretty area around the gentle slopes of the Cotswolds Hills that roughly covers three counties in the heart of England – Oxfordshire, Gloucestershire and Worcestershire. The area is famous for limestone villages (in a beautifully mellow honey-coloured hue), thatched cottages, stately homes and a gentle pace of life. Stay a little longer, however, and you'll find there's plenty more to explore. Start your trip in Oxfordshire, amid the spires of the famous university town, and from there move into the Cotswolds proper.

Highlights include Blenheim Palace (www.blenheimpalace.com) in Woodstock, home of the Duke of Marlborough and the birthplace of Winston Churchill, and the idyllic village of Stanton, 12 miles from Stow-on-the-Wold. Often described as the prettiest village in the Cotswolds, Stanton has barely changed in 300 years. The Mount Pub (01386 484316), perched on a hill overlooking the village, is perfect for a sundowner. Further south is Cirencester. It was the second-largest town in Roman Britain and boasts good ruins, including an amphitheatre. Regular markets still take place on Monday and Friday each week as they have done for over 1,000 years. Perhaps most famous of all, however, is Stratford-upon-Avon, birthplace of William Shakespeare and beautifully situated on the River Dart. Here you can visit the playwright's childhood home at Henley Street (01789 204016), attend a production at the Royal Shakespeare Theatre (01789 403444) or just soak up the atmosphere in the town.

Three Choirs Vineyard (01521 890223) offers unique weekend breaks for Londoners looking to escape the capital for a few days. It has eight well-appointed rooms that overlook the vineyards from which Three Choirs' very own wine is created, and a sumptuous restaurant offering modern British cuisine.

Bath

Located on the southern edge of the Cotswolds, but worthy of a visit in its own right, the city of Bath has a lot to offer the casual visitor, from the sweeping Georgian terraces of Royal Crescent to the famous baths after which the city is named. Bath has been declared a World Heritage Site, and at the heart of it lies the spectacularly preserved remains of the Roman Baths (01225 477725) themselves. Modern day visitors can get a taste of what it must have been like for the Romans in the recently opened Thermae Bath Spa (www.thermaebathspa.com), where you can bathe in naturally hot waters. Bath's most famous resident, Jane Austen, lived here at the beginning of the 18th century and set two of her novels, *Northanger Abbey* and *Persuasion* around the city. The dedicated Jane Austen Centre (01225 443000) offers a glimpse into her life and work, while the Regency Tea Rooms invites visitors to live the dream, in classic surroundings, complete with waitresses in period costume. There's more Georgian history to be found at Number One Royal Crescent (01225 428126), the first house to be built on Bath's most famous street and now perfectly preserved as a museum. Nearby Salisbury is home to an impressive 800-year-old cathedral, which houses Europe's oldest clock and one of the few remaining copies of the *Magna Carta*. Farleigh Hungerford Castle (01225 754026), nine miles south-east of Bath, contains a rich history, chequered with treason and witchcraft. The 16th and 17th century 'death masks' in its crypt are some of the best examples of their kind to be found in the UK. For places to stay in Bath see www.visitbath.co.uk.

The New Forest

In 1079 William the Conqueror designated the vast expanse of wild woodland to be his 'new hunting forest', and now, nearly 1,000 years later, it's not only still here, but remains largely untouched. Located in pretty Hampshire, the New Forest national park lies within an hour or two's drive of London and is best explored by foot, bicycle or on horseback. There are excellent walking routes for solo exploration, or you can join one of the regular year-round guided walks. Visit the network of pretty villages and working farms in and around the forest or discover grazing deer deep within the wooded landscape. A good place to start is The New Forest Museum & Visitor Centre (02380 283444) in the town of Lyndhurst. From there, the options are endless – in and around the forest are all manner of leisure activities, from wildlife parks and Roman ruins to historic houses and museums.

End Of The Pier

Brighton's historic West Pier, which was once a splendid example of Victorian architecture but fell into disrepair, was destroyed by high winds and fire in 2003. Its remains can still be seen from the seafront, although Brighton's other pier, the Palace Pier, continues to be a major attraction.

Brighton & Beyond

Brighton is one of the UK's most charming seaside towns (although it now has 'city' status). It's affectionately nicknamed London-on-Sea, due not only to its regular visitors from the capital, but also because of the huge number of Londoners who move there permanently. Highly urbane (the shopping in the area around The Lanes can be as good as you get in the capital) and unfailingly cheesy (Brighton Pier happily remains a tasteless stretch of fairground rides, cheap amusement centres and the inevitable sticks of Brighton rock), it remains a town eminently at ease with its dual personality. It's home to a merry band of hippies, weekend clubbers and a legendary gay scene, all of which is as appealing to its large student population as it is to its ever-increasing number of metropolitan sophisticates.

If you're only visiting for the day, you'll probably get no further than the pretty, pebbled seafront and the pier, a stroll around The Lanes and a visit to the wonderfully over-the-top, Indian-inspired Royal Pavilion (01273 290900), designed by John Nash for George IV as a summer retreat. If you stay longer, nearby Lewes, a 15 minute drive away, is worth exploring. This pretty historical town is particularly fun on Bonfire Night, when the streets fill with revellers for a notoriously fiery parade.

A short train ride from Brighton is Arundel Castle (01930 882173), home of the Duke of Norfolk, and open to the public every summer. A spectacular castle and stately home, it's beautifully situated overlooking the River Arun and dates back nearly 1,000 years. Its vaulted Fitzalan Chapel and gardens are a particular delight. Nearby Petworth House (01798 342207) is a suitably stately home and offers wonderful parklands filled with deer, but the real treasures of Petworth are a collection of paintings by Turner, who once had a studio here. The Chattri Indian War Memorial on the Downs above Patcham, just outside Brighton, is a touching monument honouring the Indian soldiers who fought for Britain during the first world war and died of their wounds at the Royal Pavilion Hospital.

Royal Pavilion

Missing The Boat

Windermere, the largest lake in the national park, was a popular home for motorised watersports such as powerboating and waterskiing – but no longer. In 2005, in a bid to restore tranquillity and safety to the lake, park authorities imposed a 10mph speed limit on powered vehicles using Windermere. The move was backed by many, but campaigned against by others who claim the ban has robbed enthusiasts of the country's best spot to enjoy powered water activities, as well as harming the local economy. You can still sail or undertake other activities on the water, but the debate over the speed restrictions are set to rumble on.

The Lake District

If city life is getting you down, then a few days of fresh air and wholesome walking in the spectacular Lake District is the perfect remedy. It's a good five-hour drive from London, but is well worth the effort. Not only is this beautiful national park in the north-west corner of England home to a large concentration of lakes, as the name suggests, it also contains a cluster of the country's highest peaks and some pretty towns and villages. The area is a haven for people who enjoy trekking – the altitude of the closely concentrated 'fells' ranges from about 2,000 to 3,000 feet, and the difficulty of hikes varies accordingly. It's also a great place to get stuck into other outdoor pursuits such as rock climbing, mountain biking and watersports – see www.lakedistrictoutdoors.co.uk for a comprehensive list of activity providers, as well as places to stay. For those seeking a less strenuous break, you'll find tranquility by spending some time on or by one of the many lakes – this is the part of the country that inspired poet William Wordsworth after all. The south-east area of the national park is home to the longest lake, Windermere, as well as the attractive town of Ambleside, but its accessibility makes it extremely popular with day trippers. If you've got the time it's worth heading further into the northern and western regions to escape the crowds – the areas around Buttermere and Loweswater get nowhere near the same volume of visitors as the south-east. The only real downside to the Lakes is the rain – weather fronts coming in off the Irish Sea make this a particularly wet part of the country, so be sure to take some waterproof gear. Look on the bright side though; getting soaked gives you the perfect excuse to dry off with a pint of Jennings in one of the many country pubs.

Edinburgh

Scotland's capital city is a beautiful place, frequently referred to as the 'Athens of the north' for the number of 18th century buildings designed in the Greek neo-classical style. First-time visitors may be surprised to discover the city is historically divided into the 'Old' and 'New' town – to the casual eye it all looks ancient – but it's a separation clearly defined by the city's main thoroughfare, Princes Street.

Princes Street lies parallel to Edinburgh's oldest street, the Royal Mile, a broad avenue that runs from the imposing Edinburgh Castle (the second-most visited historic monument in Britain after the Tower of London; 0131 2259846) to the Palace of Holyrood House (0131 5665100), a former home of Mary Queen of Scots that's still used as a residence by the Queen today.

Borrowdale

Coniston

Sitting With Arthur
*For spectacular views
of Edinburgh and
beyond take a 45-
minute hike up
Salisbury Crags to
Arthur's Seat, an
extinct volcano which
looms large over
the city.*

Along the way you'll encounter many of Edinburgh's most famous sites and monuments, from the Victorian pleasures of the Camera Obscura (0131 2263709) to the splendour of St Giles' Cathedral (0131 2259442). Look out too for the former home of the Scottish religious reformer, John Knox, on the High Street, a stark contrast to the controversial modern architecture of the new Scottish Parliament Building, which opened in 2005. Off the main drag, the imposing neo-classicism of George Street in the New Town has recently become one of the capital's most fashionable strips and is full of trendy bars and chic boutiques. Meanwhile, the pretty cobbled streets around the Grassmarket perform a similar function over in the Old Town. But if it's fashionable Edinburgh you're looking for, better head to the seaside suburb of Leith, where the once deprived docklands have been given a modern makeover and are now home to some of the most sought-after addresses in town.

Monuments and buildings aside, Edinburgh is famous for its festivals and parties. The city's annual Hogmanay celebrations are widely regarded as being some of the best in the UK, but it's the Edinburgh Festival and the concurrent Fringe Festival that are the city's biggest tourist draw. Locals batten down the hatches as the incoming performers and visitors (over a million in total) take over – the city transforms itself every August into a month-long frenzy of classical and modern arts, comedy, entertainment, and also puts on the renowned Military Tattoo. Visit then and with any luck you'll catch the city (notorious for its grey skies and bone-chilling winds) on one of its rare sunny days. For places to stay in Edinburgh, see www.edinburgh.org.

Dublin

Dublin is rich with resonance and associations. Built around the river Liffey, it's an atmospheric place, compact and easy to get to know, with plenty of quaint, cobbled alleyways, imposing stone churches and genuinely welcoming hosts. The home of literary heroes including Oscar Wilde and James Joyce, it is also renowned for the famous Guinness. Anyone who wants a taste of real literary Dublin should scour the bookshops for a copy of a real gem *Hold Your Hour and Have Another* by the late Brendan Behan. Join one of the many literary walking tours if you want to know more about Behan and co, or head out on the tiles if the 'black stuff' is your thing. Any visit to Dublin should begin with the city's oldest building, Christ Church Cathedral (www.cccdub.ie), founded in 1038 by King Sitric of Dublin, then rebuilt in stone in 1169. More impressive is St Patrick's Cathedral (www.stpatrickscathedral.ie) nearby, the largest church in Ireland, constructed on the site where St Patrick himself was said to have baptised converts.

Other historical treats include Trinity College Dublin (+353 1 6082320), home to the ancient religious illuminations *The Book of Kells*, and Dublin Castle (+353 1 6777129). For a taste of new Dublin, head to Temple Bar. This once run-down part of town on the south side of the Liffey, near Ha'Penny Bridge, has been reborn as the cultural corner, and bursts with fashionable bars and eateries, art galleries and loft-style apartments. North of the Liffey and O'Connell Street you'll find the famous Gate Theatre (+353 1 8744045), which staged Oscar Wilde's *Salome* after the play had been banned in Britain and where a young Orson Welles made his first professional appearance. Central Dublin covers a relatively small area and you can easily get around on foot – a trail around the city's literary hotspots is a good way to explore. Pick up a ticket for the Jameson Literary Pub Crawl from the Dublin Tourism Centre in Suffolk Street (+353 1 6057799) and follow in the footsteps of Joyce, Shaw, Beckett and many others. A teetotaler's alternative is the literary walk that sets off from the famous Bewley's Cafe on Grafton Street (+353 1 4960641), or skip the literary pretensions altogether and simply head for the World of Guinness exhibition at The Guinness Brewery (+353 1 4536700).

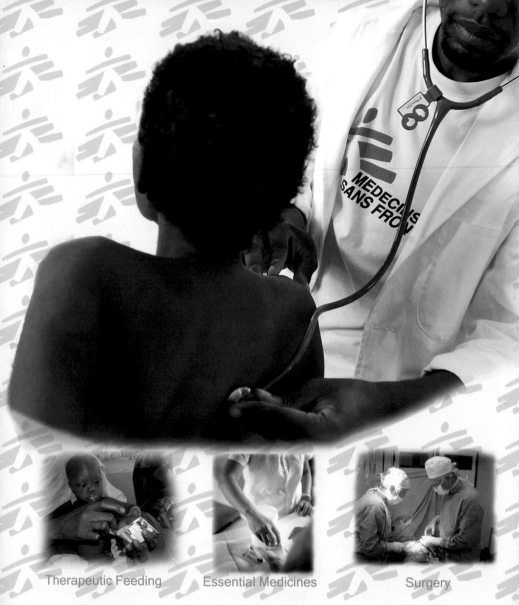

Therapeutic Feeding   Essential Medicines   Surgery

MEDECINS SANS FRONTIERES
أطبـــاء بــلا حـدود

Providing emergency medical
relief in over 70 countries.

help us help the helpless

Activities

Activities

Sports & Activities

There are so many activities, sports and courses to enjoy in the capital that you may struggle with indecision, but never boredom. London is an expensive city, but costs can be competitive and there are often cheaper options when it comes to exercise. Wherever you live, you'll never be more than a couple of miles away from a gym, health club or park for working out. Sociable sports such as football, cricket, rugby and tennis are particularly popular, while workers stressed out by the city's fast pace of life are also drawn to well-being activities such as yoga, tai chi and Pilates. What London lacks is easy access to the sea and mountains; watersports usually take place on lakes outside the capital, while snow sports are out unless you fancy Vertical Chill's man-made ice wall (see p.244). Although there are lots of green open spaces in the city, activities such as golf, horse riding and extreme sports tend to take place out of town, but usually within an hour's drive. Brits may have a reputation for grumbling about the weather but the rain doesn't deter – locals have been brought up to endure wet spectator stands and soggy trainers. This doesn't mean that you have to tolerate it though; many indoor venues cater for activities that are traditionally pursued outside.

It's a charming idiosyncrasy of British life that a number of much-loved activities can be combined with another favourite national pastime – drinking. Board games and cards are popular, and you can engage in sports such as snooker, bowling or darts while downing a pint or three.

If you're looking for a team to join or a good place to take up an activity, try www.gumtree.com or www.london.gov.uk. Alternatively, pick up a free newspaper such as *Metro*, *London Lite* or *The London Paper*, available at tube and rail stations, or buy a weekly magazine such as *Time Out*, which provides comprehensive listings. For other activities or courses see www.lastminute.com or www.hotcourses.com.

Activity Finder

American Football

Other options **Australian Rules Football** p.237, **Rugby** p.272

American football has struggled to establish a profile in the UK, despite the gloriously brief incarnation of the London Monarchs in the 1990s (the team won the inaugural World Bowl in 1991 but disbanded in 1999). In early 2007 plans to host an autumn NFL match between the Miami Dolphins and New York Giants at the new Wembley Stadium – the first time a league game will be played outside of North America – were announced to try to boost the sport's popularity here. If you're an exiled fan or player looking for some gridiron action, don't despair - there are two teams in London that play in the national British American Football League (or BAFL, a moniker some non-fans who have tried to understand the game would say is appropriate). London Olympians (www.olympiansfootball.org) are based at Crystal Palace, and London Blitz (www.londonblitz.com) play at Finsbury Park. The UK season runs from April to September, and clubs tend to recruit new members over the winter.

Art Classes

Other options **Art Galleries** p.194, **Art & Craft Supplies** p.315

Don't let your lack of technique or two left thumbs put you off – artistic skills can be learned. London has some exceptional art schools; as well as the places listed in this section, both the Central Saint Martins College of Art and Design (7514 7000) and Camberwell College of Arts (7514 6302) have good reputations. Alternatively, if drawing and painting don't get your creative juices flowing, stained-glass courses at Rainbow Glass Studios (7249 0276) might be for you – or why not give body art or ornamental woodwork a try? Both www.hotcourses.com or www.artcourses.co.uk are mines of information.

444 Chiswick High Rd
W4
⊖ *Chiswick Park*

Art 4 Fun

8994 4100 | www.art4fun.com

The premise is simple – you eat cake, drink frothy coffee or even wine (if you take your own) and decorate whatever piece of crockery, wood or glass takes your fancy. It's creative, relaxing and inexpensive, and when you've finished your work of art, it will be 'finished' for you to make it usable. Items cost from £3.50, which includes materials. Great for children's parties, hen nights and birthdays. There is another Art 4 Fun in West Hampstead (7794 0800), and both are open daily from 10:00 to 18:00.

2 Parkhurst Rd
N7
⊖ *Caledonian Road*

Islington Arts Factory

7607 0561 | www.islingtonartsfactory.org.uk

The IAF is a bustling, creative environment that encourages expression, with a warren of studios and galleries plus a cafe. There is a range of courses available, including photography, music and dance. Visual arts subjects include life drawing, painting and working with clay. The factory is open from 10:00 on weekdays, 14:00 on Saturdays and 11.00 on Sundays. Membership is a must if you want to join a class, and costs £15 a year.

Maria Assumpta
Centre, Kensington
Square
W8
⊖ *High Street*
Kensington

London School of Painting and Drawing

7240 3436 | www.thelondonschoolofpainting.org

This is a relatively new endeavour set up by artists and tutors from the Royal Society of British Sculptors and the Slade School of Fine Art, so you'll be in good company. The school welcomes all levels of experience, and prices are reasonable. A term of evening drawing classes (Tuesdays, 19:00 to 21:00) costs £160 including materials; a Saturday painting class, held on one Saturday every month, costs £55 with materials; and an intensive five-day summer school course costs £249.

235

University College
London, Gower St
WC1
⊖ Warren Street

The Slade School of Fine Art

7679 2313 | www.ucl.ac.uk/slade

Slade is arguably the most famous art college in London. As well as producing mainly contemporary art, the institute also focuses on discussing and analysing its history and practice. Slade tends to concentrate on graduate and postgraduate courses, but there are also short evening and weekend tutorials that you can sign up to, plus summer courses in painting and drawing.

Athletics

Other options **Running** p.273

There are athletics tracks, stadiums and clubs all over London. Tracks and stadiums are generally run by borough councils, which often charge a small entry fee to use the facilities; most have been upgraded in recent years and house football or rugby pitches as well as running tracks. Athletics is an excellent way to keep fit, and the cost is minimal. A running club can provide support and advice as well as a good workout; there are hundreds in the capital, ranging from fun groups to serious runners.

Ledrington Rd
SE19
⇌ Crystal Palace

Crystal Palace National Sports Centre

8778 0131 | www.gll.org

This 200-acre park, which is set to feature heavily in the 2012 Olympics, houses an impressive, internationally renowned athletics stadium that boasts a recently refurbished synthetic indoor track, a 400m eight-lane outdoor track and seating for 16,500 people. There is a small charge to use the facilities (£2.40 for adults and £1.70 for juniors). The centre is also the home ground for the South London Harriers athletics club (www.southlondonharriers.org).

Hornsey Gate,
Endymion Rd
N4
⇌ ⊖ Finsbury Park

Finsbury Park Track & Gym

8802 9139

Home to the Heathside Running Club (www.londonheathside.org.uk), Finsbury Park has two synthetic tracks – an oval 400m track with six lanes and a straight 10-lane track. There's a small cost for using the site, which is floodlit and has comprehensive facilities, including extensive seating and spotless changing rooms. Open 10:00 to 16:00 Thursdays to Mondays and 16:30 to 21:30 on Tuesdays and Wednesdays.

Artillery Way,
off Du Cane Rd
W12
⊖ East Acton

Linford Christie Stadium

8749 6758

Originally named the West London Stadium, this place was renamed in 1993 in honour of Thames Valley Harriers' most famous member and his World Championship and Olympic 100m victories. Revamped in 2005, the stadium has floodlit training facilities, a synthetic 400m eight-lane track, a 100m straight track, a field events area and rugby pitch. For more information about the club see www.thamesvalleyharriers.com.

Rhodeswell Rd
E14
⊖ Mile End

Mile End Park Stadium

8980 1885 | www.gll.org

There's a small fee to use the eight-lane synthetic athletics track at this East End stadium, which was refurbished in the 1990s. There is good disabled access and changing rooms, and athletics clubs based here include the Victoria Park Harriers & Tower Hamlets AC (www.vphthac.org.uk). Tennis facilities and football pitches are also available for hire.

Battersea Park
SW11
⊖ **Battersea Park**

Millennium Arena Athletics Track
8871 7537 | www.wandsworth.gov.uk

Previously known as the Battersea Park Athletics Track, this tired-looking site got a change of name and an overhaul a few years ago. The old pavilion was replaced with a two-storey building, which now houses changing rooms and a fitness centre. The track was upgraded to eight lanes and covered seats were fitted. A number of clubs practice here, including university clubs and the Belgrave Harriers (www.belgraveharriers.com). Opening times are 07:00 to 22:00 on weekdays, 07:30 to 19:30 on weekends. There's a £2.50 entry charge for adults.

Randolph Ave
W9
⊖ **Maida Vale**

Paddington Recreational Ground
7641 3642 | www.cannons.co.uk

The old track at this ground is now grassed over, but remains famous for having been used as a training ground by Roger Bannister who, in 1954, became the first man to run a mile in under four minutes. The new track is a six-lane synthetic one used by the Serpentine Running Club (www.serpentine.org.uk). To date, there's no seating and the track isn't floodlit, but light from the adjacent all-weather pitch seems to suffice. Open 07:00 to 21:00 on weekdays and 07:00 to 16:30 on weekends, it costs £1.10 to use the track.

Australian Rules Football
Other options **American Football** p.235, **Rugby** p.272

'Aussie rules' is a popular summer sport with London's large population of expat Australians. There are several British Australian Rules Football League teams in the capital, mainly based in west London due to the concentration of Antipodeans in this part of town. The clubs are by no means exclusive to Australians, however – anyone is welcome to join, even newcomers to the game (each team must field a certain number of non-Europeans). It's not just about the sport either – the social (read: beer drinking) side of things is just as important as the footie at most clubs, so be prepared to live up to the 'go hard or go home' Australian philosophy. For a gentler introduction, 'touch Aussie rules' is a mixed, non-contact version of the sport for people who haven't played before (see www.touchaussierules.com to find your nearest game).

Australian Rules Football Clubs

North London Lions	www.aussierules.co.uk	07715 115298
Wimbledon Hawks	www.wimbledonhawks.com	07962 816313
West London Wildcats	www.wildcatsfc.co.uk	07930 522575
Putney Magpies	www.putneymagpies.com	77067083
Wandsworth Demons	www.wandsworthdemons.com	na

Badminton
Other options **Leisure Facilities** p.292

Badminton is a much-loved game in the UK, and one in which the British excel. In London, there are many leisure centres and parks with courts and a number of clubs of differing levels; some compete in leagues and others play just for fun. It's an aerobic sport that attracts a sociable crowd as it can be played in couples. Phone 01908 268400 or visit www.badmintonengland.co.uk for more information about playing the sport. As well as the clubs detailed overleaf, there are several sports centres in east London that offer badminton including the John Orwell Sports Centre (7488 9421), Whitechapel Sports Centre (7247 7538) and York Hall (8980 2243). The cost of court hire in these venues ranges from £3 to £11, depending on age and membership.

237

Marylebone Badminton Club

www.marylebonebadminton.com

This friendly club has around 20 members and plays on Saturdays from 09:00 to 11:00. The group plays for fun (albeit of the competitive sort) and there's no league play of which to speak, so it doesn't matter if you miss the odd session. The skill level is around the intermediate mark and membership costs £25 for 10 weeks, or £5 a session for guests. It's recommended that potential members go along as a visitor first to see if their level of play matches the group.

Sobell Leisure Centre

7609 2166 | www.aquaterra.org

This centre is affiliated to the Finsbury Park Leisure Centre on Norman St (Old Street tube), which also has courts. A supervised badminton clinic meets every Saturday when juniors play from 10:00 to 12:30 and adults from 12:30 to 15:00. There's no need to book in advance and the sauna is available after play for a reduced fee. Prices for sessions range from £4 to £11. The Sobell Badminton Club plays on Tuesdays, Fridays and Sundays, and welcomes people of all ages and abilities.

Victoria Badminton Club

www.victoriabadminton.org.uk

A welcoming club that puts emphasis on competitive play, exercise and enjoyment. The group consists of about 40 people of all ages, who take over five courts from 18:00 to 20:00 every Friday. The intermediate-level club contains a good mixture of new and long-term members. Full membership is £26 for three months and a guest session costs £4. It's a relaxed club so players don't have to come every week or be there at precisely 18:00.

Basketball

London has a professional basketball club, the London Towers, and there are plenty of clubs and indoor venues in which to play. However, with so many outdoor courts dotted about the capital people tend to see basketball more as a street sport. There are over 160 clubs of various standards in London and the surrounding area, plus four main leagues that are affiliated to England Basketball (www.englandbasketball.co.uk). The best way to contact one in your area is to visit www.basketballinlondon.co.uk. There's a flourishing wheelchair basketball league for men, women and juniors in the UK too. In 2005, Birmingham – the UK's second-largest city – beat off competition from Paris and Vancouver to win the bid to host the 2010 World Wheelchair Basketball Championships. For more information about this area of the sport, visit www.gbwba.org.uk.

Beauty Training

Other options **Beauty Salons** p.297

The Carlton Institute of Beauty Therapy

01395 279968 | www.beauty-training.co.uk

Although this establishment is based in Devon, training takes place just outside London in Windsor. Carlton is the largest independent school in Britain (with nearly 20 years' experience), and trains to national and international standards. Several one and two-day courses are offered, plus longer options, and home study packages in electrolysis, massage, nails, reflexology and waxing are also available. A prospectus detailing costs and course dates can be ordered by calling 01395 279777.

47 Great Marlborough St
W1
⊖*Oxford Circus*

London College of Beauty Therapy
7208 1300 | www.lcbt.co.uk

Situated in the heart of London's shopping district, near Oxford Street and Carnaby Street, this college (which recently celebrated its 10-year anniversary) is a shining example of how much the beauty industry has grown in Britain. For the curious but not yet committed, short courses include anatomy, body massage and nutrition. For those seeking a qualification, an NVQ in beauty therapy is available, which includes work experience in real salons. Call for a prospectus.

118 Baker St
W1
⊖*Baker Street*

The Ray Cochrane Beauty School
7486 6291 | www.raycochrane.co.uk

Established more than 50 years ago, this school is well-respected globally. Excellent day courses include basic facial and manicure and pedicure, and there are twice-weekly evening classes in massage and waxing or longer full and part-time courses in both national and international diplomas. This is the first school in Britain to offer Cidesco qualifications (an international beauty association). The student salon is a cheap and cheerful place to go for a facial, so long as you don't mind being a guinea pig (don't worry, the students are overseen by a qualified therapist).

The Ray Cochrane Beauty School

Birdwatching
Other options **Environmental Groups** p.253

The great thing about birdwatching is that you can do it anywhere – all you need are birds (which you'll find practically anywhere in the UK). Only recently a rare American robin took up residence in Peckham, causing a virtual standstill in the inner-city south London neighbourhood. Generally, it's recommended that twitchers and birders tighten the straps on their binos (that's binoculars to the rest of us) and head for a park, reserve or sanctuary, of which there is a multitude in and around the capital. There are a couple of sites and birdwatching groups featured below, or visit myweb.tiscali.co.uk/calidris – an extremely useful online guide to the best birdwatching spots in the vicinity. Alternatively the Royal Society for the Protection of Birds is a passionate and helpful organisation (www.rspb.org.uk).

Birdline South East
www.southeastbirdnews.co.uk

Run by experienced birders, this organisation provides a reliable news service for south-east England. There is a phone number that people can call with details of any sightings, and the 'birdline' is updated up to 25 times per day with information from London and counties in the south-east including Kent, Hampshire and Essex. Phone 0800 0377240 to report anything you spot, or 09068 700240 to hear the latest news (calls to this number cost 60p per minute).

239

East London Birders Forum

County Arms,
420 Hale End Rd
E4
⊖Highams Park

www.elbf.co.uk
Upstairs at the County Arms in Highams Park is where you'll find the East London Birders Forum nesting – it meets there on the second Tuesday of every month at 20:00 (except in July and August). Its aim is to promote local birding and gather information on the area's avian fauna. Talks cost £1 to attend and the group also organises guided walks.

Marylebone Birdwatching Society

Gospel Oak
Methodist Church,
Agincourt Rd
NW3
⇄Gospel Oak

7485 0863 | www.geocities.com/birdsmbs
The Marylebone Birdwatching Society meets in Hampstead on the second Friday of every month between 19:00 and 21:15. Although the group is based in north London, people from all parts of the city are welcome to join. Whether you're a knowledgeable ornithologist or a novice, the society will take you under its wing. Membership is £10, which includes reduced admission to meetings, coach outings and details of special events and birdwatching holidays.

Bowling

Tenpin bowling is a popular pastime in the capital – the opportunity to have a drink or two while taking part in a sporting activity appeals to busy Londoners. People of any age can play – the game requires skill over strength, so bowling alleys are the perfect places to take children, celebrate birthdays or hold corporate events. Bowling lanes tend not to be the most tastefully decorated establishments – unless you have a penchant for gaudy, kitsch interiors – and the food often makes McDonald's look like nouvelle cuisine, but they're always fun places. Equipment can be hired on site, so all you need to take with you is the right moves. Most people participate as a means to relax but there are leagues in London if you're a serious player; contact the British Tenpin Bowling Association (www.btba.org.uk).

All Star Lanes

Victoria House,
Bloomsbury Place
WC1
⊖Holborn

Bloomsbury Bowling

7025 2676 | www.allstarlanes.co.uk
This six-lane bowling alley, diner and American cocktail bar is smaller and more intimate than nearby Bloomsbury Bowling (see below), but it is also more expensive. It runs a league, and two lanes and the cocktail bar can be hired for private parties. The alley is open until 02:00 on Fridays and Saturdays; games cost from £7.50 per person and you'll need to book in advance to avoid disappointment.

Bloomsbury Bowling

Tavistock Hotel,
Bedford Way
WC1
⊖Tottenham
Court Rd

7183 1979 | www.bloomsburybowling.com
This 1950s-style bowling alley and reasonably priced diner, which is situated in a former basement car park under a hotel, has developed a cool reputation among urbanites for its individual look and unique atmosphere. The decor is a mix of retro and modern fittings, and there are karaoke rooms for hire plus a boutique cinema. The bar is open until 01:00 on weekdays and 03:00 at weekends, with occasional live music. Prices start at £36 an hour for a lane (for up to eight people), £5.50 for a game (per person) and between £20 and £75 for a karaoke room. Call ahead for private bookings.

40

17 Queensway
W2
⊖ Queensway

Queens Ice and Bowl

7229 0172 | www.queensiceandbowl.co.uk

London's only bowling and ice-skating combo caters for groups of people who can't quite agree on what activity they want to do. It costs £6 per person per game, but there's also a £4 fee if you book in advance. The facilities are open until 23:30 seven days a week. There is also a handy bar on site and food is available. If you'd rather skate, it's good fun at the weekend when live DJs turn the rink into a cheesy ice disco; admission to this costs £9.

Boxing

Boxing in London has become much more accessible in recent years for both men and women. No longer is this aerobic and skillful exercise – renowned for building up strength, stamina and muscle tone – confined to people who want to belt the living daylights out of each other. Today, London has clubs for people of all levels, where everyone is welcome to learn the basics without acquiring a bloody nose or cauliflower ear. For women especially, the self-defence techniques boxing teaches can be a comfort. 'White-collar boxing' (see The Real Fight Club, p242) has grown notably, as stressed executives find release in a healthy, controlled environment. Equipment, such as gloves and punch bags, is usually provided but it's worth buying your own if you intend to stick with the sport. Health clubs and sports centres also have boxing or 'boxercise' classes. Serious boxers will need a signed medical certificate from the Amateur Boxing Association of England (www.abae.co.uk) before they can compete.

20 Hazellville Rd
N19
⊖ Archway

Boxing London

07956 293768 | www.boxinglondon.co.uk

No experience is needed to join this gym, which offers friendly and expert training (the owner, Enzo Giordano, was himself a super-middleweight contender). Like most boxing gyms, classes begin with a warm-up or skipping, followed by circuit training, then sparring in the ring with a qualified instructor. Oh, then there's the press-ups and sit ups. Classes are every Tuesday and Thursday evening at 19:30, and at 12:00 on Saturday; the cost ranges from £5 to £7 per session.

Archway 180,
Lambeth Rd
SE1
⊖ Lambeth North

Fitzroy Lodge ABC

7928 0146 | www.fitzroylodge.com

Fitzroy Lodge ABC is one of the oldest amateur boxing clubs in London, with qualified volunteer coaches who have experience of teaching at all levels. It provides a broad spectrum of boxing-related training, including preparing people for competition and fitness training for all ages and sexes. The club is open every day except Sunday. Times and prices vary but open training currently takes place between 09:30 and 14:00 on Mondays and Wednesdays, 07:30 and 21:00 on Tuesdays, 09:30 and 17:00 on Thursdays, 16:00 and 20:00 on Fridays, and 10:00 and 12:00 on Saturdays. The cost is £50 for annual membership, then £2 per session for adults (£5 on Saturdays).

10 Half Moon Lane
SE24
⇌ Herne Hill

McKenzie's Gym

7737 2338

Situated above the Half Moon pub, this small, friendly club caters to all levels of fitness. The owner, former British light-welterweight champ Clinton McKenzie, is a jovial, encouraging trainer who is on hand to provide guidance on the fitness machines, bags and in the ring. There's a joining fee of £100, and membership is £50 a month, but non-members can just turn up and pay £15 a session.

241

2-6 Curtain Rd
EC2
⇄ ⊖ *Liverpool Street*

The Real Fight Club

7092 9943| *www.therealfightclub.co.uk*

This 'white-collar boxing' club operates from a number of gyms and has more than 400 members. Founded in 2000, it attracts a lot of male and female professionals from the City who want something different from their exercise time (the motto is 'forget golf'). The organisation focuses on the positive aspects of boxing – courage, commitment and confidence – and has raised over £800,000 for charities. Its club fight nights have even had royalty in the audience. This class of boxing is regulated by the International White Collar Boxing Association.

13 Sherwood St
W1
⊖ *Piccadilly Circus*

The Third Space

7439 6333 | *www.thethirdspace.com*

One of London's premier private gyms, The Third Space offers high-tech equipment, top-notch instructors and a fully loaded medicine centre. Unfortunately the cost of joining reflects this: £275, plus an annual membership of £1,180. Because of its close proximity to Soho, it's very popular with media darlings. There's a competition-sized boxing ring and professional trainers on hand to help you with your technique in a group or one-on-one setting. Classes are held every other day but you need to join to participate. The gym's opening hours are 06:30 to 23:00 Monday to Friday and 08:30 until 20:30 on Saturdays and Sundays.

Bridge

Bridge isn't just a round of cards for Omar Sharif and ladies of a certain age dressed in twinsets and pearls – it's a game of skill and chance that attracts fans of all ages and experience. Its popularity probably springs from it being such a sociable game; it's played by four people, in pairs, often as part of a larger tournament. London has a number of clubs – both big and small – and associations, plus regular leagues and tournaments. There's even a bridge shop, fittingly called The Bridge Shop (7486 8222). To find a club near you, see www.bcmchess.co.uk, or for more information about the game contact the English Bridge Union (01296 317200).

Chess

To the layman, chess is a frighteningly high-brow board game played by bespectacled geniuses. To aficionados, it's an abstract game of skill and strategy, a mental sport of epic proportions. If you fit into the first category, the thought of joining a chess club is probably not going to excite you, but the hugely popular game can be very addictive once you've got the hang of it. There are chess clubs dotted around London, most of which play in competitions such as The London Chess League (www.londonchess.com). Some pubs, such as The Harrison (7916 3113) near King's Cross, also put on chess nights. Chess shops are growing in number too; The London Chess Centre (7388 0424) on Euston Road is one of the most popular. Alternatively, check out www.englishchess.org.uk, website of the English Chess Federation.

Middlesex
Community Centre,
Petticoat Square
E3
⊖ *Aldgate*

Metropolitan Chess Club

www.metchess.org.uk

The Metropolitan Chess Club, reputedly one of the oldest clubs in London, plays from 18:00 to 22:00 every Thursday. There are currently over 60 members, many playing in teams in the London and Middlesex Leagues. If you're interested in joining, go along to a club night. People of all abilities are welcome, although there are enough players of a high standard to challenge serious players. Annual subscription is around the £60 mark, with discounts for those aged under 21 or over 60.

Morley College,
61 Westminster
Bridge Rd
SE1
⊖Lambeth North

Morley Chess Club
7609 2016 | www.morleychessclub.co.uk

This club maintains a superb facility, including educational resources such as a chess library. Members meet every Friday from 18:15 and anyone is welcome, from novice to 'grandmaster'. Membership is a snip – £8 if you're enrolled at nearby Morley College and £12 if you're not. The club's website is pretty comprehensive and includes free downloadable literature on the game. You can also get one up on your next opponent by accessing moves from previous matches.

Chiswick Town Hall,
Heathfield Terrace
W4
⊖Chiswick Park

West London Chess Club
07768 940789 | www.westlondonchess.com

Founded way back in 1893, the West London Chess Club caters for players of all ages and abilities. Meetings take place in the committee room of Chiswick Town Hall at 19:15 every Wednesday night. Membership costs £50 a year and entitles you to take part in league matches as well as club friendlies or 'blitz' games. The popular junior club runs on Saturday mornings from 11:15 to 13:15.

Climbing

Despite being a sprawling metropolis with no mountains, London is estimated to be home to a quarter of Britain's active climbers. Man-made walls may not be the real thing, but they let city-bound enthusiasts hone their skills and enable beginners to have a go to see if they like it. London has three main climbing centres and an ice wall. Some sports centres, such as Westway (see p.244), also have climbing facilities. Almost all welcome differing levels of fitness, offer courses and training (both on and off site), and provide or hire out equipment. These places are a good way to make friends as they are where climbing clubs (who are usually an amiable bunch) hang out. Two groups of note are Rockhoppers Mountaineering Club (www.rockhoppers.org.uk) and North London Mountaineering Club (www.nlmc.co.uk).

Green Lanes
N4
⊖Manor House

The Castle Climbing Centre
8211 7000 | www.castle-climbing.co.uk

This venue claims to receive more annual visits than any other climbing centre in the UK, and, housed inside a former Victorian water pumping house, it's nothing if not impressive. Two floors offer 300 routes, a cave, bouldering walls and overhangs for all levels of fitness. There's the Geckos club for children (07776 176007), various introductory courses and the atmosphere is one of friendly efficiency. Opening hours are 14:00 to 22:00 on weekdays and 10:00 to 19:00 at weekends. Prices range from £5.50 to £10.50 per session, and monthly, six-monthly and annual membership passes are available.

Haverfield Rd
E3
⊖Mile End

Mile End Wall
8980 0289 | www.mileendwall.org.uk

Housed inside an old pipe engineering works, the climbing area is extensive and the centre offers a wide range of courses for beginners and professionals alike. As well as having numerous boulders to climb, there is top-roped and lead climbing and a 'monkey house' training area – great for some upside-down hanging. The centre is relaxed, informal and cheap, making it popular with younger people. Entry costs £5 for adults or up to £300 for annual membership. The wall is open from 12:00 till 21:30 on weekdays (21:00 on Friday) and 10:00 to 18:00 on Saturdays and Sundays.

Ellis Brigham,
3-11 Southampton St
WC2
⊖ *Covent Garden*

Vertical Chill
7395 1010 | www.vertical-chill.com

Inside the outdoor clothing and equipment shop Ellis Brigham stands Vertical Chill, an eight-metre ice wall which is surprisingly suitable for both novice and accomplished climbers. A beginners' ice climbing lesson is available for £40; more experienced climbers who need equipment can try 'climb & hire' sessions for £30, or if you've got all the gear you'll pay £20. All sessions last an hour and the wall is open from Tuesday to Sunday, but you're advised to book in advance to avoid disappointment.

The Castle Climbing Centre

Crowthorne Rd
W10
⊖ *Latimer Road*

Westway Climbing Centre
8969 0992 | www.westway.org

The community-based Westway Climbing Centre has a generous 2,200 square metres of wall for seasoned climbers and beginners to explore. The centre runs an extensive programme (together with ladies' nights and workshops) suitable for people of differing abilities, including those with special needs. It's open from 09:30 to 22:00 Monday to Friday (08:00 onwards on Thursdays) and 10:00 to 20:00 on weekends. A casual climb costs between £5.50 and £8 and an adult monthly pass is £37.50. The centre is occasionally closed for events.

Clubs & Associations

There are a number of expat clubs that organise business, cultural, intellectual, philanthropic, social and sporting activities events in London. The diversity of clubs depends on the country (Australia, Ireland, New Zealand, South Africa and the US are best represented), but most generally don't require you to be from that country; just having an interest is enough. Activities vary, but include wine tastings, trips, walks and talks by people from that country who have made the move to the UK. If you can't find anything to suit here, try your country's embassy or chamber of commerce, who should be able to put you in touch with more contacts.

68 Old Brompton Rd
SW7
⊖ *South Kensington*

American Women's Club of London
7589 8292 | www.awclondon.org

A well-established women's club (it's been running for over 100 years) that accepts US citizens or people with links to America. It offers a chance to meet like-minded people who want to take part in a range of activities, from day trips and creative pursuits to golf and anything that gets you involved in making the most of life in the capital. There are also online forums which cater for American expats. The London Expat American Meeting Group (see american.meetup.com/11) has more than 1,000 members and meets at least once a month. American Expats (www.americanexpats.co.uk) gives people from the US an opportunity to chat, swap tips, find American products and foodstuffs, get information about immigration and jobs and make friends. For a comprehensive list of other American groups in London see www.usembassy.org.uk.

Various locations ◄

Anglo-Danish Society
01332 517160 | www.anglo-danishsociety.org.uk

This society, which is closely linked to the Danish Embassy, aims to promote understanding and friendship between the UK and Denmark. There's a focus on education (it provides scholarships for Danish students wishing to study in the UK and details a number of educational lectures) but also arranges social activities and events, such as musical evenings and weekend stays in the country. Membership is just £15 a year.

Various locations ◄

Anglo-Finnish Society
www.anglofinnishsociety.org.uk

Meetings for this society, which nurtures relationships between the UK and Finland, take place every month except during the summer holidays. It holds many Finnish-related events, such as exhibitions, concerts and talks. Membership is a snip at £10 a year (less if you're a student or OAP) and includes a subscription to the quarterly magazine *Finn-Niche* as well as other goodies.

Swire House,
59 Buckingham Gate ◄
SW1
≥ ⊖ Victoria

Britain-Australian Society
7630 1075 | www.britain-australia.org.uk

This society helps members maintain connections with Australia. With branches throughout the UK, it's a focal point for Aussies to meet and join in with a number of events, whether it's celebrating Anzac Day, wine tasting or group outings. Yearly membership costs £20 upwards, which gives you access to the society's events both in the UK and Australia.

Lancaster Hall Hotel, ◄
35 Craven Terrace
W2
⊖ Lancaster Gate

German YMCA
7723 9276 | www.german-ymca.org.uk

Part of the worldwide Youth Hostel Association movement (see www.ymca.org.uk), this German-focused branch in the heart of London arranges activities for anyone over the age of 18 and provides advice and support to Germans living in London. There are daytime events for OAPs, Sunday concerts (known as 'Schubertiades'), and an Anglo-German circle, which meets most Thursday evenings at 19:30 at the group's Lancaster Hall Hotel base.

Gumtree
www.gumtree.com

A hugely popular online community and classifieds site, which now covers more than 60 cities in six countries. It provides information, advice and details on just about everything for Aussies, Kiwis and South Africans, and it's especially good for finding accommodation, jobs and like-minded folk to meet up with. Subscription is free and you can post an advert for whatever it is that's missing in your life.

50-52 Camden Square ◄
NW1
⊖ Camden Town

London Irish Centre
7916 2222 | www.irishcentre.org

This long-running centre has excellent links to the Irish community in London – it has been offering advice, accommodation, employment, training and information on events such as Irish bands, dances and speakers for over 50 years. There's also a 'missing persons' service for friends and relatives wishing to locate lost relatives living in the UK. The website is impressively comprehensive, and whatever it is you're looking for, you're likely to find it here.

245

29 Harley St
W1
⊖ *Bond Street*

Network Canada
07981 610005 | www.networkcanada.org

A networking group for Canadians working in London that arranges social activities such as ice hockey and an annual Thanksgiving ball. Events are usually held after work in central London, and membership, which costs £20 a year, entitles you to free or discounted access. Network Canada is also affiliated to Vandoos (www.groups.yahoo.com/group/london-vandoos), an informal social group that meets on the 22nd of every month, usually in the pub.

Various locations

New Zealand Society
07957 424004 | www.nzsociety.co.uk

What started out as a dining club for New Zealanders in London has since grown to become one of the leading expat organisations in the UK. The society fosters the relationship between the UK and New Zealand and organises events and activities for Kiwis living in London, as well as for people curious about the country. Membership currently costs £25, or £37.50 for a couple.

Voetsek!
www.voetsek.com

A comprehensive online information service for South Africans living in London, this site provides information on everything you need to know, from opening a bank account to finding out whether your driving licence is valid, and from sourcing South African doctors and dentists to getting a job. The site considers itself a one-stop-shop, and certainly does a good job. The 'cheap calls' section allows you to phone a South African landline for 5p a minute, or 15p a minute to a mobile.

Cookery Classes

In the UK, a number of celebrity chefs have demystified cooking by heralding simplicity (Jamie Oliver's modern and rustic touch), adding a touch of glamour (Nigella Lawson and her sensual cakes) or mixing creativity with science (Heston Blumenthal). You can take courses around the country run by masters: Rick Stein in Cornwall, Nick Nairn in Scotland and Raymond Blanc at Le Manoir aux Quat'Saisons in Oxfordshire – but they don't come cheap. Far better to start with a course at your local college (see www.hotcourses.com) or try one of the schools featured below. A cookery course is something you can do alone, with a partner, with friends or as a corporate activity.

Various locations

Cookie Crumbles
0845 6014173 | www.cookiecrumbles.net

Carola Weymouth, a trained chef and former food and drink editor of *Family Circle* magazine, runs a range of cooking activities, workshops and 'cookie parties' for children and teenagers. There are tea parties for the younger kids, with animal-themed or 'beach breezer' menus, and lessons aimed at teens on how to cook a three-course meal. Private parties cost £165 for six kids; workshops cost roughly £30 per child. Check the website for locations and more information.

114 Marylebone Lane
W11
⊖ *Bond Street*

Cordon Bleu Institute

7935 3503 | *www.cordonbleu.edu*

Cordon Bleu is probably the most recognised cookery institute in the world – there are 26 Cordon Bleu schools in 15 countries around the globe. Nine months of studying could gain you a 'Grand Diplome le Cordon Bleu', a chef qualification equivalent to an Oxbridge degree. The location of the school, in the heart of the West End, makes it even more popular with international students. Longer courses include 'intensive cuisine' and 'patisserie', and there are a number of day and weekend lessons in areas such as vegetarian cooking and pastry, which cost between £100 and £280.

70 Fortune Green Rd
NW6
⇌ ⊖ *West Hampstead*

Hampstead Cuisine School

0870 8964648 | *www.citrustreeproductions.co.uk*

This intimate school is hosted by Chico Francesco, a culinary traveller whose unique yet informative lessons may be more appealing to some than those offered at larger cookery schools. Chico's imagination knows no bounds and he offers an eclectic and tempting range of one-day courses and workshops, from children's cooking, wheat and dairy-free food, and from 'cooking for blokes' to the exotic-sounding 'colours, scents and flavours of Mumbai'. There's something here to match most tastes, and you're guaranteed a relaxing experience. Course prices start at around £90 for the interestingly named 'fiery peppers and lime down coconut grove' to £300 for a two-day thali, mezze and tapas extravaganza. Gift vouchers are also available.

21 St Alban's Grove
W8
⊖ *High Street*
Kensington

Leiths School of Food and Wine

7229 0177 | *www.leiths.com*

Leiths has become famous country-wide since it was featured in the *Chef School* TV series, and remains well-respected for its passion for cuisine and the quality and professionalism of its teaching staff. Courses available range from diplomas to evening, weekend and holiday programmes on subjects such as chocolate-making, game, fish and sauces, for both 'career cooks' and 'enthusiastic amateurs.' Corporate hospitality packages and wine courses are also an option. Prices vary from £40 for a specialty beer-and-food-matching evening to £15,000 for a three-term diploma. A 10-week beginners' cookery course costs £580.

5 William Blake House,
Bridge Lane
SW11
⇌ *Clapham Junction*

Mosimann's Academy

8870 8717 | *www.mosimann.com*

This converted Victorian school in Battersea was opened in 1996 by Anton Mosimann, who was responsible for providing his previous employer – London's Dorchester Hotel – with two Michelin stars. The academy offers top-notch facilities and a range of courses covering theoretical and practical aspects of food and wine. It's safe to say that you'd be learning in the presence of a master – Mosimann is fanatical about food; his collection of some 6,000 cookery books is one of the world's largest.

Cricket

In summer, cricket is played and watched all over the country, and London is no different – although you may find it's played on astroturf rather than grass. Games range from amateur friendlies to Premier League knockouts. The England and Wales Cricket Board-accredited leagues – the highest level that a club cricketer can play – were established, with some success, to close the gulf between county and club games. However, the majority of people get involved for recreational reasons and to socialise, as do the spectators who like nothing more than to watch the game on a sunny day with a jug of Pimms to hand. Check out the following clubs, or visit www.play-cricket.com or www.club-cricket.com for more details.

247

Hampton Wick Royal Cricket Club

Bushy Park,
Hampton Wick
KT1
≥ *Hampton Wick*

8977 2378 | www.hwrcc.co.uk

If you've always imagined playing cricket in lush open fields surrounded by green countryside, try this family-orientated club, set in beautiful surroundings in Bushy Park and just a short train journey form central London. The club was founded in 1863 and welcomes new players and non-playing members. There's a Saturday league, Sunday friendly teams and a Wednesday team in the summer.

Ken Barrington Cricket Centre

The Brit Oval
SE11
⊖ *Oval*

7820 5739 | www.surreycricket.com

The Brit Oval, where England won the coveted Ashes in 2005 (before surrendering them less than 18 months later), is the home of both the Surrey Cricket Club and the Ken Barrington Cricket Centre. The centre, named after the famous player, is fantastically well-equipped, with six cricket nets and indoor facilities that groups or individuals can hire. There are also professional coaching sessions for adults and juniors. Opening times are 09:00 to 22:00 Monday to Friday, while drop-in clinics run from 19:00 to 21:00 on Fridays. Call for weekend opening times and prices.

MCC Indoor School

Lord's Cricket Ground
NW8
⊖ *St. John's Wood*

7616 8500 | www.lords.org

The Marylebone Cricket Club (better known as the MCC) was founded in 1787 and calls Lord's – the world's most famous cricket ground – its home. It promotes cricket to young people and hosts the Spirit of Cricket Day, part of an international campaign to encourage sportsmanship. Regular users include Middlesex, MCC Women and Young Cricketers teams, although the facilities are open to other clubs. There's a 19-yard run-up and bowling machine, or you can book coaching sessions. Opening times vary according to the season so call ahead for details and prices.

Peter May Centre

135 Wadham Rd
E17
⊖ *Walthamstow*
Central

8531 9358 | www.gll.org

This purpose-built centre was opened in 2000 and is owned by the London Playing Fields Society. Its many facilities include six cricket nets and a range of outdoor playing fields for adult and junior cricket. It costs around £18.50 an hour to hire a lane. The centre is open from 06:15 to 22:00 Monday to Friday and 08:15 to 18:30 at weekends.

Cycling

Other options **Bicycles** p.316, **Bicycle Tours** p.223

Cycling has become a much more attractive mode of transport in London in recent years (cycle journeys rose by 100% between 2000 and 2005) – a combined result of traffic, the congestion charge, and the July 2005 bombings. In 2006, mayor Ken Livingstone invested £26 million in cycling, and more cycle paths are available than

ever before (although London still lags behind other European cities, especially Paris). There's an abundance of bike-hire shops, clubs, tracks, instructors, training sessions and organisations, some of which are listed here, as well as organised bike rides, such as the annual 54-mile London to Brighton bike ride – Europe's biggest cycling fundraiser. If you choose to cycle make sure you invest in the right gear (a helmet, lights and bright clothing), as accidents are not uncommon on busy streets. The London Cycle Network (www.londoncyclenetwork.org) produces a newsletter with new routes for cyclists, while the London Cycling Campaign (www.lcc.org.uk) lists rides and events. If you're looking for training and advice contact Cycle Training UK (7582 3535), which can arrange on-road sessions from £20 an hour.

British Legion, 97 Barry Rd SE22 ⇌East Dulwich

De Laune Cycling Club
8290 1013 | www.delaunecc.org

Founded in 1889, De Laune currently boasts over 130 members and meets at the British Legion on the first Thursday of every month. The club offers all levels and styles including road, track, cross-country and triathlons. New members are always welcome and everyone is encouraged to have a go at each discipline. Full membership will only set you back around £20 (£15 for students, £10 for 16-18 year-olds and £6 for under 16s. The club meets at the British Legion in Dulwich.

Finsbury Park N4 ⇌ ⊖Finsbury Park

Finsbury Park Cycling Club
www.finsburyparkcc.org

This club, which dates back to 1883, is based in and around north London and Hertfordshire. The club's ethos is to make cycling a rewarding and enjoyable activity, and it looks after sporting cyclists and new members of all abilities. Cyclists have the opportunity to try road racing, time trialing and track-racing and there are park events and cycling trips abroad. The club meets in Finsbury Park each week.

Herne Hill Stadium, Burbage Rd SE24 ⇌Herne Hill

Herne Hill Velodrome
www.hernehillvelodrome.co.uk

The last remaining track from the 1948 Olympics still in use today, this excellent 450m course has been threatened with closure, but at the time of writing was still up and running. Training takes place in all weather, all year round. Sessions for a range of cycling – for both children and adults – cost between £1 and £7. Bike hire is also available.

Various locations

OYBike
0845 2265751 | www.oybike.com

Hire chain-free bikes from over 60 places around Hammersmith, Kensington and Fulham on a pay-as-you-go system. The initial membership fee is £10; hire is free for the first 30 minutes, and then costs £2 an hour (up to £8 a day). Register by mobile or online before you ride. The bikes are locked to stands at various locations – you just need to phone OYBike to receive a code, key it into the lock, and away you go.

Dance Classes
Other options Music Lessons p.266

London is a superb place to learn to dance or continue with your training. Because of its multi-ethnicity, there are classes for all types of dance from around the globe. You could take an occasional drop-in (or 'open') class (usually between £3 and £10) or a course (prices vary depending on length). If you're serious about dancing, it's a good idea to become a member of one of the schools, which will give you a discount on every class you take. Contemporary dance schools tend to teach both ballet and Pilates, as these techniques complement each other. Whether it's the romance of ballroom, the passion of flamenco or tango, the exotic art of belly dancing or the urban moves of hip-hop and street, there's something to get most people's feet moving. Not only do you get to keep fit, you'll look mightily impressive every time you take to the dancefloor. The website www.londondance.com is an excellent resource to help you find out more about a particular class or style. If the thought of a lesson sounds too daunting, there are plenty of bars and clubs that put on Salsa classes, and your fee usually gets you admission to the venue afterwards. If you like to combine your dancing with a bit of fighting, you could have a go at the Brazilian martial art-dance fusion known as capoeira (www.londonschoolofcapoeira.co.uk).

ACW Dance Studio

23 Inner Park Rd
SW19
⊖ *Southfields*

8871 0890 | www.acwdancestudio.com
Whether you're 8 or 80, this relaxed, friendly studio has a class to suit you, including jive, line dancing, mambo, swing, tango and waltz. Exams can be taken here, and there are group or private lessons available plus extracurricular activities to sign up to, such as theatre trips and tea dances at the Waldorf. Classes start at £4 for members (£5 for non-members); private lessons are £24 for members (£28 for non-members).

Bollywood & Bhangra Beats

27 St Mary's Mansions,
St Mary's Terrace
W2
⊖ *Warwick Avenue*

7724 5282 | www.threebee.co.uk
This first-rate company teaches Indian-based dancing, which has become very popular in London, partly because it looks so spectacular and partly because of the city's large Asian population. Drop-in classes are available at venues across town – check the website for details. Each class costs £8 for non-members or £5 if you're a member. The organisation also provides workshops, making it a popular choice for groups of friends wanting to try something different.

Danceworks

16 Balderton St
W1
⊖ *Bond Street*

7629 6183 | www.danceworks.co.uk
A large Victorian listed building houses Danceworks, which has a good range of classes and a congenial atmosphere. There are six dance studios and a number of conventional classes (£5-£6) including ballet, Bollywood, bhangra and tap, as well as lessons to suit other tastes such as African dancing, burlesque, striptease, pole dancing and 'urban flava'. Open 08:30 to 22:00 on weekdays and 09:00 to 18:00 on weekends.

Expressions Dance Studios

39-51 Highgate Rd
NW5
⇌ ⊖ *Kentish Town*

7813 1580 | www.ExpressionsStudios.com
Expressions is a friendly and diverse school. There are a large number of classes available, including African, ballet, ballroom, breakdance, flamenco, hip-hop, Irish, jazz, jive, line dancing, pole dancing, rock and roll, salsa, street, tap and tea dance. Celebrity dancer Anton du Beke (of BBC's *Strictly Come Dancing* fame) teaches here, and celebrities have been known to use the studios. Adult membership starts from £12 a month, plus class fees. You don't need to be a member to dance here but classes are cheaper if you are.

Pineapple Dance Studio

7 Langley St
WC2
⊖ *Covent Garden*

7836 4004 | www.pineapple.uk.com
Pineapple is very popular in London, which can, on occasion, make the atmosphere a little intimidating compared with other, more down-to-earth, studios. Lately though it seems to have changed for the better. Originally situated in an old pineapple warehouse (hence the name), it's grown to provide a huge variety of dance styles (over 200 classes per week) for all ages and levels, including ballet, cheerleading, contemporary, hip-hop, jazz, latin, pop and tap, as well as singing, yoga, Pilates and martial arts. You can also book private dance lessons.

17 Duke's Rd
WC1
≷ ⊖ Euston

The Place
7121 1000 | www.theplace.org.uk

Based at the London Contemporary Dance School, this well-respected organisation offers Pilates, ballet and expressive contemporary dance for people aged five upwards. The contemporary teaching techniques are based on those of Graham, Cunningham and Limón (well-known names to dancers). Ballet classes are taught from beginner to intermediate stages and complement contemporary training. No membership is required; you can pay per class (£9.80, or £7.30 for concessions) or in blocks, although to reap the benefits, enrolling for a term of classes is recommended.

Darts

Darts is the quintessential British pub sport – beloved of those who like to drink a lot and exercise a little. You will find a dartboard and a set of 'arrows' in most traditional pubs in London; in some you can just step up to the oche and play, in others there may be more formal leagues that you can join. Darts has a certain kitsch reputation among younger Londoners thanks to the nicknames and oversized satin shirts of the game's oversized professional players, and the game is growing in popularity. Contact the Greater London Darts Association (8560 8804) if you're a serious player looking to compete regularly, otherwise ask at your local pub; if they haven't got a dartboard, they'll know someone who has.

Diving

OK, so London doesn't have quite the same climate as the Maldives, and the Thames isn't a patch on the Great Barrier Reef, but Great Britain is an island and you don't have to travel far to get to the coast from most parts of the country. As a result, there are more diving clubs, schools and courses in London than you might expect for a big city. Dive enthusiasts tend to be a fun, often slightly crazy bunch wherever you go in the world (maybe it's the nitrogen bubbles), and London's divers are no different – there's an animated social scene attached to the sport in the city. Most clubs organise trips to good diving locations, so it won't just be water-filled quarries and swimming pools if you decide to take up or carry on with the activity. If you're learning to dive in London, the two main governing bodies that you're likely to encounter are the worldwide Professional Association of Diving Instructors (PADI), and UK organisation the British Sub Aqua Club (BSAC). Both list affiliated clubs on their websites (www.padi.com and www.bsac.com).

72 Hubert Grove
SW9
⊖ Clapham North

Big Squid
7733 6966 | www.bigsquid.co.uk

If you want to learn scuba diving, continue your underwater education or just make new buddies, the stylishly named Big Squid diving school offers PADI courses, trips to dive sites (including wrecks and shark dives in the UK and abroad) and an active London-based club, which non-PADI divers are welcome to join. PADI courses are available in Clapham and Battersea for beginners and qualified divers. Choices include Open Water (£235 for a weekend at Clapham Leisure Centre), Refresher, Advanced and Divemaster courses, as well as Bubble Maker for children over 8 years old and specialty courses.

251

Ironmonger Row
Baths
EC1
⇌ ⊖ *Old Street*

Clidive

07799 628066 | www.clidive.org

This BSAC club meets every Thursday from 19:00-21:30 at the historic Ironmonger Row Baths, followed by a few pints and a chat at the Britannia Arms around the corner. The club runs domestic and overseas diving trips throughout the year, and prides itself on the friendliness of the organisation. It also owns two fully equipped dive boats and has scuba kit available for members' use. Try-dives take place approximately every three months and cost £10, which is refunded if you sign up for a course.

11 Power Rd
W4
⊖ *Gunnersbury*

London School of Diving

8995 0002 | www.londonschoolofdiving.com

This purpose-built dive centre is affiliated to PADI and arranges a variety of social and diving activities. As a member (£75 a year) you'll be invited on seasonal UK diving weekends and trips abroad, monthly seminars, pool nights such as underwater obstacle evenings, and other social events. Specialty outings include diving with sharks at the Blue Planet Aquarium in Cheshire, a weekend in Dorset, and a day trip to the world's deepest pool in Brussels, as well as non-diving activities such as climbing. A try-dive costs £25.

Central YMCA Club,
112 Great Russell St
WC1
⊖ *Tottenham*
Court Rd

YDIVE

07977 481940 | www.ydive.org.uk

A branch of the BSAC that is open to all Central YMCA members, YDIVE also accepts divers with a PADI or other diving qualification. The club meets at the YMCA on Tuesday evenings from 19:00, where it runs classroom lessons followed by pool sessions. Regular try-dive nights cost just £10 (free if you're a Central YMCA member). The first year's membership costs £294 and includes access to the YMCA gym, BSAC membership, and all training courses.

Drama Groups

Ah, the smell of greasepaint, the glare of the lights, the audience adulation... if you just can't get enough of the theatre, then joining a drama group could be for you. The capital has some very well-respected amateur groups that put on productions throughout the year, and there are no less than 250 colleges that run drama classes in the capital (see www.hotcourses.com). Just about every borough has some sort of drama activity so if you find yourself unable to resist bursting into song at inopportune moments, maybe it's time to channel your efforts and give the cat some peace.

Finchley Methodist
Church, Ballards Lane
N3
⊖ *West Finchley*

Guild Players

www.guildplayers.org.uk

The Guild Players is an amateur dramatics group affiliated to the Methodist church, although anyone can join. It runs the whole gamut in terms of style, from drama to farce, and usually puts on two productions a year, one in spring and the other in autumn. This active bunch also organises play-reading evenings, training and social events. Annual membership is £10.

Richmond Shakespeare Society

The Mary Wallace Theatre, Twickenham
TW1
⇌ ⊖ Richmond

8744 0547 | www.rss-mwt.org.uk

Not quite the Royal Shakespeare Company in terms of stature, although this highly respected amateur dramatic group has an impressive heritage. The Richmond Shakespeare Society started performing the Bard's work in 1934, and has since gone on to produce plays written by a variety of authors. Full membership (£25 a year) entitles you to participate in productions and vote at meetings, while for £10 you can get part-membership, a requirement if you want to buy tickets.

South London Theatre

2a Norwood High St
SE27
⊖ West Norwood

8670 4661 | www.southlondontheatre.co.uk

The South London Theatre is a well-known repertory-style house that produces over 20 shows a year. There are two spaces in what was once a Victorian fire station – the Bell Theatre, a traditional venue seating around 100 people, and Prompt Corner, a studio that accommodates up to 60. Membership costs £30 a year, which goes towards the theatre's upkeep and the cost of productions, and the fee entitles you to audition or work behind the scenes, attend workshops and go to social events.

Stagecoach Theatre Arts

Various locations

01932 254333 | www.stagecoach.co.uk

Stagecoach is huge. In less than 20 years it has built up a children's part-time theatre school empire of nearly 600 franchises nationwide teaching 36,000 students, plus more worldwide. Small classes usually entail three hours of drama, dance and singing taken by showbiz professionals, and each school showcases its students' work twice a year. The company also plays host to workshops and non-residential holiday programmes. There are more than 50 venues across London - check the Stagecoach website to find one in your area.

The Woodhouse Players

Welsh Church Hall, Leytonstone High Rd
E11
⊖ Leytonstone

8279 9684 | www.woodhouseplayers.co.uk

The self-styled 'friendliest amateur drama group in east London' is still going strong 20 years after it was formed. The jovial enthusiasts meet most Wednesdays and some Fridays and Saturdays with the aim of putting on up to seven main productions a year, plus smaller one-off shows. Membership fees are minimal and everyone gets to have a say in what shows are chosen. New members are encouraged to join, and you don't need to have any theatre training to get involved.

Environmental Groups

With warnings over global warming and climate change high on the world agenda, environmental concerns are becoming increasingly important to the average Londoner. One of the aims of the city's pioneering Congestion Charge (see p.154) is to cut the amount of traffic pollution, and while the general attitude towards recycling initiatives has become more positive in recent years, some boroughs are more conscientious than others, and there is definitely still room for improvement. Check out your local council's website for details about recycling or environmental campaigns in your area (www.londoncouncils.gov.uk).

If you want to do more than just your bit, there are several organisations to which you can contribute. Friends of the Earth (7490 1555) and Greenpeace (7865 8100) have the duopoly in terms of sociable, active networks – both have groups in different regions of London who assist with campaigns. For those who want to get their hands dirty, the London & West Middlesex National Trust Volunteers

253

organisation helps out with repair and maintenance projects at National Trust properties – you can sign up via the group's website, www.lwmntv.org.uk. The Women's Environmental Network campaigns on green issues from a female perspective and has three local groups in London (7481 9004).

Fishing

Fishing rivals football as the UK's most popular recreational pastime, and London's rivers, lakes and streams provide ample opportunities for avid anglers. There are any number of spots from which to choose, ranging from small ponds to reservoirs (see a comprehensive list at www.go-fish.co.uk/london.htm). Some of these are official sites which charge a day rate for fishing, others are public places where you can just turn up with your rod and packed lunch. That said, if you plan to fish in fresh water anywhere in London you'll need a licence from the Environment Agency, which you buy online (www.environment-agency.gov.uk). There are numerous angling clubs in the capital (see www.fishsoutheast.co.uk/clubslondon.htm for a selection), and beginners can choose from a good range of fishing equipment at Farlows (see p.342).

Flower Arranging

Other options **Flowers** p.330, **Gardens** p.333

For the budding artist in you, there are a number of community colleges, schools and florists that offer flower arranging or floristry courses in London. Whether you want to try this creative activity for the first time, continue a hobby or train to be a florist, you can choose anything from short evening lessons in wedding flowers to longer courses where you can gain a qualification. A good place to start is the National Association of Flower Arrangement Societies, which acts as an umbrella for floristry clubs – check out www.nafas.org.uk for details of your nearest organisation. If you want to get a qualification, community colleges tend to run floristry courses for school leavers (visit www.hotcourses.com), while specialist schools and florists (whose courses are usually more expensive) are utilised by professionals. Centrally located Floriart offers courses for those who want to take the skill up as a hobby rather than a profession, while Jane Packer Flower School Tuition (7486 1300) and McQueens (7251 5505) are two world-renowned, stylish establishments offering a full range of courses. If you'd like to try something a bit more exotic, Brunel University Arts Centre (01895 266074) runs courses in the Japanese flower arranging art of ikebana.

Football

Football is the country's most popular sport for players and spectators alike. The beauty of the game is its ability to transcend cultural and racial boundaries – thousands of people from all backgrounds come together every evening and weekend to play in their various teams. The main administrative body for the game is The Football Association (7745 4545) but, for amateurs wanting to get involved, the best website to visit is (www.londonfa.com), home of the London County Football Association, which represents over 2,500 clubs playing five-a-side, eight-a-side or eleven-a-side in the capital. Alternatively, try the Amateur Football Alliance (www.amateur-fa.com) or the Amateur Football Combination (www.amateurfootballcombination.com), two useful directories of London teams. There are a number of industry leagues, such as the Stock Exchange FA and the London Legal Football League, and most sports centres and playing grounds run informal teams – contact your local centre for details. Although traditionally a men-only sport, women's football has gone from strength to strength in recent years. There's now a national league and women's teams attached to some

Premiership clubs. The game is proving increasingly popular on an amateur level too – clubs and informal teams are always looking for new players. Check out www.ladies-football.co.uk for more information.

Various locations

The Elms
8954 8787 | www.theelms.co.uk

The Elms arranges five, six and seven-a-side football leagues for both men and women. Games are held on Monday to Thursday evenings at venues across the city, and the leagues last for 10 weeks. A weekly results and tables service as well as the participation of FA referees are all included in the fee. Teams usually play two or three matches per night.

Various locations

Goals
www.goalsfootball.co.uk

It's every schoolboy's dream to pull on his boots and run out for a game at Wembley – and you can do just that with Goals. Sadly you'll only be lacing up your astroturf boots though, as this is only near, not quite in, the national stadium. Goals' venues feature artificial, all-weather pitches and are available to hire for either league games or just a kickabout with friends. As well as at Wembley, this national company has pitches across Greater London in Beckenham, Bexleyheath, Dagenham, Dartford, Heathrow, Ruislip, Sutton and Wimbledon.

Various locations

Powerleague
www.powerleague.co.uk

This well-established five-a-side football league firm has over 300 venues across the UK, including 11 in the Greater London area. It's heavy on the corporate side, but the facilities and all-weather floodlit pitches make Powerleague a popular choice. The company runs competitive leagues, and all games have an FA-qualified referee. Social matches and coaching (for adults and children) are also available.

Various locations

Top Corner Events
7700 1888 | www.topcorner.it

Top Corner specialises in one-day industry tournaments, held across its 16 central London locations. Competitions generally include a full day's football action (up to 12 matches), FA-qualified referees, top facilities and, if you're any good, trophies. New leagues, from five-a-side through to eleven-a-side, start every month, but the location of matches can vary. The company also provides bespoke events services and sports holidays.

The home of Arsenal Football Club

255

Gardening
Other options **Gardens** p.333

London is awash with gardens, open spaces, parks and allotments. For a European city it's remarkably green, which is just as well – if the vast urban landscape wasn't interspersed with flora and fauna, the capital would be unbearably stifling. Organic gardening in particular has had a revival as people rebel against the potentially unhealthy pesticides found in many supermarket foodstuffs. For green-fingered folk, there are a number of ways to get their hands dirty, from joining a local gardening club to volunteering to clean up and maintain public spaces.

5 King James St
SE1
⊖ *Elephant & Castle*

Bankside Open Spaces Trust
7261 1009 | www.bost.org.uk

This Bankside organisation is made up of local residents, schools, community groups and businesses, all working together to provide information and lessons about gardening activities in the north Southwark area. Its aim is to encourage green spaces in the inner city, whether it's children's playgrounds, public gardens or just window boxes. Guidance will be given so you don't need to have gardening experience to volunteer.

Various locations

East London Organic Gardeners
7265 8257 | www.elog.org.uk

This organisation offers east Londoners the chance to get practical advice about organic gardening. Members are invited to attend talks and lectures on various subjects including genetically modified crops, beekeeping and seed merchants, as well as trips to places of interest. It'll cost you £5 a year to join, which also entitles you to a quarterly newsletter.

Various locations

Guerrilla Gardening
www.guerrillagardening.org

This seemingly covert operation is now an international movement. There's something of the vigilante about people who join this organisation, but its aim is simply to put a smile on city dwellers' faces. In short, followers salvage tired, ugly public spaces by planting flora and fauna at night, thus contributing to making London a more pleasant place to live. Arrangements are made via the website – sign up if you'd like to get involved.

Royal Botanic Gardens, Richmond
TW9
⊖ *Kew Gardens*

Kew Gardens Volunteers
8332 5655 | www.rbgkew.org.uk

Recently selected as a Unesco World Heritage Site, the Royal Botanic Gardens at Kew are arguably the most famous in London (see p.219). Located by the Thames near Richmond, the gardens are a must-see for visitors and a place of serene contemplation for London's busy residents. People wishing to help with the running of Kew can volunteer to take part in a number of horticultural and educational projects, or become a guide.

Various locations

North London Organic Gardeners
groups.msn.com/northlondonorganicgardeners

North London Organic Gardeners meets on the first Tuesday of every month to discuss organic gardening and all that it entails. Meetings are open to members and non-members who live in north London, and are useful for learning new techniques and swapping tips. The society also gets together at members' houses to compare notes on each others' gardens.

180 Spa Hill
SE19
⇄ *Crystal Palace*

Spa Hill Allotment Society

8653 5636 | www.spahill.org.uk

This community group invites gardening enthusiasts of all abilities to join. Most members have one of the 300 allotment plots on Crystal Palace Hill, but there's a long waiting list to get your own patch (preference is given to people who live within the immediate area). However, if you just want to go along without taking up part of the allotment, you can become a 'garden member' for just £2 a year. The society provides training and advice on gardening techniques, and also has links to the Spa Hill Organic Gardening Group.

Golf

Golf's image has changed in recent years, and is no longer confined to chequer-trousered executives. A few of the stuffier clubs maintain a depressingly patronising attitude towards women and the 'working classes', but most are welcoming. Golf courses obviously require large areas of open space, which can be at a premium in urban settings, but despite this there are several places where you can swing your driver within the capital. Facilities vary from fun venues open to beginners, such as Urban Golf and Richmond Park, to membership-only clubs with hefty fees. Equipment can nearly always be hired on site so don't let the thought of buying expensive clubs put you off. For a comprehensive list of golf courses in and around London check out the directory on www.golftoday.co.uk.

Grange Lane,
College Rd
SE21
⇄ *Sydenham Hill*

Dulwich & Sydenham Hill Golf Club

8693 3961 | www.dulwichgolf.co.uk

This 6,100 yard par 69 course is dotted with oak trees and boasts glorious views over the City of London. It's a private club, but welcomes players of an average standard during the week (weekends are strictly reserved for members). The course opens from 08:00 to dusk and the price for visitors starts at £25 for a round.

Denewood Rd
N6
⊖ *Highgate*

Highgate Golf Club

8340 3745 | www.highgategc.co.uk

Anywhere that describes itself as 'an oasis of calm amidst London's rat race' is bound to appeal, even more so because it's the nearest 18 hole venue to the centre of London. The hilly course runs to around 6,000 yards with a par of 69. All the usual facilities, such as a clubhouse, bar and pro's shop, are offered. The course is open from 08:00 until dusk. It's a members' club, but visitors can play during the week from £34 a round.

Urban Golf

The Manor House,
Friern Barnet Lane
N20
⊖ *Totteridge &*
Whetstone

North Middlesex Golf Club

8445 1604 | www.northmiddlesexgc.co.uk

Another par 69, but be warned – this course is not for the faint-hearted. It's notorious for being extremely challenging, although more seasoned golfers will appreciate its speed and difficulty. If you do make it to the 18th hole without breaking your clubs in a fit of pique, you'll be rewarded with a great view of the attractive clubhouse. Open from 08:00 until dusk seven days a week, visitors are welcome.

257

Richmond Park Golf Course

Richmond Park, Roehampton Gate SW15 ⇌Barnes

8876 3205 | www.richmondparkgolf.co.uk

Richmond Park offers two 18 hole courses: the Dukes and the Princes (the latter has panoramic views over the park). There are no membership restrictions (you pay daily, from £19 a round), which makes it a convenient choice, if a little overcrowded at times. If you are a lone player, it's possible to join other groups – at their discretion, of course. There's also a practice range, tuition (lessons cost from £20 for 30 minutes), an academy for children and a large shop. The course opens for play as early as 06:00 during summer.

Urban Golf

33 Great Pulteney St W1 ⊖Piccadilly Circus

7434 4300 | www.urbangolf.co.uk

Urban Golf is an indoor golf centre where beginners and experienced golfers can play or be coached on 52 simulated courses from around the world, without leaving central London. As well as the Soho centre, there is also one in Smithfield, Farringdon (7248 8600) – so not only are the Urban Golf venues in the coolest parts of town, they're also stylish, friendly and serve drinks and food, making them good spots for group outings. The Soho venue, on Great Pulteney Street, is open seven days a week, while the Smithfield Urban Golf is open from 10:00 until 23:30 Monday to Saturday. Booking is advisable.

Wanstead Golf Club

Overton Drive E11 ⊖Wanstead

8989 3938 | www.wansteadgolf.org.uk

The proximity of this private club to the City makes it attractive to high-flying workers, but the tricky 18 hole course isn't for beginners. Full membership costs £1,100 a year, although there are only a limited number of memberships available and you'll also need a handicap certificate and knowledge of golfing etiquette. Visitors and corporate events are welcome.

Hockey

Hockey is a serious amateur sport in the UK – clubs in London tend to be well-organised establishments rather than the 'turn up and play' set-ups found in some other participant sports. Don't be put off by the formality though – new members are always welcome, and most clubs have a number of teams for both men and women, so you should be able to find your level. Hockey teams are quite often affiliated to other sports clubs too, such as cricket and tennis, so you're likely to encounter a lively social scene when you sign up. There are many clubs in London – besides the areas listed here, check out www.englandhockey.co.uk for a comprehensive run down.

Barnes Hockey Club

Lonsdale Rd SW13 ⊖Hounslow

8748 6220 | www.barneshockeyclub.co.uk

Located just south of the Thames in south-west London, Barnes Hockey Club has several teams of different levels as well as an active social club. The hockey set-up is just one strand of club, which also runs tennis, squash, cricket, croquet, bowls and even bridge teams. It has good community links too – a nursery uses the clubhouse during the week. New members are welcome.

Blackheath Hockey Club

Rubens St SE6 ⊖Catford

www.blackheath.co.uk

If you like your hockey with a bit of heritage, then it's worth checking out Blackheath, which is reputed to be the oldest club in the world (dating back to 1840). There are several Saturday teams for men and women, and the club also has affiliated cricket and squash teams. Training and matches are played at three venues across south-east London, in Blackheath, Mottingham, and Catford (where the clubhouse is located). If you want to become a member, email steve@blackheath.co.uk.

The Carlton Tavern,
33a Carlton Vale
NW6
⊖ Maida Vale

Hampstead and Westminster Hockey Club
www.hwhc.co.uk

Based at the Paddington Recreation Ground in Maida Vale, this long-established club for men and women caters for cream-of-the-crop players right through to recreational stick wielders. Games are played on Saturdays, and there are a whopping 12 men's teams and six for women. After a trial, the club will endeavor to place you in a team that best suits your ability – although you'll have to be pretty good to force your way into the men's first team as it plays in the national Premier Division.

Horse Riding

Equestrian activities are hugely popular in Britain. The large open parks of London make riding almost as enjoyable in the city as in the countryside, but it's not a cheap leisure pursuit. It is however an excellent way to keep fit – riding not only strengthens your muscles but also improves your posture, and it gets you a little closer to nature in this sprawling metropolis. Whether you're a novice or experienced rider, it's advisable to try out a few stables to find an environment best suited to you, and make sure they treat their horses well. Equipment is generally provided, although you'll be expected to wear comfortable trousers and footwear with a small heel (don't wear trainers). The British Horse Society (0870 1202244) will be able to give you more detailed information about riding and approved schools in your area.

Empress Avenue
E12
⇌ Manor Park

Aldersbrook Riding School
8530 4648 | www.aldersbrookriding.co.uk

Cheaper but just as experienced as other London riding establishments, this small, accommodating school provides lessons in an outdoor paddock, dressage (for intermediate levels and up), British Horse Society training and tests, and pony games for children. Aldersbrook is particularly gentle on novice or nervous riders. Private lessons start from £30 an hour or £35 for groups of four or more.

63 Bathurst Mews
W2
⊖ Lancaster Gate

Hyde Park Stables
7723 2813 | www.hydeparkstables.com

These stables aren't cheap (from £49 an hour for tuition), but they cater for all abilities and ages. You can choose from weekend dressage classes, lessons in riding and stable management in two outdoor arenas, or take hacks along the 300-year-old Rotten Row in Hyde Park – one of the most famous equestrian venues in England. Open from 07:15 to 17:00 on weekdays and 09:00 to 17:00 on weekends. Advanced booking is recommended.

Lea Bridge Rd
E10
⇌ Clapton

Lee Valley Riding School
8556 2629 | www.leevalleypark.org.uk

As well as playing golf, fishing, walking or birdwatching in the 10,000 acres of wilderness that make up Lee Valley Park, you can also ride at these reputable stables.

259

Here you'll find quality instruction in riding and horse care in a safe atmosphere. Activities include riding for the disabled (see www.riding-for-disabled.org.uk), half-hour 'have-a-go' sessions for beginners, hacking on Hackney Marshes, cross-country courses, a pony club for under 21s, and social events. Lesson prices start from £17.50 an hour for adults.

Stag Lodge Stables

Robin Hood Gate, Richmond Park SW15 ⇌Norbiton

8974 6066 | www.ridinginlondon.com

Richmond Park is the stomping ground for horses and riders from these long-established, family-run stables. The horses are well-trained – a must for beginners – and the instruction is friendly. A one-hour group hack costs £25 on weekdays, £35 on weekends, and a private hack is £40 or £50. Hacks includes cantering (if you're brave enough as a beginner), although booking a two-hour ride (double the price) is recommended to get a proper look at the park. Evening lessons are available. Open every day except Mondays.

Wimbledon Village Stables

24 a/b High St SW19 ⇌ ⊖ Wimbledon

8946 8579 | www.wvstables.com

It's worth becoming a member at these stables, a short walk from Wimbledon town, to take advantage of reduced riding rates. There are private and group lessons, as well as livery, day courses, excursions, lectures and riding on Wimbledon Common and in Richmond Park. The more competitive can enter dressage and jumping competitions. British Horse Society training is also offered. The stables arrange 'desperate horse-wives' events every Wednesday, and 'horse power' riding sessions for men. Prices start from £40 an hour for a lesson for non-members.

Ice Skating

Great fun, if a little tough on the behind, ice-skating is a very sociable activity and a good place to meet friends while getting some exercise (and the occasional bruise). There are permanent ice rinks all over London, plus a number of seasonal rinks that spring up in winter. Skate hire is available from all rinks but, in general, expect to pay extra on top of the entrance fee. The sport became very popular in the 1980s after Brits Torvill and Dean won Olympic gold, and remains popular today – some 50,000 children complete a Skate UK Learn to Skate course every year. However, the sport is not an easy one to master. It requires speed, strength and grace in equal measure. If dancing on ice doesn't appeal to you, most ice rinks will have details on speed skating and ice hockey. Visit the National Ice Skating Association's website, www.iceskating.org.uk, for more information.

Alexandra Palace Ice Rink

Alexandra Palace Way N22 ⊖ Wood Green

8365 4386 | www.alexandrapalace.com

This large rink is open year round and has a capacity for 1,250 people, so if you like your rinks to be intimate this one isn't for you. There's a wide range of activities, lessons are available for almost every aspect of ice sports, and the venue is home to an amateur ice skating club (www.apskate.org.uk). The rink can be hired out and is officially approved for conducting marriages, giving a whole new meaning to the term 'white weddings'. Sessions cost between £6 and £7 for adults, or it's a fiver during happy hour (16:30 to 17:30).

Broadgate Ice Rink

Broadgate Circus,
Eldon St
EC2
Liverpool Street

7505 4068 | www.broadgateice.co.uk

Open seven days a week from late October until mid-April, Broadgate Ice Rink is an open-air venue in the heart of the City. Its location makes it a popular place to hire for corporate events, and it's also the only place in London to play host to broomball – a game played in shoes, not skates, that involves hitting a ball with rubber paddles. Skating sessions cost £6 for adults or £40 for a monthly season ticket.

Sobell Ice Rink

Sobell Leisure Centre,
Hornsey Rd
N7
Finsbury Park

7609 2166 | www.aquaterra.org

This well-equipped north London leisure centre houses a skating rink that offers a variety of sessions focused on children, including families, parents and toddlers, and after-school. There's also junior ice hockey and a six-week Learn to Skate course for a reasonable £40. For speed-shy beginners, Monday nights from 18:45 to 20:00 is a safe time to take to the ice.

Somerset House Ice Rink

Somerset House,
Strand
WC2
Charing Cross

7845 4671 | www.somersethouseicerink.org.uk

This enormously popular outdoor rink is only open from November to January, but has become an absolute must-do. The rink's attractiveness lies mainly in the stunning setting; the majestic Somerset House looks even more romantic at night, illuminated up by flaming torches and coloured lighting. Sessions are hour-long and there's often a late skate until 23:30 – but you must book tickets (from £10 per adult) in advance.

Streatham Ice Arena

386 Streatham
High Rd
SW16
Streatham Hill

8769 7771 | www.streathamicearena.co.uk

If you're ever in the mood for a spot of disco skating, there's only one place to go. Streatham Ice Arena will have you jiving across the ice with the best of them – there's a junior disco on Fridays and Saturdays from 18:00 to 20:00, and adult evening discos take place every Tuesday to Saturday from 20:00 onwards. There are also classes, a schools ice-skating programme and a shop, plus ice-hockey team the Streatham Chiefs are based here. Adult prices start from £6.

Language Schools

If you'd like to improve your English, there are numerous language schools in London. Some specifically teach English as a second language, and many also provide other language courses such as French and Spanish. Individual needs vary, so you may not need to do the whole course – prices featured tend to be either for a week or 10 weeks. Academic establishments such as colleges, universities and institutes generally offer evening language classes (see www.hotcourses.com for details), or if one-to-one home tuition appeals try Talk Languages (see below).

East London School of English

154-170 Cannon
Street Rd
E1
Whitechapel

7265 8868 | www.elsenglish.com

This welcoming school situated near the City of London and with decent transport links offers good value courses in reasonably sized classes (the average is 12 students). There are eight graded levels, from beginner to proficiency, and an extra option to take exams. A 10-week course costs £245 (or £179 for four weeks). Student services include an accommodation officer who will help you find somewhere to stay, and there's online information about opening a bank account and finding work.

French and Spanish a la Carte

97 Revelstoke Rd
SW18
⊖ Southfields

8946 4777 | www.frenchandspanishalacarte.co.uk

An intimate language school in a private house offering French and Spanish classes taught by nationals to adults and children. Courses cost £130 for 12 weeks or £250 for a week-long intensive course. For children, it costs £115 for a 14 week course (one hour a week) or £182 for a 14 week playgroup for under fives (two hours a week). Private home tuition (about £27 to £40 an hour) is available, and the school also organises language holidays abroad.

The Language Centre

University of the Arts London, 65 Davies St
W1
⊖ Bond Street

7514 7261 | www.arts.ac.uk/languagecentre

Located in the heart of London's bustling shopping district, this establishment is affiliated to the University of the Arts London – making it a good choice for those with artistic leanings who wish to learn a language. It offers a variety of English courses, as well as 10 week French, German, Italian, Japanese, Mandarin and Spanish evening classes. A 10 week English course costs £160 a week (15 hours' tuition) while a 10 week evening course costs £195. The centre can arrange accommodation for students.

London Study Centre

Munster House, 676 Fulham Rd
SW6
⊖ Parsons Green

7731 3549 | www.londonstudycentre.com

A large, well-equipped school on Fulham Road that offers English language classes at an economical price (the downside being that the classes are larger – up to 24 people). Students can start a class any Monday morning (except over Christmas and Easter, when the centre is closed); 10-week courses cost about £490. There's an accommodation and welfare officer on hand for pupils needing practical advice.

Saint George International

79-80 Margaret St
W1
⊖ Oxford Circus

7299 1700 | www.stgeorges.co.uk

This family-owned school has been running English language courses for more than 40 years. Its programme includes business English, academic English, intensive courses and summer schools (it works closely with the University of Westminster and uses the university's facilities in July and August). All are available to beginners and intermediate English speakers. A standard course starts from £180 a week, while individual tuition is available from £40 an hour. The school can also arrange accommodation.

Talk Languages

Various locations

0845 0224444 | www.talklanguages.net

A highly recommended, well-organised company offering one-to-one tuition with excellent teachers, and over 35 languages to choose from. At £24 an hour (the teacher comes to your home), this service is not only great value for money, it's flexible, which means you can do as much or as little as you need to. Alternatively, you can pay from £32 for small groups of people (from two to five per group).

Libraries

Other options **Books** p.317, **Second-Hand Items** p.345

With more than 360 public libraries in London, including specialist and academic institutions, you can readily access just about any kind of information you can think of. Most public libraries offer books for borrowing and reference, internet access, computer facilities, large print, braille, magazines, newspapers, CDs, DVDs and reading groups. In order to take out books you need to become a member by providing proof of your name and address. The libraries listed below are some of the capital's most notable, although you'll find local ones in every borough (see www.londonlibraries.org for a full list of locations).

The British Library

96 Euston Rd
NW1
⇌ ⊖ King's Cross
St. Pancras

0870 4441500 | www.bl.uk
Britain's magnificent national library houses a wealth of information (150 million items and counting), including every book published in the UK and Ireland. There's space to seat 1,200 readers, and an estimated 16,000 people use the library every day. The *Magna Carta* rests here, as does Shakespeare's first folio and some of The Beatles' song manuscripts, and there are also regular exhibitions. The library is open from 09:30 to 18:00 Monday to Friday, 09:30 to 17:00 on Saturdays, and from 11:00 to 17:00 on Sundays. It's free to enter the building, although you'll need to take two forms of ID if you want a 'reader pass'.

The London Library

14 St James's Square
SW1
⇌ ⊖ Charing Cross

7930 7705 | www.londonlibrary.co.uk
The world's largest independent lending library was built in 1841 (it maintains an imposing Victorian atmosphere) and was utilised by great writers such as George Bernard Shaw and Charles Dickens. Its huge collection – over one million books and volumes – makes it a favourite with writers, researchers and scholars alike. Membership starts at £195 a year (£105 for temporary overseas visitors, plus a deposit), or £10 a day (£30 a week) to use the facilities – this doesn't allow you to take out books, however. The library is open from 09:30 to 19:30 Monday to Wednesday and 09:30 to 17:30 Thursday to Saturday.

St Pancras Library

Camden Town House,
8 Argyle St
WC1
⇌ ⊖ King's Cross
St. Pancras

7974 5833 | www.camden.gov.uk/stpancraslibrary
If you're a regular commuter in and out of King's Cross station, this library – a short walk away – is worth a visit should your train get delayed. It houses books, newspapers, CDs and community information, and there's also internet access and photocopying facilities. Membership is free; all that's required is proof of name and address. It's open 10:00 to 19:00 on Mondays and Thursdays, 10:00 to 18:00 on Tuesdays, Wednesdays and Fridays, and 10:00 to 17:00 on Saturdays.

Westminster Reference Library

35 St Martin's St
WC2
⊖ Leicester Square

7641 1300 | www.westminster.gov.uk
This reference library is just one of 12 in the Westminster borough. You don't have to live in the area to use the facilities as they're open to anyone who's interested. It's especially good for business, law and official tomes, but also has an excellent, little-known art and design collection on the top floor, with over 40,000 books on subjects including architecture, ceramics, fashion, furniture and graphics (ring ahead for opening hours). It's child-friendly too. Open 10:00 to 20:00 Monday to Friday and 10:00 to 17:00 on Saturdays.

Martial Arts

Martial arts are so popular in London that the hardest task is not finding a club, it's choosing which type of practice to follow. There are centres that concentrate solely on particular disciplines, and many local sports centres, gyms and community facilities teach classes of some sort. A selection of the martial arts being practiced in London are aikido, chin woo, judo, ju-jitsu, karate, kendo, kickboxing, taekwondo and Thai boxing. For those who can't decide, there's mixed martial arts, which combines boxing, wrestling, and ju-jitsu (see www.cagerage.co.uk). There are many benefits to taking up a martial art; you'll learn self-defence skills (a real confidence booster, especially for women), increase energy and flexibility, relieve stress, and improve reflexes, co-ordination, self-discipline and awareness. Useful organisations include the British Judo Association (www.britishjudo.org.uk), the British Martial Arts Institute (www.bmai.co.uk) and the Martial Arts Clubs directory (www.martialartsclubs.com).

Archway Campus,
2-10 Highgate Hill
N19
⊖ Archway

Archway Ju-jitsu

07932 154007 | www.archwayjitsu.com

This north London club teaches practical techniques for defending against attackers without relying so much on strength. Classes are open to anyone aged 14 or over, regardless of ability or experience. Sessions are held Wednesday nights from 20:00 to 22:00, and Sunday evenings from 18:00 to 20:00. The cost is £4, although your first session is free.

Topnotch Health Club,
Tudor St
EC4
⇌ ⊖ Blackfriars

Chang's Hapkido Academy

07951 535876 | www.changshapkidoacademy.co.uk

Grandmaster Gedo Chang's hapkido martial arts schools focus on self-defence, confidence, balance and fitness. Hapkido is an ancient Korean discipline made up of 'hap' (body and mind coordination), 'ki' (inner energy) and 'do' (self-control and discipline). The centre teaches how to subdue an opponent without causing serious harm. It is open five days a week, offers individual and group classes for all ages, and also organises social events. There's an enrolment fee of £40, plus a £50 to £75 payment a month for classes.

Various locations

KB Kick Boxing

7681 0114 | www.kbkickboxing.co.uk

KB offers a range of classes for beginners upwards, and all provide cardiovascular workouts that concentrate on footwork, kicking and punching combinations, and defensive and offensive techniques. A hardcore soundtrack keeps students moving, plus there's yoga on the timetable for those looking for something more serene. The fee for the beginners' class is £95, which covers joining and two months of classes. There are various venues around central London.

72 Putney High St
SW15
⊖ Putney Bridge

Martial Fitness

8788 2815 | www.martialfitness.com

Martial Fitness offers kickboxing and kung fu classes for children, teenagers and adults, as well as box-fit sessions – punching and kicking techniques combined with circuit training that help burn fat and tone muscle. It is also planning to introduce the intimidating 'Do Jo Boot Camps' – 10 days of intensive fitness training and conditioning for all levels. Membership costs £75, plus extras depending on the package you choose.

Sports & Activities

Tokei Martial Arts and Fitness Centre
Lion Court,
28 Magdalen St
SE1
⇌ ⊖ London Bridge

7403 5979 | www.tokeicentre.org
One of London's leading martial arts establishments, and the only purpose-built centre in the UK, Tokei offers classes in wu shu kwan (Chinese kickboxing), judo, karate, freestyle wrestling and Thai boxing, not to mention aikido, Brazilian ju-jitsu, capoeira, hapkido, sanjuro and tai chi. If you're not exhausted from reading that list, there's also a fully-equipped gym. Membership costs £45 a month.

Mother & Toddler Activities
The days of being a stay-at-home mother are long gone for many women. In London it's not unusual for a young child and parent to have a full itinerary of activities such as music class on Monday, gym on Tuesday, yoga on Wednesday, massage on Thursday and swimming lessons on Friday. There's something to do every day of the week and, what's more, it doesn't cost a fortune. Want to talk to your baby before they can answer back? Baby Sing and Sign may be just the thing. Is your child already showing musical ability? Try Caterpillar Music (www.caterpillarmusic.co.uk) to bring out the budding Beethoven in your little one. For those who don't want to sign up for a whole course, local churches often run cheap toddler groups costing around £1 a visit, or there's always your local One O'Clock Club, a council-run initiative providing activities for pre-school children in local parks. See your local authority's website for details.

Aquababies
Kensington Sports Centre, Walmer Rd
W11
⊖ Latimer Road

01273 833101 | www.aquababies-uk.com
Aquababies promotes swimming for babies and toddlers in a safe and professional environment. This company has classes in 30 pools across London and the surrounding counties. Lessons are 35 minutes long and courses last for five weeks (£55). Each class introduces a new skill, which can be repeated if necessary.

Baby Massage
154 Kings Head Hill
E4
⇌ Chingford

8923 6452 | www.yoga4birth.co.uk
The power of massage cannot be underestimated – not only will it help you bond with your child, it will help them become more positively aware of their bodies, aid sleep, and reduce colic and other infant aches and pains. Classes are kept small (up to 10 mums, dads or carers, plus babies) and the courses last for six weeks (£72).

Monkey Music
Various locations

01583 766464 | www.monkeymusic.co.uk
There are 14 places around London (and many more outside the capital) that offer these fantastic 30 minute music classes for mums (or carers) and their children. They introduce music to small children in a way they can relate to and help develop children's musical and social skills. Classes cater for babies up to 4 years old. Courses last around 12 weeks and cost £6.50 per session. There's a joining fee of £16, and a free trial session is offered to those interested. Contact your local group via the website for times.

Sing and Sign
Various locations

01273 550587 | www.singandsign.co.uk
These classes encourage early communication between parent and child. In safe surroundings, you and your baby are invited to sing, sign, play and socialise. Various props such as instruments, puppets and pictures are used to great effect. There are classes throughout London: in Ealing (west), Wimbledon and Southfields (south-west), and Dulwich and Greenwich (south-east). A 10 week course costs £75. Contact Sing and Sign for details of the class closest to you.

The Complete **Residents'** Guide

Brockwell Lido,
Dulwich Rd
SE24
Herne Hill

Whippersnappers
7738 6633 | www.whippersnappers.org

Based at Brockwell Lido and other venues across London, Whippersnappers provides 250 under 5s with much-loved music and interactive storytelling workshops, as well as sessions for children whose first language is not English, autistic children, and those with disabilities. Each session costs £4 (£1 per extra sibling). See the website for venues and times.

Music Lessons
Other options **Dance Classes** p.249, **Orchestras** p.268, **Singing** p.274

London has thriving live music, DJ and music production scenes. Depending on your level of skill there are a range of options, from developing your proficiency with an instrument to learning about the technical and production side of the business. For a full list of music courses in the capital see www.hotcourses.com. Home tuition is an alternative if you wish to practise in your own environment (although your neighbours may not be so keen). If you'd prefer to get out there and mingle with other musicians, signing up to a school or course is the way to go.

50-52 Union St
SE1
Waterloo

London Centre of Contemporary Music
7378 7458 | www.lccm.org.uk

Based in south London, this independent, accredited music school has both degree-level and shorter courses available. It stresses the importance of being an all-rounder in order to survive a career in this notoriously competitive industry. The school specialises in bass, drums, guitar, piano, saxophone, studio production, trumpet, trombone and voice lessons, and also offers courses in funk, soul and electronica. It boasts a team of experienced teachers that have worked and studied with a string of famous artists. Prices vary; call for details.

41 Spelman St
E1
Aldgate East

The London Music School
7247 1311 | www.tlms.co.uk

A well-respected contemporary music school, with a reputation that has spread throughout Europe, this establishment is renowned for its sound and audio engineering and MIDI technology courses. It also offers a range of instrument lessons in bass, drums, guitar and keyboards and is a popular choice for DJs, musicians and songwriters who want to use technology to aid their creativity. Six-month full-time courses and 10 week part-time courses are available; ring for details and prices.

71 Strahan Rd
E3
Mile End

London Piano School
8980 0821 | www.londonpianoschool.co.uk

He may be young (he's not yet 30), but piano tutor Noel Charles knows his Mozart from his Mendelssohn. This friendly school offers classical piano and music theory to children and adults of any ability, and promises to be particularly gentle on nervous pupils. You have the option to play for relaxation or towards exams in a calming, studious environment.

266

Various locations

Music for London
0845 2262971 | www.musicforlondon.co.uk
Although this company is initially for people wanting to hire out professional musicians for events, all its musicians are skilled teachers who will happily provide home tuition. Whether it's singing, double bass or the trumpet, Music for London can put you in touch with the right tutor for your requirements. Call to discuss the various options.

226-228 Baker St
EN1
⇌ Enfield Town

North London Music Centre
8342 0807 | www.northlondonmusiccentre.co.uk
The North London Music Centre sells instruments as well as providing one-to-one training for brass, guitar, piano, percussion, strings and woodwind in a range of styles from rock to R&B. Pupils can learn at their own pace or study for recognised exams. Singing lessons are also available. Tuition (based at the centre) is available during the day and evenings and costs £24 an hour or £13.50 for 30 minutes.

Netball
Netball is one of the few sports in the UK that has a higher women's profile then men's. The leagues mentioned here consist of mainly female players, though it's possible to play in social mixed teams (see Social Sports, p.267). Netball, a variation of basketball, is played in many schools from a young age, and most universities, colleges, sports centres, gyms and some large companies have netball teams.

Various locations

Alpha Netball Club
www.alphanetball.co.uk
Alpha Netball Club was established in 1979, and encourages women of all ages and backgrounds to participate both recreationally and competitively. This friendly club currently has four teams in three adult leagues, uses qualified coaches, and provides umpiring and coaching training. Alpha welcomes experienced players from the age of 14 upwards. Venues vary, but teams usually play in Brixton, Kennington, Stockwell and other south London areas.

Broomfield Park
N13
⇌ Palmers Green

North London Netball League
www.nlnl.co.uk
Well established and well respected, this league has been running successfully for over 50 years and also provides umpiring and coaching courses. The league is made up of five divisions and hosts around 50 teams from 23 clubs. There's also a popular junior league split into three divisions: under 12s, under 13s and under 14s. The winter season runs from September to May, and the summer league runs from mid-May to the end of June. Visit the website for club information and contacts.

98 Gibbins Rd
E15
DLR ⇌ ⊖ Stratford

Social Sports
8534 8444 | www.socialsports.co.uk
Social Sports has hosted indoor and outdoor netball events since 2001. It runs mixed and ladies leagues at well-equipped venues in Docklands, Paddington, Stratford, Shepherd's Bush and Wimbledon. The focus is on the fun side of the game as well as socialising afterwards. The leagues are broken into experienced, intermediate, social and open divisions. Single players can register online (£46) – you can choose to be assigned a team or play on a 'ringer' basis.

Orchestras/Bands
Other options **Music Lessons** p.266, **Singing** p.274

Sinfonia, chamber, symphony, philharmonic – all are options available to amateur and professional musicians in London. There are a wide range of amateur orchestras to choose from – some only accept skilled musicians but others embrace players of all levels of experience. If you don't play (yet) but have always dreamed of doing so, don't fret as there are orchestras out there for beginners. Some of these are featured below, or check out www.ensemble.demon.co.uk/orchest/olondon.htm, which lists just about every amateur orchestra in the Greater London area.

Professional Development Centre, English St
E3
◉ **Mile End**

East London Late Starters Orchestra
8748 8401 | www.ellso.org.uk
A fantastic organisation that welcomes wannabe musicians with little or no experience, as well as skilled players. Beginners need to join in September and attend Saturday morning sessions, from 09:15 to 13:15, while the afternoon sessions (from 14:00-16:30) are for people of all levels of ability. Membership costs £15 a year, plus £7 a session (£10 for non-members). Beginners will need to pay extra to cover tuition fees and instrument hire.

Various locations

Lambeth Orchestra
www.lambeth-orchestra.org.uk
The Lambeth Orchestra performs a range of reasonably priced concerts, usually at St Luke's Church (West Norwood, SE27) or All Saints (West Dulwich, SE21). The charity encourages new players to join; to apply you simply need to fill in the form on the website. At the time of writing, double bass players were much sought after.

Various locations

The Learning Orchestra
www.ravel.org.uk/tlo
The Learning Orchestras provides two options for different levels of ability. The main orchestra is interested in musicians of grade five standard and above, and rehearsals take place on Thursdays between 18:30 and 21:00 at St Pancras Church House, NW1 (near Euston station). The intermediate orchestra practises at The London School of Hygiene & Tropical Medicine, Keppel Street, WC1 (Goodge Street tube) and accepts musicians of grade three level and over. Neither outfit cares too much for auditions, and both are particularly interested in people who are returning to playing after an absence.

Hinde Street Methodist Church
W1
◉ **Bond Street**

London Charity Orchestra
www.londoncharityorchestra.co.uk
This orchestra was specifically set up to play on behalf of charitable causes. Its members are a combination of students, skilled amateurs and professionals. The orchestra is always on the look out for string players and specialist instruments but anyone with grade eight or over should apply. There's no membership fee or audition process.

Lancaster Road Methodist Church
W11
◉ **Latimer Road**

Portobello Orchestra
www.geocities.com/portobelloorch
The Portobello Orchestra consists of musicians of all levels of ability. New players are welcome to join although places are dependent on what instrument you play (some orchestral sections can accommodate less accomplished players better than others without being found out). Rehearsals take place from 19:30 to 21:30 on Mondays.

Royal Orchestral Society for Amateur Musicians

Quintin Kynaston School, Marlborough Hill NW8
⊖ St. John's Wood

7333 5120

This society is the oldest of its kind in the country – it was founded by Queen Victoria's son, the Duke of Edinburgh, in 1872. He was an avid violinist and was the society's first president. Many years later, the group is still popular. The orchestra is made up of music students and amateurs and is coached by professional conductors. Rehearsals take place at 19:00 on Mondays.

West London Sinfonia

39 Mount Park Rd W5
⇌ ⊖ Ealing Broadway

8997 3540 | www.westlondonsinfonia.org

You need to be a decent player to join this orchestra – grade eight or above is required, but they're a sociable bunch so if you think you fit the bill (and especially if you're a cellist or double bass player) get in touch. Rehearsals are on Tuesday nights and the orchestra often goes abroad to play.

Photography

London is a photographer's dream. Whether you fancy being the next Annie Leibovitz or David LaChapelle or you just want to progress from shooting snaps to pictures of a more professional standard, there are more than 185 colleges that offer to teach and train you in the subject. There are a range of courses to suit all tastes, from a basic introduction to more specialised skills such as travel photography or portraiture. A lot of classes also focus on the history of photography. Advanced courses often expect a portfolio, so get snapping or sign up to an evening class if you're serious. Check out the ones below or see www.hotcourses.com for more information.

Picture Perfect

The say a picture can speak a thousand words so if you can't sum up the sights and sounds of a city in a sentence then grab a copy of one Explorer's stunning *Mini Photography Books*, which showcase unique views of each city. Make sure the next time you go on holiday you take home more than just your memories.

Barnet College

Wood St EN5
⊖ High Barnet

8266 4000 | www.barnet.ac.uk

A good option for studying art and design subjects (especially if you live north of the river) whatever your level of ability, Barnet College offers a variety of part-time weekend and evening photography courses in subjects including darkrooms and digital photography, plus various workshops. There's also a full-time BTEC National Diploma (an interview is required) for those wishing to pursue a career in photography. Call for a prospectus.

Hackney Community College

Falkirk St N1
⇌ ⊖ Old Street

7613 9123 | www.tcch.ac.uk

Based around Hackney, a hotbed of artistic activity, there are two chief centres to this college (London Fields and Shoreditch) plus other locations including the Puttnam Building (a media centre named after the film director Lord David Puttnam). This is a modern, well-equipped breeding ground for creatives that offers the chance to hone your artistic talent while equipping you with practical advice to transfer your skills to the workplace. Photography courses are based at the Shoreditch site and include a BTEC National Diploma, part-time programmes and a 10 week course for beginners.

269

61 Westminster
Bridge Rd
SE1
⇌ ⊖ **Waterloo**

Morley College
7450 1889 | www.morleycollege.ac.uk

A well-respected college that's been offering reasonably priced courses for all abilities since the 1880s. There are short courses, held over two Sundays, such as the intriguingly titled 'Holiday photography: places, faces, spaces', plus 'Photographing London'. Daytime introductory and intermediate courses are available, as well as a longer City & Guilds evening programme. Courses start from around £40 (excluding the price of film) and go up to £524 for a qualification.

17a Electric Lane
SW9
⊖ **Brixton**

Photofusion
7738 5774 | www.photofusion.org

An independent photography centre with a full range of facilities, situated in the heart of Brixton (probably one of the most colourful areas in which to take pictures in London). As well as having a studio, darkrooms and a picture library, there's a strong accent on education and training for beginners through to professional photographers wishing to further their skills. There are courses in professional development (which includes reviewing your portfolio and business practice), camera and lighting, image composition, Photoshop, retouching, and darkroom and printing; prices range from £40- £650. The gallery, where people can showcase their work, attracts thousands of visitors.

Clapham
Leisure Centre,
Clapham Manor St
SW4
⊖ **Clapham North**

Zoom In
7720 7437 | www.zoom-in.org

This not-for-profit organisation was set up 10 years ago by two professional photographers for people wishing to learn about the subject but who do not have the funds to do so. There are beginner, intermediate and advanced courses in camera basics, digital photography, film processing, technique, documentary photography, landscape and portraits, to name but a few. Prices start at around £60 for a one-off evening introductory class but courses mainly run for three or four weeks (one three-hour session a week) and start from £150. Concessions are available.

Rollerblading & Inline Hockey
Other options **Parks** p.213

London can't match the legendary sights and sounds of New York's Central Park skaters, but there's a definite buzz surrounding its rollerblading scene. Stroll through a park any day of the week and you'll see plenty of lycra-clad limbs whizzing by. Despite typical English scepticism at a 'show off' sport, more and more Londoners are throwing shapes at one of city's word-of-mouth skates. Friday Night Skate, which meets regularly at Hyde Park Corner, has gained a legendary reputation among locals and tourists. It's a 20km ride through the West End accompanied by a sound system; all you need to join in is the ability to stop your skates and take a few rough bumps. If you like skating to music, try boogieing on wheels at the Roller Disco at Canvas in King's Cross (7630 6625). Citiskate, which organises the Friday Night Skate, offers lessons to novices (www.citiskate.co.uk). For beginners and families there are more straightforward rides in Battersea and Hyde Park (www.rollerstroll.com and www.easypeasyskate.com). You can hire skates for as little as a tenner at Slick Willies in Kensington (www.slickwillies.co.uk). If you're keen to try your skating skills in a game of inline hockey, there are a couple of clubs in London that welcome new players: the Battersea Blues, who play at Battersea Youth Centre (8871 8529) every Friday from 20:00 to 21:45, and Plumstead Skater Hockey, who play every Wednesday at Plumstead Leisure Centre (8855 8289) from 20:45 to 22:15.

Sports & Activities

Rowing

Other options **Watersports** p.282

Rowing is synonymous with the Thames – it is home to the annual Oxford and Cambridge Boat Race (see p.44) which runs from Putney to Mortlake and draws a large crowd (who are also attracted by the riverside pubs). For those actually taking part in the sport there's a real sense of camaraderie and a love of London's waterways. Most clubs have both men and women's teams and welcome beginners; for a full list contact the Amateur Rowing Association (8237 6767). West of London you'll find Henley Rowing Club, a good out-of-town option that prides itself on providing facilities for all levels of ability, age or sex. It also plays a big part in the annual Henley Royal Regatta, a huge four-day competition known as much for socialising as for sport.

The Boat House,
Ferry St
E14
DLR *Island Gardens*

Blackwall & District Rowing Club

7987 3071

Steeped in history (it was formed in the mid-19th century when the boats were kept behind an inn), this club has excellent facilities including a gym, an eight-person rowing tank and hot showers, not to mention a great position on the opposite side of the river from the attractive Greenwich waterfront. The club makes good use of the 7.5 mile stretch of water between the Thames Barrier and London Bridge, where crews are able to gain experience in boat handling. Membership is £316 a year for adults.

Trafalgar Rowing
Centre, 11-13 Crane St
SE10
DLR *Cutty Sark*

Globe Rowing Club

8858 2106 | www.globerowingclub.co.uk

The warm and friendly folk at Globe Rowing Club have a passion for the lower reaches of the Thames, an area rich in maritime history. Members go out on the water every weekend, although crews training for races will be on the river most days during the summer. Recreational rowers can generally get as far as Tower Bridge or the Thames Barrier on Sundays. Subscriptions are very reasonable: full membership costs £20 a month, juniors (16 to 18) pay £7.50 a month, and beginners' sessions (which take place on Mondays) are just £3.

Staines Boat Club,
28 Riverside Drive
TW18
≥ *Staines*

Sculling for Pleasure

7917 2998 | www.scullingforpleasure.co.uk

Sculling for Pleasure claims to be the only company that focuses solely on the recreational sculler rather than training up crews for regattas, as most rowing clubs do. Sculling is rowing with two oars, for solitary or duo rowers, and requires precision and skill. It's a great way to get out on to the water without having to rely on lots of other people to participate. A session costs £30 for one-on-one coaching with an expert, and the company uses Staines Boat Club as a starting point (its offices are actually in land-locked Piccadilly). Note that Sculling for Pleasure doesn't accommodate non-swimmers.

Putney Embankment
SW15
⊖ *Putney Bridge*

Thames Rowing Club

8788 0798 | www.thamesrc.demon.co.uk

Founded in 1860, and currently claiming to be the largest and most successful organisation of its type in Britain, the Thames Rowing Club is a friendly but competitive establishment that encourages new members who are serious about the sport. There's training for men, women, juniors, novices and professionals. The club owns a large number of high-quality racing boats and has a gym and indoor rowing tank. Membership costs depend on the season.

271

Rugby

There are two codes of rugby: union and league. London has around 100 rugby union clubs with teams playing in a number of competitions and divisions. Several clubs are made up of other countrymen living in and around the city, such as London Irish and Springboks. Some clubs also have junior and women's teams. For those who just want to play recreationally, a more relaxed, local club is a better option. There's also the relatively new 'touch rugby' game, which is popular with same-sex and mixed teams. Leagues are organised by the English Touch Association; visit www.touchrugby.com for more details. If you're looking to play in your area, www.rugbyinlondon.com lists details of all types of clubs, including non-league and a gay team (King's Cross Steelers). Rugby league is more popular in the north of England but there are plenty of amateur clubs competing in the London area. The capital also has its own professional club, the London Skolars, which plays in National League Division 2 and has a number of junior teams. For more information on clubs in London, contact the British Amateur Rugby League Association (www.barla.org.uk).

Harlequin Ladies

Summers Lane
N12
⊖ **West Finchley**

Finchley Rugby Club
8445 3746 | www.finchleyrfc.co.uk

This club extends a warm welcome to new players, particularly those who are planning to relocate here (the club may also be able to assist players looking for work in London). It features players from many countries including New Zealand, South Africa and Ireland, and has a reputation for playing free-flowing rugby and a busy social calendar off the field. Finchley RC currently fields four teams of varying levels and has an over-35s team as well as a youth section. Teams train at 19:30 on Tuesdays and Thursdays.

Springhill
Sports Ground
E5
⇌ **Clapton**

Hackney RFC
07092 385079 | www.hackneyrfc.co.uk

A small, welcoming club, and one of only a handful based in east London (and the only one in Hackney borough), Hackney RFC (known as the Griffins) has two teams that play competitively and in friendlies against local sides. Facilities are basic; changing takes place at the nearby rowing club after the clubhouse burned down, but there are plans to rebuild it. The club also hopes to set up women's and youth teams. Training takes place at 19:30 on Tuesdays at Springhill Sports Ground, and also on Saturday afternoons, followed by a knees-up in The Swan pub. Fees are £5 a game.

Richardson Evans
Playing Fields,
Roehampton Vale
SW15
⊖ **Putney Bridge**

Harlequin Ladies
8410 6000 | www.harlequinladies.co.uk

It doesn't matter if you've never played rugby before, the Harlequin Ladies (affiliated to Harlequins, one of London's top professional clubs) are always on the lookout for new players for its adult and youth teams. Training takes place every Tuesday and Thursday from 19:30 to 21:00 and matches are played on Sundays. Take the number 85 bus from Putney Bridge tube to get to the ground.

London New Zealand

Acton Sports Club,
Park Place
W3
⊖ *Gunnersbury*

8546 3647 | www.lnzrugby.co.uk

This club exists to provide mainly – but not exclusively – New Zealanders with the chance to play rugby in the capital. The 2005-06 season was the most successful in the club's 80 year history with both its teams gaining promotion. London New Zealand's amateur status means that it can't source work permits for its players. Training is every Wednesday at 19:00 (meet under the floodlights) and membership is £100 annually.

Wimbledon Rugby Club

Beverley Meads,
Barham Rd
SW20
⇌ *Raynes Park*

8946 3156 | www.wimbledonrfc.co.uk

Wimbledon Rugby Club is one of the oldest in the country. It was a Wimbledon captain, LJ Maton, who drafted the first laws of the game. The club currently has three men's teams, a ladies' side, veterans' team and youth section. Men's teams play on Saturday afternoons and women's training is every Thursday at 19:30, with matches on Sunday. Newcomers are welcome to join a couple of sessions before deciding to join.

Running

Other options **Athletics** p.236

Given the amount of open spaces, river paths and parks in London it's no surprise that running is popular. There are road running, cross-country and track outfits to suit most people's tastes. Whether it's the British 10K (www.thebritish10klondon.co.uk), the women-only Race for Life 5K runs for charity (www.raceforlife.co.uk) or the Flora London Marathon (www.london-marathon.co.uk), there's always an event to train for if you need a goal to aim for. Niketown, Nike's flagship London store, organises three-mile runs for women on Monday evenings and longer runs for mixed groups on Tuesdays at 18:00 – just turn up in your gear. The website of magazine *Runner's World* (www.runnersworld.co.uk) is a useful resource.

Dulwich Park Runners

College Clubhouse,
Dulwich Common
SE21
⇌ *North Dulwich*

8670 9321 | www.dulwichparkrunners.com

This small, mixed group of 120 members meets every Tuesday and Thursday at 19:45 at its well-equipped clubhouse in charming Dulwich, before heading off to the nearby sports ground. Adult membership costs £40 (guests can try three sessions before joining) or there's an eight-week beginners' course on Saturday mornings (£30). In summer, there's an inter-club league with family-orientated events. This is an informal, affable club, and it's a gorgeous part of London in which to run.

East London Road Runners

Newham
Leisure Centre,
281 Prince Regent Lane
E13
DLR *Prince Regent*

8534 0209 | www.eastendrr.co.uk

There are a multitude of running groups in east London, perhaps because the area is so flat. This accommodating group accepts all levels and has exclusive use of Newham Leisure Centre's outdoor track on Tuesday evenings. Meet at 18:45 for coached track sessions. Lifetime membership is £10, plus £3 per session (£5 for non-members). On Thursday evenings, there's also a 'buddy system' that provides support for road runners.

Serpentine Running Club

Seymour Centre,
Seymour Place
W1
⊖ *Edgware Road*

7723 8019 | www.serpentine.org.uk

This enthusiastic and sociable club caters for all ages, nationalities and abilities, and although its focus is primarily on fun, there's plenty to offer the serious runner. There are more than 2,500 members (over half are women), and runs take place on Tuesday,

273

Wednesday and Thursday evenings, plus Saturday and Sunday mornings (the latter includes a strong family contingent). The club runs mainly in the Royal Parks (Hyde Park, Kensington Gardens, St James's Park and Green Park) but organises sessions across London, from Richmond to Greenwich. You can try before you buy; if you like it, membership costs £25 a year (on top of a £30 joining fee).

SweatyBetty Running Club

833 Fulham Rd
SW6
⊖ Parsons Green

0800 1693889 | *www.sweatybetty.com*

You only have to check out the fresh-faced and spirited beauties on SweatyBetty's website to feel compelled to join one of its runs. The company, run by women for women, started life as a sportswear outlet but has since expanded to offer sporting events and training. One-hour runs, with a trainer, take place on Mondays (13:00) from the store in Notting Hill (7727 8646), 18:15 from the Richmond shop (8948 8459), 18:30 on Tuesdays from the store in Battersea (7978 5444) and the Fulham Road store (7751 2476). These sprightly gals also have walking and yoga clubs on the go – visit the website for more details.

Scrabble

Other options **Chess** p.242

Scrabble, the classic board game which uses letter tiles to spell out words for points, was invented in the 1930s by the delightfully named Alfred Mosher Butts. Originally, his brainchild was called 'Lexico' until the rights were bought by an American lawyer, who renamed the iconic game. Since the 1950s, more than 100 million boards (in 27 languages) have been purchased, but before you start feeling sorry for Mosher Butts, he was by no means fleeced; the unemployed architect got royalties for every unit sold. Today, groups in London are organised locally and take the game very seriously indeed. The best way to get involved is to contact the Association of British Scrabble Players (anne.ramsay@blueyonder.co.uk) or the London Scrabble League (janet.bonham@tesco.net); both should be able to point you in the right direction.

Singing

Other options **Music Lessons** p.266

Singing is a great way to relax, let off steam and develop your vocal technique, and there are lessons, courses and amateur groups to be found all over London. Whether you just want to sound better in the shower, be part of a like-minded society or are serious about singing as a career, there's something to suit your needs. A selection are listed below, or check out www.choirs.org.uk.

City of London Choir

Bridewell Hall,
Bride Lane
EC4
⇌ ⊖ Blackfriars

8398 5058 | *www.cityoflondonchoir.org*

One of London's more adept amateur choral groups, the City of London Choir is made up of professionals of all ages and includes bankers, journalists, doctors, teachers and students among its 100 or so members. Rehearsals take place every Wednesday from 18:30 to 20:45 at Bridewell Hall near Ludgate Circus from September to June (excluding Christmas and Easter). It holds up to four large concerts each year as well as smaller events. Annual membership costs £115 (there are concessions) and you need to audition, although they promise to make it as painless as possible.

Sports & Activities

Various locations ◀

Pro-vocals

07771 776363 | *www.pro-vocals.co.uk*

For £60 an hour Larion van der Stolk, a professional singer/musician/songwriter/musical arranger (he's a talented man), will work out your range, show you how to breathe and project, and teach you a few songs – all of which will bring you one step closer to stardom (or at least give you the guts to get up at karaoke). The lessons are fun and focused on bringing out the best in the individual's voice rather than training you to sound like someone else, which is probably just as well. A few lessons are recommended, and group sessions are available too.

76 Stanley Gardens ◀
W3
⊖ Turnham Green

Vocaltech

8749 3131 | *www.vocal-tech.co.uk*

Excellent, experienced tutors and a variety of courses and classes with professional singers are on offer at this well-run vocal school in west London. Whether you want to study for a three-year degree, a year-long diploma, a part-time three-month certificate or private lessons, Vocaltech has a number of options, all of which will give you the necessary training to sing for your supper. The school is affiliated with Guitar-X and Drumtech, which teach guitar, bass, drums and percussion.

164 Eversholt St ◀
NW1
⇌ ⊖ Euston

Voxbox

7388 1799 | *www.singing-lessons-london.co.uk*

Voxbox is located in a hip setting and has experienced singers on hand to get the best from your vocal cords. There are four tutors who teach 'speech level singing', a form of coaching that encourages a natural vocal sound. Lessons take place between 13:00 and 22:00 and cost £30 to £45 an hour for private lessons or £125 for a six-week group course (Tuesday or Thursday evenings). Its gift vouchers make an ideal present for the budding pop star in your family. For more information call between noon and 14:00.

Skateboarding

As you'd imagine in Europe's biggest urban sprawl, there are plenty of concrete places to please those that know their ollies from their nollies. You'll find some really good official parks in town, the pick of the bunch being the super-hip BaySixty6 Skatepark under the Westway near Ladbroke Grove (www.baysixty6.com). There's also a classic 1970s skate park out at Harrow (www.harrowskatepark.co.uk), and ramps and bowls in parks all over town (Victoria Park and Alexandra Palace to name a couple). Skateboarding being something of an underground activity, many boarders utilise steps, benches and rails across the city too. The concrete curves and edges of the Southbank Centre are a famous favourite for street skaters, and if you become part of the boarding community you'll no doubt be introduced to some other top spots, but be warned – you run the risk of getting in trouble with the law if you're caught 360ing where you shouldn't be.

Snooker

Snooker and pool halls are not the most salubrious of environments, but if you like to play sport on a garish carpet surrounded by a haze of smoke with a pint close to hand, then this is the game for you. Both snooker and pool, the game's American off-shoot, are hugely popular in Britain. There are a number of 'halls' in London and nearly all offer amateur or semi-professional leagues. Many pubs also have a table or two and arrange competitions among regular drinkers. In the last few years, the arrival of the stylish Elbow Room chain has made the game more accessible to people (especially women) who would normally avoid the dingy 24 hour pool halls, even though such

275

The Complete **Residents'** Guide

clubs have developed a kitsch coolness among devotees, students and after-hour drinkers. Check out the English Pool Association (01952 641682), which organises amateur leagues and competitions. For all things snooker visit www.worldsnooker.com.

Centre Point Snooker Club

103 New Oxford St
WC1
Tottenham Court Rd

7240 6886

Don't be put off by the underground location, the drunks that frequent it, or the steeper-than-usual membership (£30 a year); you're paying for the centrality of this venue. Inside it's not too bad for your typical London snooker setting. There are seven snooker tables, plus five American and two English pool tables. Food is available and there's also a licensed bar. Its opening times (Monday to Saturday, 11:00 to 06:00, and Sundays from 15:00 to 03:00) enable you to have a game long after the pub and even clubs have shut. A pool table costs £6.70 an hour, a snooker table is £4.60.

The Elbow Room Pool Lounge and Bar

89-91 Chapel Market
N1
Angel

7278 3244 | www.elbow-room.co.uk

Popular with, well, just about everyone, but particularly loved by people in the media, the three Elbow Rooms in London are cool dives, complete with wooden floorboards and leather seating. DJs play at weekends and there are various themed events which give these clubs more of a bar feel (though that doesn't detract from the game). Times vary but, generally, opening time is noon until 02:00 or 03:00. A table (there are 10) costs between £6 and £9 an hour, plus a refundable deposit of £10. In busy periods, games are limited to one hour at a time. Visit the Elbow Room website for more information about its two other bars in Shoreditch and Westbourne Grove.

King's Cross Snooker and Pool Club

275-277 Pentonville Rd
N1
King's Cross St. Pancras

7278 7079 | www.londonsnooker.co.uk

King's Cross Snooker Club is big. At the last count there were 18 full-size snooker tables plus a separate pool hall with four tables. It attracts some real die-hards too, helped by the fact that it's open 24 hours in an area of town that never sleeps. There's a lounge, the obligatory licensed bar and food available all day, plus snooker coaching. You have to be a member to play (a steal at £15). Games cost £4.65 an hour from 16:00 to 00:00 and £3.80 at other times.

Mayfair Snooker Club

145 Upper Tooting Rd
SW17
Tooting Bec

8767 7202 | www.londonsnooker.co.uk

Bit of an institution this; mostly because snooker legend Jimmy White used to practise here. Between 11:00 and 18:00 it's £10 to play all day (or £5 for three hours). Afterwards it's £6 an hour. You have to be a member (£20 a year), but guests can be signed in. There are seven full-size American pool tables and nine snooker tables in a separate hall, as well as a bar with large-screen TV and friendly staff (unless you start dancing on the tables, that is).

Social Groups

Other options **Clubs & Associations** p.244

London is not just about shopping and drinking; it's a great place to meet people and discover new interests and hobbies. From networking and expat groups to film and book clubs, there's something on every night of the week. Unlike sports clubs or similar fixed-location activities, social clubs offer a choice of venues and events so you can choose when you go out and who to go with.

Sports & Activities

Various locations

Entertaining London

01920 830316 | www.entertaininglondon.com

Since it was established almost a decade ago, this 'leisure lifestyle club for busy people from all over the world' has grown to become London's leading club for the 18-40 age range. There are JTU (just turn up) events happening almost every day and discounted activities, including adventure weekends and skiing holidays. It's friendly and informal and provides great variety. Membership starts from £49 for three months, which gives you access to the events calendar.

9 Fitzmaurice Place
W1
⊖ **Green Park**

Junior League of London

7499 8159 | www.jll.org.uk

This is a women's community group that organises volunteer projects throughout the capital for women of all ages to roll up their sleeves and get stuck in, no matter what their ability, culture or background. If you want to work within your community and put something back into society, this is the place for you. It costs £40 to join.

Various locations

London Art Club

www.londonartclub.com

This club is for people with an interest in the arts, whether they are new to London or have lived here a while but want to expand their social circle. There's no fee, just the cost of entrance to whatever galleries, museums or theatres are visited. Most members are in their 20s and 30s and come from a variety of backgrounds, but anyone with a fondness for the arts is welcome. To join, register online and state which events you would like to experience.

Various locations

London Theatre and Restaurant Club

8542 1118 | www.ltrc.co.uk

With nearly 1,000 members (and around 15 people attending each event), this social and arts club offers days and evenings out, including trips to comedy shows, quiz nights, dance classes, tours, walks, paintball, musicals, jazz, restaurants – you name it, they do it (as long as it's in the interest of art and cuisine). There are around 40 events a month (half of which cost under £20), plus discounts for members.

Various locations

The Savvy Club

0870 0056225 | www.savvyclub.co.uk

This is a club for professionals. Consider it a social network that has access to exclusive venues and events which would be harder to experience otherwise, including celebrity restaurants, gourmet tastings and city breaks. There is a touch of the frou-frou about the people that you'll meet and the places you'll see as part of this organisation, so flaunt your success and those designer threads and you'll all get along like peas in one luxurious pod. There are no charges; just book, pay and go along for stylish, cool nights out.

Squash

Other options **Leisure Facilities** p.292

Poor old squash. A much-loved game for some, who relish the speed and agility required to play it, but seemingly loathed by others. The International Olympic Committee has yet to be convinced that it's a sport worthy of inclusion in its competition. Don't let that put you off though – it's one of the best forms of aerobic exercise. There are squash clubs all over London, mainly affiliated to tennis, lawn or health clubs (which means you have to join or be signed in as a guest). If you're serious about the sport your best bet is to join a club, where you'll find other keen competitors and a decent social scene. However, if you only want to play occasionally, booking a court at your local leisure centre is probably a better option. England Squash (www.englandsquash.com) provides details of court locations.

Plough Lane
SW17
⊖ *Tooting Broadway*

Christopher's Squash and Fitness Club
8946 4636 | www.christopherssportsclub.co.uk
One of the largest (and friendliest) squash clubs in London, Christopher's has seven squash courts and 27 internal leagues competing with each other or in inter-club competitions. There's coaching for players at all levels, and the club's ample size means that it's a good place to meet squash partners. Social 'club nights' are held on Thursday and Friday evenings. Membership is £50 a month for adults for unlimited use of the squash courts, gym, aerobics and dance classes. Open 07:00 to 23:00 on weekdays and 09:00 to 23:00 on weekends.

Haven Green
W5
⇌ ⊖ *Ealing Broadway*

Ealing Squash & Fitness
8997 3449 | www.ealingsfc.co.uk
With five well-maintained courts, including a championship glass-backed one, this is one of London's best sites for the fast and furious game. There are 50 internal leagues, from beginner to advanced, plus coaching and tournaments. Like most clubs, membership is required, but there's no annual contract and you can play before you pay. It costs £48 a month to join, which includes gym access. There's a bar too to quench that squash thirst.

Lyndhurst Gardens
N3
⊖ *Finchley Central*

Finchley Manor Squash Club
8346 1327 | www.finchleymanor-squash.co.uk
Finchley Manor was founded as a tennis club in 1881, but squash has been played here since the late 1960s. Situated in a leafy suburb, this family-orientated members' club has recently had its facilities upgraded, including a complete refurbishment of the fitness room, changing rooms and – essential for a health club – the bar. The club now has four quality courts, one of which is glass-backed with spectator seating. It runs internal leagues to suit all standards of play and competes in the winter and summer Middlesex leagues. Professional coaching is available, and there's a session for juniors on Saturday mornings.

48a Greenway Avenue
E17
⇌ *Wood Street*

Walthamstow Cricket, Squash & Lawn Tennis Club
8520 5042
This multi-facility club in north-east London was founded in 1862 and plays in a range of competitions in the competitive Essex League as well as running club championships. Squash is played daily on three courts, and facilities include modern changing rooms, saunas and sunbeds, as well as two licensed bars. There's a lively social scene, and full membership costs £144 a year, which includes use of all the facilities.

Racket Science
Squash isn't the only sport you can play on a squash court. Racketball, a slightly slower, less fierce variation using a shorter-handled racket and larger ball that is not as bouncy, is also played in the same arena. The game was invented in the US in the 1950s as 'raquetball', an alternative that made hand-to-eye coordination easier than in squash, and also allowed use of the ceiling and all wall space (the British variation, racketball, doesn't allow use of the ceiling). If you've always fancied squash but have been put off by its aggressive image, this could be the game for you.

Sports & Activities

Swimming

Other options **Leisure Facilities** p.292

Public swimming pools in London have suffered at the hands of local council budget cuts in recent decades, but the angry public response is proof that swimming and access to clean, safe pools is seen as an essential right of residents of London's boroughs. For a swim, aqua aerobics or other pool activities, or to book lessons, try your local sports centre, details of which can be found on your borough's website (www.london.gov.uk/london/links.jsp). For people who wish to learn to swim, or brush up on their technique, Swimming Nature runs professional lessons for both adults and children at a number of London pools (0870 0949597). For a comprehensive list of venues in London see www.swimmersguide.com, and for details of local swimming clubs contact the Amateur Swimming Association (www.britishswimming.org).

Acton Baths,
Salisbury Rd
W3
⇌ Acton Central

Acton Swimming Club

8992 8877 | *www.actonswimmingclub.org.uk*

This club, otherwise known as The A Team, has operated from the same swimming baths since its formation in 1904, and provides coaching sessions seven days a week for all levels – from novice through to intermediate, senior and masters. The club encourages people to take part in competitions, but also puts the accent on enjoying swimming, which is helped by the thriving social network. Contact the club for rates and a trial to test the waters.

Swiss Cottage
Sports Centre,
Adelaide Rd
NW3
⊖ Swiss Cottage

Camden Swiss Cottage Swimming Club

7974 5440 | *www.camdenswisscottage.co.uk*

This is one of the biggest and most successful swimming clubs in central London, running lessons and competitive training for children and adults from pools within the Borough of Camden and the Mallinson Sports centre in Highgate. For the masters section (a squad training programme for adults), a certain level of ability is required. Children's lessons take place Monday to Friday from 16:30 to 18:00 in Swiss Cottage and Kentish Town pools.

Various locations

Clissold Swimming Club

07891 880781 | *www.clissoldswimmingclub.org.uk*

This competitive club, which uses venues in Hackney, Shoreditch and Stoke Newington, caters for youngsters from the ages of 5 to 18 whatever their ability, from non-swimmers and beginners through to competitive swimmers. The club recently introduced water polo to its training programme. The taster sessions are free to exisitng members.

Hyde Park
WC2
⊖ Hyde Park Corner

Serpentine Swimming Club

www.serpentineswimmingclub.com

This legendary club, which was established in 1864, has special permission to use the Serpentine Lake in Hyde Park daily from 06:00 to 09:30. Members swim all year round, whether the water is warm in the summer or freezing in winter (they'll even break the ice for you to get in). The club is famous for the 'Peter Pan Christmas Day Race', a 100 yard jaunt for experienced swimmers while most people are at home unwrapping presents. If you'd like to join, meet up with the club's swimmers at 08:00 on Saturdays. Membership costs £20 a year.

279

The Complete **Residents'** Guide

Tennis

Other options **Leisure Facilities** p.292

In part because of the universal reputation of Wimbledon, tennis is seen as a quintessentially English sport. The Victorians established clubs all over London and for a time the English were world beaters, though success was patchy after the 1930s. The last time a Brit won Wimbledon may have been 1977 (Virginia Wade), but the form of Andy Murray is inspiring confidence in British tennis of all abilities. The multicultural mix of London residents means that tennis is no longer the preserve of the middle classes as it once was. It's certainly popular – three million people play regularly in the UK – which may explain the millions invested in the new National Tennis Centre in Roehampton, south-west London, which opened in early 2007. It provides exceptional facilities: 16 outdoor courts, six indoor courts, a gym, a physiotherapy centre, as well as first-class coaching and a training centre for wheelchair players.

London has tennis courts aplenty: in private clubs, public parks, and in sports centres. Below, you'll find an assortment. Alternatively, for courts in your area, try your borough's website (www.london.gov.uk) or the UK's governing body for tennis, the Lawn Tennis Association (www.lta.org.uk).

Battersea Park Rd
SW11
⇌ **Battersea**

Battersea Park Tennis Courts

8871 7542 | www.wandsworth.gov.uk

Battersea Park has a whopping 19 floodlit courts (13 hard courts, six artificial grass) available all-year round. Courts are open 08:00 to 22:00, Monday to Friday and 08:00 to 19:00 at weekends. A court costs £6.90 an hour at peak times, but it's worth getting a membership card (£22 a year for Wandsworth residents, £27 for everyone else) which enables you to book a week in advance. There's a range of coaching sessions to suit all ages and abilities, which are available as evening or weekend intensive courses. There are also week-long camps over the summer holidays.

---

93 Conway Rd
N14
⇌ **Palmers Green**

Conway Lawn Tennis Club

8882 9218 | www.conwaytennisclub.co.uk

Founded in 1925, this family orientated club is strong on community spirit. There are five courts (two are floodlit), four men's and two women's teams, plus squads for veterans and children. Club sessions take place on Wednesday evenings and Sunday mornings. Team practice is on Saturday mornings. Junior coaching takes place most days of the week. Full membership costs £140 a year, which includes free admittance for a child.

Giant Arches Rd,
off Burbage Rd
SE24
⇌ **Herne Hill**

Dulwich Sports Club

7274 1242 | www.dulwichtennis.com

This club has excellent facilities for cricket, croquet, squash and tennis, and a licensed bar with a pool table. The atmosphere is congenial and child-friendly (a must in family orientated Dulwich) and players of all abilities are welcomed. In winter, the club uses five all-weather hard courts (three with floodlights) and six grass courts in summer. Coaching is offered in a structured programme. Potential new members should visit the club at 13:30 on Saturdays and join the mixed session (bring your own racket). Yearly membership is £235 plus a £50 joining fee.

Golden Lane Leisure Centre

Fann St, Golden Lane Estate EC1 ⊖ Barbican

7250 1464 | www.cityoflondon.gov.uk

Golden Lane is a stone's throw from Barbican tube, and boasts two all-weather tennis courts, a 20 metre swimming pool and a multi-purpose indoor hall. There are tennis lessons for young and old; children's coaching takes place on Saturday mornings. There's a relaxed atmosphere to Golden Lane, and as it's the only publicly funded leisure centre in the City it is popular with companies, whose employees make the most of the amenities.

Hyde Park Tennis Centre

South Carriage Drive, Hyde Park W1 ⊖ Knightsbridge

7262 3474 | www.royalparks.gov.uk/parks/hyde_park/sport.cfm

This centre, accredited by the Lawn Tennis Association and conveniently located in central London, has six courts, a changing pavilion and a cafe for when you've worked up an appetite. Membership is available but 'turn up and play' is encouraged. There are coaching courses for both children and adults, organised tournaments and local tennis leagues. Call for opening hours.

Parliament Hill Outdoor Tennis Courts

Highgate Rd NW5 ⇌ Gospel Oak

7284 3648 | www.cityoflondon.gov.uk/openspaces

It's worth buying a registration card, which costs £11, from the on-site tennis keeper to book one of these 10 open-air courts in advance (£4.70, phone between 08:30 to 10:00). Otherwise you could just turn up, but be warned that a court may not be free. However, in quiet periods (Monday to Friday from October to March) booking isn't necessary. The courts are open seven days a week, and there's group coaching for adults and children throughout the summer.

Richmond Lawn Tennis Club

Old Deer Park, 187 Kew Rd TW7 ⇌ ⊖ Richmond

8332 6696 | www.richmondlawntennisclub.com

This is an upmarket well-established club with over 300 members, set in the Royal Deer Park next to Kew Gardens. Richmond has four all-weather courts that are available all-year round and eight grass courts open in the summer months. The club shares a pavilion (and three bars) with the London Welsh Rugby club and the Richmond Cricket Club. As well as social tennis, there's competitive tennis on offer in the Surrey League, coaching for all ages and social events throughout the year. Adult membership costs £185 a year.

Triathlon

The triathlon – swimming, cycling and running – was 'invented' in the 1970s in the US and is now an Olympic sport. Today, it's the fastest growing multi-discipline sport in the UK and one in which the Brits fare well (eight world champions and counting). Whereas the thought of three disciplines may put some people off, it needn't. Thousands of first-timers compete each year (in 2006, 45 per cent of the London Triathlon's entrants were race virgins). Distances vary so it's possible to start with a shorter event; a 'sprint', which is a ¾ km swim, 20km cycle and 5km run and work your way up to 'Ironman' level, which is a 3.8k swim, 180km cycle and 42km run. The sport's popularity is reflected in the size of the British Triathlon Association (BTA), which has over 8,500 members and 300 affiliated clubs (01509 226161, www.britishtriathlon.org). For those put off by getting wet, there's the duathlon – three legs of running, cycling and running again.

In 2006, the Michelob ULTRA London Triathlon (www.londontriathlon.com) was the world's largest triathlon, attracting over 8,000 competitors and 40,000 spectators. The 2007 event will take place in August. There are three main categories: Super Sprint, Sprint and Olympic. London Triathlon also organises The London Duathlon, which is held in Richmond Park each September.

Various locations
Crystal Palace Triathletes
8290 5320 | www.crystalpalace-tri.co.uk
A friendly, welcoming club with over 100 members, which hosts two swim nights (Tuesday at St Joseph's College, Upper Norwood and Thursdays at The Bridge Leisure Centre, Lower Sydenham), a run on Wednesday evenings at Crystal Palace Park, and a cycle ride on Sunday mornings. There are members of all levels of ability, so you decide how hard and how often you want to train. The cost of monthly membership varies depending on which month you join.

Various locations
Hillingdon Triathletes
www.hillingdontriathletes.co.uk
This active west London club caters to anyone from 16 to 60, with abilities ranging from novice through to world championship contenders. Members regularly compete in triathlons, duathlons and a number of other events, including cross country. For just £22 a year, you can swim at the club; otherwise sessions cost £4 a time. For those only interested in duathlon, membership is a mere £10.

Various locations
Serpentine Triathlon Club
www.serpentine.org.uk
This is part of the Serpentine Running Club, which, thanks to its winning central location, has over 2,000 members. There are Sunday rides from Roehampton Gate in Richmond Park, weekly runs (see Running section, p.273) and Monday swims at the Guy's and St Thomas' Hospital pool. There's no separate joining fee to take part in the triathlon activities as joining the club enables you to take part in all club training and events.

Various locations
Tri London
www.trilondon.co.uk
Based in north London, and affiliated to the BTA, this club holds regular swim, bike and runnng sessions and has a good mix of serious and casual triathletes. Swims are held on Monday and Wednesday evenings at Cally Pool (see Swimming, p.279), bike rides leave from The Clocktower, Crouch End on Sunday mornings and run times vary. The club also participates in cross country, fell racing, open-water swimming, cycling endurance events, time trials and adventure races. Membership is £43 a year for new members. If you wish to swim with the club, you'll also need to pay additional swimming club fees, which are £21 per month.

Watersports
Other options **Rowing** p.271

London may not have the clear blue waters of the Caribbean, but that doesn't prevent a flurry of activity on waters in and around city. Activities such as sailing, powerboating, canoeing, kayaking, waterskiing, wakeboarding and windsurfing take place on the Thames, in one of London's many docks, or on reservoirs and lakes outside London. Opening times vary according to season, as do membership requirements and activity costs; the following information gives a rough guide but for details contact the individual clubs or centres.

Other useful contacts include British Waterski (01932 570885; www.britishwaterski.co.uk), the UK Windsurfing Association (01273 454654; www.ukwindsurfing.com), the Royal Yachting Association (0845 3450400; www.rya.org.uk) and the British Canoe Union (0115 9821100; www.bcu.org.uk).

Albany Mews, Albany Park Rd
Surrey
⇌ *Kingston*

Albany Park Canoe and Sailing Centre
8549 3066 | www.albanypark.co.uk

Situated on the Thames between Kingston Bridge and Teddington Lock, this welcoming centre has lots to offer watersports enthusiasts in London, and off-site in south Wales and the Midlands. There's something for everyone here: dinghy sailing, kayaking, open canoeing and courses in adult sailing and powerboating, to name but a few. Albany Park also holds activity days for those wanting to practise general boating skills. It's very popular with schools and youth organisations because of the amount of courses available. Adult courses are available at weekends.

Welsh Harp (Brent Reservoir), Birchen Grove
NW9
⊖ *Wembley Park*

BTYC Sailsports
8731 8083 | www.btycsailsports.org.uk

This is a friendly, not-for-profit club with Royal Yachting Association-qualified instructors on hand to give basic, advanced and race training. A range of modern dinghies and windsurf boards are available (free to members) to enjoy on the club's 70 acres of water.

235a Westferry Rd, Millwall Dock
E14
DLR *Island Gardens*

Docklands Sailing and Watersports Centre
7537 2626 | www.dswc.co.uk

This club uses the sheltered waters of Millwall Dock, which are ideal for beginners learning watersports. Approved by the Royal Yachting Association, the training centre also takes the more experienced out onto the sometimes choppy waters of the River Thames. Sailing, rowing, canoeing, dragon boat racing and powerboating are on offer, as are sailing courses. There is also full disabled access.

Clockhouse Lane, Bedfont
Middlesex
⇌ *Ashford*

Princes Club
01784 256153 | www.princesclub.com

The Princes Club, Europe's largest waterski and wakeboard facility, is a short train ride from London. Here, you'll find two cable tows and lakes for kneeboarding, wakeboarding (the fastest growing watersport in the UK) and waterskiing, plus five boat lakes and a coaching team. There's also a gym, six squash courts, a restaurant and bar, clubhouse and shop. Wakeboarding is on offer to everyone and costs £19 an hour for non-members.

Queen Mary Reservoir, Ashford Rd
Middlesex
⇌ *Ashford*

Queen Mary Sailing Club & Sailsports
01784 248881 | www.queenmary.org.uk

The Queen Mary Sailing Club uses one of London's largest reservoirs (over 700 acres), and its elevated position makes it a prime spot for sailing and windsurfing. Members can sail, take advantage of member discounts on courses and boat hire, store their boat or board, use the clubhouse's excellent facilities and attend the club's social events. There's also a youth group, which meets on Sunday afternoons.

3-4 Shadwell Pierhead, Glamis Rd
E1
⊖ *Wapping*

Shadwell Basin Project
7481 4210 | www.shadwell-basin.org.uk

This community-focused centre was established in 1976 by local parents and has since become a superb facility for learning watersports. There are courses for adults in sailing, canoeing, and kayaking and children of all abilities (aged 9 or over) can enjoy learning the basics of canoeing, kayaking, sailing and dragon-boating. Its safety record is impeccable and the group is licensed by the Adventure Activities Licensing Authority, and approved by the British Canoe Union and Royal Yachting Association.

Rope St,
off Plough Way
SE16
⊖ Canada Water

Surrey Docks Watersport Centre
7237 5555

Based at the converted Greenland Dock, once the largest commercial dock in the world, this centre is open to beginners and experts. The centre offers a range of lessons and activities including windsurfing and powerboating (for adults), and sailing and canoeing (for all ages). To kayak you'll need to have a British Canoe Union qualification.

Wine Tasting

Once upon a time, the Brits' idea of a sophisticated dinner party included a sickly sweet Riesling or a cardboard box of plonk that the rest of Europe wouldn't wash dishes with. Thankfully, Londoners' palates are now more refined, and the vast array of wines on display in supermarkets and off-licences is proof that wine is big business in the UK. Wine-tasting evenings are sociable and fun events that anyone (who isn't pregnant, driving or under the legal drinking age of 18) can enjoy. Not only will you get to taste fine wine you probably know very little about, you'll discover *why* it's fine wine, what types go best with certain foods and – importantly – what to avoid. Whether it's your birthday, stag or hen night, anniversary, or a corporate event, wine-tasting is as enlightening as it is entertaining. Here are some options to mull over.

Garden Floor,
6 Coldbath Square
EC1
⇌ ⊖ Farringdon

The London Wine Academy
0870 1000100 | www.londonwineacademy.com

Specialising in corporate events, staff training courses, courses and workshops for the public, the London Wine Academy has a practical and enjoyable approach towards wine tasting. Courses, which are held in various venues around the capital, cost between £99 and £259, while corporate events start at £25 a head. The Academy also arranges wine tours.

9 New Oxford St
WC1
⊖ Tottenham
Court Rd

Planet of the Grapes
7405 4912 | www.planetofthegrapes.co.uk

This brilliantly named wine shop now has a tasting cellar (which holds up to 24 people) where tasting evenings are held. It can also be hired for private wine-tasting events. Here, you can savour hand-picked wines at reasonable prices. The friendly and unpretentious owners are engaging and instructive – a must if you prefer a bespoke service and an intimate setting. The shop is open six days a week from 10:00 to 20:00.

1 Bank End
SE1
≋ ⊖ *London Bridge*

Vinopolis

0870 2414040 | www.vinopolis.co.uk

Set within the arches of a Victorian railway viaduct, Vinopolis' two acres are a haven for anyone with even a passing interest in wine. There are three self-guided wine tours on offer: 'Original' (£16); 'Discovery' (£21) and 'Vintage' (£26), with each including at least five tastings of wines from all over the world. An added bonus is the location; you can sample the culinary delights of nearby Borough Market before taking a tour, or stagger along the South Bank in a happy haze afterwards.

Writing Classes

London is renowned for its media and publishing industries so it's unsurprising that there are a number of writing courses and classes available. Courses range from how to write poetry or a novel, to practical advice about writing for children or TV. Courses are typically within the English, Journalism or Media departments of universities and colleges, and course prices vary according to the length of the course and your eligibility. There are also commercial institutions that specialise in writing, but these are usually more expensive. For EU and international students of all ages, please be aware that it's unlikely you'll get fee subsidisation from the UK government (unless you're an EU citizen under 19). The London Colleges website details your rights and offers advice to EU students and international students (www.londoncolleges.com).

Keeley St
WC2
⊖ *Covent Garden*

City Lit

7492 2600 | www.citylit.ac.uk

City Lit offers over 3,000 part-time, day, evening, week and weekend courses for adults – more than any other institution in the capital. There are over 50 writing courses to choose from, including creative writing, scriptwriting, writing for children's TV and writing short stories for magazines.

University of London, New Cross
SE14
≋ ⊖ *New Cross*

Goldsmiths

7919 7171 | www.goldsmiths.ac.uk

Goldsmiths, part of the University of London, has a reputation for the unconventional. The college prides itself on encouraging creativity in individuals (which accounts for former graduates such as Damien Hirst, the enfant terrible of British art, and kooky designer Vivienne Westwood), while maintaining academic excellence. Goldsmiths offers a number of long and short creative writing courses including Writing Fiction, Writing for Performance and Script & Screen.

126 Shirland Rd
W9
≋ ⊖ *Queens Park*

The London School of Journalism

0800 838216 | www.lsj.org

The LSJ is a school approved by the National Union for Journalists that offers long distance learning. The school also holds courses in creative writing, as well as post-graduate degrees, evening and weekend classes. Courses include feature writing, writing a novel and writing a bestselling thriller. Prices vary according to eligibility. There is also a summer school.

Royal Court Theatre, Sloane Square
SW1
⊖ *Sloane Square*

Royal Court Young Writers Programme

7565 5050 | www.royalcourttheatre.com

The YWP is a programme run by the highly esteemed Royal Court Theatre, which holds writing groups for 13 to 16 year-olds and 17 to 25 year-olds interested in writing plays. No previous experience is needed, but candidates must be within the specified age range(s). All sessions are led by professional playwrights. The website is incredibly comprehensive and well worth browsing before you commit to a course.

285

Spectator Sports

If you're a sports fan but the thought of doing all that exercise tires you out, there are plenty of opportunities to watch someone else put in all the effort. Football is the most popular spectator sport in the UK, and with six Premiership clubs plus four Football League teams – Millwall, Leyton Orient, Brentford and Barnet – in London the casual fan is spoiled for choice (club supporters are slightly more partisan though – you won't catch a Spurs fan popping along to the Emirates Stadium to cheer Arsenal along on a spare Saturday). There are famous venues that play host to summer sports too, such as Grand Slam tennis at Wimbledon and international cricket at Lord's and The Oval, plus an annual athletics meet at Crystal Palace (8778 0131). You can also catch some major events for free – every spring crowds line the streets to watch competitors slog it out in the London Marathon and the Oxford-Cambridge boat race. Away from the top-level stuff, thousands of amateur matches and events take place across town every weekend – stroll down to your local park and you're likely to be able to watch teams of enthusiasts playing anything from football to frisbee.

Boxing

From bare-fist fighting in dusty pubs to multimillion pound title bouts in huge arenas, boxing is big business in London. The pugilistic tradition of public house fighting is firmly ensconced in London's history; in 1743, John 'Jack' Broughton created the first set of boxing rules after a successful career fighting in Tottenham Court Road's drinking dens. For enthusiasts The Lamb and Flag in Covent Garden and The Ring in Blackfriars were two of the most famous pubs for arranged bouts. Thankfully venues are more salubrious today. Many don't usually sell tickets directly, so check listings at www.britishboxing.net or try agencies such as See Tickets (www.seetickets.com) and Ticketmaster (www.ticketmaster.com).

One Western Gateway,
Royal Victoria Dock
E16
DLR *Custom House*

ExCel Centre

7069 5000 | www.excel-london.co.uk

This gargantuan purpose-built exhibition centre is a short, canopied walk from the DLR station of the same name. It's a regular venue for top-end boxing matches (Britain's Olympic heavyweight boxing champion Audley Harrison fought here) and is where boxing, as well as judo and weightlifting among other disciplines, will take place during the 2012 Olympics.

Old Ford Rd
E2
⊖ *Bethnal Green*

York Hall

8980 2243 | www.gll.org

York Hall is the sacred home of boxing in London, and was saved from closure in 2004 after fierce lobbying from some of the sport's biggest names. Famous British boxers Lennox Lewis and Audley Harrison learned their craft at York Hall, and it's not uncommon to see retired boxers sat ringside during bouts. Go to www.britishboxing.net for more information about scheduled fights.

Spectator Sports

Cricket

St John's Wood
W8
⊖ *St. John's Wood*

Lord's Cricket Ground

7616 8500 | www.lords.org

Owned by the Marylebone Cricket Club (MCC), the 'spiritual home' of cricket is, in financial terms, also one of the most successful. It is the home of the England and Wales Cricket Board as well as the MCC Museum. The ground hosts npower Test matches and NatWest-sponsored one-day internationals, as well county championship matches (it's the home ground of Middlesex). The website is comprehensive and includes details on various tours of the ground. Call 7432 1000 for tickets.

336 Kennington Park Rd
SE11
⊖ *Oval*

The Oval Cricket Ground

7582 6660 | www.surreycricket.com/the-brit-oval

This much-loved ground has a humble background as a cabbage and market garden. It eventually opened as a cricket ground in 1846 and is now home to Surrey County Cricket Club. It became famous for being the first English ground to host an England v Australia test match (what was to become The Ashes). The England team were soundly thrashed, but made up for it over 150 years later when the team won The Ashes here in 2005.

Equestrian

Showjumping is big in Europe, and as the Brits are a particularly horsey lot, large crowds flock to Olympia (www.olympiashowjumping.com), the home of the sport. The Equine World website (www.equine-world.co.uk) is a great place to check out upcoming showjumping and dressage events in London. The big competition of the year is the London International Horse Show, which takes place every December at Olympia, while The Horse of the Year Show (usually held in autumn; see www.hoys.co.uk) is renowned for its mix of serious competition and entertainment.

Football

London, with six teams, is the city with the highest concentration of Premiership clubs in the country. The Premiership season runs from August to May and the final of the FA Cup (the oldest football cup competition in the world) takes place in mid May. The new Wembley Stadium is due for completion in May 2007 and, as the home of English football, will host international games and showpiece finals such as the FA Cup, the Carling Cup and the Community Shield. Tickets for Premiership matches are notoriously difficult to buy; with some clubs operating schemes where only members are able to purchase tickets for home games. You can buy tickets online or by telephone through sports ticket agencies – it's not recommended that you buy tickets from touts outside stadiums as it's expensive (and illegal). Each club has different levels of membership so sometimes even members have to compete to get tickets for bigger games. Season tickets are often very difficult to obtain for bigger clubs such as Arsenal, with many having long waiting lists. However, match tickets and season tickets are more readily available – and affordable – at smaller London clubs.

Emirates Stadium,
Ashburton Grove
N7
⇌ ⊖ *Highbury & Islington*

Arsenal FC

7704 4000 | www.arsenal.com

Arsenal Football Club, previously known as Woolwich Arsenal, turned professional in 1891. 'The Gunners' moved to Highbury just before the First World War and were promoted to English football's top division a few years later where they have remained ever since (much to the joy of their fans and annoyance of rivals). The club moved to the impressive 60,000 capacity Emirates Stadium at the start of the 2006/2007 season.

Arsenal tube is a short walk away, but Finsbury Park and Highbury & Islington stations are less crowded on match days. Tickets are only available to members; contact the club for more details.

The Valley, Floyd Rd
SE7
⇌ **Charlton**

Charlton Athletic FC

8333 4000 | www.cafc.co.uk

Charlton Athletic are known as the 'Addicks' after a turn-of-the-century fish and chip shop run by Arthur Bryan – who helped fund the team and gave out haddock ('addick') suppers to the winners (and cod to the losers). Today, priority is given to members, but the club follows the Premier League fan's charter by offering 5% of home match tickets to non-season ticket holders. Renowned as a well-run community club, Charlton were the first club in the country to back the Let's Kick Racism Out Of Football campaign.

Stamford Bridge,
Fulham Rd
SW6
⊖ **Fulham Broadway**

Chelsea FC

0870 3002322 | www.chelseafc.com

Reigning Premiership champions Chelsea celebrated their 100-year anniversary in 2005. Once a struggling mid-table side, the club's fortunes have been transformed by the investment of new owner Roman Abramovich and the motivational skills of manager Jose Mourinho. The club's ability to purchase top players at will – and their subsequent success – has caused some resentment among rival fans. Tickets go on sale about a month before each fixture with the club limiting the number of tickets that season ticket holders and members can buy per game.

Craven Cottage,
Stevenage Rd
SW6
⊖ **Putney Bridge**

Fulham FC

0870 4421222 | www.fulhamfc.com

The oldest London club in the Premiership has failed to establish itself as a force to rival neighbours Chelsea, despite the financial backing of Mohammed Al Fayed, owner of Harrods (p.356). The club has also faced a continuous fight to stay at its spiritual home, Craven Cottage. The ground is situated on the north side of the banks of the River Thames, and the Oxbridge boat race (p.44) can be seen briefly from its stands.

Bill Nicholson Way,
748 High Rd
N17
⇌ ⊖ **Seven Sisters**

Tottenham Hotspur FC

0870 4205000 | www.tottenhamhotspur.com

In 1963, Tottenham Hotspur (Spurs) became the first English club to win a European trophy – the European Cup Winners' Cup. Spurs were also the first club in the 20th century to achieve the League and FA Cup Double, winning both competitions in the 1960/61 season. The rivalry between Spurs and north London neighbours Arsenal knows no bounds. Club members have a 10-day priority period in which to buy match tickets before they're made available to the public.

Boleyn Ground,
Green St
E13
⊖ **Upton Park**

West Ham United FC

8548 2748 | www.whufc.com

The 'Hammers', who returned to the Premier League in 2005, have won the FA Cup three times but never the League Championship. The club has rivalries with most London clubs, but their oldest foe is Millwall FC; this mutual dislike dates back to before both clubs were formally formed when both West Ham and Millwall were shipbuilding firms competing for the same contracts. Although priority is given to members and season-ticket holders, tickets are sometimes available on general sale.

Golf

Wentworth Rd,
Virginia Water
Surrey
⇌ **Virginia Water**

Wentworth Club

01344 842201 | www.wentworthclub.com

Wentworth Golf Course, established over 75 years ago, has played an integral part in recent golf history and presently hosts the BMW Championships (May), the PGA Championships and Wentworth Senior Masters (August) as well as the HSBC World Match Play (October). A total of 130,000 spectators visit the course every year. Tickets are available to club members first before going on general sale.

Greyhound Racing

A lot of money rides on greyhound racing – £2.9 billion to be exact. The sport that once had a relatively small following now attracts nearly four million people a year to races up and down the UK. Choosing which dog to back is the most fun for casual observers, especially as their names range from the sublime to the ridiculous. Races take place all-year round at London's top two racetracks.

Chingford Rd
E4
⊖ **Walthamstow**
Central

Walthamstow Stadium

8498 3300 | www.wsgreyhound.co.uk

Walthamstow Stadium has a typically colourful east London history. In 1933 it was founded by William Chandler whose first foray into the sport was as an illegal street bookmaker. After greyhound racing fever gripped London in the late 1920s, he opened the stadium. Today, it's open for evening racing every Tuesday, Thursday and Saturday from 18:30. Admission to the main enclosure costs £6. Children under 15 are admitted free when accompanied by an adult. Special packages (which include a meal and drinks) are also available.

Plough Lane
SW17
⊖ **Tooting Broadway**

Wimbledon Dogs

8946 8000 | www.lovethedogs.co.uk

People don't just go to Wimbledon for tennis; the borough also has one of the most popular greyhound stadiums in the UK. It's not particularly swanky, but it's big and draws a mixed, friendly crowd which includes serious punters as well as celebratory groups who fancy a flutter. Race nights are Tuesdays, Fridays and Saturdays with the first race at 19:30 during the week and just before at the weekend. Admission is £6 on all race nights; children can watch but obviously can't bet.

Horse Racing

Betting on horse racing in the UK is a huge concern – over £10bn is placed with betting shops and online bookmakers each year. It's also a massively popular spectator sport. According to the British Board of Horseracing, over six million people attended race meetings in 2005. The most prestigious and popular events tend to combine sport with socialising; the annual Royal Ascot event is renowned as much for fashion and flowing champagne as the action on the track. The UK's (and world's) most famous steeplechase is the gruelling Grand National, held at Aintree near Liverpool every April. An hour or so commute from London are three racecourses, each famous in its own right: Ascot for Royal Ascot; Kempton Park for the King George VI Chase and Sandown for the Gold Cup steeplechase.

Ascot
Berkshire
⇌ Ascot

Ascot Racecourse
0870 7227227 | www.ascot.co.uk
Probably the most famous racecourse in the world, Ascot attracts half a million visitors a year. In June, Royal Ascot (the one where ladies wear monochrome hats) brings in over 300,000 guests in just five days (during this time, Ascot's 140 strong staff swells to over 6,000). There are flat and hurdle tracks: both of which are notoriously demanding for horse and jockey. Ticket prices start from £54 for Royal Ascot.

Staines Rd East
Sunbury on Thames
⇌ Kempton Park

Kempton Park
01932 782292 | www.kempton.co.uk
Kempton Park was established in 1878, and is celebrated for its King George VI Chase, which Desert Orchid won a record four times. There's racing all-year round on the flat course, and tickets are available through its website. Prices range from £11 to £20 and concession tickets are available.

Portsmouth Rd,
Esher
Surrey
⇌ Esher

Sandown Park
01372 464348 | www.sandown.co.uk
Home to the world-renowned Gold Cup steeplechase (April) and Coral Eclipse Stakes flat race (July), Sandown also boasts a golf course, a ski centre and go-karting facilities. Races take place all year round and there are usually up to seven races a day. Tickets cost from £15 to £23 and can be bought online or by telephone (they cost slightly more at the gate).

Rugby Union

Rugby Rd
TW1
⇌ Twickenham

Twickenham
0870 4052000 | www.rfu.com
Located in the London Borough of Richmond upon Thames, Twickenham was recently expanded to seat 82,000 visitors, making it the largest rugby stadium in the UK. The stadium is home to the Rugby Football Union (RFU), and hosts England's home test matches, as well as the the Guinness Premiership Final and the Heineken Cup Final, both of which take place in May. Twickenham also hosts large-scale rock concerts (the Rolling Stones played in 2006). The Six Nations matches involving England are played every February and March. RFU members are offered priority tickets. To become a RFU member you need only join your local rugby club. Tickets for most international fixtures are limited; try www.ticketmaster.co.uk and www.soldoutevents.com but expect to pay premium prices.

Snooker
Snooker is still a massively popular sport in the UK despite its limited appearances on the nation's TV screens. There are numerous tournaments throughout the UK, but two of the biggest are the Masters in January and the Pot Black Cup in September. The World Snooker Championship takes place in April in Sheffield. For tickets try: www.soldoutticketevents.com or www.ticketmaster.com.uk. Full details of snooker tournaments are available at www.worldsnooker.com.

89 Pall Mall
SW1
⊖ Green Park

The Royal Automobile Club
7930 2345 | www.royalautomobileclub.co.uk
This private members' club hosts the Pot Black Cup, a spin-off of the well-liked TV series which ran on BBC TV from 1969 to 1986. The 2005 Pot Black tournament featured some of the world's top players including Ronnie O'Sullivan, Stephen Hendry and Jimmy White. A limited number of tickets are available through www.worldsnooker.com

290

Arena Square,
Engineers Way
HA9
⊖ *Wembley Park*

Wembley Arena

8782 5500 | www.wembley.co.uk

Wembley Arena plays host to the Saga Insurance Masters (formerly the Benson & Hedges Masters until there was a ban on tobacco advertising), a professional snooker tournament first held in London in 1975. For many players it's the biggest tournament after the World Championships. Ronnie O'Sullivan beat rising star Ding Junhui in the 2007 tournament. For tickets, call 0870 0600870.

Tennis

Palliser Rd
W14
⊖ *Barons Court*

The Queen's Club

7385 3421 | www.queensclub.co.uk

Built in 1886, and named after Queen Victoria, this well-renowned club was the first multi-purpose sports facility to be built anywhere in the world. It originally hosted many other activities including athletics, baseball and rugby. Now it focuses on tennis and hosts the Stella Artois Championships, the World Rackets Championships and the British Open. Priority tickets are given to those on its mailing list; remaining tickets are then distributed on a first come, first served basis (you can join the mailing list at www.stellaartoistennis.com). The Queen's Club also boasts 28 outdoor and eight indoor tennis courts, two real tennis courts, three squash courts and a gymnasium should you wish to join the club as a member.

Church Rd
SW19
⊖ *Southfields*

Wimbledon (The All England Lawn Tennis Club)

8944 1066 | www.wimbledon.org

The Wimbledon Championships is perhaps the world's most famous tennis tournament, attracting around half a million spectators each year. Today, players from over 60 nations compete and the event is televised to millions worldwide at the end of June and beginning of July. Because there's such high demand, the club uses a public ballot for tickets for the show courts – you'll need to enter it the year before you wish to attend. You can also obtain tickets through The Lawn Tennis Association (7381 7000; www.lta.org.uk). Also remember you can gain entry to the show courts (Centre Court and Courts 1 and 2) and outer courts on the day if you're prepared to queue (you'll need to get there as early as 04:00). Tickets also become available for the outer courts towards the end of play for a reasonable price. If you can't make it to the tournament, the Wimbledon Lawn Tennis Museum (8946 6131) contains a collection of memorabilia, interactive exhibits and a reconstruction of the men's dressing room circa 1980.

291

Leisure Facilities

There's a crossover between sport and leisure facilities in London. For example, health clubs have gyms, some gyms have spas, and sports centres can sometimes have the lot. Local authority-owned facilities tend to be cheaper than private clubs and don't require membership (though it's a cheaper option if you use them regularly) but they're generally not as plush as private establishments and more crowded, often requiring that you book ahead to guarantee a court or class.

Large chains, such as Holmes Place and LA Fitness, have the monopoly on health clubs and, while they provide excellent facilities, often ask you to sign up to a minimum of three months (sometimes a year), which if you don't have the time to attend can prove a little expensive.

Given the size of the capital, it's recommended that you join or attend a club or centre close to where you live or work, otherwise you could be adding a couple of hours travel time to your chosen activity. Fortunately, every borough in London has something to offer. The website www.fitmap.co.uk is a useful site if you're searching for a sports centre, gym or health club in your area. Don't underestimate the amenities in your local borough (a list of which can be found at www.london.gov.uk).

Sports Centres

If you're keen to get fit but balk at the steep membership prices of private gyms, check out the various sports centres across town. These tend to be owned by local authorities, who outsource the running of the facilities to leisure companies such as Courtneys (www.courtneys.co.uk), Fusion (www.fusion-lifestyle.com) and GLL (www.gll.org). Although the centres may not be as flashy or exclusive as a David Lloyd or Fitness First, what they lack in prestige is more than made up for in terms of value. You can tailor your activities to suit your interests – you usually pay for an individual session or month-by-month membership rather than a hefty year's fee – and, while the level of facilities can vary from place to place, they can include gyms, exercise studios, fitness classes, swimming pools and courts.

27 Brixton Station Rd
SW9
⊖ Brixton

Brixton Recreation Centre

7926 9779 | www.leisureconnection.co.uk

'The Rec', as it is known locally, is run by Leisure Connection, which takes care of about 80 sports and leisure centres in Britain on behalf of local authorities. The centre has just undergone refurbishment. It's a popular venue (hence the queues at peak times), and it's generally well-run and clean, although staff are not always the most helpful. Spread over six floors, facilities include a fitness suite, swimming pools, a climbing wall, an aerobics and dance studio, squash and badminton courts, plus a sauna and solarium. There's a creche too, but booking is advised. Prices are generally cheap, and if you purchase a Lambeth Leisure Card you could save even more.

Sports Centres

Arches Leisure Centre	80 Trafalgar Rd	SE10	8317 5000	www.gll.org.uk
Central YMCA	112 Great Russell St	WC1	7343 1700	www.centralymca.org.uk/club
East Ham Leisure Centre	324 Barking Rd	E6	8548 5850	www.gll.org
Elephant & Castle Leisure Centre	22 Elephant & Castle	SE1	7582 5505	www.fusion-lifestyle.com
Jubilee Sports Centre	Caird St	W10	8960 9629	www.courtneys.co.uk
New Bridge Park Community Centre	Harrow Rd	NW10	8937 3730	www.brent.gov.uk
Paddington Recreation Centre	Randolph Ave	W9	7641 3642	www.courtneys.co.uk
Queen Mother Sports Centre	223 Vauxhall Bridge Rd	SW1	7630 5522	www.courtneys.co.uk
Seymour Leisure Centre	Seymour Place	W1	7723 8019	www.courtneys.co.uk
Swiss Cottage Leisure Centre	Winchester Rd	NW3	7974 2102	www.camden.gov.uk/swisscottage

Sports & Leisure Facilities

Golden Lane Leisure Centre

Fann St, Golden Lane Estate
EC1
⊖ Barbican

7250 1464 | www.cityoflondon.gov.uk

Golden Lane is the only publicly funded leisure centre in the City, which explains why it gets packed at lunchtimes (especially the attractive pool, which draws big crowds throughout the summer). There's a gym, a decent-sized swimming pool (which offers women-only sessions on Tuesday mornings), two all-weather tennis and netball courts, a badminton court and an indoor hall. It's a relaxed venue, with helpful staff and a congenial atmosphere. You can pay as you go, or take out monthly or annual membership for discounted use.

Oasis Sports Centre

32 Endell St
WC2
⊖ Tottenham Court Rd

7831 1804 | www.camden.gov.uk

This council-run sports centre in busy Covent Garden is indeed an oasis: there are a range of facilities including squash courts, and an indoor and heated outdoor pool (which gets as crowded as the bustling streets in summer). It's got a big, modern gym and offers a range of exercise classes: aerobics, yoga and power pump, among others. You don't have to be a member to use the facilities, but if you plan to use them regularly it's probably worth joining up.

Tottenham Green Leisure Centre

1 Philip Lane
N15
⇌ ⊖ Seven Sisters

8489 5322 | www.haringey.gov.uk

This huge indoor centre is a stone's throw away from White Hart Lane, Tottenham Hotspur's football ground. It's got a large pool, a children's pool with a wave machine, a sports hall and a fitness room. There's enough space to not feel over-crowded here, a rarity for most public leisure centres, although the downside is that it's quite easy to lose your way. It's very kid-friendly and there's also a decent library. A good all-rounder, with the usual members and non-members price structure.

Westway Sports Centre

1 Crowthorne Rd
W10
⊖ Latimer Road

8969 0992 | www.westway.org/sports

Nestled underneath the A40 flyover, Westway isa well-respected centre that's strong on community participation and encouraging newcomers in all sports. It has the largest climbing wall in Britain, with excellent supervision and training to suit all levels. There are eight indoor and four outdoor tennis courts, six artificial football pitches (one is full-size), a gym with disabled access, basketball and netball courts. There's also a fitness studio that tends to attract sport rather than gym aficionados. Contact the centre for member and non-member prices available.

Gyms

London has numerous 'pure' gyms that concentrate solely on cardiovascular training, free weights and fitness classes. These places tend to be sweaty hives for fitness fans and are focused on working out and toning; they offer little else in the way of other sports and don't have pools or spa facilities (with a few exceptions), though many may have saunas, sunbeds and steam rooms to help you wind down after sessions. Typically you need to become a member, although day rates and pay-as-you-go options are available. If you want more facilities than just gym training, a sports centre (p.292) or health club (p.295) is a better bet. Prices below should only be used as a guide. Contact each club for up-to-date membership costs.

Soho Gyms

Soho Gyms are spacious places filled with natural light and banging tunes. Each gym varies slightly in size and facilities but the 'freedom tag plus' allows access to all its gyms. Facilities include good-sized gyms, cardio stations, trainers and a comprehensive schedule of classes including body pump, muay Thai kickboxing, spinning and yoga. Prices are reasonable. See www.sohogyms.co.uk for more details.

293

**Fountayne House,
Fountayne Rd**
N15
⇌ ⊖ *Seven Sisters*

Bodyworks Gymnasium

8808 6580 | www.bodyworksgym.co.uk

This 7,000sq ft men-only gym is furnished with modern, functional equipment, including barbells, cross trainers, exercise bikes, free weights, sports bikes and steppers, it also has aerobics, dance and fitness studios. If that list doesn't tire you out there are classes aplenty, including body toning, boxercise and circuit training. Fitness instructors and personal fitness programmes are also available, and membership costs from £30 a year, plus £3 per visit. Facilities are open to non-members.

42-49 St Martin's Lane
WC2
⊖ *Leicester Square*

Gymbox Covent Garden

7395 0270 | www.gymbox.co.uk

A boxing-focused gym with a free weights area, cardio space, plenty of classes and a cool atmosphere – cinema screens and nightly resident DJs provide the backdrop as you work out. Classes range from 'exotic dancing' and 'disco yoga' to 'hula hips' and 'Bollywood grooves'. The boxing ring itself is official Olympic size and there are over 25 punchbags for training. For those who need that extra push Gymbox has fully qualified 'Very Personal Trainers' to get you moving. Membership costs £49 to £68 per month, plus a one off joining fee of £100, all of which entitles you to full use of the gym's facilities. Non-members can attend some classes but prices aren't cheap – it can cost from £15 a session. There's another branch in Holborn (7400 1919).

151 Draycott Ave
SW3
⊖ *South Kensington*

KX Gym

7584 5333 | www.kxgymuk.com

KX Gym has an impressive range of equipment and facilities but it comes at a price. There's a one off joining fee of £1,500, and a year's membership costs £3,000 (which can be paid in monthly installments of £275). You need to be a member or guest of a member to use the facilities but non-members can use the spa (prices start from £90 for a one-hour massage; £80 for members). The gym also has a dedicated spinning room with 20 bikes. For resistance training there are over 100 sets of dumbbells, squat benches, leg presses and a complete range of dual axis resistance machines. The spa offers a selection of eastern and western healing therapies. Members can also make use of valet parking, a laundry service and permanent lockers.

2 Hague St
E2
⊖ *Bethnal Green*

Muscleworks Gym

7256 0916 | www.muscleworksgym.co.uk

This men-only gym is big on nurturing bodybuilders and claims to have helped more professional athletes reach peak fitness than any other gym in London. Facilities include the latest weight training and cardiovascular equipment, sunbeds and saunas. All instructors are fully trained to give nutritional advice alongside the usual workout programmes. It costs £345 for a year's membership, and £120 for a three-month membership; single workouts cost £5 for non-members.

**21-22 The Arches,
Winthorpe Rd**
SW15
⊖ *Putney Bridge*

Physical Culture Exercise & Tanning Studios

8780 2172

This women-only gym provides a safe, clean place to exercise. The gym's aim is to help customers stay active, reduce body fat, boost energy levels and, for over 40s, prevent osteoporosis. Facilities include the latest cardio and resistance gym equipment. The basic membership costs from £39.99 per month (minimum 12 month contract) and entitles you to use all equipment and facilities; this increases to £99 per month when three personal training sessions a week are included. A free trial session is offered should you wish to try it out first.

294

Health Clubs

Other options **Sports Centres** p.292

Health clubs are big business in London; not only do you have a choice of companies, but of hundreds of branches. It can be overwhelming, so it's strongly recommended that you shop around to see which club suits your needs. It's essential you read the small print as many health clubs insist you set up a direct debit and commit to a year's membership – if you don't like the club or if you move away, you may find yourself paying for it anyway (though some clubs allow you to transfer to a nearer branch). Don't be afraid to ask questions so you're certain what your membership entails, as it varies from club to club. All clubs regularly run promotions so check their websites, and ask for a free trial, which clubs usually allow (some will then give you the hard sell, but don't be intimidated by such tactics).Try not to be seduced by an expensive club unless you're sure you'll use it regularly; you might find that a smaller club or your local sports centre (p.292) will suit your needs (and your bank balance) just as adequately. The companies featured below are the major chains. Others you may want to consider are: David Lloyd Leisure (www.davidlloyd.co.uk); Fitness Exchange (www.fitness-exchange.net) and Living Well (www.livingwell.com).

Various locations

Cannons
8336 2288 | *www.cannons.co.uk*

This is a welcoming, mid-range chain that provides decently priced, well-equipped gyms for a wide variety of customers. Its central London clubs are aimed at busy workers and offer individual and corporate membership (periods are split into peak and off-peak times). Outer London clubs offer options for families and most clubs have creches. The majority of clubs have a gym (the City club also has a women-only gym), cycle studio, cardio equipment, a swimming pool, steam room, saunas, sunbeds, as well as a range of fitness classes. Opening hours vary but generally clubs are open Monday to Friday, 06.30 to 22.00 and weekends, 10.00 to 18.00. Membership varies according to the club, but expect to pay up to £83 a month in central London, plus an initial administration fee. Length of membership is flexible, but there's a minimum period of three or 12 months at certain branches. Day membership isn't possible except as a guest of a member, or during special promotions.

Various locations

Esporta
01189 123500 | *www.esporta.com*

Most of the clubs in this reputable chain are focused on family activities and have excellent facilities for both children and adults, though people without kids shouldn't be put off; there are separate changing rooms for over 16s and adult-only areas in the restaurants and bars. Every club has a gym and free weights, studios offering classes in aerobics, cycling and dancing, a pool and spa amenities including a sauna, sunbeds and steam room. Selected clubs also have squash and tennis courts, outdoor pools, beauty treatment centres (usually available to non-members too) and creches. The focus at Esporta is not only on fitness but on relaxing; there's good cafes and even free internet access for members.
Opening hours vary, but are generally 06.30 to 23.00 on weekdays and 08.00 to 20.00 on weekends. Monthly membership starts from £64 per month and enables you to use all Esporta clubs. There's a free one-day trial for potential new members.

295

Various locations

Fitness First
0870 8988080 | www.fitnessfirst.co.uk

Fitness First staff are quite the salespeople, which may explain why it's the biggest fitness company in the world. Its gyms are possibly not the most luxurious, but they're reasonably priced and unpretentious, and have all the facilities you'd expect (except for swimming pools). You'll find a gym, fitness studios (with a wide range of classes such as body combat, circuit and Pilates), beauty treatment rooms and sunbeds, saunas and steam rooms. Personals trainers are also on hand for an extra cost.

There are 48 clubs across London. Opening hours are usually Monday to Friday, 06:30 to 22:00; Saturday, 08:00 to 20:00, and various times on Sunday.

Membership prices fluctuate depending on the club. Prospective members can take out a one-day free membership but be warned that staff will try (in some cases relentlessly) to get you to join during this trial. There are numerous types of membership, including gold membership, which gives you access to all Fitness First clubs and student membership, which allows you to join for an initial three months.

Various locations

Virgin Active
www.virginactive.co.uk

Virgin Active attracts a slightly older, professional clientele, which is reflected in the steeper membership costs and a slightly more exclusive atmosphere. The chain was recently bought by Virgin Active (part of the huge Virgin conglomerate) so it's possible the present clubs will be overhauled at some stage – in appearance at least.

Virgin Active clubs offer the latest gym machines, a large range of classes including aerobics, boxercise, ballet and step, ozone-treated swimming pools, steam rooms, sunbeds and saunas. Most gyms also have women-only gyms and saunas as well.

There are over 30 clubs in Greater London. Opening hours vary between branches but Monday to Friday, 06.30 to 22.30, and weekend opening until 18:00 is typical. Annual membership costs vary significantly between each location; expect to pay around £40 and above in Greater London, and up to £130 in the centre of town.

Virgin Active

Cannons

Cannons

Well-Being

Well-Being

Taking care of yourself, whether it's with a wax, a luxurious facial, or a weekly yoga class, is common in the capital. Though London is relatively expensive, many residents have a certain amount of disposable income to keep themselves looking happy and healthy, and most will admit they need some 'me-time' and relaxation techniques to keep them sane.

Yoga, Pilates and complementary therapies are hugely popular and reasonably priced; beauty treatments tend to be pricier, especially in some of the top spas (which are often found in hotels).

Generally, such personal luxuries have become widespread and most of your colleagues and friends will have indulged or participated in at least one experience in this section, so it's worth asking around for recommendations. If you can find the time and money, you should try at least one – in such a frenetic city, these are the things that will help to keep you calm, balanced and in good shape.

Beauty Salons

Other options **Beauty Training** p.238, **Hairdressers** p.298, **Health Spas** p.299, **Perfumes & Cosmetics** p.343

Londoners are, on the whole, a well-groomed lot, and a huge number of residents (both men and women) enjoy some sort of regular beauty treatment. Some salon services, such as waxing, only take 15 to 30 minutes, making them a more affordable option than longer spa treatments. Salons come in all shapes, states and sizes; from local high-street shops that offer the basics at cheapish prices to more luxurious experiences in central London and affluent parts of town, such as Chelsea and Notting Hill. Beauty salons and nail bars in less well-off areas may not appear to be too swanky, but many are good value so keep an eye out for deals and ask around locally for recommendations. In central London prices are higher; there are offers, but you're often only paying for the convenience of a central location.

Beauty Lounge

2 Percy St
W1
⊖ Goodge Street

7436 8686 | www.beautylounge.co.uk

In this airy, chilled space you'll find friendly beauty therapists providing a wide range of affordable treatments. The salon boasts celebrity fans and is the only place in London where you can try the Ole Henriksen facial. With waxes from £10 and the ever popular 'Fake Bake' tans costing £45, The Beauty Lounge will have you feeling good and looking great at reasonable prices. You may also be tempted to buy some of the organic products available, such as celebrity facialist Susan Ciminelli's range – if it's good enough for Jennifer Lopez, it's probably good enough for you.

Groom

49 Beauchamp Place
SW3
⊖ Knightsbridge

7581 1248 | www.groomlondon.com

'One chair, two therapists, one hour' is the motto here, and they stick to it – every client is pampered by two staff during indulgent hour-long treatments. Some of the delights on offer are the Weekly Groom Hour (£105), which includes a cleanse, tone and exfoliation, massage, make-up application, manicure, pedicure and eyebrow shape; and a Retail Revival Hour (£95), which incorporates a facial, neck and shoulder massage, and hot-stone pedicure. There are also half-hour treatments for the rushed. Considering Groom has salons in swanky Knightsbridge and superior department store Selfridges on Oxford Street (7499 1199), the atmosphere is remarkably down-to-earth while the results remain fantastic. It's open daily until 20.00 making it ideal for pampering after work or a long day hammering the credit card.

400 Oxford St
W1
⊖ Bond Street

Men's Salon at Selfridges
7318 3709 | www.selfridges.com

Small but perfectly formed, this salon is a man-only zone and perfect for fellas who want to look good without getting found out doing it. The treatment rooms are hidden behind the barber shop, which makes it a good place for a quick tidy up, although not necessarily to have a spa experience. But while you're there, how about a hot and wet shave (from £35) followed by a pedicure (£27) and an eyebrow shape (£16)?

127-131 Westbourne
Grove
W2
⊖ Notting Hill Gate

Spa.NK at Space.NK
7727 8002 | www.spacenk.com

This highly revered apothecary has over 20 shops in London, and the Notting Hill branch has six treatment rooms offering massages, facials, tanning, waxing and a relaxation area. The ranges stocked are thoughtfully chosen for their innovation and high quality – it's worth buying as a treat so you can continue the good work at home. Prices start from £70 for a luxurious hour-long 'rose body cocoon' massage, and from £65 for an aromatherapy facial. There's also a treatment room in Space.NK in Soho (7734 3734) where you can have a facial, wax (£15 to 20), or an hour-long self-tan treatment with all-over exfoliation (£75).

Hairdressers

London has an excellent reputation for hair styling and, because it's a competitive market (there are hundreds of salons), there are some good deals to exploit. In recent years, more and more salons have added beauty treatments to their menus, such as manicures, pedicures, waxing and facials. Covent Garden is the place for top hairdressing companies, closely followed by Soho and Fitzrovia. The rents are high in these areas, which is reflected in steeper prices, but you're usually guaranteed a good cut and attentive service (if not, don't be afraid to ask for a free restyle). Don't neglect your local, cheaper salons though, which often employ stylists who have been trained in top salons in central London. For a cut and blow dry (also known as a cut and finish), men should expect to pay upwards of £30, women north of £45. If you use a celebrity or award-winning stylist, prepare to wave goodbye to at least £250. On the other hand, men who are happy to use a traditional local barber won't have to fork out much more than £10.

174 High Holborn
WC1
⊖ Covent Garden

Aveda Lifestyle Institute
7759 7355 | www.avedainstitute.co.uk

Is it a hairdressing salon? Is it a spa? Is it a wonderfully stylish building full of natural products that protect your hair but don't damage the planet? Actually, it's all three. At Aveda UK's flagship salon your appointment isn't just focused on cutting your hair; the approach is holistic and you'll receive a consultation and a head and shoulder massage before your cut. Top cuts, top products, top hair colouring, and you get to be kind to the earth while being made to look beautiful. Prices start at £51 for a cut and blow dry (£44 for men) and a semi-permanent colouring starts from £50. The spa offers a wide range of treatments including manicures, pedicures and hair removal.

7 Percy St
W1
⊖ Goodge Street

Charles Worthington
7631 1370 | www.cwlondon.com

Unpretentious and not overpriced for such a well-respected and well-known hairdresser, Charles Worthington also boasts an extensive product range. The space is chic and calming and stylists treat clients equally, a promise not all big name salons can deliver in London. The Broadgate branch has a spa, which offers a range of treatments including massages, manicures and pamper packages. A cut and finish

298

starts from £49 (or from £250 if you want the man himself to wield the scissors). A half head of highlights or lowlights starts at £87. There are also branches at The Dorchester, Park Lane (7317 6321), Covent Garden (7831 5303) and The Broadgate Club in Exchange Place (7638 0802).

Daniel Hersheson

45 Conduit St
W1
⊖ *Bond Street*

7434 1747 | *www.danielhersheson.co.uk*

Daniel Hersheson and his son Luke have been top of the fashion hair stylist tree for a while now and rightly so – but this level of quality doesn't come cheap. A cut and finish with a basic stylist costs around £55 (Daniel or Luke command around £250), a colour technician starts from £65 for a colour or £130 for a half head of highlights. The seats you sit in to have your hair washed are electric-powered and tilt so you're almost lying down, making it a relaxed start to your appointment, and the service is warm and welcoming. A manicure, pedicure and hair removal service is available at Conduit Street and there are beauty treatments at the branch in Harvey Nichols (7235 5000).

Headmasters

11-12 Hanover St
W1
⊖ *Oxford Circus*

7408 1000 | *www.hmhair.co.uk*

As well as its Hanover Street branch, Headmasters has 15 other franchises in London, including in Fulham, Hammersmith, Wimbledon and Richmond. Most are open until 21:00, making it easy to get a haircut after work. Rates vary but expect to pay around £50 for a cut and finish. However, there are usually special offers and customers often get money-off vouchers for their next visit. The salon in Hanover Street often offers a glass of wine to customers needing to relax after a long day.

Saco

71 Monmouth St
WC2
⊖ *Covent Garden*

7240 7897 | *www.sacohair.com*

This stylish salon has an international feel – Saco also has a presence in Montreal, Canada – and staff are trustworthy and hospitable, which makes visiting here a satisfying experience. Beauty treatments are available and there's a training school for wannabe stylists. A cut and finish starts at £48, a semi-permanent fashion colour from £45, and a half head of highlights or lowlights between £100 and £120 (depending on hair length).

Tommyguns

65 Beak St
W1
⊖ *Oxford Circus*

7439 0777 | *www.tommyguns.com*

Tommyguns is where the cool media set of Soho go to get their hair cut. Stylists regularly work on pop promos, style magazines and at fashion weeks, and these uber-trendy salons have a list of celebrity clients as long as your arm. They've got a good reputation for cutting-edge cuts, but some may find the atmosphere as intimidating as others find it exciting. A cut and finish starts from £48 for women and £37 for men. There's also a salon in Charlotte Road, Shoreditch (7739 2244).

Health Spas

Other options **Massage** p.301, **Leisure Facilities** p.292

Often seen as an extravagance in an already expensive city, spas remain popular with tourists, 'ladies that lunch' and those treating themselves. There are some spectacular spas in London, but expect to pay the price to relax in world-class surroundings. Some offer discounts to remain competitive in an increasingly crowded market, while establishments such as Porchester Spa (see below) or Ironmonger Row baths (7253 4011) offer facilities and treatments at a price that allows spa fans to visit more frequently. Whether a thoughtful gift, weekly treat or a well-deserved reward, you should be able to find a spa to suit your needs at a price that suits your bank balance.

2-3 Lancashire Court
W1
⊖ Bond Street

Elemis Day Spa
7499 4995 | www.elemis.com

With an international reputation for creating exquisite natural products, Elemis is pricey but has arguably one of the best skin care ranges around. Its flagship spa in central London is influenced by Japanese, Thai and Balinese therapies, and there are a number of special treatments available, including the Arabian Jewel Ritual (£195 for two-and-a-half hours); Ceremony of Sun (a self-tan experience, £70 for an hour); and a Time for Two couples ritual (£95 per person for one hour). One-hour massages start from £70, a one-hour facial from £70. Antenatal and detox treatments, plus manicures and pedicures, are also available.

Elemis Day Spa

27 Shorts Gardens
WC2
⊖ Covent Garden

Nickel
7240 4048 | www.nickelspalondon.co.uk

With spas in Paris, New York and San Francisco, and its own product range, Nickel is a well-known spa for men with not a hint of pink in sight. Nickel's stores are cool and masculine with none of the flowery connotations of female-orientated spas. Think of it as a barber's (you can get your hair cut) but with facials, massages, waxing and Botox treatments. A one-hour massage or facial starts from £55; a 30-minute manicure is £20. The spa is open until 21:00 on Thursday and Friday so you can be groomed in time for the weekend.

Porchester Centre,
Queensway
W2
⊖ Bayswater

Porchester Spa
7792 3980 | www.westminster.gov.uk/leisureandculture

This spa is situated in the art deco Porchester Centre, which is also home to a gym, pool and exercise classes. The building has a faded grandeur, but it's hardly the epitome of luxury – although it has been lovingly refurbished recently. There are two Russian steam rooms, three Turkish hot rooms, a sauna, plunge pool and a relaxation lounge – and because the Porchester is a public spa, run by Westminster council, it's affordable. Treatments start from £22 for a half-hour massage and £40 for an hour. For £59 a month the 'ultimate spa' membership gives you unlimited use of all the facilities in the centre, including certain days at the spa. A quirky, affordable gem, it has women-only days on Tuesday, Thursday and Friday, with men only on Monday, Wednesday and Saturday. Sundays are mixed.

12 Floral St
WC2
⊖ Covent Garden

The Sanctuary
0870 7703350 | www.thesanctuary.co.uk

Although some say the tropical-themed Sanctuary is looking a tad jaded these days, it's still the most famous women-only spa in London. The infamous swing over the atrium pool is still there, plus a whirlpool, saunas, steam rooms, a meditation suite, koi carp lounge and treatment rooms. There are a range of convenient spa packages available for days (from £67), evenings (from £43), expectant mums (£145) and 'girl's delight' for two (£335). Treatments are affordable – the 50-minute aromatherapy full-body massage costs £60, and the 45-minute hamman rasul (a Turkish mud chamber) costs £39. It's also worth checking the website for special offers. The restaurant is licensed, which makes the venue popular with groups whose intentions are to splurge, not purge.

The Spa at Mandarin Oriental

66 Knightsbridge
SW1
Knightsbridge

7838 9888 | www.mandarinoriental.com/london

Renowned for being one of the top spas in London (at top-end prices), and a celebrity favourite, this is pure indulgence. The serene Eastern-inspired rooms induce a Zen-like state in even the most stressed client, yet the thorough massages ensure that you leave revitalised. What adds to the experience is the 'Heat & Water Oasis' – the sanarium, the amethyst crystal steam room, vitality pool with hydro-jets, and a relaxation area with changeable lighting to suit your mood. To use the Oasis, you'll need to book two hours of treatments at around £100 an hour. Day programmes, including treatments, use of the facilities, and lunch at The Park restaurant, cost from £350 – but if you've got the cash to spare, this pampering experience is well worth it.

Massage

Other options **Leisure Facilities** p.292, **Health Spas** p.299

Waxing and tanning treatments are relatively inexpensive in London, but more luxurious treatments such as facials and massages are rather more pricey. Expect to pay between £50 and £70 for a one-hour massage. Besides beauty salons and spas, some tanning and hairdressing salons offer massages, or check the websites below for practitioners in your area (who will often travel to you). Several places have sprung up in central London that offer 10 or 30-minute back or foot rubs, making them a great way to de-stress after a tiring day. Massage may still be seen as an expensive treat, but the benefits are great for both body and mind. Clare Maxwell-Hudson, who runs a massage school, provides a list of qualified therapists at www.cmhmassage.co.uk, as does www.embodyforyou.com.

Cucumba

12 Poland St
W1
Oxford Circus

7734 2020 | www.cucumba.co.uk

A true urban pit stop, Cucumba provides convenient, affordable beauty treatments that people can fit into their everyday schedule – situated just off Oxford Street, so you can easily combine beauty therapy with retail therapy. There's the £7.50 top-up in under 10 minutes; a 10-minute quick fix for £10; a 20-minute pit stop for £18.50; a 30-minute Cucumba for £27.50; or a 45-minute Cucumba deluxe for £40. There are a variety of massages, facials, waxing, manicures and pedicures on offer, a juice bar and gift vouchers available. Open all week, but Sunday is by appointment only.

Pure Massage Fulham

3-5 Vanston Place
SW6
Fulham Broadway

7381 8100 | www.puremassage.uk.com

Pure Massage believes that there are huge benefits from regular massage and accordingly concentrate on nothing else. There are reflexology, back, foot and pregnancy treatments to choose from; an hour starts from £65, or go for a reasonably priced combo such as a back massage with face reflexology (£75). Pure Massage also offers 'massage your stress' and 'baby massage' courses. Closed on Sundays. There's also a branch in Fenwick department store on New Bond Street (7629 9161).

65-67 Brewer St
W1
⊖ Piccadilly Circus

Relax Soho
7494 3333 | www.relax.org.uk

Relax works in the same way as Walk-in Backrub (see below), except you lie down – though there's the option for a chair massage should you wish. Popular with the media set in Soho, this friendly centre has a calming atmosphere. The company uses and sells natural products and even has a flower delivery service. A 10-minute chair massage costs £10, a one-hour massage starts from £60, and there's a variety of choice – from Swedish to Indian head massage. There's also a branch at the BBC in White City (8811 8844). Open seven days a week.

Various locations

Walk-in Backrub
7436 9875 | www.walkinbackrub.co.uk

For under a tenner you can get a 10-minute backrub in specially designed massage chairs – you'll be amazed what a difference a few moments make – or try a 20 or 30-minute massage. Full body shiatsu treatments and foot rubs for aching shoppers are also available at these handy massage drop-in centres (no appointment is required), plus there are a range of massage-related products and gift vouchers available to buy online and in-store. There are five outlets of this great chain in central London: Neal's Yard, Covent Garden (7836 9111); Selfridges on Oxford Street (0870 8377377); Kingly Court, off Carnaby Street (7436 9875); Charlotte Place, off Goodge Street (7436 9876) and in Harrods, Knightsbridge (7730 1234).

Meditation

There's no shortage of meditation classes and centres in London. No longer attached to the hippy hook of the 1960s, the practice is growing in popularity with the mainstream. Meditation involves clearing the mind, focusing and breathing correctly; its aim is to help a person embrace change, discover self awareness and develop spiritual insight. There are a number of different teachings from various schools including Buddhism, Christianity, and Zen, and alternative methods such as the mantra-based or transcendental meditation. Check out www.meditateinlondon.org.uk, a comprehensive site for those interested in the practice, which includes a list of classes across the city.

36 Shorts Gardens
WC2
⊖ Covent Garden

Inner Space
7836 6688 | www.innerspace.org.uk

Affiliated to the Brahma Kumaris World Spiritual University (www.brahmakumaris.org.uk), which has 4,000 branches in more than 70 countries, Inner Space is set in tranquil surroundings in Covent Garden. There are ongoing lunchtime and early evening courses in practical meditation from Monday to Thursday, plus lunchtime and evening classes at Templeton House in the City. Courses are free, but donations are always welcome. Also on offer are programmes in creative meditation, positive thinking, self esteem and time management. The website is a useful resource that includes lecture archives, and the centre also holds talks in Islington.

The Old Courthouse,
43 Renfrew Rd
SE11
⊖ Kennington

Jamyang Buddhist Centre
7820 8787 | www.jamyang.co.uk

Jamyang is a charity that instructs people on the teachings of Tibetan Buddhism. It has grown over the last 20 years and now cites visits from a number of Tibetan teachers, including the Dalai Lama. There are two meditation rooms, overnight accommodation, a garden, and a bookshop – the proceeds of which go towards bringing meditation into the lives of the local community. Introductory classes cost

£5, as do meditation classes – or alternatively you can just drop in for some quiet time. Other activities arranged by the centre include philosophy classes, regular pujas (chanting ceremonies), Tibetan language and art classes.

The London Buddhist Centre

51 Roman Rd
E2
Bethnal Green

0845 4584716 | www.lbc.org.uk

The London Buddhist Centre is a large, well-known venue (it's housed in a former fire station, and hard to miss) run by the Friends of the Western Buddhist Order. Here, they practice two disciplines: metta bhavana (the 'development of loving kindness') and 'mindfulness of breathing'. As well as regular weekly classes for different levels of experience in Bethnal Green, and Saturday sessions in Covent Garden, the centre organises talks, retreats, introductory weekends and events. Classes cost from £3 to £7.

The Wren Clinic

Idol Lane
EC3
Monument

7283 8908 | www.wrenclinic.co.uk

This centre for 'natural health and counselling' is located in the City in a Grade I listed church tower, designed by Sir Christopher Wren. The clinic has a number of consultation rooms and offers an extensive choice of therapies including meditation in relaxing surroundings. Six times a year, a 'silent mind' course is taught over two Saturday afternoons and is suitable for beginners who wish to learn successful meditation techniques, and more experienced practitioners wanting to try a new angle. The course costs £99.

Pilates

Other options **Yoga** p.306

Closely associated with yoga and based around the principles of flexibility, posture and strength, this body-conditioning method is popular with athletes because it helps to prevent injury, increases body awareness and alignment, and eases movement. There are myriad Pilates classes in London for all abilities, including in gyms, health clubs and places that offer yoga or dance. While there is sometimes equipment involved depending on the type of class, it's possible to practice Pilates on a mat, and so it's easy to study at home. Also, because it's gentle (although not necessarily easy), pilates is suitable for children and older people, but you need to stick at it to get results. It's not aerobic so don't expect to sweat. Do check that the practitioner is qualified; the Pilates Foundation website – www.pilatesfoundation.com – is full of good advice and tips, as well as listing teachers and classes in London.

Bodywise

119 Roman Rd
E2
Bethnal Green

8981 6936 | www.bodywisehealth.org

This Buddhist charity has been operating for 20 years and offers yoga (including pregnancy and postnatal), Pilates, tai chi, and complementary therapies. Pilates classes are led by a specialist teacher and former dancer, who vouches for the power of this body conditioning method as it helped her recover from a back injury. A six-week course starts from £51 (paid in advance), while drop-in classes run every Saturday morning and cost between £7 and £9.

Kings Cross Studios

154 Caledonian Rd
N1
King's Cross St. Pancras

7837 7111 | www.kingscrossstudios.co.uk

Kings Cross Studios offers Pilates within a programme tailored specifically for the individual client. New clients get free initial consultations followed by a private session for a full assessment of their needs, progressing to further private or studio-based sessions. Programmes focus on ante and postnatal requirements, overall body conditioning, postural issues and muscular stress and tension. The studio's philosophy is that each client has a unique set of requirements, which are met while maintaining the highest standards of teaching. You'll need to book classes – private sessions cost £50 an hour and studio lessons cost £28 for 90 minutes. Courses are available in blocks of five or 10.

4 Mandeville Place
W1
⊖ Marylebone

Pilates off the Square
7935 8505 | www.pilatesoffthesquare.co.uk

Established in 1986, Pilates off the Square offers classes and private lessons for all ages and levels of fitness. Classes are tailored to fit the individual and are suitable for both body conditioning and rehabilitative exercise. There are two studios as well as changing facilities. 'Early bird' and lunchtime classes cost £20 for an hour, while a private session is £50. You can book a set of 10 90-minute studio sessions for £235, or 10 private sessions for £450.

Reiki

Reiki is a Japanese healing therapy that is not attached to any religious belief. Pronounced ray-kee (which means 'universal life force energy'), a practitioner will move their hands above parts of your body to rechannel blocked or negative energy. It's a balancing therapy for a multitude of conditions – physical, emotional and mental – and can also help sleep patterns and restore energy levels. The UK Reiki Federation lists practitioners around London, and many of these do home visits. See www.reikifed.co.uk.

68 Exmouth Market
EC1
⊖ Angel

Central for Health
7689 3717 | www.centralforhealth.co.uk

Central for Health is a complementary therapy clinic based in trendy Clerkenwell in the heart of the East End. Reiki is available from a choice of three fully qualified practitioners, each with different approaches so it's well worth reading their online profiles to decide which one is right for you. Reiki is said to help with a range of conditions including chronic fatigue, insomnia and multiple sclerosis among others, and aims to provide customers with a sense of physical relaxation as the healing energy does its work. Sessions start from around £25 for half an hour or £45 for an hour, depending on the practitioner.

10a Station Parade
NW2
⇌ ⊖ Willesden Green

CHAIM Centre
8452 0900 | www.chaimcentre.com

One of London's top centres for complementary health, the Centre for Complementary Health and Integrated Medicine offers reiki plus 30 other therapies, and gives advice on treatments in a friendly, professional way. Traditional reiki is used by qualified staff to treat problems such as backache and muscle pain, and costs from £25 for 30 minutes rising to £60 for 90 minutes. Sessions run on Monday, Tuesday and Friday afternoons and Tuesday and Thursday evenings (appointments are necessary). If you're interested in learning more about reiki, you can also attend workshop courses.

9 Lister House,
11-12 Wimpole St
W1
⊖ Bond Street

W1 Reiki
7323 6853 | www.w1reiki.co.uk

Recommended by *Tatler* magazine and fashionista Isabella Blow, among others, leading reiki professional Yu Chou provides safe, non-invasive treatment in a calm environment. Reiki therapy is offered to people of all ages, from expectant mothers to the elderly; even newborn babies can benefit. A full treatment lasts between 45 and 90 minutes, and a professional practitioner will discuss your requirements on your first visit before creating your personal plan. Prices start from £39 for a 45-minute therapy covering the essentials. Clients booking eight sessions or more get a discount, and there's a refund policy if you're not totally satisfied with the treatment.

Tai Chi

Tai chi is a unique activity that almost anyone can participate in and benefit from; its slow, measured movements stimulate the natural flow of chi (energy), which relieves stress, increases flexibility, aids balance, builds confidence and raises awareness. Because it's non-aerobic, tai chi is excellent for older people or people suffering from an illness or condition. In London it's almost as popular as yoga; classes can be taken in gyms and health clubs but, if you're serious, a centre or instructor devoted to the discipline is more likely to teach you the philosophy behind it. Both the Tai Chi Union for Great Britain (www.taichiunion.com) and Tai Chi Finder (www.taichifinder.co.uk) are excellent resources for finding out more about the discipline and the teachers and classes in your area.

144 Kensington Park Rd
W11
⊖ Notting Hill Gate

Andrew Popovic Oriental Healing
7193 1237 | www.chiworks.org

Andrew Popovic's Oriental Healing in Kensington Park Road runs weekly tai chi classes at the nearby Etheline Holder Hall. These friendly classes are small so students get individual attention, and are available to beginners and intermediates. A six-hour beginner's course runs every couple of months, over three consecutive weeks, and costs £60; private tuition costs £60 an hour. Retreats and workshops are also on offer.

Maybank Rd
E18
⊖ South Woodford

John Ding International Academy of Tai Chi Chuan
8502 9307 | www.taichiwl.demon.co.uk

This organisation was set up by John Ding, a master who claims his ancestry can be traced back to the creator of the Yang style of tai chi, Yang Lu Chan. Ding and other instructors teach classes for all abilities at the full-time centre in South Woodford and in Limehouse (8502 9307). Beginners' classes start from £10.

Various locations

London School of Tai Chi Chuan
8566 1677 | www.taichi.gn.apc.org

This school is part of an international body that has teachers in over 30 cities around the world. In London, its teaching locations are in Soho, Marylebone, and Golders Green, and the school also organises summer holiday courses abroad. For beginners, the 37-posture Yang-style short form is usually taught in 30 one-hour classes, in three separate sections over 10 weeks; each block costs £80 (alternatively, weekend intensive training is offered).

Various locations

The Tai Chi Centre
07944 880072 | www.thetaichicentre.co.uk

The Tai Chi Centre holds classes, provides one-to-one sessions and conducts workshops at a variety of venues in south London including Clapham, Colliers Wood and Tooting. Beginner courses usually last for six weeks and take place in the evening (£80). A Sunday class (15:00 to 19:30) is open to all (students who have missed an evening class can attend for free). Workshops are also held throughout the year in London and Scotland.

Yoga

Other options **Pilates** p.303

Like Pilates, yoga is very popular in London. It's unbeatable for improving posture and flexibility and has the added bonus of focusing the mind and releasing stress. These days you're just as likely to practice yoga in a light and airy urban space with underfloor heating as you are in a drafty church hall. There are a number of centres, gyms and health clubs that offer classes, so it's worth trying a few venues first as they vary in size. You may prefer the atmosphere of a large class to the intimacy of a smaller one, or some centres may not have enough (or too much) of a spiritual slant for you.

Astanga Yoga London

Dharma Shala,
92-94 Drummond St
NW1
Euston Square

07747 824178 | www.astangayogalondon.com
There are five instructors at this centre, all teaching the astanga system. Classes run Monday to Friday in the morning and evening (apart from Friday evening), plus Sunday morning. There are also weekend courses for beginners. A block of five classes costs £45; drop-in classes are £12. Programmes follow the Mysore method unless otherwise stated. Private tuition is also available.

Innergy Yoga Centre

Acorn Hall, Kensal Rd
W10
Ladbroke Grove

8968 1178 | www.innergy-yoga.com
This well-established centre differs from many of the new studios that have sprung up in that it offers substance over style. Situated in a church hall, Innergy may not be as swanky as others but it maintains a legion of faithful devotees. There are between three and five classes per day; lunchtime classes (12:30 to 13:30) from Mondays to Thursdays cost £8; other classes, workshops and evenings cost between £10 and £15.

Iyengar Yoga Institute

223a Randolph Ave
W9
Maida Vale

7624 3080 | www.iyi.org.uk
There are two large studios in this light, open space in an attractive part of London. Iyengar offers 10 classes a day here including beginners, over 59s, pregnancy, children (seven years and over), intermediate and remedial (or people with joint problems). The institute also offers regular events such as workshops and intensive weekends. Classes cost between £8 and £13 (less if you're a member, which costs £50 a year) and there are free taster sessions and classes for the unemployed.

The Shala

80 Caistor Mews
SW12
Balham

8674 7887 | www.sangamyoga.com
Formerly known as The Sangam Yoga Centre, the renamed Shala, which has moved from Battersea to Balham, offers astanga yoga to beginners and intermediates, as well as antenatal, postnatal, baby and Mysore self-practice classes. Single classes cost £11, a Mysore self-practice block of five classes costs £45, and the astanga beginners' course is £90 for a month. Massages, yoga holidays and workshops are also available.

Triyoga

6 Erskine Rd
NW3
Chalk Farm

7483 3344 | www.triyoga.co.uk
Triyoga offers affordable classes in an attractive building in a number of disciplines, including astanga and iyengar, as well as Pilates, pregnancy classes, massage, acupuncture and a kids' club. Classes run daily from 06:00 to 22:00 (Saturday from 08:00; Sunday from 09:00). There are two other branches: Neal's Yard (7483 3344) and Soho (7483 3344). All venues are shoe and mobile phone-free zones, which is a welcome relief for most London residents looking for an excuse to switch off and kick back.

Great things can come in small packages…

Perfectly proportioned to fit in your pocket, this marvellous mini guidebook makes sure you don't just get the holiday you paid for, but rather the one that you dreamed of.

New York Mini Visitors' Guide
Maximising your holiday, minimising your hand luggage

BIGGEST CHOICE OF BOOKS

MAGIC CHOICE OF BOOKS

EXCITING CHOICE OF *BOOKS*

 Phenomenal choice of books

UNBEATABLE CHOICE OF BOOKS IN FULL COLOUR

SPECIAL CHOICE of books

THRILLING CHOICE OF BOOKS

Encyclopedic choice **of Books**

 BALANCED CHOICE OF BOOKS

 FANTASTIC CHOICE OF BOOKS

BORDERS.

Shopping

Shopping

Code Breaker

We've included a London postcode by each entry in this section to help you locate the shops, markets and department stores. The map on p.458 shows which area of town each one covers.

Introduction

Home to Oxford Street, the world's longest shopping thoroughfare, and more than 40,000 stores, including the world's largest fashion store, Topshop, London offers quality and sheer quantity, as well as unmatched variety. Specialist outlets selling rare and bespoke items sit alongside hip, individual boutiques, department stores and scores of high-street shops.

Prices are broadly comparable to other cosmopolitan European cities; higher than Prague, but lower than Stockholm. Most prices include UK Sales Tax (VAT), currently at 17.5%. Exempt items include food, books, newspapers and magazines and children's clothes.

You can easily spend a fortune here if you choose, but London is still a fabulous place for bargain hunting if you know where to look. Most tourists and plenty of residents head straight to Oxford Street, home of high-street fashions, sports shops, bookshops, chemists, fast food joints and, increasingly, cheap shops selling imported clothing and warehouse overs. Nearby Tottenham Court Road is a hotspot for electrical goods and home furnishings, while Portobello Road in west London is lined with antiques and vintage clothing shops, and has a bustling market on weekends. Knightsbridge, Kensington and Mayfair are among the most upmarket areas: Knightsbridge's famous Harrods store is still a draw with visitors and moneyed locals alike. Like the celebrated bookshop Foyles, Harrods is more than 100 years old and a symbol of London's

What & Where to Buy – Quick Reference

Alcohol	313	Eyewear	330	Luggage & Leather	338	Shoes	345
Art	314	Flowers	330	Medicine	338	Souvenirs	347
Art & Craft Supplies	315	Food	331	Mobile Telephones	339	Sporting Goods	348
Baby Items	316	Gardens	333	Music, DVDs & Videos	339	Stationery	349
Beachwear	316	Gifts	333	Musical Instruments	341	Tailoring	350
Bicycles	316	Hardware & DIY	334	Outdoor Goods	342	Textiles	350
Books	317	Health Food	334	Party Accessories	343	Toys & Games	351
Clothes	319	Home Furnishings & Acc	335	Perfumes & Cosmetics	343	Wedding Items	352
Computers	328	Jewellery & Watches	336	Pets	345		
Electronics & Home App	328	Lingerie	337	Second-hand Items	345		

Clothing Sizes

Women's Clothing

Aust/NZ	8	10	12	14	16	18
Europe	36	38	40	42	44	46
Japan	5	7	9	11	13	15
UK	8	10	12	14	16	18
USA	6	8	10	12	14	16

Women's Shoes

Aust/NZ	5	6	7	8	9	10
Europe	35	36	37	38	39	40
France only	35	36	38	39	40	42
Japan	22	23	24	25	26	27
UK	3.5	4.5	5.5	6.5	7.5	8.5
USA	5	6	7	8	9	10

Men's Clothing

Aust/NZ	92	96	100	104	108	112
Europe	46	48	50	52	54	56
Japan	S	-	M	M	-	L
UK	35	36	37	38	39	40
USA	35	36	37	38	39	40

Men's Shoes

Aust/NZ	7	8	9	10	11	12
Europe	41	42	43	44.5	46	47
Japan	26	27	27.5	28	29	30
UK	7	8	9	10	11	12
USA	7.5	8.5	9.5	10.5	11.5	12.5

Measurements are approximate only; try before you buy

January Sales

The best time to pick up a bargain in expensive London – especially on the high street – is during the January sales. Many start as early as Boxing Day, mostly in big electrical and furniture stores, and last until the end of the month. Department stores such as Selfridges and Harvey Nichols offer some of the best deals, but sharpen your elbows as this is a fiercely competitive business.

continually flourishing shopping scene. Shopping malls and high-street clothing stores offer good value for money and have frequent sales; the massive Blue Water centre in Greenhithe, Kent is a popular out-of-town destination. Markets and second-hand shops are plentiful. Charity shops are the cheapest, while vintage clothing stores and exchanges sell quality discounted designer gear to savvy locals.

Borough Market is famed for its organic food, and there are many specialist wine shops in the capital (Londoners do like a tipple). Major supermarket chains such as Tesco and Sainsbury's seem to open new stores every few months, and the competition keeps prices healthy, if not exactly cheap.

Shopkeepers in London tend more towards disinterested than pushy, although staff in small boutiques are usually friendly. You're only likely to be given the hard sell in shops offering imported goods – often leather – where the staff may hail from cultures with different selling styles. Otherwise, London really just sells itself.

Online Shopping

If you order goods online from outside of the EU, it's classified as importing and should be declared to HM Customs & Excise, who will probably charge you for customs duty and VAT. Some online sales companies pay these duties for you, so check the small print. Exempt items include those costing less than £18 (excluding alcohol, tobacco and perfume) and personal gifs worth less than £36. DHL (www.dhl.co.uk) and Parcelforce (www.parcelforce.co.uk) provide full details. Many websites take payment in other currencies with certain overseas credit cards and will deliver internationally. Branded packaging means they may be subject to customs inspections at their destination.

Websites That Deliver

- **www.amazon.co.uk** – music, DVD and books
- **www.play.com** – music and DVD
- **www.abebooks.com** – books
- **www.mothercare.com** – mother and baby
- **www.boots.com** – pharmacy
- **www.cd-wow.co.uk** – music
- **www.jessops.com** – photography
- **www.figleaves.com** – lingerie
- **www.linksoflondon.com** – jewellery

Refunds & Exchanges

Shops must refund faulty goods as long as you have proof of purchase (preferably a receipt). Ask to speak to the manager if the shop assistant appears unwilling to honour this agreement. If you simply change your mind, or a garment doesn't fit, most companies will offer an exchange or a credit note and sometimes, a refund – if the item is in the same condition in which you bought it and hasn't been worn. Marks & Spencer allows you to exchange items bought from their overseas stores in London, but this isn't typical. You normally have 28 days after purchase to return goods, but this can differ. Most shops will have a sign by the till explaining their policy – if not, ask at the time of purchase.

Consumer Rights

It is against UK law for shops to have a 'no refund' policy. To make a complaint, contact the Consumer Direct advice service on 0845 4040506 or go to www.consumerdirect.gov.uk. Make sure you have the full details of the trader and purchase to hand. Consumer Direct is also handy for additional queries about your consumer rights.

Shipping

Residents rarely make big savings shipping large goods from London to overseas – it can be costly, and few purchases are significantly cheaper in the UK. Major stores including John Lewis, Selfridges and Harvey Nichols will ship large items internationally, although not to BFPO (British Forces) addresses, and Harrods will only ship items that are exclusive to the UK. Harrods, Selfridges and John Lewis use standard courier services for items too large to send by Royal Mail, and Harrods charges an extra 2% administration fee based on weight. Airmail is usually the only option, and does not include heavy items being carried up to an apartment from the street. It's cheaper to use a shipping company such as DHL (www.dhl.co.uk), CityLink (www.city-link.co.uk), Parcelforce (www.parcelforce.com) and www.wedelivertheworld.com – many stores will send to their UK addresses for forwarding to an international destination. Typically, shipping companies will only deal with items that have been pre-packed for international shipping – although www.sendit.com provides a list of online retailers who will ship to your country of choice.

How to Pay

Most London shops only accept pounds sterling, but a few take euros and list both currencies on their price tags. Cash, credit cards, debit cards and cheques are usually accepted, although small shops and market stalls may only take cash. Debit and credit cards are increasingly popular, especially as many supermarkets offer a cashback facility when you use your debit card to pay. The chip and PIN system is almost universal (customers type a personal identification number into a machine), but if you don't have a PIN, a few vendors will allow you to sign instead. Visa and Mastercard are the most commonly accepted debit/credit cards, but most outlets accept Visa Electron, Maestro (previously Switch), Solo, American Express and some less common cards such as Diners Club and JCB. Furniture store IKEA charges less if you pay by debit card than by credit card, but this is rare.

Bargaining

Other options **Markets** p.367

Unless goods are ex-display or damaged, it's not customary to haggle for prices in London shops, but markets, antiques shops and electrical goods stores are the exceptions. Electrical retailers may offer a discount if you pay in cash, and food markets often lower prices at the end of the day. In markets, it's acceptable to ask for a 'best price', particularly for second-hand goods. If you make an offer, start low, but not ridiculously low as they may not take you seriously. Make sure the stallholder knows you're a savvy resident, and try walking away to see if they lower their price. But bear in mind that shops in London are rarely short of business and are unlikely to be desperate for your custom.

312

Alcohol

Other options **Drinks** p.373

You can buy booze, as Londoners usually call it, at supermarkets, off-licences, corner shops and specialist wine stores all over London, as well as at all airports. Prices aren't desperately competitive compared with much of Europe, but there's a wide range of beers, spirits, wines and ciders available. Supermarket wines start at around £1.99 a bottle, but you'll need to spend around £5 for anything of a reasonable quality, and more for fine wines. Bottles of spirits are usually £10 or more, and a six pack of beer costs around £4. Off-licences have a better selection, but are more expensive, unless you take advantage of the nifty bulk offers that chains offer.

Berry Bros & Rudd

3 St James's St
SW1
⊖ Green Park

7396 9600 | *www.bbr.com*

This family run business has been going since 1698. You can spend thousands in Berry Bros & Rudd's ancient cellars, but if that sounds a bit daunting, you can still pick up a basic bottle of wine for around £5. Staff will put mixed cases and Christmas gift parcels together for you, and will also offer deals for corporate event organisers. There is also a factory outlet in Basingstoke, Hampshire if you're prepared to travel for a good deal.

Gerry's Wine and Spirits

24 Old Compton St
W1
⊖ Leicester Square

7734 2053

A Soho institution, this tiny off-licence on Old Compton Street is bulging with unusual wines and spirits including the super-strong, much-publicised absinthe (approach at your peril). Many Soho types head here for its great selection of international vodkas and tequilas at reasonable prices, as well as various obscure bitters. If you need a quirky, unusual present for a drinker, or a talking point at a boozy dinner party, this is a safe bet.

Oddbins Fine Wine Store

41a Farringdon St
EC4
⇌ ⊖ Farringdon

7236 7721 | *www.oddbins.com*

An offshoot of the Oddbins chain, the Fine Wine branches specialise in more exclusive products and offer a constantly changing range. Particularly good for Australian and New Zealand wines, it also stocks an interesting selection of port and unusual whiskys. Customers are typically wine devotees who know their stuff, rather than students looking for a cheap bottle of plonk for a party, but staff are generally happy to advise the less knowledgable.

Oddbins

395 The Strand
W2
⊖ Embankment

7240 3008 | *www.oddbins.com*

This is a major chain of off-licences with a good range, if unconventional opening hours in some of its smaller stores. Prices are competitive and there are frequent offers: deals have included 20% off when you buy six bottles of selected wines; buy two, save £10 on selected malt;, and reductions from £14.99 to £9.30 on clearance lines.

313

Pitfield Beer Shop
0845 8331492 | *www.pitfieldbeershop.co.uk*
Founded in 1980, Pitfield has produced some award-winning beers including Dark Star (now renamed Black Eagle). A few years ago it decided to ditch its shop in north London and go online, where you can shop for more than 500 types of beer. International brews are a speciality, and Pitfield also offers organic, vegan and vegetarian-friendly real ale. There's also a delivery option, or you can save money by picking up a bottle from one of its stalls at a farmers' market.

1 Bank End
SE1
⇌ ⊖ *London Bridge*

Vinopolis
0870 4444777 | *www.vinopolis.co.uk*
A bit of a tourist trap, albeit a classy one, Vinopolis is a huge wine centre near Borough Market with a museum and tasting rooms as well as a shop selling fine wines from around the globe. It also sells whisky, wine gadgets and gifts, and has regular events such as 'welcome to wine', a tasting session aimed at wine novices, cocktail and whisky masterclasses and seasonal wine tastings.

Art
Other options **Art & Craft Supplies** p.315, **Art Classes** p.235, **Art Galleries** p.194

The art scene in London is positively thriving, with British artists such as Damien Hirst and Tracey Emin attracting massive international attention in recent years. You can buy any type of art here, from traditional landscapes to conceptual sculptures. East London has long been a hot spot for artists, with Hoxton galleries such as the White Cube (p.190) holding public previews of work from high-profile artists including Jake and Dinos Chapman and Gilbert and George. In Fitzrovia, Windmill Street's many independent galleries showcase both established and up-and- coming artists and have regular previews. You can pick up a Warhol or Picasso at Westbrook Gallery (7580 1151), who also offer bespoke art for your home (7580 1151). The Frieze Art Fair in October (www.friezeartfair.com) has become an important date on any serious art buyer's

calendar, and the Affordable Art Fair in Battersea Park (www.affordableartfair.co.uk) caters for budget buyers with paintings from new artists, of which many are priced under or around £100. You can also shop online for contemporary fine-art at sites such as www.artlondon.com or www.londonart.co.uk. And if you're really strapped for cash, most homewear stores sell cheap prints of works of art to adorn your walls, while museum and art gallery shops offer prints of works in their exhibitions.

Art & Craft Supplies

Other options **Art Classes** p.235, **Art Galleries** p.194, **Art** p.314

26-28 Broadwick St
E1
⇌ ⊖ *Liverpool Street*

Cowling & Wilcox Ltd.

7734 9557 | www.cowlingandwilcox.com
This large established Soho shop is moving with the times and supplies an increasing amount of products to graphic designers alongside more traditional fine-art and craft materials. Especially good for paper and card, it aims to stock materials you wouldn't find in your average high-street store. Discounts are offered for bulk buys, and students get a reduction. There's a local delivery service should you get over-excited and buy more than you can carry.

12 Percy St
W1
⊖ *Tottenham Court Rd*

Daler Rowney

7636 8241
This is small, friendly store, formerly owned by the art material manufacturers Daler Rowney. It can be found in an arty area off Tottenham Court Road, near the many upmarket art galleries of Percy Street and Windmill Street. Oils, watercolours, acrylics, inks and pastels are available in abundance, as are easels, brushes and the original Daler Rowney range. Helpful advice is available from the friendly staff.

105 Great Russell St
WC1
⊖ *Tottenham Court Rd*

L Cornelissen & Son

7636 1045
This atmospheric, delightfully old-fashioned establishment dates back to 1855, and is chock full of jars of exotic art supplies including pigments and pastels. You can buy your pigments by the bag, with 50g costing you around £5. The store claims to have more than 20,000 items in stock, so it's a good bet for serious artists, and, as you might expect, the staff know their stuff.

Various locations

London Graphic Centre

www.londongraphics.co.uk
With three branches in London, London Graphic Centre is one of the major art suppliers in the city. Its flagship Covent Garden store boasts over 20,000 products and claims to be the largest independent art store in Europe. It's a fantastic place to shop for good buys in card and paper, cutting tools, paints and specialist materials for arts such as screen and block printing. Its website lists art colleges, artist sites and links to other useful resources.

Various locations

Paperchase

www.paperchase.co.uk
This funky, fashionable chain does a nice line in art supplies as well as its trademark greetings cards, gifts and Christmas decorations. The Tottenham Court Road branch has an entire floor dedicated to paper, cards, embellishments and more. Even if you're not an artist, Paperchase's stylish printed paper is likely to tempt you to get out the glue. Prices are reasonable, with flocked paper starting at £3, and moulding kits for £4.50.

Baby Items
Other options **Kids Clothing** p.325

Most new mums' first stop is Mothercare, which has 24 stores across London and is a great all-round store for baby basics – it sells everything from nappies and food to cots and toys. Prices are not the cheapest in the market (similar items can be found for less at www.kiddicare.com) but they are competitive. It also has good in-store feeding and changing facilities. John Lewis (p.358) doesn't have its own baby brand, but stocks a range of competitively priced big brands including Mamas and Papas and Baby Bjorn, and you can rely on staff for objective advice. Many well-off young parents prefer selective boutiques, and up-and-coming areas are increasingly peppered with high-end kids' stores such as Soup Dragon in Crouch End (see Kids Clothing, p.326) and JoJo Maman Bébé in Clapham (www.jojomamanbebe.co.uk). Try supermarket chain Sainsbury's (p.359) for an excellent range of foods at competitive prices, including Heinz baby food, Hipp Organics and Plum Baby Superfood. Most other chemists and supermarket chains stock baby food and milk.

Beachwear
Other options **Sporting Goods** p.348, **Clothes** p.319

High-street shops and department stores usually only stock beachwear between May and September, which perhaps isn't surprising given London's far-from-tropical climate. Sports shops and specialist surf shops stock and display them all-year round – try Notting Hill's London Beach Store (7243 2772), which also stocks kites, eyewear and more. The popular, slightly upscale Sweaty Betty (www.sweatybetty.com) has 12 London shops selling beach and fitness clothing, with bikinis starting at around £25. Quiksilver (www.quiksilver.com) is another well-known surf brand with a great selection of beachwear and wetsuits for both men and women. The best prices are found in high-street stores such as Next (p.320), Topshop (p.321), Marks & Spencer (p.359), and particularly New Look (p.320) and H&M (p.319), where you can usually pick up a bikini for less than £10. Try the autumn sales in September and October for real bargains. Department stores such as Selfridges (p.358) also have a good range.

Bicycles

51 Gray's Inn Rd
EC1
⊖ *Chancery Lane*

Condor Cycles
7269 6820 | *www.condorcycles.com*
Condor has a great workshop, its own range of road bikes and fields teams in numerous biking competitions. Staff are knowledgeable, and prices are reasonable; its website offers gift ideas for less than £10. There's a good range of clothing, including the excellent label Assos. In fact, Condor is one of the few retailers in London to stock the Assos women's range.

Brody House,
Strype St
E1
⊖ *Aldgate*

Cycle Surgery
7373 3088 | *www.cyclesurgery.com*
This excellent chain has six branches in London and stocks mountain bikes, road bikes, clothing and accessories at competitive prices. Cycle Surgery's efficient maintenance is especially good value, and staff offer sound advice. There are also plenty of workshop tools on sale should you be up to the job yourself. Check its website for details of clearance sales; older models are sometimes on offer for £100 less than the original price. The store also sells fully serviced ex-demonstration bikes at good prices, and has a decent selection of kids' bikes.

Various locations

Evans Cycles

www.evanscycles.com

With branches all over the city, Evans is London's largest chain of bike stores. Shops can get very busy, meaning staff don't always have the time to give you thorough service. Serious bikers tend to steer clear of these stores, leaving its relatively steep prices and crowded shopfloors to the less initiated. That said, there's a good range of bikes and accessories available, and it does have good sales. Many branches offer repairs and services.

123 Essex Rd
N1
⊖ *Angel*

Mosquito Bikes

7226 8765 | www.mosquito-bikes.co.uk

Specialising in speedy bikes for serious enthusiasts, Mosquito offers a top range of Italian bikes and very personal customer service. Staff are happy to custom make your bike and are just as helpful to small spenders as they are to big ones. You can book a personal bike fitting for £90, which will be refunded if you spend more than £2,000 (you get £40 off if you buy a bike costing more than £1,000).

52-54 Tooley St
SE1
⇄ ⊖ *London Bridge*

On Your Bike

7378 6669 | www.onyourbike.com

This London branch of the small family owned chain claims to be the largest bike shop in Europe. Customers rave about the good, honest sales staff who offer great service and reliable repairs. The range of bikes, clothing, and accessories is deservedly popular and among the best in the capital. Brands stocked include Trek, Mezzo, Marin, Brompton and Cannondale, and there is the occasional freebie for cyclists during special in-store promotions.

Books

Other options **Second-Hand Items** p.345, **Libraries** p.262

4 Blenheim Crescent
W11
⊖ *Ladbroke Grove*

Books For Cooks

7221 1992

A charming independent bookshop aimed at budding chefs, Books For Cooks was founded by cookery enthusiast Heidi Lascelles in 1983 with the aim of stocking as many different cookbooks as she could find. As a result, the shop has an excellent selection, and it even smells delicious – there's a kitchen at the back that serves different dishes each day that customers can taste for a reasonable price. If you just want to sit, read and take in the atmosphere, there's a well-worn and comfy sofa.

203-207 Oxford St
W1
⊖ *Oxford Circus*

Borders

7292 1600 | www.bordersstores.com

The US book chain is doing a storming trade in central London, with several floors covering all popular subjects in its massive store near Oxford Circus tube. It also sells CDs and magazines, and hosts free gigs and book signings. Perhaps best of all, you can escape the West End hustle and sit and read in its cafe to your heart's content; you could fill several hours here easily.

179 Shaftesbury Ave
WC2
**⊖ Tottenham
Court Rd**

Forbidden Planet

7420 3666 | *www.forbiddenplanet.com*
A one-stop shop for science-fiction geeks and an enjoyable browse for anyone remotely interested in cult books, comics, film and television, the recently expanded Forbidden Planet has a spectacular selection of graphic novels, sci-fi and fantasy books and DVDs. It also sells collectables related to comics, movies and TV shows, such as *The Lord Of The Rings* figurines. There's also regular signings and special events that attract salivating fans.

**113-119 Charing
Cross Rd**
WC2
**⊖ Tottenham
Court Rd**

Foyles

7437 5660 | *www.foyles.co.uk*
Foyles is probably London's most famous book store, and has supplied generations of Londoners since opening in 1906. The building is huge, and the selection almost overwhelming. Text books of all kinds can be found here, as well as fiction and specialist areas including gay & lesbian, alongside an impressive collection of printed music. Its ordering service is excellent and vows to supply any book in print. There's a also a jazz shop and cafe on the first floor.

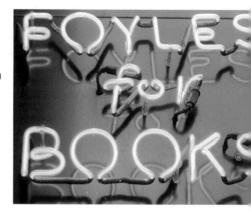

187 Piccadilly
W1
⊖ Piccadilly Circus

Hatchards

7439 9921 | *www.hatchards.co.uk*
This is an old-fashioned, high-end bookshop with five floors of literature and frequent book signings from big names, as well as seasonal customer events including prize draws and author appearances. It sells a wide range of signed first editions, making this a good spot for unusual presents; a recent £50 buy was the limited edition, signed and slipcased version of Lauren Bacall's *By Myself And Then Some*. Excellent sections include art, architecture, biography and fiction.

32 The Broadway
N8
⇌ ⊖ Finsbury Park

Prospero's Books

8348 8900
This small independent store, an offshoot of Muswell Hill Bookshop (8444 7588), is hot on food and drink. Prospero's also stocks a good line in local authors, local history and science, and like many small bookshops offers an atmospheric, relaxed alternative to large chain stores. Mobile phones must be switched off, meaning this has the feel of a good old-fashioned bookshop rather than a grab-your-money enterprise.

12-14 Long Acre
WC2
⊖ Leicester Square

Stanfords

7836 1321 | *www.stanfords.co.uk*
Well-established bookshop specialising in travel books and maps, with an increasing section of CD-Rom maps. This is the place to go if you need a detailed road map for somewhere obscure – or a Christmas present for that difficult male relative. Look out for three-for-two offers on selected maps and books. Stanfords also hosts events such as the Voluntary Services Organisation's recruitment drives.

Various locations ◄

Waterstone's

www.waterstones.com

One of the UK's largest and most respected book chains, Waterstone's stocks most categories you can think of and often has three-for-two offers on new titles. Consequently, it's popular with travellers searching for airport reads, and cost-savvy Christmas shoppers. Sections include crime, education, poetry and drama, sport, and health and wellbeing. Its stores also stock a good range of stylish greetings cards, and hold regular book signings from established and up-and-coming authors and celebrity writers: Courtney Love popped up at its Piccadilly store to promote her diaries.

Clothes

Other options **Tailoring** p.350, **Sporting Goods** p.348, **Shoes** p.345, **Lingerie** p.337, **Beachwear** p.316

High Street

481-483 Oxford St ◄
W1
⊖ Oxford Circus

H&M

7493 8557 | www.hm.com

H&M's motto is to bring its army of fans 'fashion and quality at the best price'. And with Viktor & Rolf joining Karl Lagerfeld and Stella McCartney in creating a line for this high-street chain you can't argue with its fashion credentials. The McCartney range almost caused a riot when stock sold out in a matter of hours. Detractors say the H and M stands for 'hit and miss' and it's true that this two-floored flagship store on the corner of Oxford Street and Regent Street can be muddled, but if you want to follow the latest (men's, women's and kid's) trends and not spend a fortune, this is where to do it.

Various locations ◄

Karen Millen

0870 1601830 | www.karenmillen.com

A cut above many of its high-street neighbours, Karen Millen offers women striking designs, with fitted skirts and tops, well-tailored suits, lush fabric and beautiful evening-wear. Heavy, fine knits are a speciality. It's always a pleasant browse, although you'd be pushed to find anything here much less than £50, except in its tempting post-Christmas sales. Also owned by the same company is the cheaper, slightly younger-skewed Oasis (www.oasis-stores.com) and Coast (www.coast-stores.co.uk), which focuses on special occasion wear, and is particularly useful for off-the-peg bridesmaid dresses.

Various locations ◄

Mango

7434 3694 | www.mango.com

The Spanish women and kids' chain has proved to be a big hit in London, with several branches popping up over the city. Prices tend to be slightly higher than in Spain, but still often good value for colourful clobber. There's also a branch in Covent Garden, but the Oxford Street store is, perhaps surprisingly, more spacious and a calmer place to browse and try on clothes without having to deal with long queues.

216 Oxford St ◄
W1
⊖ Oxford Circus

Miss Selfridge

7927 0188 | www.missselfridge.co.uk

Miss Selfridge is where teenage girls flock for their fashion coming-of-age. This high-street heavy has stores throughout the city, supplying the fashion conscious with every style seen trotting down the catwalk – all downsized and made affordable (tops and trousers hover around the £30 mark, while little else is more than £50). This Oxford Street branch is directly linked to Topshop, and can become a bit of a pushy thoroughfare to its oversized Arcadia sister. As well as selling clothing, jewellery and accessories, Miss Selfridge also offers vintage Biba pieces and worn-in leather boots. Be warned that it's not just the customer base that's prepubescent – sizes are a bit on the wee side too.

Various locations

Next
0844 8448333 | *www.next.co.uk*
This dependable, if not exactly fashionable, high-street chain sells clothes and accessories for men, women, children and babies, and also has an extensive shoe department and homewares section. Its popularity may have dipped in recent years, but its bumper sales remain incredibly popular and competitive affairs, where people queue overnight for big discounts. For some inexplicable reason Next also has a swimwear sale whatever the season.

Various locations

New Look
0500 454094 | *www.newlook.co.uk*
Cheap, cheerful and – if you shop carefully – fashionable, New Look is a godsend for trendy young women on a budget. It's quick to pick up on catwalk trends, and has a fast turnover of clothing such as funky t-shirts (from around £5) and dresses (from £20). There are also some great buys to be had in the shoe section, where prices can be as low as £5. Friday nights and Saturdays get very busy with girls looking for pretty, glam party threads.

King's Mall, King St
W6
⊖ *Hammersmith*

Primark
8748 7119 | *www.primark.co.uk*
Rock-bottom bargain buys used to be an embarrassment in some London circles, but a £12 Primark jacket is now a badge of pride for many – especially if someone mistakes it for a designer label. The chain used to only run from out-of-town locations, but an Oxford Street branch opened in April 2007. Men, women and children are catered for, but don't expect a relaxing shopping experience, more of a frenzied one. Most women, at least, will reason that bargains like these are worth fighting for.

Various locations

Reiss
7323 6300 | *www.reiss.co.uk*
Seen as slightly more grown up than some of its high-street peers, Reiss follows catwalk trends to produce high-quality fashion for men and women. Shoes and accessories (including leather bags and luggage) are also available, while its suits, knitwear and coats are highly recommended. Prices are reasonable given the quality of the clothes and staff are more friendly and helpful than in some other London chains.

222 Oxford St
W1
⊖ *Oxford Circus*

Topman
0845 1214519 | *www.topman.com*
Remembering its days of 1980s grey flecked suits, some British men still dismiss Topman, but they're missing out. This is now the best place on the high street for stylish men's t-shirts; think edgy graphic patterns that wouldn't look out of place in a designer store at four times the price. Topman is also hot on jeans and accessories, and undercuts many a high-street rival on items such as flip-flops. There is men's jewellery for the brave, too. This two-levelled flagship store on Oxford Street is huge and is packed at weekends.

216 Oxford St
W1
Oxford Circus

Topshop
0845 1214519 | www.topshop.com

Massively popular, and literally massive, this women's clothing store has a huge range of fashionable threads, from glam ranges to vintage valuables – a veritable heaven for the fashion weary and the style wired. There are many concessions here including Faith shoes and Calvin Klein underwear. The quality is excellent, especially considering the prices (between £30 and £40 for jeans) and there's a decent vintage section, although this – like the accessories floor – is on the pricey side for the high street. If you're not sure what suits you, Topshop offers a style advice service, and if it all gets too much, there's a cafe where you can take a break.

84-86 Regent St
W1
Piccadilly Circus

Uniqlo
7434 9688 | www.uniqlo.co.uk

Regarded as the Japanese equivalent of Marks & Spencer, Uniqlo offers basic casual threads for men and women at extremely competitive prices. Designs are simple, although there are a few more flourishes in its range than when the store(s) first opened to mixed reviews a years ago. This flagship Regent Street branch sets the tone; big, plain space full of primary coloured clothing that will rarely cost more than £30. It's particularly good for t-shirts, jumpers and essentials including socks.

20 The Market
WC2
Covent Garden

Whistles
7487 4484 | www.whistles.co.uk

This is a popular upscale bohemian-led women's chain, favoured by ladies who like to be swathed in beautiful flowing garments and opulent fabrics. It's more expensive than many stores – £100 or so for trousers – but its elegant designs are unique and long lasting. Whistles recently launched a limited edition range called Collectables – only 100 are made of each design – which is available in its King's Road, Westbourne Grove and St Christopher's Place branches, as well as in Selfridges (you'll find Whistles gear in some department stores too).

Various locations

Zara
www.zara.com

Overtaking Hennes & Mauritz (H&M) as Europe's biggest fashion retailer, Zara, with large stores on both Regent Street and Oxford Street, has not left London off its world domination map. Its rails boast wide ranges for women, men and children, with cosmetics also on offer. Zara, though equally reasonably priced and up-to-the-minute as its closest competitors, is slightly more conservative; while Topshop designs shout 'See me, I'm so hot right now!', Zara's clothes are more likely to whisper office chic and understated elegance.

Designer

205-206 Sloane St
SW1
Knightsbridge

Alberta Ferretti
7235 2349 | www.albertaferretti.com

This classy store in the heart of London's upmarket Knightsbridge showcases the Italian designer's pretty creations over two floors. She's recently expanded her traditionally girly, bohemian line, to enter more sophisticated retro territory. A tailored jacket could set you back a cool £500, so it's certainly not cheap, but if you're dressing for a big occasion and are aiming to impress, Alberta Ferretti should do the job. Accessories are also available.

321

53-55 New Bond St
W1
⊖ *Bond Street*

Miu Miu

7409 0900 | *www.miumiu.com*

Favoured by upmarket, fashionable Londoners, Miu Miu is an offshoot of famous Italian designer Prada and stocks sleek designs for women in sumptuous fabrics and bold colours, in an enjoyably extravagant setting. There's an alteration service available so you can get the perfect fit, and you can ship overseas (many customers are jet-setting types, as you'd imagine). Its handbags and shoes are equally world-renowned, with prices often running well into the hundreds.

17-18 Old Bond St
W1
⊖ *Bond Street*

Prada

7647 5000 | *www.prada.com*

Showcasing the Italian designer's trademark sleek, dark designs with a modern edge, this is a suitably luxurious yet minimally decorated store favoured by wealthy young trendies and numerous famous showbusiness folk. The funky Prada Sport label is available here, as are menswear, shoes and bags. Price-wise, it's exclusive stuff: a lovely Prada deerskin handbag will set you back somewhere in the region of £700. There's another branch on Sloane Street (7235 0008).

30 Bruton St
W1
⊖ *Green Park*

Stella McCartney

7518 3100 | *www.stellamccartney.com*

The daughter of Beatle Paul McCartney, Stella has built up a strong reputation as an excellent eccentric British designer and is a favourite with her fellow celebrities who are happy to splash out £100s for her feminine designs and animal-friendly fabrics (no leather or fur is used in her designs). McCartney's pal Kate Moss models in the designer's adverts and other celebs seen at Stella events include Gwyneth Paltrow and burlesque model Dita Von Teese.

44 Conduit St
W1
⊖ *Oxford Circus*

Vivienne Westwood

7439 1109 | *www.viviennewestwood.com*

The punk pioneer is still churning out challenging designs, most of which feature in bias-cut dresses and tartan fabrics. This flagship store stocks diffusion labels Red Label and Anglomania as well as the main women's label, Gold Label and menswear. Westwood also does eyewear, bags, shoes, jewellery and perfume. There's another store in Davies Street (7629 3757), and Westwood stock in department stores Liberty, Selfridges, Harrods as well as World's End on King's Road (7352 6551). As for prices? Well if you have to ask how much it costs, you probably can't afford it.

Boutique

9 Nelson Rd
SE10

Joy

8293 7979

If you're looking for that quirky item that everyone will comment upon, men's and women's boutique Joy is a good bet. And it's better value than many of its kind – a tweed asymmetrical skirt goes for around £55, for example, and a men's t-shirt around £25. Look upstairs for a mouthwatering selection of party dresses and ball gowns. Staff are helpful and friendly and the late opening hours suit full-time workers.

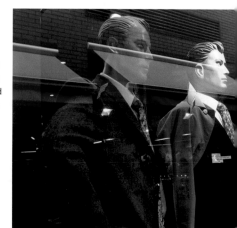

65 Monmouth St
WC2
⊖ **Covent Garden**

Koh Samui
7240 4280

This light and airy little boutique stocks a choice range of designer labels (including Chloé, Balenciaga and Dries Van Noten), and has helpful, unpretentious staff. Koh Samui's loyal customers love this place for its careful selection of unusual designer gear; head here if you're looking to splash out on an eye-catching dress for a wedding that (hopefully) no-one else will be wearing. It also stocks beautiful jewellery. Look out for designer bargains during its sales.

176 Upper St
N1
⊖ **Angel**

Labour of Love
7354 9333

Labour of Love harks back to Upper Street's days as a boutique-led enclave before the chain stores moved in. Head here for a carefully selected range of quirky clothing from some lesser-known, up-and-coming designers, and you'll be surprised by the pleasing emphasis on quality cuts and stylish accessories. It helps that this is also a welcoming environment in which to shop. It's on the pricey side (most things are around £100 or more), but it's worth it if you're prepared to pay for something unusual, and you might snap up a half-price bargain in its sale.

105 Great Eastern St
EC2
⇌ ⊖ **Old Street**

Wink
7608 2323

The essence of Hoxton hip, this attractive little shop near Old Street tube is crammed full of funky new designs and accessories for both men and women. You'll find established names such as Conscious Earthwear, Hysteric Glamour and Maharishi here, alongside up-and-coming designers and Wink's own distinctive label. This is a great place to find an unusual t-shirt or a colourful print dress, and Wink also offers accessories and cool clothes for designer kiddies.

Urban

121-123 Long Acre
WC2
⊖ **Covent Garden**

All Saints
7836 0801 | *www.allsaints.co.uk*

One of the more urban fashion chains in London, All Saints does a good line in funky designs for both men and women, recently with a rocky edge; think sprayed knitwear, fatigued t-shirts and tops emblazoned with dramatic gothic crosses. T-shirts start at around £40. It has seven stores around London, and the label is also stocked in department stores Harrods and House of Fraser. Check its website for details of upcoming sample sales.

17 Shorts Gardens
WC2
⊖ **Covent Garden**

Boxfresh
7240 4742 | *www.boxfresh.co.uk*

Baggy jeans and t-shirts typify London label Boxfresh, which stocks hip gear for both sexes from £25. These urban designs, in mostly muted colours, aren't the kind that stop traffic, but they do have a relaxed sense of cool. Its new footwear collection recently launched at this Covent Garden store, which opened in 1992 and has been followed by a rash of streetwear stores in the Seven Dials area since.

41 Kensington High St
W8
⊖ **High Street Kensington**

Slick Willies
7225 0004

While some skate shop staff seem to take pride in having attitude, Slick Willies adopts the more sensible approach of being friendly and helpful. The shop is near Hyde Park, the second home of many in-line skaters, and duly stocks a good range

323

of gear and street clothing along with skating equipment. If you can't wait to show off your new threads, you can hire skates here for £10 per day, and nip off to Hyde Park for the afternoon.

200 Oxford St
W1
🚇 *Oxford Circus*

Urban Outfitters

7907 0800 | *www.urbanoutfitters.co.uk*

The hip clothing and accessories store may not be as cheap in London as it is back in the US, but it's still an enjoyable place to browse, with its emphasis on stylish spaces and luxurious layouts. Both sexes are well served with edgy designer gear from the likes of Fornarina, Diesel and Nike, and the homeware and gifts sections are full of kitsch fripperies begging to be taken home. There are also large branches in Covent Garden (7759 6390) and High Street Kensington (7761 1001).

Vintage

12 Camden Passage
N1
🚇 *Angel*

Annie's Vintage Clothes

7359 0796

Head down this cobbled backstreet off Upper Street to Annie's if you're after an unusual vintage frock for a big night out, or even your wedding day. There's a glittering selection of well-chosen garments from the 30s onwards, many of which surpass current day designs in terms of quality and sheer glamour. You may also be able to find a vintage handbag to match in its excellent selection of accessories. Fashion designers have been known to pop by in search of striking one-offs.

21 Goodge St
W1
🚇 *Goodge Street*

Bang Bang

7631 4191

A treasure trove for fans of rare vintage pieces, Bang Bang clutters its shelves with Prada shoes and handbags and its rails with a mix of designer and classy high-street pieces. It only sources individual and striking stock (bear this is mind when you're trying to flog back your rejects). Embroidered jackets, corsets and leopard print often feature. Prices are pretty reasonable, from £5 to £10 for high-street stuff, and £50 to £100 for designer, and the careful selection process does pay off.

6 Monmouth St
WC2
🚇 *Covent Garden*

Pop Boutique

7497 5262 | *www.pop-boutique.com*

This kitsch retro second-hand store serves students well with its 60s and 70s bulk buy-ins, including logo t-shirts, velvet and leather jackets, tracksuit tops and jeans from all eras. The prices are appealing too, and more in line with markets such as Camden than most Covent Garden outlets. Pop does its own brand of retro clothing, and is run by The Vintage Clothing Company, who supply vintage gear for women's high-street chain Topshop and other outlets throughout the UK.

87 Lower Marsh
SE1
🚆 🚇 *Waterloo*

Radio Days

7928 0800

One of those lovely shops that transports you back in time, Radio Days is packed with odds and ends from the 40s, 50s and 60s as well as the odd 1920s piece. Good buys include men's silk dressing gowns and beaded dresses from around £20. You can also pick up intriguing vintage magazines from the 20s through to the 80s as well as vintage tableware and, of course, the titular radios.

98 Portland Rd
W11
⊖ **Holland Park**

Virginia
7727 9908
Lace, feathers and pretty dresses decorate this exclusive boutique that specialises in pre 50s designs. Prices often run into the hundreds – sometimes even thousands – but if you can afford it, a splurge at Virginia does feel like a treat, especially as pieces are usually in amazing condition. You might want to dress up for a trip to Virginia though; it can be a bit daunting walking into this immaculate, extravagant place dressed in scruffy jeans and a t-shirt.

Fetish & Alternative

153 King's Rd
SW3
⊖ **South Kensington**

Ad hoc
7376 8829
Soho sadly lost its Ad hoc store a few years back, but there's a survivor on the King's Road, and lots of fun it is too. This jumbled, eclectic and edgy shop is full of quirky delights and is a great place for goths, fancy dressers and fetish fans alike. Feather boas, masks and wigs mingle among PVC dresses and provocative t-shirts. Prices are lower than many specialist shops, so it's a good bet for a bargain.

131 King's Cross Rd
WC1
⇌ ⊖ **King's Cross St. Pancras**

Breathless
7278 1666
One of London's friendlier fetish shops, this recently relocated and enlarged store has divine designs for men and women. Expect to find red and black latex corsets, killer heels and high-waisted rubber breeches for men. Uniforms are a feature, and there's a made-to-measure service. Staff are happy to give you advice, and while the location is quite central, it's not in the middle of a shopping district, so it's less likely to attract curious tourists and passers-by. So you can try on those rubber breeches without the fear of prying eyes.

41 Old Compton St
W1
⊖ **Leicester Square**

Paradiso
7287 2487
In a prime position on the corner of London's famously gay Old Compton Street, Paradiso stocks quality fetish gear for both sexes – and anyone in between. Rubber, leather and PVC are the standard fabrics for catsuits, trousers, t-shirts, skirts, shorts and dresses, although you can pick up an ornate satin basque for a pretty penny. Elaborate jewellery designs and sex toys also feature. Be warned that female staff tend towards the suitably haughty.

Kids Clothing

Various locations

Baby GAP
www.gap.com
Kids up to the age of 4 are catered for in Baby Gap, with trousers from around £10 and tees from £6, dresses from £10 and babygros from £5. The clothes are essentially mini versions of adult GAP designs; t-shirts come in lots of bright colours and dresses are frequently pink. Like GAP Kids, which offers similar, slightly more expensive clothing for older children, this is a good place for well-made basics. Stores are up to usual GAP standards, bright and clean though sometimes difficult to navigate with a buggy. Staff are efficient and helpful.

Various locations

Boots

www.boots.com

Like Mothercare, the pharmacy chain Boots does trendy, hardwearing clothes for babies and toddlers at excellent prices. babygros cost around £10 for a pack of three, with tracksuits at £14 and tees at around £4, while dresses and trousers start at the £8 mark. Not all Boots stores stock baby clothes though, so it's best to call up your local branch to check first (shops are usually very busy) and grab a helpful member of staff if you get lost.

Various locations

Mothercare

www.mothercare.com

An excellent all-round chain for kids' clothes, with prices starting at £8 to £10 for trousers and jeans, £5 to £10 for t-shirts, jumpers and cardigans, £8 for dresses and £10 for three pre-packed babygros. Stores have a huge range of sizes and styles that are as practical as they are fashionable. Look out for its adorable mini combats, distressed jeans, pretty dresses and funky slogan tees. Staff are friendly and stores are bright and clean. All the shops have a changing and feeding area which you can use even if you're not making a purchase.

50 East Dulwich Rd
SE22
⇌ Peckham Rye

Raisin

7635 9377

If your little darling deserves nothing but the best, head for Raisin and its range of boutique kids' clothes. Trousers cost around £30, while cashmere jumpers start at £40. Raisin typically stocks only one of each size, which gives it an extra feeling of exclusivity, although it may order or repeat stock. As a result, 'yummy mummies' flock here and compete to buy the coolest clothes for little Jasmine and Joshua.

27 Topsfield Parade
N8
⇌ Hornsey

Soup Dragon

8348 0224

Soup Dragon aims to provide beautiful and unusual clothes that you won't find on the high street, and it usually delivers. Both parents and indulgent gift-givers will find it hard to leave empty-handed, and will be tempted by slogan tees (from £15) and trendy outfits in a wide variety of colours and sizes. Colourful hoodies start at around £14, and there's funky knitwear for boys and girls at around £15. It also does fancy dress outfits for special occasions. There's another branch in East Dulwich (8693 5575).

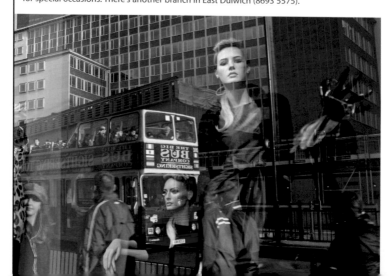

Unusual Sizes

Various locations

Evans
www.evans.ltd.uk
Probably Britain's best-known larger women's chain, Evans supplies women in sizes 16 to 32 with fashionable high-street clothing at high-street prices. It also has petite and tall ranges, and offers a good selection of lingerie (bras go up to 50H) and shoes. Well-trained staff are on hand with advice about what suits you best and you can book a personal style consultant in many stores (check its website for more details).

Various locations

High & Mighty
www.highandmighty.co.uk
Big and tall men can stride confidently through the doorway of High & Mighty, which has been specialising in unusual sizes since 1956. It has a decent range of suits as well as casual shirts and t-shirts from quality brands including Ben Sherman, Umbro, Cottonfield and Animal in sizes L, XL and XXL. Prices are reasonable – t-shirts start from £20. Its online store has a range from Polo by Ralph Lauren.

21-25 Chiltern St
W1
⊖ Baker Street

Long Tall Sally
7487 3370 | www.longtallsally.com
Long Tall Sally is the UK's leading taller women's brand. The stores were launched in 1975 by Judy Rich, who persuaded manufacturers to start making fashionable clothes longer, and in special designs for her stores. Shop here for classic, flattering designs for the taller woman, where skirts and trousers start at £35. Long Tall Sally also has a concession in House of Fraser (p.358).

Accessories

Various locations

Accessorize
www.monsoon.co.uk/icat/accessorize
This rather marvellous chain store stocks tempting accessories in small branches throughout central London. Keeping a close eye on current trends, it is packed floor-to-ceiling with glittery scarves, shiny handbags and sparkling rings, as well as seasonal favourites such as sunglasses and woolly hats. Prices aren't bad, with clutch bags from £15, and it has a section for glamorous little girls. Check out its Trocadero store (7287 8673) for the real bargains; it seems to have a permanent sale.

117 Regent's Park Rd
NW1
⊖ Chalk Farm

Beatrix Ong
7449 0480
This is the former Jimmy Choo designer's flagship store, which is frequented by many Primrose Hill celebs (mostly British actresses with plenty of time to rest – and lust after handbags). If you've got a spare few hundred pounds, the suede and leather bags are gorgeous, and regularly feature in the pages of upmarket fashion magazines. Metallics such as bronze and gold have featured heavily in Beatrix Ong designs lately.

Various locations

Claire's Accessories
www.clairesaccessories.net
Undercutting Accessorize, this international chain does a swift trade in bags, hats, hair clips and hen night paraphernalia aimed at teens, tweens and the young at heart. Many older women take advantage of its funky designs and rock-bottom prices (purses and phone holders cost just a few pounds). It holds regular sales, and you can also get your ears pierced here.

327

3 Ellis St
SW1
⊖ **Sloane Square**

Lulu Guinness

7823 4828 | www.luluguinness.com

Make like a real glamour puss and pop into this chic store that stocks the designer's trademark 50s inspired handbags, as well as kitsch powder compacts, umbrellas, scarves and fragrance. Lulu Guinness claims to blend 'schoolgirl, vamp, and granny' in her extravagant, often humorous designs, some of which have ended up in museums. Floral designs mix with studs and stripes for that quirky, post-modern, anything-goes look. Most handbag prices run into the hundreds of pounds.

31 Monmouth St
WC2
⊖ **Covent Garden**

Orla Kiely

7240 4022 | www.orlakiely.com

Every London girl worth her fashion salt knows the name Orla Kiely, and the experienced designer is still turning out bold, colourful designs for handbags, hats and accessories as well as clothing. Prices start from £100. You'll find Orla Kiely stock in many other stores, but this shop on Monmouth Street has the widest selection and a luxurious feel. Typical customers are wealthy women and style-conscious shoppers in search of a one-off treat.

Computers

Other options **Electronics & Home Appliances**

London moves with the times when it comes to computers and tends to launch new products roughly in line with the US. Prices in the capital can be as much as 20% more than in the US, although they're comparable with Asia. Most large high streets have both independent computer stores and major retailers. Head for Tottenham Court Road for dozens of shops selling PCs and Macs, such as MicroAnvika (7467 6000), where notebooks start from £430, Macs from £680 and desktop computers from £300. Sony (www.sony.co.uk) and Apple (www.apple.com/ukstore) both have their own brand stores; Apple's new outlet on Regent Street is very well stocked (7153 9000). Most major retailers such as PC World (www.pcworld.co.uk) and Dixons (www.dixons.co.uk), who have stores throughout London, sell a variety of brands – desktop computers at PC World start from £230, laptops from £350. Computer fairs are a great place for good deals (check www.britishcomputerfairs.com for details of those in London). For repairs, most people use a local repair shop or send it back to the manufacturer. Apple and Toshiba

Computers		
Apple	W1	7153 9000
Apple Repair Shop	E1	0870 220202
Evesham Technology	W1	7468 1010
MicroAnvika	W1	7467 6000
PC World	EC3	0870 2420444
Sony Centre	W1	0845 6340350

offer international warranties as standard, but be aware that some stores and manufacturers only offer this as an optional upgrade. If you're taking a computer out of UK, check store customer services to see if you can get VAT back.

Electronics & Home Appliances

Other options **Computers**

Stores tend to stock all the big electronics brands, and the major department stores (p.355) such as John Lewis, Selfridges, Debenhams and House of Fraser have an exclusive department dedicated to electronics. Supermarkets such as Tesco and Sainsbury's are increasingly dabbling, and the independent shops on Tottenham Court Road cover a whole spectrum. Retailers such as Dixons, Currys and Comet all

328

have a presence in most large London high streets (quick tip: look out for sales of ex-display items). If you're taking goods abroad, bear in mind that while smaller electronic items such as iPods and cameras will be suitable for use in other countries with the correct plug adaptors, and that TVs come in different standards (the UK uses PAL, 24 frames to a second while the US uses NTSC, 29 frames to the second, and voltage can differ). For second-hand goods, try www.ebay.co.uk , www.gumtree.com, *Loot* magazine (www.loot.com) and supermarket noticeboards or local shop windows. For iPods and accessories, head to the Apple store, Virgin Megastore, John Lewis, Amazon and Comet. To get the best deals, check online comparison sites such as www.kelkoo.co.uk.

Various locations

Currys
0870 6097911 | *www.currys.co.uk*
Currys' London stores offer a range of items from stereos to cameras, and all at cheap prices. You can reserve an item online to pick up in-store, or arrange home delivery. Promotions include deals of the day and price cuts on ex-display models, and you can spread the cost of payments with its finance options. Hi-fi stereos start at less than £100, televisions at £130 and cameras from as little as £30. You can buy the 'whatever happens' after-sales protection on all items up to a year from the date of purchase.

Various locations

Dixons
0870 6097905 | *www.dixons.co.uk*
This is an excellent all-round chain for electrical goods, from home appliances such as irons and toasters to televisions, stereo equipment and computers. Dixons has a price match policy where it checks prices against 15 other retailers including Comet, Argos, Jessops and Sainsbury's – if you can find it cheaper elsewhere, Dixons will lower the price. Accordingly, portable stereos start at a reasonable £20, compact digital cameras start at £30 and LCD televisions at £130. Home delivery is possible, just ask in store for more details. Dixons offers insurance against breakages and finance options for easier payments.

Unit 1a The Eye,
Proctor St
W1
⊖ **Holborn**

Jessops
0845 4587136 | *www.jessops.com*
Mainly known for selling cameras, Jessops also stocks camcorders, MP3 players, printers and sat nav systems. Prices are very reasonable: digital SLR cameras start at around £380, digital camcorders from £90, MP3 players from £45 and LCD televisions from £400. Jessops usually offers an online 'deal of the day', and you can get reductions on in-store display stock. Stores are split into four areas: camera hardware, accessories, digital photo centre and customer service. Staff are well-trained and knowledgeable about each camera's functions. Home delivery is offered as is after-sales insurance.

278-306 Oxford St
W1
⊖ **Oxford Circus**

John Lewis
7629 7711 | *www.johnlewis.com*
John Lewis has an excellent electrical goods department that sells big names at competitive prices. Items tend to be at the top end with televisions starting at £350 for a 19 inch LCD TV. All TVs come with a free five-year guarantee. Cameras start at £160 and iPod nanos go for £99. In addition to the manufacturers' guarantee, John Lewis also provides a free second-year service guarantee on larger electrical items, portable audio items, DVD equipment, computers and other items.

329

2 London Bridge Walk
SE1
⇌ ⊖ *London Bridge*

Richer Sounds

7403 1201 | www.richersounds.com

Richer Sounds is a very popular small chain that sells hi-fi equipment and flat-screen televisions. Staff are extremely helpful, and you can call ahead to reserve items if you spot a bargain on its website. Home delivery is available, with prices depending on the size of the item. The store offers two levels of extended warranty: Panel Protection for LCD and plasma screens and Supercare for other items. There is a 45-day cooling off period for both services. LCD televisions start at £250, portable DAB radios from £40 and home cinema systems from £140.

Eyewear

Other options **Sporting Goods** p.348

Even the short-sighted can find opticians in most of London's prominent shopping areas, with major chains on nearly every high street. There are many independent vendors, such as the excellent Mallon & Taub on Marylebone High St (7935 8200) and small chain David Clulow (www.davidclulow.com) who specialise in fitting contact lenses. Major chains can afford to offer big discounts and promotions, such as a free second pair of designer glasses if you spend more than £99 (as seen recently at Boots, www.boots.com) or half-price glasses if you are a member of the Contact Lenses by Post scheme, a recent feature at Dolland & Aitchison (D&A). D&A also has a digital photography service that lets you see what you look like in different styles (www.danda.co.uk). Most opticians offer eye-testing between £10 and £20, with some customer exceptions (mainly the unemployed and children). All opticians sell glasses, prescription sunglasses and contact lenses and many will customise with reflective lenses, memory flex frames or super-thin glass for higher prescriptions. Contact lenses come in all types, from daily wear to monthly and yearly wear, soft and hard. Despite London's climate, sunglasses are big business and there are dedicated shops such as the Sunglasses Hut (7287 5273). Designer brands on offer include Prada, Ray Ban, Oakley, D&G and start from around £80. Fashion shops such as Topshop, Oasis and Warehouse all stock their own ranges of sunglasses, with price tags closer to the £15 mark, with styles often inspired by the bigger designers. You can also get fairly convincing fakes from cheap, unbranded stores on high streets including Oxford Street.

Flowers

Other options **Gardens** p.333

14 Clifton Rd
W9
⊖ *Warwick Avenue*

Absolute Flowers

7286 1155

This simple, eye-catching flower shop blossomed out of a stall on nearby Portobello market run by owner Halley Newstead. Absolute Flowers will arrange gorgeous bouquets for Mother's Day, Valentine's Day, birthdays, anniversaries, weddings and just about any occasion you care to mention. Prices start at a reasonable £25, and the shop offers a delivery service. While there, pop next door to see Absolute's furniture shop – a fragrant place to browse for stylish homeware and accessories including candles and lamps.

60 Upper St
N1
⊖ *Angel*

Angel Flowers

7704 6312 | www.angel-flowers.co.uk

Angel Flowers on Islington's trendy Upper Street recently made the top five in *Tatler* magazine's list of florists, which is not surprising given its fashionable decor and exotic stock, which is imported from Dutch markets four times a week. It does functional as well as elaborate arrangements, delivers for both corporate and private customers and has the best selection of oversized cacti in the capital. You can order gift bouquets in person, by phone or through its online shop (www.angel-flowers.co.uk). Wedding flowers are one of the shop's specialities.

Bloomsbury Flowers

29 Great Queen St
WC2
⊖ Covent Garden

7242 2840 | *www.bloomsburyflowers.co.uk*

Some people complain that central London has a lack of excellent flower shops, but this Covent Garden store is surely an exception to the rule. Run by Stephen Wicks and Mark Welford, both ex-Royal Ballet dancers, Bloomsbury offers a choice of seasonal flowers and an emphasis on scent as well as style in its bouquets. Friendly staff are happy to help, and customers are encouraged to call first and have a chat about which type of flowers they're looking for.

Wild At Heart

49a Ledbury Rd
W11
⊖ Notting Hill Gate

7727 3095 | *www.wildatheart.com*

A delightfully English flower shop with a fittingly fashionable Notting Hill vibe, Wild At Heart stocks fresh, high-quality blooms and provides for the fashion industry and boutique hotels, as well as local customers after tied bunches and table arrangements. It also has its own school where you can learn about plants and flower arranging, although if you tell your partner you're going to 'Be Wild At Heart' classes, they might start to worry. It also sells a range of interiors and homewares including pottery, blankets and tables. There is another branch based at the Great Eastern Hotel near Liverpool Street station (7618 5350).

Food

Other options **Health Food** p.334

The UK is becoming increasingly aware of the benefits of organic food, and as usual London has been leading the way. Many specialist stores have sprung up in recent years, and companies such as UK5 Organics (www.uk5organics.org.uk) will deliver to your home. Organic-lead markets such as Borough Market (see Markets, p.367) are responding to the demand for fresh, seasonal and locally sourced produce, and are hugely popular with locals. The London Farmers' Markets website (www.lfm.org.uk) has details of regular markets all over the capital, listing stallholders and their produce.

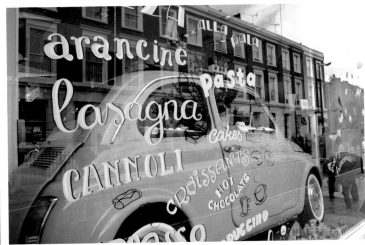

All its markets, such as Marylebone and Primose Hill, are part of the National Association of Farmers' Markets, who stipulates that farms must be within 100 miles of London. And with the fresh, organic boom, it's no surprise that Health food shops have never been more popular (see Health Food, p.334).

Quality meat is readily available from London's independent butchers; try the famed Ginger Pig in Marylebone for excellent pork and bacon from the owners' farm, carved before your eyes (7935 7788). Also popular is Randalls in Fulham (7736 3426), which offers quality cuts including Aberdeen sirloin and delicious racks of lamb. Both of these are quite pricey, however. Try family butcher Frank Godfrey in Highbury (7226 9904) for pure-bred Aberdeen Angus beef at reasonable prices. That said, everybody likes a tasty treat, and independent establishments such as sweet shop Hope and Greenwood in East Dulwich (8613 1777) and chocolatier Rococo on King's Road (7352 5857) provide for sweet tooths in search of a special selection. The latter is known for its delicious organic chocolate, so you can indulge without troubling your conscience too much.

Harrods Food Hall

87-135 Brompton Rd
SW1
⊖ *Knightsbridge*

7730 1234 | *www.harrods.co.uk*

Few forget their first visit to the food hall at Harrods, an opulent showcase of fragrant goods that attracts just as many spectators as shoppers. There's plenty of choice behind the elaborate displays – the meat and fish counters are expansive, and the range of gourmet chocolates, pastries and other fineries extremely tempting. Unless you're part of the wealthy Holland Park set, you won't find yourself popping here for a weekly shop, but it's certainly an experience and a great place to stock up on choice ingredients for that special dinner party.

Harvey Nichols Food Hall

109-125 Knightsbridge
SW1
⊖ *Knightsbridge*

7235 5000 | *www.harveynichols.com*

A bit like Harrods' younger, trendier sister, Harvey Nichols has a more sleek, more modern looking food hall, but it's no less exclusive – or expensive for that matter. Specialising in its own-label products in branded packaging, it stocks delicious oils and sauces along with staples such as meat and cheese and a great selection of wines. Again, if you can afford to shop here every week, you've really made it. Still, it's always fun to pop in for a treat or a stylish present for that foodie friend.

La Fromagerie

2-3 Moxon St
W1
⊖ *Baker Street*

7935 0341 | *www.lafromagerie.co.uk*

Head to La Fromagerie in Marylebone or Highbury Park to sample an impressive range of cheese from around the world, or to discuss your cheeseboard requirements with the helpful and knowledgeable staff. If you're keen to learn, there are tutored tastings in the Marylebone branch, which you can also hire out for private dinners and cocktail parties. As the name suggests, this place is most famous for its incredible variety of cheeses, but it also stocks fruit and vegetables delivered from markets in France, Italy and across the UK each week, to compliment your fromage. There's also a tempting range of home-made seasonal jams, chutneys, freshly baked bread, biscuits and cakes.

Patisserie Valerie

Various locations

www.patisserie-valerie.co.uk

This much-lauded patisserie has branches in Covent Garden, the City, Kensington, Knightsbridge, Marylebone, Soho and Belgravia. The fact that these areas are mostly well-to-do should give you an idea of the quality – and prices – on offer. A small chocolate, strawberry and banana gateau starts at £18 and goes up to £140 for the 16-

inch version (that's got to be some party). Its gateaux, tarts and pastries are decorative and divine, while the store celebrates seasons in style, filling windows with hand-made chocolate eggs at Easter, and chocolate hearts around Valentine's Day.

Selfridges Food Hall

400 Oxford St
W1
⊖ **Bond Street**

0870 8377377 | *www.selfridges.com*

There is a strong international flavour to Selfridges' impressively stocked food hall, which tends to favour practicality over showy displays. If you're hankering after the food of your home country, the chances are they'll have it here – European, Middle Eastern, Japanese, Chinese and Indian foodstuffs are all stocked in abundance. You'll also find an impressive range of meats and cheeses at the impressive deli counter. It's also more competitively priced than many swanky department stores, even more reason to pick up a bottle or two from its excellent wine and spirits department while you're at it.

Villandry

170 Great Portland St
W1
⊖ **Great Portland St**

7631 3131 | *www.villandry.com*

Villandry's impressive gourmet emporium takes food very seriously, sourcing high-quality products from the world over. There's plenty of European wines, cheeses, olive oils, vinegars, and hams, plus local produce such as pickles and chutneys, fresh fruit, vegetables and herbs – not forgetting its range of delectable chocolates. Villandry also offers hampers for special occasions. There's free delivery in central London for orders more than £75 (which isn't too hard to rack up), but if you can't wait, you can eat in-store either at its restaurant, or charcuterie bar. Recent offers included a choice of six charcuterie plates with a matching glass of wine for just over £10.

Gardens

Other options **Hardware & DIY** p.334, **Flowers** p.330

Private gardens are pretty thin on the ground in central London, so many garden stores are found further out of town. The Sunshine Garden Centre in leafy Muswell Hill is an excellent stop for flowers, garden tools, furniture and outdoor heating and lighting (8889 4224). Elaborate ornaments can be found at Crowther of Syon Lodge near Sloane Square (7730 8668) where prices start at £1,000. RK Alliston (0845 130 5577) near Parsons Green has a wonderful selection of more reasonably priced accessories such as plant pots and bird houses, while The Conran Shop in Marylebone (7723 2223) is a good bet for stylish garden trinkets and books. If you know what you want and you can't find it anywhere, companies such as Garden Architecture (7385 1020), also in Parsons Green, will tailor-make sculptures, pots and so on to order. For basics, try larger out-of-town supermarkets and DIY stores, such as B&Q (www.diy.com) and Focus DIY (www.focusdiy.co.uk).

Gifts

There is no excuse to go to a birthday party empty-handed in London as you can buy gifts of all shapes, sizes and price ranges across the city. Department stores are a good first-stop for easy recipients. Debenhams stocks a useful range of accessories and reasonably priced

333

jewellery for men and women. American Retro in Soho (7734 3477) is the perfect place for liberal friends who have everything – there's a healthy selection of stylish photography books from publishers Taschen, as well as designer cufflinks and other trinkets. Perfect Presents (7512 9440) in Canary Wharf offers more traditional gifts such as picture frames, silver and toys, and Grace & Favour in East Dulwich (8693 4400) does a lovely line in tempting homestuffs at reasonable prices. For slightly more expensive interiors and quirky accessories such as a bull's horn coat hook and embroidered purses go to Graham & Green (p.335) in either Ladbroke Grove, Chalk Farm or Sloane Square. Try Lush's various stores (www.lush.com) for the best selection of bathtime treats. Showroom 64 (7636 2501) north of Oxford Street offers a selection of funky slogan babygros – the gift of choice for many a new London child (although the little darlings may not fully appreciate the £20 you spend on it).

Art Attack
London's world-renowned galleries and museums offer rich pickings for the curios shopper and souvenir hunter. As well as selling exhibition-related items, many offer books, homeware, gadgets and stylish stationery. The Design Museum's range of quirky toys, books and cool kitchenware is one of the best.

Hardware & DIY
Other options **Outdoor Goods** p.342

If you're doing up a house or just tidying up a few rough edges, you'll find lots of DIY shops scattered around the city, with slightly fewer in the city centre. Larger out-of-town supermarkets often stock basic domestic hardware, and there are several chains such as B&Q (www.diy.com) and Homebase (www.homebase.co.uk) dedicated to the avid DIY-er. B&Q has huge branches and a vast inventory of home and garden products at reasonable prices; power drills start at £12. If you're looking for bargains, household chain Robert Dyas (www.robertdyas.co.uk) has five branches in London with knockdown prices on everything from screws to hammers and all that is fiddly in between. A 51 piece screwdriver set costs about £6. Leyland SDM (www.leylandsdm.co.uk) has competitive prices on quality tools and wall paints, while Buck and Ryan (www.buckandryan.co.uk) on Southampton Row offers a good line in power tools and lighting supplies, and are happy to advise both the trade and public. Windmill Tool and Hardware (7580 5712) is a typical local hardware store in a central location, and has a great range of brass fixtures and fittings. For other specialists, try James Phelps for plumbing (7485 9504) and FADS (www.fads.co.uk) for paint.

Health Food
Other options **Health Clubs** p.295, **Food** p.331

There is no excuse for a poor diet in London – at least if you're willing and able to pay a bit extra. Chains such as Planet Organic (www.planetorganic.com) have huge stores full of fresh organic products, as well as supplements and specialist ranges for those with conditions such as wheat intolerance. Fresh & Wild (www.freshandwild.com) is another very popular chain with several London branches stocking carefully sourced meat, cheese, and vegetables, as well as skincare products. One of the UK's most established high-street health food chains is Holland & Barrett (www.hollandandbarrett.com). Its many London stores stock a good range of supplements and healthy snacks. GNC also has six London branches selling vitamins, protein powders and more. Increasingly, supermarkets are stocking gluten-free ranges, although you may have to hunt around the store to track them down. They also have own-brand health-conscious ranges such as Marks & Spencer's Count On Us, and many sell calorie-counting brands such as Weight Watchers. Sports stores such as LA Muscle (8965 1177) in Harlesden also stock supplements, and clinics such as The Nutrition Coach (0845 0502442) near Great Portland Street give excellent advice on eating wisely and choosing supplements to tackle any health issues.

Home Furnishings & Accessories

Other options **Hardware & DIY** p.334

Various locations

Argos

0870 6003030 | *www.argos.co.uk*

Argos has always been popular with Christmas shoppers after cheap toys, games and jewellery, but recently it has expanded its range and quality of furniture in competition with IKEA. Argos keeps prices low by having small stands from which you can browse a catalogue, make a note of your choice, pay at the till and then collect your goods from a counter. A quick and easy home delivery service is provided on internet orders, so the website is more useful if you're ordering large items. Argos is especially hot on storage; you can get shoe cupboards for less than £40 and desktop DVD holders for less than £3.

Various locations

Graham & Green

0845 1306622 | *www.grahamandgreen.co.uk*

This family business has branches in Ladbroke Grove, Chalk Farm and on the King's Road, and does a stylish line in smaller furnishings and home items such as lamps and cushions and brightly coloured Moroccan leather pouffes for around a hundred pounds. If you're after home products that dinner guests will drool over, Graham & Green is a good bet, and not extortionate when it comes to pricing; its 'antique' wine glasses were recently priced at £18 for four.

Graham & Green

Various locations

Habitat

0844 4991116 | *www.habitat.net*

Founded by Terence Conran in the 60s, Habitat was probably the first UK store to provide affordable, stylish furniture. It's now now owned by the IKEA group, but it's a slightly classier affair than its Swedish cousin, however, and prices reflect that: coffee tables usually run into the hundreds, for example, although prices on smaller items such as kitchenware and lampshades can be much more competitive. Habitat stores in Tottenham Court Road, Regent St, King's Rd, High St Kensington, Hammersmith and Finchley Road are beautifully designed and are always pleasant places to browse.

Various locations

Heal's

www.heals.co.uk

An established London outlet with branches in Tottenham Court Road and King's Road, Heal's is a high-end furniture and home accessories store with mouthwatering designs in sofas, occasional tables and lighting. It has a great gifts section and sells stylish coffee table books, cool kitchenware and designer bath accessories. Most items are exclusive to Heal's. It also offers a bespoke sofa service; you can pick your fabric and your style from a range provided, although most designs would look best in a large, spacious home – something most of its well-heeled customers probably possess.

353

Various locations ◀ **IKEA**

0845 3551144 | *www.ikea.com*

Londoners flock to IKEA in search of basics, bargains and the odd quirky piece of design. From wine bottle racks for £3.49 to double bed frames for £300, prices are always competitive, making IKEA a popular destination for those moving into a new home. The company was founded in Sweden in 1943, and now has three huge stores on the outskirts of London, in Croydon, Wembley and Edmonton. Most products are flat-packed and packaged for self-assembly, and home delivery isn't included in the price, so you're best off driving there and being prepared to do some work when you get home. If you can, avoid weekends and especially bank holidays when the stores are full of families. Kids can always head for the play area, however, and stressed parents to the cheap and cheerful cafe.

Purves & Purves

8838 0200 | *www.purves.co.uk*

This classy establishment used to live on Tottenham Court Road, but it's now online only, having been forced off the high street by higher rates – and what they bristlingly call 'the onslaught of cheap products from eastern manufacturers'. Nothing about Purves & Purves is cheap; it stocks top furniture brands such as Vitra, Magis and Driade, and prides itself on quality – recent items include a Magis Bombo stool in metallic silver for just under £300. A haven for style, if not bargains.

Various locations ◀ **Warren Evans**

7693 8988 | *www.warrenevans.com*

These popular London bed specialists are a bit more expensive than high-street outlets, but customers rave about the quality. It offers a good delivery and assembly service and a broad choice of colours and styles, while it's also worth checking its website for special offers. Among its biggest sellers is a luxury coil spring mattress, which sells for around £135. Its organic, individually pocket sprung mattress costs more in the region of £700. Warren Evans has branches in Camden, Battersea and Hammersmith.

Jewellery, Watches & Gold

Other options **Markets** p.367

11 Hatton Garden ◀ **Arlington & Co**
EC1
⊖ Chancery Lane

7405 4402 | *www.arlington-co.com*

Hatton Garden is known as London's top spot for diamonds, and Arlington & Co is widely regarded as the jewel in its crown. A family business, it specialises in certified diamonds and quality coloured stones set in 18ct gold or platinum. Arlington is proud of its customer service, and takes a keen interest in shoppers and their requirements. As such it's a useful place for nervous proposers who have the cash, but not the diamond know-how.

41 Exmouth Market ◀ **EC One**
EC1
⇌ ⊖ Farringdon

7713 6185 | *www.econe.co.uk*

A fashionable jewellers favoured by celebrities and style magazines, EC One now has two branches, in Westbourne Grove and its original store in Exmouth Market. Stocking jewellery from more than 50 international designers, EC One keeps a close eye on catwalk trends. An elegant Miranda Rashidan cuff bracelet was recently priced at £450, and a Neissing engagement ring (with tension set diamond) from £1,520. The store also offers a wedding collection and bespoke service.

**178a Westbourne
Grove
W11
⊖ Notting Hill Gate**

Fiona Knapp

7313 5941 | www.fionaknapp.com

Colour is key in the stylish store of this New Zealand designer; bright gems are a feature in her designs that range from retro to modern. Much of it will cost you a couple of thousand pounds, but if money is no object and style paramount, this is the place to go shopping for that distinctive brooch, ring or pair of earrings. Fiona Knapp is a favourite of numerous style magazines such as *Vogue* and *Arena*, and the Sunday supplements of many a national newspaper.

Various locations

H Samuel

www.hsamuel.co.uk

If a price tag of more than £100 brings you out in a cold sweat, head for H Samuel, one of the UK's largest high-street jewellers with branches throughout London. Something of a no-frills establishment, it stocks a good range of watches, rings, necklaces, earrings and gifts at low prices (Crystal Cufflinks cost £13). It also stocks jewellery from well-known fashion brands – a DKNY ladies' red leather strap watch costs £80, and Ben Sherman square cufflinks £15. You can get a similar range of jewellery at many UK department stores and fashion shops too.

**25 Old Bond St
W1
⊖ Green Park**

Tiffany & Co.

7409 2790 | www.tiffany.com

Tiffany has made a huge success of marketing itself as *the* luxury international jewellers, and this large, elegant store is duly packed with inquisitive window shoppers as well as seriously loaded folk just picking up something for the weekend. It is also a popular spot to splash out on an engagement ring; you can schedule a private in-store consultation, or browse online. Pricing varies according to the diamond – an engagement ring could set you back anywhere from £700 to (deep breath) £700,000. Tiffany estimates a one-carat will be between £6,675 and £26,300. Stylish watches go for around £1,000, although you can snap up a key ring for a mere £60 if you're determined to possess Tiffany on a (relative) budget.

Lingerie

Other options **Clothes** p.319

Marks & Spencer (p.359) has reigned supreme in the mid-priced underwear department for many years, supplying everything from sexy thongs to podgy-bits-control pants. It has a measuring service and an increasingly broad range of sizes, with regular, no-frills bras starting at £9. Most department stores (p.355) have a decent lingerie section – Selfridges (www.selfridges.com) is particularly comprehensive and stylish, if more expensive than M&S, and stores such as Bhs (www.bhs.co.uk) offer ranges with lower prices, as do many larger supermarkets (p.359). Chains such as La Senza (www.lasenza.com) stock trendy bras, bikinis, panties, pyjamas and more (bras start at £15), although its Oxford Street store can be hectic. Agent Provocateur offer luxurious, high-end designs in a boudoir setting with prices to match

337

(www.agentprovocateur.com), and the small chain Rigby & Peller (see Shopping Areas, p.363) provides old-school designer lingerie. Bras are usually around the £50 mark, which may seem expensive, but you're paying for precise measurements and quality material.

of a good halloween

Luggage & Leather
Other options **Shipping** p.312

The Personal Touch
If you don't have the time but you do have the money, personal shopping services are plentiful among London's department stores. Dedicated staff in Harvey Nichols, Harrods and Selfridges will discuss your requirements, bring you clothes to try on, keep you refreshed, then gift-wrap and deliver your chosen items – all for a premium price, of course.

Leather is not especially cheap in London, unless you head for the Brick Lane area in the East End where there are a number of dedicated shops such as A M Leather (7729 2600) selling men's and women's jackets and trousers. A pair of leather jeans costs £50. Markets such as Exmouth Market are worth browsing for leather handbags, including designer imitations. High-street women's fashion shops and department stores tend to sell a limited amount of leather clothes, with trousers and jackets starting from £80, and a good selection of leather handbags from £10, and wallets from £3. Larger out-of-town supermarkets are also worth checking out. Suitcases are available in department stores, with the high end of the market served by luxury brands such as Louis Vuitton (www.louisvuitton.com), where prices start at around £400. Henry Tompkins leather (www.htleather.co.uk) offers a bespoke service and will custom make leather handbags to your requirements. Order online or see his products at Custom Leather in Camden market (7482 1407).

Medicine
Other options **General Medical Care** p.140

Sofa so Good
Nearly all furniture stores (p.335) stock leather sofas. One of the biggest chains, DFS, has a number of branches on the outskirts of London and has regular discounts and offers (www.dfsonline.com).

You can usually find a chemist when you need one, particularly in built-up areas with high streets and small parades of shops. And where there's a high street, there's generally a Boots (p.326) not far behind. It has an efficient pharmacy service for prescriptions and stocks most over-the-counter medication. Superdrug (www.superdrug.com) often offers reductions on common pain killers, vitamins and so on, and many of its branches have a pharmacy counter. Independent pharmacists such as Garden Pharmacy in Covent Garden (7836 1007) are also relatively common. Less easy to find are 24 hour pharmacies such as Zafash Pharmacy on Old Brompton Road (7373 2798). Phone NHS Direct (0845 4647) for your nearest. You can buy standard painkillers such as paracetamol in garages, corner shops and supermarkets, and stronger brands in chemists – although you'll have to get a prescription for the really strong stuff. Most prescriptions come with a fixed charge of £6.65, although some patients including the over 60s are exempt. Qualified in-store pharmacists will also advise, although they're usually careful to tell you to see your doctor for anything that could be remotely serious.

Mobile Phones

Other options **Telephone** p.136

Almost every London high street has a number of mobile phone stores, often sponsored by the major networks such as The Orange Shop (www.shop.orange.co.uk) and the O2 Store (www.o2.co.uk). A popular independent choice is Carphone Warehouse (www.carphonewarehouse.com), a large chain of stores stocking many different brands and accessories, with frequent special offers. You can arrange a contract with a mobile phone provider and get a SIM card in-store. Be aware that prices don't vary wildly between stores. If you already have a contract with a network such as Orange or Vodafone and are looking for a new phone, you can usually check in-store if you're due for a cheap or free upgrade. You can also buy phones in electronic stores such as Dixons (p.329) and Currys (p.329), as well as Virgin Megastores (p.340) and larger supermarkets such as Tesco (p.360) who have their own mobile phone packages. Guarantees and insurance are usually available for an additional fee. Second-hand mobile phones can be bought at sites such as www.ebay.co.uk and www.secondhand-mobilephones.co.uk – but if you're offered a really cheap second-hand mobile in a small shop or market, you may want to question where it's come from.

Music, DVDs & Videos

Despite the advent of CDs and MP3s, vinyl is alive and well in London, with specialist records shops spread all over the capital. Soho and the surrounding streets are full of independent music shops frequented by DJs keen to snap up the latest underground releases, and musos systematically scouring the racks for rare second-hand gems. Berwick Street alone is home to Reckless (7434 3362), Sister Ray (7287 8385), Mister CD (7439 1097), Music And Video Exchange (7434 2989), and more including Mr Bongo, Sounds Of The Universe/Soul Jazz and Selectadisc on Broadwick Street. Vinyl is also stocked in chains such as Virgin and HMV, although CDs and DVDs are more popular with your average punter. Prices can be very competitive if you know where to look. Videos, however, are fast dying out, and are more likely to be found secondhand on auction sites such as www.ebay.co.uk than in stores.

Various locations

Fopp

www.fopp.co.uk

A relatively recent addition to the UK's music chain stores, Fopp is an addictive place to browse, with rock-bottom prices and an atmosphere that feels less corporate than its largest competitors. Near the entrance of its large Tottenham Court Road store, you'll find CDs and DVDs separated into sections according to price; the £5 section isn't full of tat, just classics that have been knocking around for a while. New releases start at £8. Fopp also sell books, and its larger branches have cafes. Look out for news of live performances from the likes of UK bands Dirty Pretty Things and The Kooks.

Various locations

HMV

www.hmv.co.uk

Even with Virgin nipping at its heels, HMV is, as its slogan indicates, the 'top dog' when it comes to high-street music, with two big stores on Oxford Street and more across the capital. Stocking CDs, DVDs, books, games and accessories, it also has a limited vinyl section with an emphasis on dance music. Check HMV's website for offers of the week.

DVDs Online

The popularity of online music and DVD sites is growing all the time in the UK. These are some of the most popular:
www.play.com
www.amazon.co.uk
www.cd-wow.com
www.hmv.co.uk

33

51 Poland St
W1
◉ **Oxford Circus**

Phonica

7025 6070 | *www.phonicarecords.co.uk*

Genuine vinyl enthusiasts flock to this Soho shop for its fantastic selection and equally enthusiastic staff. With decks, sofas and comfy chairs, it's a popular hang-out spot and a place to discover new tunes. The racks are filled with 12inches in genres including house, electronia, hip hop, breaks, funk, reggae, Latin, folk, rock, nu Jazz and many obscure, ever-evolving categories. Prices start from £5. You can also shop online (www.phonicarecords.co.uk).

130 Talbot Rd
W11
◉ **Notting Hill Gate**

Rough Trade

7792 3490 | *www.roughtrade.com*

Rough Trade began life in Notting Hill in 1976 and cottoned on quickly to the punk scene, before starting its own label and signing the hugely successful indie band The Smiths. It now has a Covent Garden store, and both this and the original shop have become legendary among vinyl fans. Now, of course, Rough Trade also sells CDs, and has an unparalleled selection of esoteric indie music. Expect to pay between £5 and £6 for a 12 inch. As with many specialist music stores, staff tend to be on the snobby side, so be careful you don't ask for the latest Britney album.

94 Berwick St
W1
◉ **Oxford Circus**

Sister Ray

7287 8385

If you're desperately searching for that elusive new wave track from 1984, Sister Ray is a good bet. It stocks an excellent selection of hard-to-find vinyl from decades gone by, as well as more up-to-date indie, jazz, electronica, techno, trance and drum and bass. Unlike most music stores, no format is considered too old for Sister Ray – you can buy cassettes and videos as well as CDs and DVDs. Prices are very competitive: LPs usually go for less than £10, and it has a great reduced section with prices sometimes as low as a pound. You can also order online at www.sisterray.co.uk.

74-75 Warren St
W1
◉ **Warren Street**

Sterns

7387 5550 | *www.sternsmusic.com*

BBC Radio 1 DJ Andy Kershaw raves about Sterns – pop in and you'll see why. The friendly, lively store specialises in world music, with a particularly impressive selection of African releases from Zaire, Zimbabwe, Senegal, Ghana and Cameroon (it has the largest selection of African music outside of Paris – 3,000 titles at the last count). Sterns also has its own labels (Sterns and Earthworks) and regularly collaborates with African artists, and sells these recordings and other releases on its comprehensive website.

Various locations

Virgin

www.virginmegastores.co.uk

A massive national and international chain established by entrepreneur Richard Branson, Virgin stocks a huge range of CDs, games, books, vinyl, DVDs, MP3 players and all manner of accessories. Many shops also have a cafe and a section selling Virgin mobile phones and products. You'll find a Virgin Megastore on Oxford Street as well as in Croydon, Piccaddilly Circus and Liverpool Street. The one on Oxford Street has a huge musical instrument section downstairs where you'll often see and hear frustrated drummers. A busy, big-bucks place, this is a world away from Soho's cosy little independent record shops, but it's a good place for bargains in the sales. The complete *Sex And The City* box set was reduced from £129.99 to £49.99 in a recent sale.

40

Musical Instruments

Other options **Music Lessons** p.266, **Music, DVDs & Videos** p.339

27 Denmark St
WC2
⊖ **Tottenham
Court Rd**

Andy's Guitar Centre & Workshops

7916 5080 | www.andysguitarnet.com

Tourists, film crews and musicians flock to Andy's, which has been going strong since 1978. Four floors house an excellent selection of guitars and equipment, and Andy's also has a repairs workshop in case you've been playing too hard. There's a drum and amp centre as well. Female guitarists particularly love this place, finding it much friendlier than some of its more macho, sneery neighbours. There is a hire service (hence the film crew interest), and guitar lessons are regularly available.

152-160 Wardour St
W1
⊖ **Oxford Circus**

Chappell

7432 4400 | www.chappell-bond-st.co.uk

Chappell has been around since 1811 and is widely considered to be the most comprehensive music shop in London; it has a huge range of instruments across all disciplines, as well as a large printed music section. Charles Dickens was apparently a fan. Chappell is well known for pianos, keyboards, brass and woodwind, as well as a few things that weren't around in Dickensian times, such as mics, amps and mixers. Prices are competitive; student violins start at around £70 and more professional models cost from £300 (this includes case, bow and rosin). Silent, plug-in equipment such as electric violins are usually rigged up and connected to headphones so you can have a play. Pianos – everything from uprights to grands – are regularly tuned.

10 Golden Square
W1
⊖ **Piccadilly Circus**

Footes

7287 4634 | www.footesmusic.com

Footes specialises in orchestral instruments including drums, trumpets, saxophones and violins, and it also sells accessories and offers a repair service. Run 'for musicians by musicians', Footes accordingly has staff who know their stuff and are happy to advise on buying an instrument, whether you're a pro or just starting out. Footes has been in business since 1920, and claims to have the largest selection of drums, percussion, woodwind, brass and string instruments in central London and its online store will deliver anywhere in Europe.

24 Rathbone Place
W1
⊖ **Tottenham
Court Rd**

Hobgoblin Music

7323 9040 | www.hobgoblin.com/london

This busy shop claims to have 'London's best choice of folk instruments', and there's no debating its impressive range of guitars, world percussion instruments and recorders, as well as its on-site repair workshop. Staff tend to be knowledgeable old hands who are especially down with the folk and Celtic scene. It's not all acoustic though – Hobgoblin also specialises in Yamaha electric guitars and amps, and sells CDs, books and accessories.

92-94 Charing Cross Rd
W1
⊖ **Leicester Square**

Macaris

7836 2856 | www.macaris.co.uk

Macaris has counted celebrities both past and present among its customers, from the late Joe Strummer of The Clash to Chris Martin of Coldplay. The main focus is guitars and basses, but it also sells brass and woodwind and more unusual string instruments such as banjos, ukuleles, mandolins and harps. It frequently runs special sales and weekly discount specials, and you can part-exchange your old instrument for a new one. Classical acoustic guitars start at £59, and starter electric guitars from £99. Macaris is also a great place to pick up musical gifts, such as a metal kazoo for just £3.

341

8-11 Denmark St
WC2
⊖ *Tottenham
Court Rd*

Rose Morris
7836 0991 | www.rosemorris.com
Set over six floors, this is the megastore of Denmark Street, the Mecca of musical instruments. Rose Morris stocks quality guitars, digital pianos and synths from brands such as Fender, Ibanez, Godin and Yamaha. You can get machine heads, pick ups and more in its parts shop. Check its website for special offers such as free products thrown in when you buy a guitar. As well as stocking instruments, Morris offers a good accessories section, with guitar tuners and straps from £17, as well as videos, DVDs and sheet music from films, shows, singers and bands. If you're itching to make sweet music, check out the ads on its noticeboard.

Outdoor Goods
Other options Sporting Goods p.348, Hardware & DIY p.334

Various locations

Blacks
0800 665410 | www.blacks.co.uk
One of London's most popular outdoor clothing chains, Blacks is brilliant for camping supplies. Stores are laid-out intelligently, and fully trained staff are ready to answer your queries (although you might have to form an orderly queue at the weekend). Blacks also delivers, which is quite a handy service if you're thinking of buying the whole works, including tents, sleeping bags, rucksacks, hiking boots, fleeces and camping accessories. Brands stocked include Camelback, Karrimore, Stormshield and Victorinox. This is a useful place for women to shop for reasonably trendy outdoor gear at decent prices, with micro fleeces starting at around £30.

9 Pall Mall
SW1
⊖ *Piccadilly Circus*

Farlows
7484 1000 | www.farlows.co.uk
If you're preparing for a stylish weekend at your country pad – or someone else's country pad – Farlows is the place to shop. This massive store specialises in a range of outdoor equipment and clothing including air guns, fishing tackle, waterproofs and luggage, as well as clothing, accessories and footwear for men and women – including the classic Hunters' green Wellington boots, which have adorned the feet of wealthy country folk for decades. Customer service is excellent. Farlows sister company, Sportfish (www.sportfish.co.uk), sells fly fishing equipment, clothing and accessories.

Various locations

Field & Trek
0870 7771071 | www.fieldandtrek.com
Field & Trek stocks everything you need to keep you safe, dry and toasty on a camping trip: tents, survival gear, waterproofs, footwear, hats, gloves and first aid kits. It sources quality brands from around the world and trains staff to give useful advice to customers – whatever their experience of the camping scene. Field & Trek also has an award-winning online mail-order service.

30-32 Southampton St
WC2
⊖ *Covent Garden*

The North Face
7240 9577 | www.thenorthface.com
This US chain aimed at younger customers is one of London's most popular sports stores, largely thanks to its excellent range of fleeces, footwear and equipment (it also has its own brand of clothing). The products are squarely aimed at climbers, mountaineers, skiers, snowboarders, hikers and endurance athletes, as well as outdoorsy types looking for a cosy fleece (you'll see a lot of no-nonsense barmen in this label). This relatively new two-level store in Covent Garden is well designed and has a great range. Prices are competitive considering the quality; insulated waterproof men's boots start from £50.

10 Henrietta St
WC2
⊖ *Covent Garden*

Rohan
7831 1059 | *www.rohan.co.uk*

Rohan's hardwearing trousers were quite the thing in yuppie London circles in the 80s, and they still do roaring trade in outdoor gear for men and women. Typical Rohan customers travel widely and lead an active life in all weather conditions – the sort of Londoners who holiday in the Lake District. This should give you a hint as to cost. Rohan clothing is not cheap – its new self-heating vest is around £150 – but the range and quality is impressive. The clothes tend to use materials that are light, easy to pack and which wash and dry quickly. Ranges have tended towards practicality, but a new women's design team has been introduced in an effort to woo more fashionable customers who want to saunter into a cool bar after a hard day's rambling.

4 Mercer St
WC2
⊖ *Covent Garden*

Snow & Rock
7420 1444 | *www.snowandrock.com*

Snow & Rock may not be the cheapest place to shop for outdoor gear, but it is definitive when it comes to ski, as well as skating, mountain and snowboard clothing. You'll find a huge range of clothing and footwear, accessories, skates, skateboards, skis, boots and snowboards. This four-floor flagship store is particularly well-stocked (there are other smaller stores in Holborn, Kensington and Chelsea). It also caters for kids, with snow boots starting at around £22. There's also a coffee shop, web cafe and a fitting/service centre.

Party Accessories
Other options **Parties at Home** p.450, **Party Organisers** p.450

If you're planning a small bash, most supermarkets and department stores stock basic party accessories, such as paper plates and cups, party hats and balloons, as well as seasonal ranges such as Halloween masks, Christmas decorations and Santa hats. John Lewis (p.358) has a good selection, as does toy store Hamley's (p.351) which has a fancy dress section for kids (little and big) at reasonable prices. Angels on Shaftesbury Avenue (7836 5678) is a respected fancy-dress hire shop for adults with prices ranging from around £10 for a basic Superman outfit to £100 for an elaborate former film star's costume. Try South London's Balloon & Kite company (8946 5962) for general supplies. If you're hoping to impress, check yell.com for local companies who offer party catering, children's entertainers and DJ hire. Many bakeries, such as Daisy Cakes Bake Shop in Greenwich (8248 3047), make cakes and pastries to order.

Perfumes & Cosmetics
Other options **Markets** p.367

Boots (www.boots.com) and Superdrug (www.superdrug.com) are the first stops for many price-savvy Londoners shopping for cosmetics and perfumes. Boots is slightly more upmarket – it has better quality brands and stocks its own decent but affordable range. Superdrug specialises in fun and colourful make-up sets for teens, as well as staples such as lipstick and foundation from bargain brands such as Collection 2000 and Miss Sporty. Most department stores (p.355) have sizeable perfume and cosmetics departments and offer advice and makeovers. Spas and beauty salons stock quality ranges for a price, and there are a good number of dedicated cosmetics stores catering for both women and, increasingly, men. Afro beauty products are available in special stores such as Dalston's Sade Bodycare

343

(7254 1313) and AfroEurio Hair & Beauty on Uxbridge Road (8579 9595). Alexandra Palace in north London also plays host to an annual Afro Hair & Beauty exhibition (www.afrohairshow.com).

174 High Holborn
WC1
⊖ **Covent Garden**

Aveda Lifestyle Institute

7759 7355 | www.avedainstitute.co.uk

The name may be rather grandiose, but this huge beauty salon is worth a look if you're a fan of Aveda's environmentally aware products, with their emphasis on recycled plastic packaging and refills. The quality is good, and the prices upper end, but not extortionate; you'll pay around £10 for handcream or shampoo. If you'd rather not do it yourself, pop in for an expert manicure, pedicure, facial or massage in a relaxing environment. There's also a small selection of jewellery on offer.

374 Oxford St
W1
⊖ **Bond Street**

The Body Shop

7409 7868 | www.thebodyshop.co.uk

Since the 80s this British chain has been world-renowned for its reasonably priced products that are both environmentally and animal friendly. It's a no-fuss kind of place, but its lipsticks are a strong point (costing around £8) and there's a good men's section too. Fragrances tend towards the heady (you can usually whiff a White Musk girl a mile off), but its scented moisturisers are more subtle; a delicious smelling coconut caress gift bag goes for around £15. If you're shopping for a cheapish girlie present, you won't go far wrong here.

210-220 Regent St
W1
⊖ **Oxford Circus**

Liberty

7734 1234 | www.liberty.co.uk

This plush boutique store prides itself on its customer service, and its cosmetics counter is no exception; staff take time to find out about you before advising on the most appropriate products. All the beauty and body products are now housed in its lovely Tudor building on Great Marlborough Street. There's a good selection of edgy brands such as Nars, Shu Uemura and Kiehl. You may pay for the gorgeous packaging, but a splurge here feels like a treat.

55 Neal St
WC2
⊖ **Covent Garden**

Shu Uemura

7836 5588

A popular haunt for London trendies, Shu Uemura stocks its own range of hip bright colours of eye shadow, lipstick and quality skincare products in this flagship store. Prices are what you'd expect: blushers cost around £10 and mascara £16.
It is renowned for its eyelash curlers; if you ask nicely staff might let you try before you buy. If your own eyelashes simply aren't good enough, get some falsies fitted inside the store at the Tokyo Lash Bar.

299 Upper St
N1
⊖ **Angel**

Space NK

7704 2822 | www.spacenk.co.uk

Space NK's fashionable stores stock numerous cosmetics brands, from staple all-rounders such as Elizabeth Arden and Lancaster to brands such as Barielle, who specialise in hand and foot creams, the famous Kiehl's, whose lotions and potions work wonders with dry, weather-beaten skin and stylish shower gels and creams from ultra-healthy REN. Men are catered for as well as women – sensitive shavers could do well to shop here – and there are bath products and fragrances as well as skincare and cosmetics. Prices range from £10 to more than £100.

Pets

Other options **Pets** p.132

There are a number of pet stores in London, although you won't find many in the centre of town. One exception is the Aquatic Design Centre, which sells both common and exotic fish (7580 6764). For furry creatures, try Chiswick Pets (8747 0715) or Blackheath's Pets At Home (8469 9130). Many Londoners prefer to choose a needy cat or dog from a rescue home such as the world famous Battersea Dogs & Cats Home (7622 3626). The website www.dogshome.org has useful information about registering and vaccinating your pet, as well as the Pet Passports Scheme that allows you to take your pet abroad without having to go through quarantine. To pamper your new pooch, splash out on accessories, clothing and designer bowls head to Mungo & Maud near Sloane Square (7952 4570). Most department stores (p.355) and supermarkets (p.359) offer more basic pet supplies.

Second-Hand Items

Other options **Books** p.317

Credit to the Nation
The UK is the most enthusiast spender on credit in Europe, owing an average of £8,500 per household, excluding mortgages. It's an addiction which shows no sign of abating. At the end of 2006 the UK's total personal debt stood at £1,268 billion, and was increasing by a staggering £1 million every four minutes.

Going secondhand is your best bet for a true London bargain or a rare find. Charity shops such as Oxfam (www.oxfam.org.uk), Save The Children (www.savethechildren.org.uk) and Cancer Research (www.cancerresearchuk.org) are plentiful on London streets, particularly outside of the centre. They usually stock clothing, books, household goods, toys, music and DVDs, while Oxfam also has specialised book and music stores. Check the local press for details of weekend car boot sales, where people sell their unwanted stuff. Not only is this great for a rummage, but it's also an ideal place to barter. You can offload your own surplus at both car boot sales and charity shops, as well as advertising anything from old washing machines

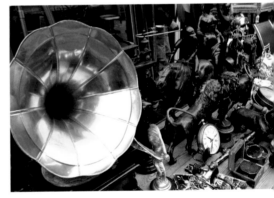

to unwanted jumpers online at www.loot.com, which is also a daily classifieds newspaper whose sections include electrical, music, travel, home and garden and property. Most corner shops and supermarkets also charge a small fee for advertising on their noticeboards.

Shoes

Other options **Clothes** p.319, **Sporting Goods** p.348, **Beachwear** p.316

London may not be as cheap as some of its European neighbours when it comes to shoes, but it still sells plenty of them. And just about any type of footwear is available. There are the dedicated trainer shops of Covent Garden, the value high-street shoe chains of Oxford Street, the high-end designer emporiums of Chelsea and

345

Knightsbridge, and the reliable large sections in most department stores – House of Fraser (p.358) has a particularly good range. Georgina Goodman in Green Park (7499 8599) will custom-make delectable shoes for both men and women from £600. At the other price extreme, women's high-street fashion store New Look (p.320) is excellent for cheap, trendy buys. Kids are catered for in children's clothing shops such as GAP kids, Next and Mothercare (see Kids Clothing, p.325), as well as by chains such as Clarks. High-end shoe stores usually offer repair services, and there are many dedicated shoe repair places throughout the capital that will re-heel and mend within a day or two – sometimes even while you wait.

201 Regent St
W1
⊖ **Oxford Circus**

Church's Shoes
7734 2438

Church's Shoes is an established brand specialising in hand-made formal men's shoes – it's been manufacturing them at its Northampton factory since 1873. Church's stock some women's designs, but it's the gents that really flock to its store in Burlington Arcade for well-made, comfortable and typically British designs made from top-quality leather. Given the quintessential British look on offer, it also attracts numerous customers from abroad who are looking to take home a slice of classic Brit style.

Various locations

Clarks
www.clarks.co.uk

An established quality high-street chain, Clarks is the kind of good old-fashioned store associated with smart brown men's brogues – although there's much more to this store than that. You can get funky knee-high women's boots for around £70, or men's ostrich print leather shoes from designer Oliver Sweeney for a similar price. Kids' shoes come in half sizes and a range of widths, and staff are happy to fit and advise on style and comfort.

49-51 Old Church St
SW3
⊖ **South Kensington**

Manolo Blahnik
735 2386

Status symbols, works of art and tools of seduction; Manolo Blahnik shoes are anything but practical – hence their sexy reputation that has entered popular culture thanks to shows such as *Sex And The City*. Stilettos, in a glorious array of colours and fabrics, are the main attraction. Its Chelsea shop can be a bit daunting (you have to ring a doorbell, and staff can be on the snooty side) but Manolos aficionados usually leave with smiles on their faces – and their wallets a few hundred pounds lighter.

Various locations

Office
www.office.co.uk

In the summer, sparkly heels and strappy sandals scream out of the shop windows of this popular, fashionable chain, which also does classic, simple designs, especially in winter when many Brits favour comfort over full-on glamour. Smart men's lace-ups go for around £60, women's pixie boots around £40, and trainers from £30. Office also has a discount shop on St Martin's Lane in Covent Garden that's well worth checking out for warehouse overs and discounts on last season's merchandise.

60 Neal St
WC2
⊖ **Covent Garden**

Offspring
7497 2463

This dedicated trainer shop (on London's top trainer street) is an offshoot of Office, and is a heaven for sporty types – or even those who just want to look fashionably sporty without having to put in the effort. All the main brands for both men and women are stocked here, including Nike, Adidas, Converse, Puma, Reef, Reebok and New Balance.

If you're after the latest design hot from the factory, chances are they'll have it here in this bright and funky store, which specialises in street and skate trainers. Most prices are RRP, but check out its sales for good deals.

Various locations

Shellys
www.shellys.co.uk

In a prime location on the corner of Oxford Circus, Shelly's flagship store has floors of men's and women's shoes at reasonable prices (from around £20) and in fashionable designs, sometimes pre-empting other high-street stores when it comes to trends. The latest styles are in demand and shift quickly, so it pays to ask them to reserve a pair for you if you're unsure. Partly because of its location, this store can get very busy, but it's calmer in other outlets such as the one in Covent Garden.

Souvenirs
Other options **Gifts** p.333

Where there are tourists, there are souvenir shops in London. Central shopping and entertainment locations such as Piccadilly Circus, Covent Garden and Oxford Street are all well served, as are areas with museums, especially South Kensington and attractions such as the Tower of London and Buckingham Palace. Common shops include The London Souvenir (7242 9032) and Fancy That of London (7925 2647). Typical London souvenirs – Beefeater dolls, Union Jack tea towels, model London buses and the classic 'My Boyfriend Went To London And All He Bought Me Was This Lousy T-shirt' tops – are regarded as decidedly tacky by residents. That said, such gifts may be appreciated by young relatives, and they're lapped up by many visitors. Museum and art gallery shops often stock much classier souvenirs, although they're typically more related to exhibitions than London itself. As is the way, airports are a good bet for last-minute souvenir shopping.

Sporting Goods
Other options **Outdoor Goods** p.342

Canada Water Retail
Park, Surrey Quays Rd
SE16
⊖ Surrey Quays

Decathlon
7394 2000 | www.decathlon.co.uk
Decathlon is a massive store with an excellent selection of equipment at very competitive prices, where women's walking shoes by Kelenji go for as little as £8. Almost every imaginable sport is catered for, from watersports to golf and from cycling to badminton. Children's sports are also covered, so you can protect those little rugby players' teeth with Kipsta kids' gum shields for as little as £1. The free Decathlon card offers invites to events and preview evenings, and rewards customers with points every time they make a purchase.

Various locations

JD Sports
0870 8730300 | www.jdsports.co.uk
Previously known as a bit of a downmarket tracksuit warehouse, JD is smartening up its image while retaining a reputation for sports-inspired and street clothing. The brand is hot on trainers, sweaters and jackets and should make youngsters happy by keeping up with trends in football boots and replica kits. Accessories such as sweatbands are also available, and JD has its own brands – McKenzie for men and women, and youth label Carbrini. Other brands stocked include Adidas, Nike, Reebok, Puma and Timberland. Prices are very competitive; you can expect to buy Adidas trainers for less than £50.

38-42 King's Rd
SW3
⊖ South Kensington

King's Road Sporting Club
7589 5418
If you're a woman who's serious about swimming, head for King's Road Sporting Club, which does a great line in swimwear separates, allowing you to mix and match to get your favourite combination of colour and style. If you're travelling abroad to warmer climes, this is also a useful stop as it stocks swimwear all-year round. 'Activewear' is sourced from the US and, to a lesser extent, Europe. Brands include One Step Ahead, Perfetto, Venice Beach, USA Pro and Manuka.

24 Lower Regent St
SW1
⊖ Piccadilly Circus

Lillywhites
0870 3339600
Lillywhites used to be a London institution, but since being acquired by chain Sports World it's become a little less exclusive than its grand exterior would imply. Previously known for quality goods at high prices, it now plays host to tourists milling around Piccadilly Circus. Most customers flock here for good value football shirts (around £40) and rugby gear, as well as skiing, snowboarding and tennis equipment – although quantity rather than quality now seems to be the rule. There are frequent sales, but the store layout, crowds and stock levels can make for a frustrating shop.

236 Oxford St
W1
⊖ Oxford Circus

Nike Town
7612 0800 | www.nike.com
As the name suggests, this flagship store is a detination in itself and can take half a day to explore. The stylish layout sees areas devoted to different sports such as running, basketball and golf, with a three-storey projector screen showing sporting images in the middle. You can find all Nike's clothing and equipment here; the store has 70,000 sq ft of shopping space, which includes the largest women's sports clothing and footwear area in Europe. Look out for its nifty shoe box dispenser which sucks your new trainers from the store room through a clear tube into the shop. Stylish gimmicks aside, it can get busy and a bit bewildering so avoid peak shopping times if you can.

Totally Fitness

108 Crawford St
W1
⊖ Oxford Circus

7467 5925 | www.totallyfitness.co.uk

Totally Fitness does a lot of its trade online, but you can check out its range of equipment in this London showroom and now also on the fifth floor of Harrods (p.356). The store supplies equipment to gyms, so it knows its stuff, but it also caters to a London public keen to get fit at home or on the run. Totally Fitness offers an astonishing range of heart rate monitors aimed at different disciplines (the popular Polar range starts at around £150), as well as yoga, boxing equipment, bikes, rowers and treadmills. The Baker Street store also incorporates Totally Games, which sells pool tables, table tennis tables and more.

Stationery

Ordning & Reda

168a King's Rd
SW3
⊖ South Kensington

7351 1003 | www.ordning-reda.com

This Swedish company, part of the Bodum group, claims to supply paper products that 'awaken creativity' and its bold, simple designs are certainly eye-catching. As you expect from its location on the King's Road, its products are aimed at fashionable young things prepared to spend a little more than high-street prices, with cloth-bound notebooks costing just less than £10. As well as selling paper and envelopes, Ordning also stocks, diaries, boxes, binders, address books, bags and cards. There's also an Ordning & Reda concession in Selfridges (see p.358).

Paperchase

Various locations

www.paperchase.co.uk

With a fantastic selection of greetings cards, Paperchase is the first stop for many a trendy middle class Londoner preparing to attend a birthday party, engagement do, christening or civil partnership. Styles range from classic black and white photography to ironic kitsch humour and cartoon spin-offs; the main problem here is deciding which to plump for. Paperchase also offers paper and card for design use at reasonable prices, as well as accessories so you can make your own. Linen address books start at £8, while 10 'thank you' cards start at £4. Also see Art & Art supplies (see p.315).

Ryman

Various locations

www.ryman.co.uk

This chain is an efficient provider of office and everyday stationery and of particular use to anyone who works at home. It also offers student discounts to encourage the inner bookworm. Offering basic binders, display books, files and desk tidies, Ryman allows you to keep your affairs in order at a reasonable price. Its stores also stock a good range of pens, paper, computer accessories, birthday cards, glue, post-it notes and more.

Scribbler

Various locations

www.scribbler.co.uk

Cute, fun and funky designs dominate in Scribbler's colourful central London stores that sell greeting cards, gifts, wrapping paper and a choice range of pens, paper and envelopes. Kitsch retro designs (ironic 50s and 60s reproductions are a feature) and stylish photography cards dominate. If you're the sort of person who likes to send a bunch of 'thank you' cards decorated with close-up photos of Liquorice Allsorts, Scribbler is your place. And it'll only cost a little more than a fiver.

349

40 New Bond St
W1
⊖ *Bond Street*

Smythson

7629 8558 | *www.smythson.com*

One of London's most famous, and famously expensive, stationers, Smythson supplies royals and rich folk who delight in its high-quality stylish designs. Naturally, you can have your envelopes and paper personalised here, or you can choose from Smythson's watermarked ready-to-write range (from £9 for 50 sheets). You'll also find photo albums and frames, leather handbags and jewellery boxes, special occasion cards, diaries and leather desk and office accessories.

Tailoring

Other options **Textiles** p.350, **Souvenirs** p.347, **Clothes** p.319

London's Savile Row is world famous for its gentlemen's tailors, where the rich and famous go for bespoke clobber. Suits are the main focus, and well-established companies include Gieves & Hawkes (7434 2001) and Henry Poole & Co (7734 5985). You can choose your own design – Henry Poole has over 4,000 different patterns, and prices start at around £2,000. Don't panic because outside Savile Row prices are cheaper; suits start at £800 at Tony Lutwyche on Berwick St (7292 0649), and £500 at George's Tailors (8341 3614). Emma Willis (7930 9980) on Jermyn Street will create bespoke shirts for women as well as men from about £200 and women's tailoring specialist Pamela Blundell (07788 100836) is favoured by the likes of Kylie Minogue – prices start at £1,600. If you're looking for tailor-made curtains to suit your bedroom and your budget, there are lots of companies that offer bespoke curtains, blinds and soft furnishings, such as south London's Alison Doney (8870 7793). Most dry cleaners offer an affordable alteration/repair service. Golden Touch (7831 6222) in Holborn is among central London's cheapest and A1 Express Tailors in Soho (7437 2710) is also a good bet for speedy, reasonably priced alterations. See Weddings (p.352) for dedicated wedding tailors.

Textiles

Other options **Tailoring** p.350, **Souvenirs** p.347

Whether you're looking for silks, cottons, linen or chiffon, London won't disappoint. For the best buys, try independent shops. Prices are low on Brick Lane, where stores and stalls offer a colourful choice, and slightly higher around Soho's Broadwick Street and Berwick Street, where The Cloth House (7287 1555) sells silks from from £6 per metre.

Shops around Sloane Square stock top-end fabrics at top-end prices: try Cath Kidston for bright floral linens from £22 per metre (7584 3232), or head to Parson's Green for House Couturier, where silk velvet upholstery starts at £49 per metre (7371 9255, by appointment only).

Textiles are also available in department stores such as John Lewis (p.358) and Liberty (p.358), and IKEA (p.336) now sells cheerful print fabrics at low prices. Try the street markets on Southall Broadway and Portobello Road (Saturdays) for cheap, quality fabrics. Sunday's Brick Lane market is famous for its bargain price silks. You may need to search through lower quality rolls, but there are some amazing finds if you look hard enough. For an indication of quality, check the thread count; the higher the better. Also look at how the fabric feels and flows, and grab a handful of cloth; the quicker the wrinkles drop out, the better the fabric. Material is typically sold by the metre and width is fixed at around 115cm or 140cm. Heavy-duty upholstery tends to cost more than dressmaking fabrics, although bridal fabric and silks can be very expensive.

Toys & Games

181 King's Rd
SW3
⊖ South Kensington

Daisy & Tom
7352 5000 | www.daisyandtom.com
This Chelsea toy store has been trading for the last 10 years, catering for babies through to pre-teen children, and aims to provide and all the latest toys before other shops. Beautifully crafted dolls houses sell for around £80, while F2 Ferrari-style toy cars will cost closer to £400. But there are cheaper buys to be had, such as hand-crafted wooden toys from £20 and cuddly bears from £6. Staff are extremely friendly and seem to genuinely love children. There's even a regular puppet show and an in-store carousel for kids between the ages of 2 and 10.

188-196 Regent St
W1
⊖ Oxford Circus

Hamleys
0870 3332455 | www.hamleys.com
Mention 'toys' and 'London', and most people will think of Hamleys. Its Regent Street store has a whopping seven floors of toys, gadgets and games for all ages. There's an enormous range of products, including an own-brand line of toys. Staff are well-trained; you'll often see them demonstrating toys such as bubble-blowing machines and remote-controlled cars. Each floor is dedicated to specific lines or ranges: interactive (e.g. Lego) in the basement; soft toys on the ground floor; games on the first floor, pre-school on the second; girls' toys on the third; models on the fourth and boys' toys on the fifth. Hand-puppets start at £5, action figures and dolls from £7. If you're gift shopping, there's something for every price range and taste. As well as modern gadgets, Hamleys also stocks old favourites such as fuzzy felt, Scalextric and Play Doh. Just be prepared to spend an hour or so here – especially if you've got kids in tow.

107 Lillie Rd
SW6
⇌ ⊖ West Brompton

Patrick's Toys & Models
7385 9864 | www.patrickstoys.co.uk
This family run firm has been trading in London for over 50 years, and it duly has a traditional feel. The model department specialises in rocketry, planes, cars, sci-fi and military items (Patrick's is the main agents in London for Hornby and Scalextric). There's also a great range of outdoor toys and go-karts (if that all sounds a bit hectic, there is a good number of more sedate toys and games). Staff are enthusiastic and knowledgeable, as you would expect from such a well-established store.

19 Beak St
W1
Oxford Circus

Playlounge

7287 7073 | *www.playlounge.co.uk*

This popular store sells design-conscious toys for teenagers and children. It also caters for big kids who love their comics; it's well known for its collection of beautifully crafted comic books. Head here to browse for collectables as well as comics, pop-up books and cuddly toys. Build-your-own Bonsai kits start at £15, Little Uglys soft toys start at £10 and various books cost from £11.

760 Old Kent Rd
SE15
New Cross Gate

Toys R Us

7732 7322 | *www.toysrus.co.uk*

Toys R Us is a great place for value toys and games for all ages, from babies to teenagers. Stores are enormous, with products from all major brands including Leapfrog, Umbro, Fisher Price and Lego. Prices are very competitive, with BMX bikes from £75, Lego kits from £3 and Crayola stamp sets from £4. Customer service isn't bad, although it can be difficult to find staff when you need them. The website has a buyer's guide and offers free standard delivery on orders of more than £150.

Wedding Items

There's no shortage of wedding dress shops in London. Popular and central off-the-peg sources include Debenhams (www.debenhams.com), Browns Bride (7514 0056/57), Berketex Bride (7766 0100) and Caroline Castigliano (7636 8212). Further out in Hornsey, Mirror Mirror Couture (8348 2113) has very helpful staff, and stocks its own designs as well as those of Justine Miriel, Pronovias and more. If you really want to splash out, try a bespoke service from Ana Cristache (www.anacristache.co.uk) or Johanna Hehir (www.johanna-hehir.co.uk) – check out www.wedding-directories.com for more information. Plus-size brides are catered for at Voluptuous Brides (07930 496604) in Brixton. It's also worth attending events such as The Designer Wedding Show (www.designerweddingshow.co.uk), held at Battersea Park, for an overview of the market, ideas and potential savings.

For wedding shoes, try the reasonably priced wedding collections in LK Bennett (www.lkbennett.com), Faith (www.faith.co.uk) and Next (www.next.co.uk.). Gina near Bond Street (7409 7090) is popular but expensive (from £300 a pair). Chains and department stores including John Lewis, Debenhams, Argos, Heals, Habitat, Harrods and Selfridges have wedding list services (nearly all are online so there's no excuse for you or your guests to arrive empty-handed). They also have formal clothing suitable for attending weddings and civil partnership cermonies. Most good stationery shops (see p.349) carry a wedding range, and Tottenham Court Road specialist store Confetti (0870 7747177) has a large selection of invitations and 'thank you' cards.

Places to Shop

The following section helps you decide where to shop in London. Whether it's for staple groceries at the supermarket, a second-hand bargain at one of the capital's famous markets or a one-off piece of clothing at a high-end department store such as Selfridges, you'll find the lot and everything in between listed below under the following categories: shopping malls, department stores, supermarkets, independent shops, streets and areas to shop, and markets.

Shopping Malls

Most central London boroughs have a shopping centre or arcade, although outside of the West End many are a trifle dilapidated and have a limited range of stores. The most modern and comprehensive are Whiteleys (see p.355) and Brent Cross, both easily accessible by public transport and with ample parking facilities. Bluewater, on the outskirts of London, is also immensely popular and tends to make for a full day out as opposed to just a quick visit. Shops are varied; big name stores sit next to boutiques and independents, and traditional shops nestle next to modern, up-and-coming brands. The idea is to keep you there all day, so the facilities are impressive: foodcourts with at least five/six decent outlets, cinema complexes, children's play areas and hairdressing salons. Opening hours are also designed to pack 'em in. All three malls open seven days a week from 09:00 to 22:00, with shops typically opening from 10:00 to 20:00, except on Sunday (opening hours range anywhere between 10:30 to 18:30). Parking is usually free at some shopping centres (Brent Cross has 6,500 spaces), with longer waits at weekends, peak hours such as lunchtime and during the sales season. In central shopping centres, such as Whiteleys, parking can be pricey.

Greenhithe
Kent
⇌ Bluewater

Bluewater

0870 7770252 | www.bluewater.co.uk

With more than 330 stores and restaurants and three leisure villages, Bluewater considers itself equal to the West End in quality and range. And with stores including Armani Exchange, Aldo, All Saints, Calvin Klein Jeans, Clarks, Currys, Jaeger, Mango, Levis and just about every other high-street name you can think of, they could well be right. Parking is free at Bluewater, which has 13,000 spaces, but during especially busy times it can take almost an hour to get out of the car park and back on to the main road. There is a train station nearby, though, and your day ticket includes the price of the shuttle service from Greenhithe station to Bluewater. Voted the best mall by Tommy's baby charity, Bluewater's services include feeding areas, a creche and children's play area. There are also 50 acres of surrounding parkland to explore and a multiscreen cinema.

Brent Cross
NW4
⊖ Hendon Central

Brent Cross Shopping Centre

8202 8095 | www.brentcross.co.uk

This huge north London shopping centre is home to large branches of major chain stores including Boots, Waitrose, M&S, Fenwick, John Lewis, H&M and WH Smith among many others. You can shop here for menswear, womenswear, food and drink, books, electrical goods, gadgets, toys, perfume and make-up, jewellery, shoes, confectionary, music and movies and furniture. There's a huge variety of shops, and the clientele is very mixed, so expect to see wealthier shoppers mingling with bargain hunters. The atmosphere is friendly but businesslike; quick spending is the mission here. There's an information desk run by efficient staff who speak a number of languages. Facilities for parents and children include free buggy loan, and family friendly restaurants that will warm bottles or provide highchairs on request. It can get very crowded, so avoid peak shopping times.

353

Croydon Whitgift

8686 0297 | *www.whitgiftshopping.co.uk*

Croydon was recently voted the third best place to shop in London outside of the West End, and the Whitgift is easily the best of the area's shopping centres. There are 120 stores including big names such as M&S and Allders, as well as specialist stores such as Famous Memorabilia, Sew 'n' Sew and Websters Pen Shop. The layout of the arcade can be a bit confusing, so you'll need to get your bearings pretty quickly. The atmosphere is definitely more urban and edgy, but the shops are clean and well-run. There are two car parks and numerous restaurants.

Lakeside

01708 694320 | *www.lakeside.uk.com*

Lakeside was one of the first American-style shopping centres to open in the UK, and it's still one of the big boys, with two levels of stores and a third level devoted entirely to a foodcourt. Stores include typically well-known names such as Burton, Cards Galore, Clarks, Dorothy Footlocker, H&M, Hallmark Cards, HMV and La Senza. There are 13,000 free car parking spaces, although some spaces are a bit of a walk to the main precinct. If you want to offload the kids on a Saturday morning, the cinema shows supervised kids' films at 10:30. There's a Sproggs creche for children aged 2 to 7 on level three, which is staffed by fully qualified childminders. There's also a baby centre with change facilities, a feeding area and a play area, as well as complimentary pushchair hire if you've forgotten yours.

N1 Islington

7359 2674 | *www.n1islington.co.uk*

Contrary to reports, Islington isn't just about designer boutiques. The main thoroughfare, Upper Street, now has its own shopping mall with chain brands such as Borders and fashion shops including Next and Oasis. It's not huge – to give you an idea, the car park has 100 spaces and costs £2.30 per hour – but there is room for a nine-screen Vue cinema. Restaurants including Wagamama, Yo! Sushi, Starbucks reflect the increasingly middle-class area. Children are welcome, although there are no special facilities other than baby changing.

The Plaza

7637 8811 | *www.plaza-oxfordst.com*

They don't come much more central than The Plaza, a small Oxford Street shopping centre combining big high-street names such as Oasis, Warehouse, Games Workshop and WH Smith with lesser known independent stores. The foodcourt is basic but functional – you can have a coffee at Bbs Coffee and Muffins, a baked potato at Spudulike or a Margarita at Pizza Hut Express. There's also a Holmes Place health club and a walk-in Medicentre, as well as toilets and baby-changing facilities. Unsurprisingly, there are no parking facilities.

Surrey Quays Shopping Centre

7237 5282 | *www.surreyquaysshoppingcentre.co.uk*

For a basic weekly shop, Surrey Quays more than does the job. Don't expect exclusivity, but do expect a comprehensive line-up of high-street stores (48 in total) including Bhs, Tesco, Mothercare, Boots and electronic retailers Currys. Food, clothing, sports items, toys, toiletries, electrical goods, books and jewellery can all be found here, and the benefit of its size is that it's never too busy. There is free parking for 1,400 cars, including disabled and parent and child parking, and loads for kids including an indoor children's play area, a creche and a discovery planet activity centre for children up to the age of 10. This isn't free but entrance starts at £3.50 and includes some free food and drink.

29-41 Earlham St
WC2
⊖ **Covent Garden**

Thomas Neal Centre
7240 4741

Known as a trendsetters' heaven, this funky arcade sells labels aimed at young and wealthy folk. Originally a warehouse, the building has been considerably gentrified and is home to designer boutiques for men and women, as well as beauty emporiums and a couple of cute little cafes. It brings together stores not known for their presence in bigger shopping centres, such as Fred Perry, Paul Frank and Quiksilver. Staff mirror the clientele and you'll find several 'resting' actors holding court at some of the more boutiquey stores. Parking is non exisitent – this is the West End after all.

151 Queensway
W2
⊖ **Queensway**

Whiteleys
7229 8844 | www.whiteleys.com

Set in a splendid old building, the relatively central Whiteleys is not your typical bland shopping centre; it has a touch of class more reminiscent of an old-style department store. It was originally just one store opened by William Whiteley in its current location in 1911. The atmosphere is a bit like a village – albeit a large, wealthy one, where you might bump into a neighbour doing the weekly shop. Stores include fashion chains H&M, Karen Millen and Tie Rack, beauty shops Beauty Base and Body Shop, and practical stores such as opticians Vision Express and mobile phone store Vodafone. Parking starts at £1.50 per hour.

Department Stores

London is world-famous for its department stores. Selfridges, Harvey Nichols and Harrods are familiar to many foreign visitors, and some of them have a presence in cities as far-flung as Hong Kong. Most of the city's department stores have a huge range of goods, making them an efficient one-stop-shop for gift-shoppers and fashion fans keen to see all the latest ranges under one roof. They're not all national or international chains, though; outside the centre you'll find local independent department stores such as Morleys of Brixton (7274 6246). These places don't always have the vast selection available in the well-known stores, and can be on the relatively shabby side, but they often have more of a community feel and offer a useful service to locals keen to avoid the trek into the city centre. If you're department store-hopping, larger out-of-town shopping centres are a good bet, but the bigger stores tend to be clustered around the West End, on high streets such as Oxford Street. Knightsbridge is known for its two upmarket emporiums: Harvey Nichols supplies wealthy shoppers with designer gear, while the vast Harrods is pretty much a day out, and has a nice line in posh nick-nacks proudly packaged in its famous carrier bags. While Harrods and Harvey Nichols are known for exclusive stock and prices, and Selfridges and Liberty are a cut above, you won't find that prices differ dramatically in mid-market stores such as John Lewis, Bhs (www.bhs.co.uk) and Debenhams (www.debenhams.com). As a result, stores offer loyalty schemes and other incentives to win trade. John Lewis, for example, regularly checks prices at other stores to make sure they're the cheapest and will refund the difference if you find the same item cheaper. Liberty offers loyalty cards to customers spending more than £100 in-store. Also look out for details of shopping evenings in the press; sometimes readers of glossy magazines can spend an evening shopping without the hustle and bustle that usually accompanies a trip to a London department store. You might even get a glass of bubbly to make it an even more pleasurable experience.

181 Regent St
W1
⊖ **Green Park**

Fortnum & Mason

7734 8040 | www.fortnumandmason.com

This upper class store was founded by one of Queen Anne's entrepreneurial footmen in 1707, who sold spare royal candle wax to set up shop. Historically, the store has royal approval, and has held a number of royal warrants personally approved by a member of the royal family. By the 1800s, Fortnum & Mason was firmly established as London's major supplier of exotic and fine foods, and is still a specialist in caviar, cheese, chocolate and sweets, teas and coffees from around the world, as well as wine and spirits and hampers. There's a quirky department devoted to food oddities with interesting histories such as Pusser's Dark Navy Marmalade (£5.90 a jar) which was created to commemorate Nelson's victory over the French at Trafalgar. Caviar starts at £12.95 a jar and pates at £4.95 a jar. Kids can be entertained at special storytelling afternoons (book in advance), and there are three civilised restaurants.

87-135 Brompton Rd
SW1
⊖ **Knightsbridge**

Harrods

7730 1234 | www.harrods.co.uk

Famously opulent Harrods actually has more humble beginnings – it was originally a wholesale grocer in London's East End in the 1830s. It moved to larger premises 20 years later in Knightsbridge (where it remains to this day) after which it broadened its remit considerably. Having changed hands several times, Harrods is now owned by the Al Fayed family, and still stocks anything and everything on its seven floors. Departments include fashion, food and drink, children's clothes and toys, sports equipment and home furnishings. Harrods is not as expensive as you might think, with Harrods towels starting at £3, Harrods pocket address books from £7 and charm key-rings for £12. At the other end of the scale, however, it stocks designer clothes and jewellery at astronomical prices. Harrods has a staggering 28 restaurants offering a la carte to oysters and champagne. There are six family friendly eateries including Planet Harrods and Mo's Diner.

109-125 Knightsbridge
SW1
⊖ **Knightsbridge**

Harvey Nichols

7235 5000 | www.harveynichols.com

Borne out of a Sloane Square linen shop in 1813, Harvey Nichols is now the toast of the privileged classes and continues to expand across the UK and internationally with stores in Edinburgh, Leeds, Riyadh, Dubai and Hong Kong.
Wallets are emptied in men's and women's fashion and accessory departments, a foodhall, a furniture emporium and beauty hall. Stocking many limited-edition items, the store is proud of its exclusive image and is aimed at a wealthier crowd. This is where Anya Hindmarch Pablo Logo travelbags sell for £345, Chanel limited-edition compacts from £22 and Culti sofas for close to £4,700. The famous fifth floor hosts a restaurant, cafe and bar where London's 'ladies who lunch', well, lunch. Bookings can be made online in advance and it now has introduced a special, healthy children's range. Personal shoppers are available by appointment, and there's a Daniel Hersheson Salon on the fourth floor should your require some serious pampering.

Need Some Direction?

The *Explorer Mini Maps* pack a whole city into your pocket and once unfolded are excellent navigational tools for exploring. Not only are they handy in size, with detailed information on the sights and sounds of the city, but also their fabulously affordable price mean they won't make a dent in your holiday fund. Wherever your travels take you, from the Middle East to Europe and beyond, grab a mini map and you'll never have to ask for directions.

Harrods

Lakeside

The Plaza

Heal's

Harvey Nichols

Various locations ◄

House of Fraser
0870 1607268 | *www.houseoffraser.co.uk*

With more than 61 outlets, House of Fraser is one of the UK's biggest department store chains. Most of these trade as House of Fraser, but Army & Navy, Binns, Dickins & Jones, Dingles, and Rackhams are also owned by the chain. They're hot on fashion clothing, make-up and homewares and also stock big-name electrical goods, accessories and food. Prices are very competitive: perfume gift sets from brands such as Benefit and Stella McCartney start at £25, Gaggia coffee makers start from £135 and DKNY bags retail at £59.99. Some branches of House of Fraser have mother and baby rooms for changing and feeding. Other facilities include a free courier service within the Square Mile (City store only), complimentary personal shoppers and an alterations service. The Oxford Street and Victoria branches have restaurants.

Various locations ◄

John Lewis
0845 6049049 | *www.johnlewis.com*

John Lewis opened his first store on Oxford Street in 1864 and in 1905 bought his second store, Peter Jones, in Sloane Square. By 1999 there were 25 John Lewis department stores across the UK, and it's safe to say that the brand now has an enviable reputation in the UK. The company has an interesting mission statement, too, which states that 'the happiness of its members' is the partnership's ultimate purpose, presumably reasoning that happy workers equals happy shoppers. And happy they usually are, thanks to a huge range of departments including audio and TV, computing, electrical, fashion, beauty, furniture, home and garden, nursery, sports and toys. Prices aren't cheap but John Lewis has a strong reputation for customer service and stocking quality brands. The stores typically have two cafes to choose from and there are baby-changing facilities.

210-220 Regent St ◄
W1
♻ **Oxford Circus**

Liberty
7734 1234 | *www.liberty.co.uk*

The aesthetically pleasing Liberty store began trading in 1875, selling ornaments, fabric and objects of art from the Orient. Founded by Arthur Liberty, who opened the shop thanks to a £2,000 loan, the store used to occupy a house on Regent Street, where it now fills two properties, which are joined by a walkway. Arthur Liberty's idea was to bring beautiful things to ordinary people, and he duly sourced fabrics and fine goods from Java, Persia and India. Today, the store offers gorgeous stationery, accessories, homewares, and men's and women's designer clothing, with prices perhaps not so accessible to 'ordinary people' any more. The beauty range has the most reasonably priced stock, with soaps and potions retailing at £4/£5 upwards. There's a tea room on the ground floor, and also the boutiquey Art Bar Cafe where furniture is eclectic and some of the pieces can be found for sale in-store. Other facilities include a gift-wrapping service, florist and personal shopping. There is also a Liberty concession in Terminal 3 of Heathrow Airport.

400 Oxford St ◄
W1
♻ **Bond Street**

Selfridges
0870 8377377 | *www.selfridges.com*

Selfridges opened in 1909, and has been credited with putting Oxford Street on the world retail map. Back then it had a Silence Room with a sign reading: 'Ladies will refrain from conversation!'. These days it's a rather more laidback and carefree affair and sells high-street and designer fashion for women, men and children who are freely allowed to converse. There is an excellent cosmetics floor, as well as homewares, electricals and gourmet food departments. Prices are reasonable given the high quality: Goldstar baby boots sell for £20 and Rimowa luggage starts at £380. But a trip

358

to Selfridges isn't just about shopping. Here, you can have your nails done, get your bike repaired, get your ears pierced or book a trip to the theatre. There are also five stylish cafes, three bars, four restaurants and several snack bars. There's a baby change area, and a Santa's grotto at Christmas too. Look out for Selfidges' spectacular Christmas-themed windows and regular events, including live music.

Supermarkets

Various locations ◄ ### ASDA
www.asda.co.uk
ASDA's marketing campaigns always focus on value for money, and its known for offering money-saving deals on good quality food. The 'ASDA Price' promotion gives you selected goods at very low prices while stock levels last, while 'multisave' allows you to buy more than one of an item and get discounts. ASDA also has a commitment to ethical trading and British Food, sourcing more than 90% of its fresh food line within the UK. ASDA's 14 London branches concentrate on food, drink, groceries and flowers. Home delivery is available and costs £3.99 for all orders, although there is a minimum spend of £25 required.

Various locations ◄ ### Iceland
www.iceland.co.uk
'Cheap' is probably the first word that springs to mind when considering this supermarket chain and it probably likes it that way; families and students keen to grab a bargain flock to Iceland. Frozen foods are the main focus (hence the name) and families on a budget cram their freezers full of goodies. Alcohol and fresh goods at very reasonable prices are also available, and some stores also sell electrical items. There are 10 branches in London, all in less expensive neighbourhoods such as Brixton. Iceland also offers free home delivery if you spend more than £25 in-store, something unheard of among other supermarket chains.

Various locations ◄ ### Marks & Spencer
www.marksandspencer.com
While privileged shoppers use the food section of M&S department stores for their weekly food shop, others pop in for a tasty treat to supplement their cheaper supermarket shop, or for its range of sandwiches and snacks at lunch hour.
Both here and in M&S supermarkets, prices are higher than the leading supermarket chains, but the own-brand quality and range is excellent. There are more than 50 stores on London's high streets and in various shopping centres throughout the capital, with some Simply Food stores based in major London train and tube stations for those wanting a quick shop on the way home from work. Some of the larger M&S stores have cafes, although its online ordering service concentrates on clothing, lingerie and homewares rather than food.

Various locations ◄ ### Sainsbury's
www.sainsburys.co.uk
A quality supermarket chain, Sainsbury's is known for its Taste the Difference range which aims to source good food at sensible prices. Despite being overtaken by Tesco as the most popular chain in the UK, Sainsbury's has a very noticeable presence in London thanks to its Sainsbury's Central and Sainsbury's Local stores as well as its larger superstores in the suburbs, which can be found on high streets, in business parks or shopping centres. Sainsbury's also operates low-cost chain Savacentre. Most high-street Sainsbury's are devoted to food, wine and grocery shopping, but at larger stores and

359

Savacentres you can buy white goods, clothes and electrical items at very competitive prices. There are restaurants and coffee shops at some larger superstores. Sainsbury's online offers banking services, insurance, gas and electricity, as well as home delivery.

Various locations

Tesco
www.tesco.com
Renowned for cheap prices on a huge range of goods, international chain Tesco has recently overtaken its competitors to become the most popular UK supermarket, and you'll see hundreds of branches in shopping centres, high streets and business parks all over London. Smaller branches are known as Tesco Metro and Tesco Express, with the latter found in petrol stations. Stores stock food, wine and groceries at competitive prices, and there are clothes, cookwares and electrical goods in many bigger stores. Some larger branches have coffee shops and restaurants. Tesco also offers financial services such as insurance, loans and banking, and its online ordering service is very popular with customers shopping for anything from contact lenses and furniture to electricals and baby buggies. Delivery costs between £3.99 and £5.99 depending on your chosen delivery time.

Various locations

Waitrose
www.waitrose.com
Waitrose is known for its quality food, and you tend to find its branches in wealthier areas of London such as the newly revamped Brunswick Centre near Russell Square. Fresh produce arrives daily from all over the world and bread is baked on the premises. Its selection of wine and spirits is probably the best of all the supermarkets, and it stocks more luxury (read expensive) items than any other chain. There is a focus on organic food as

well as basic groceries. Stores are well designed and offer a surprisingly pleasant shopping experience at non-peak times. There are also books to browse and a good selection of toiletries, so you can grab your bathroom necessities at the same time as your weekly food shop.

Independent Shops
While you'll hear Londoners complaining about the onslaught of the high-street chain – and it is true that their presence is on the increase – there are still a good number of charming independent shops, some responding to this very complaint. Quality food and drink emporiums are big business in wealthy areas such as Chelsea, as are fashionable boutiques in Notting Hill and music shops in Soho. Some do struggle to keep up with rising rents, but there are established family firms such as James Smith & Sons on New Oxford Street (aka 'The Umbrella Shop', 7836 4731) that are established enough to survive.

Not big, but very clever…

Perfectly proportioned to fit in your pocket, this marvellous mini guidebook makes sure you don't just get the holiday you paid for but rather the one that you dreamed of.

London Mini Visitors' Guide
Maximising your holiday, minimising your hand luggage

21a Jermyn St
W1
♦ **Green Park**

Bates Hats

7734 2722 | www.bates-hats.co.uk

A delightfully old-fashioned establishment that kits out natty men (or 'discerning gentlemen' as it calls them) in hats of every conceivable kind. Well, probably not baseball caps. Bates offers these gents a range of formal hats, bowlers, top hats, tweed caps, panamas, and straw boaters. The planter panama with a wide brim starts at £60. Staff are experts naturally and will advise you on how best to treat your hat (you should avoid pinching the front of a Panama, you know).

61 Endell St
WC2
♦ **Covent Garden**

Coffee, Cake and Kink

7419 2996 | www.coffeecakeandkink.com

One of the more cosy cafes in Covent Garden, Coffee, Cake and Kink offers a niche line in fetish literature, fairtrade coffee and sumptuous slices of organic cake. The array of art and accessories on display is mostly available to buy should you be in the mood for a little eroticism. On Friday nights, customers can bring their own booze, but will be charged a £5 corkage fee. There also toys and a few fetish dolls to fill any gaps in conversation.

83 Marylebone High St
W1
♦ **Marylebone**

Daunt Books

7224 2295 | www.dauntbooks.co.uk

Housed in an imposing 19th century building, this bookshop wows allcomers and has gained a loyal following among both residents and repeat visitors. Travel is the shop's speciality. Books are well organised by area, so you can find novels about Italy alongside non-fiction guides to the country. This is a great place to come if you're preparing for a holiday and want to be well informed about the region before you arrive. Staff are very helpful and know the store and stock inside out.

24 Cheshire St
E2
♦ **Shoreditch**

F-Art

www.f-art.uk.com

You don't get much more Shoreditch than F-art (see what they did there?). This gallery, shop and art space sells a range of self-consciously quirky bits and bobs including pictures, posters and illustrations from local creatives. F-Art also offers a contemporary art and furniture sourcing service, as well as bespoke framing for those edgy prints.

Daunt Books

Heywood Hill

10 Curzon St
W1
⊖ Green Park

7629 0647 | www.heywoodhill.com

With an eccentric manager and even more eccentric arrangement of books, Heywood Hill is a rare antidote to London's large chain stores. The shop has well-read staff and a rich literary heritage (comic author Nancy Mitford worked in the shop during the second world war). Heywood sells new, second-hand and antique books, a combination rarely seen in the capital.

International Magic

89 Clerkenwell Rd
EC1
⊖ Chancery Lane

7405 7324 | www.internationalmagic.com

More of an institution than a mere shop, International Magic is the meeting place for tricksters from all over the world. Its founder, Ron MacMillan, was a world famous magician, and the store, which also organises the International Magic Convention, is still run by members of his family. As well as a variety of magic props, there are magic books and DVDs on sale. The shop also runs a beginner's magician course.

Sh!

57 Hoxton Square
N1
⇌ ⊖ Old Street

7613 5458

While many Soho sex shops are on the seedy side, this Shoreditch emporium is quite the opposite and welcomes women with its girly pink design. In fact, men are only allowed if they're with a woman, so there are no furtive pensioners in macs here. Sex toys, kinky outfits and erotic literature are all sold at reasonable prices, and staff are helpful and matter-of-fact about sexual matters. After all, they've probably seen everything by now.

Streets/Areas to Shop

There are many different areas to shop in London, and each comes with its own character. If comparison shopping for high-street fashions, the world-famous Oxford Street is a must. A short walk away, Tottenham Court Road's cluster of electrical stores take the leg work out of hunting for the right computer/TV/iPod, while nearby Soho's independent music shops have bags of character. London also has glamour in spades; Bond Street and Knightsbridge's designer stores invite people watching, wistful window shopping and decadent splashing out. If you're after something particular, you can bet there's a corner of London that has the necessary specialists, whether it's Brick Lane for textiles or Piccadilly for tailoring. Further out of town, shopping centres such as Lakeside Thurrock, Bluewater and Brent Cross avoid central London's major stumbling blocks: limited, expensive parking and the weekday Congestion Charge. Your best bet for stress-free London shopping is to get up early, put on your comfy shoes, hop on the bus or tube then hit the streets.

Angel

N1
⊖ Angel

This pleasant shopping area is easily accessible from the centre of the city and is popular with 20 and 30 somethings with a bit of cash to splash. Most of the action is based around Upper Street, where high-street stores mix with boutiques, flower shops, cool bars, restaurants, record shops and estate agents (there are plenty of desirable residencies for sale around here). There are fine interior and design boutiques further along Upper Street away from Angel tube – Aria, Atelier Abigail Ahern and Oliver Bonas are three of the most quirky and desirable. Here, you'll also find Space NK for all your apothecary needs. And keep your eyes wide open for the mouthwatering delights of Soi 5 sweet shop (7354 4666). Head for Camden Passage and The Mall on Upper Street for antiques, or Push on Theberton Street for maternity

361

wear. St John Street is worth a look for second-hand shop Dress For Less. The N1 Islington (p.354) off Upper Street provides the most viable option for parking.

W1
⊖ *Bond Street*

Bond Street

If one thing characterises the Bond Street area, it's wealth. Split in two halves, New Bond Street and Old Bond Street, it's lined with expensive designers such as Prada, Louis Vuitton, Armani, Versace and Ralph Lauren, and populated by designer-clad jet-setters and celebrities. Understated old school glamour is the favoured look, although famous jewellery shops such as Tiffany's (p.357), Cartier and Asprey and Gerrard attract a wider variety of window shoppers. For less expensive fashion, head to South Molton Street, which is good for shoes, and also hosts youthful designer store Browns. Smart restaurants and hotels are de rigeur in the New Bond Street area and near famous auction house Southeby's – although by Bond Street tube on Oxford Street, it's more a case of burger joints and boozers. On-street parking is limited, but you'll notice that most regulars have chauffeurs anyway.

NW1
⊖ *Camden Town*

Camden

Camden is constantly abuzz with tourists, teenagers, goths and tramps. This is where middle-class shoppers rub shoulders with shady -looking locals as they browse for bargains in Camden High Street's many clothes stores. Shoes are a speciality, and are often cheaper than shops on Oxford Street; styles lean towards the young and edgy, with alternative styles (punk, goth, emo, fetish) well covered. Perhaps because of the colourful locals, charity shops such as Mind have interesting stock, and Camden is also a good bet for fancy dress shopping (try Escapade on Camden High Street, 7485 7384). The pubs and restaurants are equally vibrant, with many pubs hosting up-and-coming bands. Camden Town tube is exit-only on Sunday afternoons, but the area is well served by buses. Parking is restricted, and the car park on Pratt Street fills up quickly.

Canary Wharf

E14
≥ ⊖ *Canary Wharf*

www.mycanarywharf.com
This large shopping centre in the regenerated Canary Wharf area is a one-stop-shop for clothing, stationery, food, music, eyewear and more. Karen Millen, Monsoon, Reiss and Oasis are typical of the high-street stores featured here – don't expect quirky individual boutiques, although there are high-end retailers such as Bang & Olufsen (home entertainment) and Mont Blanc (stationery). There's also the flagship store for the quality supermarket Waitrose, which was awarded Store Design Of The Year by *Retail Week* in 2003. Three underground public car parks make Canary Wharf more accessible than central shopping areas, and there are plenty of bars and restaurants serving the many workers in the area.

Covent Garden

W1
⊖ *Covent Garden*

While originally best known for its market, Covent Garden has become a haven for clothes shoppers thanks to the designer boutiques and high-street fashion stores that have sprung up both in the central pedestrianised piazza and throughout the surrounding streets. Mexx, French Connection, Firetrap, Hobbs, Paul Smith and Ted Baker are all within easy walking distance of

each other. The latter two are in Floral Street, a particularly charming side-street near a charming pub, the Lamb & Flag (7497 9504), a respite from the crammed touristy boozers around Long Acre, Covent Garden's own mini-high street. Another oasis from crowded shopping streets is Neal's Yard, a delightful little pedestrianised area with health food shops, street boutiques and restaurants spilling out onto a courtyard. Neal Street itself is the best place in London for trainer shoppers; Offspring and Foot Locker being two of the best stores. Nearby Seven Dials offers street fashions from Fred Perry, Boxfresh, Adidas and Stussy. The area gets very busy at weekends and in early evenings, in part due to the many theatres in the area. Public transport is your best bet – walk 15 minutes from Charing Cross or Tottenham Court Road if you want to avoid the packed tube stations of Covent Garden and Leicester Square.

High Street Kensington

W8
⊖ *High Street Kensington*

High Street Ken', as locals often abbreviate it, packs in the department stores and high-street shops in a slightly less overwhelming fashion than Oxford Street. In Barkers arcade, the accent is on exclusive designer gear, while chains such as River Island and Miss Selfridge dominate the main street, with a proliferation of shoe shops and mobile phone stores on the north side. Kensington Church Street mixes high-end boutiques and antiques with bargain clothes shops and the famous Patisserie Valerie (p.332). If you're after more than pastries, there's always somewhere to whet your whistle in the area, but it may not be of the highest quality, unless you head for Babylon (7937 7994) in the spectacular surroundings of The Roof Gardens. There's car parking in Hornton Street, but it's expensive, reflecting the upmarket tone of the area and neighbouring Knightsbridge.

365

SW7
⊖ Knightsbridge

Knightsbridge

One of London's poshest shopping areas, Knightsbridge attracts wealthy shoppers and daytrippers keen to experience famous upmarket department store Harrods. The massive store is worth a look for its specialist fashion floors and spectacular food hall, while smaller rival Harvey Nichols boasts three floors of designer gear and a popular bar. Head for Sloane Street for more upmarket fashions, and to Hans Road for Rigby & Peller, an old-fashioned lingerie boutique that specialises in made-to-measure. There are five large car parks within walking distance, but as with everything else in Knightsbridge, don't expect them to be cheap.

W1
⊖ Baker Street

Marylebone High Street

An upmarket but accessible alternative to nearby Oxford Street, Marylebone is a good bet for specialist shops, such as La Fromagerie cheese shop (p.332) and Ginger Pig organic butchers (both off the high street on Moxon Street), and independent bookshop Daunts (p.362), which has a good range of travel and cookery books. The Conran Shop is a stylish place to browse for gifts and furniture, and the high street's charity shops are a cut above the rest, although they know the worth of their designer clothes and price accordingly. There's no shortage of gastropubs and restaurants, and there are three NCP car parks and two Masterparks within walking distance.

W11
⊖ Notting Hill Gate

Notting Hill

There's a fashionable, edgy vibe to this area which takes in both swanky upmarket residences and run-down council housing that used to dominate in years gone by. Perhaps as a result, it's popular with affluent trendies and kids looking for street style. Notting Hill is known for pricey fashion boutiques such as The Dispensary (7221 9290), antiques shops on Portobello Road and music shops such as the second-hand Music and Video Exchange on Pembridge Road. Excellent florist Wild at Heart (p.331) and boutique jeweller EC One (p.336) can be found further towards Westbourne Grove, where many shoppers seek out its fashionable bars, pubs and restaurants, and the comfy Electric Cinema, which has a funky design and sofas for two. On-street parking is pricey and limited – try walking from a car park in nearby Bayswater Road.

W1
⊖ Oxford Circus

Oxford Street

London's busiest shopping street is a mecca for tourists and locals after big-name brands and, increasingly, bargains. Many fashion stores have sales every few weeks, and with chains such as Zara, Mango, Marks & Spencer, New Look and H&M, comparison shopping is easy to do in an afternoon – that's if you can handle the crowds. Saturday afternoons, especially near Christmas, are heavy with human traffic – entire families, often – while weekday mornings are the quietest. The top end of Oxford Street, towards Bond Street tube station, has department stores including John

Lewis, House of Fraser and Selfridges, while Regent Street (which cuts across Oxford Street) offers more high-street fashion, designer stores and the famous Hamley's toy shop. Oxford Street is also worth a look for lingerie shops, record stores, bookshops such as the excellent and comprehensive Borders, and cheap temporary shops selling warehouse overs; you never know what you might find among the tat. There are restaurants and bars aplenty in the streets shooting off Oxford Street – head south for Soho and north for Fitzrovia.

Markets
Other options **Bargaining** p.312

Almost every major area of London has some kind of market, be it clusters of small food stalls or a huge covered fashion market. Camden and Portobello Road are two of the biggest, and a huge draw at weekends. While Portobello Road specialises in antiques and clothing, Camden is known for its alternative fashion and furniture. Flower lovers head for Columbia Road in Bethnal Green on a Sunday, while foodies flock to Borough on Fridays and Saturdays for produce both local and imported. While most street

markets in London are free, a few smaller ones – such as discount design fairs – may charge a few pounds for entry. Many markets combine static stalls with moveable ones on certain days of the week. Days and opening times vary, but most major markets are popular on weekends and you'll need to visit early to get the best deals. Market stallholders tend to be friendlier than your average high street shop assistant and bargaining is accepted, if not welcomed and anticipated.
You can tour old-fashioned cockney markets with London Street Market Tours (see www.dockland.co.uk).

Berwick St
W1
⊖ *Piccadilly Circus*

Berwick Street Market
If you're after a traditional London market experience in the centre of town, head to Soho's Berwick Street for the all-day market (open Monday through to Saturday). Here, you'll find fruit and veg sellers who've been working here for most of their lives, and they've got the patter to prove it. You can usually rely on the produce to be fresh and decent value. It's a good spot to pick up fish as well as fruit and veg, and there's an array of cheap goods such as CDs and accessories to browse once you've picked up your supper. The local market trader pub was transformed into a trendy gastropub, The Endurance, a few years ago, but this and other watering holes nearby still attract a lively mix of stallholders, media types and other local workers (some of whom may include ladies of the night – this is right next to Soho's red light district, after all).

367

Borough Market

8 Southwark St
SE1
≕ ⊖ *London Bridge*

7407 1002 | *www.boroughmarket.org.uk*

Borough, the toast of the middle classes, has become massively popular in recent years thanks to its specialist stalls selling fresh, often organic food and drink. Fine wines, ports and ciders are readily available, and you'll find unusual meats such as ostrich. Stop off for a cider or sample some cheese before grabbing your lunch at Brindisa, which has eager punters queuing up for its grilled chorizo sandwiches. There's imported produce as well as homegrown, and while prices are rarely rock-bottom, the quality is typically excellent. The buzzing nearby pubs also add to the weekend atmosphere. Free entry, open Friday and Saturday afternoons until 16:00.

Brick Lane Market

Brick Lane
E2
⊖ *Shoreditch*

While Brick Lane's street market errs on the cheap and cheerful, selling second-hand clothing, furniture and cut-price toiletries, the 'Sunday UpMarket' in the Old Truman Brewery, Ely's Yard is another story. Stylish homewares, jewellery, fashions and hand-made accessories are the pick, and there are music stalls and plenty of international food. The punters reflect Brick Lane's increasingly hip image, meaning the area is now almost as well known for its fashion as it is curry houses (there are many textile stores here too). Look out for signs for temporary for its designer clothing sales in the surrounding streets.

Broadway Market

Broadway Market
E8
⊖ *Bethnal Green*

www.broadwaymarket.co.uk

A relatively small market full of character, Broadway mixes farmers' market stalls with trendy clothes and accessories. It's a lovely spot to browse for that must-have handbag, cushion or hat before picking up some unusual cheese, meat, mushrooms or even chocolate or cake for dinner. You can usually try before you buy – quite useful given that the range can almost be overwhelming. There are also a few flower stalls selling colourful bunches to brighten your dinner table. Pop into the Dove pub (7275 7617) to sample its wild boar burgers and extensive Belgian beer list. Free entry, open Saturday 11:00 to 15:00, May to November.

Camden Market

Camden High St
NW1
⊖ *Camden Town*

Undoubtedly London's most vibrant market, Camden is a collection of different markets based around Camden High Street. Camden Stables Market on Chalk Farm Road is one of the most popular, selling vintage clothing, alternative fashion, antiques, furniture, quirky crafts and tempting international takeaway food. Like most of Camden's markets, it's a mixture of street stalls and permanent buildings – converted old stables, in this case. Camden Lock nearby has stalls specialising in hand-crafted products, while Canal Market, overlooking Regents Canal, offers accessories, music, jewellery, collectables and more. Buck Street market on Camden High Street is popular with teens shopping for t-shirts and jewellery, as is the indoor Electric Ballroom on Camden High Street and the former fruit and veg market on Inverness Street. The best bargains tend to be shoes and second-hand goods: the edgy designer boutiques are more about exclusive designs. Weekends are busiest, when all stalls are open, although many open seven days a week. Entrance is free to all markets.

Columbia Road Flower Market

Columbia Rd
E2
⊖ *Bethnal Green*

This is a cheerful and colourful way to spend (an early) Sunday morning. Crammed into one long street, the market boasts a staggering variety of flower and plant stalls, where cut flowers jostle for space with garden furniture and pot plants. The market has a dedicated fanbase who travel from across London and beyond each weekend. It is bustling as early as 09:00, which can be quite overwhelming to newcomers, but green-fingered shoppers will find it well worth the trip. It remains the best place in London to pick up a relatively cheap and fresh bunch, either for the dining table or visiting in-laws. Traders are friendly and may well cut you a deal, particularly at lunchtime when the market is starting to wind down – although early-bird deals are possible too, when the range is more extensive. Prices are competitive (a clematis will cost £5) and there's all manner of exotic and rare plants and shrubs.

105a Commercial St
E1
⇌ ⊖ Liverpool Street

Old Spitalfields Market
www.visitspitalfields.com
'Spitalfields', as it's commonly known, has become a fashionable, friendly alternative to Camden Market, albeit one that's considerably smaller. Its stalls are housed under one large roof and offer original designs in the fields of interiors, fashion, arts and craft, as well as food – its original product dating from the 1600s. There are stalls all week except for Saturdays: deli on Wednesdays (also, records and books on the first and third Wednesday of the month); antiques on Thursdays; fashion and art on Fridays. But it's Sundays, with their bohemian mix of hand-crafted gifts, quirky clothing and vintage gear, that are most popular. The accent is on the individual. This is where to come for an unusual print t-shirt that you won't find on the high street.

Portobello Rd
W11
⊖ Notting Hill Gate

Portobello Road Market
www.portobelloroad.co.uk
Antiques dominate the south end of this long, fashionable west London street that hosts market stalls every Saturday, both on the road and in its arcades. Rare vintage costumes, militaria, brass, books, jewellery and paintings can all be found. Food stalls dominate further down the street, followed by clothing and jewellery in a wide range of styles and price ranges. Funky fashions typify the Portobello Green arcade (look out for youthful designs from Preen in particular) and many more hip designers do brisk business under the large canopy nearby. Stallholders tend towards the efficient rather than chatty, but haggling is worth a try.

369

Going Out

Going Out

Going Out

London boasts one of the most vibrant and diverse social scenes in the world, where a bona fide mix of people come together to have a great time. From cosy homely pubs to beautifully designed bars, there are venues for all tastes and budgets. Certain areas have their own distinct vibes with faithful followings. For an eclectic blend of trendy and trashy, Soho still delivers. Within it, Old Compton Street is home to a vibrant gay scene where chic and chichi rub shoulders. Join the retro-funk artists and creative types in lounge bars and banging clubs in the 'new cool' Hoxton and Shoreditch. Super-clubs, such as legendary Ministry of Sound, are slowly losing favour to their shoe-cupboard-sized cousins where DJs set trends in a more intimate and laid-back atmosphere. Fulham and King's Road are good enough for young royalty and offer choices from cheery pop to dark dance, but some bars can be a bit pretentious and full of wannabes and *Big Brother* Z-listers. Mayfair is still the setting for designer-clad beautiful people slinking between the VIP lounges of sexy-looking bars and private members' clubs. Upper Street offers the highest concentration of restaurants and bars; forget the chains and discover more than 100 venues packed on to one street. In the backstreets around Oxford Street, hidden bars come alive after dusk offering jazz and live music – audiences at 100 Oxford Street have enjoyed performances ranging from The Sex Pistols to The White Stripes. Head south to Clapham 'village' where a growing crowd of young professionals kick back for nights of cheesy tunes and booze. Like many capital cities social hours are dictated by office hours; there's a weeknight rush from 18:00 to 23:00, but at the weekends things tend to get going from 21:00 and last well into the early hours.

Code Breaker

We've included a London postcode by each entry in this section to help you locate the restaurants, bars and clubs. The map on p.458 shows which area of town each one covers.

Eating Out

Travel the length and breadth of London and you travel the world in cuisines. Such is the diversity of the dining scene that modern British food is classed as just another category among the nations represented on the plate – you really are bound only by your appetite and sense of adventure. The colourful legacy of trade and immigration has left strong bastions of ethnic food: 'Banglatown' in Brick Lane and Spitalfields for Bangladeshi and Indian cuisine, Brixton for Caribbean food and of course Chinatown for Cantonese specialities. The unfavourable climate means there is no street-food culture to speak of, instead dive into any fish & chip shop or try a kebab house for a late night shish. The dark years of culinary dross are firmly in London's history. Today, a new generation of chefs, hungry for success in this ravenous city, is creating waves and new foodie fashions on the restaurant and gastropub scene. You'll be able to sample innovative menus that use the best local and international produce available without breaking the bank. If you do want to splash out, Michelin stars are generously scattered around, with chefs now more famous than their celebrity guests – the likes of Gordon Ramsay, Marco Pierre White, Jamie Oliver, Nobu Matsuhisa and Giorgio Locatelli are all competing for the 'it' crowd. Advance booking is recommended but many

Dress Code

Most people opt for a relaxed, casual look, but after-work drinking means the 'suits' are omnipresent and you won't feel out of place if you want to flash some bling. A few fine-dining restaurants keep their tired 'no jeans' policy and some clubs still refuse entry to people wearing trainers. Football shirts or colours are not permitted in some bars or pubs.

Discounts

Because competition is tough across London's restaurants, bars and clubs, you will often find lunch, pre-theatre and weeknight discounts – even in the most exclusive restaurants. There are dozens of free loyalty and privilege cards available, such as the 'passport' from myvillage.com or in listings magazines such as Time Out, *which will shave a few pounds and pence off your bill. Book ahead at www.toptable.co.uk for discounts at hundreds of London's leading eateries.*

popular places will not take reservations for peak times on Friday and Saturday, operating a first-come-first-served system instead. Standard opening hours are 12:00 to 16:00 and 17:00 to 00:00 Monday to Saturday, with limited opening on Sundays. In central London children and babies are welcome in restaurants and bars but often not after 20:00. Fortunately this is a city of villages where you'll find friendly places guaranteed to welcome the little ones with open arms at any time. In the run up to Christmas and new year, office parties often take over large sections of restaurants, limiting access, and sometimes service, for individual diners.

Delivery

Delivery and takeaway menus are posted through the letter box a couple of times a week, mostly, but not exclusively, for Indian and Chinese food. If you prefer something more sophisticated you can entertain at home without the hassle of shopping and cooking using one of the many home-catering services available. They can simply deliver your choice of food or come to your house, cook in your kitchen, serve and even do the washing up before they leave (see p.450). Supermarkets such as Waitrose (see p.360) also provide party catering services that can be arranged online and delivered at your requested time.

Restaurant Timings

Although London competes with the continent in terms of the quality of its cuisine, the cold nights and traditional opening hours mean its restaurants have not adopted the dining hours of their European neighbours. Restaurants are busiest between 19:30 and 21:30; many are often unwilling to take reservations beyond 23:00. If you want to eat after midnight outside of Soho the choice may be limited to chippie, Chinese or Indian. Sunday closure is common, especially in the evening, and many restaurants and bars also closed on public holidays. Pubs and bars offering food will have notices of when their kitchens close, but these times vary massively so look out.

Bring Your Own

A number of smaller, independent restaurants in London do not have a licence to serve alcohol. However, a majority of them operate a 'bring-your-own' policy where you can take beers and wine and be charged a negligible 'corkage' fee – often great value when you consider the price of wine in the city's restaurants.

Drinks

Alcohol is sold in corner shops and off-licences until 23:00 and in some supermarkets 24 hours a day. Staff at Oddbins and French off-licence Nicolas and are good at wine recommendations, although you might want to make friends with the merchants at Majestic or Vinopolis as they can offer great deals on mixed cases. The spirit sections of larger Waitrose stores are incredibly extensive.

The minimum legal age for buying alcohol and drinking in public places is 18, and photo ID may be required to make a purchase if staff believe you look suspiciously young. Even if you have gained entry to a pub or club, you may again be asked to prove your age at the bar before being served, especially if you look younger than 21.

Cuisine List – Quick Reference

African	376	French	393	Moroccan	405
American	377	Greek	395	Polish	406
Arabic/Lebanese	378	Indian	395	Russian	406
British	378	International	398	Seafood	408
Caribbean	383	Italian	399	Spanish	408
Chinese	384	Japanese	401	Thai	409
European	387	Latin American	402	Turkish	410
Far Eastern	390	Mediterranean	404	Vietnamese	411
Fish & Chips	392	Mexican	405		

373

The Complete **Residents'** Guide

Children aged 14 or over can enjoy a glass of wine with a meal in a restaurant but may not be present in an establishment that serves alcohol unless accompanied by an adult over the age of 18. Prices across London vary greatly but are generally higher than anywhere else in the UK. You will usually pay less in pubs than bars but expect to hand over about £2.50 for a pint, around £4 for speciality or foreign brews and at least £5 for a cocktail. A spirit and mixer will usually set you back around £3.50 but something like a vodka and Red Bull will rarely come in under a fiver. Some bars charge absolutely scandalous prices for glasses of wine so work out what everyone wants first; it is always cheaper to buy a bottle and share it.

Hygiene

Since the Freedom of Information Act was introduced, The Food Standards Agency and local authorities in London publish the results of all their hygiene inspections for restaurants, cafes, pubs and other food outlets. Most places are safe and clean but to avoid food poisoning steer clear of street vendors, and trust your eyes and nose.

Hidden Charges

Service charges in restaurants and bars are discretionary but many will add 12.5% to your bill unless you instruct them otherwise. If you get a bread roll before your starter it is probably free, but if a basket of bread or prawn crackers is placed on the table expect to pay for it. Likewise when offered water expect to pay for a bottle unless you specify you would like a glass or jug of tap water.

Tax, Service Charges & Tipping

The standard value-added tax (VAT) charge is 17.5% and is included in the price of any item or service you pay for. A service charge is different to VAT – it's usually added on to restaurant bills, at around 12.5% of the cost of the meal. However, it is not compulsory to pay it, and if you feel the service has been poor you have the right to reduce, or not pay, the added charge. Tipping is becoming increasingly common, but is still not expected outside of restaurants and bars, and also not if you've already paid a service charge. Generally people tip waiters (and less so bar staff) about 10%, while most people tip their taxi drivers £1 or so depending on the cost of the journey. It is common for restaurants to pool tips and divide them.

Vegetarian Food

Almost all menus now include a couple of vegetarian options, but for those wanting something more adventurous than mushroom risotto there are over 100 pure vegetarian, vegan and organic meat-free havens to choose from. Boring brown nut bakes have been replaced by innovative dishes served with style and imagination; from tapas and grazing menus to six-course chef's specials. Many wholefood and health-food shops also have hot and cold food counters where you can grab a bite for a couple of quid after doing your shopping. Manna in Chalk Farm (7722 8028), established more than 40 years ago, is the oldest vegetarian restaurant in the capital, while Indian food has long been the best choice of ethnic cuisines for vegetarians - but with places such as Eat and Two Veg on Marylebone Road (7258 8595) boasting American-diner-style dishes, and Mildreds (0871 2238079) in Soho offering an imaginative burger of the day alongside great tagines and organic wine, perceptions and expectations are slowly changing. Vegetarian restaurants are becoming increasingly popular with those who have special diets or food allergies as they offer gluten or yeast-free alternatives not found elsewhere.

Food on the Go

London is a busy place – people are always in a hurry, dashing from home to work, meeting to meeting, or shop to shop. For many, that leaves little time to stop and eat, hence the multitude of outlets and chains catering for the 'food on the go' market. You can't walk more than a couple of blocks in central London without seeing at least one sandwich shop, such as a Pret a Manger or Eat, or a Costa Coffee or Starbucks coffee house. You can sit in or take away at most places, where a bite and a drink won't leave you much change from a fiver. Food options range from baguettes, ciabattas and panini to salads, soups and sushi. There are other similar chains too, the sight of which will become familiar in no time at all, plus plenty of quality independent, local companies. If you're after something quick but a little less healthy, McDonald's, Burger King and Kentucky Fried Chicken all make their presence felt throughout the capital.

Sunday Lunch

The roast is one of the last bastions of British dining culture. Served on Sundays at pubs and gastropubs, it is simple food but, when done right, completely majestic. A roast meat, usually beef or lamb, occasionally pork and chicken, is accompanied by 'all the trimmings' – namely slow-roasted English root vegetables such as potatoes, parsnips and carrots, plus broccoli, cauliflower and peas mixed and matched according to season and availability, and a towering crisp yorkshire pudding drizzled with thick gravy. The test of a good roast is how tender the meat is and how tall, puffy and crisp the yorkshires are. Spoon a little horseradish sauce and mustard with beef, mint sauce with lamb, and redcurrant jelly with chicken to complete the experience.

The Yellow Star

This natty yellow star is our way of highlighting places that we think merit extra praise. It could be the atmosphere, the food, the cocktails, the music or the crowd – but whatever the reason, any review that you see with the star attached is somewhere that we think is a bit special.

Restaurant Listing Structure

The number of eating and drinking venues in London is simply staggering – you could go out to a different place every night of the year for a decade and still only have scratched the surface. Reviewing every restaurant and bar would require a collection of work to rival the *Encyclopaedia Britannica* in volume, so instead our Going Out section brings your attention to a cross-section of places that are definitely worth a visit. Each review attempts to give an idea of the food, service, decor and atmosphere. Restaurants have been categorised by cuisine (in alphabetic order).

Independent Reviews

All of the outlets in this book have been independently reviewed by a food and drinks writer who is based in London. Their aim is to give clear, informative and unbiased views of each venue, without any back-handers, hand-me-downs or underhandedness. If any of the reviews in this section have led you astray, or if your favourite local eatery doesn't grace these pages, then drop us a line on info@explorer-publishing.com.

Explorer Recommended

Best of British		Cheap Eats		Fine-Dining		For Couples	
Butlers Wharf	379	African Kitchen	376	Cinnamon Club	396	Almeida	393
Inn the Park	380	Arancina	413	Club Gascon	393	Gordon Ramsay	395
Roast	382	Busaba Eathai	409	Hakkasan	385	Pétrus	394
Savoy Grill	382	Canela	402	Maze	398	Sardo Canale	400
St John	383	Ooze	400	Ubon	402	Troubadour	430

African

Other options **Arabic/Lebanese** p.378, **Moroccan** p.405

77 Askew Rd
W12
⊖ *Shepherd's Bush*

Adam's Café
8743 0572
Rich tagines, fluffy couscous and other fabulous dishes from Tunisia, Morocco and north Africa are served as faithfully to the originals as possible at this family-run restaurant. The decor is bright and colourful, with mosaics on the wall and skylights above drenching the guests in a warm glow. The staff are genial, enthusiastically explaining the differences in flavours and aromas of the cuisine and making each guest feel as if they have been personally invited to the restaurant. On the menu, skewers of marinated grilled fish of the day make a good alternative to meat dishes with a few, mainly pastry-based, vegetarian options. Finish with platters of baklava-style desserts dripping with honey or fresh citrus sorbets. For under £10 you can have the 'menu rapide' – one course served with mint tea or coffee, perfect for a quick lunch. If you have the time, three courses will set you back less than £20.

102 Drummond St
NW1
⊖ *Euston Square*

African Kitchen Gallery
7383 0918
The walls and windowsills in this tiny treasure-trove restaurant-cum-gallery are adorned with tribal masks and artwork, but the real jewels are its owners. They proudly serve generous portions of cinnamon-infused plantation beef, jerk chicken swimming in thick black juices and blackened tilapia fish, freshly made in their home kitchen and reheated on site to order. Vegetarians won't be disappointed with the array of dishes made from cassava, sweet potato and plantain. Bring your own booze for a miniscule corkage fee or enjoy the restaurant's fiery ginger beer. In the summer, when the six candlelit tables inside are full, people spill out on to the street and the tiny patio behind. Those unable to find a place can order their favourites to take away, with coconut-laced rice and peas included for the already bargain prices. While you wait, check out the counter – laden with tempting bites from moreish salt cod fritters and sweet coconut balls to guava flan.

Africa Centre,
38 King St
WC2
⊖ *Covent Garden*

Calabash
7836 1976
In the basement of the Africa Centre, just off Covent Garden, you'll find this small restaurant that gives diners the opportunity to explore many of the continent's wonderful cuisines. Some of the more traditional ingredients that are not found on supermarket shelves in the UK make appearances – fufu made from ground cassava flour, injera made from teff and the increasingly familiar okra, yam and plantain. The stews are rich and filling and the portions are very generous; you may want a Kenyan tusker beer or South African pinotage to help wash it down. The decor is very simple and plain but the occasional troupe of drummers start up and breath new life into the room. At Calabash, you get great value for money, faultless cuisine, and swift, friendly service, all while enjoying a culinary tour of Africa in the heart of London.

196 Caledonian Rd
N1
⊖ *Caledonian Road*

Merkato
7713 8952
Fenced in on an otherwise ugly Caledonian Road is this oasis of Ethiopian aromas and tastes. The hubbub of chatter from the local Ethiopians and other laid-back guests seems to work in time to African music in this cafe-styled restaurant. Staff are happy to make recommendations for the uninitiated and guide you through names such as doro wot (chicken stew) and shiro (lentil stew). Platters of soft sourdough

Restaurants

serve as the communal plate with dishes spooned on top for you and your party.
The red juices soak through giving off the kind of heat that starts in your mouth
then moves on to punch out your sinuses. Balance the heat with a glass of tej, sweet
honey wine, or a cold beer. A final fragrant experience comes in the form of a cup of
coffee, freshly roasted and passed round for all to smell before being ground and
served with popcorn.

48 Westow Hill
SE19
⇌ Crystal Palace

Numidie
8766 6166 | www.numidie.co.uk
Named after the ancient nation of Numidie, equivalent to modern day north-eastern
Algeria and parts of Tunisia, this small restaurant looks – in a certain light – like a
souvenir shop. It is filled with knick-knacks, newspaper cuttings and Algerian
memorabilia, and Serge Ismail, the owner, is justifiably proud of his backgrounds and
what he has created. It is a wonderful neighbourhood restaurant that other districts
would be jealous of. The cuisine is predominantly north African with a post-colonial
nod to the French. Dishes include merguez in fiery harissa, terrine of aubergine and
jambonette of pigeon as well as warming tagines, meats that melt in the mouth and
fluffy couscous. Desserts are worthy of much merit so try them if you can leave
enough space after the generous main courses. House wines, like the rest of the menu,
are very reasonably priced making this the restaurant of choice for family feasts,
evenings with friends or romantic dinners for two.

American

275 Portobello Rd
W11
⊖ Ladbroke Grove

Babes n Burgers
7727 4163 | www.babesnburgers.com
Perhaps it's time to lose the 'Babes' part of this restaurant's name now that the child-
friendly area out the back has been replaced with a bar. Still, the main reason you
come here is for burgers and that's what you get: beef, veggie, chicken or fish served
between a bun with a side order of crispy salty fries. The restaurant has cottoned on to
the requirements of a new generation of burger eaters and offers healthy options with
halloumi cheese toppings, sprouting salads or wok-steamed vegetables as side orders.
The wheat-free baps will set you back an extra £1.50, which seems reasonable, but
swap it for a 'no carb' option (a large lettuce leaf) and you have to pay the same. There
are healthy smoothies and completely unhealthy but delicious icecream milkshakes to
satisfy any sweet tooth. Service can be a little haphazard but the atmosphere is fun,
especially when Portobello Road Market is in full swing (p.369).

12 Moor St
W1
⊖ Leicester Square

Ed's Easy Diner
7434 4439 | www.edseasydiner.co.uk
Ed's is a 1950s-style American diner in all its glory. Black-and-white chequered tiles
and red leather stools with mini jukeboxes on every table make it a fun place to stop
and recreate scenes from *Grease* while out in the West End. Stacks of pancakes come
with slivers of crunchy bacon and maple syrup, while thick malted milkshakes are
made in traditional flavours as well as greedy butterscotch, coffee and banana, or
peanut butter. There is a great range of juicy inch-thick Irish steak burgers or chicken
and veggie alternatives with classic toppings, or you could always try a hot dog or
bowl of steaming hot chilli with your fries. If all of this is making you worry about your
waistline, fear not; the green menu outlines all the nutritious values of Ed's products
from the fat and protein in its burgers to the vitamins in the salads. There are also
branches at Piccadilly Circus (7287 1951), Covent Garden (7836 0271) and on King's
Road (7352 1956).

377

The Complete **Residents'** Guide

75 Wapping High St
E1
Wapping

Lilly's
7702 2040

The best of the Big Apple comes to the heart of Wapping, offering friendly locals and American food junkies a taste of the modern USA. Burgers and big grills sit alongside sauteed pacific prawns and caesar salads as well as more Mediterranean-influenced dishes. Deep aubergine walls combine with the elegant wooden tables and floor to create a stylish dining room that is a far cry from the typical chrome-filled burger bar you might expect. Prices are mid-range and the atmosphere is relaxed which suits this crowd-pleasing cuisine. Child-friendly service and excellent quality ingredients make this the perfect local family restaurant. And with desserts such as white chocolate icecream profiteroles with hot chocolate sauce, adults will be just as happy as the kids.

Arabic/Lebanese
Other options **African** p.376, **Moroccan** p.405, **Turkish** p.410

182-184 St John St
EC1
Farringdon

Darbucka
7490 8772 | www.darbucka.com

Music, dance, drinking and dining are all enjoyed at Darbucka. This is a party place happy to accommodate large groups looking for a fun rather than sophisticated gourmet experience. Picture mint tea, mezze and shisha pipes under a canopy of white tents and you'll get the gist of this Arabian extravaganza. The menu offers Lebanese hot and cold mezze, skewers and meats from the grill accompanied by fluffy couscous, as well as stews and roast fish. Fresh salads are exactly that, not drowned in dressing or straight from the packet as is often the case in budget restaurants, while the fruit salad makes a refreshing alternative to the sickly sweet baklava. Downstairs in the world music bar there are comfy cushions on which to slump and enjoy the belly dancers.

313-319 Old St
EC1
Old Street

Shish
7749 0990 | www.shish.com

This is cuisine from the ancient Silk Road brought to one of the trendiest streets in London. The bright and colourful setting attracts a funky young crowd, hungry for the restaurant's delicious signature grilled kebabs. The atmosphere is informal and relaxed with couples, friends and parties coming to sit on the banquettes, tables or by the hot grills to see and smell the chefs in action. Delicious mezze of taboule, borak and dumplings are perfect for sharing as a starter. Shish, including marinated lamb, chicken or halloumi cheese served with salad and fluffy couscous or chips, are the main event and there is a great range of wraps including a crunchy and flavourful falafel. Staff are charming and efficient even during the worst Saturday night frenzy, and the food is reasonably priced for the area and the style of restaurant. As this part of town is famed for its nightlife this is a fun place to start the evening with a bite to eat and a few cocktails.

British
Other options **Fish & Chips** p.392

350 King's Rd
SW3
South Kensington

Bluebird
7559 1129 | www.conran.com

Fresh clean design is at the core of the beautiful first-floor dining room of the Bluebird Brasserie. A high glass roof floods light into the crisp white room, which is decorated with framed photographs capturing times past in a restaurant that is absolutely 'now' – you would expect nothing less from successful restaurateur and design guru Sir Terence Conran. Bluebird's chefs also have an eye for the aesthetic as the inventive British cuisine is exceedingly well presented. It is obvious after just one mouthful, but the knowledgeable staff will happily assure you, that the ingredients, sourced from small farms and producers across the British Isles, are of the highest quality. And what could be more authentic than Cornish crab, crackled pork, strawberries and elderflowers or the great knickerbocker glory?

Boxwood Café

The Berkeley, Wilton Place
SW1
⊖ Knightsbridge

7235 1010 | www.gordonramsay.com

Boxwood serves the kind of sublime quality dishes you'd expect from a restaurant in the Gordon Ramsay group, and adds its own sense of fun. Choose from veal and foie gras burgers with chips, mini icecream cones in silver stands or seriously dark chocolate fondue with fluffy marshmallows, fruit kebabs and biscotti. You'll find young families relaxing here on Sundays, well looked after by helpful staff. The clean lines of the chic interior also make this a calm retreat from a day out in Knightsbridge, and with a three-course set lunch costing just £21, you can suspend the guilt of the money you've just spent shopping. If you're feeling more decadent, try the six-course 'taste of Boxwood' menu, accompanied by a bottle of wine.

Butlers Wharf Chop House

36e Shad Thames
SE1
⊖ Tower Hill

7403 3403 | www.chophouse.co.uk

Homegrown produce is cooked to perfection in this delightfully relaxed restaurant that overlooks the very British Tower Bridge. Wood pigeon and Cornish razor clams are among the delectable starters you can choose from, followed by steak and kidney pudding with oysters and Suffolk pork loin tenderly cooked. Dishes you would normally associate with hearty comfort food and country cottages are quite at home in the oak-lined dining room or on the riverside terrace. The ingredients are as fresh as they are indigenous and are treated superbly by head chef Shannon Whitmore. Butlers has not minimised any of the charm or intense flavours of these rustic favourites, but still made them accessible and appealing to urbanites. Wines on the restaurant's very extensive list come from as near as Sussex and as far away as New Zealand, but you can also order a very traditional English beer to accompany your meal.

Cockneys Pie and Mash

314 Portobello Rd
W10
⊖ Ladbroke Grove

8960 9409

For less than a fiver you'll get great meat, fish and vegetable pies plus the statutory scoop of mash served with greenish gravy. You have to know your ones and twos here though as you place your requests in terms of how much you want: one pie with two scoops of mash, or maybe you want two pies and one scoop of mash with liquor? If they ask you if you want one lump or two, however, they are not talking about the mash, but the number of sugars to put in your tea. Whatever you order, your plate will be handed to you across the counter, then you take it to one of the tables stocked with the essentials – vinegar and ketchup. This is real East End food that is not lost on the good people of west London.

Local Cuisine

British cuisine has undergone a revolution but most will still argue that, done well, you can't beat a 'propa' fried English breakfast or fish & chips piled into waxed paper and doused in salt and malt vinegar. Foods that enjoy as much notoriety but less popularity are jellied eels, best served in East End caffs. It's in that neck of the woods that you'll find the best pie and mash shops serving little parcels of heritage with mashed potatoes, mushy peas and liquor. At the opposite end of London, and the social scale, order afternoon tea in one of the elegant hotels and tea rooms of Mayfair; expect your earl grey to come in silverware, cucumber sandwiches to come 'crusts off' and the bill to be more than you bargained for. An institution of culinary culture to round off every week is the traditional Sunday roast with all the trimmings, which you'll find served in almost every gastropub in town.

St James's Park
SW1
⊖ **St. James's Park**

Inn the Park

7451 9999 | *www.innthepark.com*

No ordinary park cafe, Inn the Park is a beautiful, natural restaurant that is as suitable for lunch with the kids as for a three-course business dinner. The wooden structure lies low on the north-east side of the park's horizon, overlooking 'Duck Island' and the lake. During the day it is bustling and bright as breakfasts are served followed by wedge sandwiches and hot food such as home-made meat pies and soups from the 'grab and go' section. Settle in for a gourmet lunch of high-class British dishes served with large old-fashioned cutlery and cute bee-embossed glasses in one of the large booths or on neat wooden tables. When night falls it becomes even more stylish and sophisticated, but also intimate and romantic thanks to starry lights from the London Eye and the nearby fountain. The barman also happens to be a genius when it comes to creating unique cocktails.

6 Old Court Place,
Kensington Church St
W8
⊖ **High Street**
Kensington

Maggie Jones's

7937 6462

This is homely, rustic British cooking in a simple but sophisticated restaurant. Maggie Jones isn't actually the owner's name, it's Princess Margaret's married name, used when she and her husband courted at this restaurant. Regular Kensingtonites, as well as a generous handful of American tourists, have been coming for decades to enjoy sublime cuisine amid the quaint and faintly eccentric English decor of hanging baskets, old crockery, cooking pots and dark wood panelling. A doorstop slice of farmhouse bread and pat of golden butter whets the appetite as you choose from the menu. Expect to find skillfully cooked classics such as potted shrimp, haunch of venison and game pies, as well as a variety of dishes cooked to traditional recipes using fresh, regional produce. House wine is served in 1.5 litre measures and you will only pay for what you actually drink. There is a sense that the helpful and amiable staff really want you to relax and enjoy the night, not just get through their shift.

87 Tower Bridge Rd
SE1
⇌ ⊖ **London**
Bridge

Manze Pie and Mash Shop

7277 6181 | *www.manze.co.uk*

This is a celebration of Englishness and a fantastic old-fashioned eatery, where you'll find green-and-white tiles on the walls, formica tables and a pearly king or queen if you're lucky. The business was established in 1902 by Michele Manze, the present owner's grandfather. The Peckham branch, the third in his small empire (there's also one in Sutton), was awarded a Blue Plaque in 1995. The secret of its success is plain for all to see: fantastic ingredients, kept simple and made into outstanding dishes by people who care about their job. You can see old machinery still in use and even older traditions proudly practised. The menu is straightforward – meat pie served with scoops of fresh mashed potatoes drowned in green liquor, all made to a secret family recipe. There is a 'new' vegetarian pie made with soy mince, or for an alternative to beef try the deliciously moist and tasty stewed or jellied eels washed down with a glass of sarsaparilla or a mug of tea. Either way, it will set you back just a few quid.

2 Queen's Crescent
NW5
⊖ **Chalk Farm**

Monkey Chews

7267 6406

Nestling at the back of a friendly neighbourhood bar is this cosy little dining room that serves home-made British food. The menu is simple and offers dishes that will warm your soul and make you want to settle in all night. Spit-roast lamb with rosemary and thyme and butchers' Lincolnshire sausages with garlic mash and gravy are among the firm favourites with young locals, who treat it like a home from home. This is a relaxed and welcoming place where conversations are leisurely and the dining is hassle free.

A good way to round off a meal is to slip into the bar afterwards for a few drinks and, from Thursday to Saturday, listen to musicians play live sets.

123a Clarendon Rd
W11
➍ *Notting Hill Gate*

Notting Grill
7229 1500 | www.awtrestaurants.com

TV chef Antony Worrall Thompson has created a relaxed dining room serving simple British fare. Starters include plenty of 1980s restaurant classics such as prawn and avocado and smoked salmon, which have not gone out of fashion for a reason. Main courses are meat focused. Thick and juicy steaks are cooked to your preference, as per the cooking guide detailed on the menu, and served with traditional dressings. There are no chef secrets here, just a sincere care for what you are eating. You can find out the provenance of all of the organic, locally sourced produce; descriptions of meat, for example, come with details of the amount of fat on the meat and what texture to expect. This is a great place for foodies, but is just as popular with couples, families and groups that have something to celebrate.

Tower 42,
25 Old Broad St
EC2
➔➍ *Liverpool Street*

Rhodes 24
7877 7703 | www.rhodes24.co.uk

Fittingly situated on the 24th floor of the tallest building in London, with breathtaking views of St Paul's Cathedral, the Gherkin and the London Eye, this restaurant celebrates the best of old and new British cooking. The dining room would feel small and intimate were it not for the wall-to-ceiling glass walls that expose you to the world outside (anyone who is afraid of heights might not want a window table). This is dining at the high end of the spectrum in all senses. The comprehensive menu includes fresh and fragrant as well as rich and indulgent dishes to suit all palates but one thing overrides them all – a sense of great simplicity and style. The ingredients are sourced, where possible, from the UK, and there are superb world wines to match.

28-30 Rivington St
EC2
➔➍ *Old Street*

Rivington Bar and Grill
7729 7053 | www.rivingtongrill.co.uk

Nestled among the galleries of Hoxton is the Rivington Grill, its popularity confirmed by its recent redevelopment which has swallowed up the old deli to create more space for diners. The restaurant offers sublime breakfasts from chelsea buns to black pudding with duck egg, as well as lunch and dinners of wonderfully fresh fish, seafood and game served in a humble, homely style. Its simplicity is even more appealing in an area where try-hards overdo kitsch and modernity at the expense of real taste. The people who eat at Rivington know good food and good produce – the sort who would normally buy it themselves from Borough Market or their local butcher's to cook at home, if only they had the time. Thankfully they don't and are keeping the Rivington in business for the rest of us who can't be bothered to pretend.

381

Roast

The Floral Hall, Stoney St SE1 ⊖ Southwark

7940 1300 | www.roast-restaurant.com

Based in the elegantly refurbished flower hall of Borough Market (p.368), Roast offers a 180-degree view of characterful London architecture; a glimpse of St Paul's, the green rafters of the marketplace, and the old pubs and narrow winding streets surrounding this hub of activity. Early birds who have seen the market in full swing can relax for a leisurely breakfast. Lunch and dinner are finer affairs with the menus reflecting the best of British produce. Orkney rare-breed beef, tender lamb shanks and roast game are masterfully cooked and served without pretension (you can even ask for a dollop of mustard, mint sauce and horseradish cream on the side). Wines can be recommended to suit your choice of food but, in the very finest British tradition of uncompromising manners, the barman will be just as happy to recommend cocktails to accompany your meal should you prefer. Afternoon tea, served from 13:30 to 17:30, is also a delight.

The Savoy Grill

The Strand WC2 ⇄ ⊖ Charing Cross

7592 1600 | www.gordonramsay.com

Here you'll find outstanding cuisine, impeccably served in an imposing art deco-styled dining room, and a distinctly modern British menu. From a man (Marcus Wareing) who has prepared dessert for the Queen one would expect nothing less than perfection – and it is delivered. During the week, businessmen and shoppers retreat from the hustle and bustle of the West End to enjoy long lunches of sublime dishes such as seared fat scallops with smooth sherry caramel followed by braised pork cheeks. Evenings are more elegant and intimate affairs, with theatre-goers enjoying pre or post-show food, and romancing couples sliding closer together in the booths that edge the room. There is no pomp, but just enough ceremony to make you feel special. Weekend menus are well priced at £25 a head for three courses. For the best view in the house book the chef's table; the glass front keeps the heat and fracas of the huge kitchen out but the preparation of the fabulous dishes in sight.

Smiths of Smithsfield

67-77 Charterhouse St EC1 ⇄ ⊖ Farringdon

7251 7950 | www.smithsofsmithfield.co.uk

Open from 07:00 to service the workers of the famous meat market nearby, Smiths serves hearty all-day breakfasts, brunches, lunches, dinners and drinks in an impressive building that stood empty for 40 years. Big open windows and blasted brickwork give it a New York loft conversion style, where friends gather to share fun and fine food. Sandwiches come with traditional fillings such as roast beef, horseradish and watercress or ham, mature cheddar and sweet mustard on wedges of fresh crusty bread. Other dishes such as corned beef hash and meat pies sit alongside fresh blends from the juice bar. If you're looking for a relaxing drink and a bite to eat, the ground floor has comfy sofas and low tables. On the first floor there is a slightly more formal dark oak dining room with well-polished service, while the top floor offers a luxurious restaurant with views across the city.

Restaurants

26 St John St
EC1
⇄ ⊖ *Farringdon*

St John Bar and Restaurant

7251 0848 | www.stjohnrestaurant.co.uk

Fergus Henderson has single-handedly stopped London's restaurant-going public from turning their noses up at cuts and entrails of animals that would normally end up in a stockpot or worse. St John showcases such delicacies as tripe, bone marrow, kidney and heart, cooked to perfection by chefs according to simple British recipes. Cleverly combined with seasonal vegetables and delicious sauces these ingredients really are a cut above the average steak or leg roast. As well as the meats there is a range of interesting fish and seafood such as smoked eel, skate and langoustines. Wines are available by the glass, half and full bottle and if you really like what you are drinking you can buy any of the bottles to take away at a reduced rack rate. The restaurant is based in an old smoke house (there is a bar area in one chimney and the kitchen in the other) that retains much of its old character despite its lick of fresh white paint.

Caribbean

42-44 Kingsland Rd
E2
⇄ ⊖ *Old Street*

Anda da Bridge

7739 3863

The most exciting flavours from the Caribbean find their way to Anda da Bridge. Patties, the finest jerk pork and even jerk snapper are among the favourites, as are 'brown down chicken stew' and the classic saltfish and ackee. If you have any space left after the generous portions then the boozy flambe or dense black cake can serve as both dessert and drink. If you are looking for more lubrication, there's a wide selection of dark and intense rums, Caribbean beers and fresh fruit cocktails. It does feel more like a bar than a restaurant but as long as you don't mind ordering and collecting your own drinks the rest will come to you. Food is reasonably priced and the atmosphere is hot. Resident DJs play a mixture of soul, reggae, R&B and rare grooves but special guest nights bring out the dancehall, basement reggae and soka.

12 Acre Lane
SW2
⊖ *Brixton*

Bamboula

7737 6633

This small and charming Caribbean restaurant showcases tasty foods that will make you want to come back for more. The jerk chicken, curried goat and patties are all spectacular but for those who want to go beyond the steadfast favourites there are stews made from oxtail and dumplings, ackee and saltfish, as well as plenty of plantain, yam, salads and tender callaloo. This is unpretentious fare served with a smile. The interior is as you would expect of a Caribbean restaurant in London; bright, colourful and bursting with character. There is always reggae music playing to keep the staff moving and the wide range of customers grounded. If you've got a big appetite you can guarantee 'satisfaction' with the namesake menu, a lunch or dinner of chicken, rice and peas, plantain and a soft drink, but if it's gargantuan you could try the 'hungry man' menu. Whatever you order you can bet it will be outstanding value for money.

10-12 Kentish Town Rd
NW1
⇄ ⊖ *Kentish Town*

Mango Room

7482 5065 | www.mangoroom.co.uk

Fresh blues, bright pinks, exotic flowers and bowls of shiny mangoes make a colourful setting for this modern Caribbean restaurant. Chargrilled jerk chicken, curried goat, saltfish and ackee are all cooked with a delicate hand. As you would expect, fish dominates the menu with sea bass, snapper and kingfish as well as more familiar salmon and tuna served with fresh coconut, mango or peanut sauces. At lunchtimes lighter snacks such as salt cod, plantain and sweet potato fritters can be ordered with a fresh green side salad or sticky 'ebony' wings. Sit under large oil paintings of Caribbean landscapes listening to vintage reggae and ska with a rum in your hand and, were it not for the grey skies and cold breeze outside, you could actually be eating your dinner in the islands.

12 Clapham High St
SW4
**⊖ Clapham
Common**

Roti Joupa
7627 8637
Trinidadian cuisine that you won't get in many places outside of the Caribbean is offered at Roti Joupa, much to the joy of the local Trini expats and new Clapham devotees. You'll find all the favourites from this fabulously diverse cuisine – roti (a kind of flatbread made with wheat flour), split peas, dalpuri and paratha, callaloo, and dense sweet black cake laced with lashings of Caribbean rum. This is just a small restaurant but it is jam-packed with character and delicious smelling food, which is really cheap and filling. The infamous 'all-fours' card game tournaments heat up the atmosphere on a few evenings a month – so check the boards for notices and you could be entertained by the colourful characters while you dine.

Chinese
Other options **Far Eastern** p.390

51 Marchmont St
WC1
⊖ Russell Square

China House
7713 0866
So long as you're not put off by the paper tablecloths and oversized heater in the middle of the room, you'll find some of the best dishes this side of Canton with authentic prices to match at China House. Mixed starters of sticky spare rib with soft meat that falls off the bone, spring rolls filled with duck and Chinese mushrooms and spicy satay chicken demonstrate that remarkable care and attention has been paid in preparing these staple dishes. Prawn ho fun in black bean sauce and crispy fried chilli beef are generously sized and tasty with no trace of gluten or oil slicks. The one-dish

specials such as roast crispy pork with steamed rice suit the local Chinese clientele as well as passing tourists and students keen to take advantage of the £3.50 takeaway special offer available on 49 different dishes.

17 Wardour St
W1
⊖ Oxford Circus

Chuen Cheng Koo
7734 3281
This restaurant is just like those you find in China: large and loud with endless rooms and a ubiquitous trolley service offering a fantastic range of choices. There are so many that you can try something new every time; enjoy the crispy taro cakes, fluffy white char siu bao or rice-

noodle wrapped prawns in sweet soy sauce. Or stretch to chicken's feet, sticky rice parcels with dried shrimp and scallops washed down with pots of hot jasmine tea. Set the pace as fast or as slow as you like, as the silk cheong sam dressed staff will bring their trolleys round again and again, loaded with freshly fried morsels and steaming bamboo baskets. You can dine from the a la carte menu here in the evening, but more fun is to be had at lunch and throughout the afternoon, in true Cantonese style.

Drunken Monkey

222 Shoreditch High St
E1
⇌ ⊖ *Old Street*

7392 9606 | www.thedrunkenmonkey.co.uk

A funky interior filled with silk lanterns and purple neon lighting makes a suitably cool setting for this Shoreditch den of excellent dining. Open until midnight, it's a great place for friends to share baskets of fresh and fabulous steamed, grilled or fried dumplings, buns and spring rolls or generous portions of noodles. The informal style of dining and laid-back mood pulls in a mixed crowd of Old Street fans, who also come to listen to the DJs play rare grooves, and sip superb cocktails such as the 'black buffalo' or 'simian features' with basil, pineapple and passion fruit. There is a happy hour every day and regular special offers on drinks so you can try to live up to the restaurant's name. But the focus is, and should remain, the food.

Hakkasan

8 Hanway Place
W1
⊖ *Oxford Circus*

7907 1888

This Michelin-starred Chinese restaurant is one of the best fine-dining options in the capital. The restaurant is stunning; sprays of exotic flowers welcome you at the door, from where you are lead into a dimly lit charcoal slate-lined room, with furniture softened by rich oriental embroidered fabrics. The cuisine is deserving of its reputation. Lean and light ostrich, venison and quail feature on the menu as well as the more traditional Chinese pork, duck and seafood dishes. Wines are expertly recommended by the sommelier to match your meal. Your tastebuds will be in heaven for the evening, though your wallet might hurt for a while longer. For a lighter (and cheaper) taste of Hakkasan, dim sum and cocktails are served in the bar area, which gets busy at the weekends. If you're looking for a more intimate affair lunch is your best bet.

Ken Lo's Memories of China

65-69 Ebury St
SW1
⇌ ⊖ *Victoria*

7730 7734 | www.memories-of-china.co.uk

This restaurant is imprinted on the minds of locals, not because of the bold red banners which welcome you, but thanks to consistently high ratings and positive reviews. Food and decor are elegant and traditional, and there's an easygoing atmosphere; dress up or down and you'll feel comfortable. The cuisine is classic Chinese in the UK; from sticky spare rib starters and crab and sweetcorn soup through to szechwan crispy duck with pancakes. These dishes are cooked with a more delicate touch than the average takeaway and are light, well presented and slime free. Ken Lo may not transport you to a faraway land but it is far enough away from Victoria station to escape its hectic surrounds and dreary chain bars and restaurants. There is also another branch on Kensington High Street.

385

Holiday Inn Express,
Bugsby's Way
SE10
⊖ **North Greenwich**

Peninsula

8858 2028 | www.mychinesefood.co.uk

Chinese families queue up here every weekend to enjoy dim sum as they know it best. Steamed, fried and grilled little bites and deliciously smooth cheung fun are accompanied by musty bo-lay or jasmine tea. As most of the people who dine here are Chinese, it is worth following their lead when it comes to ordering, especially if you find yourself going for the same things time and again. Everything is reasonably priced and the service is great, although don't expect too much of a personal touch when it reaches its busiest times on Saturday and Sunday lunchtimes. Dim sum is served daily before 17:30 as is the tradition, but Peninsula also offers an a la carte menu with more commonly known Chinese dishes from sizzlers to stir fries. Specialities such as chicken's feet, snails, shark's fin, marinated duck tongues, braised eel and delicately cooked cuttlefish are among the Chinese diners' favourites.

45 Great
Marlborough St
W1
⊖ **Oxford Circus**

Ping Pong

7851 6969 | www.pingpongdimsum.com

This sleek, oil-slick-black eatery offers dim sum to a trendy London crowd at affordable prices. With a first-come-first-serve policy, space at the bar can be tight, but the cocktails are divine. Kumquat mojitos are especially moreish, with peach and chilli ice tea a perfect virgin drink (although annoyingly a 12.5% service charge is added just to slide the drink across the bar). The 24 page menu has photos to show you what's what, and staff are good at advising on the contents of the many little parcels. Sitting on round tables makes it easier to chat in the fun and informal atmosphere, and the set menus for eight people or more are exceedingly generous with 19 different pieces of dim sum to try – incentive enough to plan your next party here. If it's full when you arrive, there are five other Ping Pongs across the West End and west London.

40-42 Baker St
W1
⊖ **Baker Street**

Royal China

7487 4688 | www.royalchinagroup.co.uk

Patience is a virtue that will certainly be rewarded if you join the queues on Sunday for this legendary dim sum – there is a no-reservations policy which is efficient at getting even large groups seated within half an hour or so. The spacious dining room is animated with flying golden geese on the walls and loud conversation. Follow the Chinese tradition and dine on the large round tables with friends and family; the more people there are the more dishes you can sample and the more reasonable the bill. You can order a range of the better-known dim sum, from pork puffs and prawn siu mai to har gau, but don't miss the delightful fried yam paste with dried meat, mushroom and dried shrimp cheung fun or crab noodles. Service throughout the meal is immaculate but not intimate, although endless top-ups of jasmine tea do come with a smile.

15-17 Broadwick St
W1
⊖ **Oxford Circus**

Yauatcha

7494 8888

Enjoy delicious Chinese morsels day, and now night, courtesy of Alan Yau's Michelin-starred Yauatcha. Clean and pure dim sum of the highest quality based on Hong Kong specialities are offered alongside an adventurous range of parcels including ostrich dumpling, venison puffs or wagyu beef cheung fun. The Cantonese love fish and seafood, something clearly reflected in the delicate scallop shumai, roasted cod with lily flower, and steamed sea bass served with duck egg. Staff will help you to avoid over-ordering, and recommend a balanced menu. When it comes to dessert, Chinese restaurants are usually known for eggy or over-sweet cubes or tarts, but these are neither – just sexy, sensual and very feminine. They can be ordered to accompany a pot of blue tea or to takeaway in delicate boxes.

European

Other options **French** p.393, **Greek** p.395, **Italian** p.399, **Mediterranean** p.404, **Russian** p.406, **Spanish** p.408

35 Pembridge Rd
W11
⊖ Notting Hill Gate

12th House

7727 9620 | www.twelfth-house.co.uk

An astrological – yes, really – restaurant, bar and cafe that is not as mysterious as you might expect. Fine modern European cuisine is served to a diverse range of guests in this unique little place. Downstairs, the dark wood walls and tightly packed tables make it a snug place to sip a glass of wine, cocktail or hot toddy. Upstairs, the restaurant serves inch-thick steak and out-of-this-world lamb shank. Sharing platters are fun to nibble on, perhaps while one of you prepares for your astrology and tarot readings to be done by the resident expert. The 12th House styles itself on 18th century coffee houses and wants to bring back the tradition of discussing charts, life, love and business in an elegant setting. If you don't have a full chart to discuss, the staff will ask you your star sign then deliver you a card with your horoscope on it.

74 Blackfriars Rd
SE1
⇌ ⊖ Blackfriars

Baltic

7928 1111 | www.balticrestaurant.co.uk

If the idea of the Baltic conjures up images of ice and simple food then you'll be blown away by the warm atmosphere and intricate dishes offered by this restaurant. Amber backlit walls, golden chandeliers and red splash paintings set a rich tone for sophisticated diners. You can enjoy a cocktail or straight shot of one of over 40 types of vodka on offer in the bar while you wait for your table. Once in the large sky-lit restaurant, you can indulge in blinis with caviars to suit your taste and budget, before moving on to blood-red beetroot soup. The wild boar is particularly notable.

17 Nelson Rd
SE10
DLR Cutty Sark

Bar du Musee

8858 4710 | www.bardumusee.com

Bar du Musee has French styling, French staff, and a French ambience, but offers a modern, European menu. A conservatory-style dining area filled with red velvet chairs and decorated with scenes of the Champs Elysee on the walls confirms the Franco feel. The bar serves wine by the glass from an extensive list, as well as cigars. Some of the dishes, such as the warm goat's cheese salad, can be likened to a chic Parisienne – light and very well dressed. Food is served to a soundtrack of soft jazz, while the staff are gracious and offer well-informed wine recommendations. In summer you can easily spend a lazy day under the shade of one of the white canopy umbrellas.

105 Falcon Rd
SW11
⊖ Southwark

Fish in a Tie

7924 1913

You don't have to wear a tie or even eat fish to love this restaurant. The winning formula is good food served at outstanding value in a friendly atmosphere by intelligent and good humoured staff who care about you, the restaurant and their reputations enough to ensure you come back again. The menu is simple with juicy soft

38

lamb, flavourful chicken and, of course, fish dishes all generously portioned and well executed. The wine list offers a range of decent choices for different budgets and tastes, desserts are filling and very moreish and the coffee is excellent. To freshen your palate at the end, nibble on your free slice of watermelon. The management has kept the interior simple too: fresh bright walls and fairly tightly packed little tables with candlesticks in wax-drenched old wine bottles.

Claridge's, Brook St
W1
⊖ Bond Street

Gordon Ramsay at Claridge's
7499 0099 | www.gordonramsay.com

The staff here possess charm and charisma, a rarity in fine-dining restaurants. Their welcome will set you at ease in the serene art deco-styled dining rooms while still making you feel as glamorous as the guests in the suites above. Fortunately you don't need the wealth to match as a set lunch menu offers three courses for just £30, extraordinary value for such exquisite cuisine. Main choices include pot-roast belly of pork with baby artichoke and braised turbot with caviar, and stand-out desserts such as fig and almond tart with a grape sorbet round the meal off. Talented head chef Mark Sargeant watches over proceedings, and you can even request a seat in the heart of the kitchen at the chef's table while enjoying an eight-course tasting menu tailored just for you.

89 Royal Hill
SE10
⇌ DLR Greenwich

The Hill
8691 3626

Tucked into the corner of a backstreet in central Greenwich is The Hill, a beautiful pub and restaurant. Come for drinks at the bar and chat with the locals, sip a good cup of coffee with your daily paper while admiring the oil paintings for sale, or sit at one of the tables in the raised section of the brasserie for a delicious lunch or dinner. The wide menu offers excellent vegetarian and healthy options as well as chic brasserie and comforting gastropub classics. It gets busy most evenings and all day at weekends so it's advisable to book to avoid disappointment. Management and bar staff are warm and kind, making the atmosphere relaxed, unpretentious and unthreatening. A lovely garden at the back has been tastefully decked and filled with plants, and there's the essential barbecue for those long summer evenings.

16 Hoxton Square
N1
⇌ ⊖ Old Street

Hoxton Apprentice
7749 2828 | www.hoxtonapprentice.com

Nothing about the food and service in this restaurant is amateur. The menu offers a wide range of well-prepared and beautifully presented modern European dishes cooked by chefs who, like the front of house staff, are gaining skills and qualifications for life in this training restaurant. Wind down after your hard day's work in the light, open rooms and enjoy 'beer and bruschettas' from 17:00 to 19:00 every day, or tuck in to a generous main course such as pan-fried salmon fillet served with pea puree, lemon potatoes and vanilla oil or the tenderloin of pork, poached in marjoram milk, with garlic mash. All the money made at the restaurant goes to the Training for Life charity so you can feed your soul too while you dine.

1 West St
WC2
⊖ Leicester Square

The Ivy
7836 4751 | www.the-ivy.co.uk

The most celebrated dining room among London's glitterati, The Ivy has been entertaining actors and theatre lovers in the heart of the West End since 1917. Everyone who is anyone wants to get a table. The staff extend a warm welcome and genuine thoughtfulness that makes each guest feel spoiled and relaxed at the same time. The decor of dark woods and white table linen is simple and elegant, and is lifted by the hubbub of conversation and laughter. With dishes including wild rabbit salad, fillet of red deer, caviar and a healthy amount of foie gras, it is clear this is no ordinary menu for ordinary people – and that's exactly why you should try it. Pre-theatre and weekend set lunch menus make it accessible to those on a tighter budget. The waiting list is long but when your time comes it feels like a red letter day.

Kanteen

K West Hotel and Spa, Richmond Way W1
⊖ Shepherd's Bush

0870 0274343 | www.kanteen.co.uk

Contemporary chic in the form of brightly coloured glass panels, modern art and luxurious leather furniture sets the scene for suitably modern cuisine. During the

week, the media set from the nearby BBC studios come to enjoy business lunches from the express menu, safe in the knowledge that if they don't get their starter, main course and coffee served within an hour they will get the whole lot free of charge. In the evenings, things can be rather more indulgent as guests happily while away the hours eating in the restaurant before drinking all through the night in the K-Bar lounge, which remains open 24 hours a day. The menu offers the sort of uncomplicated dishes that would suit any taste with a good range of vegetarian and generous salad dishes alongside pasta and the usual main courses of fish, lamb, beef, chicken and pork. Weekend brunch is a pricey affair and aimed more at hotel clientele than passers by.

Little Bay

140 Wandsworth Bridge Rd SW6
⊖ Fulham Broadway

7751 3133 | www.little-bay.co.uk

Value is often the exception not the rule when it comes to eating in London, but the Little Bay chain, which also has branches in Kilburn, Battersea, Farringdon and Croydon, has it covered. The great thing about its ornate rooms, pleasant atmosphere and professional service is that you are not made to feel that this is a cheap option. Starters are simple, fresh and tasty, main courses generous and rich with classics such as moules mariniere or rib-eye steak, and desserts suitably indulgent, and there is also a range of light dishes. There are daily specials to reflect the season and availability of produce but the menu is wisely limited in the number of choices it offers, ensuring the dishes it does serve are of the highest standard. The fare, much like the restaurant, is satisfyingly more imaginative than one would expect for the price.

Menier Chocolate Factory

51-53 Southwark St SE1
⇌ ⊖ London Bridge

7378 1712 | www.menierchocolatefactory.com

This former chocolate factory has been converted into a gallery, theatre and restaurant. The main dining room is a tribute to its industrial age, with tall ceilings, oak beams and stripped pillars decorated with a charming collection of antique clocks and other furnishings. A few large sofas and tables around the edge of the room make it

389

feel cosy and comfortable for snacks and drinks, with a raised central platform for the dining area. The menu is appealing, with a mix of fusion and modern British dishes. If you want to keep it simple you can't go wrong with the burgers and fat, hand-cut chips, appetisers and light bites, which are perfect with a pint. Prices are reasonable, and you can watch a show for £27.50, including two courses. There is live jazz every third Thursday and the garden offers a quieter alternative to the riverfront during the summer months.

130 Regents Park Rd
NW1
⊖ *Baker Street*

Odette's
7586 5486

Every area has its old established restaurants, patronised by knowledgeable locals and curious passers-by, and Odette's in Primrose Hill is a classic. It is green fronted with huge baskets of flowers, tables on the pavement in summer, and a small conservatory. There are a few eating areas; choose the pretty mirrored dining room and you're in for stunning views of the park, or alternatively venture down into the more intimate wine cellar. Tables are laid with crisp white cloths, and polished silver and glass reflect light around the room. The menu offers modern European cuisine with a light French accent, all elegantly presented and accompanied by a wine list with choices to suit different budgets. The restaurant has a really relaxed atmosphere despite its popularity, and this is one old classic that's likely to be around for a while longer.

161 Wardour St
W1
⊖ *Oxford Circus*

St Moritz
7734 3324 | www.stmoritz-restaurant.co.uk

Fondues haven't been a staple of the dinner party scene since the late 1980s but the original Swiss dish served in this rustic restaurant is worth revisiting. There are five traditional cheese options to choose from including fondue forestiere with rich wild mushrooms, and fondue valaisanne with gruyere and vacherin cheeses cooked with tomatoes and white wine. There is also an oil fondue for dipping meat and a fondue chinois, a stock hotpot that quickly braises fine slices of beef. Of course that is not the sum of Swiss cuisine; cured and dried meats feature heavily on the menu as well as pastas and potato bakes, perfectly accompanied by a range of Swiss wines. The decor is alpine chalet and the people fun and inviting – all perfect for warming the soul during a cold, damp London winter.

Far Eastern
Other options **Chinese** p.384, **Japanese** p.401, **Thai** p.409, **Vietnamese** p.411

132-136 St John St
EC1
⇌ ⊖ *Farringdon*

Cicada
7608 1550 | www.rickerrestaurants.com

The original link in a small chain of pan-Asian restaurants, Cicada marries the idea of fine-dining with a passion for the delights of the Far East. Each small dish is a joy to the eye and the palate. Japanese gyoza and Chinese shumai dumpling starters whet the appetite for a sublime beef or roast duck dish, and there are also Korean kimchee, Thai curries and Vietnamese roasts on the menu. You can order 10 dishes for just over £22, good value given the time and ingredients that go into each individual dish. Although fusion food has gone through cycles of popularity, this is one place that has never slipped out of fashion. Cicada is a sparkling, sexy and fun place to dine, and the seductive cocktails are expertly blended.

Restaurants

Camden Market,
Chalk Farm Rd
NW1
⊖ Camden Town

Gilgamesh

7482 5757 | www.gilgameshbar.com

Gilgamesh lives up to its epic name. Two statues of the mythological hero-king sit overlooking the biggest dining room in London. Staggered across the large space is a VIP suite, Babylon bar and oriental tea room, and capacity for 600 patrons. The British museum meets neon nightclub look really works, underlining a sense of flamboyance and fun shared by all who drink or dine here. Young staff in tight-fitting, trendy black hoodies with tan leather belts look after the glamorous crowd and serve cocktails, wine and sake from lengthy lists. The food offers the best of Asia: crisp squid with dipping sauce is hot and perfectly sticky, and the sea bass is moist and delicious, but even simple dishes such as fresh scallop and yellowfin tuna sashimi take on a sense of drama when served with fanned bamboo over dry ice.

54-56 Great Eastern St
EC2
⇌ ⊖ Old Street

Great Eastern Dining Room

7613 4545 | www.greateasterndining.co.uk

There are a few modern twists that make this pan-Asian menu stand out from the fusion crowd – soft-shell crab salad with sweet tamarind and lotus root is sensuous and exotic, the aubergine and lychee curry subtly fragranced and watermelon and Thai basil-infused cachaca shower-fresh. Although Shoreditch regulars might grab a plate of chilli squid and a beer during the day, the restaurant really comes alive at night. The decor is dark and music loud so is best enjoyed with friends who will be happy to spend the rest of the evening drinking cocktails in the bar upstairs or dancing until the early hours in the strictly dress-down club beneath.

7 Sheaveshill Parade
NW9
⊖ Colindale

Jakarta

8205 3335 | www.jakartarestaurant.co.uk

The flavours of south-east Asia are brought together in harmony in this beautiful restaurant, which is decked out in Balinese statues and artwork. Rijtafel – meaning 'rice table' – is a selection of seven or eight of the most popular dishes, a great option if you're not sure what to order from the extensive but inexpensive menu. Fiery fresh soups with rich coconut bases and generous amounts of seafood, followed by spicy nasi (rice) or mee (noodle) goreng, chilli roast duck or whole roasted sea bream are among the traditional specialities. Jakarta clearly has the balance right as it is usually busy with couples and families.

2a Kensington Park Rd
W11
⊖ Notting Hill Gate

Nyonya

7243 1800 | www.nyonya.co.uk

Despite sitting on one of the most popular thoroughfares in Notting Hill, this fabulous restaurant, set on two floors for informal and communal dining, remains relatively undiscovered. Those familiar with Chinese, Thai and Malay food will recognise the ingredients but the presentation is discernibly different; there is an emphasis on the aesthetic and the delicacy of flavour is second to none. The restaurant's glass front floods light on to diners while they enjoy delicate dishes of otak-otak (fish seasoned with coconut and spices and steamed in banana leaves) or street hawker food such as nasi goreng and laksa lemak (spicy coconut noodles). If you can't decide on dessert, the kuih is perfect, offering bite-sized portions of elaborately baked cakes and puddings.

6-8 Southwark St
SE1
London Bridge

Silka

7378 6161 | www.silka.co.uk

Tucked underneath Borough Market is this sophisticated and soothing pan-Asian restaurant. Horizontal stripes across its bright white walls stretch the room and give it a sense of space, making the subterranean venue attractive for daytime as well as evening dining. There is a delicious range of curries, grilled and stir-fried dishes with a heavy emphasis on Indian-style cuisine. The 'Ayurvedic platter', which is made up of 'low-fat energy food', has been designed with health in mind and, unusually for an Asian restaurant, there is a delicious selection of salads. Don't worry if you have a large appetite because portions are generous. There is a cheap buffet lunch running from Wednesday to Friday that attracts the office crowd, while on other days there is a set lunch menu which is also very reasonably priced.

78-79 Leadenhall St
EC3
Aldgate

Singapura

7929 0089 | www.singapura-restaurants.co.uk

Maureen Suan Neo brings the very feminine style of Malaysian cooking known as nyonya to the male-orientated quarter of the City. The spacious restaurant is modern and a little stark with its white walls and black balustrades, but this simple layout seems to attract plenty of business at lunch and in the evening. The menu also offers dishes from Thailand, Vietnam and Singapore, such as delicate spring rolls with crisp vegetables, spicy nasi goreng and thick nutty satay. There is plenty of healthy fish and vegetarian dishes for those who prefer a lighter lunch or dinner, and even a vegan set menu. House wines are well priced and there's a decent choice to suit different tastes and budgets.

Fish & Chips

Other options **British** p.378

7-8 Leigh St
WC1
Russell Square

North Sea Fish Restaurant

7387 5892

This popular traditional 'chippie' offers a range of fabulous fresh fish, as well as pies and the classic battered sausage. If you fancy your fish unbattered, the staff are happy to serve it lightly grilled with a wedge of lemon, or simply dusted with flour and pan fried at your request. Portions are generous and prices are reasonable – you can have your takeaway supper wrapped and ready for about a fiver. If you dine in the restaurant you will be served by women in chequered pinnies and hats, but be prepared to pay a premium for your seats. Much better to grab a takeaway and plonk yourself on the bench out front.

67-69 Norwood Rd
SE24
Herne Hill

Olley's Fish Experience

8671 8259 | www.olleysfishexperience.com

Fish & chips is taken very seriously by owner Harry Ziazi and his team. Every element of your meal is as fresh as possible, with ingredients stored at the optimum temperature to guarantee perfection. The light batter coating the 13 delicious types of fish seems neither too thick nor too thin. Chips have been pre-blanched then fried to ensure they are crisp on the outside and fluffy on the inside and are not over-salted. And it's not all deep frying and fat; you can also have your fish grilled with a spice paste or steamed with a little ginger and spring onion and served with new potatoes and broccoli. If you do want to indulge in the full works try Olley's legendary pea fritters, with a pickled egg or gherkin on the side. The restaurant is popular with people of all generations and backgrounds, who come to take away or sit in the rustic-styled interior, where exposed bricks and wood add to the quaint charm – staff even wear pinnies and straw hats.

French

Other options **European** p.387

30 Almeida St
N1
⊖ *Angel*

Almeida

7354 4777 | *www.almeida-restaurant.co.uk*

This is French regional cuisine at its simplest and best, offered by the reliable Conran group. Pre and post-theatre menus give early and late diners gourmet choices often limited by traditional fine-dining opening hours. Dishes on the set menu are recommended with wine by the glass, carefully matched to bring out their flavours. You are of course free to choose from an extensive wine list if you prefer, and the sommelier will skilfully guide you through. The trolley of tarts wheeled round for dessert is a fine spectacle. Although it is all quite pricey, you are paying for the quality. If you want a repeat performance in your own home, head chef Ian Wood runs cookery masterclasses from the restaurant.

57 West Smithfield
EC1
⇌ ⊖ *Farringdon*

Club Gascon

7796 0600 | *www.clubgascon.com*

Pascal Aussignac is a young chef who likes to move with the times. His superb menu offers modern and inventive dishes such as foie gras popcorn as well as time-honoured classics. Portions are nouvelle cuisine in size and the format of the menu has changed in keeping with the new fashion for tasting menus; guests are encouraged to order three or four dishes per person and share them with their fellow diners. The restaurant has updated its thinking in terms of atmosphere too; it is refreshing to find a French fine-dining restaurant that doesn't care if you wear jeans to dinner – although the old-fashioned values of good service and elegant decor are thankfully retained. Club Gascon is not reinventing French cuisine, more fine-tuning it.

1 Poultry
EC2
⊖ DLR *Bank*

Coq d'Argent

7395 5000 | *www.conran-restaurants.co.uk*

A beautiful glass rooftop glitters with the lights of the Square Mile, making Coq d'Argent a beautiful, romantic place to dine in the heart of the City. The atmosphere is formal but warm, with staff ensuring guests feel welcome and special. Lunch is a more business-orientated affair with plenty of suits and a hum of work-related chatter, but there also tends to be groups of ladies meeting with friends to redress the work/play, masculine/feminine balance. The evenings are quiet and intimate and you can wind down at the end of the week with a Sunday lunch that offers distinguished regional French cuisine accompanied by the tinklings of jazz musicians. There is an excellent value menu too – a 'prix fixe' for two and three courses if you want to watch your budget – and the spacious roof gardens offer spectacular views.

30-31 Clerkenwell Green
EC1
⇌ ⊖ *Farringdon*

Dans le Noir?

7253 1100 | *www.danslenoir.com*

London has finally seen the light on this sensory dining experience, following its huge success in Paris. After sipping beautifully presented champagne cocktails in a dimly lit lounge your blind waiter or waitress will lead you to a pitch-black dining room. What feels quite challenging at first soon becomes fun as you successfully pour your first glass of wine in the dark and find the bread basket. Eating the surprise menus becomes an intriguing communal experience as your ears tune in to all the voices in the room. Wonderful textures and aromas take over visual pleasures and if you choose to ditch the cutlery and eat with your hands you'll find the ingredients actually enhanced by the darkness. This isn't perhaps the place for a first date, but a very unique dining experience that comes highly recommended.

24 Inverness St
NW1
⊖ Camden Town

Haché
7485 9100 | www.hacheburgers.com

With thick juicy chopped (hache) 100% Aberdeen Angus steak in a ciabatta roll, peppery rocket and a side of crisp, lightly salted fries, burger and chips doesn't get much better than this.

Toppings are classified by regions and style, so there's Canadian sweet bacon and cheddar cheese, Catalan chorizo and chilli, and portobello mushrooms and basil. Tuna steak and fresh vegetables make fine alternatives to beef, or if you're on a health kick you can opt for a low-carb burger (you can even have it without the roll and with plenty of salad). Ditch the burger completely and go for one of Haché's mammoth salads and you may have space for a supremely tasty dessert such as dense Belgian chocolate fudge brownie or creme brulee. The simple interior is lit by dripping chandeliers and fairy lights, and the genial service attracts a discerning young crowd from near and far.

36d Shad Thames
SE1
⊖ Tower Hill

Le Pont de la Tour
7403 8403 | www.conran-restaurants.co.uk

Fine food enjoyed in style by the riverside is a very French affair, but you don't have to get on the Eurostar to enjoy it. Le Pont de la Tour has been a fixture on one of the prettiest stretches of the South Bank for many years; its simple and classy decor helps focus guests' attention on the wonderful views outside. There is also a live pianist to entertain you while you sip a few cocktails at the bar. The menu offers French cuisine with a light touch. There is a heavy emphasis on fresh seafood and fish but the meat dishes, though limited in choice, are delicious. Those on a tighter budget can still enjoy the feel of the restaurant at a fraction of the price with the bar and grill menu, daily specials and the 'menu du marche', which offers the best seasonal produce crafted into fantastic dishes. On Sundays, Mondays and Tuesdays, wine is also priced the same as it is in the restaurant shop, making it accessible to all.

**The Berkeley,
Wilton Place**
SW1
⊖ Knightsbridge

Pétrus
7235 1200 | www.gordonramsay.com

Dining at Pétrus feels more like an invitation to an elegant and opulent stately home than a night at a restaurant. The maitre d' welcomes you into a room that feels more like a jewellery box with its richly coloured walls delicately lit by black crystal chandeliers, and you settle down for some serious fine-dining. The senses are excited by the modern French cuisine, imaginatively created and lovingly prepared by top chef Marcus Wareing. It goes without saying that the wine list is extraordinary. Expert staff introduce each dish with flair and ensure you have everything you need without intruding. If you think it's too good to be true you're welcome to go in to the kitchen to meet the chefs and see the action. Seeing and tasting truly is believing.

Restaurants

68 Royal Hospital Rd
SW3
⊖ *Sloane Square*

Restaurant Gordon Ramsay
7352 4441 | www.gordonramsay.com
Despite having three Michelin stars, this Gordon Ramsay restaurant showcases the best in fine-dining without being showy. Clean lines, soft cream walls and mirrors reflect light around the newly refurbished room. Staff are models of graceful professionalism with service flowing as smoothly as the champagne. Dishes of delectable art are created to thrill the eye as much as the palate. The quality of each ingredient – from the frogs' legs to the velvety pigeon served with foie gras – is evident with every mouthful and reflects impeccable sourcing. Price means dining here is often reserved for special occasions but you can expect nothing less than mastery in the kitchen and magic in the dining room.

Greek
Other options **European** p.387

89 Regents Park Rd
NW1
⊖ *Chalk Farm*

Lemonia
7586 7454
You know a Greek restaurant is good when it is full of Greeks. Extended families with kids in tow mix happily with the Primrose Hill glitterati to enjoy humble, home-style cuisine. Like any Greek mama would insist, the portions are generous and traditionalism rules on the menu. Juicy lamb kleftiko melts in the mouth and hare stifado is a moist and flavourful delight. The scented honey dripping with baklava and pistachio nuts accompanied by a thick creamy coffee make for the perfect end. The waiters and waitresses, many of whom have been with the restaurant since its early days, treat you like one of their own, with smiles and affection bouncing off the leaf-covered walls. One of the few remaining family-run restaurants where you can still have a fabulous meal with a glass of wine for under £20.

14-15 Hoxton Market
N1
⇌ ⊖ *Old Street*

The Real Greek Mezedopolio
7739 8212 | www.therealgreek.com
Since 1999, trendy Hoxtonites have crammed through the Real Greek's glass doors to enjoy authentic souvlaki and horta at its marble mezze bar before dancing the night away in nearby clubs. The smell from the chargrills hits you as soon as you walk in, with a satisfyingly meaty aroma filling the air. Mezze is a winning choice to share or to hoard all for yourself. Smoky and peppery feta and tangy Santorinian fava dips make a welcome change to the usual hummus and taramasalata and are perfect accompanied by a carafe of wine from the all-Greek wine list. Main courses mostly come off the grill and can be accompanied by even more fresh and appetising dips or a proper Greek salad. Prices are higher than a real taverna, but you pay for consistent quality and a fun experience, as well-suited to a romancing couple as a band of friends.

Indian

136-140 Herne Hill
SE24
⇌ *Herne Hill*

3 Monkeys
7738 5500 | www.3monkeysrestaurant.com
A bright white restaurant with a few purple walls and an eclectic mix of photos give this Indian restaurant a rather modern industrial feel. The food is also modern, with several twists and turns on the old favourites. Dishes are well presented in ceramic pots and platters, all emblazoned with the 3 Monkeys logo. The professional staff know their menu and clientele well, and try their best to ensure your experience is above ordinary. The ambience depends on the night of the week; Monday to Thursday is generally quiet, while the weekend is lively. The restaurant is spacious, so you never feel as though it is too packed.

395

The Complete **Residents'** Guide

Amaya

Halkin Arcade,
Motcomb St
SW1
Hyde Park Corner

7823 1166 | *www.realindianfood.com*
Amaya's two large tandoor ovens stand proudly for all to see in the open kitchen of this Indian grill. The rest of the dining room is a big, bright, colourful space naturally lit through the glass roof and, at night, by large chandeliers. The venue is loud and lively most nights of the week, perfect for dining with friends. There is also a trendy cocktail bar and lounge area for pre or post-dinner drinks. Amaya is part of the new breed of Indian restaurant, presenting cuisine in the modern way: tapas-style small dishes served as a grazing menu. The tasting menu is a good option if you want to try the house specialities or any new dishes, and the fish and shellfish are highly recommended. Food is light and fresh and the wine list has been created to match the food rather than by traditional regions and styles.

The Cinnamon Club

The Old
Westminster Library,
30 Great Smith St
SW1
St. James's Park

7222 2555 | *www.cinnamonclub.com*
The curry house has certainly evolved in the UK, but at The Cinnamon Club it has been taken to dizzying heights. Set in the sympathetically converted Westminster Library, it whispers grace, elegance and class. Traditional Indian ingredients are cleverly combined with local produce to bring the best of both worlds to diners. This is a popular place to see and be seen, especially among A-list celebrities and music royalty, but even so the food remains the most impressive sight. There are so many exciting dishes and ingredients on the menu that it can be quite hard to order, so perhaps leave it to the experts and opt for the seven-course gastronomic menu with wine recommended by the sommeliers. After indulging in such fine food you can end your evening in the appropriately decorated Library Bar, a nod to the original reading room that stood in its place over 100 years ago.

Cumin

255 Finchley Rd
NW3
Finchley Road

7764 5616
This fresh new restaurant with its bold, bright, modern photographs depicting colourful scenes and people of India is attracting a new breed of curry lovers who don't need six pints of lager before they eat. Dining is on communal-style tables laid with spices in a large dining room. The atmosphere is at its most vibrant in the evenings and, although it does get very busy, the open room makes you feel that there is plenty of space to breathe. There is a large range of vegetarian and succulent seafood dishes as well as grilled meats and classic curries. Staff are friendly and good at steering you through the maze of different flavours.

Gufaa

39 Upper St
N1
Angel

7354 5465
Nestled between gift shops and cafes on Upper Street, Gufaa is hard to spot, save for its keyhole sign which welcomes you. Inside it feels like an anglicised 'Indian' of old, without the chintz. Instead, cream and maroon walls with dark wooden tables are cleanly laid out while music moves from sitar to smooth trance beats. The thali for under a tenner is a great deal at lunchtime and fills the restaurant with office workers. Rather than sticking to the old favourite chicken tikka massala, try chicken stuffed with potato, almonds and spices then cooked in yoghurt or one of the chef's recommendations. Gosht lamb with rich coconut and heady chilli sauce is wonderful, as is murgh sagrana laced with cream and about a dozen spices. Fish marinated in saffron and herbs and roasted in a clay oven provides an appetising option for the health conscious.

167-169 Wardour St
W1
⊖ **Tottenham Court Rd**

Imli

7287 4243 | www.imli.co.uk

It's not uncommon in an Indian restaurant to order a few dishes to share, but Imli takes this one step further by offering 'modern Indian tapas'. This is not just a new gimmick but culinary wizardry. A choice of dozens of innovative dishes, brought to the table as and when they are ready, give you and your fellow diners the freedom to sample Indian cuisine with an original twist. Alongside rich curries are dishes such as grilled chicken served with cumin mash and coriander chutney. Lighter paapdi chaat (crisp puffed wheat, sprouting beans and potatoes covered with yoghurt and tangy chutney) or the very un-Indian seafood platter of fried squid, juicy prawns and salmon fishcake sits happily alongside traditional curries. Three of these dishes per person are enough, but try to squeeze in a dessert too. The black salt and raspberry sorbet gives a hit of sulphur before delivering a burst of fresh fruity flavour. Like the rest of the restaurant, it is unusual but delightful.

9 Marshall St
W1
⊖ **Oxford Circus**

Masala Zone

7287 9966

Brits have taken Indian cuisine into their hearts and homes, so the popularity of this quick, cheap and cheerful Indian restaurant, which also has outlets in Islington and Earls Court, should come as no surprise. It is geared towards busy workers and eaters on a budget, but what is striking is the quality and range of dishes at such a competitive price. You can get two courses for £7.95 and three for £9.45, and portions are generous. There is no boring formula to the food, which is served at communal tables surrounded by folk art. Authentic specialities come from all regions of India, with street-food-inspired starters and sumptuous main dishes. The Ayurvedic thali, devised to suit diabetics, is revolutionary for Indian restaurants in the UK.

45 London Wall
EC2
⇌ ⊖ **Moorgate**

Mehek

7588 5043 | www.mehek.co.uk

This fresh, simple and well-designed restaurant in the heart of the City offers a hard-working crowd respite and refreshment. Pinks and yellows will soften your mood in a place whose name means 'fragrant'. There is a bar area that gives guests the opportunity to have a few drinks and share an Indian tapas selection of tasty vegetarian, fish or meat morsels and densely filled samosas. The main restaurant menu offers traditional cuisine from all regions of India prepared with a delicate touch and finesse, as well as more innovative dishes such as duck served in banana leaf or Goan-style prawn curry in a baby coconut. The staff are attentive but not in your face and the prices are not excessive – good news in an area where restaurants often charge according to their clients' salaries, not to their standards of food or service.

Banglatown

Recently renamed Banglatown, the Brick Lane area in east London is famed for its concentration of colourful curry houses and restaurants. This hot-bed of Bangladeshi cuisine is favoured as much by City boys after a few beers as it is by tourists and locals. Some restaurants operate a bring-your-own alcohol system so check beforehand if you want a drink with your meal. Preem (7247 0397), City Spice (7247 5755) and Gram Bangla (7377 6116) are just three stand-out restaurants in the area – or ask around for local recommendations.

39

34 Highgate Hill
N19
Archway

The Parsee
7272 9091 | www.the-parsee.com

At the bottom of Highgate Hill, behind a slightly shabby exterior, is this great Indian restaurant that has been keeping the folks of Highgate and Archway happy for years. The decor is simple and modern, with black-and-white photos on the walls and tidy black tables dotted around a small room. Talented chef Cyrus Todiwala offers a few standard Anglo-Indian dishes alongside fantastic Parsee specialities. Opt for the latter and you won't be disappointed. Delicate fragrant dishes made with generous amounts of fish or meat blended together with fruits, nuts and spices represent the richness of this complex style of cooking. Regional dishes from coastal India also feature on the menu, giving customers more than the average curry house experience without charging a fortune for the privilege.

784 Holloway Rd
N1
Holloway Road

Sitara Indian Restaurant
7281 0649

Modern jazz and Indian food might not be your typical combination but it's one that works at Sitara. Its owners are clearly trying to break the mould for Indian food, now as familiar to most British palates as fish & chips. The fact that this restaurant has been popular for more than 10 years shows it has succeeded in doing what many people found shocking. In fairness, this is more a jazz-Indian restaurant than an Indian-jazz restaurant; the music is loud and the service not always consistent but the balti and tandoori dishes are good and the vibe more buzzy than your run-of-the-mill curry house. Fun rather than quiet conversation should be on the menu if you choose to dine here.

International

10-13 Grosvenor Square
W1
Bond Street

Maze
7107 0000 | www.gordonramsay.com

Supremely talented chef Jason Atherton has created inspired Asian-influenced French cuisine, served Spanish tapas style in a restaurant which feels more New York than Mayfair. But confused he is not – superb-looking dishes such as Orkney scallops roasted with spices are perfectly balanced and presented with the flair of a fashion designer. In contrast to the tight control of the kitchen, the interior designer has let his imagination, and Gordon Ramsay's budget, run away with him, and to great success. A huge glass wave sweeps over the bar, while dark wood, contorted iron and coloured glass all help to create a fun atmosphere for fine-dining, where you can enjoy spectacular cocktails before, during and after your grazing experience.

50 Hampstead High St
NW3
Hampstead

Toast
0871 2074172

When the rest of the street is quiet, you will always find a buzz surrounding Toast. It offers drinking and dining in trendy but elegant surroundings, in keeping with the new breed of Hampstead residents. There is a definite eye for style in this bar and restaurant. The choice of food and drinks available almost any time of day is huge, and the vibe is just as great for afternoon tea and scones as it is for a dinner party with friends or a few cocktails and spring rolls on a Friday night. Whenever you go you will get honest food served by efficient, relaxed and friendly staff who will go out of their way to make sure you can get a table as soon as possible, and, once ensconced, help you enjoy your time with them.

Italian

Other options **European** p.387, **Mediterranean** p.404

Angela Hartnett at The Connaught

16 Carlos Place
W1
⊖ Bond Street

7592 1222 | www.gordonramsay.com

Angela Hartnett has won a place among the finest chefs in Britain, a Michelin star and respect in what is considered a man's world, but there is still something delightfully feminine about her restaurant. The interior of the two main dining rooms has relaxed the stiff-upper-lip tone set by the surrounding hotel, although you can indulge in Regency and Georgian glass, gold and glamour if you desire private dining. The food warms the soul with a delicate balance of British and Italian-influenced dishes. Leave yourself in her capable hands for an outstanding eight-course tasting menu that includes dishes such as beautiful duck ravioli served with white asparagus. The sommeliers poised to recommend wines to accompany your menu from their lengthy list are approachable and helpful. Sunday brunch and lunch offers mean you can enjoy the high level of cuisine and service on a smaller budget.

Caravaggio

107-112 Leadenhall St
EC3
⊖ DLR Bank

7626 6206 | www.etruscagroup.co.uk

Caravaggio is big, bold and full of life; how appropriate that opera singer Luciano Pavarotti opened the restaurant back in 1996. Since then it has made its name among neighbouring business people for excellent lunches that can be served within the hour, and as a great venue for parties held in one of the balcony rooms of this former bank. It is bustling and busy most of the time and the atmosphere lively and fun. The cuisine is classic Italian with great antipasti, pastas and risottos as well as a healthy share of meat dishes. The wine list comprises an array of Italian varieties from different regions that you won't find on the standard trattoria menu. Service is well dressed and polished, and the art deco design inviting.

Fifteen

15 Westland Place
N1
⇌ ⊖ Old Street

0871 3301515 | www.fifteenrestaurant.com

Jamie Oliver's famous restaurant is still attracting a flurry of guests long after the hype surrounding his TV programme died down. The concept for the show and the restaurant was to give 15 young wannabe chefs from disadvantaged backgrounds a chance to build a career in catering. The results have been impressive. The trattoria, with dried chillies hanging from the rafters, has a typically relaxed vibe and serves simple rustic food including pastas, pan-fried fish and grilled meats. Downstairs is the fine-dining restaurant whose decor is a mix of New York subway and Tate Modern. The cuisine has a more modern Mediterranean feel and uses fresh, seasonal ingredients. The service is immaculate but not stiff, and the atmosphere always animated. You can walk in to the trattoria without a reservation but there is little hope for a seat in the restaurant if you haven't booked.

La Porchetta

141 Upper St
N1
⊖ Angel

7288 2488

If it was in Italy, La Porchetta would be full of young people out to grab a cheap, quick pizza with friends. Conversations are animated and loud, the waiters are happy to chat, flirt and laugh with you as they fly about the room, and the music pumps through the speakers. The pizzas are made with fantastic ingredients to traditional recipes – no ham and pineapple on thick crust here, just beautiful thin dough with fresh toppings, baked for a few minutes in stone ovens. The pastas and salads are wholesome and generous, and coffee is short, dark and strong. In typical Italian

399

fashion, this is a child-friendly restaurant, and day and night, seven days a week, families and friends come in for healthy, fast food. La Porchetta also has branches in the City (7837 6060), Holborn (7242 2434), Muswell Hill (8883 1500), Finsbury Park (7281 2892) and Chalk Farm (7267 6822).

62 Goodge St
W1
⊖ Goodge Street

Ooze
7436 9444 | www.ooze.biz

A risotto bar is a fresh concept for a dish as old as Italy, but Ooze does it well. Purists have the choice of classics such as pumpkin, hazelnut and sage, or salmon with braised fennel, but those who want to challenge their taste buds and preconceptions will not be disappointed by the chef's innovative creations. Sliced sirloin steak served with red onion, wine and peppery rocket is rich but somehow not heavy on the palate or stomach. The 'all-day breakfast' served as smoky pancetta risotto topped with roasted cherry tomatoes, spicy bocconcini sausage and poached egg will surprise and delight even the greatest sceptics. Low salt, low fat and low carb choices are marked, and if you want a quick working lunch that won't leave you snoozing throughout the afternoon your dish can be cooked without butter or parmesan. The atmosphere is fun and the decor a soft mint-green, light enough to freshen any gloomy London day.

287 Upper St
N1
⊖ Angel

Ottolenghi
7288 1454 | www.ottolenghi.co.uk

The displays of salads, roasted vegetables, grilled fish and breads that greet you when you walk in to this delicatessen-cum-restaurant are sensational. Against the all-white background of the simple interior, the Mediterranean-influenced dishes look like they have been set up for a food magazine shoot. Diners sit for brunch, lunch or dinner on long communal tables, or you can take away – sometimes necessary as lunchtimes can be really busy. This is nothing like a standard sandwich shop, so expect to pay a little more than usual for the quality of the ingredients and the chic surroundings. The bakers also do their best to ensure you don't leave without something sugary by displaying a mouth-watering array of meringues, moist cakes, biscuits and sweets by the till.

42 Gloucester Ave
NW1
⊖ Camden Town

Sardo Canale
7722 2800 | www.sardocanale.com

Sister to the original Sardo in Fitzrovia, Sardo Canale offers all the modern style of Sardinia on Regent's Canal. Chic glass, mirrors and distressed concrete are accompanied by attractive staff who bring you baskets of bread to enjoy while you drool over the choices of regional food and wines. The Mediterranean island of Sardinia is known for the quality of its seafood, and Sardo Canale doesn't disappoint, serving delicious fish dishes such as tuna, swordfish carpaccio, and spaghetti alla bottarga dressed with quality pink mullet roe. Meat courses include hearty traditional sausages, delicate veal roasts and beautifully pink pan-fried liver with balsamic vinegar. This is Italian food that Italians want to eat. Desserts such as sebadas – pastry filled with fluffy white cheese and drizzled with honey – demonstrate perfectly how to combine simplicity and elegance on a plate.

Japanese

Other options **Far Eastern** p.390

47 Museum St
WC1
⊖ Holborn

Abeno

7405 3211 | www.abeno.co.uk

The first restaurant in the country to serve okonomiyaki, where each table has its own metal hot plate upon which a blue-capped Japanese waiter or waitress will cook your dish. The heat from the plates means a cold Japanese beer or sake is very welcome. Gyoza starters have interesting combinations, including tofu and avocado, and the noodle dishes are filling and tasty. The signature okonomiyaki is basically an omelette made with cabbage, spring onions and a combination of other ingredients such as chicken, bacon, seafood or fish, and covered with a sweet sticky barbecue sauce and mayonnaise. Sounds confusing, and not particularly appetising, but tastes outstanding. As this is Japanese cuisine the price is higher than your average omelette, but you won't find many like it unless you're willing to fly first. You can also try Abeno Too on Great Newport Street, near Leicester Square tube station.

265 Eversholt St
NW1
⊖ Mornington Crescent

Asakusa

7388 8533

Sitting at a sushi counter watching a master at work is just one of the reasons that people queue outside this Japanese restaurant. Unremarkable inside, Asakusa focuses on the most important things in Japanese cuisine: freshness and simplicity. The range of fish is particularly impressive and the presentation of each dish immaculate. Beers are served ice cold and sake served warm, just as they should be. If you visit later in the evening, the businessmen can get a bit rowdy, all adding to the impression that Asakusa wouldn't be out of place in downtown Tokyo. The Japanese customers who dine here en masse clearly know a good thing when they find it. If you want to join them it's better to book in advance.

139 Wardour St
W1
⊖ Oxford Circus

Gama

0871 0751189

Many of the oriental restaurants concentrated around Chinatown focus their attentions on the needs of English diners, but Gama is different. It is mostly frequented by young Japanese and Koreans which can only mean one thing: they are doing the authentic stuff right. The bulgogi, a Korean-style barbecue, is one of its strongest performers, but if you feel like pushing the boat out try yuk we – raw beef served with gama sauce. Being understood can be a bit difficult unless you speak Korean or Japanese, but these hurdles can be overcome with smiles and the help of your fellow diners. It's a relaxed canteen-style diner, and is great value for money. If you want to carry on partying then join your fellow diners downstairs at J's Lounge for late-night cocktails and very unoriental salsa music.

15-17 Brunswick Square
WC1
⊖ Tottenham Court Rd

Hare and Tortoise Noodle and Sushi Bar

7278 4945 | www.hareandtortoise-restaurants.co.uk

One-plate wonders are the speciality of this busy eatery, which was popular long before the regeneration of the Brunswick Centre into Bloomsbury High Street. Thankfully, though all around it has changed, and it now calls itself a noodle and sushi bar rather than noodle and dumpling bar, the menu and service are as good as ever. Grab a huge bowl of soba or udon soup, fried noodles or rice dish with a range of vegetarian, fish, seafood and meat options, or one of its special roasts for under a fiver. Ebi gyoza, filled with fresh fat prawns, is just £3.50 and platters of sushi are very generous compared with the miserly boxes sold in many restaurants and supermarkets today.

401

34 Westferry Circus
E14
⊖ **DLR** *Canary Wharf*

Ubon
0870 2238090

The younger sibling of the critically acclaimed Nobu, Ubon serves signature dishes from sushi and sashimi to wagyu beef and black cod in miso. The contemporary and spacious dining room is simple and tasteful and showcases stunning panoramic views. The atmosphere is just as suitable for a classic bento box lunch with colleagues as a luxurious party with friends or a quiet dinner for romancing couples. Dishes are made of the finest ingredients and crafted with aesthetics as much as flavour in mind. Some of the more unusual Japanese ingredients are available for those who want to be a little adventurous, including sea urchin and smelt eggs. The good-humoured staff make you feel at ease and look after guests with care. There are a couple of adjoining stylish bar lounges where you can enjoy cocktails or sip sake before and after dinner.

223 Portobello Rd
W11
⊖ *Ladbroke Grove*

Ukai Sushi Bar
7727 8222

Small, dark and sexy, this modern sushi bar is well worth a visit should you be browsing in Notting Hill. Slip inside and choose to sit on the blocks or bench either side of the restaurant for lunch or dinner. Service is fast and as friendly as the language barrier will allow, but it's all pretty straightforward. The menu is authentic Japanese: delicious miso soup, steaming bowls of noodles and some of the best sushi and sashimi in town. Jasmine and green teas come in delicate pewter pots that can be topped up for as long as you want. The bill will come as a pleasant surprise – it is rare for quality Japanese cuisine to cost this little in London.

5 Raphael St
SW7
⊖ *Knightsbridge*

Zuma
7584 1010 | www.zumarestaurant.com

Beauty and taste go hand in hand with Japanese cuisine but Zuma is the London master of this art. It comes at a premium but this is clearly not a deterrent as Londoners are fighting for reservations. If you do get in, expect the sublime; sushi and sashimi of the highest order, dishes from the robata grill and specials such as black cod or whole lobster tempura accompanied by one of 30 types of sake. If you're uninitiated in Japanese food or just want a hand, your personal waiter will happily design a menu around your tastes. The main dining room has a lively canteen vibe with black tableware, bamboo furniture and paper lanterns. Those who can get a seat at the sushi bar can ogle the incredible speed and dexterity of the talented chef. You can also hire a kotatsu, a traditional private dining room where you sit around a modern sunken table – a rather more comfortable option than the old Japanese tatami mats.

Latin American
Other options **Mexican** p.405

33 Earlham St
WC2
⊖ *Covent Garden*

Canela
7240 6926

Just off Seven Dials sits this popular but delightfully different spot for the local lunchtime crowd. Despite its stripped cafe decor, Canela should not be overlooked for an informal evening meal. Pots of thick black feijoada and the daily changing chef's special, such as chorizo and chicken stew, simmer to the side of the large chiller cabinet, ready to be served with freshly baked cheese bread or mountains of rice. There is a welcome array of wheat and gluten-free cakes and breads to go with healthy fresh ginger or herb infusions, or, if you prefer, indulgent vegetarian dishes such as lasagne oozing cheese and rich tomato sauce. This is a laid-back joint where table service can be a little slow, but once you've had a couple of zesty caipirinhas all is quickly forgiven.

72 Upper St
N1
⊖ Angel

Cuba Libre
7354 9998

Cuba Libra packs in the crowds for classic cocktails, music and food from the largest, most individual Caribbean island. The eclectic menu is not particularly authentic, but does great Caribbean and Latino-influenced dishes. Tapas and paella are the most popular with groups who have come to eat, drink and be very merry. Staff do their best to keep up with the torrent, somehow managing to keep a smile on their faces when people start shouting above the music. Hover by the small bar at the back of the restaurant for a delicious mojito or two after dinner and it won't be long before your hips shake to the sound of the sexy salsa music. Management are smug about the popularity of this restaurant and, although this can be annoying when it comes to booking, it is clear why.

91-93 Great
Eastern St
EC2
⇌ ⊖ Old Street

Favela Chic
7613 5228 | *www.favelachic.com*

A South American slum may not be the most appropriate name for a restaurant and bar frequented by the moneyed and uber-cool Shoreditch crowd, but at least Favela Chic follows the theme through well. Walls are covered in corrugated iron, brightly coloured chipboard and a whole host of other detritus. For all its post-modern irony and statements about culture and society (which no doubt accounted for its success in Paris over the last 10 years) London's Favela Chic is a fun place to go. The Brazilian music is fantastic and the cachaca-based cocktails are great pre-dinner warmers. The menu choice is limited but dishes such as the thick dark and flavourful feijoada – a Brazilian classic – have been recreated well. It is not a cheap place to eat and drink, and you can't linger too long at the table before it is whipped away to make space for dancing, but if you want to kick back and dine with a difference, this is one Shoreditch slum that is well worth considering.

100 Wardour St
W1
⊖ Oxford Circus

Floridita
7314 4000 | *www.floriditalondon.com*

Despite the garish mirrored pillars, neon signs and salsa music, style over substance this is not. While lithe dancers swing and sway in front of the great in-house band, the chefs sweat to deliver chargrilled lobster with garlic and parsley, and spit-roast sucking pig with lime and oregano plus black beans on the side. The cured hand-dived scallops served with beluga caviar, probably not seen in Cuba since Hemingway discovered the daiquiri, are expensive but worth the indulgence. It seems a prerequisite that the sexy staff, dressed in tight black dresses and well-tailored shirts, be as proficient on the dancefloor as they are at serving, but don't be persuaded to leave your table without sampling the sumptuous desserts such as coconut creme caramel or warm banana and toffee tart served with cinnamon icecream, or at least ordering another mojito – you can always work the excess off later.

403

1 Bell Inn Yard
EC3
⊖ **DLR** *Bank*

Gaucho Grill
7626 5180 | www.gaucho-grill.com

With testosterone levels in the City reaching epic levels it's no surprise that Gaucho Grill is the preferred dining spot for the red-blooded male to hunt down some meat. Its unassuming entrance takes you down into the old vaults of the Bank of England, which have been stylishly converted with dark woods and cow-hide stools into a modern, clean-cut restaurant. Gaucho attracts crowds from offices across the Square Mile and there is a blur of business talk, blue shirts and striped ties at lunchtimes. The main draw is of course the exceptional Argentinian beef from cows that graze on the vast and fertile grasses of the Pampas. Aside from the meat, Gaucho sources naturally organic ingredients direct from Argentina – potatoes that develop slowly on the hillsides of the Andes, Patagonian lamb, Ushuaian crab and trout from Bariloche. There are sharing platters or the 'bespoke' private dining service, excellent cocktails and a fine and rare wine collection – ideal if you're dining on the company expense account.

77-78 Upper St
N1
⊖ *Angel*

Rodizio Rico Churrascaria
7354 1076 | www.rodizio.co.uk

This is the best 'all you can eat' option for ravenous carnivores in London. The name, roughly translated as 'rotating barbecue', sums up what this restaurant is about – a wide selection of meats, grilled, griddled and roasted to perfection. Order a set menu, which can also include treasures from the sea, sit back and relax. 'Passadores', otherwise known as waiters, come round to your table with platters of freshly cooked meat for you to indulge in, and they'll keep coming until you tell them to stop. You may find the better cuts of meat are offered later when your appetite may have diminished a bit, but don't be afraid to ask for specific things if you want them – the staff are friendly and will oblige if they can. Fill whatever room is left on your plate at the salad bar, which offers fresh vegetables and other traditional accompaniments.

Mediterranean
Other options **European** p.387, **Greek** p.395, **Italian** p.399, **Spanish** p.408

45 Ledbury Rd
W11
⊖ *Westbourne Park*

Beach Blanket Babylon
7229 2907

Be amazed by the baroque decadence at this Georgian house in Notting Hill. Beach Blanket Babylon invites London's wealthiest young socialites to fluff their feathers and put on their finest displays – and you can almost smell the money when you walk in. There are church doorways, statues and gargoyles aplenty to add fantasy to any evening. The chapel, crypt and scullery serve as restaurant areas, each a bare brickwork candlelit cavern with greenery winding wildly around the room. The menu offers modern Mediterranean cuisine accompanied by a wallet-busting wine list. Cocktails are beautiful and fresh and the champagne list is, of course, extensive. Ladies can inspect the vintage costume jewellery for sale in the stunning glass cabinets while they powder their noses.

8 Theberton St
N1
⊖ *Angel*

Mem and Laz
7704 9089

Be careful or you'll knock your head on the dozens of colourful glass lanterns on the ceiling of this little local restaurant. Take a great big breath as you walk in and smell the meat sizzling on the grill as it wafts through the room. Reasonably priced dishes come from all nations touched by the Mediterranean. Filo pastries filled with feta and herbs followed by rich and deliciously creamy moussaka or kleftico transport you to a Greek island in seconds. The Turkish owners do what they know best – kebabs, grills and fresh fish steaks. It's heaving on Friday and Saturday nights and busy with locals even in the late afternoon, but still feels intimate enough for a romantic evening for two. It is the sort of place you could bring anyone; partner, boss, friends, even your granny.

Mexican

Other options **Latin American** p.402

2 Jamestown Rd
NW1
⊖ *Chalk Farm*

Arizona

7284 4730 | www.arizona-camden.8m.com

Impossible to miss along one of the main streets of Camden, the Arizona frontage sticks out like a fountain on the desert plain. This is Tex Mex cuisine served as it should be: big, bold and lively, with Mexican hats on the walls and sawdust on the floor. The menu has exactly what you would expect – hot sticky wings, sizzling steaks, burritos and fajitas, all ready to be washed down with plenty of cold Corona beer. People often come here to party, so after 23:00 expect your table to be whipped away to make room for dancing revellers. Staff are friendly and the cocktails are good value, with a happy hour every day.

103 Hampstead Rd
NW1
⊖ *Hampstead*

Mestizo Restaurant & Tequila Bar

7387 4064 | www.mestizomx.com

No dust on the floor or plastic cacti here, this is Mexican fine-dining with a Mayan touch rather than the cheap American interpretation. The deep red walls, simple black furniture and glowing orange bar conjure images of a soft Mexican sunset. The menu kicks off with traditional tapas, which you can order as a starter or combine to create a grazing menu. Main courses are classics such as mole poblano or verde, and the desserts are equally authentic in style and flavour. Afterwards, head downstairs into the appropriately named 'Downstairs' bar and choose from the fantastic range of tequilas and 'mestizos', accompanied by salsa or Latin jazz.

Moroccan

Other options **African** p.376, **Arabic/Lebanese** p.378

38 Queensway
W2
⊖ *Queensway*

Bedouin

7243 3335

Shisha pipes bubble away in this little Moroccan restaurant, filling the air with mint and apple aromas. Bedouin is a humble but reliable restaurant showcasing the best bits of Moroccan customs and dining culture without shouting about it. The manager and waiters are lighthearted and friendly and only too happy to help. There are dancers and live music on some nights, but the main focus is the unfailingly good food. Whatever your tastes or dietary preferences, there are dishes to suit. You can make up a grazing menu from the wide number of starters or order a few of the generous house special main courses. Wine served by the glass is reasonable, but Bedouin's teas are a much more refreshing and economical way to wash down the spices.

189 Upper St
N1
⊖ *Angel*

Maghreb Moroccan Restaurant

7226 2305 | www.maghrebrestaurant.co.uk

Shorn of shisha pipes, glass lanterns and scatter cushions in its bright and simple decor, Maghreb won't transport you to the narrow streets of Marrakesh; it lets the food do that. Baked duck pastillas and harira soup made with tomato, celery, coriander, chick peas, ginger, cinnamon and saffron are traditional regional dishes recreated with style and passion. The tagines, from vegetarian lentil to pumpkin and

405

spiced fish to succulent rabbit show how fantastic a homely stew can really be. Couscous dishes are piled high with grilled meats, sausages and vegetables, and desserts are sticky and sweet. The reasonable prices and friendly service confirm this place as one of the best Moroccan restaurants in town.

Souk Bazaar

27 Litchfield St
WC2
⊖ *Leicester Square*

7240 1796 | www.soukrestaurant.co.uk

The opulence of Moroccan dining comes to London at Souk Bazaar and nearby sister restaurant Souk Medina (1a Short's Gardens). Dining is on low tables with comfortable, colourful sofas and pouffes beautifully accessorised with silk cushions and delicately lit by ornate lanterns and candles. The rich, fragrant scents of Morocco fill the air, producing an intoxicating aroma of fruits and flowers with a hint of apple tobacco. The reasonably priced set menu offers delicious starters including spicy aubergine dish zaalouk or herby taboule, followed by a speciality tagine or a sweet sticky baklava and mint tea, or choose from the exquisite dishes on the a la carte menu. Round your meal off in style by reclining with a shisha pipe. The downstairs section has a fun vibe, with guests relaxing on floor cushions while being entertained by belly dancers and loud music.

Polish

Other options **European** p.387, **Russian** (below)

Wodka

12 St Albans Rd
W8
⊖ *High Street Kensington*

7937 6573 | www.wodka.co.uk

This spot in a quiet residential area of Kensington sells Polish vodkas and eastern European foods to illustrious locals. The name and the extensive list of vodkas do not represent the best thing on the menu – the food is the real focus of well-deserved attention. Smoked duck with spring onion and horseradish is rich and tangy, the pan-fried trout with almonds and creamy butter is delicate and light. The monthly changing menus include seasonal ingredients that reflect the cuisines of different regions. Each is as carefully balanced as the decor, with its red prints and warm glowing candles reflecting against the industrial grey-and-white walls.

Russian

Other options **European** p.387, **Polish** (above)

Potemkin Russian Restaurant and Vodka Bar

144 Clerkenwell Rd
EC1
⇌ ⊖ *Farringdon*

7278 6661 | www.potemkin.co.uk

Cobalt blue walls combined with burgundy and gilt mirrors reflect the light and add a touch of traditional glamour to this modern space. Russian expats love it for its authentic cuisine and exuberant style. Smoked fish and caviar is served at a remarkably reasonable price, while staff are sweet and helpful at explaining the intricacies of the dishes. Begin with a starter accompanied by one of 130 vodkas, including a delightful range of herb and spice-flavoured options. Sturgeon features among the specialities on the menu, a rarity for London and a delight on the palate. Three courses with vodka and breads costs around £20, which is excellent value given the size of the portions.

Trojka

101 Regents Park Rd
NW1
⊖ *Chalk Farm*

7483 3765

Antique mirrors, stained-glass windows and ornate frames are brought to life by the bustle of local Russians and eastern Europeans who frequent Trojka. Live Russian music is performed on many nights of the week by men whose ruddy cheeks suggest one too many frozen vodkas. The cuisine is interesting and well executed though perhaps a

When you're lost what will you find in your pocket?

Item 71. The half-eaten chewing gum

When you reach into your pocket make sure you have one of these minature marvels to hand… far more use than a half-eaten stick of chewing gum when you're lost.

Explorer Mini Maps
Putting the city in your pocket

little clinically presented. Dill herring with Russian salad, blinis with caviar and main courses of goulash or stroganoff will satisfy newcomers, while less-familiar dishes from traditional Polish, Jewish and Ukrainian kitchens are on offer for the experimental.

Seafood

The Boulevard,
Imperial Wharf
SW6
🚇 *Fulham Broadway*

Deep
7736 3337 | *www.deeplondon.co.uk*
Swedish husband and wife Christian and Kerstin Sandefeldt have brought their signature style and panache with all things fishy to this large and spacious development at Imperial Wharf. The well-designed, modern restaurant offers fantastic fish and outstanding seafood in true Scandinavian tradition; mussels, herring, crayfish and prawns all have the fresh flavour of the sea (and all have been sourced ecologically). If you don't want to eat fish, you can choose from the first-rate meat dishes on the menu (look out for the wood pigeon, venison and other game). There are lots of fish-friendly wines and 18 akvavits to accompany your meal.

188 Westbourne Grove
W11
🚇 *Notting Hill Gate*

FishWorks
7229 3366
Fishmonger out front and informal fish restaurant out back has proved a winning formula for FishWorks, which has branches all over the south of England. You can almost smell the sea when you walk into its pretty white and blue restaurant in Notting Hill. The fresh taramasalata is delicious and a perfect treat while you decide which one of the many mouthwatering platters of seafood and fish you'd like to order. The service is smart and relaxed and the staff are experts in wine recommendations to match your catch. It's not as cheap as your local chippie but this is an underwater world away, and with seasonal lunch menus with a glass of wine for under £20 you can enjoy the treasures of the deep without that sinking feeling when you get the bill.

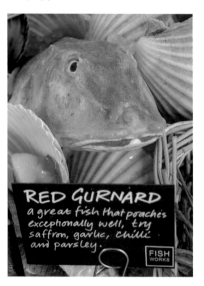

RED GURNARD
a great fish that poaches exceptionally well, try saffron, garlic, chilli and parsley.
FISH WORKS

Spanish
Other options **European** p.387, **Mediterranean** p.404

Beaufort House,
15 St Botolph St
EC3
🚇 *Aldgate*

Barcelona Tapas Bar y Restaurante
7377 5111 | *www.barcelona-tapas.com*
The Gaudi-inspired design of this tapas bar is a ray of sunshine amid the grey office blocks of the City. Colourful tiles and lizards don the walls, watching over the crowd as they enjoy mouthfuls of croquetas and tortilla. The quality of the ingredients is impressive and there are diverse dishes from different regions of Spain with wines to match. Happy hour sees a range of tapas to accompany drinks, served free of charge as they would be in Spain. If you want to enjoy a full spread, booking a table is recommended, especially at lunchtimes and early evenings towards the end of the week when everyone wants to wind down with easy but tasty food.

Cantaloupe

35-42 Charlotte Rd
EC2
⇌ ⊖ **Old Street**

7729 5566 | www.cantaloupe.co.uk

This restaurant offers a whole day's worth of dining, fun and drinks. Start at the front area complete with DJ and slouchy leather sofas for reclined drinking, then make a beeline to the back to discover the dining area, set apart from the main room. You can slide into booths to enjoy the predominantly Spanish and South American menu. Sharing platters of hams, cheeses, warm flatbreads and croquettes makes for an excellent starter, while main courses are generous and full of Iberian flavours. Stay on for desserts such as dulce de leche with cinnamon icecream berries, and don't worry about the calories either – if you book in advance you can get free entry to Cargo (p.440) around the corner for a spot of boogieing. After a heavy night of drinking and dancing, refuel with a Cantaloupe brunch; you can opt for a traditional English or stick with the Spanish theme.

Mesón don Felipe

53 The Cut
SE1
⇌ ⊖ **Waterloo**

7928 3237

In a corner of Southwark sits one of the oldest tapas restaurants in London, bursting at the seams with noisy diners enjoying fabulous Spanish food at the bar. Adding to the conversations is the sound of flamenco and classical Spanish guitarists playing from a small platform overlooking the square room. With its flaming red walls and conviviality, you could be in any local restaurant anywhere in Spain. All the regulars can be expected: wafer-thin jamon serrano; paprika-red chorizo; fat green olives stuffed with anchovies; patatas bravas; and grilled sardines glistening in olive oil. There are also seasonal specials, fresh seafood and interesting vegetarian options, and Spanish wines come by the carafe to help it all go down. The service is fast and the turnover big, but the staff know exactly what it takes to ensure their guests leave happy and so don't push you to move on.

Thai

Other options **Far Eastern** p.390, **Vietnamese** p.411

Blue Elephant

4-6 Fulham Broadway
SW6
⊖ **Fulham Broadway**

7385 6595 | www.blueelephant.com

Tropical plants and gold pagodas sit alongside golden statues and waterways in this expansive eating arena, creating a lavish scene for regal Thai food. The extensive menu has all the old favourites, such as mussaman, green and red curries, and tom yam soup, plus speciality dishes. Unusually for a Thai restaurant the dessert list is long and full of deliciously sticky or fresh and fruity dishes. Enjoy drinking coconut juice, or one of the many cocktails based on the fruits and seasonal flavours of Thailand. Set menus suit different budgets, and while none are particularly cheap they are very cheerful and worth splashing out on. There is a real sense of theatre in this restaurant, and a waterside table offers beautiful views – although the rest of the room is so elaborately decorated and the food so well crafted that you'll feel like you're actually in Thailand wherever you sit.

Busaba Eathai

106-110 Wardour St
W1
⊖ **Oxford Circus**

7255 8686

Every night of the week queues of people in search of fabulous Thai cuisine stretch under the awnings of this Wardour Street restaurant run by Alan Yau, the man who brought London Hakkasan (p.385) and Yauatcha (p.386). Tables are communal and often cramped but that doesn't detract from the simple, well-priced dishes from the grill, wok or curry pot. Yellow or mussaman duck curries are worth it for a change to green chicken, and the fish is a speciality. A no-reservations policy means many head down early to guarantee a place at the table, but at least turnover is fast. The staff offer menus and do their best to keep you smiling rain or shine, but with a reputation as golden as Yau's you're guaranteed great food that's well worth waiting for.

45 Pitfield St
N1
⇌ ⊖ *Old Street*

Charlie Wright's International Bar
0871 2230905
A lively night out is guaranteed at Charlie Wright's. It may be a bar but it's also undeniably one of the most fun places to eat Thai food in London. Step inside and you'll be hit by the fragrance of spices and fresh herbs as well as the sight of people excitedly playing table football and dancing. This place breaks the rules for restaurant and pub dining – in fact it has made up its own, much to the delight of Shoreditch regulars. Chicken penang seems to be a local favourite to the extent that the familiar nod to the barman accompanied by 'the usual' takes on a different meaning. There is an inventive cocktail list to accompany your meal, plus Thai beers and a range of Belgian brews. Jazz bands play on Sunday while at other times DJs spin an eclectic mix of tunes. It's a far from glamorous setting, but anyone who has been to Thailand will recognise the excellent cuisine, served in a laid-back atmosphere.

119 Upper St
N1
⊖ *Angel*

Isarn
7424 5153
Small but perfectly formed, Isarn sits quietly and peacefully among the hubbub of Upper Street. Fresh ingredients are beautifully cooked and presented in ornate plates, cups, glasses and boxes, while black furniture shines under the light of huge lampshades and delicate lines of butterfly motifs cast pretty shadows. The £5.90 khantok lunch set is one of the best options on the menu, and includes spring rolls, fish cakes or soup and steamed jasmine rice to accompany main courses of green curry, chargrilled beef with chilli or tamarind chilli chicken. Owner Tina Juengsoongneum has an eye on the aesthetics at all times at this family-run restaurant, which is no surprise when you discover her brother is the illustrious restaurateur Alan Yau.

The Halkin Hotel,
5 Halkin St
SW1
⊖ *Hyde Park Corner*

Nahm
7333 1234 | *www.halkin.como.bz*
Gold surrounds you in this fabulous restaurant in the new and rather exclusive Halkin Hotel – it's on the pillars, draped over the windows and around the necks of most of the diners. But perhaps it is Australian chef David Thompson who has the golden touch, since he's won the restaurant a Michelin star. His menu is based on royal, specialist, regional and ancient Thai recipes that have been collected over decades, giving guests a wonderful choice of dishes served with the lightest hand. The mood is quiet and relaxed early on when the restaurant is filled with people enjoying business lunches. It's not until later that the noise and activity levels pick up, making it a fun and lively place to match the fine cuisine.

Turkish
Other options **Arabic/Lebanese** p.378

107 Upper St
N1
⊖ *Angel*

Gallipoli Bazaar
7226 5333 | *www.cafegallipoli.com*
Brass platters, shisha pipes and bazaar music will soon make you forget the idea of an intimate dinner for two and have some serious fun. Fill your table with hot and cold mezze dishes such as smoky and smooth aubergine baba ganuus, crunchy kisir with

nuts and cracked wheat, and spicy sucuk izgara sausage, all of which are perfect for sharing. The signature 'kebap' platter is a generous mixture of grilled chicken, seasoned lamb and fresh fish that can be tailored to your tastes. Vegetarians will enjoy flaky light pastry around soft herby cheese or the peppery falafel, as well as traditional stuffed and stewed aubergine dishes. The full mezze menu of 12 dishes is great value at under a tenner each, and other set-menu options make group dining easy. Gallipoli has two equally good sister restaurants further along Upper Street, but book early as they all fill up fast.

72 Borough High St
SE1
⊖ Borough

Tas
7403 7200 | www.tasrestaurant.com

When a restaurant succeeds in making the simplest of authentic dishes sublime, you can trust that the rest of the meal will be great. Start a meal in Tas with hummus and crunchy kisir on warm soft flatbread and you'll see why it has earned a great reputation for serving very well-priced Turkish food. Although traditional in essence, the dishes are inventive. There is an intense depth of flavour in the casseroles and floral fragrance of the light pilaffs. Vegetarian options are plentiful and all the food is wholesome, healthy and natural. It gets busy on both floors for lunch and dinner seven days a week so expect the atmosphere to be lively, especially later when the live music and performers begin to entertain. The experience is completed with more simple things done well – fresh mint tea, thick and creamy coffee and sticky sweet baklava. There are other branches in Farringdon, Waterloo and Bloomsbury.

Vietnamese
Other options **Far Eastern** p.390, **Thai** p.409

326 Upper St
N1
⊖ Angel

Nam Bistro
7354 0851

Some of the best cuisines around the world are served in humble surroundings by unassuming staff – and this is exactly how Nam Bistro offers its Vietnamese fare. There are no frills, just plastic tables, kind and attentive service and honest dishes that give you a flavour of the east without challenging your taste buds or your wallet. The excellent mixed starters such as satay skewers, prawn toast and spring rolls are not dissimilar to ones you might find in modern Chinese restaurants, but the main courses really showcase Vietnamese specials: fresh rice rolls and succulent beef in thick sauces, sticky rice, and creamy desserts flavoured with exotic fruits. Two people can comfortably eat for less than £15 each, which makes Nam Bistro ideal for both those seeking interesting cuisine on a shoestring budget and Upper Street revellers looking for a quick bite before a big night out.

86 St John St
EC1
⇌ ⊖ *Farringdon*

Pho

7253 7624 | www.phocafe.co.uk

Upon their return from travels round Vietnam, Steve and Jules Wall were surprised to find that nobody in London was serving the healthy and wholesome noodle soup that is the staple breakfast, lunch or dinner in the south-east Asian country. Pho is a meal in a bowl consisting of noodles combined with a range of meats, seafood or vegetables and served with fresh herb salad (seasoned to taste by the individual diner). The simple but colourful surroundings of bare-brick walls with bright orange chairs complement this street food. At the main counter you can see the chef preparing the bowls and takeaway noodle boxes, and creating intensely fragrant stocks. A nod to Vietnam's French colonial heritage sees the menu include crusty breadsticks filled with lemongrass chicken or hot beef, and there are crepes served with prawns and beansprouts. The prices are as cheap as they could be in this part of town, and all the dishes can be enjoyed with a cold beer from Vietnam or Laos.

134 Kingsland Rd
E2
⇌ ⊖ *Old Street*

Sông Quê

7613 3222

This cheap and cheerful restaurant offers diners the chance to taste some of London's best Vietnamese cuisine. Give yourself plenty of time to wade through the menu, which contains a vast array of dishes, although whatever your choice the standard is high. The noodle soups (pho) are served with bunches of fresh herbs and dressings on the side, bahn xoe crepes are filled with juicy prawns, pork and fresh bean sprouts, while the crispy fried squid and sweet roasted baby quail are both excellent. Service is fast and could use a little polishing, but you'll struggle to find such good value for money elsewhere. Sông Quê is great for a quick, healthy soup at lunchtime or a lavish dinner with friends. Finish with one of the excellent desserts and an exquisitely smooth ca phe (coffee).

Pho

Deep

Cafes & Coffee Shops

London has a serious caffeine addiction – or so it would seem from the number of chain coffee shops opening on the high street every week. Independent cafes and tea rooms are finding it increasingly hard to compete, but are thankfully still fighting their corner with faithful regulars unwilling to give up either their home-baked food or mug of British 'builders' brew'. In old-style cafes, or 'caffs' as they are known locally, time stands still. Their formica tables, tiled walls and glass counters manned by charming or often characteristically grumpy ladies and gents ready to serve you tea or coffee with your 'full English' breakfast remain a great tradition. As for an evening cafe culture, the UK has not quite caught up with the continent, but Londoners are working on it, thanks mainly to Italian and Arab proprietors. Food varies massively from simple home-style sandwiches and baguettes to gourmet cooking, and is usually Mediterranean in style and cheaper than in pubs and restaurants. A recent trend for food shops and delicatessens to have a few tables where customers can relax is also a welcome addition.

14 Old Compton St
W1
Oxford Circus

Amato
7734 5733 | www.amato.co.uk

Falling in love with Amato is easy to do. The cafe is an institution on Old Compton Street and has a place in the heart of many a Londoner. The mood is relaxed and welcoming, the art deco-inspired interior spacious and stylish, and the charming staff make it a perfect setting to spend a leisurely afternoon sipping 'proper' coffees and nibbling on delicious cakes with friends. It is not as cheap as the chains but has more character and charm in one cup than the rest put together. There's also an array of chocolates and sweet marzipan creations in a glass counter at the front of the shop that look desirable enough to melt anyone's heart.

19 Pembridge Rd
W11
Notting Hill Gate

Arancina
7221 7776

It's hard to wander past the orange Fiat sliced in half in the window of this little Notting Hill cafe without wanting to pop in. Step inside and you can expect a warm greeting from the smiley staff standing ready to serve behind a long bright counter filled with delicious Sicilian treats. The cafe's namesake, arancini (rice balls with different fillings rolled in golden breadcrumbs and deep fried), is the speciality of the house. Other dishes to try are the baked pastas and pizzas. You can grab a slice to go or head upstairs with your tray to find a space in the small dining room. This is a good place to come for a cheap but very healthy bite on the way home, and a relaxing place if you want to sit and tap away on your laptop. Despite the fast service and the quickly prepared food, there's no rush once you sit down – as is the Sicilian way.

27 Upper St
N1
Angel

Art to Zen
0871 3320569

Relax with a cup of herbal tea and a slice of cake in this peaceful cafe. The food is fresh and healthy with plenty of soups, bakes and big pastas to fill you up. Puddings on the menu are reminiscent of a country kitchen rather than a city cafe, with deliciously sticky custard and soft, whipped cream to top them all. The staff are sweet and will let you linger long after your coffee grinds are visible at the bottom of your cup. People come here to chat, read and even work, perhaps inspired by all the artwork on display and for sale. There is also live music on some evenings to complete the creative vibe.

413

22 Frith St
W1
⊖ **Leicester Square**

Bar Italia

7437 4520 | www.baritaliasoho.co.uk

All the ingredients for a fantastic Italian cafe are here: intense dark espressos, loud conversation, passionate punters screaming about football, and a panino or two made with fresh prosciutto crudo and nothing else. Bar Italia is open until the early hours of the morning and has become a favourite among clubbers, especially those spilling out of Ronnie Scott's Jazz Club, who want a quick bite and a good coffee before heading home. Whatever time of day or night there is a great atmosphere and the food is delicious. There's a range of Italian delicacies to eat in or take away, and the cafe's shelves are filled with tempting grocery items. It's not cheap but you're paying for authenticity.

4 Blenheim Crescent
W11
⊖ **Ladbroke Grove**

Books for Cooks

7221 1992 | www.booksforcooks.com

A few bookshops have cottoned on to the fact people might want to linger over a cup of something while they flick, but Books for Cooks takes the idea to another level. The owners use a test kitchen at the back to try out recipes from the hundreds of books stocked in the shop (p.317). If approved, the dishes go on to the menu to be enjoyed by anyone who swings by. There are cakes and bakes, soups and stews and a whole host of other things to nibble and munch. The menu changes daily according to the latest release and the produce available in nearby Portobello Road Market (p.369). Here's a shop that takes its subject very seriously; if you visit early lunchtime any day of the week you will find all the staff sat around the large table eating together.

86 Royal Hill
SE10
⇄ DLR **Greenwich**

Buenos Aires Café and Delicatessen

8488 6764

Popular with local 'yummy mummies' stopping off for herbal tea and a gossip during the day, and the new breed of Greenwich young professionals at the weekend, this cafe deli offers more than the average. Authentic Argentinian goods fill the shelves, where you'll find yerba mate, a tea with health and medicinal properties relatively undiscovered by most Brits. You can pick up some picadas to whip out for a party from the freezers, while fresh seafood and bowls of fantastic pasta with bright green pesto reflect the strong Italian influence in Argentinian cuisine. There is also a good range of meats and cheeses.

11-13 Old St
EC1
⊖ **Barbican**

De Santis

7689 5577

Go to any cafeteria or bar in Milan and customers will rush in, hover at the bar to knock back a shot of espresso on their way to or from work, and perhaps grab a pastry. The same scenes are played out in Shoreditch at De Santis. You can expect superb sandwiches with simple deli-style fillings that are fresh and flavourful, including slices of prosciutto crudo, mortadella or some salami. Bread is baked fresh on the premises every day. There is a pleasant terrace at the back and a laid-back, softly lit lounge room downstairs – but to suck in the real feeling of Italy, sit around the high rosewood tables or perch on the stools at the bar. If you choose to linger for longer than a panino there are plenty of menu options that will fill your stomach and warm your heart, including handmade pizzas and focaccias, pastas, stews, salads and vegetables.

332 Bethnal Green Rd
E2
⊖ **Bethnal Green**

E Pellicci

7739 4873

Once a meeting place for the notorious Kray brothers and their gang, E Pellicci is an unmistakable and unforgettable East End cafe. The owner Nevio Pellicci, born above the cafe 80 years ago, and his son know almost all of the people who come through the door and seem genuinely enthused to see every one. Generations have been

Cafes & Coffee Shops

coming for killer breakfasts, egg and chips or just a mug of tea and a bit of toast. Those who feared it would go the way of so many other glorious 1950s cafes bought out by monotonous chains can rest assured now that the building has been awarded Grade II listed status. Outside, its original lettering and a red neon sign hangs overhead, while inside the open, impressive and intricate art deco-style wooden interior is a delight.

Frizzante@Hackney City Farm

Hackney City Farm,
1a Goldsmith's Row
E2
⊖ *Bethnal Green*

7739 2266 | *www.frizzanteltd.co.uk*
From farm to table in under 100 metres – you can't get fresher free-range eggs with your toast than this. Popular with families because of its fantastic location, Frizzante serves Mediterranean cuisine and cafe staples. The food is perfect for kids, with an array of delicious pizzas and pastas as well as creamy moussaka and wholesome roasted vegetable salads, and the walls are brightly covered with children's paintings and drawings. The child at heart can tuck into the 'big farm breakfast' with bacon and all the trimmings, or juicy burgers with jacket potatoes and salad. This is the perfect place to bring children (and adults) who are too used to seeing their food sliced and shrink wrapped. There are plenty of vegetarian options plus a seasonally changing specials menu, and if you've been really good you can have one of the heavenly cakes or desserts.

The Gate

Triyoga, 6 Erskine Rd
NW3
⊖ *Chalk Farm*

7586 0025
Just because it's in a yoga centre doesn't mean you have to know your alfalfa from your sprouting mung beans – this restaurant simply serves good food that just happens to contain no meat. The first Gate restaurant in Hammersmith received much critical acclaim, and this one is equally worthy of praise. Taking inspiration from cuisines across the world, the menu contains sumptuous and inviting dishes. Snacks such as butternut and cashew samosa or Indo-Iraqi potato cake precede warm root salad, aubergine teppanyaki or thick porcini polenta. The decor is as fresh as the food, and the staff are relaxed and helpful. Open seven days a week until 18:00, this is a wonderful place to brunch or lunch.

Grocer on Elgin

6 Elgin Crescent
W11
⊖ *Ladbroke Grove*

7221 3844
Gourmet food is available to eat in or take away in this modern grocer-meets-cafe. If you opt for the former, you can sit at one of its high coffee bars, little tables or along the bench in the modern frosted conservatory at the back of the shop. It's all very urban and minimalist in contrast to the country kitchen food shops that you'll find nearby. Staff who know their stuff dress in long black aprons to match the slick black-and-white decor, while a huge coffee machine bubbles away to serve tasty little espressos. There are wonderfully elegant, diverse and interesting dishes on offer until late in the evening, making Elgin's a great place to stop off for dinner after a long day.

Konditor and Cook

10 Stoney St
SE1
⇌ ⊖ *London*
Bridge

7407 5100 | *www.konditorandcook.com*
This fabulous German-inspired bakery can be classed as a cafe if you count the two small tables outside. Whatever you want to call it, it is worth a visit for the fabulous cakes, tarts, biscuits and breads prepared daily. It sells ranges of healthy or indulgent muesli, as well as great coffee for a morning treat. Pop by for lunch and you can also choose from fresh and interesting salads, deep-filled sandwiches and bagels, again with fresh organic and tasty ingredients that are a world away from their supermarket equivalents. The kitchen prepares a fresh pot of soup and a couple of wholesome hot

415

The Complete **Residents'** Guide

dishes every day at lunchtime; get there early to guarantee a choice as this is a popular place for local office workers. Some of the cakes and biscuits seem expensive at first glance, but the quality is outstanding, they look beautiful and the intense flavours speak for themselves.

22 The Pavement
SW4
⊖ *Clapham Common*

Macaron
7498 2636

Chocolat meets *Moulin Rouge* in this fabulous cafe-patisserie. The burlesque red-lipped staff transport you to another time and place. At the back of the shop you can see into the kitchen, where the suitably podgy and extraordinarily talented baker will be kneading dough in his white overalls and hat, engulfed by a cloud of flour. You can enjoy a rich cafe creme or an aromatic tea at the communal table at the rear of the shop, or alternatively you can sit on one of the tables on the pavement outside. You could be tempted by the macaroons or a cream-filled pastry, or you might want to make up a bespoke box of chocolates. If you prefer something savoury, the tartines and fresh loaves are delicious and, although more expensive than your average loaf, you'll get the quality and intense flavour you may have forgotten real bread had.

50-52 Brushfield St
E1
⇌ ⊖ *Liverpool Street*

Market Coffee House
7247 4110

With crumpets, cakes and creaking floorboards, this cafe on the corner of Spitalfields market is an oasis of country calm in the middle of the City. Traditional English food and drinks are served on wobbly tables with mismatched old chairs to the sound of Radio 4, and the walls are lined with old copies of the *The Spectator* magazine. You can enjoy home-made soups, a fish supper with a fresh ginger beer or a wedge of cake with a cup of hot chocolate for a very reasonable price in priceless surroundings. It helps that the genteel staff seem to nurture their customers rather than just serve them. The cafe and its tables on the pavement outside are always full on a Sunday, but it's quieter during the week, especially around breakfast time when you can enjoy your loose-leaf tea and buttered crumpet in relative peace and quiet.

42 Gloucester Ave
NW1
⊖ *Chalk Farm*

Melrose and Morgan
7722 0011 | *www.melroseandmorgan.com*

Melrose and Morgan is a grocer and kitchen that unleashes that 'kid in a sweet shop' joy within. Colourful cup cakes, muffins and tarts, along with healthier bowls of fruit, salads and vegetables, are prepared throughout the day and laid out on the large central table – so pull up a stool and fill your plate. You can also help yourself to the delicious pates, mousses, cold meats and terrines from the fridge to go with freshly baked bread. The majority of the foods are sourced from the British Isles and, because Melrose and Morgan goes direct to individual farms and producers, the staff are able to tell you where everything comes from. This is a great place to pick up a hamper in the summer for alfresco dining on the hill, or for naughty winter treats.

2 Park St
SE1
⊖ *Borough*

Monmouth Coffee Company
7645 3585 | *www.monmouthcoffee.co.uk*

The smell of rich, fresh roasted beans wafts out of this open-fronted coffee shop. Whole-bean coffee is delivered daily from the firm's roasting site in Covent Garden, and trained baristas know how to pour the perfect espresso or frothy cappuccino. Different varieties and exotic blends are displayed for you to smell and try before you buy. You can take your coffee away or drink in on stools by the windows or along the large communal wooden table in the middle of the shop. Pots of golden butter, honey and jams are laid on the table to go with the fresh baguettes. If you prefer

416

something even sweeter, there is a fantastic range of French pastries and chocolate. It gets phenomenally busy when Borough Market is in full flow, but the queue is definitely worth it.

2a Neal's Yard
WC2
⊖ **Covent Garden**

Neal's Yard Salad Bar
7836 3233

Those looking for a healthy lunch or a wide choice of vegan and vegetarian bites should find their way through the lanes off Covent Garden to Neal's Yard. A range of fresh organic salads and home-made soups can be accompanied by a doorstop of freshly baked bread or wheat and gluten-free corn breads and polenta muffins. Portions are generous and there are interesting Lebanese, Portuguese and Brazilian dishes on the menu. The fresh juices and smoothies are a real treat on a hot day, giving you an instant boost of natural energy and a feeling that you have been good to yourself. The premises are split, with half of the seating upstairs and half in an open room across the square. Ordering a takeaway is cheaper, and there are usually a few tables outside and bench seats around the courtyard.

8 Denman St
W1
⊖ **Piccadilly Circus**

New Piccadilly Café
7437 8530

This much-loved Italian-owned cafe is engaged in a constant battle with the multinational chains churning out lattes to the busy working masses. But its decor is holding its own – the place is filled with silk flowers, old movie and show posters, and original 1950s fittings including formica tables with little banquettes and red lamps that shine over them. The charming proprietor, Lorenzo Marioni, whose father Pietro founded the cafe, serves cheap and delicious British favourites or a great plate of spaghetti to an ageing band of customers, and a few new fans who have discovered the wonders that lie behind the bright signs in the window. Postcards from grateful guests and regulars line the back of the counter, a small token of thanks for great service and years of friendship. You can see people breathe a sigh of relief when they sit down here, and for a place that has let time stand still it is still very much in demand.

Bishop Square,
37 Brushfield St
E1
⇌ ⊖ **Liverpool**
Street

Patisserie Valerie
7247 4906 | www.patisserie-valerie.co.uk

It's hard not to notice the fabulous fairytale cakes and sweet creations in the window of this beautiful cafe and patisserie. If the tiers of icing and chocolate truffles alongside mouthwatering marzipan sweets and cream-filled cakes don't tempt you in, then perhaps the delicious Italian icecreams will. Valerie is popular all day and evening, but especially at lunchtimes when people from nearby offices need something to cheer themselves up. The ciabatta bar is great for a takeaway, the coffee is superb and the staff are all friendly and animated, as you would imagine for an Italian family-run operation. The 60-seat brasserie is open until 20:00 serving fresh dishes from pastas to steaks with a selection of wines and bottled beers, and is great for a quick dinner after a hard day's work.

76 Royal Hill
SE10
⇌ **DLR Greenwich**

Royal Teas
8691 7240 | www.royalteascafe.co.uk

This is a local favourite for lazy weekend breakfasts. It's a cosy space with patches of exposed brickwork and antique wooden tables and chairs, and has a surprisingly fresh and light atmosphere. You can order porridge with jam or honey, or an American or old-fashioned English breakfast from the cooks-cum-wait staff, while house specialities come at a very reasonable price. Tempting large, moist cakes are on display by the counter, ready to be served with your choice from the great selection of teas

417

that are stored in a big old chest of drawers, or coffee freshly ground to order. Seasonal main dishes such as potato spinach and mascarpone gratin will stay on the menu for a couple of days, but the favourites always come back.

48 Brushfield St
E1
⇌ ⊖ **Liverpool Street**

S&M Cafe

7247 2252 | www.sandmcafe.co.uk

Despite the name there's nothing kinky going on here, unless gorgeous grilled sausages and mash really does it for you. This little cafe decked out in 1950s-style black-and-white tiles serves comfort food with a smile, something which is clearly needed judging by the amount of people who frequent it. You can order from a range of more than 20 varieties of sausage, four types of fluffy mash and three gravies, accompanied by mugs of tea or something a bit stronger. Other well-loved British dishes such as toad-in-the-hole, shepherd's pie, and trifle or apple crumble served with custard are 'just like grandma used to make'. There are other branches on Portobello Road (8968 8898) and Essex Road (7359 5361).

175 Westbourne Grove
W11
⊖ **Notting Hill Gate**

Tea Palace

7727 2600 | www.teapalace.co.uk

Regal purple and rich cream set the tone at Tea Palace. The dozen or so small tables that sit alongside displays of tea and teapots are fresh and welcoming. Relax and enjoy a pot of some of the finest blends of tea from around the world or fresh herbal, citrus or fruit infusions. And why not accompany afternoon tea with a naughty-but-nice slice of cake, or perhaps a savoury dish such as a smoked salmon terrine? If you want the full works, the 'palace tea' or the 'champagne tea', which include an array of finger sandwiches, cakes and scones with clotted cream, will rival any Mayfair hotel for class, style and sumptuousness. It is a lovely place to treat your mother, or your granny for that matter, and with dishes including gressingham goose and salad with a green-tea dressing, the lunch menu is also good enough for royalty.

226 Westbourne Grove
W11
⊖ **Notting Hill Gate**

Tom's Delicatessen

7221 8818

Tom Conran's delicious little deli and cafe is full of fantastic food and fun surprises. The American-diner-style decor has 1950s memorabilia piled high in showcases, and booths that have been made from reclaimed public transport seating. Beautiful locals come to have leisurely brunches and lunches here most days of the week, but at the weekend it is particularly busy so it is worth coming early. The large communal dining table downstairs is inviting, as are the delicious hot dishes, stuffed sandwiches and freshly baked pizzas on offer. The food is not exactly cheap, but this is a trendy posh place with an eclectic edge – you won't find many other London cafes topping their smoked salmon bagels with caviar.

14 Neal's Yard
WC2
⊖ **Covent Garden**

World Food Café

7379 0298 | www.worldfoodcafe.net/wfc

If you crave the kinds of food you tasted while travelling the globe you should make a beeline for the World Food Café. You climb the stairs from street level to reach the bright dining room, which is open for lunch only. A large U-shaped counter dominates, behind which the chefs prepare dishes daily in their humble kitchen. They create thalis from India, Egyptian falafels, curries from Thailand and stews from South America, plus many other dishes. There are plenty of lassis and juices to drink, and you're welcome to bring your own alcohol. The room is light and airy, the cuisine vegetarian and mostly healthy. It's a lot pricier than you would have paid when you were wearing your backpack, but the atmosphere makes up for it.

Drinking

Pubs and bars are the lifeblood of London. Turn any corner and the chances are you'll spot a familiar wooden sign hanging from a pole or flashing neon in the window drawing you in for a drink. Londoners go to the pub to gather their thoughts, shelter from the wet weather, or spend their hard-earned cash having fun with friends and family. Whatever your style you'll find a place to suit, from old man's boozer to champagne cocktails in designer chic surroundings. The country's long-standing licensing laws, which saw most places stop serving alcohol at 23:00, have recently been relaxed, a change most evident in hotel bars. It's not only opening times that have expanded in recent years – tastes have too. London abounds with specialist beer bars, wine bars, vodka bars and cocktail bars, but old-fashioned English pubs, with their hand-pulled pints of draught bitter and ales, still draw enough punters to keep the tradition going strong.

Door Policy

Great British Beer Festival

Fans of real ale, bitter and blinding hangovers descend on Earls Court Exhibition Centre every August for the Great British Beer Festival. Over 65,000 eager drinkers attend the four-day event, enjoying beers, lagers and ciders from all over the world.

Door policies vary according to venue and area, and even day of the week. At some low-key bars and pubs, you'll have no trouble walking in at any time, regardless of group size or what you're wearing, while others will have restrictions of some sort on most nights. Busy venues in the centre of the city or on regional high streets generally have burly bouncers on the doors from Thursdays through until the end of the week, primarily to keep potential troublemakers out, with large groups of lads or people who've had too much to drink the main cause of suspicion. You may also be turned away if you look under the legal drinking age – 18 – unless you can produce a valid form of ID such as a driving licence or Proof of Age card (www.portmangroup.org.uk). You won't have to pay to get into most pubs and bars unless they're staying open late, in which case you may have to shell out a few pounds after 22:00. Clubs almost always charge to get in (see p.440), although the earlier you get there the cheaper it is likely to be. Some also have a dress code (see p.372). If you're heading for a night out at a particular venue, it's always safest to phone ahead to check exactly what the policy is to avoid disappointment.

Explorer Recommended

Cocktails		Real Ale		Gastropub		DJ Bars	
25 Canonbury Lane	431	Earl of Lonsdale	423	The Anchor and Hope	420	Bar Vinyl	431
Floridita	403	The Market Porter	426	Cat and Mutton	422	Big Chill House	432
Gilgamesh	391	The Opera Rooms	427	Lock Tavern	426	Home	435
Kinky Mambo	442	Owl and Pussycat	427	The Peasant	427	Lockside Lounge	435
Loungelover	435	Princess Louise	428	White Swan Pub	430	Medicine Bar	436

Pubs

Other options **Bars** p.431, **Nightclubs** p.440

55 Charterhouse St
EC1
⇌ ⊖ Farringdon

Abbaye
7253 1612

Belgian bars are famed for their beers and mussels, and Abbaye knows where its strength lies. Half-kilos of mussels come in six different styles, and there is Belle-Vue, Leffe and Hoegaarden on tap, flavoured beers such as the increasingly popular Früli, chocolate or banana Floris, and a more sedate range of other ales, lagers and bitters. Moody lighting, large candelabras and gilt mirrors set a dark tone in the bare-bricked bar, and there is live jazz music on Wednesday nights to raise the roof – get in early to guarantee a table. You may even feel moved to offer thanks for the beer given the amount of religious-themed decor. If beer is not your drink of choice try the flavoured gins or another shot from Abbaye's impressive range of spirits.

63 Abbey Rd
NW8
⊖ St. John's Wood

The Abbey Road
7328 6626

No Beatles memorabilia here, just modern furniture and a great menu that attracts an upmarket crowd. Having changed more than just its name back to the original from The Salt House, this gastropub has its detractors as well as its fans. But if you like your pint served by friendly staff, your table to be covered in white linen, and a lengthy wine list, then this is the place for you. Nostalgia does have its place here though, and many regulars choose to settle in on one of the long sofas to let the live jazz take them back to another time and place, probably before they had to think about mortgages or congestion charges. The canopied terrace is a big draw in summer, with a jug of Pimms and lemonade the perfect accompaniment.

11 Princess Rd
NW1
⊖ Chalk Farm

The Albert
7722 1886

Victorian architecture, rich red walls on the outside and wood panelling inside create an old-pub welcome with a simple, fresh feel. The Aussie bar staff are charming, giving The Albert a family-friendly atmosphere that is not at all pretentious, and the range of beers and bitters certainly won't burn a hole in your pocket. You can drink alfresco in summer in the pretty beer garden or on a street-side table, or huddle next to one of the big gas heaters in winter. This is not a gastropub but it does serve good food with an upmarket twist – although the meat pie and fish & chip nights are firm favourites with locals. Tuesday is quiz night.

36 The Cut
SE1
⇌ ⊖ Waterloo

The Anchor and Hope
7928 9898

An hour-long wait for a table is not uncommon for this fantastic gastropub, but it's worth every second as the British cuisine and tasty pints are outstanding. Cornish coast crab, lamb shoulder cooked for 30 hours, casseroles to share, plump duck, and fine aged beef with seasonal vegetables are all available without taking out a bank loan for the privilege. Despite the high-class cuisine, The Anchor and Hope has managed to retain the feeling of a pub rather than a restaurant, something many places struggle to achieve. The staff are full of smiles and the selection of wines and ales are fairly priced. There is a no-booking policy, but you can avoid the rush by eating late or early, or join the others hovering over plates of tasty tapas at the bar.

The Bountiful Cow

51 Eagle St
WC1
⊖ *Holborn*

7404 0200

This rather tight space on the corner of a Holborn backstreet has been cleverly transformed into a gastropub with a modern interior and a lavish menu. Funky metal stools reach up to the polished laminate-wood bar, the walls are lined with red leather banquettes, and booths separate the tables. Get your chaps on for a bovine theme – there are posters of cartoon cowgirls and old adverts on the walls, and plenty of meat on the menu. Vegetarians beware: fine steaks, burgers and roasts take centre stage in this operation. Request a table on the lower level of the pub and you can look through the window at the chefs going about their work. The beers are plentiful, with a few good draughts on the menu including Adnams and Broadside, while jazz music creates a mellow atmosphere.

The Bridge House

218 Tower Bridge Rd
SE1
⇄ ⊖ *London Bridge*

7407 5818

Popular after work for a supper of generous proportions and at weekends with locals filling up on fabulous breakfasts and late lunches, The Bridge House has changed its menus and upped its game over the past year. As well as the usual spirits and bottled beers, there is now a fantastic range of wines chalked on to the board above the spacious bar. The variety of ales on tap will keep any beer-lover happy, and the staff can very competently describe each one, even giving samples if you are still unsure which to choose. Bar snacks are visible in big glass jars and include dangerously good chilli puffs, bombay mix and a range of flavoured nuts. There is a restaurant downstairs and a space for private parties upstairs but, with plenty of tables or sofas, the smart-casual main room is the best place to sit and enjoy the fine British cuisine.

The Bull

13 North Hill
N6
⊖ *Highgate*

0845 4565033 | *www.inthebull.biz*

Catering to the demands of increasingly affluent locals, this once-derelict Grade II-listed building has been transformed into a gastropub, one that's definitely more gastro than pub, but that's what the Highgate set seems to want. The large cream chandelier-lit rooms adorned with blood-red pictures of bulls and toreros suggest a Spanish connection, but the menu offers French-influenced cuisine of the highest standards, created by a Michelin-starred chef. There is a large terrace with outdoor heaters for the cold winters, sun shades for the balmy month(s), a private dining room for small functions and an American pool table. For those who want to go to the pub for a beer rather than foie gras, The Bull does pull some excellent pints, including Timothy Taylor and Highgate Special bitter, as well as an array of guest ales, foreign beers and draught and bottled lagers.

Camden Arms

1 Randolph St
NW1
⊖ *Camden Town*

7267 9829 | *www.thecamdenarms.com*

Said to be haunted by the spirit of Lieutenant-Colonel Fawcett, the victim in Britain's last-ever fatal duel, held here in 1873, the only noticeable thing that goes bump in the night are the speakers. Pink neon backlights the windows, a square bar stands proud, and an interesting mix of lampshades brighten the deep aubergine walls while the two fireplaces at either end of the pub warm the toes and souls of all who enter. Creative types lounge happily on the scattered furniture, enjoying beers, wines, cocktails and sexy canapes from the British menu. The outdoor bar and barbecue bring in the crowds from Camden Market in the summer (p.368), and if you want exclusivity climb the spiral staircase to the spacious white private rooms, which are available for hire.

421

225 Portobello Rd
W11
⊖ **Ladbroke Grove**

The Castle
7221 7103

The Castle is a refreshingly dark, rough-around-the-edges little pub. Most evenings it is full of students and scruffy youngsters planning to put the world to rights – as soon as they finish their pints. The entertainment is top notch, with live music on Wednesdays in the form of acoustic, rock, hip-hop and rap acts. Customers turn DJ on Thursdays with the 'bring your own records' night. The range of bottled and on-tap beers seems to keep everyone happy, although it can get pretty busy around the large bar. The kitchen offers standard pub dishes such as burgers, sandwiches, roasts, and a few other deviations that are very well turned out – more than can be said for most patrons.

76 Broadway Market
E8
⊖ **Mile End**

Cat and Mutton
7254 5599 | *www.catandmutton.co.uk*

As the gentrification of pubs spreads across town, even Hackney's Cat and Mutton has turned gastro, much to the pleasure of local 'bohos' and young professionals. It has gone for a stylish, minimal feel with a black ceiling, schoolroom furniture, banquettes and bare brickwork – but its best feature is the food. The daily changing menu is chalked on to a board for hungry patrons to ponder. There's a decent range of vegetarian choices and gastropub food that is surprisingly unfussy, including dishes such as gazpacho, rock oysters, sea bream and a great Sunday roast. Head up a set of pretty spiral stairs to find a more formal, quieter dining room, which can be a pleasant refuge from the masses on busy weekends. Staff are sweet and the pub declares itself dog and child-friendly, though only until 20:00 (for children that is, not dogs).

26-28 Ray St
EC1
⇌ ⊖ **Farringdon**

The Coach and Horses
7278 8990 | *www.thecoachandhorses.com*

At a time when other pubs are stripping faster than a Soho dancer, the Victorian interior to this beautiful pub remains delightfully unchanged. Plaster mouldings on the ceiling, etched glass and wood panelling give the venue character and a friendly feel. The management has created a fun atmosphere and coupled it with seriously good menus. The beers and ales are well looked after, and the range includes Young's Special, London Pride, Adnam's and Wells Eagle IPA. There's a small patio under bright orange awnings at the back, which is a haven for workers in the summer.

142-144 Commercial St
E1
⇌ ⊖ **Old Street**

Commercial Tavern
7247 1888

Cabbages serve as candlestick holders in the new and eccentrically refurbished Commercial Tavern. Its outrageously flamboyant owners have lovingly added their own sense of style, from polka dot tables to a myriad of mirrors, but more importantly they've created a welcoming atmosphere. After a day scouring Old Spitalfields Market (p.369) you can enjoy banter at the bar or relax in an ex-barber's chair. There's a range of ciders available in bottles and Black Sheep and Scrumpy on tap alongside real ales and reasonably priced wines. The blinds are often closed and the room is dimly lit,

422

making you feel as though you've stepped into another time zone. In an era of chain pubs and themed bars it's fantastic to see something a bit different, and with tunes from Elvis to *The Sound of Music* playing no one is trying to be too clever. Retreat to the pool table if you're feeling overwhelmed, but ask yourself this – why have one chandelier when you can have 16?

Coopers Arms

87 Flood St
SW3
South Kensington

7376 3120

This Victorian-style backstreet pub has plenty of charm and a relaxed atmosphere, ideal for a Sunday reading the papers by the fire while nursing a pint of ale. The selection of Young's ales is pretty good, as is the wine list, which caters to the affluent crowd from the surrounding area. The food is modern European and good quality for the money. The open bar area feels light and airy, and the plants and pine furniture add a sense of space. Most big football matches are screened here, especially ones involving Chelsea. Large parties are catered for in a private room upstairs.

Drayton Arms

153 Old Brompton Rd
SW5
Gloucester Road

7835 2301

Never judge a London pub by its exterior. Outside are ornate stone carvings and high windows, a few wooden benches and large plants scattered on the pavement in a slightly European style. Walk inside and it is very eclectically British: a retro haven of random, colourful light fittings and a mix of furniture and dark patterned wallpaper. It's a laid-back pub that focuses on beers, live music, interesting food and creating a relaxed atmosphere where people are not competing to be seen or heard. Beers on draught include Spitfire, Hoegaarden, Früli, Canadian Sleeman and Adnams. The wine list is well priced and the Sunday roast brings them in from miles around. It is, after all, what's on the inside that counts.

Earl of Lonsdale

277-281 Westbourne Grove
W11
Ladbroke Grove

7727 6335

Massive lanterns hang outside the doors of this corner pub that is straight out of a Dickensian novel. Instead of being stripped and refurbished in the modern fashion, this place has recreated the glory of an 'olde worlde pub', thankfully without becoming a parody of itself. The Earl has all the traditional trimmings: velvet, gold and plenty of wood, and there are cosy snugs set aside for smoking, dining and drinking, each separated by four-foot high doors. The food is good and staff helpful. Because this is a Samuel Smith pub the drinks are reasonably priced, with plenty of real ales and bitters to choose from. If that's not enough there are open fires in the back room to warm your toes on a winter's day and a lovely garden out the back for the summer months.

The Elk in the Woods

37 Camden Passage
N1
Angel

7226 3535

Find this treasure of a tiny pub surrounded by antique shops and quirky boutiques and you'll feel a million miles away from neighbouring Upper Street. Grab a laid-back brunch with friends or just tuck yourself in for an afternoon of drinking and chatting in one of its big armchairs. With waiter service you won't even have to disturb yourself to go to the bar. The gastropub-style menu offers slightly unusual dishes along with the best of modern pub grub, so you can choose from rabbit stew or sea bream as well as roasts, curries and sausages. Snacks seem pricey for the size of portion but the sharing platters are so appetising that they're worth stretching the budget for. You may not spot an elk inside, but this place is certainly a diamond in the rough.

423

65 Gloucester Ave
NW1
⊖ *Camden Town*

The Engineer

7722 0950 | www.the-engineer.com

A gastropub in the heart of Primrose Hill, opened in 1995 by an actress and an artist, The Engineer has plenty of glamour and personality while still delivering exactly what you might want from a pub – great beers, an extensive wine list by the glass and bottle, and fabulous food. Filled with large vases full of fresh flowers, vats of olives behind the bar, designer wallpaper and antique mirrors, the attention to detail is evident in all elements of the design – particularly the luxurious private dining rooms. The breakfast menu offers fresh fruit platters and smoothies as well as grilled kippers and the 'full English'. There is also a children's menu and crayons to keep the little ones happy while the grown-ups have a drink with friends inside or on the patio.

North Rd
N6
⊖ *Highgate*

The Gate House

8340 8054 | www.upstairsatthegatehouse.com

At the top of Hampstead Lane and North Road sits the oldest, largest and most imposing pub in Highgate. Black beams are a striking feature on the outside, as is an old oak bar on the inside, and there are dozens of photos showing scenes of village life from yesteryear. The only evidence you'll find of it being a Wetherspoon pub are the fruit machines and curry nights, but don't let them put you off. Inside you'll find a pleasant mix of ages and social types enjoying a huge array of beers, wines and spirits. Hand-pulled ales with peculiar names such as Peggotty's Porter and Conservation Bitter, as well as Old Rosie cider, sit happily alongside foreign brews such as Leffe and Kirin. Pop 'Upstairs at the Gatehouse' to the aptly named theatre, which puts on plays and music from established and up-and-coming artists.

**60 Greenwich
Church St**
SE10
DLR *Cutty Sark*

The Gipsy Moth

8858 0786

If you've never been out in Greenwich this is a good place to start. Just opposite the famous Cutty Sark, this pub's big garden is a hit in the summer – but it's a pity that it closes at 21:30. The crowd on an average evening represent the sort of young professionals who are flocking to set up home in this beautiful part of town. The conservatory, set for diners, is delicately lit with fairy lights, but the menu is a far more macho affair. Chicken and ham pie, sausage sandwich with roasted red onion, and steak and chips with tarragon mustard are among the generous main courses. If you want to nibble while you drink, the smoked fish sharing platter makes a welcome change from tortilla chips – fresh flaked salmon, prawns in their shells, smoked trout and peppered mackerel all come with ciabatta bread.

**2 Castlehaven Rd,
Camden Lock**
NW1
⊖ *Chalk Farm*

The Hawley Arms

7428 5979 | www.thehawleyarms.com

The Hawley Arms is home to a refreshingly mixed clientele of local Camden types, music buffs and average Joes, and offers a fun and frolicsome atmosphere. Polaroids of happy customers linger on the wall behind the bar, tall glass jars of snacks are reminiscent of sweet shops of old, and the jukebox plays a range of good tunes. Outside, the roof terrace is busy come cloud or shine, and inside there is a large bar, leather sofas and a polished wooden floor. Some of the polish could be better used to buff up the service, although this is mainly due to the number of punters who want to get in on the action. The range of ales, from IPA to Old Bob, should keep most discerning beer drinkers happy, while others will be content with a good choice of wines, ciders, cocktails and spirits. The Sunday roast is a big winner.

115 Upper St
N1
⊖ Angel

The King's Head
7226 1916 | www.kingsheadtheatre.org

Drop in any day of the week and you'll be entertained, not just by the musicians that come on stage every night from 22:00, but also by the actors and comedians who have made this place their second home. There's a theatre through the back and the punters propping up the bar are as likely to be in for auditions as a quick pint – that's the beauty of this unique pub. People of all ages, types and tastes mix, mingle, chat and laugh together, and thespians, bohemians and romantics all share tales over a few drinks. The walls are a hall of fame of actors past and present, and faded beauty rubs shoulders with new hopefuls. The old saying 'if it ain't broke don't fix it' applies here to the Victorian cash register still pinging behind the bar, as well as to the venue itself.

90 Gloucester Ave
NW1
⊖ Chalk Farm

The Lansdowne
7483 0409

Sash windows, high ceilings, chunky wooden tables, green tiles and a cosy fireplace give The Lansdowne a distinctive old-pub feel, but the drinkers that frequent it are anything but traditional – here you'll find the Primrose Hill set, kitted out in low-slung jeans and designer T-shirts, catching up on gossip and lounging over a glass of merlot. The service can be irregular but always well intentioned, and if you're content to people-watch while you wait, there won't be a problem. You can dine downstairs, but if you prefer white table cloths head upstairs to the small restaurant serving excellent modern fare plus home-made pizzas, pastas and legendary steaks. This is a lovely place to while away a Sunday after an invigorating walk in Regent's Park or on Primrose Hill.

35 Chalk Farm Rd
NW1
⊖ **Camden Town**

Lock Tavern

7482 7163 | www.lock-tavern.co.uk

Retro-chic is the order of the day in this uber-trendy Camden pub. In contrast to the surrounding grimy streets, the Lock proves to be a well-polished haven. DJ sets ensure the house is packed every night with a playlist aimed at true music aficionados, but somehow everyone is made to feel at home. Through the kitchen hatch come steaming dishes of gorgeous meat pies, pastas, and sausage and mash, but outshining the rest are the roast dinners served with towering yorkshire puddings and all the traditional trimmings. There are plenty of bottled beers to choose from and a few ales and bitters on tap to accompany the lagers. Wine and cocktails are a little steep but at least there is a decent choice. Have enough of them and you'll soon discover the unisex toilets. The walled pub garden and conservatory act as quiet refuges from the music, and will soon become one for smokers too (see p.372).

36 Drury Lane
WC2
⊖ **Covent Garden**

Lowlander Grand Café

7379 7446 | www.lowlander.com

Look through the door of this beer cafe any night of the week and it will be buzzing. The reason city types and students come is for the choice of over 100 Belgian and Dutch beers and ales all served in the correct glasses, flutes or casks. Management do their best to maximise tables in the main biergarten-style bar and in the overlooking restaurant area, which means it can feel a little bit crammed and noisy but provides a great excuse to share tasting notes with your neighbours. Fortunately, waiter service means you won't have to fight the crowds to get to the bar and the menu descriptions really do help those who don't know their Dupont from Duimpje. If you need something to soak up the alcohol try the cheese or charcuterie boards or the more generous and delectable moules frites or duck breast with wild berry sauce.

9 Stoney St
SE1
≈ ⊖ **London Bridge**

The Market Porter

7407 2495 | www.themarketporter.co.uk

As the name suggests, market workers have been coming to this pub for generations. Open from 06:00, it has as much character as the most chipper of 'barrow boys'. It's busy during peak times, such as after work, while traders, tourists and locals all crowd in on Fridays and Saturdays when the busy Borough Market is open (see p.368). It can be hard to fight your way to the bar, but when you get there you won't be disappointed with the range of real ales available – there are 10 beers and cider on tap, as well as many bottled varieties. Drinks are sold at proper pub prices too, rather than the inflated bar prices that you'll find in most London establishments. Food is served in the bar and there is a decent restaurant upstairs, but this is more of a drinkers' pub.

28 Leigh St
WC1
≈ ⊖ **Euston**

The Norfolk Arms

7388 3937 | www.norfolkarms.co.uk

Nowhere is the ongoing transformation of King's Cross more evident than at The Norfolk Arms. Ragged carpets, the heavy smell of stale beer and miserable service have been replaced by elegant tables inside and out, chequered napkins and hanging chillies. There is little of the old pub left, except for a beautiful fresco of a Victorian lady and a fireplace, but it has scrubbed up well. The Spanish-influenced menu is cheerfully served by the staff, and you can choose from dishes such as charcuterie, oysters or a wedge of moist cake from the 'kitchen table'. There is also an extensive chalkboard list of wines, and delicious roasts are served up on Sundays. The outside tables are packed in the summer.

Pubs & Bars

29 St Martin's Lane
WC2
⊖ Leicester Square

The Opera Rooms at The Chandos
7836 1401

Leicester Square and its surrounds are teaming with tourists and bright bars, so it's refreshing to see the traditional Opera Rooms still thriving. Take the winding stairs to the side of The Chandos pub and follow the old Victorian pictures up until you reach two small rooms. There are comfortable large sofas and low tables in the main bar area, perfect for groups of people to spread out and relax, and more intimate tables in the room next door where on winter days the fire is lit. Samuel Smith enthusiasts can appreciate the cask ales, and the rest can simply appreciate the very reasonably priced spirits and wide-ranging wine list. Food is available from 09:00 until 20:30, from breakfast right through to pies, baguettes and other pub fare.

34 Redchurch St
E2
⇌ ⊖ Old Street

Owl and Pussycat
7613 3628

A 16th-century boozer that has survived waves of modernisation on the edges of cool Shoreditch. No stripped walls or floorboards in sight, just thick carpet and velvet seats. A relaxed crowd of workmen, old regulars and newcomers frequent this charming pub. The huge open fire is lit to warm the room in the winter months, and there is even a traditional bar billiards table. Good pub food is offered, with a carvery upstairs serving pork, lamb and beef roasts plus all the trimmings. Tables in the garden at the back make a lovely place to sip a glass of shandy or cider in the summer, but it's only small and its reputation as a great alternative to the trendy Shoreditch night spots and backstreet bars is spreading.

240 St John St
EC1
⇌ ⊖ Farringdon

The Peasant
7336 7726 | www.thepeasant.co.uk

The scarlet and black of The Peasant have seduced many a Londoner, and the joints continue to be legendary among gastropub lovers. Vintage posters of Mediterranean resorts, movies and musicians are as equally well placed on the deep red walls downstairs as they are on the soft cream walls upstairs. Draught beers include Bombadier, Watt Tyler, Budvar and Leffe as well as a few organic ciders, and tapas and light bites come as separate dishes or platters that are big enough to share. Order lunch in the bar or the main restaurant upstairs and you won't be disappointed. Brunch and Sunday lunch bring in a swarm of regulars, all eyeing the soft sofas or window seats. A patio at the back, filled with foliage and flowers, is opened during summer but is small so it's best to book. During the long cold winter the staff take pity on the soggy souls who enter, and often light the fire.

35 Old Church St
SW3
⊖ South Kensington

The Pig's Ear
7352 2908 | www.thepigsear.co.uk

A good-looking pub for good-looking people, The Pig's Ear has made a fine job of bringing pub culture into the 21st century. It has stripped out the fuss and nonsense and left a bright, spacious bar with plenty of seating and a smattering of paintings. As long as you're not on a budget you'll have a fantastic time. The Pig's Ear Ale sits alongside a fair few draught brews, and there is also a good selection of Belgian bottled beers and a comprehensive wine list. In the evenings it gets really busy with a very Chelsea crowd (think men in wealthy slacks and brogues), but during the day it has a more relaxed vibe with a few people dropping in for a bite to eat and a beer after shopping on King's Road.

42

*The Complete **Residents'** Guide*

82 Middlesex St
E1
Aldgate East

Poet
7422 0000

A bust of Shakespeare welcomes all to Poet. The large room is nicely decorated with chandeliers and funky lampshades and has a lively atmosphere most nights. It gets busy at lunchtime when the City types crave a beer and a plate of pub grub, so it's best to book a table to guarantee a place. It then peaks again after work hours when the girls tend to let their hair down with a large glass of pinot grigio while the boys move on to vodka Red Bulls. For those who want a more serious drink there is a decent wine list and a range of beers on tap including Greene King, IPA, Morland, Flowers and Budvar. The big screen shows major sporting events, and there is a small courtyard at the back where summer barbecues are cooked.

11 Pembridge Rd
W11
Notting Hill Gate

Prince Albert
7727 7362

Just off the main drag near Notting Hill tube station you'll find one of the best pubs in the area. A few candles, a huge chandelier hanging from the ceiling to the left of the bar and amber lights all glow gently, but the Prince Albert remains remarkably dark, especially its back room which is almost pitch black. Perhaps the low lighting is one of the reasons this place is so popular with dating couples and after-work drinkers. You can nibble on its well-priced fresh bar snacks or order good organic food prepared by the chef in the open kitchen out front. Alongside regular draught and bottled beers, there's an impressive selection of Belgian beers with the increasingly popular strawberry Frülli on tap.

76-78 Paul St
EC2
Old Street

The Princess
7729 9270

The Princess is an old-fashioned pub with a modern menu. The main room is usually busy with a mixed crowd of suits from Moorgate, arty students and trendy young professionals, and the place tends to have a lazy Sunday lunch feel whenever you go in. The impressive high windows make it feel spacious, and flowers and plants soften the masculine pub feel. The spiral staircase leads to an even roomier, more glamorous dining room where couples and groups of friends come to eat among the artwork and sculptures – you can even purchase an oil painting here if you wish. If you're more interested in buying drinks than art, fear not: there is a good range of beers on draught and an extensive wine list.

208 High Holborn
WC1
Holborn

Princess Louise
7405 8816

A rather unexpected beauty lies behind the thick wooden doors of the Princess Louise. Look up and the intricate plasterwork, painted and repainted over the years with thick red layers, is glorious. On the walls are gilt mirrors, stunning tiles made by Simpson & Sons, detailed stained glasswork by Morris & Son, and joinery thought to be by Lascelles – all considered the finest craftsmen of the late 1800s. The partition walls that once separated the women from the men and the rich from the poor have been taken out but the rest, thankfully, remains intact. Even the toilets are said to be listed. The clientele is a mix of young creative professionals, suited gents and older regulars, all enjoying relatively cheap drinks (including guest ales) and traditional pub food such as pork pies, ploughman's platters and bags of scratchings.

65 Kentish Town Rd
NW1
⊖ *Camden Town*

Quinn's
7267 8240

You'll find Belgian and German beers galore in what is most definitely still a pub, not a bar. Hover by the large fridges and one of the friendly landlords will happily give you the lowdown on each and every one, detailing the origin, flavours and style – no mean feat when there's over 100 bottles. You can order your beer by number which saves on embarrassing pronunciations, and comes in especially useful once you've sampled a couple. Despite the predominance of foreign beers, Quinn's is still an Irish pub, but happily there's no faux paraphernalia, just dark wood, comfortable tables and bar stools. The food is good and the drinks are not as expensive as you might expect – all of which makes up for the pub's hideous yellow-and-blue paint job.

52 Royal Hill
SE10
≷ **DLR** *Greenwich*

Richard I
8692 2996

This is an old-style drinkers' pub where you can still buy a round and get change from a tenner. There is a main bar room and a smaller snug as well as plenty of seating on the terrace at the front. The garden out back is great in the summer and the heaters scattered around mean you can even brave it in the winter. The food is straightforward and reasonably priced and the pub does good barbecues, which are especially popular after the Guy Fawkes fireworks display on Blackheath in November. As a Young's pub there is a great range of ales and beers on tap as well as a decent selection of bottled beers. It gets busier as the weekend progresses and more of the locals decide to take a load off their feet and enjoy a few relaxing pints.

116 Wardour St
W1
⊖ *Oxford Circus*

The Ship
7437 8446

This massively popular old-style pub is crammed every night of the week. Media and fashion types from nearby offices come to get away from over-designed bars with overpriced drinks, but once they've left the pub tends to fill up with punks and old rockers. Inside it's comfortable and a little worn around the edges but by no means tatty, with some old features such as its etched windows, decorative glass behind the bar and carved woodwork reminding you of old-fashioned boozers. There are no DJs here, just great music chosen by the landlords; the noise level rises as the evening goes on reflecting the good time being had by all. If you're looking for a quieter time to come and gather your thoughts, or pen a song like The Clash did under the staircase here, come on a weekday lunchtime.

7 Portobello Rd
W11
⊖ *Notting Hill Gate*

Sun in Splendour
7313 9331

The window panes of this large pub beg you to peer through, and with humorous signs out front you know this is going to be a funky, tongue-in-cheek place. The Sun is a breath of fresh air for those who like laid-back modern drinking holes that still feel like proper English pubs: not too much stripped furniture, no gastronomic, astronomically priced dishes on the menu, just great drinks and an atmosphere to match. It's full of young people who look as though they shop at the local market, and you get the feeling that if you're a local this is the sort of place where everyone knows your name. Follow the jungle scenes painted on the wall to the not-so-secret garden where you can sit under the glass roof on one of the battered old sofas kept warm with the outdoor heaters and lit by the moonlight (clouds permitting).

429

263-267 Old Brompton Rd
SW5
⊖ Earl's Court

The Troubadour
7370 1434 | www.troubadour.co.uk

The Troubadour boasts a fantastic cafe, delicatessen, club and gallery, each with its own individual style and character. The licensed cafe, with its stained-glass windows, dark wood panels, tankards hanging from the ceiling and red velvet seating, is reminiscent of old bohemian coffee houses. It's a great place to meet friends for a few drinks, a relaxing meal or simply to read the paper while listening to the great jazz and classical music. Staff are really laid-back and friendly and would never dream of hurrying you to move on (it's open from 09:00 until midnight so there's plenty of time to enjoy it). The club in the cellar of the cafe is home to more great music featuring live bands and solo artists who write and perform their own music. Former Troubadours include Jimi Hendrix, Bob Dylan, Joni Mitchell and Paul Simon. Different sessions run throughout the week, with unsigned bands on a Wednesday.

28 North Hill
N6
⇌ ⊖ Victoria

The Victoria
8340 4609

Flower baskets dripping with colour, racing green and cream tiles from street to roof, a few wooden tables on the outside and hand-pumped beer on the inside – what more could you ask of a north London pub? The Victoria has been freshened up by new management, and although they've stripped out the thick carpet, they've left the pub's character in touch. Local residents of all ages relax in the amicable atmosphere of this small comfortable venue. The prices are good for the area, the food is simple and tasty and the beer garden is attractive, especially in the summer. While all around have turned gastro, The Victoria has managed to retain what is great about traditional English pubs – friendly people and good beer in welcoming surroundings.

108 Fetter Lane
EC4
⊖ Chancery Lane

White Swan Pub and Dining Room
7242 9696 | www.thewhiteswanlondon.com

The major reworking of the Mucky Duck into the beautiful White Swan Pub and Dining Room has proved a hit with the legal types who are always looking for an exciting but classy place to drink around Chancery Lane. The main room, with its open mezzanine areas, is a vision of dark wood on white walls. Upstairs the dining room is resplendent in style and elegance. There is a rush-lunch menu to cater for the businessmen and women who want fine-dining rather than soggy sandwiches and crisps but don't have the time to linger. In the evenings, the atmosphere relaxes as people wind down. The quality ingredients on the menu have been well treated by the chef and come well presented on the plate. There are guest ales, draught lagers and plenty of bottled beers to choose from, but if you're dining you should take advantage of the wine list, which boasts 150 choices from around the world.

White Swan Pub and Dining Room

7 Shepherdess Walk
N1
⇌ ⊖ Old Street

William IVth
8119 3012

There is a fresh feel to this pub and it has nothing to do with the recent paint job. Candlelit tables and white chairs share the space with a couple of welcome leather sofas, armchairs and pub moggy Joanna. Upstairs is like a 1930s schoolroom (it's nicknamed the 'geography room') – each table has its own glass desk-lamp, and the walls are covered in maps and posters. Rather than a place for lectures, the room shows the occasional football match on a large drop-down screen. The beers include draught Black Sheep and Flowers IPA and the wine list has a good range of varieties and prices. The nostalgic pub menu showcases produce sourced from local markets and dishes of a bygone era – lamb shank with mash and mint sauce, pork pie with piccalilli or roast chicken with seasonal vegetables and a meat platter containing the finest of nearby Spitalfields.

Quiz Nights

Think you've got what it takes to scoop the top prize on *Who Wants to be a Millionaire*, or reckon you can do better than some of the slow-witted contestants on *The Weakest Link*? If so, you can put your grey matter to the test by taking part in one of Britain's favorite pub pastimes, the quiz night. Hundreds of venues across the capital run these popular events on a weekly basis. The format usually consists of teams of friends huddling round a table, scratching their heads or furiously scribbling on their answer sheets as the landlord or quiz MC reads out the questions. The format is split into categories such as general knowledge, current affairs, entertainment and sport,

Quiz Nights			
Bushranger	8743 3016	Sunday	W12
Islington Tap	7704 8304	Sunday	N1
The Duke of Argyll	7437 6819	Monday	W1
The Fox	8788 1912	Monday	SW15
The Cleveland Arms	7706 1759	Tuesday	W2
The Haven	8997 0378	Tuesday	W5
OSP	8748 6502	Tuesday	W6
Paragon	8742 7263	Tuesday	W4
The Mucky Pup	7226 2572	Wednesday	N1
Duke of Edinburgh	7326 0301	Thursday	SW9

with breaks between rounds so you can get in a round. There's usually a nominal entry fee of £1-2, which goes into a prize fund for the winner and runner up. It's a fun, social way to spend an evening, although expect to be frustrated as you rack your brain for that elusive answer that you *know* you know, if only you could remember it…

Bars
Other options **Pubs** p.420, **Nightclubs** p.440

25 Canonbury Lane
N1
≋ ⊖ **Highbury & Islington**

25 Canonbury Lane
7226 0955
Tucked between designer furniture shops, this place is full of neo-baroque decadent glamour and delicious drinks; it's all about lifestyle. Bottles of exotic and expensive liquor stretch up to the ceiling on glass shelves, and, at night, the bare backlit walls glow red – this could be the backstage lounge for a catwalk show. Staff seem to enjoy getting to know their customers as there are lots of happy regulars, but drinks are not cheap; this is the place to come to indulge. Cocktails range from bright and colourful to sexy and seductive, while the music is cool and the room just dark enough – a great combination in what feels like an exclusive club off the well-trodden Upper Street route.

6 Inverness St
NW1
⊖ **Camden Town**

Bar Vinyl
7681 7898
Cool kids and tourists come to this legendary bar to drink and flick through the record collection of its award-winning basement shop (at the same time). It has a relaxed mood during the day with DJs beginning to play from 14:00. In the evenings, the tempo builds to deliver exactly what's needed after a long day. Staff are great fun and help keep

431

things lively, pulling Hoegaarden and Budvar by the gallon to satisfy thirsty punters. The menu offers simple but tasty food, from salads and ciabattas to fresh pizzas. Considering the type of venue and its popularity it all remains reasonably priced.

57-59 Charterhouse St
EC1
⇌ ⊖ *Farringdon*

Beduin

7336 6484 | www.beduin-london.co.uk

Champagne, dancing and shisha pipes are the main draw for this Arabian-themed bar and nightclub. The vibe is animated and the place is very accommodating to larger groups that want to celebrate in style. There are only a couple of beers available, but plenty of cocktails and spirits to choose from. There's a range of excellent tapas-style dishes on the bar menu, but if you want to create your own party feast you can order a selection of hot and cold pastries, skewers and goujons to pick at all night for a fixed price. Guest DJs from some of London's best nightclubs play sophisticated house sets from Wednesdays through to the weekend.

29-33 Heddon St
W1
⊖ *Piccadilly Circus*

Below Zero and Absolut Ice Bar London

7478 8910 | www.belowzerolondon.com

Inspired by the popularity and, pun intended, cool status of Swedish ice hotels, Absolut has brought the first permanent ice bar to the UK. Kept at five degrees below zero you can't stay for long before you begin to lose the feeling in your feet – and that has nothing to do with the amount of vodka you drink. In fact, you'll be limited to a 40-minute slot – long enough for hypothermia to set in, but you won't be fully exposed as your entry fee includes a thermal poncho and gloves to handle your vodka-filled ice glass. Be warned, a refill costs £6, and other drinks are expensive, but this is an experience that can't be replicated anywhere else in the country. After your icy blast, thaw out with some warm hospitality in the lounge and restaurant at Below Zero.

257-259 Pentonville Rd
N1
⇌ ⊖ *King's Cross*
St. Pancras

The Big Chill House

7684 2019 | www.bigchill.net

Following the success of its bar in Brick Lane, The Big Chill House has opened in King's Cross. Set on what used to be the 'wrong side' of the Thameslink station, the Big Chill House is another sign of the area's fast and furious regeneration. As its name suggests, this is a friendly and relaxed bar where a young crowd come to hear chilled dance and enjoy a few drinks with friends. It's big, with three floors of dancing and drinking

space, and the layout encourages groups to mix, mingle and lounge on large sofas, low tables and big cushions. There is a terrace which is perfect for sunny days and moonlit nights when you want to get some fresh air.

15 Atlantic Rd
SW9
⊖ *Brixton*

Brixton Bar and Grill

7737 6777 | www.bbag.me.uk

A smooth place with a polished team behind it. A predominantly young and trendy crowd are attracted by the slinky cocktails, fantastic array of wines, champagnes, beers on draught and straight-up shots from the extensive drinks list. People also come to enjoy fabulous tapas, seafood, vegetarian specials or snacks such as kumara chips, fish fingers or mezze dishes to share. Music is strictly soul and funk, and on Tuesdays you can play backgammon. There are low banquette seats as well as a long, high table and bar stools in a room that is gently candlelit. This is a refreshingly different type of bar for the area – it has been well received by the locals and now has a firm following of friendly regulars.

43 Exmouth Market
EC1
Angel

Café Kick

7837 8077 | *www.cafekick.co.uk*

This little cafe near Exmouth market is home to some passionate football players – 'babyfoot' players to be precise. In France and Italy, this game is played day and night by both schoolkids and adults, and on their return from travelling around Europe the owners decided to bring a piece of the action back to London with them, along with some other great European elements. Expect boisterous behaviour in the front of the bar where there are three tables. A game costs just 75p with a winner-stays-on policy if all the tables are busy. Out back there is a more relaxed atmosphere, except if a match is being shown on the big screens. Babyfoot is thirsty work so luckily there is a great range of beers and wines on offer. There are also fine Portuguese hotpots, salads and soups, which prove especially popular with the local market-stall holders. But if you just want a few nibbles to keep your energy levels up for the main match, opt for the platters of cheese or charcuterie. The bar's younger and bigger sibling, Bar Kick, can be found in Shoreditch.

58 Porchester Rd
W2
Royal Oak

Cherry Jam

7727 9950 | *www.cherryjam.net*

Wooden booths are laid out around a slick asymmetrical bar in this cherry-red little venue. The vibe is laid-back funk with high-end cocktails, fine wines, champagnes and international beers. In the early evening people come straight from the office to drink away their stresses and enjoy the chilled-out music, but at the weekend things get really hot. A mix of live bands and DJs play tunes from Brazilian samba to house, electro and soul. Once a month, the legendary Book Slam takes place, where award-winning novelist and hip-hop journalist Patrick Neate hosts an evening of literature, acoustic music and spoken-word performances. To feed your stomach as well as your soul, tuck into the mouth-wateringly fresh pan-Pacific cuisine.

89 Westbourne Park Rd
W2
Westbourne Park

The Cow

7221 0021 | *www.thecowlondon.co.uk*

When this old Irish pub on Westbourne Park Road was revamped by Tom Conran, it quickly became known for its fantastic oysters and Guinness. Now it seems more famous for the crowds of people who come to enjoy the oysters and Guinness than the food and drink that attracted them in the first place. The small venue is perennially swamped with customers, but if you do manage to get in and find a seat you'll be pleased with the range of fresh crustacea and Belgian beers on the menu. There are also a couple of real ales, cider served over ice, and plenty of wines to choose from. It's quite expensive but if you're into people watching this is a great place to come as it is filled with music and media types, artists and actors.

84-86 Great Eastern St
EC2
Old Street

The Foundry

7739 6900 | *www.foundry.tv*

Former banks turned into bars are not unusual in the UK, but this one has been given a different treatment than most. Walk in and you'll find yourself surrounded by a myriad of paintings and photographs on the wall, including your own staring back at you from

433

a TV screen, snapped by the CCTV cameras at the door (for entertainment rather than security purposes). The bar in the basement features remnants of the bank vault, with its original high-density concrete walls, but is now used as an exhibition space. Poetry readings and art and sound installations attract very creative people, and, until recently, The Libertines were the resident band. If you want a bar that sums up the bohemian side of the area, you'll find it at The Foundry.

Freedom

60-66 Wardour St
W1
⊖ Piccadilly Circus

0871 3325262

Freedom is a flamboyant and fabulous bar that hosts art exhibitions, film premieres and glamorous after-show parties. Upstairs the stylish and wildly colourful cocktail bar is popular for leisurely daytime drinking with a few tasty snacks on the side, and the atmosphere gets livelier as the evening draws in. Dancing is the name of the game in the large basement club, with three poles for people to work their magic on. An open-house policy that welcomes gay and straight people is in operation. The DJs are hot, while the decor and dancing are as exotic as the fish in the massive tank along the wall – expect mirror balls, bare chests and a night of fun.

The Green

74 Upper St
N1
⊖ Angel

7226 8895 | *www.the-green.co.uk*

This small, minimalist bar is popular with the after-work crowd, who are possibly enticed by the regular two-for-one drinks offer between 16:00 and 19:00. Whatever brings them in, the manager plays a great host, creating a fun and friendly atmosphere. The Green is a gay bar but has a relaxed attitude, so people of any sex and sexuality will feel comfortable. There is a good range of foreign bottled beers and ciders, and a few on tap, plus an impressive selection of wines and champagnes for such a small establishment. Cocktails are well made with fresh ingredients, and the same care and attention are clearly put into the food. Bloody marys and 'The Green brunch' are sure to help you get over your Sunday hangover on what it calls 'slack sabbath'.

Greenwich Park Bar and Grill

1 King William Walk
SE10
DLR Cutty Sark

8853 7860 | *www.thegreenwichpark.com*

Just across the road from Greenwich Park is this relaxed, stylishly designed bar. Drinks are well priced for the surroundings and the menu uses the best quality ingredients for simple and enticing food. The eggs benedict and other American breakfasts are good brunch options, rib-eye steak sandwich is great for lunch, and you can't go wrong with the spring lamb or jumbo prawns for dinner. You can dine in either the bar or the first-floor restaurant, which features aquamarine walls and hand-painted murals. The top-floor lounge is available for private parties and pre-dinner cocktails if the main bar downstairs is crammed, which it tends to be at the weekends. If the park has left you wanting to stay outside, there is also a small but perfectly formed patio courtyard.

101-106 Leonard St
EC2
🚆 ⊖ **Old Street**

Home

7684 8618 | *www.homebar.co.uk*

Decked out in slouch-inducing armchairs, the description 'lounge bar' is appropriate here because you'll feel like you've moved in – although the place is larger than one any artsy Hoxtonite could afford to live in. The relaxed atmosphere, created by chilled music and soft amber lights, is remarkably unpretentious given the bar's reputation as the place that created the 'boho' hip scene. The three open-planned rooms offer plenty of space for groups of friends, but seem just as appropriate for a romantic date. The tempo picks up between Thursdays and Saturdays, with DJs mixing their beats as smoothly as the bartenders do cocktails. Try the lemongrass martini or a 'dark and stormy' made from Cuban rum, ginger and lemon juice. Many have tried to replicate this winning formula, but there really is no place like Home.

233 Shoreditch High St
E1
🚆 ⊖ **Liverpool Street**

Light Bar

7247 8989 | *www.thelighte1.com*

The Light Bar attracts City types in trainers for beers, cocktails and good music. It's a bar, restaurant and club so it's easy to spend the whole evening here. There is a good range of bottled beers from Duvel and Kasteel Cru to strawberry Früli, as well as some specialist draught ales and a wide selection of cocktails and spirits. It gets hectic at the bar but there are plenty of slim, tall tables in the spacious bare-brick main room on which to rest your drinks. The high ceilings and concrete floors help the loud music bounce around to sometimes deafening levels. Outside in the summer the chunky wooden tables, benches and chairs are packed. To keep everyone fuelled there are salads, wraps, burgers and deli platters for sharing. There's also a Sunday brunch and traditional roast lunch if you've overdone it the night before.

75-89 West Yard
NW1
⊖ **Camden Town**

Lockside Lounge

7284 0007

This stylish DJ bar, which overlooks the Regent's Canal, has a fantastic boardwalk balcony that beckons you in for a cocktail or three. Gently lit and decorated with funky photos of typical Camdenites, this long bar is far from the world of incense sticks and gothic corsets that surrounds it. Come and relax with a pint, order from the mouthwatering menu and click on your laptop for some free Wi-Fi surfing during the day. In the evenings, let the DJs entertain you with their favourite tracks. On Sundays there is often live music in the form of percussion bands belting Brazilian beats or nu-jazz. Inside, the bar is filled with a relaxed mix of friendly and very happy customers.

1 Whitby St
E2
🚆 ⊖ **Liverpool Street**

Loungelover

7012 1234 | *www.loungelover.co.uk*

A favoured bar among east London trendies, Loungelover is flamboyant, artistic and decadent. The interior is filled with golden palm chandeliers, hippo heads, resplendent gilt mirrors and lush velvet. Old and new come together well as the burlesque sexy reds and Regency-style chairs sit alongside cool blue glass-topped tables and perspex. Expect to be teased by the names on the cocktail list, which is split by genre rather than spirit: 'virgin', 'lotus position' and 'hot lover'. They are exceptionally good (if a little expensive) and the canape menu, including caviar and wild boar, is suitably glamorous. The only drawback is that you cannot simply swing into Loungelover for a drink on a whim as it operates a fairly tight booking system.

435

181 Upper St
N1
Angel

Medicine Bar

7704 8056 | www.medicinebar.net

One of the forerunners of the DJ-bar concept, Medicine has a following of firm believers. The music and atmosphere is plugged in, but not in-your-face, and the crowds really go for it at the weekend. The temperature rises on the dancefloor and upstairs, so the bar gets phenomenally packed – staff do their best to keep up but it can take a while to get served. Medicine caters for a funkier crowd who want to make some noise while listening to top tunes. The dress code is strictly laid-back, so the suits tend to steer clear. You won't want to leave, but note that if you do the doormen can get a bit heavy and won't let you back in, even if you pop out for just a moment.

45 Lavender Hill
SW11
Clapham Common

Mishmash

7326 7455 | www.mishmashbar.co.uk

Bright purple and red walls, colour-changing lanterns and pink sofas fill the room in this stylish bar. Add the exotic wallpaper and screens showing scenes from *Barbarella* and the 70s kitsch setting is complete. Music ranges from funky disco to 80s pop and Ibizan house, while on Sunday you can relax to R&B tunes. The bar food is an Italian selection: tasty pizzas, calzones and panini. Groups are particularly well catered for with grazing menus and a bottle service – pre-order a bottle of spirits and it will be

delivered to your table in an ice bucket along with mixers and glasses, saving you time (but not necessarily money, unless everyone in your party was planning on drinking double shots all night). The mouthwatering cocktail list, with a two-for-one offer running from 17:00 until 20:00, will help you wind down after work, and encourage you to stay until the early hours.

183-185 Wardour St
W1
Oxford Circus

Nanobyte

7734 0037 | www.nanobytebar.com

The bright lighting and spacious interior give Nanobyte a relaxed atmosphere that attracts a laid-back crowd, rare for such a central

location. The Pimms on tap also helps to draw in the drinking connoisseurs. Beers include IPA, Spitfire, Piretti, Warsteiner and a few guest ales, plus the usual standards, and there are plenty of wines to choose from. Freshly prepared food is served most of the day. Brunch and tapas snacks are available, as are sharing boards, while bigger dishes for those with serious appetites include beer-battered fish & chips, thick sausage and cheesy mash. The service is good, especially if you're rushing in for a working lunch, and the reasonably priced cocktails make it a popular place to come in the evening – get in early to grab a table.

283 Westbourne Grove
W11
Notting Hill Gate

Negozio Classica

7034 0005 | www.negozioclassica.co.uk

Sophisticated Italians in London come in droves to enjoy the fineries of their homeland. The wines laid in wooden cases against all the walls clearly show that this is a shop, but it's also an arena for the owners to show off about all things good in Italy. The produce has been carefully sourced from artisanal producers, and the staff really

436

know what they are talking about. Stand at the long bar to sample some of the wines, or take one of the tables at the front of the shop to enjoy a glass or bottle with a platter of select cheeses served with a few pickles, apple, a sample of salamis, crostini or classic bruschetta. The bar attracts an older crowd of wine aficionados who love to discuss the finer things in life.

Occo

58 Crawford St
W1
♁ **Edgware Road**

7724 4991 | *www.occo.co.uk*

Opulence is everywhere in this contemporary Moroccan-influenced bar and lounge. The large oyster-coloured main bar is busy most nights of the week, but is especially popular from Thursday to Sunday. If you prefer something a little more intimate, slip into the deep-red 'boudoir' with its ornate Moroccan silver lantern. The main party area is the subterranean lounge, Mim. Bordered with low tables, cushions and candles, there is plenty of space to dance to the live music or DJs. The staff are inviting, and the cocktails are sophisticated and delicious – try specials such as fig bellini, made with champagne, honey, vodka and fig puree. Whatever your preferred tipple, the mixologists are happy to tailor to your taste.

Opal

36 Gloucester Rd
SW7
♁ **Gloucester Road**

7584 1118 | *www.opalbar.co.uk*

The owners claim feung shui chic sets the tone for Opal, but the vibe feels more like wild fruit at this exciting Kensington bar. Sharing is big here – large, deliciously crafted cocktails are created so that four to eight people can drink from the same glass. Gems to try include a 'miss kensington', an 'opal fizz' or even an 'inga from sweden'. If you have to keep an eye on your budget this is not the place to come, as most people in Opal are interested in decadence at any price. DJs play R&B, and there is also an Arabic night. Expect to get up close and personal on the dancefloor and at the bar as people here want to party hard – and take everyone with them.

OQO

4-6 Islington Green
N1
♁ **Angel**

7704 2332

This minimalist venue offers Chinese tapas and cocktails, and is one of the most alluring new venues in the area. Hover somewhere along the 40-foot-long bar, lit with an amber glow, and you can watch the staff shake and stir while the chefs package neat parcels of prawns for you to snack on. OQO is a nice place to go for a few drinks early on in the evening before heading off to a restaurant or a club. The seating – black-and-white square leather stools and benches – gets a little uncomfortable after a while, but it does mean you can pull up as many as you need for groups of friends. Friday and Saturday nights tend to be standing-room only.

Pool

104-108 Curtain Rd
EC2
⇌ ♁ **Old Street**

7739 9608 | *www.thepool.uk.com*

If you want a funky place to come and shoot some pool this is a good bet. Tables are free on Sunday, but the rest of the week you pay per hour or half-hour. If you are a regular sharp shooter you can get a 'hussla' card and collect stamps to gain a free hour's play and entrance into proper competitions. If you're worried about the colour of your money the three happy hours, from 17:00 until 20:00, offer two-for-one deals on selected cocktails, beers and shooters. Even when the happy hours are over the drinks are reasonably priced. If you've worked up an appetite, the kitchen does a tasty line in noodles, soups and stir fries as well as platters of won ton parcels to pick at while you play. Films are shown on the big screen downstairs (you have to sign up to watch them, but they're free and the good people at Pool will let you know when they're on).

43

2 Tabernacle St
EC2
⇌ ⊖ **Old Street**

Sosho

7920 0701 | www.sosho3am.com

All the ingredients for an excellent bar have been mixed to perfection at Sosho: a stylish and spacious interior that's comfortable and beautiful; excellent cocktails that don't feel like a complete rip off; and music that makes you want to dance. Not surprising then that it gets completely packed from Thursday through to Saturday. The crowd come from both sides of the east divide – trendy, arty patrons from Shoreditch and Hoxton, and hard-nosed City punters – but all seem to get along famously, slinking into the soft sofas and lounge chairs or cutting some rug to the salsa tunes in the cosy downstairs room. If you want to be sure of having somewhere to rest your drink, you can book a table at no extra charge.

Borough Market
SE1
⇌ ⊖ **London Bridge**

Wine Wharf

7940 8335 | www.winewharf.com

Part of the Vinopolis empire on the South Bank, the Wine Wharf is a modern bar with exposed brick, metal, and wooden beams that give it a characteristic warehouse feel. Customers seem to be executives on expense accounts and those who really know their plonk from their pinot. If you're looking to join the ranks of the wine connoisseurs you can opt for a tray of five glasses for a small tasting session of specially selected whites and reds, all for £10. Staff are, as you would expect, passionate about wine and very knowledgeable, happy to share all they know if you're interested. If wine is not your tipple of choice, there are also a few imported beers and a selection of brandies. Tasty bar bites include welsh rarebit and crepes alongside the usual nuts and crisps. The full lunch menu has sharing platters of oysters and charcuterie alongside light pasta, fish and steaks.

2a Southwark Bridge Rd
SE1
⇌ ⊖ **London Bridge**

Zacudia

7021 0085 | www.zakudia.com

Want to feel like you're *really* in London? Then head to Zacudia, where you can sip a 'southwark sling' while looking out over St Paul's and the Thames. This light, clean-cut bar gets busy in the evenings with city slickers and cultured types who have come straight from the neighbouring Tate Modern. Seating is on green-and-red suede stools, and occasional tables make it easy to move around and extend your group. The menu offers tasty global food including fiery fresh Thai beef salad and juicy steak burgers, as well as generous sharing platters. Resident DJs play soul, jazz, funk, hip-hop and house on Thursday, Friday and Saturday nights.

Karaoke Bars

White Bear Yard, 25a Lisle St
WC2
⊖ **Leicester Square**

Imperial China

7734 3388 | www.imperial-china.co.uk

A Chinese restaurant first and foremost, with a decent reputation for Cantonese cuisine, Imperial China also has private rooms for hire where people can eat and sing, making it a good option for parties and celebrations. The accent here is on Chinese culture – you cross a wooden bridge over a pond to get to the location – though fortunately, if you're not Chinese, the songs are mainly in English. Rooms can hold up to 30 people and costs £30 per person for the set menu and karaoke. Open from 12:00 until 23:00 every day.

Late London

In 2005, a 24 hour alcohol licence law came into effect, meaning pubs, bars and clubs could serve drinks around the clock. In reality the law had remarkably little impact on traditional pubs across the capital, many of which extended trading times by one or two hours at most. Thankfully, a lot of bars have extended their licences and now stay open until 02:00 or 03:00, with clubs going strong until 04:00 or 06:00.

Pubs & Bars

7-9 Cranbourn St
WC2
⊖ **Leicester Square**

K-Box
7287 8868 | *www.k-box.co.uk*

It may not be the swankiest (that accolade goes to Lucky Voice), but it's probably London's biggest 'pure' karaoke venue. Like Lucky Voice, the rooms are fitted with touchscreen karaoke systems, there's Asian food on the menu, and a bar. A room holding eight people costs from £35 to £60 per hour, depending on the time and day. K-Box is open from 18:00 until 03:00 Thursday to Saturday and 18:00 until 23:00 during the rest of the week.

Various locations

London Karaoke
7241 4660 | *www.londonkaraoke.co.uk*

This company travels to locations (usually bars, but also private venues) to host karaoke evenings. You can hire the gear yourself too, the price of which includes delivery and collection plus a demonstration on how to use it. With over 8,000 songs to choose from, there's bound to be something for even the most reluctant performers.

52 Poland St
W1
⊖ **Oxford Circus**

Lucky Voice
7439 3660 | *www.luckyvoice.co.uk*

Probably the coolest venue in London to sing your heart out in, this bar (co-owned by Martha Lane-Fox, the entrepreneur who set up Lastminute.com) has an underground but hip vibe, and serves top-notch cocktails and sushi. The nine rooms can fit up to 12 crooners at a time, and all have touchscreen monitors and 5,000 songs to choose from. It's a popular place, so it's advisable to book ahead. Prices start from £20 per hour for a room holding up to four people (£60 an hour for eight people on weekends). Open from 17:30 until 01:00 Monday to Thursday, 15:00 until 01:00 on Fridays and Saturdays, and 15:00 until 22:30 on Sundays.

Nightclubs

Other options **Pubs** p.420, **Bars** p.431

London is a clubbers' paradise, with every taste, budget and fetish catered for. DJs set trends that send ripples across the world's music scene, and the style of clubs has changed with these fashions – hard-house mega-clubs have been overtaken in popularity by smaller, underground venues playing break-beats and electro. There are still huge venues spread over a few floors where you can dance until dawn though, or if you prefer to have a few drinks and end up shuffling on to the dancefloor there are plenty of bars with late licences playing mainstream and retro tunes. Entry is generally free to these type of venues before 22:00 or 23:00, with charges from £5 after that. For the more serious clubs, entry costs between £12 and £15. Door policy can be tough if you're with a big group of men or seem a little too drunk.

256-260 Old St
EC1
⇌ ⊖ **Old Street**

Aquarium

7251 6136 | www.clubaquarium.co.uk

This is the only nightclub in town with a swimming pool and a whirlpool bath, so you'll have to coordinate your swimwear as well as your shirts. Lifeguards watch as revellers splash and frolic in the water, but this is no municipal pool so they get to see plenty of inventive strokes. You can dry yourself with a fluffy towel and pop to the rooftop garden to recuperate before hitting the dancefloor. It's 10 years since Aquarium opened but the theme nights are still as popular as ever, with the infamous 'Carwash' bringing out 70s silver platforms and hotpants aplenty. The Adonis Cabaret and Creme de la Creme nights also fill the two dancefloors with 80s cheese, garage, pop and the occasional bit of bhangra beat or ragga. This club has a sense of humour, but if you don't there are plenty of other places on Old Street that would suit you.

49 Chalk Farm Rd
NW1
⊖ **Chalk Farm**

Barfly

7691 4244 | www.barflyclub.com

An institution in the music world, Barfly is one of the hottest places to see soon-to-be-big new bands. The bare-brick walls still manage to be battered every night of the week by the savvy crowds who come in to see some of the 1,000-plus live acts that play every year. When it all gets going, you can guarantee it will be hot and sweaty. The bar staff try their best to hear your order over the music, but you'll have to shout at least three times. It's not all guitar music though, as Barfly makes sure clubbers get their fix with Adventures Close to Home, Casino Royale and Transmission nights all making monthly Friday and Saturday appearances.

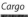
Cargo

Kingsland Viaduct,
83 Rivington St
EC2
⇌ ⊖ **Old Street**

Cargo

7749 7844 | www.cargo-london.com

A converted railway arch plays host to some of the best new dance music in town. Regular nights have become legendary: Wah Wah features soul, funk, jazz, hip-hop, latin and boogie; Andy Smith, who made his name as Portishead's tour DJ, brings you The Document, and Manchester-born Mish Mash plays a party mix of hip-hop and funk. The atmosphere is electric and the people really friendly. Drinks are not the usual club rip-offs, instead there are large bottles

of cruzcampo to share, regular two-for-one offers, and even pub prices during pub hours. Sizzling summertime takes things outdoors into the garden for a barbecue and a cooler breeze. Cargo is part of the Cantaloupe group (p.409) so nibbles are guaranteed to be good, and the small cafe to the left of the entrance keeps hungry clubbers going until dawn.

200 York Way
N7
≥ ⊖ *King's Cross*
St. Pancras

Egg
7609 8364 | *www.egglondon.net*

Set in the industrial end of King's Cross station, the three-floored Egg stands out like a lily on a stagnant pond. The beautiful club is full of beautiful people armed with sunglasses on heads and ready to dance through until Sunday afternoon. The huge ground floor has an industrial bare-brick look, while the middle floor, with its neon blue bar, leads on to a stunningly manicured terrace and garden. Outside there are balcony decks, a bar and hammocks by a paddling pool. Egg showcases the best of global clubbing culture: residencies include European DJs at Jet and Chicago house with legend Robert Owens. The best alternative, electro-clash, rock and hard dance music is incorporated in the Synthetic Culture set. The club has a sexy, sassy attitude, and keeps it in check with a pretty heavy dress code at the door – no polo shirts or branded sportswear.

7 Torrens St
EC1
⊖ *Angel*

Electrowerkz
7837 6419 | *www.electrowerkz.com*

Things can get pretty messy at Electrowerkz – and that's just how everyone wants it to stay. Club nights include the supreme reggae 100% Dynamite event hosted by Soul Jazz, Warp Records nights, and the notorious Slimelight on Saturdays, which is the biggest goth night in London. You have to apply for membership by showing your face at the door, so make sure you get your best black leather on and polish those piercings. As the name implies, Electrowerkz is also home to some awesome electronica music. Although the venue is just off the City Road, the club has an air of warehouse rave. Drinks are cheap and while the people may be less shiny than most clubs in this neck of the woods, they are pretty happy – and that includes the bar staff and doormen, who make this place somewhere you want to keep coming back to.

77a Charterhouse St
EC1
≥ ⊖ *Farringdon*

Fabric
7336 8898 | *www.fabriclondon.com*

Fabric has always been at the cutting edge of music fashion in London. Energy levels are high and the new talent is as raw as the meat that used to be sold in this Victorian archway. The club has gone for a minimalist mood, making room for serious dance space. The sound system in the two massive rooms will make every cell in your body shake to drum and bass, hip-hop, electro-minimal and house. It's regularly filled with about 1,500 people, but if you want to hide away from the mass you can squeeze up the stairs to the little attic room and lose yourself. Tickets range from £12 to £15, but become a member for £6 a month and you get a discount at the door and a separate queue to jump in. The superb Fabric CDs are also sent to you every month.

44

1 Town Hall Parade
SW2
Brixton

The Fridge
7326 5100 | www.fridgerocks.com

A building that has been lovingly restored in all its 1930s glory is home to one of the longest-running independent clubs in London. Keen on not letting people get too settled with any one perception of the place, the club is constantly innovating and setting trends. Look out for the fridges over the front doors, go-go dancers, and TV screens hanging from the burnt ceiling. It's still one of the main clubbing attractions in Brixton, bringing a genuine mix of people from across the city to hard dance parties. All kinds of people, from gay to straight and everything in between, mix it up on the floor to big-name DJs, who play from 22:00 every night. The Fridge Bar next door often hosts after-party parties for revellers who just can't stop. There is live music on Tuesdays, with open-mic sessions for the bold and brave.

146 Clapham High St
SW4
Clapham Common

Infernos
7720 7633 | www.infernos.co.uk

Disco fever is brought kicking and screaming into the 21st century at this incredibly popular venue. The club is mainly frequented by drunk 30-somethings who want to recreate their student days. Wild groups of ex-rugby boys playing drinking games and City girls who want to rip off their suits and pull down their hair fill this place to breaking point most nights of the week, but especially so at the weekends. It's easy to lose people in the crowd, but if you do, you may find them in the Piano Bar, Shooter Bar or the VIP room. It's free to get in before 22:00 and the drinks are cheap, hence so many flushed purple faces and fuzzy eyes. The music is strictly cheese so come armed with a sense of fun and no pretences.

144-145 Upper St
N1
Angel

Kinky Mambo
7704 6868 | www.kinkymambo.co.uk

What lies behind the big blacked-out windows of Kinky Mambo need not be a mystery. Let the big bouncers welcome you in, which they'll do with a surprising smile, and you'll quickly discover what the pink neon sign has drawn you into. Nothing too 'kinky', just 'elegant debauchery' – meaning lots of fun nights, from salsa to burlesque, regular DJs and live music, which all make this place, and everyone in it, really move. The extravagant bar features chandeliers, thick carpet, vases filled with flowers, pink walls and bright pink lights that are dimmed as the evening progresses. If that's not glitzy enough, try one or two of Kinky's 150 delicious cocktails, shaken or stirred by top-notch mixologists using unusual flavours and ingredients. The entry charge varies depending on the night, but is never more than a few pounds.

1a Camden High St
NW1
Camden Town

Koko
7388 3222 | www.koko.uk.com

Restored to its former theatrical glory, Koko is one of the top clubs in the capital. Metal pipes and glow-sticks have been replaced by gilt decor, Greek gods and a rich purple-and-red colour scheme. The sound system and lighting are excellent but expect to pay premium prices for your drinks and entry. There is a definite sense of glitterati glamour in dancing the night away here; if you shimmy on to one of its balconies you'll be rewarded with a great people-watching spot. On Friday nights, Club NME plays, but Koko also hosts fantastic live entertainment from the likes of Madonna through to music award shows.

70 Upper St
N1
⊖ Angel

Ladybird
7359 1710

A new club on this ever-changing high street offers something European in flavour. French owned, this club, bar and restaurant invites new musicians to test their original tunes upstairs on the small stage rather than piping in music. Behind the velvet curtains downstairs there is a different vibe, darker and more soulful. DJs play in this intimate room packed with people shaking loose the shackles of the week until 04:00 – the latest licence for this kind of venue in the area. Ladybird is aimed at a more sophisticated clientele looking for a friendly place to talk, drink and dance. It may be just up the road from chain bars such as Walkabout or Pitcher and Piano but it feels a million miles away.

8-10 Brewer St
W1
⊖ Piccadilly Circus

Madame Jo Jo's
7734 3040 | www.madamejojos.com

Sensational cabaret, comedy, club nights and live music performances all take place in the crimson red boudoir that is Madame Jo Jo's. The decor has a black stocking and soft velvet grungy glamour, with retro interiors that conjure images of burlesque from a bygone era. The unique experiences, ostentatious style and gaudy character of the club bring in celebrities, musicians and Soho's finest for nights of debauched fun. Club nights that celebrate the diverse include Keb Darge's Deep Funk, 80s electro-kitsch at The Glitz, and indie and rock at White Heat, as well as French house, hip-hop and northern soul. Drinks are delectable and not outrageously priced, and it's only £6 to get in before 23:00.

Guest Lists
You don't have to be a VIP to get on the guest list for many clubs and bars. Simply call in advance to put you and your guests' names down or register online at sites such as www.viewlondon.co.uk. You can gain entry to private members' clubs by signing up to guest list services such as guestlist.me.uk or exclusivelondon.co.uk.

St Matthews Church,
Brixton Hill
SW2
⊖ Brixton

Mass
7738 7875 | www.mass-club.com

The worshippers that come in from the cold to Mass at the converted St Matthews church tend to have a different kind of spirit in mind to regular churchgoers. This spacious club has a reputation for hard and heavy underground music, from R&B and house right through to trance and grime. Three large rooms usually fill up quickly for the various club nights, which include Tasty, Torture Garden, Trouble on Vinyl and Valve. Top artists include Norman Jay, Ed Real, Skinnyman, Grooverider, Chris Liberator and Graham Gold, while reggae master David Rodigan brings people across town on a Wednesday for his sessions. Drinks are reasonable and the entrance fee not too outrageous for such wicked, sinful nights.

103 Gaunt St
SE1
⊖ Elephant & Castle

Ministry of Sound
0870 0600010 | www.ministryofsound.com

This legendary club still has a huge following in London, and attracts a string of homegrown and international DJ talent. The lighting and sound systems outclass and outshine the rest, and perhaps that's why Ministry is still the biggest brand in clubbing, delivering where it counts: the dancefloor. Be it in the main or the busy balcony bar, the crowd is hands-in-the-air happy until 07:00 on Saturday nights/Sunday mornings and 05:00 on Fridays. Ministry is loyal to those who helped make it, so there are special nights and parties for all those old ravers out there. If you're a 'cristal clubber' you can book a table in the VIP lounge for the night. The club host will escort you from your limo to the door, you'll have access to a private dancefloor suspended above the main arena, and drinks will be brought to you by your own waitress all night long.

Neighbourhood

12 Acklam Rd
W10
⊖ *Ladbroke Grove*

8960 9331

The triple-stack turntables at Neighbourhood have been worked by the hands of some of the best DJs in the industry. Residents Pete Adarkwah, Jafar and Brazilian expert DJ Harv, plus regular club nights from Felix de Housecat and Andy Cato, attract clubbers from all over the nation to this spacious west London venue. You'll find live shows from some big names too. This is not the sweaty hardcore club style where everyone is too wasted to talk; people seem to look out for each other here. Spread over two floors, the modest surroundings and furnishings let the details such as spectacular lighting and great sound take centre stage. It has a sociable, fun atmosphere that makes everyone want to come to this Neighbourhood.

Notting Hill Arts Club

21 Notting Hill Gate
W11
⊖ *Notting Hill Gate*

7460 4459 | *www.nottinghillartsclub.com*

Every night of the week the Arts Club plays host to different acts and, like a chameleon, takes on the colours of each one perfectly. There are live gigs and DJ sets playing Scandinavian sounds, alternative hip-hop, break-beats, indie, punk, soul and groove. These are not your average performances by average people – high-octane celebrities and musical legends put on shows and club nights that others attempt to follow. It's open until 02:00 seven nights a week, with two sessions on Saturdays. Expect your fellow clubbers to be wild but unpretentious, and the bar to serve drinks with ethics in mind; alongside local brews and ciders are beers from Turkey, Peru and even Lapland. If you get in to the club before 18:00 entry is free, after that you can expect to pay about £5.

Oliver's Jazz Bar

9 Nevada St
SE10
DLR *Cutty Sark*

8858 5855

Deep in the soul of Greenwich is this subterranean treasure of a club. Live jazz and blues are played to a mixed crowd of music lovers. The only clue to its existence is a small metal gateway entrance tucked away behind the Spread Eagle pub. Descend into a hot, smoky bar to the sound of a deliciously smooth voice coming from the depths of the singer's lungs, accompanied by an old boy skillfully manning his bass, and another tinkling his piano. There is no glamour except the glint in their eyes, but this is the sort of club everyone wants to find. Drinks come at pub prices and there are tables for about 20 people, all swaying and shuffling their feet until the early hours. The venue is a late-night jewel that once found is never forgotten.

Plastic People

147-149 Curtain Rd
EC2
⇌ ⊖ *Liverpool Street*

7739 6471 | *www.plasticpeople.co.uk*

This little basement club prides itself on hosting some of the most progressive nights, bringing out the freshest sounds and newest beats to a hungry London crowd. R&B, drum and bass, hip-hop, broken beats, future jazz and techno take centre stage throughout the week. DJ Abdul Forsyth and guests bring Balance to Saturday nights, Fridays see the Future Sound of the Underground with Forward, while CDR showcases

44

tracks in the making from UK and world DJs. Londoners have responded to their call to dance with fervour, as the place is packed every weekend. These people know how to do clubs – and, for them, it has nothing to do with slick decor or gimmicks.

47 Frith St
W1
⊖ Tottenham Court Rd

Ronnie Scott's Jazz Club
7439 0747 | www.ronniescotts.co.uk
Generations of music lovers have visited the legendary Ronnie Scott's. Scott broke new ground back when Americans weren't allowed to play in the UK by persuading the Musicians' Union to let in the talent – and now Brits can't get enough of them. Some of the true greats have donned the stage, from Zoot Sims to Ben Webster. Today's talent is still outstanding, and the atmosphere euphoric. Come to dine on the fine cuisine or just sit with a drink in the tiered seats overlooking the stage – you'll be entertained all evening. Guests, musicians and staff are all smiles, and no one can help tapping their feet and swaying their hips to the riffs and rhythms. There is a fantastic mix of generations, from old timers who saw the doors open to those who are making their first foray into the world of jazz. Open until 03:00.

162 Tufnell Park Rd
N7
⊖ Tufnell Park

Tufnells
7272 2078 | www.tufnellsclub.com
New ownership has given this popular place, formerly called Progress Bar, a fabulous makeover. No more garish flock wallpaper, just simple lines and a well-stocked bar to keep everyone smiling. Tufnells is a huge venue frequented by a great mix of people, with live music three nights a week and occasional impromptu gigs. There is a DJ spinning from Thursday to Sunday with a strictly 'no cheese' music policy so expect good tunes and a laid-back atmosphere. The service at the bar is quick and the prices are relatively cheap. A new menu has been recently introduced and gigs are listed on the Tufnells website so you can check out the night's line-up before heading over.

63b Clerkenwell Rd
EC1
≥ ⊖ Farringdon

Turnmills
7250 3409 | www.turnmills.co.uk
Londoners can be a fickle crowd – although many turned their back on Turnmills when some shinier new clubs opened in the area, now they are coming back with their tails between their legs and wry smiles on their faces ready to party like it's 2000. The Gallery, which has been called a 'crowd pleaser', is not the most progressive of nights, but there's nothing wrong with that. Matt Hardwick brings trance back to the fold and Marcel Woods sneaks techno in through the back door. The decor is dark with a Mediterranean edge to it. Away from the main room you can nestle into the alcoves, but if you're trying to get served at the bar you could have a bit of a fight on your hands. Queues for entry can be long and frustrating, but a text ticket system works well and means you can jump right in.

174 Camden High St
NW1
⊖ Camden Town

The Underworld
7482 1932 | www.theunderworldcamden.co.uk
Directly opposite Camden tube station and tucked under the Worlds End pub is a club that has become as famous as the prodigious bands that have graced its stage. Some nights it is the realm of long-haired, goatee-bearded moshers, on others indie kids clad in vintage clothing, but more often than not it's full of clubbers in low-slung jeans and skinny T-shirts. Whatever the night, The Underworld can be relied on for a great atmosphere and down-to-earth fun. Hundreds of people crowd in to dance and drink during its Silver, Pump up the Volume and Nasin club nights until the wee hours, making the air thick with sweat and the floor stickier than treacle. You can get tickets for the venue's numerous gigs from the pub upstairs or from its website.

Gay & Lesbian

The well-established gay and lesbian scene in London is better described as a gay community, with dedicated barbers, clothing shops and health clubs, as well as estate agents, travel agents and solicitors. Although many of the most popular bars and clubs are still based in Soho, specifically Old Compton Street, the 'out' scene is by no means limited to W1. From the Black Cap in Camden (0871 2230886) to West Five in Ealing (8579 3266), there are more gay places than ever before, each with an individual vibe – laid-back cafes to flamboyant burlesque and cabaret. Attitudes have also come a long way. The colourful Pride parade marches through the streets every summer, culminating in a wild party in Hyde Park that attracts huge crowds. A great way to tap in to what's hot and happening is to pop in to the Prowler store (7734 4031) on Soho's Brewer Street, or check out websites such as www.gay.com and www.gingerbeer.co.uk.

54 Old Compton St
W1
Leicester Square

The Admiral Duncan
7437 5300

The Admiral Duncan has risen triumphantly from the ashes and dust after the nail bomb attack of 1999, which ripped it apart and killed three people, to become a symbol against oppression and prejudice. It's now one of the most visited gay pubs in Soho and has a vibrant atmosphere with a familial feel. There is a small dancefloor, the decor is fresh and bright and the music is good. In summer, punters spill on to the pavement outside.

4 Carlisle St
W1
Tottenham Court Rd

Candy Bar
7494 4041 | www.thecandybar.co.uk

The ground floor of this lesbian venue is popular for a quick post-work drink, while the lounge upstairs offers a more relaxed vibe. After a few delicious cocktails most slip downstairs to the bijou club. DJs, live acts and even karaoke are all there to entertain you, but if that isn't enough to tickle your fancy then perhaps the pole dancing and strip shows will – Candy Bar was the first UK club to have such licensed lesbian entertainment. Gay men are welcome as guests.

53 Old Compton St
W1
Tottenham Court Rd

Comptons of Soho
7479 7961

There's not much room to breathe in this pub, which is slap in the middle of Soho, and that's why people like it. Since coming out 20 years ago it has built a reputation for being fantastic for people watching. It attracts an older crowd and has a heavy cruisey atmosphere downstairs, especially at weekends, but the Soho Club Lounge upstairs is a little more relaxed. The Sunday Lunch Club runs every week from 13:00 until 16:00 and serves classic roasts to a backdrop of old movies.

66 Wardour St
W1
Tottenham Court Rd

Freedom
7734 0071

Once a gay club through and through, Freedom now has an open-door policy regarding the sexuality of its patrons. Behind the sheet-glass windows the decor is wild, with frills and dripping chandeliers alongside zebra stripes. The street-level bar is always busy but it's the basement bar that really comes to life at night. Whether it is hosting an after-show party, exhibition or premiere or it's just another night of the week, Freedom always pulls in the crowds.

Gay & Lesbian

Astoria, 157 Charing Cross Road
WC2
⊖ Tottenham Court Rd

G-A-Y
7434 0403 | www.g-a-y.co.uk

G-A-Y prides itself on its camp style and cruisey atmosphere. As London's (and possibly Europe's) largest gay venue it offers a range of fun and flashy nights out. Starring alongside its regular house nights on Thursdays are big-name performers who you would normally expect to see headlining a festival; Kylie Minogue, Bjork and Westlife have all played G-A-Y's Big Night Out, held on Saturdays. Fridays see Camp Attack and cheesy tunes from the 70s, 80s and 90s, while Mondays host the Pink Pounder when entry, you guessed it, is just a pound.

The Arches, Villiers Street
WC2
⇌ ⊖ Charing Cross

Heaven
0871 3323352 | www.heaven-london.com

Billed as the most famous gay club in London, Heaven is not for the faint hearted. The music goes through your bones and the dancing doesn't stop all week. Nights such as Extreme Euphoria, Fruit Machine and its infamous party night Heaven Saturday have tempted punters to Heaven for over 25 years. Popcorn on Monday nights promises five rooms and three floors worth of Ibiza-style clubbing. The bars (all seven of them) stay open until 06:00 – should you have Tuesdays off.

12 Old Quebec St
W1
⊖ Marble Arch

The Quebec
0871 9842888

Opened in 1946, The Quebec claims to be the oldest gay bar in London and has a certain gentleman's club charm. Its seemingly winning formula of entertainment and good drinks means it remains popular with gay men of all ages. The entertainment throughout the week ranges from karaoke and cabaret to special guest appearances and quiz nights. The pub's two bars are open until 02:00 Mondays to Thursdays, and later at weekends.

372 Kennington Lane
SE11
⇌ ⊖ Vauxhall

Royal Vauxhall Tavern
7737 4043 | www.theroyalvauxhalltavern.co.uk

Vauxhall village has grown in popularity and style, and the Royal Vauxhall Tavern is at the heart of it all. The recent refit has breathed fresh air and light into the place but it still has the same reliable atmosphere. Live music performances get the crowd going at Duckie on Saturday and there are no quiet Sunday pints with the papers here; DJs play classic house and dance anthems to keep you moving all weekend. There are also stand-up comedy, jazz and cabaret nights, as well as bling-tastic bingo.

25 Frith St
W1
⊖ Leicester Square

Rush
7734 9992 | www.rush-soho.com

Rush rivals Candy Bar in the boutique clubbing stakes and attracts a crowd of sexy successful women looking for like-minded people. Its Player and Mint nights have become legendary on the lesbian scene, but it's not just its cocktail lounge and club that catch the eye. The cafe and restaurant serves decent coffee, smoothies and brunch in case you've overdone it in the same venue the night/morning before.

11 Walkers Court
W1
⊖ Tottenham Court Rd

Soho Revue Bar
7439 4089 | www.sohorevuebar.co.uk

Glamorous evenings of pure delight are the order of the day here. The decadent interior is sexy and fun with pink leather benches in the piano bar lined up facing the stage. Drag queens, live musicians, special guest DJs and hot dancers entertain the crowds every week. Cocktails are as fresh and tasty as the punters who pour through the doors every week. The Revue Bar captures quintessential Soho; sex, entertainment and unadulterated fun.

Cinemas

Film buffs won't be disappointed by the number and diversity of cinemas in London. Most of the modern multiplexes, such as Vue, Odeon and Cineworld, tend to stick with mainstream Hollywood and British films, but there are plenty of excellent venues that screen world and arthouse films – the various Curzons, Picturehouses and Screens are the most well known. If you're feeling peckish at the pictures, most places offer the standard range of American snacks – nachos drenched in cheese, hot dogs, chocolates, popcorn and fizzy drinks – all sold at extortionate prices. If you want to bring your own, you'll need to hide it as many cinemas won't allow you to take in anything not bought on the premises. Alternatively, if you'd prefer to sit in a comfy chair and drink beer or wine, try venues such as the Electric or the Gate. Film fans with small children are catered for at the Barbican Centre, where babies are welcome at 12:00 on Mondays. For a 3D experience at the UK's largest screen, check out the Imax cinema at Waterloo.

The British Film Institute holds a hugely popular festival across London each year, showcasing new films from around the world. The ICA, Barbican, and National Film Theatre on the South Bank also host a wide variety of festivals and seasons, with hundreds of screenings and special talks. Brit flicks and Hollywood blockbusters tend to come to the big venues of Leicester Square to premiere, with fans crowding up to the barriers to catch a glimpse of their favourite actor or actress walking the red carpet.

Cinemas			
Independent			
BFI Imax	SE1	7902 1234	www.bfi.org.uk/incinemas/imax
Ciné Lumiere	SW7	7838 2144	www.cine-lumiere.org.uk
Clapham Picturehouse	SW4	7498 3323	www.picturehouses.co.uk
Curzon Cinema (Soho)	W1	7495 0500	www.curzoncinemas.com
Electric Cinema	W11	7908 9696	www.electriccinema.co.uk
Gate	W11	7727 4043	www.picturehouses.co.uk
National Film Theatre	SE1	7928 3232	www.bfi.org.uk/incinemas/nft
Prince Charles Cinema	WC2	7437 7003	www.princecharlescinema.com
Renoir Cinema	WC1	7837 8402	www.curzoncinemas.com
Rio Cinema	E8	7254 6677	www.riocinema.ndirect.co.uk
Science Museum Imax Theatre	SW7	0870 8704868	www.sciencemuseum.org.uk/imax
Screen On The Green	N1	7226 3520	www.screencinemas.co.uk
Multiplex			
Cineworld	Various	0870 7772775	www.cineworld.co.uk
Odeon	Various	0871 2244007	www.odeon.co.uk
Vue	Various	8396 0100	www.myvue.com

Comedy

From slapstick and general silliness to controversial and highly political, the British comedy scene is incredibly diverse – and London showcases more rib-crackingly good, groaningly bad and absurdly ugly comedy than anywhere else in the world. Venues range from shiny big specialist clubs to smoky pubs and seedy backrooms, and comedians here aren't afraid to engage the audience in banter. Many of the London clubs give new talent the opportunity to shine or flop, and old talent the chance to perform new material. University Student Union comedy nights are a good place to catch newcomers to the scene – easy audiences there usually help comics find their feet and practice their heckling comebacks. More well-known venues that guarantee a good standard of comedy and a great night out include

Entertainment

The Comedy Store (7344 0234), Lee Hurst's Backyard Comedy Club (7739 3122), and Jongleurs (0870 7870707). Finally, like a phoenix from the flames, cabaret has recently risen to thrill audiences again. Acts across town now pull in a mixed crowd for fun and fancy-dress frolics.

Live Music

The live music scene in London is positively electric, showcasing the greats from around the world and giving a solid platform for home-grown talent. You'll find Olympic-sized concert venues hosting billion-pound shows right through to intimate gigs in pubs and dusty clubs across the capital every night of the week. London is one of the first cities on the tour schedule for many international stars, but arguably the most exciting side of the capital's music scene is the smaller gigs where new and well-established bands like to get close to their audiences. Many up-and-coming artists also try their material on the unforgiving public in the form of busking. A lot of the brave souls on the streets and underpasses of London are incredibly talented – you could be looking at a superstar in the making. Touts hang around concert arenas charging way over the odds for last-minute tickets; beware the legitimacy of what they sell. The best way to check what's on and ensure you get a ticket is to buy weekly listings magazines such as *Time Out* or check online. Price can vary massively, but websites such as meanfiddler.com and even auction site eBay tend to give the best last-minute deals.

Live Music Venues

Jazz & Blues			
12 Bar Club	WC2	7916 6989	www.12barclub.com
Ain't Nothin' But... Blues Bar	W1	7287 0514	www.aintnothinbut.co.uk
Jazz After Dark	W1	7734 0545	www.jazzafterdark.co.uk
Jazz Cafe	NW1	0870 0603777	www.jazzcafe.co.uk
Octave	WC2	7836 4616	www.octave8.com
Ronnie Scott's Jazz Club	W1	7439 0747	www.ronniescotts.co.uk
Major Concert Venues			
Astoria	WC2	7434 9592	www.carling.com/music
Carling Academy Brixton	SW9	7771 3000	www.brixton-academy.co.uk
Carling Academy Islington	N1	0905 0203999	www.islington-academy.co.uk
The Forum	NW5	7284 1001	www.meanfiddler.com
Hammersmith Apollo	W6	8563 3800	www.carling.com/music
Royal Albert Hall	SW7	7589 8212	www.royalalberthall.com
Royal Festival Hall	SE1	0870 3804300	www.rfh.org.uk
Shepherds Bush Empire	W12	8354 3300	www.shepherds-bush-empire.co.uk
Wembley Arena	HA9	8782 5500	www.wembley.co.uk
Independent Venues			
100 Club	W1	7636 0933	www.the100club.co.uk
Arts Theatre	WC2	7836 3334	www.theartstheatre.co.uk
Barfly	NW1	7691 4244	www.barflyclub.com
The Boogaloo	N6	8340 2928	www.theboogaloo.co.uk
The Borderline	W1	7534 6970	www.meanfiddler.com
Dingwalls	NW1	7428 0010	www.dingwalls.com
Dublin Castle	NW1	7485 1773	www.thedublincastle.com
Mean Fiddler	WC2	7434 0403	www.meanfiddler.com
Metro Club	W1	7437 0964	www.blowupmetro.com
Roundhouse	NW1	7424 9991	www.roundhouse.org.uk
Scala	N1	7833 2022	www.scala-london.co.uk

449

The Complete **Residents'** Guide

Theatre

Only New York's Broadway comes close to rivalling London's West End as the world capital of theatre. London theatres produce more shows than anywhere else – over 12 million people attend on average each year, spending about £250 million on tickets. Budget-busting musicals such as *Phantom of the Opera* and *Mary Poppins* are the most popular attraction for tourists in Theatreland, while Hollywood's leading lights clamour to land roles in plays. *The Usual Suspects* star Kevin Spacey even holds the position of artistic director at The Old Vic (0870 0606628). The websites www.thisistheatre.com and www.londontheatre.co.uk provide comprehensive listings of productions and venues. Beyond the West End the scene is just as lively, and the calibre of drama and dance productions outstanding. Shakespeare's Globe (7902 1400) on the South Bank pays homage to the country's most famous playwright. The original Globe staged the Bard's plays some 400 years ago, and this reconstruction recreates the atmosphere superbly – you can stand in the pits or sit on the round wooden benches. You can also take in some Shakespeare at another unusual venue in the summer, the Open Air Theatre (0870 0601811), beautifully set in the heart of Regent's Park. All over the capital you can see small theatre companies putting on productions at fringe venues, including cafes and pubs such as the Troubadour (p.430) and The King's Head (p.425).

Tickets for all types of shows can be purchased direct from the venues, as well as through agencies such as Ticketmaster – although expect to pay a hefty booking fee to these kind of operators. If you're looking for a cheap last-minute deal or returns from a sold-out show, your best bet is to head to Leicester Square. Here you'll find several outlets offering cut-price deals on that day's performances, as well as restricted-view seats. The 'tkts' booth in the centre of the square is The Society of London Theatre's official discount outlet (there's also one in Canary Wharf).

Parties at Home

Going out on the town can put a strain on both your stamina and your wallet, so occasionally it's nice to let the action come to you by throwing a party at home. As in cities the world over, dinner parties are a popular way for friends to get together and socialise in a more relaxed, intimate environment. Chances are that you'll end up going to a fair few house parties while you're in London too – you'll usually bump into someone on a Friday or Saturday night who knows someone that knows someone who's having a party somewhere in town. If you end up being entertained in a person's home, either as an invited or uninvited guest, it's bad manners not to take along some kind of beverage, be it wine, beer or spirits. Other types of bashes that you may want to host or attend include perennial favourite the fancy dress party, or a party for your kids.

Party Organisers & Caterers

If you like the idea of hosting a party, but get worn out at the thought of all the effort and planning that goes with it, there are several firms that will do the catering for you, or even organise the whole thing, including entertainment. Options and costs vary depending on whether you want a lavish affair for 100 guests, or a simple yet elegant dinner party for six. A useful directory of party companies of all shapes and sizes can be found at www.partyoffers.co.uk, or if you're looking for entertainment for a kids' party try www.childrenspartyshows.co.uk. The huge Angels fancy dress shop on Shaftesbury Avenue (7836 5678) is a great place to start if you're looking for a costume.

Party Organisers & Caterers	
Alison Price & Company	7840 7640
Amirage Caribbean Cuisine	07711 624267
Food Unlimited	8659 8000
Penni Black	0800 3896107
Target London	01708 868109
Twizzle Parties	8789 3232

Small but indispensable…

Perfectly proportioned to fit in your pocket, this marvellous mini guidebook makes sure you don't just get the holiday you paid for but rather the one that you dreamed of.

Hong Kong Mini Visitors' Guide
Maximising your holiday, minimising your hand luggage

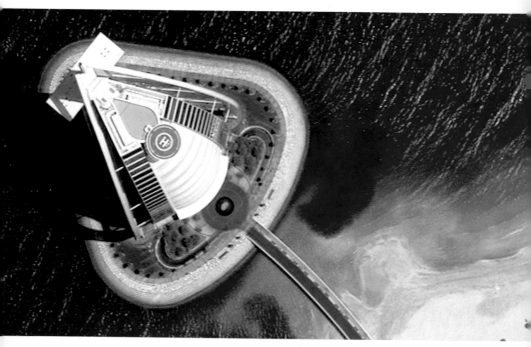

Maps

Maps

User's Guide

This section has nine detailed maps of London, with each split into various areas. They are intended to help you get your bearings when you first arrive, and give you an idea of where some of the attractions and venues listed in the main chapters of the book can be found.

The overview on p.461 shows where these areas are. They are blown up, at a scale of 1:10,000(1cm=100m). Some of the things you can find marked on the map are the main hotels from the General Information chapter (see p.2) onwards, department stores, hospitals, museums and parks. See the legend below for an idea of which is which. You'll also find London Underground and overland rail stations marked on the map. There is a full tube map on the inside back cover to help make journeys easier.

Throughout the London Explorer, shops, restaurants and other places of interest are listed with their postcode area. For an overview of which part of town each postcode covers see p.458, and the exploring and residential area maps on p.78 and p.166 respectively.

Throughout the street and underground station indexes, you'll see some map references listed next to various locations in the following format: 4-A5. The first number is the map number, and the other two digits refer to the grid location on the map. To get the bigger picture, the map on p.458 gives a postcode map. There's also a map of the UK on p.457.

Need More?

This Residents' Guide is a pretty big book – it needs to be to be pack in all the information you need when you live in a city such as London. But unless you've got huge big pockets, it's not the ideal size for carrying around with you when you're out and about.

With this in mind, Explorer has created the *London Mini Map* as a more manageable alternative. This handy little fold-out map packs the whole city into your pocket, and is an excellent navigational tool. It is part of a series of Mini Maps that includes cities as diverse as New York, Barcelona, Dublin, Sydney, Dubai and Paris. Wherever your travels take you, grab an Explorer Mini Map and you'll never have to ask for directions again. To find out more about Explorer's nifty range of visitor's and residents' guides, log on to www.explorerpublishing.com, or nip into any good bookshop.

More Maps

Beyond these maps and the very nifty London Mini Map, the definitive map of London is the A-Z, which comes in various shapes and sizes and is available from most bookshops, petrol stations, newsagents and some supermarkets. You can also pick up free tube maps from all London Underground stations.

Online Maps

There are a few websites that have searchable maps of London: Schmap maps (see www.schmap.com and download London) is one of the more useful. Hardcore map fans tend to like Google Earth (download from http://earth.google.com) for its satellite images, powerful search facility and incredibly detailed views, but the street directory isn't very detailed.

Map Legend

H	Hotel	Main Highway	
+	Hospital	Major Road	
★	Theatres	Secondary Road	
M	Museum	Other Road or Track	
	Water	A3211	Road No
	Park/Garden		Petrol Station
	Shopping	Knightsbridge	Tube Station
	Education	Waterloo	Train Station
	Built-up Area	P	Parking
		• New Zealand	Embassy/Consulate
		PIMLICO	Area Name

Street Index

Street Name	Map Ref	Street Name	Map Ref	Street Name	Map Ref
Abbey St	11-C2	Charing Cross Rd	6-F3	Gt Eastern St	5-B4
Abingdon St	10-A2	Chelsea Br Rd	9-B4	Gt George St	
Albany Rd	11-C4	Chesham Pl	9-B2	Guildford St	4-A4
Albany St	3-C2	Cheshire St	5-D4	Hackney Rd	5-C2
Albert Embankment	10-A4	Chiswell St	4-F4	Hampstead Rd	3-D3
Aldersgate St	7-E1	City Rd	5-A4	Harper Rd	10-F2
Aldgate High St	8-C2	Clerkenwell Rd	4-C4	Hatton Garden	7-C1
Aldwych	7-B2	Clive Eaton Gate	9-B3	Haymarket	6-F3
Alie St	8-C2	Club Row	5-C3	Herrick St	9-F3
Atterbury St	9-F4	Cockspur Sq	6-F4	High Holborn	7-A2
Baker St	6-B1	Columbia Rd	5-C3	Hobart Pl	9-C2
Baring St	4-F1	Commercial Rd	8-D2	Holborn Viaduct	7-D1
Bath St	4-F3	Conduit St	6-D3	Horseferry Rd	9-F3
Bayham St	3-D1	Crowndale Rd	3-E1	Houndsditch	8-B2
Baylis Rd	10-C1	Cumberland Gate	6-A3	Humphrey St	11-C3
Bayswater Rd	6-A3	Curtain Rd	5-B3	Hyde Park Cor	9-C1
Bedford Sq	6-1F	Delancey St	3-D1	Islington Gn	4-D1
Belgrave Pl	9-C2	Druid St	11-B1	Jamaica Rd	11-C1
Bermondsey St	11-B1	Duke St Hill	8-A4	James St	6-C2
Bernard St	4-A4	Duke's Pl	8-B2	John Islip St	9-F4
Bethnal Green Rd	5-C4	Dunbridge St	5-E4	Kennington Lane	10-D4
Bevis Marks	8-B2	Eagle Wharf Rd	4-F1	Kennington Park Rd	10-D4
Bishop's Way	5-F1	East Rd	5-A3	Kennington Rd	10-C2
Bishopsgate	8-B1	East Smithfield	8-D3	King Edward St	7-E2
Blackfriars Rd	10-D1	Ebury Bridge Rd	9-C4	King's Cross Rd	4-B2
Pitfield St	5-A3	Eccleston St	9-C3	King's Rd	9-A4
Bloomsbury St	6-F1	Eccleston Br	9-D3	Kingsland Rd	5-B1
Bloomsbury Way	7-A1	Edgware Rd	6-A2	Kingsway	7-B2
Borough Rd	10-E2	Essex Rd	4-D1	Lambeth Palace Rd	10-B2
Borough High St	10-F1	Euston Rd	3-D4	Lambeth Rd	10-A3
Botolph St	8-C2	Euston Underpass	3-D4	Langham Pl	6-D1
Braham St	8-C2	Eversholt St	3-E2	Leman St	8-D2
Bressenden Pl	9-D2	Farringdon Rd	7-D1	Liverpool Rd	4-C1
Brick Lane	8-C1	Farringdon Rd	4-C4	London Bridge	8-A3
Brick Lane	5-C4	Fetter Lane	7-C2	London Wall	7-F1
Bridge Rd	7-F4	Finsbury Pvt	8-A1	London Wall	8-A1
Bridge St	10-A1	Garden Row	10-D2	Long Acre	7-A3
Broad Sanctuary	9-F2	Gloucester Pl	6-A1	Long Lane	10-F1
Brompton Rd	9-A2	Goodge St	6-E1	Lower Sloane St	9-B4
Brunel Rd	11-F1	Goodman's Stile	8-D2	Lower Thames St	8-A3
Buckingham Gate	9-D2	Goswell Rd	4-D2	Mandela Way	11-C4
Buckingham Palace Rd	9-C4	Gower St	6-F1	Mans Yd	8-C3
Bunhill Row	4-F4	Gr. George St	9-F1	Mansell St	8-C2
Byward St	8-B3	Gracechurch St	8-A3	Mare St	5-E1
Cable St	8-D3	Grafton Way	3-E4	Marshalsea St	10-F1
Caledonian Rd	4-B1	Grange Rd	11-C2	Marsham St	9-F3
Calthorpe St	4-B4	Gray's Inn Rd	7-C1	Marylebone Rd	6-A1
Calvert Ave	5-B3	Great Portland St	6-D1	Millbank	10-A4
Cambridge Heath Rd	5-F3	Great Dover St	10-F2	Minories	8-C2
Camden High St	3-D1	Great Queen St	7-A2	Monmouth St	6-F2
Camden St	3-E1	Great Smith St	9-F2	Montague St	6-F1
Catlin St	11-E4	Grosvenor Pl	9-C2	Moorgate	8-A1
Chancery Lane	7-C2	Grosvenor Cr.	9-B1	Mortimer St	6-D1
Chapel Lane	8-D2	Grovs Gdns	9-C2	New Bond St	6-D3

Street Index

Street Name	Map Ref
New Fetter Lane	7-C2
New Kent Rd	10-E3
New North Rd	5-A2
New Oxford St	6-F2
Newgate St	7-E2
Newington Butts	10-E3
Newington Causeway	10-E2
Northumberland Av	7-A4
Oakley Sq	3-E2
Old Bethnal Green Rd	5-E2
Old Ford Rd	5-F2
Old Kent Rd	11-B3
Old St	5-A3
Orchard St	6-B2
Osborn St	8-D1
Outer Circle	3-A1
Oxford St	6-B2
Paddington St	6-B1
Pall Mall	6-E3
Pancras Rd	3-F2
Park Rd	3-A4
Park Lane	6-A3
Park Crescent	3-C4
Parkway	3-C1
Parliament St	10-A1
Penton Rise	4-B2
Pentonville Rd	4-B2
Percival St	4-D3
Piccadilly	6-D4
Pimlico Rd	9-B4
Pitfield St	5-A3
Pont St	9-A2
Portland Pl	6-C1
Portman Sq	6-B2
Prescot St	8-C3
Prince Albert Rd	3-A1
Puddle Dock	7-D3
Queensbridge Rd	5-C1
Raymouth Rd	11-F3
Regent St	6-D3
Regent's Park Rd	3-B1
Rolls Rd	11-D4
Roman Rd	5-F3
Rosebery Ave	4-C4
Rotherhithe New Rd	11-F4
Rotherhithe Tunnel	11-F1
Royal College St	3-E1
Royal Hospital Rd	9-B4
Royal Mint St	8-D3
Russell Sq	6-F1
Sclater St	5-C4
Seymour St	6-A2
Shaftesbury Ave	6-F3
Shepherdess Walk	4-F2

Street Name	Map Ref
Shoe La	7-D2
Shoreditch High St	5-B3
Skinner St	4-D3
Sloane Sq	9-B3
Sloane St	9-B3
Southamton Row	7-A1
Southwark Bridge Rd	10-E1
Southwark Park Rd	11-D3
Southwark St	7-F4
Squirries St	5-D3
St Bride St	7-D2
St Giles High St	6-F2
St Martin's Pl	6-F3
St. Andrew St	7-D1
St. George's Rd	10-D2
St. James St	6-D4
St. Margaret St	10-A2
St. Pancras Way	3-E1
St. Thomas St	11-B1
Stamford St	7-C4
Strand St	7-A3
Swinton St	4-B3
Thayer St	6-B1
The Cut	10-D1
The Highway	8-F3
Theobalds Rd	7-B1
Tooley St	8-A4
Tottenham Court Rd	6-E1
Tower Bridge	8-C4
Tower Bridge Rd	11-B1
Tower Hill St	8-C3
Union St	10-F1
Upper St	4-D1
Upper Thames St	7-F3
Upper Woburn Pl	3-F3
Vallance Rd	5-D3
Vauxhall Bridge Rd	9-D3
Vere St	6-C2
Victoria Embankment	7-A4
Victoria Park Rd	5-F1
Victoria St	9-E2
Walworth Rd	10-E3
Warner Pl	5-D2
Waterloo Rd	10-C1
Welbeck St	6-C2
Westminster Br Rd	10-D2
Wharfdale Rd	4-A2
Whitechapel High St	8-C2
Whitechapel Rd	5-F4
Wigmore St	6-B2
Woburn Pl	3-F4
Wormwood St	8-A1
York Rd	10-B2
York Way	4-A1

Shetland
Islands
∘ Lerwick

Orkney Islands
Thurso ∘
Wick ∘
Stornoway ∘

∘ Uig
Elgin ∘ ∘ Fraserburgh
Inverness ∘ Peterhead
Kyle of Lochalsh ∘
Mallaig ∘ **Aberdeen**
SCOTLAND
Forfar ∘
Oban ∘ **Dundee** ∘ Arbroath
Perth ∘ St Andrews
Stirling ∘ Glenrothes
Greenock ∘ **Glasgow** **Kirkcaldy**
Edinburgh
Motherwell Berwick upon Tweed
Campbeltown ∘
Ayr ∘
UNITED KINGDOM
Derry ∘ Coleraine
Strabane ∘ Larne ∘ Stranraer **Newcastle**
NORTHERN ∘ Bangor **Carlisle** **upon Tyne**
IRELAND **Belfast** Maryport ∘
Enniskillen ∘ ∘ Lurgan Whitehaven ∘ **Darlington** ∘ **Middlesbrough**
Armagh ∘ Newry ∘ Isle of Man ∘ Kendal ∘ Scarborough
IRELAND Douglas ∘ ∘ Barrow in Furness
∘ **York**
Blackpool ∘ **Leeds**
Dublin **Preston** **Kingston upon Hull**
Holyhead ∘ **Liverpool** **Manchester** **Sheffield**
Dun Laoghaire Conwy ∘ Flint ∘ **Lincoln**
Limerick ∘ Wrexham ∘ **Stoke on** **Derby** Boston ∘
Trent **Nottingham**
Waterford ∘ Aberystwyth ∘ **Leicester** **Norwich** ∘ **Great**
Birmingham ∘ **ENGLAND** **Yarmouth**
Cork ∘ **WALES** **Northampton** ∘ **Cambridge** **Lowestoft**
Haverfordwest ∘ Carmarthen ∘ **Ipswich**
Pembroke Dock ∘ **Newport** Gloucester ∘ **Oxford** ∘ **Luton**
Swansea Swindon ∘ Chelmsford ∘
Cardiff **Bristol** ∘ Bath **London** **Southend on Sea**
Taunton ∘ **Reading**
Guildford ∘ Maidstone ∘ Dover ∘ Calais ∘
Southampton **Brighton**
Exeter Poole ∘ **Bournemouth** Hastings ∘
Plymouth ∘ ∘ Torquay Weymouth ∘ **FRANCE**

North Sea
Atlantic Ocean
Irish Sea
English Channel

100km

The Complete **Residents'** Guide

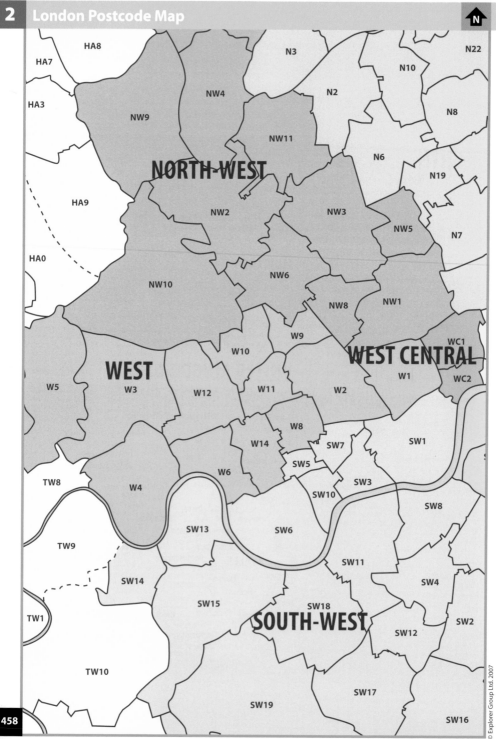

London Explorer 1st Edition

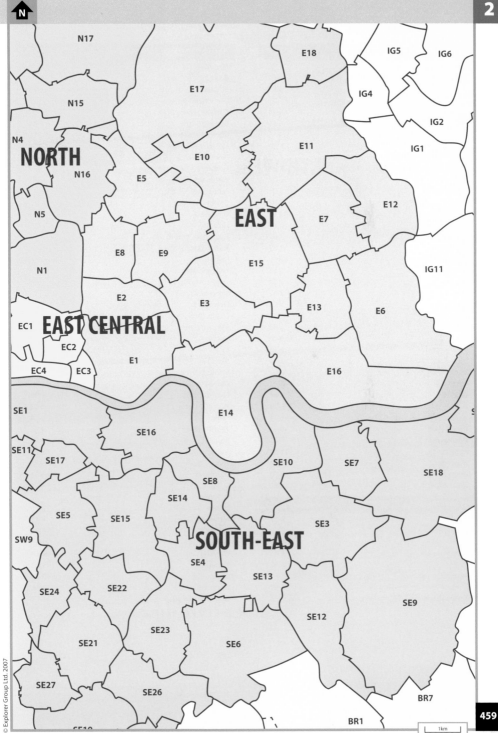

NORTH

EAST

EAST CENTRAL

SOUTH-EAST

N17

N15

N16

N4

N5

N1

E17

E18

E10

E5

E11

E7

E12

E8

E9

E15

E2

E3

E13

E6

E1

E16

E14

EC1

EC2

EC4

EC3

IG5

IG6

IG4

IG2

IG1

IG11

SE1

SE11

SE17

SE16

SE8

SE10

SE7

SE18

SE14

SE5

SE15

SW9

SE4

SE3

SE13

SE24

SE22

SE12

SE9

SE23

SE6

SE21

SE27

SE26

BR7

BR1

1km

© Explorer Group Ltd. 2007

Area and London Underground Index

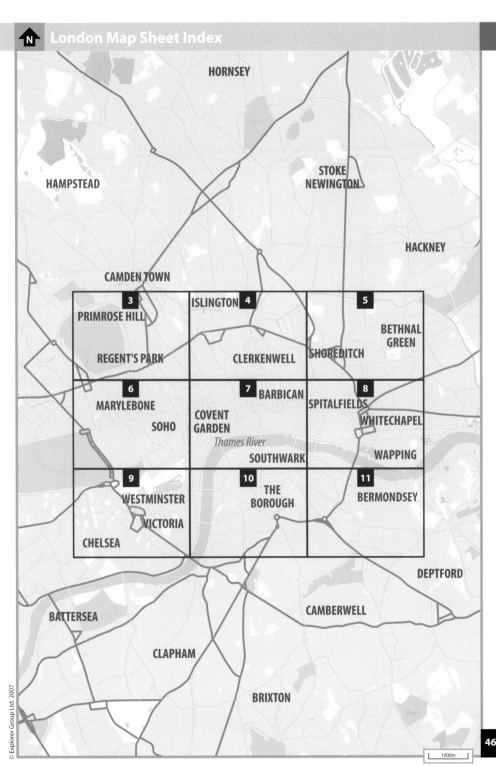

HORNSEY

STOKE
NEWINGTON

HAMPSTEAD

HACKNEY

CAMDEN TOWN

3
ISLINGTON **4**
5

PRIMROSE HILL

BETHNAL
GREEN

REGENT'S PARK
CLERKENWELL
SHOREDITCH

6
7 BARBICAN
8

MARYLEBONE
SOHO
COVENT
GARDEN
Thames River
SPITALFIELDS
WHITECHAPEL

SOUTHWARK
WAPPING

9
10
11

WESTMINSTER
THE
BOROUGH
BERMONDSEY

VICTORIA

CHELSEA

DEPTFORD

BATTERSEA
CAMBERWELL

CLAPHAM

BRIXTON

461

1000m

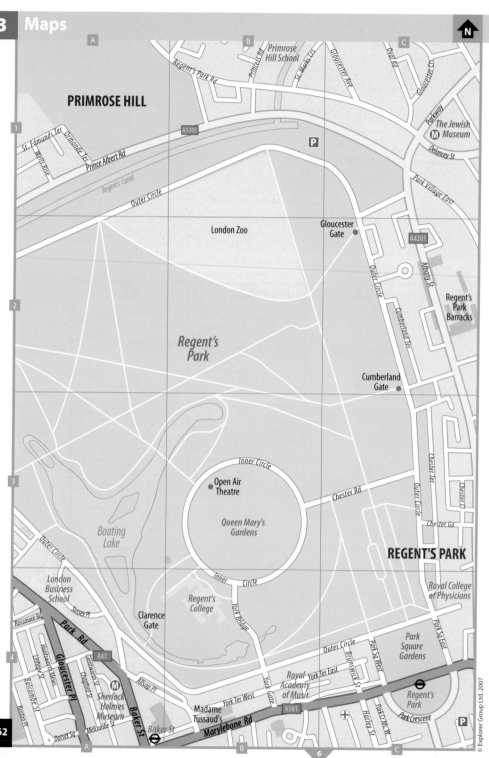

PRIMROSE HILL

Primrose Hill School

Regent's Park Rd

St. Edmunds Ter

Oppidans Ter

Regent's Park Rd

Prince's Rd

St. Marks Crs

Gloucester Ave

Oval Rd

Gloucester Crs

A5205

Regent's Canal

Prince Albert Rd

Outer Circle

Parkway

The Jewish Museum

Delancey St

Park Village East

P

London Zoo

Gloucester Gate

A4201

Outer Circle

Albany St

Regent's Park Barracks

Cumberland Ter

Regent's Park

Cumberland Gate

Chester Ter

Inner Circle

Open Air Theatre

Chester Rd

Chester Cl

Outer Circle

Chester Ga

Queen Mary's Gardens

REGENT'S PARK

Boating Lake

Inner Circle

Royal College of Physicians

London Business School

Sussex Pl

Regent's College

York Bridge

Clarence Gate

Outer Circle

Park Sq West

Park Sq East

Park Square Gardens

Rossmore Rd

Park Rd

Gloucester Pl

A41

Glentworth St

Chagford St

Allsop Pl

York Ter West

York Ter East

Brunswick St

York Gate

Royal Academy of Music

Regent's Park

Humewick Mews

Balcombe St

Ivor Pl

Huntsworth Mews

Linhope St

Transept St

Sherlock Holmes Museum

Baker St

Melcombe St

Madame Tussaud's

A501

Marylebone Rd

Park Cres. W.

Harley St

Park Crescent

Park Cr. E.

Dorset Sq

P

A   B   6   C

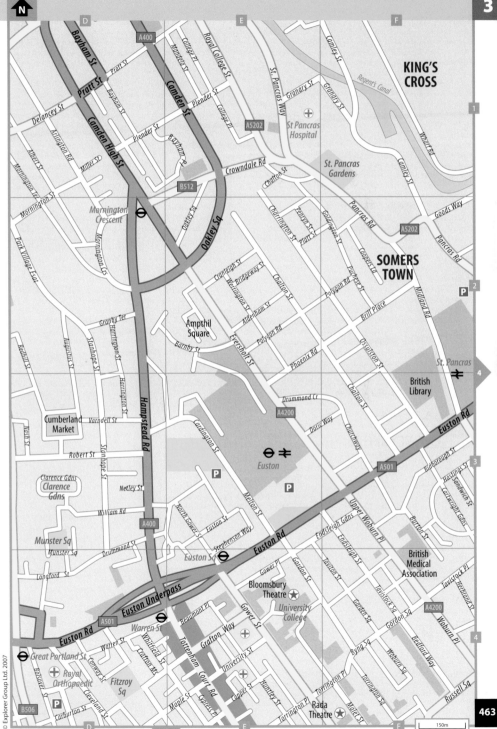

KING'S
CROSS

SOMERS
TOWN

St Pancras
Hospital

St. Pancras
Gardens

British
Library

St. Pancras

Ampthil
Square

Cumberland
Market

Clarence Gdns
Clarence
Gdns

Munster Sq

Euston

British
Medical
Association

Bloomsbury
Theatre

University
College

Euston Underpass

Warren St

Great Portland St

Royal
Orthopaedic

Fitzroy
Sq

Rada
Theatre

150m

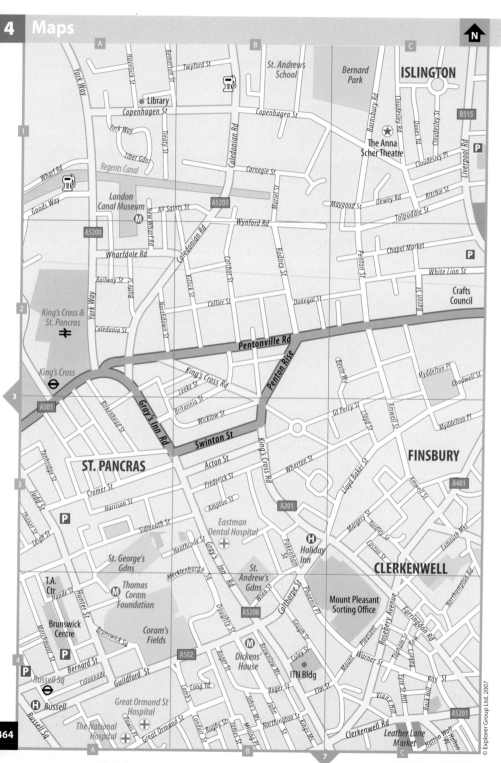

London Explorer 1st Edition

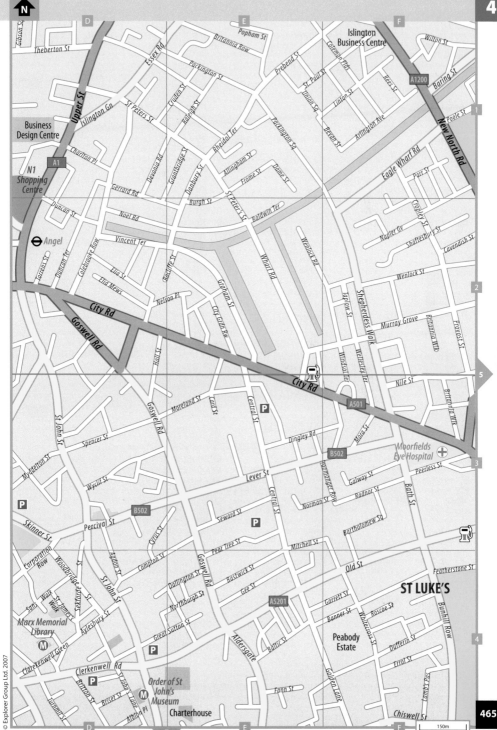

Theberton St
Gibson Rd
D
Popham St
E
Britannia Row
Prebend St
Coventry Flds
F
Wilton St
Islington Business Centre
Essex Rd
Packington St
St Paul St
Rees St
Baring St
A1200
New North Rd
Poole St

Upper St
Islington Gn
St Peters St
Cruden St
Rheidal Ter
Packington Sq
Union Sq
Linton St
Arlington Ave
Bevan St
Eagle Wharf Rd
Parr St
Crosley St

Business Design Centre
A1
Charlton Pl
Raleigh Rd
Devonia Rd
Greenbridge Ct
Danbury St
Frome St
Hume St
Allingham St
Napier Gv
Shaftesbury St
Cavendish St

N1 Shopping Centre
Duncan St
Noel Rd
Burgh St
Spreets St
Baldwin Ter
Wenlock St

Angel
Vincent Ter
Graham St
Wharf Rd
Wenlock Rd
Taplow St
Shepherdess Walk
Wenlock St

Torrens St
Duncan Ter
Colebrooke Row
Ella St
Ella Mews
Radcliffe St
Nelson Pl
City Gdn Row
Murray Grove
Britannia Wlk
Provost St

City Rd
Goswell Rd
Hall St
City Rd
Windsor Ter
Wellesley Ter
Nile St
Britannia Wlk

St John St
Spencer St
Wyclif St
Goswell Rd
Moreland St
Carl St
Central St
P
Dingley Rd
A501
Moira St
B502
Moorfields Eye Hospital
Peerless St

Myddelton St
P
Skinner St
Percival St
B502
Cyrus St
Lever St
Seward St
Central St
Ironmonger Row
Galway St
Norman St
Radnor St
Bath St

Corporation Row
Woodbridge St
Aylesbury St
St John St
Compton St
Dallington St
Pear Tree St
Bastwick St
Gee St
Mitchell St
Bartholomew Sq
Old St
Garrett St
Featherstone St
Bunhill Row

Sans Walk
St James's Walk
Marx Memorial Library
M
Clerkenwell Green
Aylesbury St
Great Sutton St
Northburgh St
A5201
Bartic St
Banner St
Whitecross St
Roscoe St
ST LUKE'S
Dufferin St
Errol St

Clerkenwell Rd
P
P
Britton St
Briset St
M
Order of St John's Museum
Charterhouse
Aldersgate
Fann St
Golden Lane
Peabody Estate
Chiswell St

Albion Pl

© Explorer Group Ltd. 2007

150m

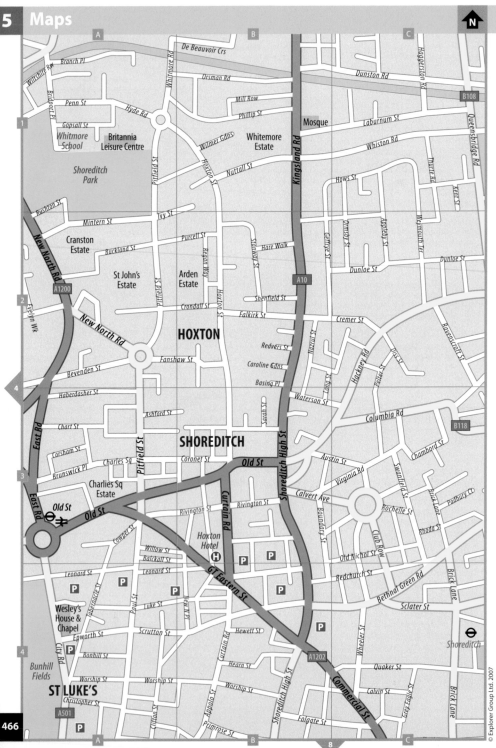

London Explorer 1st Edition

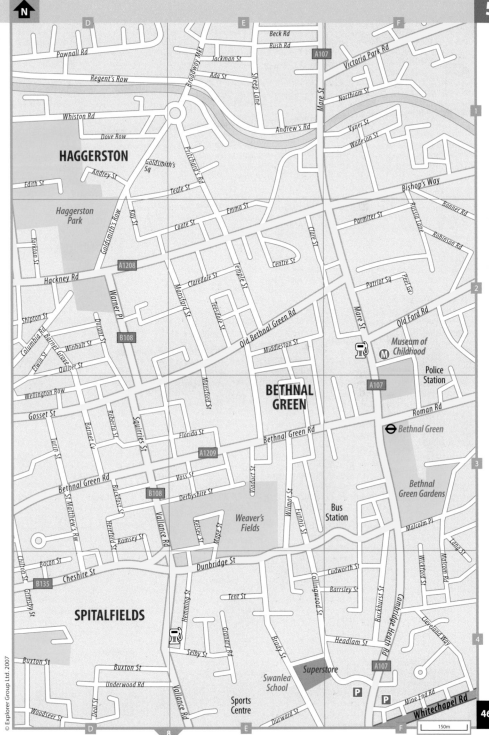

Pownall Rd

Regent's Row

Whiston Rd

Dove Row

HAGGERSTON

Edith St

Andrey St

Goldsmith's Sq

Broadway Mkt

Pritchard's Rd

Tackman St

Ada St

Beck Rd

Bush Rd

A107

Victoria Park Rd

Northiam St

Andrew's Rd

Mare St

Vyner St

Wadeson St

Bishop's Way

Bonner Rd

Teale St

Russia Lane

Robinson Rd

Haggerston Park

Yorkton St

Goldsmith's Row

Kay St

Coate St

Emma St

Clare St

Centre St

Parmiter St

Peel Gro

Patriot Sq

Hackney Rd

A1208

Warner Pl

Claredale St

Temple St

Mansford St

Teesdale St

Old Bethnal Green Rd

Patriot Sq

Old Ford Rd

Shipton St

B108

Durant St

Middleton St

Mare St

Columbia Rd

Barnet Grove

Winholt St

Quilter St

Museum of Childhood

M

Elwin St

Police Station

Wellington Row

Mansford St

A107

Roman Rd

Gosset St

Roberta St

Squirries St

Florida St

Bethnal Green Rd

Bethnal Green

Barnet Gv

BETHNAL GREEN

Turin St

A1209

Vass St

Bethnal Green Rd

Buxton St

Viaduct St

Wilmot St

Funnis St

Bethnal Green Gardens

B108

Derbyshire St

Malcolm Pl

St Matthew's Rw

Vallance Rd

Parker St

Weaver's Fields

Lang St

Marcom St

Hereford St

Ramsey St

Bus Station

Clifton St

Bacon St

Dunbridge St

Cudworth St

Wickford St

Cleveland Way

Grimsby St

B135

Cheshire St

Tent St

Collingwood St

Barrsley St

Buckhurst St

Cambridge Heath Rd

Hemming St

SPITALFIELDS

Granary Rd

Brady St

Headlam St

Buxton St

Buxton St

Underwood Rd

Selby St

Swanlea School

Superstore

P

A107

Mile End Rd

P

Woodseer St

St James

Vallance Rd

Sports Centre

Durward St

Whitechapel Rd

150m

N

London Explorer 1st Edition

© Explorer Group Ltd. 2007

Dorser Clo
Marylebone Rd
A501
Westminster Council House
York St
Bickenhall St
Porter St
University of Westminster
Luxborough St
Nottingham St
Beaumont St
Marylebone High St
Devonshire St
Devonshire Mews West
Devonshire St
Harley St
Devonshire Clo
China
Grafton St
Bulford St

Samaritan Hospital
Knox St
Upper Montagu St
Crawford St
York St
Paddington St
MARYLEBONE
Weymouth St
Wimpole St
Harley St
Harley Mews
New Cavendish St
UAE
Weymouth St
Weymouth Mews
Portland Pl

Crawford St
Wyndham Pl
Montagu Ms N
Montagu Pl
Dorset St
Clay St
Crawford St
Dorset St
Chiltern St
Manchester St
Thayer St
New Cavendish St
Marylebone St
Wimpole Ms
Harley St
Mansfield St

Bryanston Pl
Montagu Sq
Montagu Pl
Gloucester Pl Mews
Blandford St
George St
Wallace Collection
M
Bulstrode St
Welbeck St
Queen Anne St
Wimpole St
Harley St
Wigmore St

Bryanston Ms W
Bryanston Pl
Montagu Sq
George St
George St
A Adam St
Manchester Sq
Marylebone Lane
Wigmore Hall
A5204
P

Seymour Pl
Brown St
George St
Gt Cumberland Pl
Portman Clo
Heinz Gallery
M
Fitzhardinge St
Duke St
Wigmore St
Welbeck St
John Lewis

Stourcliffe St
Seymour Ms
Wythburn Pl
Brunswick Ms
P
Portman Sq
Edwards Mews
Orchard St
James St
Picton Pl
Stratford Pl
Old Cavendish St
Vere St
Dering St

Edgware Rd
Upper Berkeley St
Montcalm
H
Berkeley Ms
Churchill
H
P
Portman Sq
Barrett St
Bond St
Oxford St
South Molton St
Molton La
Woodstock St
Brook St

Seymour St
A5
New Quebec St
Portman St
Portman Ms
Selfridges
A40
Gilbert St
Weigh House St
Davies St
Brook St
Claridge's
H
Brook's Mews
Avery Row

Marble Arch
Old Quebec St
Thistle Marble Arch
Oxford St
North Audley St
Balderton St
Binney St
Duke St
Argentina
Three Kings Yd.
Grosvenor St

Connaught Pl
Bayswater Rd
Marble Arch
Cumberland Gate
North Row
Park St
Green St
Lees Pl
P
Grosvenor Sq
Brook St
Mount Row
Grosvenor St
Grosvenor Hill
Bourdon St

North Carriage Drive Ring
Speakers' Corner
Park Lane
Dunraven St
Green St
Woods Mews
Upper Brook St
US
Roosevelt Memorial
Britannia
P
Carlos Pl
P
Berkeley Sq

Brook Gate
Grosvenor Gate
P
Grosvenor House
Culross St
Upper Grosvenor St
Le Meridien Grosvenor House
H
Adam's Row
Connaught
H
Mount St

A4202
MAYFAIR
P
Park
Aldford St
South Audley St
Farm St
Chesterfield Hill
Hill St
Hay's Mews
Charles St
Claridge Ms

Dorchester
H
South St
Deanery St
Tilney St
P
Malaysia
Curzon St
Washington
H
Hay's Ms
Waverton St
Hertford St
White Horse St
A4

Hyde Park
Park Lane
Stanhope Gate
Market Ms
Shepherd St
Brick St

Achilles Statue

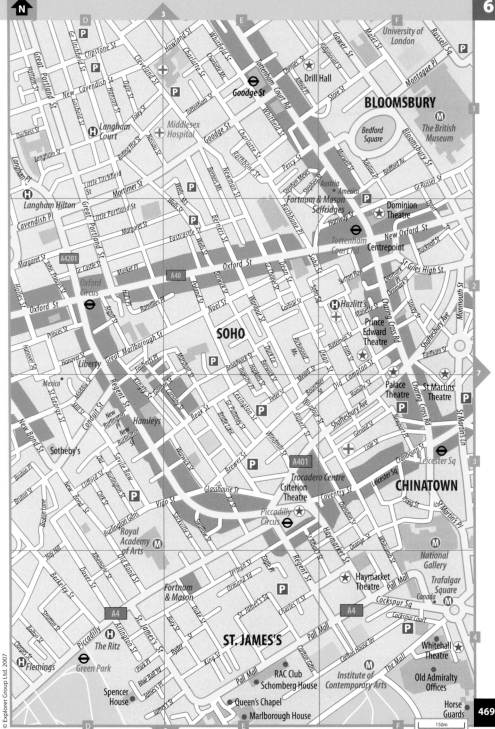

N

D · 3 · E · F

BLOOMSBURY

Gr. Titchfield St · Clipstone St · Howland St · Whitfield St · Tottenham Court Rd · Chenies St · Ridgmount St · Gower St · Malet St · Russell Sq · University of London

Great Portland St · Hallam St · New Cavendish St · Cleveland St · Charlotte St · Charlotte Mews · Store St · Montague Pl

Goodge St · Drill Hall

New Cavendish St · Hanson St · Cleveland St · Tottenham St · Bedford Sq · Bloomsbury St · The British Museum

Duchess St · Langham St · Langham Court · Rolling Hse St · Maple St · Middlesex Hospital · Goodge St · Charlotte St · Percy St · Stephen Mews · Bedford Av

Langham Hilton · Mortimer St · Little Titchfield · Great Portland St · Little Portland St · Wells St · Berners St · Newman St · Rathbone Pl · Austria · America · Fortnum & Mason · Selfridges · Dominion Theatre

Cavendish Pl · Margaret St · Eastcastle St · Hanway St · New Oxford St · Bucknall St

Margaret St · A4201 · Gt. Castle St · Market Pl · A40 · Oxford St · Poland St · Dean St · Soho St · Centrepoint · Tottenham Court Rd · Denmark St · St Giles High St · Monmouth St

Oxford Circus · Oxford St · A40 · Berwick St · Noel St · Wardour St · Sutton Row · Denmark St

Princes St · Hanover St · Ramillies Pl · Carlisle St · Hazlitt's

SOHO · Prince Edward Theatre · Charing Cross Rd · Earlham St · Shaftesbury Ave

Liberty · Great Marlborough St · Foubert's Pl · Broadwick St · Hopkins St · Brewer St · Meard St · Dean St · Romilly St · Palace Theatre · St Martins Theatre

Mexico · Regent St · Kingly St · Carnaby St · Lexington St · Bridle Lane · Bateman St · Old Compton St · Frith St · Gerrard St · St Martin's Ln

New Burlington St · New Burlington St · Hamleys · Beak St · Warwick St · Great Pulteney St · Windmill St · Wardour St · Shaftesbury Ave · Newport St · Leicester Sq

Conduit St · Savile Row · Hanover St · Glasshouse St · A401 · Trocadero Centre · Cranbourn St · CHINATOWN

Clifford St · Cork St · Vigo St · Brewer St · Criterion Theatre · Coventry St · Leicester Sq · St Martin's Pl

New Bond St · Old Bond St · Sackville St · Piccadilly Circus · Lisle St

Burlington Gdns · Royal Academy of Arts · National Gallery

Hay Hill · Dover St · Albemarle St · Jermyn St · Regent St · Haymarket · Haymarket Theatre · Trafalgar Square

Berkeley St · St James's St · Ormond Yd · Pall Mall · Cockspur St · Canada

Bruton St · A4 · Duke St · Charles St · A4 · Cockspur Court

Stratton St · Arlington St · St James's Sq · Piccadilly · Whitehall Theatre

The Ritz · Clarg Pl · Duke St · King St · Bury St · Carlton House Ter · Old Admiralty Offices

Flemings · Green Park · Blue Ball Yd · ST JAMES'S · Pall Mall · Institute of Contemporary Arts · The Mall · Horse Guards

Spencer House · RAC Club · Schomberg House

Queen's Chapel · Marlborough House

150m

469

N

A · B · 4 · C

HOLBORN

Russell Sq
A4200
Old Gloucester St
Bedford Pl
Montague St
Bloomsbury Sq
Bloomsbury Way
Bloomsbury St
Great Russell St
Gilbert Pl
Russell St
Museum St
Bury Pl
Southampton Row
Bawtry St
New North St
New Oxford St
New Oxford St
High Holborn
Town Hall
Newton St
Stukeley St
High Holborn
Martlett St
Parker St
Great Queen St
Oasis Sports Centre
Betterton St
Freemasons Hall
Wild St
Neal St
Endell St
Keeley St
Kemble St
Drury La
Sardinia St
Portsmouth St

Theobald's Rd
Jockey's Fields
Bedford Row
Red Lion Sq
Princeton St
Red Lion St
Sandland St
Emerald St
Proctor St
Fisher St
Covent Garden
Renaissance Chancery Court London
Whetstone Park
Lincoln's Inn Fields
Lincoln's Inn Fields
Gate St
Kingsway
Remnant St
Royal College of Surgeons
Portugal St
London School Of Economics
Clements Inn
St Clement's La

Gray's Inn Gardens
Raymond Bldgs
Gray's Inn Rd
Portpool Lane
Verulam St
St Cross St
Baldwin's Gdns
Leather Lane
Hatton Garden
Greville St
A5200
Prudential Bldg
Chancery Lane
High Holborn
High Holborn
London Weather Ctr
Silver Vaults
Staple Inn
Southampton Bldgs
Stone Bldgs
Chancery Lane
Cursitor St
Bream's Bldgs
Star Yd
Carey St
Bell Yd
Sir John Soane's Museum
Lincoln's Inn Hall
Royal Courts of Justice
Strand
B400
Fetter Lane
New Fetter Lane
Neville St
Dr Johnson's House
Mitre Court
Twinings
St Clement Danes Church
Middle Temple La
Inner Temple Hall
Inner Temple
Inner Temple Gdns
Middle Lib. Middle Temple
A3211

COVENT GARDEN
Mercer St
Shelton St
Long Acre
Floral St
Bow St
King St
Covent Garden Market
Henrietta St
Southampton St
Exeter St
New Row
Maiden Lane
Chandos Pl
Bedford St
Bedford Ct
Police Station
William IV St
St Martin's Lane
Royal Opera House
Bow St Courts
Russell St
Catherine St
Tavistock St
Wellington St
Burleigh St
Wellington St
London Transport Museum
Waldorf Hilton
One Aldwych
Aldwych
Aldwych
Bush House
India House
Australia House
Australian High Comission
Indian High Comission
King's College
Courtauld Institute Gallery
Somerset House
Gilbert Collection
Surrey St
Arundel St
Temple Pl
Milford Lane
Essex St
Temple
Embankment
Victoria
Blackfriars Millennium Pier

Farnham St
Langley St
Covent Garden
A4200
A4

Strand Palace
Savoy Row
Zimbabwe House
Savoy Pl
Savoy Way
Savoy St
Adam St
John Adam St
Strand
Carrick La
Savoy
Savoy Pier
River Thames
Oxo Tower

Charing Cross
Villiers St
Playhouse Theatre
Players Theatre
Craven St
Northumberland Av
Japan
South Africa
Great Scotland Yard
Whitehall Pl
Old War Office
Horse Guards Avenue
A3212
Victoria Embkt. Gdns
Victoria Embankment
Victoria Embkt. Gdns
Embankment
Embankment Pier
Rail Bridge
Cleopatra's Needle
Festival Pier
Waterloo Bridge
A301
Queen Elizabeth Hall, Purcell Room
Southbank Centre
Royal Festival Hall
Jubilee Gardens
Belvedere Rd
London Imax
Gabriel's Wharf
Bernie Spain Gdns
The London Television Centre
National Theatre
Upper Ground
Duchy St
Coin St
Stamford St
A3200
SOUTH BANK
Doon St
Cornwall Rd
Aquinas St
Theed St
Exton St
Roupell St
Brad St

London Explorer 1st Edition

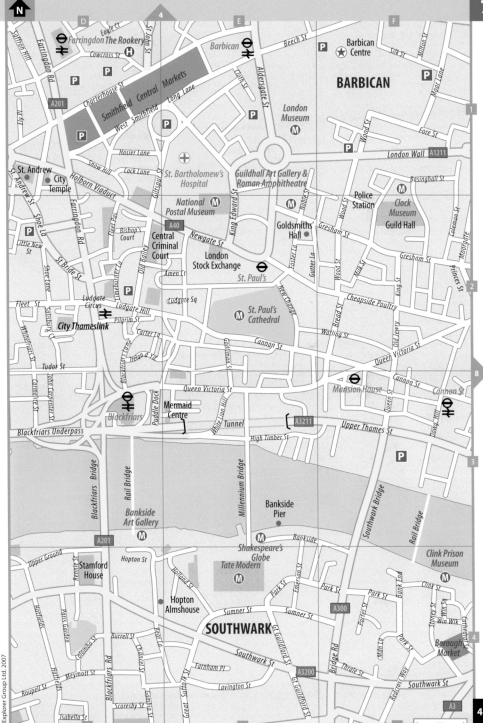

N

Saffron Hill

Farringdon Rd

A201

Ely Pl

St. Andrew St

Holborn Viaduct

Farringdon Rd

Shoe La

Little New St

Fleet St

Salisbury Sq

St Bride St

Whitefriars St

Shoe La

Tudor St

Carmelite St

John Carpenter St

Eagle Ct

Cowcross St

Farringdon The Rookery

Charterhouse St

Chaterhouse St

Smithfield Central Markets

West Smithfield

Hosier Lane

Snow Hill

Cock Lane

St. Bartholomew's Hospital

St. Andrew

City Temple

Bishop's Court

Central Criminal Court

Fleet La

Limeburner La

Old Bailey

Blackfriars Tunnel

Puddle Dock

Blackfriars

Blackfriars Underpass

Blackfriars Bridge

Rail Bridge

Upper Ground

Rennie St

Hatfields

Paris Garden

Colombo St

Hatfields

Meymott St

Roupell St

Isabella St

Stamford House

Hopton St

Holland St

Bear La

Burrell St

Blackfriars Rd

Great Suffolk St

Scoresby St

A201

Bankside Art Gallery

Hopton Almshouse

Sumner St

SOUTHWARK

Southwark St

Farnham Pl

Lavington St

A3200

Gt Guildford St

Gt Guildford St

Long Lane

John St

Clerk St

Aldersgate St

Barbican

St John St

Charterhouse St

King Edward St

Newgate St

Amen Ct

Ludgate Sq

Ludgate Hill

Pilgrim St

Carter La

Ireland Yd

Ludgate Circus

City Thameslink

Ludgate Circus

National Postal Museum

A40

London Stock Exchange

St. Paul's

St. Paul's Cathedral

Cannon St

Queen Victoria St

Mermaid Centre

White Lion Hill

Tunnel

High Timber St

A3211

Millennium Bridge

Bankside Pier

Shakespeare's Globe

Tate Modern

Bankside

Park St

Sumner St

A300

Emerson St

Porter St

Holland St

Beech St

Barbican Centre

Silk St

Milton St

Moor Lane

P

BARBICAN

London Museum

Wood St

Fore St

London Wall

A1211

Basinghall St

Police Station

Clock Museum

Guild Hall

Noble St

Gresham St

Goldsmiths' Hall

Foster La

Gutter La

Wood St

Milk St

Bread St

Watling St

New Change

Cheapside Poultry

King St

Old Jewry

Queen Victoria St

Mansion House

Cannon St

Queen St

Garlick Hill

Upper Thames St

Southwark Bridge

Rail Bridge

Clink Prison Museum

Bank End

Clink St

Stoney St

Park St

Park St

Borough Market

Win Wlk

Cathedral St

Redcross Way

Southwark St

Bridge Rd

Thrale St

Guildhall Art Gallery & Roman Amphitheatre

Gresham St

Princes St

Moorgate

Coleman St

A3

150m

© Explorer Group Ltd. 2007

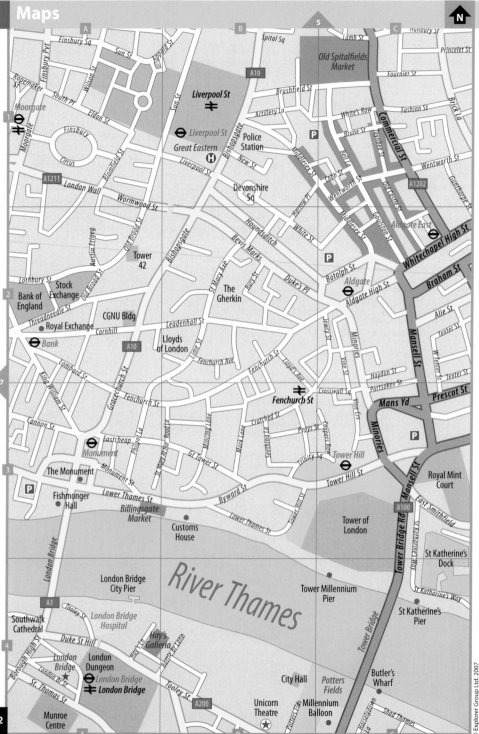

London Explorer 1st Edition

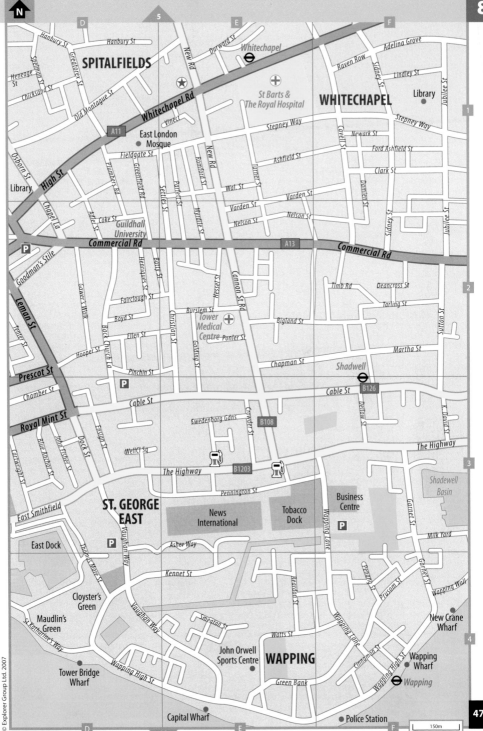

SPITALFIELDS

Hanbury St

Hanbury St

New Rd

Durward St

Whitechapel

Raven Row

Adelina Grove

Lindley St

Heneage St

Greatorex St

Old Montague St

St Barts &
The Royal Hospital

WHITECHAPEL

Library

Jubilee St

Spelman St

Chicksand St

Whitechapel Rd

Sidney St

Stepney Way

A11

Vinect

East London
Mosque

High St

Chapel La

Fieldgate St

Greenfield Rd

Fordham St

New Rd

Parfett St

Settles St

Stepney Way

Cavell St

Newark St

Ford Ashfield St

Clark St

Library

Osborn St

Adler St

Coke St

Myrdle St

Wat. St

Ashfield St

Damien St

Sidney St

Jubilee St

Guildhall
University

Commercial Rd

Varden St

Varden St

Nelson St

Nelson St

A13

Commercial Rd

Leman St

Goodman's Stile

Lower's Walk

Henriques St

Fairclough

Barry St

Hessel St

Cannon St Rd

Christian St

Burslem St

Tower
Medical
Centre

Bigland St

Timb Rd

Deancross St

Tarling St

Martha St

Sutton St

Tenter St

Boyd St

Back Church La

Ellen St

Golding St

Ponler St

Chapman St

Shadwell

Hooper St

Pinchin St

B126

Prescot St

Chamber St

Cable St

Cable St

Royal Mint St

Dock St

Ensign St

Swedenborg Gdns

B108

Dellow St

The Highway

Blue Anchor

John Fisher St

WellCl Sq

The Highway

B1203

Shadewell
Basin

East Smithfield

ST. GEORGE
EAST

Pennington St

News
International

Tobacco
Dock

Business
Centre

Wapping Lane

Garnet St

Milk Yard

East Dock

Thomas More St

Vaughan Way

Asher Way

Kennet St

Reardon St

Penang St

Prusom St

Garnet St

Wapping Wall

Cloyster's
Green

Vaughan Way

Smeaton St

Watts St

Wapping Lane

New Crane
Wharf

Maudlin's
Green

St Katherine's Way

Wapping High St

John Orwell
Sports Centre

WAPPING

Green Bank

Cinnamon St

Wapping High St

Wapping
Wharf

Wapping

Tower Bridge
Wharf

Capital Wharf

Police Station

150m

© Explorer Group Ltd. 2007

473

N

The Serpentine

6
Park Lane

Queen Elizabeth Gate

Piccadilly

Green Park

Wellington Museum, Apsley Hse

Hyde Park Corner

Hyde Park Corner

Old Park Lane

Hamilton Pl

Down St

Albert Gate

South Carriage Dr

Knightsbridge Underpass

Wellington Arch

Constitution Hill

Hyde Park Barracks

South Carriage Dr

The Lanesborough

Buckingham Palace Gardens

Knightsbridge Green

Berkeley

Duplex Ride

Knightsbridge

Grosvenor Cr

A302

Hertford St

The Halkin

Grosvenor Pl

Harvey Nichols

Sloane St

Harriet Walk

Lowndes Sq

Wilton Cr

Wilton Pl

Halkin St

Chapel St

Chester St

Chester St

Chester Ms

Wilton St

Brompton Rd

Knights Bridge

Pakistan

Basil St

Basil St

Pavilion Rd

Jumeirah Carlton Tower

Hyatt Carlton Tower

Motcomb St

West Halkin St

Belgrave Ms N

Belgrave Sq

Germany

Spain

Norway

Belgrave Ms S

Belgrave Pl

Eaton Ms N

Hobart Pl

Gros Gdns

A4

Harrods

Hans Rd

Hans Cr

Hans Plz

Hans St

Denmark

Lowndes St

Chesham Pl

Finland

Lyall St

Hyatt Mews

Eaton Pl

Belgrave Ms S

Eaton Ms

Eaton Sq

Eaton Row

KNIGHTSBRIDGE

Pont St

Pont St

Chesham St

Eaton Mews North

Eaton Sq

Lower Belgrave St

Eaton Sq

Chester Sq

Eccleston St

Hans Pl

Walton St

Cadogan Sq

Pavilion Rd

Cadogan Pl

Cadogan Lane

W Eaton Pl

Eaton Pl

Eaton Mews South

Chester Sq

Chester Sq

Ebury Ms N

Eccleston St

BROMPTON

Lennox Gdns

Clabon Ms

Moore St

Cadogan Gdns

Sloane St

Cadogan Pl

Ellis St

Eaton Ter

Minera Ms

Chester Row

BELGRAVIA

Eaton Ms S

Chester Ms

Chester Sq

Elizabeth St

Ebury Ms

Ebury St

Ebury Sq

Eccleston Pl

Colonnade Walk

Milner St

Moore St

Cadogan Gate

Cadogan Gdns

Sloane Ter

Clive Eaton Gate

5th Eaton Pl

Caroline Ter

Gerald Rd

Elizabeth St

Morgan House

Elizabeth Br

Eccleston Br

Buttery Way

Rawlings St

Draycott Pl

Bray Pl

Symons St

Sloane Sq

Sloane Square

Bourne St

Graham Ter

Francis Holland School

Ebury St

Buckingham Palace Rd

Victoria Coach Station

Police Station

Rosemoor St

Cadogan St

Draycott Ave

Sloane Ave

Elystan Pl

King's Rd

Walpole St

Cheltenham Ter

Lower Sloane St

Sloane Gdns

Hathair St

Pimlico Rd

Semley Pl

Ebury Br

Barnabas St

Ebury Br

A3217

Royal Ave

St Leonard's Ter

Franklin's Row

Royal Hospital Rd

A302

Chelsea Bridge Rd

A313

Turpentine Rd

Smith St

Burtons Court

Ranelagh Gardens

CHELSEA

Chelsea Barracks

Ebury Bridge Rd

London Explorer 1st Edition

A   B   C

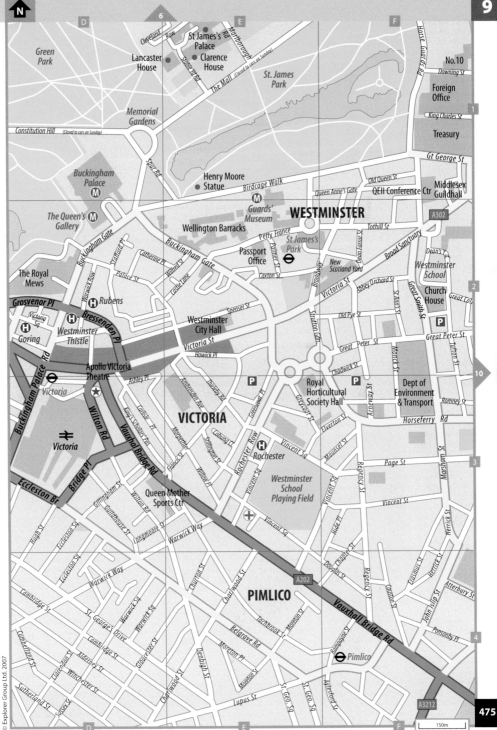

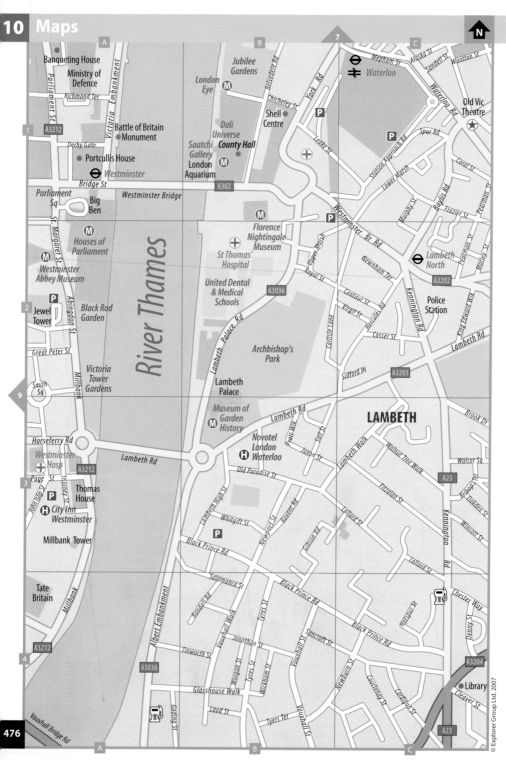

N

Banqueting House
Ministry of Defence
Richmond Ter
Parliament ST
A3212
Derby Gate
Victoria Embankment
Battle of Britain Monument
Portcullis House
Westminster
Bridge St
Parliament Sq
Big Ben
St. Margaret St
Houses of Parliament
Westminster Abbey Museum
Abingdon St
Jewel Tower
Black Rod Garden
Great Peter St
Millbank
Victoria Tower Gardens
Smith Sq
Horseferry Rd
Westminster Hosp
A3212
Page St
John Islip St
Thames Rd
Thomas House
City Inn Westminster
Millbank Tower
Tate Britain
Millbank
Vauxhall Bridge Rd

Jubilee Gardens
London Eye
Belvedere Rd
Chicheley St
Shell Centre
York Rd
Dali Universe
Saatchi Gallery
County Hall
London Aquarium
A302
Westminster Bridge

River Thames

Florence Nightingale Museum
St Thomas' Hospital
United Dental & Medical Schools
Upper Marsh
Royal St
A3036
Lambeth Palace Rd
Archbishop's Park
Carlisle Lane
Lambeth Palace
Museum of Garden History
Novotel London Waterloo
Old Paradise St
Pratt Walk
Salt St
Lambeth Rd
Tuxon St
Lambeth Rd
A3203
Sidford Pl
LAMBETH
Lambeth Walk
Walnut Tree Walk
Fitzalan St
Lambeth High St
Whitgift St
Newport St
Raven Rd
Tyers St
Gibson Rd
Pollard St
Black Prince Rd
Salamanca St
Randall Rd
Vauxhall Walk
Tyers St
Black Prince Rd
Newburn St
Jonathan St
Tinworth St
Morgan St
Tyers St
Wickham St
Vauxhall St
Sancroft St
Courtenay St
Black Prince Rd
Harleyford Rd
Glasshouse Walk
Laud St
Tyers Ter
Vauxhall St

Mepham St
Waterloo
Alaska St
Sandell St
Wootton St
Old Vic Theatre
Station Approach Rd
Spur Rd
Coral St
Tower Marsh
Murphy St
Boylis St
Frazier St
Pearman St
Westminster Br Rd
Lambeth North
A3202
Newnham Ter
Kennington Rd
Hercules Rd
Cosser St
Police Station
Lambeth Rd
King Edward Walk
Centaur St
Virgil St
Brook Dr
Watcot Sq
A23
Bishop's
Cladden St
Wincott St
Kennington Rd
Lollard St
Chester Way
Denny St
Cardigan St
A3204
Library
Cleaver St
A23

London Explorer 1st Edition

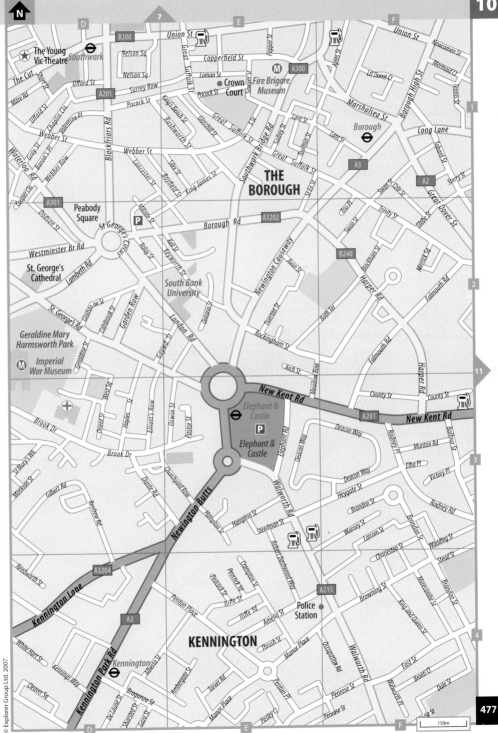

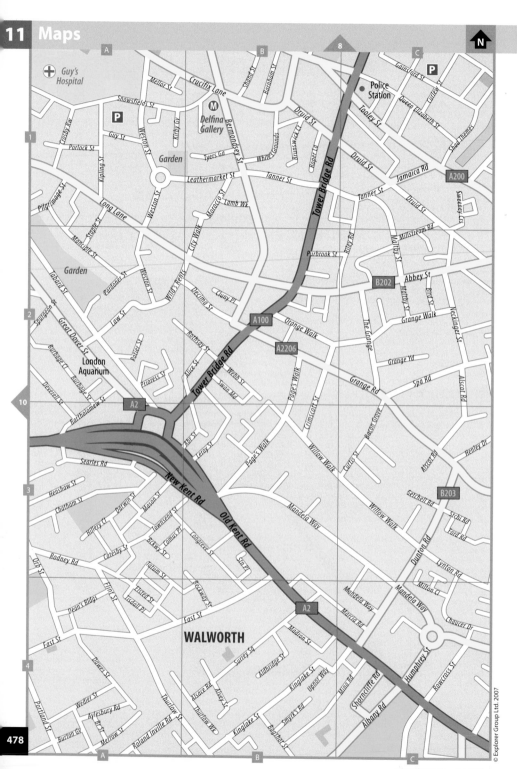

London Explorer 1st Edition

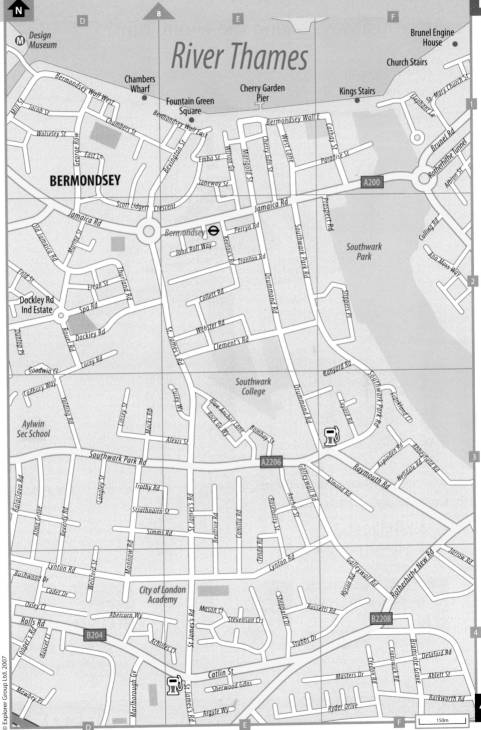

Are you always taking the wrong turn?

Whether you're a map person or not, these pocket-sized marvels will help you get to know the city… and its limits.

Explorer Mini Maps
Putting the city in your pocket

Index

Index

485

487

Index

London Explorer 1st Edition

Notes

The *London Explorer* Team
Lead Editor Sean Kearns
Deputy Editor Tom Jordan
Editorial Assistant Ingrid Cupido
Lead Designer Jayde Fernandes
Cartographer Zainudheen Madathil
Photographers Victor Romero, Sean Kearns,
Tom Jordan, Janetta Willis, Ben Robards

Publisher
Alistair MacKenzie

Editorial
Managing Editor Claire England
Lead Editors David Quinn, Jane Roberts, Matt Farquharson,
Sean Kearns, Tim Binks
Deputy Editors Helen Spearman, Katie Drynan, Tom Jordan
Editorial Assistants Ingrid Cupido, Mimi Stankova

Design
Creative Director Pete Maloney
Art Director Ieyad Charaf
Senior Designers Alex Jeffries, Motaz Al Bunai
Layout Manager Jayde Fernandes
Designers Hashim Moideen, Rafi Pullat,
Shefeeq Marakkatepurath, Sunita Lakhiani
Cartography Manager Zainudheen Madathil
Cartographer Noushad Madathil
Design Admin Manager Shyrell Tamayo
Production Coordinator Maricar Ong

Photography
Photography Manager Pamela Grist
Photographer Victor Romero
Image Editor Henry Hilos

Sales and Marketing
Area Sales Managers Laura Zuffa, Stephen Jones
Marketing Manager Kate Fox
Retail Sales Manager Ivan Rodrigues
Retail Sales Coordinator Kiran Melwani
Distribution Executives Abdul Gafoor, Ahmed Mainodin,
Firos Khan, Mannie Lugtu
Warehouse Assistant Mohammed Kunjaymo
Drivers Mohammed Sameer, Shabsir Madathil

Finance and Administration
Administration Manager Andrea Fust
Accounts Assistant Cherry Enriquez
Administrator Enrico Maullon
Driver Rafi Jamal

IT
IT Administrator Ajay Krishnan R.
Software Engineers Roshni Ahuja, Tissy Varghese

Explorer Publishing & Distribution
Office 51B, Zomorrodah Building, Za'abeel Road
PO Box 34275, Dubai, United Arab Emirates
Phone: +971 (0)4 335 3520, **Fax:** +971 (0)4 335 3529
info@explorerpublishing.com
www.explorerpublishing.com

Contact Us
Reader Response
If you have any comments and suggestions, fill out
our online reader response form and you could win prizes.
Log on to **www.explorerpublishing.com**

General Enquiries
We'd love to hear your thoughts and answer any questions
you have about this book or any other Explorer product.
Contact us at **info@explorerpublishing.com**

Careers
If you fancy yourself as an Explorer, send your CV (stating
the position you're interested in) to
jobs@explorerpublishing.com

Designlab and Contract Publishing
For enquiries about Explorer's Contract Publishing arm
and design services contact
designlab@explorerpublishing.com

PR and Marketing
For PR and marketing enquries contact
marketing@explorerpublishing.com
pr@explorerpublishing.com

Corporate Sales
For bulk sales and customisation options, for this book or
any Explorer product, contact
sales@explorerpublishing.com

Advertising and Sponsorship
For advertising and sponsorship, contact
media@explorerpublishing.com

Quick Reference

Main Hotels

Claridge's	7629 8860
Covent Garden Hotel	7806 1000
The Dorchester	7629 8888
Great Eastern	7618 5000
Hazlitt's	7829 9888
Hoxton Hotel	7550 1000
Jumeirah Carlton Tower	7235 1234
K West	0870 0274343
One Aldwych	7300 1000
Renaissance Chancery Court London	7829 9888
The Ritz	7493 8181
The Rookery	7336 0931
The Sanderson	7300 1400
The Savoy	7836 4343
St Martins Lane	7300 5500

Airport Information

Gatwick	
Lost Luggage	01293 503162
Airport Information	0870 0002468
Heathrow:	
Lost Luggage	8745 7727
Airport Information	0870 0000123
London City	
Lost Luggage	7646 0088
Airport Information	7646 0088
Luton	
Lost Luggage	01582 405100
Airport Information	01582 405100
Stansted	
Lost Luggage	01279 663293
Airport Information	0870 0000303

Useful Numbers

Ambulance	999
Anti-terrorist Hotline	0800 789321
Crimestoppers	0800 555111
Electricity Emergency (EDF)	0800 0280247
Fire	999
Gas Emergency (National Grid)	0800 111999
Greater London Authority	7983 4000
Lost Property (Transport)	0845 3309882
Missing Persons Helpline	0500 700700
NHS Direct	0845 4647
Operator (UK)	100
Operator (International)	155
Police (Emergency)	999
Police (City of London)	7601 2222
Police (Metropolitan)	7230 1212
Transport Information (Bus)	0845 3007000
Transport Information (Road; AA)	09003 401100
Transport Information (National Rail)	0845 7484950
Transport Information (Tube)	7222 1234
Water Emergency (Thames Water)	0845 9200800

Banks & Credit Cards

Abbey	0800 5…
Allied Irish Bank (GB)	01895 27…
Barclaycard	0870 1540…
Barclays	0800 400100
Egg	0845 1233233
Goldfish	0870 5111444
Halifax	0845 7203040
HSBC	0845 7404404
Lloyds TSB	0845 3000000
MBNA	0800 062062
NatWest	0800 200400
Royal Bank of Scotland	7409 0599
Woolwich	0845 0700360

Public Holidays

New Year's Day	Jan 1
Good Friday	Apr 6 (2007); Mar 21 (2008)
Easter Monday	Apr 9 (2007); Mar 24 (2008)
May Day	May 7 (2007); May 5 (2008)
Spring	May 28 (2007); May 26 (2008)
Summer	Aug 27 (2007); Aug 25 (2008)
Christmas Day	Dec 25
Boxing Day	Dec 26

Consulates

Argentina	7318 1300	W
Australia	7379 4334	WC
Austria	7235 3731	SW i
Belgium	7470 3700	SW1
Brazil	7499 0877	W1
Canada	7258 6506	W1
China	7299 4049	W1
Denmark	7333 0200	SW1
Greece	7221 6467	W11
Finland	7838 6200	SW1
France	7073 1000	SW1
Germany	7824 1300	SW1
India	7836 8484	WC2
Iran	7225 3000	SW7
Italy	7312 2200	W1
Japan	7465 6500	W1
Jordan	0870 0056952	W8
Lebanon	7229 7265	W8
Malaysia	7235 8033	SW1
Mexico	7499 8586	W1
Norway	7591 5500	SW1
Oman	7225 0001	SW15
Pakistan	7664 9200	SW1
Russia	7229 8027	W8
South Africa	7451 7299	WC2
Spain	7235 5555	SW1
Sri Lanka	7262 1841	W2
Thailand	7589 2944	SW7
Turkey	7591 6900	SW7
United Arab Emirates	0870 0056984	SW7
United States	7499 9000	W1